Canon Callaway

Izinyanga Zokubula

Divination As Existing Among the Amazulu in their Own Words

Canon Callaway

Izinyanga Zokubula
Divination As Existing Among the Amazulu in their Own Words

ISBN/EAN: 9783743423534

Manufactured in Europe, USA, Canada, Australia, Japa

Cover: Foto ©Lupo / pixelio.de

Manufactured and distributed by brebook publishing software (www.brebook.com)

Canon Callaway

Izinyanga Zokubula

The Folk-Lore Society,

FOR COLLECTING AND PRINTING

RELICS OF POPULAR ANTIQUITIES, &c.

ESTABLISHED IN

THE YEAR MDCCCLXXVIII.

Alter et Idem.

PUBLICATIONS
OF
THE FOLK-LORE SOCIETY.
XV.
(1884.)

Officers of the Folk-Lore Society,
1884-1885.

PRESIDENT.
THE RIGHT HON. EARL BEAUCHAMP, F.S.A.

VICE-PRESIDENTS.
A. LANG, M.A.
W. R. S. RALSTON, M.A.
EDWARD B. TYLOR, LL.D., F.R.S.

COUNCIL.

EDWARD BRABROOK, F.S.A.
JAMES BRITTEN, F.L.S.
Dr. R. BROWN.
EDWARD CLODD.
SIR W. R. DRAKE, F.S.A.
G. L. GOMME, F.S.A.

ALFRED NUTT.
PROFESSOR A. H. SAYCE, M.A.
EDWARD SOLLY, F.R.S., F.S.A.
WILLIAM J. THOMS, F.S.A.
W. S. W. VAUX, M.A.
HENRY B. WHEATLEY, F.S.A.

DIRECTOR.—WILLIAM J. THOMS, F.S.A.

TREASURER.—SIR WILLIAM R. DRAKE, F.S.A.

HONORARY SECRETARIES.
G. L. GOMME, F.S.A., 2, Park Villas, Lonsdale Road, Barnes, S.W.
A. GRANGER HUTT, F.S.A., 8, Oxford Road, Kilburn, N W.

AUDITORS.—John Tolhurst, F.S.A. J. S. Udal.

BANKERS.—Union Bank of London, Charing Cross Branch.

FOLK-TALE COMMITTEE.—Messrs. Apperson, Britten, Blind, Clodd, Hartland, Nutt, Lang, Ralston, Sonnenschein, Wheatley, Solly, Wake, Gomme.

The Religious System of the Amazulu.

IZINYANGA ZOKUBULA;

OR,

DIVINATION,

AS EXISTING AMONG

THE AMAZULU,

IN THEIR OWN WORDS,

WITH

A TRANSLATION INTO ENGLISH,

AND NOTES.

BY

THE REV. CANON CALLAWAY, M.D.,
Loc. Sec. A.S.L.

"I cannot but admire the incuriousness of so many travellers who have visited Dahome and have described its customs without an attempt to master, or at least to explain, the faith that underlies them."—BURTON.

NATAL:
JOHN A. BLAIR, SPRINGVALE;
DAVIS AND SONS, PIETERMARITZBURG;
ADAMS AND CO., DURBAN.
CAPETOWN:
J. C. JUTA, WALE STREET.
LONDON:
TRÜBNER AND CO., 60, PATERNOSTER ROW.

1870.

UNKULUNKULU;

OR,

THE TRADITION OF CREATION

AS EXISTING AMONG

THE AMAZULU AND OTHER TRIBES

OF

SOUTH AFRICA.

Unkulunkulu a s' aziwa. Yena umuntu wokukqala; wa dabuka ekukqaleni. Umfazi wa- | Unkulunkulu is no longer known.[1] It is he who was the first man;[2] he broke off[3] in the be-

[1] *A s' aziwa = ka s' aziwa*, is no longer known, that is, to us; or as it is said in other accounts, "A si sa m azi," We no longer know him. There no longer exists amongst us any knowledge about him. The same expression is used when speaking of the man from whom the *isibongo* (surname) of a house or tribe is derived, *ka s' aziwa*. He is lost to memory, nothing is known of him or his deeds.

[2] This is the constant statement in the traditions of Unkulunkulu. It has been said that by *umuntu* we are to understand simply a *person*. But *umuntu* means a *human being*. And it is more in accordance with the religious system of the natives to give it that meaning here. They are ancestor-worshippers, and believe that their first ancestor—the first man—was the creator. Unkulunkulu means the old-old-one, the most ancient man. In like manner Arjuna addresses Krishna as, "Thou first of the gods, the most ancient person." *(Hardwick. Christ and other Masters. Vol. I., p. 242.)* And the king Satravata addresses "Hari, the preserver of the universe," thus, "O first male; the lord of creation, of preservation, of destruction!" *(Id., p. 314.)*

[3] *Dabuka*, to separate, or to spring or break off, from something by fissure or division. Thus the swarming of bees is an *ukudabuka*. The division of small tribes from larger ones—as the small tribes of

B

ke a si m azi ; nabadala abantu a ba si tsheli ukuti wa be e nomfazi.

Si zwa ukuba ku tiwa Unkulunkulu wa dabula izizwe o*h*langeni.

ginning.[4] We do not know his wife; and the ancients do not tell us that he had a wife.[5]

We hear it said, that Unkulunkulu broke off[6] the nations from Uthlanga.[7]

Umahhaule and Unjan from the Abambo, the large tribe of Usingela; or as the Americans from the English—is spoken of as an *ukudabuka*. So if a village has become large, and the eldest son leaves the paternal kraal, and commences a new centre, that too is an *ukudabuka*. So the different kind of cattle, English, Dutch, and Zulu, are said respectively to have sprung from *(dabuka)* the English, Dutch, or Zulu. It is also said of trees. So of the Reformation it would be said that the **Reformed Churches** sprang from *(dabuka)* that of Rome; and **Dissenting Churches** from that of England. Or what is perhaps more to the point, the mode in which Minerva was produced from Jupiter's head was an *ukudabuka*. As we shall see below, according to the Hindu mythology, primitive man was produced by a division *(ukudabuka)* of the substance of Brahma. The use of the word necessarily implies the pre-existence of something from which the division took place. When it is said therefore that Unkulunkulu broke off in the beginning, we must understand either that he broke off from an eternal or at least pre-existent spiritual being, or from an eternal or at least pre-existent material being. When it is said, *wa dabuka eluhlangeni* (he broke off from uthlanga), we may have the intimation of an eternal spiritual being, a belief in whom formed a part of the creed of the ancestors of the Amazulu; and when it is said, *wa dabuka emhlabeni* (he broke off from the earth), it cannot be doubted that we are to understand it as intimating a belief in the eternity—at least in the pre-existence—of the world.

[4] *Ekukqaleni.* In the beginning. There is the same obscurity in the Zulu use of this phrase as in our own. We must understand it here as meaning, *in the beginning of the present order of things,* and not, from all eternity.

[5] But, as it will be presently seen, a first woman is by many associated with the first man, that is, Unkulunkulu is said to have had a wife.

[6] *Dabula.*—My native interpreter maintains that although above it is said that Unkulunkulu is not known to have had a wife, yet that this phrase implies it. But this is scarcely borne out by the fact that in other accounts he is said to break off cattle, &c., from Uthlanga. It seems rather that we are to understand that at first Unkulunkulu broke off, and having broken off, became the means of breaking off all other things.

[7] *Ohlangeni.*—*U'thlanga* is a reed, strictly speaking, one which is capable of "stooling," throwing out offsets. It thus comes, metaphori-

UNKULUNKULU. 3

Ku tiwa wa tuma unwaba; wa ti, "Hamba, lunwaba, u ye u yokuti, Abantu ma ba nga fi." Lwa hamba unwaba, lwa hamba kancinane, lwa libala end*h*leleni; lwa hamba lwa d*h*la umuti, o igama lawo ku ubukwebezane.[9]

Wa za Unkulunkulu wa tuma intulo ngasemva kwonwaba, se lu hambile ngesikati esipambili unwaba. Ya hamba intulo, ya gijima, ya tshetsha kakulu, ngokuba Unkulunkulu e tize, "Ntulo, u fike u ti, Abantu a ba fe." Ya hamba ke intulo, ya ti, "Ngi ti, Ku tiwa, Abantu ma ba fe." Ya buya intulo, ya fika kunkulunkulu; lwa ba unwaba lu nga ka fiki, lona lwa tunywa kuk*q*ala; lona lwa tunywa ku tiwa, ma lu yokuti, "Abantu ma ba nga fi."

It is said he sent a chameleon; he said to it, "Go, Chameleon, go and say, Let not men die." The chameleon set out; it went slowly;[8] it loitered in the way; and as it went, it ate of the fruit of a tree, which is called Ubukwebezane.

At length Unkulunkulu sent a lizard[10] after the chameleon, when it had already set out for some time. The lizard went; it ran and made great haste, for Unkulunkulu had said, "Lizard, when you have arrived, say, Let men die." So the lizard went, and said, "I tell you, It is said, Let men die." The lizard came back again to Unkulunkulu, before the chameleon had reached his destination, the chameleon which was sent first; which was sent, and told to go and say, "Let not men die."

cally, to mean a source of being. A father is the *uthlanga* of his children, from which they broke off. Whatever notions the ignorant of the present day among the natives may have of the meaning of this tradition, it may be concluded that originally it was not intended to teach by it, that men sprang from a reed. It cannot be doubted that the word alone has come down to the people, whilst the meaning has been lost. Comp. M. Casalis' account of the religious notions of the Basutos, p. 240.

[8] Hence their saying, "Ukuhambisa kwonwaba," To go like a chameleon, i. e., to go slowly. They say also *ukunwabuzela*.

[9] *Ubukwebezane.*—A shrub which bears clusters of berries of a purplish colour and sweet taste. This fruit is much liked by children.

[10] *Intulo = intulwa*, the Amalala *inulwa*. The tradition lives among the natives to the present time, and is manifested by the dislike they entertain for the chameleon. It is frequently killed. But it is used as a medicine; among other uses it is mixed with other things to doctor their gardens, that the birds may not destroy the corn; it is employed because it went slowly, and therefore will prevent the birds

Lwa za lwa fika, lwa momeza, lwa ti, "Ku tiwa, Abantu ma ba nga fi!" Ba ti abantu ba ti, "O! si bambe izwi lentulo; yona i si tshelile, ya ti, 'Ku tiwa, Abantu ma ba fe.' A si sa li zwa elako. Ngezwi lentulo abantu b' oza 'kufa."

At length it arrived and shouted, saying, "It is said, Let not men die!" But men answered, "O! we have heard the word of the lizard; it has told us the word, 'It is said, Let men die.' We cannot hear your word. Through the word of the lizard, men will die."[11]

from hastily entering the gardens! But the lizard is an object of much greater hatred, and is invariably killed if the person who sees it is able to kill it; but it is very cunning, and, as they say, "escapes only by its cunning." As they kill it they say, "Yiya! i sona lesi 'silimane esa gijima kukqala sa ya 'kuti, 'Abantu a ba fe.'" Let be! This is the very piece of deformity which ran in the beginning to say that men should die.

[11] This tradition of the origin of death has a strong resemblance to the Hottentot account. But there it is the Moon—a Hottentot god, according to Kolb, *(The Present State of the Cape of Good Hope, (Medley,) Volume I., page 95)*—which sends an insect to man with the message:—" Go thou to men, and tell them, ' As I die, and dying live, so ye shall also die, and dying live.'" The insect, meeting with the hare, entrusts the message to him; but when he reaches man, he says, "I am sent by the Moon to tell you, 'As I die, and dying perish, in the same manner ye shall also die, and come wholly to an end.'" *(Bleek's Hottentot Fables, p. 69.)*

This account is, however, a promise of renovation through death. The New Zealand legend again may be compared, where we meet with rather a foreshadowing of redemption through One destroying death by passing through it, than an account of the cause of death entering into the world. Maui is made liable to death by some accidental omission of a part of the baptismal ritual,—a cause as trivial as the delay of the chameleon, or the false message of the hare.

Maui was an abortion; he was born as his mother was passing along by the sea-shore. She cut off the long tresses of her hair, and bound him up in them, and threw him into the foam of the sea, and after that he was found by his ancestor Tama-nui-ki-te-Rangi, and by his care developed into a man. As yet there was no death. But Maui's father, "from mistake, hurriedly skipped over part of the prayers of the baptismal service, and of the services to purify Maui; he knew that the gods would be certain to punish this fault, by causing Maui to die, and his alarm and anxiety were therefore great." Maui having transformed by enchantments Irawaru, his sister Hinauri's husband, into a dog, and Hinauri having girded herself with an enchanted girdle had cast herself into the sea, and been swept away by the tide, he was obliged to quit the village where Irawaru had lived,

Wa ti Unkulunkulu wa ba nika abantu amatongo; wa ba nika izinyanga zokwelapa nezokubula; wa ba nika nemiti yokwelapa itongo. Wa ti Unkulunkulu, "Uma umuntu e gula e netongo, e banjwe itongo, wo hlaba inkomo, ni bonge itongo; umuntu u ya 'kupila, m' esuka e banjwe itongo."

Unkulunkulu gave men Amatongo;[12] he gave them doctors for treating disease, and diviners; he gave them medicines to treat diseases occasioned by the Itongo.[13] Unkulunkulu said, "If a man is ill, he being affected by the Itongo, you shall kill a bullock and laud the Itongo; the man will get well if he has been affected by the Itongo."

and so returned to his parents. His father said, "Oh my son, I have heard from your mother and others that you are very valiant, and that you have succeeded in all feats that you have undertaken in your own country, whether they are small or great; but now that you have arrived in your father's country, you will perhaps at last be overcome." On asking "what he could be vanquished by?" his father replied, "By your great ancestress Hine-nui-te-po." But he answered, "Lay aside such idle thoughts, and let us both fearlessly seek whether men are to die or live for ever." Maui pleads that he had subdued Tamanui-te-Ra (the sun), and had rescued much land by drawing it up from the sea. His father admits the truth, and bids him go boldly to visit "his great ancestress," who, he knew, would be the cause of his death. Maui set out on his journey, taking "every kind of little bird" as his companions. Maui and his companions found Hine-nui-te-po asleep. Maui told them that he was about to creep into the old chieftainess, and warned them not to laugh until they saw him "just coming out of her mouth; then they might shout with laughter if they pleased." When he entered the old chieftainess, "the little birds screwed up their tiny cheeks, trying to suppress laughter; at last, the little Tiwakawaka laughed out loud with its merry cheerful note," and the old woman awoke, and killed Maui. This was the cause of the introduction of death into the world. Hine-nui-te-po being the goddess of death, had Maui passed safely through her, then no more human beings would have died, but death itself would have been destroyed. *(Grey. Polynesian Mythology, p. 16—58.)*

[12] *Itongo,* p. *Amatongo.*—An *itongo* is properly the spirit of the dead,—a disembodied spirit. The notion that it is in the form of a snake, or becomes converted into a snake, is probably something superadded to the original tradition. But all these questions will be discussed when we come to the "AMATONGO."

[13] *Ukwelapa itongo,* lit., to treat an itongo, that is, diseases which are occasioned by the itongo, as *uthlabo,* which appears from the description to be pleurodynia; one case I was called to see was pleurisy.

Wa ti, "Ni ya 'kubona futi na sebusuku, ni ya 'kupupa; itongo li ya 'ku ni tshela into e li i tshoko." Wa ti, "Li ya 'ku ni tshela ucukomo."

Itongo li hlala kumuntu omkulu; o yena o li pupayo ku 'munumuzana; li ti, "Ni nga hlaba inkomo, u ya 'kusinda umuntu." I hlatshwe inkomo e tshiwo itongo; a ti loku umuntu ku be se ku tiwa, "U za 'kufa," a sinde; ku bonakale ke ukuti lo 'muntu u be e banjwe itongo. I ya kitshwa inyongo ngapakati enkomweni,[14] a telwe ngayo inyongo; ku bongwe, ku tiwe, "Uma si bone ukuti itongo, a si bone ukuba a pile namhla nje; ku ya sa kusasa nje u se i dhla inyama; si ya 'kubona ke ukuti itongo. Okunye loku, a si yi 'kuvuma enhliziyweni zetu ukuti itongo; si ya 'kuti, i 'kufa nje; a li ko itongo kuyena emzimbeni wake. Uma si bone ukuti ku kona itongo, si ya 'kubona ngokuba a pile, si bonge ke. I kona si ya 'kuhlaba inkomo eziningi, si bonge ke etongweni, si bone ukuti itongo lakwiti li lungile."

Uguaise Mdunga (an Ilala).

He said, "You will see also by night, you will dream; the Itongo will tell you what it is it wishes." He said, "It will also tell you the bullock it would have killed."

The Itongo dwells with the great man; he who dreams is the chief of the village; it says, "Should you kill a bullock, the man will get well." The bullock which the Itongo mentions is killed; and although people were thinking that the man would die, he gets well; and so it is clear that the man was affected by the Itongo. The gallbladder is taken from the bullock, and the man has the gall poured on him; they give praise and say, "In order that we may see that it is the Itongo, let us see him get well this very day; and at the very dawn of tomorrow eat meat; so we shall see that it is the Itongo. On the other hand, we shall not admit in our hearts that it is the Itongo; we shall say, it is disease only; there is no Itongo in his body. If we see that it is the Itongo, we shall see it by his getting well, and so we shall give thanks. Then we will kill many cattle, and laud the Itongo, and see that the Itongo of our house is good."

---

[14] *Enkomweni.*—I preserve this word because it is formed regularly. The Zulus say *enkomeni;* the Amalala *eyomweni.*

Abadala ba ti Unkulunkulu u ng' Umvelinqangi, ngokuba be ti wa vela kukqala; be ti u u/langa lwabantu lapa kwa dabuka abantu kulo. Ku tsho abadala ukuti u kona Unkulunkulu; w' enza abantu bokukqala, abadala bendulo; ba fa abadala bendulo, kwa sala abanye aba zalwa i bo, amadodana, e si zwa ngabo ukuti kwa be ku kona abadala bendulo ab' azi ukudabuka kwezwe. Ka ba m azi

The old men say that Unkulunkulu is Umvelinqangi,[15] for they say he came out first; they say he is the Uthlanga from which all men broke off.[16] The old men say that Unkulunkulu is;[17] he made the first men, the ancients of long ago;[18] the ancients of long ago died; there remained those who had been begotten by them, sons, by whom we hear that there were ancients of long ago who knew the breaking off of the world.[19] They

[15] *Umvelinqangi*, the first out-comer.

[16] Let the reader note that here three names are applied to the first man, Unkulunkulu, Umvelinqangi, and Uthlanga. *Unkulunkulu* expresses antiquity, age, lit., the old-old one, as we use great in great-great-grandfather. *Umvelinqangi* expresses priority; the first out-comer. *Uthlanga*, potential source of being. Neither must this be regarded as a contradiction to the statement lower down, "Wa vela lapa abantu ba dabuka kona o/langeni," He came out where men broke off from Uthlanga. For Unkulunkulu, the first man, sprang from—came out of—broke off from—a previously existing uthlanga or source of being, the nature of which is quite beyond the native philosophy; and having come out, he became the uthlanga or source of being of entire humanity.

[17] *U kona*, is. We must not, however, understand this as a declaration of the ancients that Unkulunkulu has a present existence. But they mean to say, "Unkulunkulu was a *reality;* that which we say of him is not a fable, but a fact. Unkulunkulu is a reality; he made us, and is, as it were, in us his work. We exist because he existed." That this is the meaning we gather not only from the interpretation of it by natives, and from other accounts of the same tradition, but from the statement made below, "B' ezwa ngokutshiwo ukuti Unkulunkulu wa be kona," They heard it said that Unkulunkulu was, or used to be; the tense necessarily implying that he exists no longer.

[18] *Abadala bendulo*, the ancients of long ago,—not merely ancients, but the ancients of primitive times; those who formed the first races of mankind.

[19] The natives profess to be unable to give any account of the origin of things; but refer to a period when the ancients understood the history of creation.

Unkulunkulu; a ba m bonanga ngame*h*lo; b' ezwa ngokutshiwo ukuti Unkulunkulu wa be. kona. Wa vêla lapa abantu ba dabuka kona o*h*langeni. Wa zala abantu bendulo; ba fa, ba shiya abantwana babo; ba zala abanye, amadodan' abo, ba fa; ba zala abanye, ukuba tina si ze si zwe ngonkulunkulu. Okoko betu aba si tshelayo izindaba zikankulunkulu nezendulo.

Ngi tshele uma ngesikati samanje ku kona abantu aba kuleka kuye Unkulunkula na?

Ka ba ko. Ba ya kcela ematongweni; ba wa dumise ukuba a ze a ba sindise.

Amatongo a ng' obani na?

Amad*h*lozi, abantu ab' esuke be file; ba fe k*q*ede, ba buye ba guk*q*uke ba be amatongo, ba hhuluzele ngesisu, ba se be ti abantu abadala, "Itongo." Igama lalo li inyoka; inyandezulu igama layo inyoka.

Ku be se ku gula umuntu, ku se ku yiwa enyangeni, ku yiwa 'kubulwa; ku be se ku tiwa, "Amatongo a ze 'kukcela izinko-

did not know Unkulunkulu; they did not see him with their eyes; they heard it said that Unkulunkulu was. He came out where men broke off from Uthlanga. He begat the ancients of long ago; they died and left their children; they begat others, their sons, they died; they begat others; thus we at length have heard about Unkulunkulu. It was our ancestors who told us the accounts of Unkulunkulu and of the ancients of long ago.

Tell me if at the present time there are any who pray to Unkulunkulu?

There are none. They pray to the Amatongo; they honour them that they may come and save them.

Who are the Amatongo?

The Amadhlozi, men who have died; when they have died, they change again and become Amatongo, and crawl on their belly, and so the old men call a dead man so changed an Itongo. It is called a snake; Inyandezulu[20] is the name of the snake.

When a man is ill, they go to a doctor to divine; and it is said, "The Amatongo have come to ask for cattle, that a bullock should be

---

[20] A large, green, harmless snake, which for the most part is observed in trees. It frequently enters the native huts.

mo, ukuze ku hlatshwe inkomo." I b' i s' i ncwatshelwa endhlini, ukuba a i dhle; se ku vulwa umnyango, ba nga i dhli ngalesi 'sikati, ba i dhle ngolunyo usuku. Kusihlwa ku lale abafana endhlini, ba i linde inyama. Ku ya sa kusasa i s' i ya pekwa, ku butane abantu, ba ze ba i dhle, ba ze 'ku i dhla inhloko. Be se ba ya hlakazeka ba ye emizini yabo; ku be se ku sala abasekaya. Ku be se ku pekwa isifuba esi za 'kudhliwa amakosikazi nabantu bonke basekaya.

Se ku butwa amatambo onke enkomo, umnikazinkomo e se wa tshisa, ukuba abatakati ba nga wa tati, ba ye 'ku w' elapa, ba m bulale, a buye a gule futi.

killed." The flesh of the slaughtered bullock is put together in a hut, that the Amatongo may eat; the door is shut, and the people do not eat the meat at the time, but on the morrow. In the evening boys sleep in the hut and watch the meat. In the morning the flesh is boiled, and men assemble to eat the head. They then separate and go to their own villages; and those of the family where the bullock has been killed remain. Then the breast is boiled, which will be eaten by the chieftainesses and by the people of the family.

All the bones of the bullock are collected, and the owner of the cattle burns them, that wizards may not take them, and apply medicines to them and injure the man who was sick, and he become ill again.[21]

Kwa ku tiwa ekukqaleni, abafundisi be nga ka bi ko, uma si buza tina, si ti, "Amatshe 'enziwe ini na?" ku tiwe, "'Enziwe Umvelinqangi." Ku tiwa tina bantu si pume emhlangeni lapa sa

It was said at first before the arrival of missionaries, if we asked, "By what were the stones made?"—"They were made by Umvelinqangi." It is said that we men came out of a bed of reeds,[22] where we had our origin."[23]

[21] This account was given by a refugee recently arrived from Zululand, whose name I do not know.

[22] *Umhlanga* is a bed of reeds. We must not confound *umhlanga* with *uhlanga*. Umhlanga is the place where they broke off—or out-came—from Uhlanga.

[23] *Vela*, had our origin,—*out-came*, equivalent to "were created." It does not mean merely appearing.

vela kona. Si buze, si ti, "Ilanga l' enziwa ini na?" ba ti, "L' enziwa Umvelinqangi." Ngokuba tina be si buza, si banciuyane, si ti, abadala ba ya z' azi izinto zonke ezi sem*h*labeni; kanti ka ba z' azi; kodwa si nga ba pikisi, ngokuba si ug' azi nati.

Kwa ti se si semabuneni Amabunu a wa si tshelanga ukuti, "Inkosi i kona pezulu;" kodwa wona e tsho e ti, tin' abantu abamnyama si ya 'kutsha; kodwa a e tsho e ti, tin' abantu abamnyama a si nawo umoya, si fana nenja, yona e nge nawo umoya.

Ba be tsho abadala, abafundisi be nga ka bi ko, ba ti, "Izinto zonke z' enziwa Umvelinqangi, zonke." Kodwa a ba m azi uma ubani na. Kodwa ba *h*lala ngokubonga izinyoka; na manje ba ya bonga zona; a ba k' ezwa; na

When we asked, "By what was the sun made?" they said, "By Umvelinqangi." For we used to ask when we were little, thinking that the old men knew all things which are on the earth; yet forsooth they do not know; but we do not contradict them, for neither do we know.

When we were with the Dutch they did not tell us that there is a Lord above; but they said that we black people should be burnt; and that we have no spirit,[24] but are like a dog, which has no spirit.

The ancients used to say before the arrival of the missionaries, that all things were made by Umvelinqangi; but they were not acquainted with his name.[25] But they lived by worshipping[26] snakes; and they still worship them; they do not yet hear; and even now

---

[24] *Umoya*, spirit. The native who related this tale, though not a Christian, had lived with whitemen from his childhood, and for some years with a missionary. The untaught native would not use *umoya* (wind, air) in the sense of spirit, as this man uses it. They would apply it to the air we breathe, but not to the spirit or soul of man. Neither do they use itongo, idhlozi, isituta (ghost), or isitunzi (shade), of any power animating the body, but only of something,—a new or distinct existence,—which comes out of the body when dead.

[25] Many misunderstandings of native traditions have arisen from the enquiry, "Unkulunkulu ubani na?" meaning who or what is Unkulunkulu. It really means, "What is his *name*?" The native cannot tell you his *name*, except it be Umvelinqangi.

[26] *Bonga*, worship. It is necessary to give *bonga* this full meaning here, and not to restrict it to the offices of *praising* or *thanking*. It is equivalent to *pata*, which is used for all and every kind of adoration and worship.

manjo lapa abafundisi be kulumayo, ba ti, "Insumansumane ; into nje ngokudhlala." A ba tsho ukuti, ku kulunywa izindaba ezi k*q*inisileyo.

Lapa ku hlatshwa, ku ya bongwa inyoka kuk*q*ala, anduba ku hlatshwe inkomo. I ti se i hlatshiwe ya hlinzwa ; ku tabatwe inyama encinyane enonileyo, i ye 'kubekwa endhlini, emsamo ngodengezi ; ku bekwe umlilo pezu kwodengezi. Uma ku tshe inyama yenkomo, ku dhle amatongo (uma 'eze a ze 'kudhla inyama yenkomo). I tutwe inyama yenkomo, i bekwe endhlini. Lapo ku kona inyama ku hlale umuntu a be munye, ngokuba ku tiwa ku za 'ku fika amadhlozi, a ze 'kudhla inyama. Ku ti kusasa a si boni lapa amadhlozi e dhlile kona; si bona izito zenkomo zi pelele zonke, nenyama e b' i sodengezini a i dhliwanga 'luto; i sa hlezi njengaloku i be i njalo; a si boni 'luto olu dhliweyo.

Kodwa si buza si ti, "Amadhlozi a dhla ni na? loku inyama ku sa si sa i bona yonke," ba ti abadala, "Amatongo a ya i kota." Si nga bi namandhla oku ba pikisa, si tula, ngokuba ba be badala ngapambili kwetu, be si tshela izinto zonke, si zi lalele ; ngokuba si tshelwa zonke, si zi vume, si zi

when the missionaries speak, they say, "It is a fable ; a plaything." They do not admit that what is spoken is the truth.

When they slaughter cattle, they first praise the snake, and then the bullock is killed. When it is killed they skin it ; and a little of the fat[27] is taken, and put in the upper part of the hut on a sherd ; and fire is placed on it. When the flesh of the bullock burns, the Amatongo eat (if they do come to eat the flesh of a bullock). The flesh of the bullock is taken and put in a house. One man stays in the house where the flesh is put, for it is said the Amatongo will come and eat flesh. But in the morning we do not see where the Amadhlozi have eaten ; we see the limbs of the bullock all there, and the meat that was on the sherd has not been eaten by any thing ; it remains just as it was; we do not see any that has been eaten.

But when we ask, "What do the Amadhlozi eat? for in the morning we still see all the meat," the old men say, "The Amatongo lick it." And we are unable to contradict them; but are silent, for they are older than we, and tell us all things, and we listen ; for we are told all things,

---

[27] The fat of the cawl or omentum is used with incense.

vume kodwa, si nga boni ka*h*le ukuba ba k*q*inisile ini na.

Uma ku ya ngena inyoka end*h*lini a i bulawa; ku tiwa, "Id*h*lozi likabani," ku tshiwo igama lomuntu owa fayo; ku tiwe le 'nyoka i pume kuye okufeni kwake. I yekwe, i *h*lale njalo end*h*lini. Ku tatwe imbuzi, ku *h*latshwe yona, ku *h*latshiswa inyoka. A i bonwa umuntu lapa i se i muka.

Abantu abamnyama lapa be hambayo ba ya dumisa inyoka. Lapa umuntu e limala wa sinda, a gwaze inkomo, ngokuba e bonga id*h*lozi, e ti li m sindisile. Lapa umuntu e zuza nezinkomo, a bonge inyoka, a ti, i yona e m nikileyo izinkomo eziningi.

A ti o nga se nayise, a ti, lapa e za 'ku*h*laba inkomo, a bonge uyise, a ti, uyise a ka m bheke njalo, a mu pe konke a ku tandayo, a mu pe izinkomo namabele,—konke.

Ukuma umuntu e gula ku bulwe ezinyangeni; inyanga i fike i ti, ma ba d*h*le inkomo. Ba i d*h*le inkomo, i ti inyanga umuntu u ya 'kusinda. Ba ti se be i d*h*lile inkomo, a nga sindi, a fe, ku tiwe, "U ya bizwa abapansi." Ku

and assent without seeing clearly whether they are true or not.

When a snake comes into a house it is not killed; they say, "It is the Idhlozi of So-and-so," mentioning the name of a man who is dead; it is said the snake came out of him at his death. It is left, and remains always in the house. They take a goat and sacrifice it, sacrificing to the snake. No one sees it when it goes away.

When black men are on a journey they honour the snake. When a man is injured and gets well, he kills a bullock, for he thanks the Idhlozi, thinking that it has saved him. When a man obtains cattle also, he thanks the snake, thinking it is the snake which has given him many cattle.

A man whose father is dead, when he is about to kill a bullock, worships his father, praying him to look on him continually, and give him all that he wishes, and give him cattle and corn,—every thing.

When a man is ill, they enquire of diviners; the diviner comes and tells them to eat a bullock. And they eat a bullock, the diviner saying that the man will get well. If when they have eaten the bullock he does not get well, but dies, they say, "He is summoned by those who are beneath."[28] They

---

[28] *Abapansi*, i. e., the Amatongo, they who are beneath. Some

tiwe, "U bulewe amad*h*lozi ngokuba e tanda um' 'eze 'ku*h*lala kuwona."

Uma kubantu abamnyama ku fe umuntu, ku ya kalwa kakulu, kw enziwe umsindo omkulu. Ku ti e se la*hl*iwe, ku tatwe izinto zake zonke, zi baselwe umlilo omkulu, ku nga bi ko na lodwa uto lwake a be lu binca emzimbeni wake olu salayo; zi tshiswe zonke, ngokuba ku y' esatshwa ukubinca impa*hl*a yomuntu ofileyo.

UFULATELA SITOLE.

say, "He has been killed by the Amadhlozi because they wish the man to go and dwell with them."

When any one dies among black men, they lament very much and make a great noise. And when he is buried, all his things are taken, and a large fire kindled to burn them; not a single thing which he wore on his body is left; all is burnt, for they are afraid to wear the property of a dead man.

Ku tiwa ekukulumeni kwabantu abamnyama, uma umuntu w enza indaba emangalisayo abantu a ba nge namand*hl*a oku y enza, noma uku i k*q*eda uma imbi, ba tsho ke, "Au! yeka! abantu bansondo b' enza nje."

Noma izulu li ya na kakulu imivimbi eminingi, li veza ukumangalisa, ku tshiwo ngokuti, "La na izulu lansondo!" njalo futi.

Na ngom*hl*aba futi uma u lukuni ekulimeni, ku ya tshiwo ku tiwe, "Au! wa ba lukuni, um*hl*aba wansondo!"

In the speech of black men, when a man does a wonderful thing which other men cannot do, or brings a bad matter to a good issue, men say, "Au! go to! the people of Unsondo[29] do thus."

Or if the heaven rains excessively great torrents, and causes wonder, it is also constantly said, "How the heaven of Unsondo rains!"

And of the earth also, if it is hard to dig, it is said, "Au! how hard it is, the earth of Unsondo!"

natives say, so called, because they have been *buried beneath the earth.* But we cannot avoid believing that we have an intimation of an old faith in a Hades or Tartarus, which has become lost and is no longer understood. *Subterraneans* is an exact translation of *abapansi,* and as we proceed we shall find that similar characteristics and actions are ascribed to the Amatongo as to the Subterraneans in the mythology of other people.

[29] *Abantu bansondo,* or it is sometimes said, *bakansondo.*

Okunye futi, uma u kona umuntu omuhle impela, abantu ba tanda ukumangala ngaye, ba ti, "Au! wa ba muhle, umuntu wansondo."

Futi, uma ku puma impi, i ya 'kuhlasela enye inkosi, ku ya tshiwo ngamakosi, ku tiwe, "Au! Ai! amakosi ansondo wona, ngokuba na ngesikati sokwinhla a ya kipa impi, na ngesobusika a ya kipa impi."

Okunye, ku tiwa abantu ngabafazi, ngokuba abafazi ba nokuma kwabo, a tsho amadoda a ti, "Au! Ai! Abafazi bansondo."

Ku njalo ke ekupeleni si zwa kungati Unsondo lo umuntu ngezwi lokuti, "Unsondo wa fa e yaleza e ti, 'Nampa abantu ngokuti na ngokuti.'" Si ti ke nga-

Besides also, if there is a very handsome man, whom people like to make a wonder, they say, "Au! how beautiful he is, a man of Unsondo."[30]

Again, if an army goes out to invade another king, it is said of kings, "Au! No! they are kings of Unsondo, for in the time of firstfruits and in the time of winter they lead out their army."

Again, men say it of women, for women have their characteristics, and the men say, "Au! No! Women of Unsondo."

So finally we hear that Unsondo is, as it were, a man by the saying which is used, "Unsondo died uttering this his last word, 'Those are men because they are so and so.'"[31] Therefore we say that this

---

[30] *Uthlanga* is also used to express beauty. "Si tshele ni uhlanga oluhle lapa lwentombi," Tell us which is the prettiest girl here. They also say, "Inkosi yohlanga," that is, a chief who refers his descent to Uthlanga, that is, to him whom they regard as the creator or source of all things. We may compare this with διογενης βασιλευς of Homer.

[31] By this we are to understand that at his death Unsondo uttered a prophecy of the future of his children, telling them by what kind of conduct, good and bad, they would be characterised. Thus it is said not only of a good man, "Wa muhle! umuntu wansondo!" How good he is! a man of Unsondo! to express the perfection of goodness, but also of the wicked, "Au! wa mubi! umuntu wansondo!" O! how wicked he is! a man of Unsondo! to express utter wickedness. We may compare this with the Hebrew idiom, which without being identical is remarkably similar; that of designating any thing of surpassing excellence as God's, e.g. "A very great trembling," lit., a trembling of God (1 Sam. xiv. 15); and in Gen. xxxv. 5, "The terror of God (that is, an exceeding great terror) was upon the cities." *(See Gesenius.)*

loko Unsondo lo Unkulunkulu lowo, e si ti wa fa; ngokuba lelo 'lizwi lokuti, "Unsondo wa fa e yalcza," si ti ku u yena lowo, a ku ko mumbc.

Kepa abanye abantu ba ti Unsondo izwi nje lokupela kwendaba; a ku 'siminya; kepa lona ngokuma kwalo li ya ku shiya loko 'kutsho kwabo, li veze ukqobo.

Ngi li shiyile futi izwi eli tshiwoyo Unsondo; a si namandhla okuti la vela esizweni esitile; li izwi e si vele li kona njalo; a li litsha, lidala kakulu; a si b' azi ubudala balo.

UMPENGULA MBANDA.

Unsondo is the same as Unkulunkulu, who, we say, died; on account ot that saying, "Unsondo died uttering his last word," it is he indeed, and not another.

But some say that Unsondo is nothing more than the last word of a matter; it has no allusion to a fact; but the use of this saying sets at naught that word of theirs, and brings out a person.

But I have omitted one thing about this word Unsondo; we cannot say it had its origin in a particular tribe; it is a word which was in constant use when we were born; it is not a new word; it is very old; we do not know its age.

In illustration and confirmation of the above I insert the following. Returning from the Umzimkulu with a young Ibaken for my guide, I availed myself of the opportunity to discover whether there existed among the Amabakca the same traditions as among the Amazulu. I therefore requested him to tell me what he knew about the tradition of the chameleon. He told me the ordinary tale, but instead of saying it was sent by Unkulunkulu, he said, " Kwa tunywa unwaba," There was sent a chameleon. I enquired by whom it was sent. He replied, " By Unsondo."—" And who was he?"—" He was he who came out first at the breaking off of all things (ekudabukeni kwezinto zonke)."—" Explain what you mean by ekudabukeni."—" When this earth and all things broke off from Uthlanga."—" What is Uthlanga?"—" He who begat (zala) Unsondo."—" You do not mean then a reed, such as those in that bed of reeds in the valley?"—" No; but Uthlanga who begat Unsondo."—" Where is he now?"

"O, ka se ko. Njengaloku ubaba-mkulu ka se ko, naye ka se ko; wa fa. Wa fa, kwa vela oku-

"O, he exists no longer. As my grandfather no longer exists, he too no longer exists; he died.

nye oku bizwa ngokunye. Uhlanga wa zala Unsondo; Unsondo wa zala okoko; okoko ba zala okulu; okulu ba zala obabamkulu; nobabamkulu ba zala obaba; nobaba ba si zala tina."

When he died, there arose others, who were called by other names. Uthlanga begat Unsondo; Unsondo begat the ancestors; the ancestors begat the great grandfathers; the great grandfathers begat the grandfathers; and the grandfathers begat our fathers; and our fathers begat us."[32]

"Are there any who are called Uthlanga now?"—"Yes."—"Are you married?"—"Yes."—"And have children?"—"Yebo. U mina e ngi uthlanga." (Yes. It is I myself who am an uthlanga.)—"Because you have become the father of children?"—"Yes; I am an uthlanga on that account." As he said this he tapped himself on his breast.

Kodwa mina ngi ti labo ba kqinisile ngokuti Unkulunkulu Umvelinqangi. Kepa le 'ndawo a ba i tshoyo ngokuti wa e nomfazi, a ngi i zwanga. Loko e nga ku zwayo ukuti abantu ba vela kunkulunkulu, njengokuba wa b' enza ngokuba-ko kwake; a ku tshiwongo ukuti Unkulunkulu wa e nomfazi. I loku e si kw aziyo.

But for my part I say they speak truly[33] who say that Unkulunkulu is named Umvelinqangi. But as for what they say respecting his having a wife, I have not heard of it. What I have heard is this, that men sprang from Unkulunkulu, as if he made them because he existed (before them);[34] it was not said that Unkulunkulu had a wife. This is what we know.

Kepa ukubongwa, ba kqinisile labo aba tshoyo ukuti, ka bongwa-

And as regards worship, they speak truly who say, he was not

---

[32] This portion I wrote at his dictation in my study; the rest from memory.

[33] The native thus begins his statement because I had previously read to him what other natives had said on the subject.

[34] He means by this that he had heard that Unkulunkulu was the first that existed, and that existing he made others. But we shall see by and bye that this man is mistaken. Unkulunkulu is supposed to have a wife.

nga ; nami ngi ya ba vumela. A si ko ukubonga loko, uma abantu be bona izinto, noma imvula, noma ukud/la amabele, be be tsho abantu ukuti, " Yebo, lezi 'zinto z' enziwe Unkulunkulu." Kepa a ba banga nalo izwi lako lokuti, " Ngi n' enzele lezi 'zinto ukuze ni ng' azi ngazo." Wa z' enza ukuba abantu ba d/le, ba boue nje. Ngemva kwaloko ba ba nako uku zi pendula, zi be ezamad/lozi. Ba m amuka Unkulunkulu lezi 'zinto.

Kukqala sa bona ukuba s' enziwa Unkulunkulu. Kepa lapo si gulayo a sa m pata, a sa kcela 'luto kuyena. Sa pata labo e si ba bonile ngame/lo, ukufa kwabo noku/lala kwabo nati. Ngaloko ke izinto zonke sa kqala uku zi kcela emad/lozini, noma amabele,

worshipped ;[35] and I agree with them. For it is not worship, when people see things, as rain, or food, such as corn, and say, " Yes, these things were made by Unkulunkulu." But no such word has come to them from him as this, " I have made for you these things that you might know me by them." He made them that men might eat and see them and nothing more. Afterwards they had power to change those things, that they might become the Amatongo's. They took them away from Unkulunkulu.[36]

At first we saw that we were made by Unkulunkulu. But when we were ill we did not worship him, nor ask any thing of him. We worshipped those whom we had seen with our eyes, their death and their life amongst us. So then we began to ask all things of the Amadhlozi, whether corn,

[35] A mistake has no doubt often arisen on the question of whether Unkulunkulu is worshipped by the natives or not, from the failure to recognise the fact that there are many Onkulunkulu ; and the statements of natives have been wrongly supposed to be contradictory. The Unkulunkulu *par excellence*, the first man, is no where worshipped. No *isibongo* of his is known. The worship, therefore, of him according to native worship is no longer possible. But the Onkulunkulu of tribes and houses, whose *izibongo* are still known, are worshipped, each by his respective descendents.

[36] He means by this that he is not sure whether in the beginning they worshipped him or not ; but they no longer worship him, but the Amatongo, and thank the Amatongo for the things which they believe were created by Unkulunkulu.

D

noma abantwana, noma izinkomo, noma ukupila. Kwa kqala ngaloko ukuba ku bonakale ukuba Unkulunkulu ka se nayo indodana yake e nga m dumisako; kwa swoleka ukubuyela emva, ngokuba abantu b' anda, ba hlakazeka, ba bambana ngezindhlu zabo; ka ba ko o ti, "Mina ngi se i leyo 'ndhlu yakwankulunkulu."

Unkulunkulu kutina bantu abamnyama u njengohlanga lombila. Lona lu nga veza isikwebu, si kiwe, lu shiywe lona; lu sale lu bola kuleyo 'ndawo; iziuhlamvu zaleso 'sikwebu zi Onkulunkulu bezindhlu e se zi ya bongana zodwa njengokulandelana kwokumila kwazo esikwebini. Ku njalo ke ukulahleka kwezibongo zikankulunkulu.

or children, or cattle, or health. By that it began to be evident that Unkulunkulu had no longer a son[37] who could worship him; there was no going back to the beginning, for people increased, and were scattered abroad, and each house had its own connections; there was no one who said, "For my part I am of the house of Unkulunkulu."

To us black men Unkulunkulu is as a stalk of maize. It may produce the ear, it be plucked, and the stalk be left, and decay in the place where it grew; the grains of the cob are Onkulunkulu of houses, which now worship those only of their own family according to the order of their growth on the cob.[38] It is on this account that the praise-giving names of Unkulunkulu are lost.

[37] This implies that he had a son; but the *isibongo* or praise-giving name of Unkulunkulu is lost; by the process of time and many wanderings, other names have been taken up, each house having its own *isibongo*.

[38] He here uses a metaphor comparing men, or their houses, to the grains on an ear of maize; Unkulunkulu is the stalk, which having done its work dies; the seeds are the men, who sprang from him and became centres of families, each having its distinct family name or isibongo, and the children of successive generations worship those who preceded them. But the native adds as I am making this note, "Lelo 'zwi lokuti izinhlamvu zi bongana zodwa loko ukuti i leyo 'nhlamvu endhlini yayo se i unkulunkulu enzalweni yayo, leyo na leyo njalo," As for the saying, Each grain worships those which belong to itself, it means that each grain in its own house is an unkulunkulu to its offspring, each to its own offspring throughout.— Thus although the First Out-comer, Unkulunkulu, is not worshipped, other Onkulunkulu are worshipped, that is, their names are known and used in acts of adoration. But we shall see this more clearly by and bye.

Futi le 'nkosi e pezulu a si i zwanga ngabelungu. Ku be ku ti ngesikati sc*h*lobo, uma izulu li ya duma, ku tiwe, " I ya d*h*lala inkosi." Ku ti uma ku kona ow esabayo, ku tiwe abakulu, " W esaba nje. U d*h*le ni yenkosi na?" I loko ke e ngi tshoyo ngako ukuti le 'nkosi e si i zwa ngani ukuba i kona, sa si i zwile pambili.

Kepa i nge njengonkulunkulu lowo, e si ti w' enza izinto zonke. Kepa yona si ya i biza ngokuti inkosi, ngokuba si ti, yona i pezulu. Unkulunkulu u pansi; izinto lezi ezi pansi z' enziwe u ye. Si nga tsho 'luto ngaleyo inkosi e pezulu, 'kupela loko e si ku tshoyo kumuntu ow esabayo, ukuti, " W one ni yenkosi?" S' azi loko ukuba o y onileyo u ya tshaywa i

And the King which is above[39] we did not hear of him [first] from whitemen. In summer time, when it thunders, we say, " The king is playing."[40] And if there is one who is afraid, the elder people say to him, " It is nothing but fear. What thing belonging to the king have you eaten?" This is why I say, that the Lord of whom we hear through you, we had already heard of before you came.

But he is not like that Unkulunkulu who, we say, made all things. But the former we call a king, for we say, he is above. Unkulunkulu is beneath; the things which are beneath were made by him. We said nothing about that king which is above but that which we say to a man who is afraid, " What have you injured which belongs to the king?" We know that he who has sinned against him is struck by him;[41]

[39] *Inkosi* may be translated king, lord, chief, &c. And we may either say, the king, lord, chief, &c., which is above,—or the king of heaven,—or the heavenly king.

[40] Is playing, or sporting, not angry. He is enjoying himself, as their chiefs do on great festivals, when it is said, " Inkosi i d*h*lala umkosi," The chief is playing a festival.

It is worth noting that So or Khevioso is the thunder god of the West African natives; and, says Capt. Burton, " according to Barbot, on the Gold Coast, (I have heard the same everywhere from that place to the Camaroons,) ' when it thunders they say the Deity—with reverence be it spoken—is diverting himself with his wives.' " *(Burton. A Mission to the King of Dahome. Vol. II., p. 142.)*

[41] That is, by lightning.

yo ; kepa si ng' azi 'luto olu nga si sindisa ekutshayweni. Si nga boni nakcula e lona s' ona ngalo kuyo na kunkulunkulu. Si ti, "Si lungile, loko e si kw enzayo konke si ku nikwe Unkulunkulu."

Kepa leyo 'nkosi e pezulu e sa y azi ngokuba izulu li duma, si ti, "I ya d*h*lala inkosi," a si tsho nokuba i vela kunkulunkulu. Unkulunkulu si ya tsho yena ukuti u ukuk*q*ala ; yona a si kw azi okwayo. Kwa *h*lala ilizwi kodwa lezulu lelo ; a s' azi ukuhamba kwayo nemibuso yayo. Ukutshaya loko e sa kw aziyo, ngokuti kumuntu ow esabayo, "Ini ukuba w esabe lapa inkosi i zid*h*lalela ? W one ni kuyo na ?" Kupela. A ku *h*langani loko 'kwazi kwetu nokukankulunkulu nokwayo. Ngokuba okukankulunkulu, si nga ku landalauda ; okwayo si nge ku lande kakulu, ku nga ba kancane nje. S' azisa

but we know nothing that can save us from being smitten. Neither do we see in what respect we have sinned either in his sight or in that of Unkulunkulu. We say, "We are righteous, for all that we do we were permitted to do by Unkulunkulu."[42]

And as regards that heavenly king whom we know because the heaven thundered, saying, "The king is playing," we do not say also that he springs from Unkulunkulu. We say that Unkulunkulu was first ; we do not know what belongs to that king. There remained[43] that word only about the heaven ; we know nothing of his mode of life, nor of the principles of his government. His smiting is the only thing we knew, because we said to a man who was afraid, "Why are you afraid when the king is playing for his own pleasure ? What sin have you done in his sight ?" That is all. There is no connection between our knowledge of Unkulunkulu and of him. For we can give some account of what belongs to Unkulunkulu ; we can scarcely give any account of what belongs to the heavenly king. We know

---

[42] That is, we live in accordance with the laws and conditions of our nature.

[43] This implies that there might have been once other words which are now lost.

okukankulunkulu, ngokuba yena wa be kona kulo 'm*h*laba, izindaba zake si nga zi landa. Ilanga nenyanga sa ku nika Unkulunkulu lapa, nezulu li kona sa li nika Unkulunkulu. Kodwa leyo 'nkosi, noma i *h*lezi kulo, a si tshongo ukuti elayo ; ngokuba sa ti konke kw enziwe Unkulunkulu.

Ku nge ti ngokuba nam*h*la si zwa si tshelwa i ni ngale 'nkosi e pezulu, si k*q*ale ukuba si ti konke okwayo ; loko okwalabo aba si tshelayo ; tina sa si nga tsho ukuba y' enza konke, sa si ti Unkulunkulu kupela. Kepa tina bantu, noma abanye abafundisi ba si tshela ngokuti le 'nkosi u ye Unkulunkulu lowo, tina a si tshongo ukuba Unkulunkulu u pezulu ; sa ti, wa ba, wa fa; kupela okwetu.

UMPENGULA MBANDA.

much of what belongs to Unkulunkulu, for he was on this earth, and we can give an account of matters concerning him. The sun and moon we referred to Unkulunkulu together with the things of this world ; and yonder heaven we referred to Unkulunkulu. But we did not say that the heaven belonged to this king, although he dwells there ; for we said all was made by Unkulunkulu.

It is not proper, because we now hear from you about that king of heaven, that we should begin to say all is his [as though that belonged to our original opinions] ;[44] that knowledge is theirs who tell us ; for our parts, we used not to say that the king of heaven made all things, we said that Unkulunkulu alone made them. And we black men, although some missionaries tell us that this king and that Unkulunkulu is the same, did not say that Unkulunkulu was in heaven ; we said, he came to be,[45] and died ; that is all we said.

[44] He means to say, It would not be right because you have told us what we did not before know about a heavenly Lord, that we should claim to have known more than we really did before you came. We knew nothing about him, but that he dwelt above, and presided over the thunder.

[45] This is the exact meaning of *wa ba*. He came to be, that is, came into being.

Loku 'kutsho kwabantu abamnyama ukuti Unkulunkulu, noma Uhlanga, noma Umenzi, lelo 'zwi linye. Kepa loku 'kutsho kwabo a ku nanhloko; ku amanqindi nje. Ngokuba izindaba zonke ezi ngaye Unkulunkulu, kubantu abamnyama a ku ko 'muntu kubo, noma amakosi wona, e namandhla okuveza indaba, ukuba nabantu ba i kqonde ukuma kwayo uma i mi kanjani na. Kepa ukwazi kwetu a ku si kqubi ukuba si ku bone izimpande zako lapa ku mila kona; a si lingi uku zi bona; uma ku kona o kcabangayo, ku be kuncinyane nje, a yeke, a dhlulele kw a ku bona ngamehlo; na loko a ku bona ngamehlo ka kqondi 'kuma kwako uma ku mi kanjani na. Ku njalo ke ukuma kwaleyo 'ndaba kankulunkulu e si i tshoyo. Si ti si ya kw azi e si ku bona ngamehlo; kepa uma ku kona aba bona ngenhliziyo, ba nga si kupa masinyane kuloko e si ti si ya ku bona noku ku kqonda futi.

Ukuma kwetu kwokukqala na lezo 'zindaba zikankulunkulu si nge zi hlanganise naloku 'kuhamba kwetu e sa ba nako ngemuva kwa-

When black men say Unkulunkulu or Uthlanga or the Creator they mean one and the same thing. But what they say has no point; it is altogether blunt.[46] For there is not one among black men, not even the chiefs themselves, who can so interpret such accounts as those about Unkulunkulu as to bring out the truth, that others too may understand what the truth of the matter really is. But our knowledge does not urge us to search out the roots of it; we do not try to see them; if any one thinks ever so little, he soon gives it up, and passes on to what he sees with his eyes; and he does not understand the real state of even what he sees. Such then is the real facts as regards what we know about Unkulunkulu, of which we speak. We say we know what we see with our eyes; but if there are any who see with their hearts, they can at once make manifest our ignorance of that which we say we see with our eyes and understand too.

As to our primitive condition and what was done by Unkulunkulu we cannot connect them with the course of life on which we entered when he ceased to be.

---

[46] It is altogether blunt. The natives not only use our saying that a thing is without point, but also the opposite, it is blunt,—that is, it does not enter into the understanding; it is unintelligible.

ke. Indhlela yake Unkulunkulu ngokweduka kwetu ku njengokuba a i zi kitina; i ya le lapo si ng' aziko.

Kepa ngi ti mina, uma ku kona umuntu o ti u namandhla okwazi izindaba zikankulunkulu, ngi nga ti u ya z' azi njengokuba si mw azi, ukuba wa si pa konke. Kepa loku 'ku si pa kwake a ku nandhlela kitina yalezi 'zinto e si nazo. Ngaloko ke uma e ti umuntu u ya z' azi indaba zake, e tsho ngaloko e si ku bonayo, ngi nga ti ku nga ba kuhle uku mw azi kwake ukuba a ngene kuleyo 'ndhlela lapa nati si tshoyo ukuti Unkulunkulu, Umvelinqangi, wa si pa izinto zonke, e si pa ngokuba e ti kakulu u si pa nje, nokuba si be abantu, 'enzela ukuze si be nento e yona a s' enzela yona.

Ku ngaloko ngi ti mina ka ko 'muntu pakati kwetu o nga ti u ya z' azi izindaba zikankulunkulu;

The path of Unkulunkulu, through our wandering, has not, as it were, come to us; it goes yonder whither we know not.

But for my part I should say, if there be any one who says he can understand the matters about Unkulunkulu, that he knows them just as we know him, to wit, that he gave us all things. But so far as we see, there is no connection between his gift and the things we now possess. So then if any one says he knows all about Unkulunkulu, meaning that he knows them by means of what we see, I should say it would be well for him to begin where we begin, and travel by the path we know until he comes to us; for we say, Unkulunkulu, the First Outcomer, gave us all things, and that he gave them to us and also made us men, in order that we should possess the things which he made for us.[47]

I say then that there is not one amongst us who can say that he knows all about Unkulunkulu;

---

[47] This is a most difficult piece of Zulu, which has been necessarily translated with great freedom; a literal translation would be wholly unintelligible to the English reader. I have produced the above translation under the immediate direction of the native who first dictated it to me. What he means to say is this, that they really know nothing more about Unkulunkulu than that he made all things, and gave them to mankind; having made men proper for the things, and the things proper for the men; but that there is not known to be any connection between the present state of things and the primitive gift of the creator.

ngokuba si tsho ngaloku ukuti, "Impela se s' azi igama lodwa lake ; indhlela yake a yona e s' enzele ukuze si hambe ngayo, a si sa i boni ; se ku mi ukukcabanga kodwa ngezinto e si zi tandayo ; kulukuni ukuzahlukanisa nazo, se si m enza ikæoki, ngokuba ububi lobo si bu tanda ngokwetu si ya namatela kakulu kubo ngokuzikqinisa." Uma ku kona izwi eli ti, "Le 'nto a i fanele ukuba u nga y enza ; uma u y enza, u ya 'kuba u ya zihlaza ;" kepa si y enze ngokuti, "Loku y' enziwa Unkulunkulu le into na, ububi bwayo bu ngapi na?"

Njengaloku sa zeka abafazi abaningi ngokuti, "Wau ! si nge zincitshe kuloku 'kudhla okungaka Unkulunkulu u si pe kona ; a si zenzele nje." Kepa lelo 'zwi lokuba uma si tanda ukungena ebubini si ngena ngaye, si be njengabantu aba sa pete ukutsho kwake ; kanti se si tula si zenzele kodwa, s' enza ngaye ; kepa a si s' azani naye Unkulunkulu, na loko a tanda ukuba si kw enze ngoku s' enza kwake.

for we say, "Truly we know nothing but his name ; but we no longer see his path which he made for us to walk in ;[48] all that remains is mere thought about the things which we like ;[49] it is difficult to separate ourselves from these things, and we make him a liar, for that evil which we like of our own accord, we adhere to with the utmost tenacity." If any one says, "It is not proper for you to do that ; if you do it you will disgrace yourself ;" yet we do it, saying, "Since it was made by Unkulunkulu, where is the evil of it ?"

Just as we married many wives saying, "Hau ! we cannot deny ourselves as regards the abundance[50] which Unkulunkulu has given us : let us do just what we like." And if we wish to enter into sin, we enter into it in his name, and are like people who are still in possession of his word ; but we do not really possess it, but do our own will only, doing it in his name ; but we have no union with Unkulunkulu, nor with that which he wished we should do by creating us.

[48] That is, we are not acquainted with any laws which he left us for the regulation of our lives.

[49] That is, we do not trouble ourselves to ask what he willed or what was his purpose in creating us, but simply do just what pleases us, and make our own wills the measure and determiner of our actions.

[50] Lit., abundance of food.

A si banga nako, tina bantu abamnyama, ukuba si bone ubukulu bukankulunkulu, nokuba wa si tanda ngokuba wa s' enza. Kepa yena si ya m bonga ngezwi lokuba uma si ya d*h*la si y' esuta, noma si ya dakwa, noma si ya zenzela loko e si tanda ukuzenzela; si se njengabantwana be shiyiwe uyise nonina; bona se be ya 'kuzenzela loko a be be nga yi 'ku kw enza, uma uyise u se kona nonina; kepa ba se be kw enza, ngokuba be ti, i*h*lane, a ba bonwa 'muntu.

Uku m bonga kwetu Unkulunkulu i loku, ukuba uma ku kona umuntu o funa uku si sola ngokuti, loku si kw enza ngani na, si ya 'kuti kuye masinyane, " Kepa, loku wena u ti, a ku fanele uma kw enziwe; kepa okubi Unkulunkulu wa ku veza ngani?" A yeke omunye. Ku njalo ke uku m bonga kwetu. A si m bongi ngokuba si ti Unkulunkulu ka si londe njalo end*hl*eleni yake ukuba si ngu ko*hl*wa i yo; se si m bonga ngokudakwa na ngokwesuta lezo 'zinto e si z' enza ngobubi.

We black men could not see the greatness of Unkulunkulu, nor that he loved us by creating us. And we worship[51] him when we eat and are filled, or when we get drunk, or do our own will in matters in which we love to have our own will; and are now like children who have no father or mother, who have their own wills about things which they would not do, if their father and mother were still living; but they do it, for they imagine they are in a wilderness where no one can see them.

This is the way in which we worship Unkulunkulu. When any one would find fault with us, asking us why we do so-and-so, we should say to him at once, "But since you say it is not proper that this thing should be done, why did Unkulunkulu create what is evil?" And the other is silent. That is how we worship him. We do not worship him by praying Unkulunkulu to keep us ever in his path, that we might never forget it; but we now worship him by drunkenness and a greedy pursuit of those things which we do by our own wickedness.[52]

---

[51] This is said ironically in contradiction of statements which are sometimes made that Unkulunkulu is an object of worship.

[52] All this is intended to show that the name of Unkulunkulu is only used as an excuse for evil, and never as an incentive to do good.

Kepa a ku ko 'zibongo e si m bonga ngazo njengaloku amadhlozi si wa bonga ngezibongo zokuti nokuti nokuti. Ku njalo ke ngi ti mina, uma ku kona o tshoyo ukuti, "Yebo, uma u funa indhlela kankulunkulu, ngi se nayo," ngi nga ti, "O, indaba kanti i sa hlelekile, si se za 'uke si bone lapo s' ahlukana kona nankulunkulu; si bone nokutsho kwetu ngokuti, ' Unkulunkulu lezi 'zinto wa z' enza nje, ngokuba zinhle.' "

Ngi ti mina Unkulunkulu ka se njengomenzi, ngokuba si y' ona ngaye, si mw enza o yena a s' enzele ububi bonke; kanti a ku njalo, ku se ku njalo ngokuba lezo 'zinto se kulukuni ukuzahlukanisa nazo, si sizakale ngokuti, "O, a ku 'keala noma ku tiwa ng' enze kabi; kepa mina ngi ti Unkulunkulu wa e nge 'kuvezi okubi, noma be tsho, kuhle nje."

I loko ke ukutsho kwami e ngi tsho ngako uma umuntu e ti, "Ngi se nonkulunkulu, izindaba zake." Ngi ti bonke abantu ba nga tanda ukuba lowo 'muntu o tsho njalo, 'ke b' eze 'ku m bona noku mu zwa; loku tina se si ze si bonge amadhlozi nje, ngokuba si

But there are no praise-giving names with which we praise him similar to the great number of them, with which we praise the Amadhlozi. For my part, then, if any one says, " Yes, if you seek the path of Unkulunkulu, I am still acquainted with it," I should say, " O, the matter, forsooth, is now set in order, now we shall see where we separated from Unkulunkulu; and perceive too what we meant by saying, ' Unkulunkulu made these things because they are good.' "

For my part I say that Unkulunkulu is no longer like the Creator, for we sin in his name, and maintain that he made all evil for us; but it is not so, but it now appears to be so, because it is now difficult to separate ourselves from those things, and we are helped by saying, " O, it is no matter, although they say I have done wrong; but I say Unkulunkulu was unable to create what is evil, and although they say it is evil, it is really good."

This, then, is what I maintain, if any one says he understands all about Unkulunkulu. I say all men would be glad to go to the man who says this to see him and to hear him; for in process of time we have come to worship the Amadhlozi only, because we knew

koʜlwe ukuba si nga ti ni ngonkulunkulu; loku si nga s' azi nokwaʜlukana kwetu naye, nezwi a si shiya nalo. I ngaloko si zifunela amadʜlozi, ukuze si libale si nga ʜlali si kcamanga ngonkulunkulu, ukuti, "Unkulunkulu wa si shiya;" nokuti, "U s' enzele ni na?"

Sa zenzela ke amadʜlozi etu, nabanye awabo, nabanye awabo. Se si fulatelene abanye nabanye; a ku se ko o ti, "Dʜlozi lakwabani." Bonke se be ti, "Dʜlozi lakwiti, ekutinitini, u ngi bheke.' Ku njalo ke ukuma kwetu.

Na kulawo 'madʜlozi a si nasiminya; ngoba na labo 'bantu e si ba bongayo, si bonga abantu aba te nabo b' emuka kulo 'mʜlaba, ba be nga vumi ukumuka, ba b' ala kakulu, be si kataza ngokuti a si ba funele izinyanga zoku b' elapa, se si tanda ukuba ba tshone. Na kulezo 'zinyanga si ya ya kuzona si nyakeme ngamazwi a ba si ʜlaba ngawo. Kepa uma e se e file si kqale ukukala nokuzitshaya pansi,

not what to say about Unkulunkulu; for we do not even know where we separated from him, nor the word which he left with us. It is on that account then that we seek out for ourselves the Amadhlozi, that we may not always be thinking about Unkulunkulu, saying, "Unkulunkulu has left us;" or, "What has he done for us?"

So we made for ourselves our own Amadhlozi, and others made theirs for themselves, and others theirs for themselves. And now we have turned the back one on the other; and no one says, "Spirit of such a family." But all now say, "Spirit of our family, of such a tribe, look on me." Such then is our condition.

And as regards the Amadhlozi we do not possess the truth; for as regards the men we worship, we worship men who, when they too were departing from the world, did not wish to depart, but were very unwilling to depart, worrying us excessively, telling us to go and seek doctors for them, and that we wished them to die. And we go to the doctors with sorrowful countenances on account of the words with which they have pierced our hearts. And when one has died we begin to weep and to throw ourselves on the ground to

ukubonakalisa ukuba si dabukile; si be si nga tandi ukuba a si shiye; naye e be nga tandi ukuba a si shiye. Kepa s' ahlukaniswe ukufa.

Ku ti ngangomso loku izolo si be si kala, ku velo isikcana somhloyana, si ti, " Ake si ye 'kuzwa uma loku ku velo nje, ku vela ngani, loku izolo si lahle Ubani." Kepa ku tiwe izazi, "O, Ubani lowo e ni m lahlileyo izolo, u ti, u ti." Kepa si kqale ukuba si m bonge, loku izolo si kalile, a si ku bonanga ukuba u ye 'kuhlangana nabanye abafileyo, ukuba ba s' enzele ugango olukqinileyo olu nga yi 'kufohlwa na ukufa. Lokupela wona amadhlozi si ti ukufa ku kuwo; uma o nga vumi, ku nge ngene. Kepa na loko si ku tsho nje; a si ku bonisisi; uma si funa ukuba si ku kqonde kahle, si y' ahluleka, ngokuba laba 'bantu e si

show that we are sorrowful; we do not wish him to leave us; neither did he wish to leave us. But we have been separated by death.

And on the morrow after the day of our funeral lamentation, if there arise some little omen,[53] we say, " Just let us go to the diviner and hear of him, since this thing has happened, for yesterday we buried So-and-so."[54] And it is said by the knowing ones, " O, that So-and-so, whom you buried yesterday, says so-and-so." And we begin to worship him, although the day before we wept and did not see[55] that he had gone to unite with the rest of the dead, that they might make a strong rampart around us which shall not be penetrated even by death. For we say that death is in the power of the Amadhlozi, and if they do not wish, it cannot enter. And that too we say merely; we do not thoroughly understand it; if we seek thoroughly to comprehend it, we do not succeed, for the men

---

[53] Such as a dog mounting on a hut, or a snake coming and taking up its abode in it. We shall hereafter give an account of their "OMENS."

[54] They suppose the omen is sent to warn them of something respecting the dead, either that he has been killed by witchcraft, or that he has sent it to comfort them by the assurance of his continued regard for them, he being one of the spirits.

[55] Yesterday they saw death only and the loss of their friend; now an omen makes them believe in his continued existence, and that he has united with other spirits to be the rampart of his people.

ti ba si mele, b' a*h*lulwa isifo; kepa si tsho kubantu nabo ab' e-muke kulo 'm*h*laba, be nga tandi uku u shiya; ba donswa ngamand*h*la okufa; a ba tshongo nokuti, " Ni nga si kaleli, lokupela tina si ya 'ku n' enzela ugange ukuze ni nga fi." Ba fa nabo be nga tandi ukufa.

Kepa uma si ba *h*labisa, si ti, "Ukufa okutile a ku pele," ku nga peli, si k*q*ale ukupikisana nabo noku ba pika, ukuti, " A wa ko amad*h*lozi; noma abanye be ti a ko, kepa mina ngi ti awakiti a fa njalo; a ku kona na linye; si ya zihambela nje; a si sizwa 'd*h*lozi."

Kepa na nam*h*la nje ku se njalo; si ya wa vuma, si wa pika; si sa hamba emkatini waloko; a ku ka bi ko okonakona; si z' enza izigabavu njalonjalo; uma si nen*h*lan*h*la si ti, "A kona;" uma si nezinsizi si ti, "A wa ko. Si zipilela nje; a si sizwa 'd*h*lozi."

whom we say are our defenders were conquered by disease; and we say they are our rampart to protect us from death, who have themselves left the world, not wishing to leave it; they were dragged away by the power of death; and they did not tell us not to weep for them, because they were about to make a rampart around us to preserve us from death. They too died against their wish.

But when we sacrifice to them and pray that a certain disease may cease, and it does not cease, then we begin to quarrel with them, and to deny their existence. And the man who has sacrificed exclaims, " There are no Amadhlozi; although others say there are; but for my part I say that the Amadhlozi of our house died for ever; there is not even one left; we just take care of ourselves; there is not a single Idhlozi who helps us."

And it is thus to the present time; we acknowledge them and deny their existence; we still walk between the two opinions; there is not as yet any certainty; we are constantly making fruitless efforts; when we are prosperous we say, " There are Amadhlozi;" if we are in trouble we say, " There are not. We owe life to ourselves alone; we are not helped by the Idhlozi."

Ku njalo ke na nam*h*la nje. Kwaba pakati kwobunzima uma u buza u ti, "Bani, nam*h*la nga ku fumana u nje, lokupela niua ni ti ni namad*h*lozi ?" a nga ti uku ku pendula, "O, wena kabani, ngi yeke nje; a ualabo aba nawo; mina a ngi nalo. Ngi ya bona manje li kona id*h*lozi eli ko eli tanda uma umuntu a ze a be mpofu, a k*g*ede izinto zake." Kepa ku tiwe lapo ku kona id*h*lozi a ku ko 'd*h*lozi.

Uma u d*h*lulela ngapambili kwaba se nen*h*lan*h*la, u ti um*h*laumbe u za 'kuzwa izwi li linye nalo; kepa uma u kuluma nabo nged*h*lozi, u nga ba u ba tunukile, ukuba ba ku tshele ubu*h*le bed*h*lozi, noku ba siza kwalo. U fike

So it is to the present time. If you ask of those who are in trouble, "So-and-so, how is it that I find you in this state, since you say you have Amadhlozi ?" he may say in answer, "O, Son of So-and-so, just leave me alone; the Amadhlozi dwell with those who have them; as for me, I have no Idhlozi. I now see that there is a kind of Idhlozi that wishes a man to become poor, and make an end of his property."[56] Thus it is said by those who believe in the Idhlozi, that it has no existence.[57]

If you pass onward to those who are in prosperity, you think perhaps that you shall hear one and the same word there too; but when you speak with them about the Idhlozi, you bring up old thoughts,[58] and they speak to you about the excellence of the Idhlozi, and the assistance it has given them. You have come to a place

---

[56] That is, by sacrificing to the Amadhlozi, and by paying the diviners and doctors.

[57] Even those who really believe in the Amadhlozi, irreverently deny their existence in time of trouble. Compare with this the following extract from the French ballad, Lénore:—

—"O ma fille! invoquons le Createur suprême;
   Ce qu'il tait est bien fait; il nous garde et nous aime.—
—Et pourtant son courroux nous accable aujourd'hui,
   A quoi sert d' implorer ses bontés souveraines?
   A quoi sert de prier? les prières sont vaines,
   Et ne montent pas jusqu' à lui."

[58] Lit., You perhaps open an old sore; as we say, We have opened his satirical vein, &c.,—that is, have set off on a subject on which they are fond of speaking.

lapo idhlozi li kona kakulu, u kqale ukubona ukuti, "O, kanti okonakona a ku ka fiki; loku ku se ukwesuta ukuti li kona; na loku ukuti a li ko ku vela ngezinsizi."

UMPENGULA MBANDA.

where there is great faith in the Idhlozi, and you begin to see that the people do not yet possess the very truth of the matter; for it is fulness which declares that the Itongo exists; whilst affliction says, it does not exist.[59]

ABANTU abadala ba ti, "Kwa vela Unkulunkulu, wa veza abantu. Wa vela emhlangeni; wa dabuka emhlangeni." Si ti tina bantwana, "Umhlanga u pi na owa vela Unkulunkulu na? Lo ni ti, 'U kona umhlanga,' u kulipi ilizwe na? Loku abantu se be li hamba lonke 'lizwe, u kulipi ilizwe, umhlanga owa dabuka Unkulunkulu u kulipi ilizwe na?" Ba ti ukupendula kwabadala, ba ti, "A si w azi nati; ba kona abadala futi aba tsho umhlanga nabo a ba w azi njalo, umhlanga owa dabula Unkulunkulu." Ba ti ba kqinisile

THE old men say, "Unkulunkulu came into being,[60] and gave being to man. He came out of a bed of reeds; he broke off from a bed of reeds." We children ask, "Where is the bed of reeds out of which Unkulunkulu came? Since you say there is a bed of reeds, in what country is it? For men have now gone into every country; in which of them is the bed of reeds from which Unkulunkulu broke off?" They say in answer, "Neither do we know; and there were other old men before us who said that neither did they know the bed of reeds which broke off[61] Unkulunkulu." They say they speak the

[59] The reader should note that this is an account derived from an educated, intelligent, Christian native.

[60] Came into being,—sprang up,—appeared,—had an origin; with a slight shade of difference in meaning *vela* is used in the same way as *dabula*.

[61] Here my MS. says *dabula*, which makes Umthlanga the active agent in the origin of Unkulunkulu, just as Uthlanga is constantly represented in other forms of the tradition. But the native teacher thinks it a mistake for *dabuka*, a repetition of what is said just above.

u kona um/langa; ba ti ba kqinisile bona ukuti u kona; kodwa tina si ti, "A u ko; loku ilizwe eli nawo si nga l' azi a ba nga li tsho ukuti li sekutini." Ku tiwa Unkulunkulu wa vela, wa zala abantu; wa veza abantu, wa ba zala.

Si ya kuleka kunkulunkulu, si ti, "Ka ngi bheke njalo Unkulunkulu wetu," owa zala aukulu, ukuti obaba-mkulu. Ngokuba owa zala ubaba-mkulu ukoko wami; owa zala ubaba-mkulu kababa Unkulunkulu kambe o pambili.

Kepa lapa a ngi sa kulumi ngalowo 'nkulunkulu owa vela em/langeni; ngi ya kuluma ngonkulunkulu ow' elamana nokoko wami. Ngokuba izind/lu zonke zi nokoko bazo ngokwelamana kwazo, nabo onkulunkulu bazo.

Abadala ba ti, "Um/langa u kona." Kepa upi na um/langa na? A ba tsho ukuti Unkulunkulu, owa vela em/langeni, u kona.

truth in saying, there is a bed of reeds; but we say, there is not; for we do not know the land in which it is, of which they can say, it is in such and such a country. It is said, Unkulunkulu came into being, and begat men; he gave them being; he begat them.

We pray to Unkulunkulu, saying, "May our Unkulunkulu ever look upon us." [The Unkulunkulu] who begat our grandfathers. For he who begat my grandfather, is my great-great-grandfather; and he who begat my father's grandfather is Unkulunkulu, the first of our family.[62]

But here I am no longer speaking of that Unkulunkulu who came out of the bed of reeds; I am speaking of the Unkulunkulu who belonged to the generation preceding my great-great-grandfather. For all families have their great-great-grandfathers by their orders of succession, and their Onkulunkulu.

The old men say, "The bed of reeds still exists." But where is that bed of reeds? They do not say that Unkulunkulu, who sprang from the bed of reeds, still exists.

[62] I have hitherto given the several forms of the tradition in the order of time in which they were written, with the exception of the account given by the young Ibakca, p. 15. This (1860) was the first intimation I received that there are many Onkulunkulu, that each house has its own, and is an object of worship, his name being the chief *isibongo* or surname, by which the Spirits or Amatongo of his family are addressed.

Ba ti, "Ka se ko Unkulunkulu, owa vela emhlangeni." Ba ti, "A si m azi uma u pi na."

Utshange isibongo sakwiti; yena a kqala abantu bakwiti, unkulunkulu wetu, owa kqala indhlu yakwiti. Si kuleka kuyena, si ti, "Matshange! Nina bakwatshange!" Si kuleka kuye uma si tanda 'luto e si lu funayo; si kuleka nabakwiti kwatshange. Si ti uma si tanda inkomo, si ti, "Nina bakwiti." U tole inkomo. "Nina bakwiti, bakwatshange, bakwadumakade!"

UNGQETO WAKWATSHANGE.

They say that Unkulunkulu, who sprang from the bed of reeds, is dead. They say, "We do not know where he is."

Utshange is the praise-giving name of our house; he was the first man of our family,—our Unkulunkulu, who founded our house. We pray to him, saying, "Matshange![63] Ye people of the house of Utshange!" We pray to him for anything we wish to have; we and all of the family of Utshange pray to him. If we wish to have cattle, we say, "Ye people of our house."[64] [And if you pray thus] you will get cattle. We say, "Ye people of our house, people of the house of Utshange, people of the house of Udumakade!"

UMFEZI, a native living in the neighbourhood, called on me. I had never spoken to him on the subject of Unkulunkulu; I availed myself of the opportunity for gaining information. It was very difficult to write anything *seriatim;* I was therefore obliged to content myself by writing what I could, and remembering what I could.

He said, "Unkulunkulu wa vela emhlangeni." Unkulunkulu sprang from a bed of reeds.

But he did not know where the bed of reeds was. But, "Wa vel' enzansi," that is, by the sea; that is, the bed of reeds from which he sprang was by the sea-side. He also said, "Kwa dabuka abantu,

[63] Matshange! that is, a plural of Utshange, meaning all his people.

[64] The prayer is either in this simple form of adoration, the suppliant taking it for granted that the Amatongo will know what he wants; or the thing he wants is also mentioned, as "Ye people of our house! cattle."

be datshulwa Unkulunkulu." Men broke off, being broken off by Unkulunkulu. He added,

Abany' abantu ba ti, ba boħlwa inkomo. Abanye ba ti ba dabuka etsheni ela kqekezeka kabili, ba puma. Unkulunkulu wa ba kqezula etsheni.

Some men say that they were belched up by a cow.[65] Others that they sprang from a stone[66] which split in two and they came out. Unkulunkulu split them out of a stone.

When asked if they prayed to Unkulunkulu, he replied,

Ka ba ko aba kcela kunkulunkulu. Ba kcela kubakubo nje.

There are none who pray to Unkulunkulu. They pray to their own people only.

I enquired what they said about thunder; he said,

Si ti, "O nkosi, si dhle ni? S' one ni? A s' oni 'luto."

We say, "O Lord, what have we destroyed? What sin have we done? We have done no sin."

He also related the following legend of the manner in which Amabele (native corn) was introduced as an article of food:—

The first woman that Unkulunkulu produced had a child before any of the rest. There was another woman who was jealous when she saw her with a child, and hated her and wished to poison her. She looked about her to find some plant possessed of poisonous properties; she saw the Amabele, which at that time was not cultivated, but grew like the grass. She plucked the seeds, and gave them to the woman. She watched, expecting to see her die; but she did not die, as she had hoped, but grew plump, and better-looking than ever. At length she asked her if the Amabele was nice. She replied, "Nice indeed!" And from that time the women cultivated Amabele, and it became an article of food.

[65] We are not to understand this as a tradition of the origin of men. It is a saying among the natives when they see an exquisitely handsome man, or when they wish to flatter a chief, to say, "Ka zalwanga; wa boħlwa inkomo nje," He was not born; he was belched up by a cow; that is, he did not go through the ordinary and tedious and painful process of being born, but came into being already a perfected man.

[66] Compare this with the Jewish simile, "Look unto the rock whence ye were hewn," that is, to Abraham, their father. (Isaiah li. 1, 2.) Here again we have the notion of Unkulunkulu being the *means of helping the human race into being*.

The next legend gives an account of the mode in which men first became acquainted with food, and of two female Onkulunkulu; the two following give—the first an account of the origin of medicines, and the second of two male Onkulunkulu.

Mina nolala, kwa ti lapa ngi se umfana omncinane kakulu, ng' ezwa indaba ngendoda yakwiti endala. Unok*q*opoza wa ti :

Kwa ku kona ekuk*q*aleni abafazi be babili em*h*langeni ; omunye wa zala umuntu om*h*lope, nomunye wa zala omnyama. Labo 'bafazi bobabili ku tiwa i bona be Unkulunkulu wamandulo. Kepa um*h*langa lowo sa u buza ; ka tsho ukuti u sekutini ; wa ti, "Nami ngi u zwe ngabadala ; a ku ko 'muntu o y aziyo indawo yalo 'm*h*langana." Futi tina bantwana aba zalwa abadala si be si nge njengabanam*h*la nje ; bona be zikataza ngokufunisisa ukwazi : tina si be si nga buzi kumuntu omkulu ; uma e si tshela indaba, si be si zwa nje ngokuba sa si iziula ; si ya bona manje loko e nga sa si ku buza, a sa ku buza ngobuula betu.

I, Unolala,[67] [say] that when I was still a very little child, I heard numerous old tales of our people. Unok*q*opoza said :

There were at first two women in a bed of reeds ; one gave birth to a white man, and one to a black man. It is said that these two women were the Unkulunkulu[68] of the primitive men. And as regards that bed of reeds, we enquired of him, but he did not say, it is in such a place ; but he said, "I too heard it of the old men ; no man knows the situation of that bed of reeds." Further, we children who are the offspring of men of old were not like those of the present time, who worry themselves with finding out knowledge : for our parts we used not to question a great man ; when he told us a tale we used just to listen because we were fools ; we now see that which we ought to have enquired about, but about which we did not enquire because of our folly.

Kepa labo 'bafazi ba zala aba-

And those women gave birth to

[67] A common mode of commencing a narrative.

[68] He here speaks of the two women as being *one unkulunkulu* of primitive men. So in conversation with another heathen native, he spoke of the first man and first woman, together, as *one unkulunkulu*.

ntwana, ku nge ko 'kudhla okudhliwayo. Ba bona amabele nombila namatanga, ku vutiwe. Umfazi wa ka itanga, wa li peka, wa funza umntwana, e nga tsho ukuba ukudhla, e ti ubuti, kumbe a nga fa masinyane, a nga zinge e m kataza ngokukala, e kalela ukudhla. Kepa lelo 'tanga la m kulupalisa umntwana; wa kqabuka umfazi nomunye ukuti, "O, kanti si ti ukufa nje, kanti ukudhla." Kw' aziwa ke amabele nombila namatanga ukuba ukudhla kanti. Ba wa dhla, ba kulupala. Ba wa vuna, ba wa londoloza, ba sizakala.

UNOLALA ZONDI.

children, there being no food which was eaten. They saw corn, and maize, and pumpkins; they were all ripe. One of the women took a pumpkin and boiled it, and gave her child a mouthful, not regarding it as food, but poison, and thinking perhaps he would die at once, and no longer worry her without ceasing by his crying, when he was crying for food. But the pumpkin fattened the child; and the other woman looked and said, "O, forsooth, we thought it was nothing but poison, and in fact it was food." Thus then it became known that corn and maize and pumpkins are food. They ate them and became fat. They harvested them and hoarded them and were helped.

EKUKQALENI kwa tiwa, "Insimu y' esuka, i sukela pezulu."[69] Kepa ke wa ti omunye umfazi, wa ti, "Ma si muke, si yosika umhlanga." Wa fika wa t' omunye, wa ti ukuba ba u sike umhlanga, "I ni ke na?" wa ti, "Nendhlela eyani na?" Wa vela umuntu, wa ti, "Eyetu." Wa tsho e se sesizibeni emanzini. Wa ti omunye, "U si buza nje: a u s' azi ini na?" Wa ti, "Si hlezi lapa nje, si hlezi emzini wetu." Kwa tiwa, "Ni ng' abakwabani nina na?" Wa ti, "Si

ONCE on a time in the beginning, a woman said, "Let us go and cut reeds." Another said when they were cutting reeds, "What is this? And of what is this the path?" A man appeared and said, "It is ours." He said this, he being still in the pool, in the water. Another said, "You ask of us: do you not know us? We are just living here in our kraal." They asked, "Of what nation are you?" He replied, "We are the people of

[69] A mode of beginning a fiction.

ng' abakwazimase." "Inkosi yenu ng' ubani ?" "Usango-li-
ngenzansi." "Kupuka ke. Po,
ni ḣlalele ni ngapansi, abantu se
be ngapezulu nje na?" Ba ti,
"Si ḣlezi nemiti yetu." "N' enza
ni ngayo na?" "S' elap' amakosi." B' emuka ke abafazi, ba ya
'kutshela inkosi. Ba ti, "Nampa
'bantu. Be ti, ng' abakazimase.
Ba ti, b' elapa amakosi. Ba ti,
umuntu o ng' eza 'ku ba tata, a
ng' eza nenoni, a fike a li tshise
ngapezu kwesiziba. Uzimase ka
yi 'kukupuka nemiti naa ku nga
tshiswa inoni."

Ya fika ke leyo 'nkosi, ya ba
nenkomo, ya ḣlatshelwa kona, kwa
tshiswa inoni. Wa kupuka ke
Uzimase nemiti yake, w' elapa ke
emakosini.

Wa ti ke naa e ya 'kumba imiti,
wa binca isikaka, 'esaba uba ku
vele amapambili esifazeneni. Kepa ke ba ti ukuvela, abakubo aba
be puma kukqala ba ti, "U ya u
fikile ke lesi 'sikakana." Ba ti
abakwiti, "U ya se ba ḣlezi ngapezulu ke la 'malembana." Se ku

Uzimase." "Who is your king?"
"Usango-li-ngenzansi."[70] "Come
up then. But why are you living
underground, since people are now
living above?" They said, "We
are living here with our medicines." "What do you do with
them?" "We administer medicines to kings." So the women
went away to tell the king. They
said, "Behold, there are men.
They say they are the people of
Uzimase. They say they administer medicines to kings. They say
the man who goes to fetch them
must take fat, and burn it on the
bank of the pool. Uzimase will
not come up with his medicines if
fat is not burnt."

So the king went with an ox,
and it was slaughtered at that
place, and the fat was burnt. And
so Uzimase came up with his
medicines, and administered medicines among kings.

When he went to dig up medicines, he put on a petticoat, fearing to expose himself to women.
But on his appearance, the people
who came up first said, "This
little petticoat has at length come."
Our people said in reply, "These
little picks are living above."[71] So

[70] Lower-gate-man.

[71] This shows that the natives believe in a succession of emigra-
tions from below of different tribes of men, each having its own
Unkulunkulu.

bangwa imiti ke nabakupuka ngapansi naba ngapezulu. Ba ti kwabakwiti, "Abakwasikakana." Ba ti ke kwabakubo, "Abakwalembe."

Ba be zalwa indoda nje; indoda leyo Umbala. B' a*h*luka ke; abanye ba hamba kwenye, nabanye ba hamba kwenye.

Ngi ti ke Uzimase Unkulunkulu wakwiti. A ngi m azi omunye Unkulunkulu wabantu. Kodwa nowakwiti w' a*h*luka o*h*langeni o kw' a*h*luka kulo abantu bonke. Abanye ba ti uma si buza, "Lwa lu 'mibala 'miningi;" ba ti, "Ngen*x*enye lwa lum*h*lope, ngen*x*enye lumnyama, ngen*x*enye lu nama*h*lati." Si ti ke tina, "Nga ba be bona ubuhhwan*q*a lobu, be ti i*h*lati njalo." Ba ti abantu laba naye wa ba veza ngoku ba zala.

USHUNGUIWANE ZIMASE.

there was a dispute about medicines between those who came up from below and those who were already above. Our people were called, "People of the little petticoat." And they called them, "People of the pick."

They were begotten by a man; that man was Umbala. They separated from each other; and some went in one direction, and some in another.

I say, then, that Uzimase is the Unkulunkulu of our tribe. I do not know another[72] Unkulunkulu of all men. But the Unkulunkulu of our tribe was derived from Uthlanga, from whence all people were derived. Some say in answer to our enquiries, Uthlanga was of many colours; they say, "He was white on one side, on the other black; and on another side he was covered with bush." So we say, "Perhaps they spoke of the hairiness of his body, and so called it bush."[73] And people say that he too gave them existence by begetting them.

[72] That is, his name.
[73] Compare this with the fabulous monster Ugung*q*u-kubantwana (*Nursery Tales*, p. 176), or Usilosimapundu (*Id.*, p. 185).

ABANYE ba ti omunye Unkulunkulu wa vela pansi; omunye w' eḥla nenkungu pezulu. A ba m kqondanga lowo ow' eḥla nenkungu. Ba ti, umḥlope ukupela kwake. Ba ti, " Kw' eḥla Ungalokwelitshe." Ba ti, labo abapansi ba m etuka. Wa ti yena, " Ni ng' etuka ni, loku nami ngi umuntu, ngi fana nani nje na ?" Ba ti, kwa tatwa izinkomo lapa 'eḥlele kona; wa ḥlatshiswa; ba ti kodwa, ka zi dḥla; wa dḥl' okwake a fike nako. Wa ḥlala, wa ḥlala, wa ḥlala, wa ḥlala lapo ke. Kwa buya kwa vela inkungu, wa nyamalala, a ba be be sa m bona.

SOME say, one Unkulunkulu came from beneath; and another descended from above in a fog. They did not understand him who came down in a fog. They say he was altogether white. They say, "There descended Ungalokwelitshe."[74] They say, those who were beneath started on seeing him. He said, " Why do you start at me, since I too am a man, and resemble you ?" They say, cattle were taken at the place where he descended, and they slaughtered them for him; but they say he did not eat them; he ate that which he brought with him. He stayed there a long time. Another fog came, and he disappeared, and they saw him no more.

Nga ngi zwa le 'ndaba kumadigane, uyise-mkulu kamdutshane, inkosi enkulu yamabakca. Nga ng' isikcaka sake esikulu.

USHUNGUIWANE ZIMASE.

I heard this tale from Umadigane, Umdutshane's grandfather, the great chief of the Amabakca. I used to be his chief servant.

Two natives, perfect strangers to us both, came up as I was asking Umpengula some questions on the subject of the previous statements. They overheard what I was saying, and asked, "Are you talking about the origin of men ?" I replied that was the subject of our conversation, and asked if they could tell us any thing about it. The elder of them replied, " Ba vela emḥlangeni," They sprang from a bed of reeds.

I asked what he knew of Unkulunkulu; he replied,

[74] That is, He-who-came-from-the-other-side-of-the-rock.

Wa ba veza abantu, naye e veziwe em*h*langeni. | He gave origin to men, he too having had an origin given[75] him from a bed of reeds.

I asked, " Wa vezwa ubani na ?" Who gave him an origin ? He said he did not know ; and added,

Unkulunkulu wa tshela abantu wa ti, " Nami ngi vela em*h*langeni." | Unkulunkulu told men saying, "I too sprang from a bed of reeds."[76]

I asked how men were produced, and got for a reply only a repetition of the statement that they sprang from a bed of reeds.—I asked if he had heard anything of a woman ; he replied,

Unkulunkulu wa vela em*h*langeni, nomfazi wa vela em*h*langeni emva kwake. Ba 'bizo linye ukuti Unkulunkulu. | Unkulunkulu sprang from a bed of reeds, and a woman (a wife) sprang from the bed of reeds after him. They had one name, viz., Unkulunkulu.[77]

I then took him to my study, and wrote the following at his dictation :—

S' EZWA ku tiwa Unkulunkulu wa vela em*h*langeni. Kwa vela indoda kukqala ; ya landelwa umfazi. Ku tiwa Unkulunkulu bo- | WE heard it said Unkulunkulu sprang from a bed of reeds. There first appeared a man, who was followed by a woman. Both are

[75] This is the nearest rendering we can give to *veziwe ;* it is equivalent to *created.* It is passive, and necessarily implies an agent by which he had an origin given to him. No native would hear such a phrase as " Naye e veziwe," He too having had an origin given him, without putting the question, By whom ?

[76] Unkulunkulu was an unbegotten though a created man. He was the first man ; by this statement he is to be understood as deprecating the ascription to himself of something higher and more exalted. He is, as it were, telling his children the history of creation as he had witnessed it. They appear to be desirous of making him the creator ; but he replies, " No ; I too sprang from the bed of reeds."

[77] This is very precise. The first man and woman sprang, the man first and then the woman, from the bed of reeds ; and both are called by one name, Unkulunkulu ; that is, Great-great-grandparent. According to Moses, the male and female were both called Adam. (Gen. v. 3.)

babili. Ya ti, "Ni si bona nje si vela emhlangeni," i tsho kubantu aba vela ngemva. Abantu bonke, ku tiwa, abantu bonke ba vela kunkulunkulu, yena owa vela kukqala.

Ku tiwa Unkulunkulu wa vela emfundeni, lapo kwa ku kona umhlanga emhlabatini lapa. Abantu ba vela kunkulunkulu ngokuzalwa.

Umvelinqangi u yena Unkulunkulu. Umhlaba wa u kona kukqala, e nga ka bi ko Unkulunkulu. Wa vela kuwo emhlangeni.

Izinto zonke za vela naye Unkulunkulu emhlangeni; konke, nezinyamazane namabele, konke ku vela naye Unkulunkulu.

Wa li bona ilanga se li bumbeke, wa ti, "Nant' ubakqa olu za 'ku ni kanyisela uba ni bone." Wa bona inkomo, wa ti, "Nanzi inkomo. Dabuka ni, ni bone inkomo, zi be ukudhla kwenu, ni dhle inyama namasi." Wa bona inyamazane, wa ti, "Inyamazane

named Unkulunkulu. The man said, "You see us because we sprang from the bed of reeds," speaking to the people who came into being after him. It is said all men sprang from Unkulunkulu, the one who sprang up first.[78]

It is said Unkulunkulu had his origin in a valley where there was a bed of reeds in this world. And men sprang from Unkulunkulu by generation.

Umvelinqangi is the same as Unkulunkulu. The earth was in existence first, before Unkulunkulu as yet existed. He had his origin from the earth in a bed of reeds.

All things as well as Unkulunkulu sprang from a bed of reeds, —every thing, both animals and corn, every thing, coming into being with Unkulunkulu.

He looked on the sun when it was finished,[79] and said, "There is a torch which will give you light, that you may see." He looked on the cattle and said, "These are cattle. Be ye broken off,[80] and see the cattle; and let them be your food; eat their flesh and their milk." He looked on wild animals and said, "That is such an

---

[78] He is called "he who sprang up at first" to distinguish him from the many other Onkulunkulu who in the progress of generation sprang up after him.

[79] Lit., worked into form as a potter works clay.

[80] The simile here is that men were existing as young bulbs ready to separate from the parent bulb.

yokuti." Wa ti, "Ind*h*lovu leya." Wa ti, "In*q*umba leya." Wa u bona umlilo, wa ti, "U base ni, ni peke, n' ote, ni d*h*lo ng*a*wo inyama." Wa ku bona konke, wa ti, "Ukuti nokuti konke."

animal. That is an elephant. That is a buffalo." He looked on the fire and said, "Kindle it, and cook, and warm yourself; and eat meat when it has been dressed by the fire." He looked on all things and said, "So-and-so is the name of every thing."

Kwa vela indoda, kwa vela umfazi. Kwa tiwa Unkulunkulu bobabili igama labo. Ba vela elu*h*langeni, u*h*langa lolu olu kemanzini.[81] U*h*langa lw' enziwa Umvelin*q*angi. Umvelin*q*angi wa milisa utshani, wa veza imiti, wa veza zonke izilwane nenkomo, nenyamazane, nenyoka, nenyoni, namanzi, nentaba.

W' enza u*h*langa; u*h*langa lwa

There sprang up a man and a woman. The name of both was Unkulunkulu. They sprang from a reed, the reed which is in the water. The reed was made by Umvelin*q*angi. Umvelin*q*angi caused grass and trees to grow; he created all wild animals, and cattle, and game, and snakes, and birds, and water, and mountains.

He made a reed;[82] the reed

---

[81] *Olu kemanzini.*—The *k* is used among some tribes, as the Amakuza, the Amalala, &c., instead of *s*, as among the Amazulu.

[82] The account here given of Uthlanga is peculiar. The native who gave it, clearly understood by it a reed. Yet one cannot avoid believing that he did not understand the import of the tradition. It is said that Umvelin*q*angi made the reed, and that the reed gave origin to Unkulunkulu and his wife. It is said also that Umvelin*q*angi begat them with a reed *(nohlanga)*; and from a reed *(eluhlangeni).* Both these forms are used of the female in generation. A child is begotten from the woman, or with her. And it is the belief of the native teacher that the real meaning of this tradition is that Umvelin*q*angi made Uthlanga, a female, and with her became the parent of the human race. Uthlanga, therefore, in this form of the tradition, has a feminine import; whilst in others it has a masculine. Yet the same men in speaking of the origin of Umvelin*q*angi (pronounced by this tribe Umvelik*q*angi) said he sprang from Uthlanga.—There is really no contradiction in such statements. For the term Uthlanga is applied not only to the Primal Source of Being, but to any other

veza Unkulunkulu nomfazi wake. | gave origin to Unkulunkulu and source of being, as a father, or to a mother, as in the following sentence:—

| U*h*langa lwend*h*lu yakwabani ubani? Ku tshiwo igama lendoda e in*h*loko yaleyo 'nd*h*lu. A i 'lu*h*langa yodwa; inye nowesifazana; ngokuba a ku ko 'lu*h*langa lwendoda yodwa e nge ko wesifazana. | Who is the Uthlanga of such a family? They answer by giving the name of the man, who is the head of that house. But he is not the Uthlanga by himself; he is the Uthlanga in conjunction with the female; for there is not a man who is an Uthlanga by himself, there being no female. |

Compare this with the following legends of the Hindus, where Brahma corresponds with Umvelinqangi; and where there is the same confusion between Brahma, the Creator,—the First Man,—"and the male half of his individuality." Umvelinqangi is both the Primal Source of Being and the First Man; he is the creator of the first woman and her husband. And Satarupa, "the great universal mother," is equivalent to Uthlanga, the female Unkulunkulu,—the great-great mother of the human race:—

"According to one view, Brahma, the God of Creation, converted himself into two persons, the first man, or the Manu Swayambhuva, and the first woman, or Satarupa: this division into halves expressing, it would seem, the general distinction of corporeal substance into two sexes, and Satarupa, as hinted by the etymology of the word itself, denoting the great universal mother, the one parent of 'a hundred forms.'" *(Hardwick. Op. cit., Vol. I., p. 297.)*

"As the old traditions of their ancestors were gradually distorted, the Hindus appear to have identified the first man (Manu Swayambhuva) with Brahma himself, of whom, as of the primary cause, he was the brightest emanation; while Satarupa, the wife and counterpart of Manu, was similarly converted into the bride of the creative principle itself. Brahma, in other words, was 'confounded with the male half of his individuality.'" *(Id., p. 305.)*

A similar apparent contradiction to that which runs throughout these Zulu legends is also found in the Myth of Prometheus, who though a man—the son of Japetus—is said to be the creator of the human race:—

"Sive hunc divino semine fecit
Ille opifex rerum, mundi melioris origo:
Sive recens tellus, seductaque nuper ab alto
Æthere, cognati retinebat semina cœli.
Quam satus Iapeto, mistam fluvialibus undis
Finxit in effigiem moderantum cuncta deorum."

(Ovid.)

Unkulunkulu wa zala abantu bendulo. Unkulunkulu wa ti, "Mina 'nkulunkulu nomfazi wami si ng' abakamvelin*g*angi. Umvelilin*g*angi wa si zala no*h*langa lu semanzini." Wa ti ekuveleni kwake, "Si ya 'kulw' impi, si gwazane ngemikonto, ku bonakale aba namand*h*la, ow a*h*lulayo omunye; a z' a ti ow a*h*lula omunye a be u yena o inkosi enkulu; ow a*h*luliwe a be umfokazi. Bonke abantu ba ya 'kuya kwo inkosi ow' a*h*lula omunye."

Umvelin*g*angi wa e umuntu owa zala Unkulunkulu clu*h*langeni lu semanzini, owa zala umfazi wake.

Unsukuzonke Memela.

his wife. Unkulunkulu begat primitive men. Unkulunkulu said, "I, Unkulunkulu, and my wife are the offspring of Umvelin*g*angi; he begat us with a reed, it being in the water.[83] At his origin he said, "We will fight and stab each other with spears, that the strongest may be manifest who overcomes the other; and he who overcomes the other shall be the great king; and he who is overcome shall be the dependent. And all people shall wait upon him who is the king who overcomes the other."

Umvelin*g*angi was a man who begat Unkulunkulu by a reed whilst it was in the water, and who begat his wife.

Abadala a ba tshongo ukuba i kona inkosi pezulu. Unkulunkulu a si m azi Unkulunkulu ukuba u nezwi lake. Si pata amatongo. Unkulunkulu izwi lake e sa li patayo elokuti a kona amatongo.

The ancients did not say there is a Lord in heaven. As for Unkulunkulu, we do not know that he left any word for man. We worship the Amatongo. The word of Unkulunkulu which we reverence is that which says there are Amatongo.

[83] *It being in the water.*—That is, according to the notion of the narrator, the reed which Umvelin*g*angi made and by which he begat the first parents of the human race, was in the water. It is probably only another way of saying men sprang from a bed of reeds. But some forms of the tradition represent tribes at least, if not the human race, as being born in or derived from the water. See p. 36.

Si nga sa vela elu*h*langeni ; a s' azi lapa sa bunjwa kona. Tina bantu 'bamnyama sa vela kunye nani 'belungu. Kodwa tina 'bantu 'bamnyama ukuvela kwetu sa vela sa nikwa izinkomo namagejo okulima ngemikono nezikali zokulwa. Kwa tiwa ke, "Okuningi ; se ni ya 'kuzenzela." S' emuka ke, s' eza neno. Nina 'belungu na sala nezinto zonke ezin*h*le nemitoto futi e si nga banga nayo tina.

Sa si va uma si i zekelwa bobaba, be ti nabo ba i va, ba ti, kwa k*q*ala kwa vela umuntu o indoda ; kwa vela emuva umfazi. Kwa ti ngemva kwa vela inkomo ; ya vela i kamba nenkunzi ; kwa ti emva injakazana, kwa ti emva kwa vela inja e induna ; kwa ti ngemva zonke ke izilwanyane ezincinane lezi, nezind*h*lovu, zi vela ngambili njalo.

Kwa ti ngemva kwa vela 'libele ; li ti 'libele uba li vele li ti nya, wa ti lo 'muntu kumfazi, "Ku 'nto o ku bona nje ke, mfazi ndini, e si za 'ku ku d*h*la. Si za 'ud*h*la. Nanti 'libele."

It is as though we sprang from Uthlanga ; we do not know where we were made. We black men had the same origin as you, whitemen. But we black men at our origin were given cattle, and picks for digging with the arms, and weapons of war. It was said, "It is enough ; you shall now shift for yourselves." So we departed, and came in this direction. You whitemen staid behind with all good things and with laws also which we did not possess.

We used to hear it said by our fathers, they too having heard of others, that a man first came into being ; and then a woman after him. After that a cow came into being ; it appeared walking with a bull. After that a female dog, and after her a dog ;[84] and after that all the little animals, and elephants ; all came into being in pairs.

After that corn came into being. When the corn had come to perfection, the man said to the woman, "That which you now see, true[65] woman, is something for us to eat. We shall eat at once. Behold corn."

[84] It is worth notice that the female of animals is represented as preceding the male.

[65] *Ndini*, here translated *true*, is a word rarely met with ; it is used as an appendage to a vocative ; it ascribes reality or speciality to the name to which it is appended. "Mfazi ndini," Thou who art my wife indeed,—*very* wife. Should a bridegroom address the bride thus, it would be an insult, and imply a loss of virtue, and if not founded in truth, would be resented probably by absolute refusal to marry.

Wa buza umfazi, wa ti, "Li ya 'wenziwa njani ukudhliwa kwalo na?" Ya ti indoda, "Lok' u li bona li mile nje ke, ma li yokusikwa. Tat' intonga, u li bule; funa 'litshe, funa elinye li be imbokondo."

Ya ti ke, "Tata, nanku umhlaba, u u bumbe, u z' 'utela 'manzi."

Wa se yena ke e gaula umtana, uluzi; wa se e pehla umlilo ke. Wa ti ke, "Basa ke; se ku za 'upekwa ke." Be se kw' epulwa ke, se ku telwa esitsheni. Ba ya dhla ke bona ke; ba ti ke, "A si zoze sa fa uma si dhle lo 'muti."

Wa ti ke inkomo ke wa zi tshenisa ukuti zi za 'udhla ingca. Wa zi tshenisa izinyamnazane lezi e zi kombisa yona ingca. Wa ti, ma zi nga hlali ekaya lapa.

Ku te mhlenikweni ku dabuka umuntu, wa ti ukwenza emhlangeni apa, wa ti, a ba ku bonanga ukudabuka kwabo; ba bona se be kqukqubele nje emhlangeni, be nga boni 'muntu owa ba veza.

Umhlanga lo ku tiwa ukwenza

The woman asked, saying, "In what way shall it be eaten?" The man replied, "Since you see it growing thus, let it be cut. Take a rod, and thrash it; find a stone, and then find a second that it may be an upper stone."[86]

He said, "There is clay; take it and mould it, and pour water into the vessel."

For his work, he cut down a small tree, the uluzi; and obtained fire by friction. He said, "Make a fire; we can now cook." The food when cooked was taken out of the pot, and put into a vessel. And so they ate, and said, "We shall never die if we eat this corn."

He told the cattle to eat grass; and he told game the same, pointing out to them the same grass. And he told them not to remain all at home.[87]

On the day the first man was created he said, as to what happened to them in the bed of reeds, that they did not see their own creation. When he and his wife first saw, they found themselves crouching in a bed of reeds, and saw no one who had created them. As regards the bed of reeds, on

[86] Viz., for grinding.
[87] Viz., that all were not to be domestic animals.

kwawo umhla ba vela wa kquma; wa t' u dabukile, kwa se ku puma bona ke. Kwa se ku dabuka lwenkomo ke nazo zonke izilwane.
UGXUMELA.

the day they came into being, it swelled,[88] and when it had burst they came out. After that there broke off the uthlanga[89] of cattle and of all other animals.

UKOTO, a very old Izulu, one of the Isilangeni tribe, whose father's sister, Unandi, was the mother of Utshaka, gave me the following accounts:—

NGI ti mina, Unkulunkulu s' azi yena o zala Utshaka; Usenzangakona o zala Utshaka. Ngasemva kukasenzangakona kambe se ku yena Utshaka. Utshaka ka zalanga yena; ka bonanga e ba nabantwana Utshaka. Kwa buya kwa bekwa Udingane. Kwa buya ba bulala Udingane, ba beka Umpande namhla nje, e nga zalanga omabili lawo 'makosi Utshaka nodingane.

I SAY for my part that the Unkulunkulu whom we know is he who was the father of Utshaka; Usenzangakona was Utshaka's father. After Usenzangakona comes Utshaka. Utshaka had no children. After him Udingane was made king. After that they killed Udingane, and made Umpande king to this day, those two kings, Utshaka and Udingane, having no children.

[88] This makes it perfectly clear what the natives understand by Unkulunkulu coming out of the earth. The earth is the mother of Unkulunkulu, the first man, as of every other creature. Compare Milton:—

"The Earth obeyed, and straight
Opening her fertile womb, teemed at a birth
Innumerous living creatures, perfect forms
Limbed and full grown."

Compare also *Ovid. Met.*, B. I., l. 416—421.—This, too, corresponds with the Scripture account of Creation; Gen. i. 20, 24. It is also philosophically correct to refer the origin of things secondarily to the earth. The material organisms of all living things consist of elements derived from the earth. The poetic imagination, to which time and space impose no limits, represents as occurring at a point in time what, it may be, took myriads of years for its production in accordance with laws imposed on the Universe by the fiat of the Creator.

[89] Lwenkomo, i. e., uthlanga. This is worth noting, the uthlanga of cattle,—that is, either the reed—primal source—from which they came; or it may mean, the first pair from which all others sprang.

Ujama kambe o zala Usenza-ngakona, uyise waotshaka, u yena o Unkulunkulu. Ba kona Omve-

Ujama was the father of Use-nzangakona, the father of the Utshakas; it is he who is Unku-lunkulu.[90] There are Omvelinga-

[90] As the question has been raised whether the natives do not call the First Man, or Being, Unkulunkulu, and an Ancestor Ukulu-kulu, in order to prevent all misunderstanding I asked him if he was not speaking of Ukulukulu. He replied Ukulukulu and Unkulu-nkulu is one and the same word; the Amazulu say Unkulunkulu; other tribes Ukulukulu; but the word is one. I enquired what he meant by Unkulunkulu; he answered,

Si bambisise clikakulu o zala ubaba; kepa si ti ukulu ke lowo. Kepa a be kona Unkulunkulu yena o pambili.

We have employed the word great [father] to designate the father of our father; and we call that man great [father]. And there was a great-great [father], to wit, one who was before him.

A si kulumi ngamand/la ukuti Unkulunkulu; si kuluma ngobu-dala kakulu. Ngokuba leli 'lizwi lokuti ukulu a li tsho ukuti mu-dala kabili, li ti mudala kanye; kepa uma ind/lu yalowo i pinda i zale amadodana, a se ya 'kuti nge-lobubili igama, a /langanise neli-kayise nelalowo, a ti unkulunkulu, ukuti omdala kakulu.

We do not speak of power when we say Unkulunkulu, but espe-cially of age. For the word great does not say he was old by twice, but he is old by once; and if the children of that man has children, they will speak by the reduplicated name, and unite their father's name with his, and say Unkulu-nkulu, that is, one who is very old.

What has been said above, then, together with what is here stated, is sufficient to settle all doubt on the subject. I shall not therefore give all the similar statements derived from a great number of different natives to confirm the fact, that by Unkulunkulu or Uku-lukulu they mean a great-great-grandfather, and hence a very ancient man much further removed from the present generation than a great-great-grandfather. Hence it is applied to the founders of dynasties, tribes, and families. The order is as follows:—

Ubaba, my father
Ubaba-mkulu, or Ukulu
Ukoko
Unkulunkulu

Umame, my mother
Umame-mkulu, or Ukulu
Ukoko
Unkulunkulu

Ukoko is a general term for Ancestor who preceded the grandfathers. And Unkulunkulu is a general term for Ancient Men, who "were first" among tribes, families, or kings. See Appendix.

linqangi. Si be si zwa Undabawakakubayeni. Abona aba zala Ujama.

ngi.[91] We used to hear of Undaba,[92] the son of Ukubayeni. They were the ancestors of Ujama.

As it was quite clear that he understood my question on the subject of Unkulunkulu to have reference to the names of the immediate ancestors of the Amazulu, I asked him if he knew anything about the first man. He replied:—

Kwa tiwa kwa puma abantu ababili o*h*langeni. Kwa puma indoda, kwa puma umfazi. Be ti kwa puma yonke imisebenzi le e si i bonayo, neyezinkomo neyokud*h*la,—konke ukud*h*la loko e si ku d*h*layo.

It was said that two people came out of a reed.[93] There came out a man and a woman. At their word[94] there came out all those works which we see, both those of cattle and of food,—all the food which we eat.

[91] Let us note this plural of Umvelinqangi; and that the Omvelinqangi are the fathers of the generation preceding that of the Onkulunkulu; that is, they are the fathers of the Onkulunkulu; that is, the great-great-great-grandfathers.

Usobekase, a petty chief over a portion of the Amabele, when speaking of the origin of things, said they were made by Umvelinqangi; that there was a first man and a first woman; they were Abavelinqangi, and that men sprang from them by generation. He did not use the word Unkulunkulu at all.—Umkqumbela, also, a very old man of the Amangwane, spoke of the Omvelinqangi in the plural, and used the word as strictly synonymous with Unkulunkulu, and, like that word, applicable not only to the first man, but to the founder of families, dynasties, tribes, &c.

[92] The origin of Undaba is thus given by Uncinjana, an Ibele:—

Undaba wa dabuka kupunga, wa zala Usenzangakona. Usenzangakona wa dabuka kundaba, wa zala Utshaka. Undaba Unkulunkulu.

Undaba sprang from Upunga, and was the father of Usenzangakona. Usenzangakona sprang from Undaba, and was the father of Utshaka. Undaba is the Unkulunkulu.

The attention of the Zulu scholar is directed to the use of *dabuka* in this statement.

Whilst travelling lately among a wholly uncultivated tribe, on asking what they meant by the *ukudabuka* of men from Unkulunkulu, they replied, "Ba dabuka esiswini sake," They broke off from her bowels; that is, of the first female Unkulunkulu.

[93] Or, from Uthlanga.

[94] In this remarkable sentence the origin of things is ascribed to the joint word of the man and woman.

He said he did not know their names.—I asked what the natives said of a Creator. He answered :—

Si vele ku tshiwo ku tiwa, "Inkosi i pezulu." Be si zwa ku njalo ke ekuveleni kwetu; inkosi ya be i konjwa pezulu; a si li zwanga ibizo layo; si zwa kodwa ku tiwa inkosi i pezulu. Si zwa ku tiwa umdabuko wezwe kwa tiwa inkosi e pezulu. Ngi te ngi mila kwa ku tiwa umdabuko wezwe u pezulu; abantu be komba pezulu njalo. U koto Mhlongo.	When we were children it was said, "The Lord is in heaven." We used constantly to hear this when we were children; they used to point to the Lord on high; we did not hear his name; we heard only that the Lord is on high. We heard it said that the creator of the world[95] is the Lord which is above. When I was growing up it used to be said, the creator of the world is above; people used always to point towards heaven.

[95] This and two or three other statements are the only instances I have met with of the word Umdabuko for the source of creation, but its meaning is evident. It is equivalent to Umdayi of the Amakqwabe, the Umdali of the Amakxosa, and the Umenzi of the Amazulu.

Umdabuko, however, is derived from *ukudabuka*, to be broken off (see Note 3, page 1), and therefore has a passive signification, and thus differs from Umenzi and Umdali, which are active. It more resembles Uthlanga, and though in some places apparently used for an active creator, would mean rather a passive, though potential source of being,—passive, that is, as a female, or as a seed, which have however wrapped up in them potentially the future offspring.

We may compare with this the legend of the Bechuanas :—

"Morimo, as well as man, with all the different species of animals, came out of a hole or cave in the Bakone country, to the north, where, say they, their footmarks are still to be seen in the indurated rock, which was at that time sand. In one of Mr. Hamilton's early journals, he records that a native had informed him that the footmarks of Morimo were distinguished by being without toes. Once I heard a man of influence telling his story on the subject. I of course could not say that I believed the wondrous tale, but very mildly hinted that he might be misinformed; on which he became indignant, and swore by his ancestors and his king, that he had visited the spot, and paid a tax to see the wonder; and that, consequently, his testimony was indubitable. I very soon cooled his rage by telling him that as I should likely one day visit those regions, I should certainly think myself very fortunate if I could get him as a guide to that wonderful source of animated nature. Smiling, he said, 'Ha, and I shall show you *the*

Ungwadi, Ujani, Umasumpa, Umatiwana, Uzikali, ubaba. Ungwadi unkulunkulu. Ujani a zala Umasumpa. A ti Umasumpa a zala Umatiwana. A ti Umatiwana a zala Uzikali. A ti Uzikali a zala abantwana. Wa zala Ungazana, wa zala Umfundisi. A si b' azi abanye. Unzwadi wa zala Uswanalibomvu. Uswanalibomvu wa zala Ungabazi.

Izizwe zouke zi nonkulunkulu wazo. I leso si nowaso, na leso si nowaso njalo. Unkulunkulu wakiti Ungenamafu noluhlongwana nosangolibanzi. Ukugcina ku tiwa "Nkosi" kumatiwana, okwa vela Onkulunkulu bakwiti. Ba vela be pete umkonto ukuba ku ponswane, si dhlane inkomo. Ba vela emdabukweni. Umdabuko

Ungwadi, Ujani, Umasumpa, Umatiwana, Uzikali, our father. Ungwadi is Unkulunkulu. Ujani was the father of Umasumpa. Umasumpa was the father of Umatiwana. Umatiwana was the father of Uzikali. Uzikali had many children. He had Ungazana and Umfundisi. We do not know others. Unzwadi was the father of Uswanalibomvu. Uswanalibomvu was the father of Ungabazi.

All nations have their own Unkulunkulu. Each has its own. The Unkulunkulu of our tribe is Ungenamafu and Uluthlongwana and Usangolibanzi.[96] At last men said "King" to Umatiwana, in whose house the Onkulunkulu of our tribe were born.[97] At their birth they handled spears that they might be thrown, and we eat each other's cattle. They sprang from the Umdabuko.[98] The Um-

footsteps of the very first man.' This is the sum-total of the knowledge which the Bechuanas possessed of the origin of what they call Morimo, prior to the period when they were visited by missionaries." *(Missionary Labours and Scenes in South Africa. Moffat, p. 262.)*

See also a corresponding legend among the Basutos:—

"A legend says that both men and animals came out of the bowels of the earth by an immense hole, the opening of which was in a cavern, and that the animals appeared first. Another tradition, more generally received among the Basutos, is, that man sprang up in a marshy place, where reeds were growing." *(The Basutos. Casalis, p. 240.)*

[96] That is, at a certain period the tribe divided into three, each having its own Unkulunkulu. So Umahhaule, who has formed a small tribe, says, in a few years he shall be an Unkulunkulu.

[97] That is, the Onkulunkulu whose names he has given not only belonged to the Amangwane, but to the family of Umatiwana.

[98] Umdabuko, Creator. See above, Note 94.

owa s' abela izinto zonke, wa si patisa nezihlangu.

ULUDONGA (an Ingwane).

dabuko is he who gave us all things, and gave us shields also to carry.

IN the neighbourhood there is a very old woman, with whom I had some casual conversation which appeared to be calculated to throw some light on their traditions; I therefore sent Umpengula to obtain from her a connected statement. On his return he related the substance of her remarks as follows:—

UNINA kabapa u ti :—Kwa ti ekuveleni, lokupela Utshaka u te e ba indoda e ngena ebukosini, sa si kqala ukwenda ngaleso 'sikati; kepa ngi be ngi za ngi zwa ku tiwa, "Amabele lawa e si wa dhlayo a vela emhlangeni; kwa ku umhlanga; ku vutiwe, ku bomvu." Kepa abantu ba zinge be bona into e bukeka emhlangeni. Ba za ba ti, "Ake si zwe uma le into i ini na." Ba wa ka, a dhliwa. Kwa tiwa, "O, kanti, ku mnandi, ukudhla." A goduka ke, a ya 'kulinywa.

Si kuluma ngaloku 'kuvela kwamabele, si ti, " Kwa vela pi loku na?" kepa abadala ba ti, "Kwa vela kumdabuko owa dabula konke. Kepa si nga m azi." Si zinge si buza si ti, "Lowo 'm-

THE mother of Ubapa says:—At first, that is, when Utshaka was a man and was entering into the kingdom; we girls were beginning to marry at that time; I used continually to hear it said that the corn which we eat sprang from a bed of reeds; there was a bed of reeds; when it was ripe it was red. And people saw constantly a beautiful thing in the bed of reeds. At length they said, "Just let us taste what kind of a thing this is." They plucked it, and ate it, and said, "O, forsooth, it is good, it is food." So it was taken home[99] and cultivated.

When we spoke of the origin of corn, asking, "Whence came this?" the old people said, "It came from the creator who created all things. But we do not know him." When we asked continu-

---

[99] Lit., The corn went home and was cultivated; that is, became a cultivated article of food.

dabuko u pi na ? Loku amakosi akwiti si ya wa bona ?" kepa abadala b' ale 'ukuti, " Na lawa 'makosi e si wa bonako, u kona umdabuko owa wa dabulayo."

Kepa si buze si ti, " U pi na ? Ka bonakali nje. U pi na ?" kepa si zwe bobaba be komba pezulu, be ti, " Umdabuko wako konke u pezulu. Futi ku kona nesizwe sabantu kona." Kepa si nga ze sa bona kahle ukuba lowo 'mdabuko u ya 'uze a bonwe nini na. Ku be ku tiwe njalo, ku tiwa, " Inkosi yamakosi."

Si zwa futi ku tiwa uma izulu li dhle izinkomo kwabani, ku tiwe, " Inkosi i tate izinkomo kwabani." Futi si zwe ku tiwa uma li ya duma, abantu ba zimise isibindi, ngokuti, " I ya dhlala inkosi." Kepa si ze sa kula ku i loko njalo.

Kepa ngonkulunkulu ka m vezanga ngokwake. Kepa ngi be ngi linga uku m kombisa kuye, a-

ally, " Where is the creator ? For our chiefs we see ?"[100] the old men denied, saying, " And those chiefs too whom we see, they were created by the creator."

And when we asked, " Where is he ? for he is not visible at all. Where is he then ?" we heard our fathers pointing towards heaven and saying, " The Creator of all things is in heaven. And there is a nation of people there too." But we could not well understand when that Creator would be visible. It used to be said constantly, " He is the chief of chiefs."[1]

Also when we heard it said that the heaven had eaten[2] the cattle at such a village, we said, " The Lord has taken the cattle from such a village." And when it thundered the people took courage by saying, " The Lord is playing." That was the state of the matter till we grew up.

But as for Unkulunkulu, Ubapa's mother did not mention him of her own accord. But I tried to direct her attention to him, that she might speak of him of her

---

[100] By this is meant, that they denied the existence of a Creator whom they could not see ; and declared their belief that their kings, whom they could see, were the Creators of all things. Just as at the end this old woman declares that the whitemen made all things.

[1] *Inkosi* may be rendered chief, king, lord. We can therefore say either Chief of Chiefs,—or King of Kings,—or Lord of Lords.

[2] That is, the lightning had struck.

zitsholo ngokwake. Kepa kwa ba | own accord.³ But I could not get lukuni loko ukukuluma ngokwake. | her to mention him of her own

³ This is a very common occurrence. Very old Amazulu, when asked about Unkulunkulu, are apt to speak, not of the first Unkulunkulu, but the onkulunkulu of their tribes.

Mr. Hully, a missionary for some years connected with the Wesleyans, went up to the Zulu country as interpreter to Mr. Owen, in 1837. He says the word Unkulunkulu was not then in use among the natives; but that Captain Gardiner introduced it to express the Greatest, or the Maker of all men. Mr. Hully refused to use it in this sense. He allowed that the word *kulu* meant great, but denied that Unkulunkulu existed in the language to express that which Capt. Gardiner wished. But he persisted in using it through a young man named Verity.

The following remarks from Captain Gardiner's work appear to justify this statement of Mr. Hully:—

"The conversation which took place I will now relate, as nearly as I can, in the precise words:—

"'Have you any knowledge of the power by whom the world was made? When you see the sun rising and setting, and the trees growing, do you know who made them and who governs them?'

"Tpai (after a little pause, apparently deep in thought)—'No; we see them, but cannot tell how they come: we suppose that they come of themselves.'

"'To whom then do you attribute your success or failure in war?'

"Tpai—'When we are unsuccessful, and do not take cattle, we think that our father' [Itongo] 'has not looked upon us.'

"'Do you think your father's spirits' [Amatongo] 'made the world?'

"Tpai—'No.'

"'Where do you suppose the spirit of a man goes after it leaves the body?'

"Tpai—'We cannot tell.'

"'Do you think it lives for ever?'

"Tpai—'That we cannot tell; we believe that the spirit of our forefathers looks upon us when we go out to war; but we do not think about it at any other time.'

"'You admit that you cannot control the sun or the moon, or even make a hair of your head to grow. Have you no idea of any power capable of doing this?'

"Tpai—'No; we know of none: we know that we cannot do these things, and we suppose that they come of themselves.'" *(Narrative of a Journey to the Zoolu Country. Capt. Allen F. Gardiner, R.N.; undertaken in 1835, p. 283.)*

He thus speaks of a tribe on the Umzimvubu:—

"On the subject of religion they are equally as dark as their

Nga za nga m gnznlela ibizo lika-nkulunkulu; kepa yena wa bona wa ti, "A! u yena pela lowo 'mdabuko o pezulu owa e tshiwo abadala." Kepa Ubapa wa ti, "Ai! u se kqala ukupambanisa amazwi. Izolo u be nga tshongo njalo kumfundisi. Unkulunkulu u be m kombisa pansi. Kepa manje u se m kombe pezulu." Kepa wa ti yena, "Ehe! wa buya w' enyuka, wa ya pezulu." Wa yeka leyo 'nd/lela yake yokukqala, wa ngena ngokuti, "Kanti Unkulunkulu u yena lo o pezulu. Futi nabelungu laba kanti i bona amakosi aw' enza konke."

accord. At length I mentioned the name of Unkulunkulu; and she understood and said, "Ah! it is he in fact who is the creator which is in heaven, of whom the ancients spoke." But Ubapa said, "No! she now begins to speak at cross purposes. She did not say this to the Missionary yesterday. She said Unkuluukulu was from beneath. But now she says he was from above." And she said, "Yes, yes![4] he went up to heaven afterwards." She left the first account, and began to say, "Truly Unkulunkulu is he who is in heaven. And the whitemen, they are the lords who made all things."

neighbours the Zoolus. They acknowledged, indeed, a traditionary account of a Supreme Being, whom they called Oukoolukoolu" [Ukulukulu] "(literally the Great-Great), but knew nothing further respecting him, than that he originally issued from the reeds, created men and cattle, and taught them the use of the assagai. They knew not how long the issitoota," [isituta] "or spirit of a deceased person, existed after its departure from the body, but attributed every untoward occurrence to its influence, slaughtering a beast to propitiate its favour on every occasion of severe sickness, &c. As is customary among all these nations, a similar offering is made by the ruling chief to the spirit of his immediate ancestor preparatory to any warlike or hunting expedition, and it is to the humour of this capricious spirit that every degree of failure or success is ascribed." *(Id., p. 314.)*

[4] That is, she assents to the statement that Unkulunkulu sprang from the earth. But asserts also that he is the heavenly Lord, of whom she has been speaking.

This account is in many respects very remarkable. It is not at all necessary to conclude that the mind of the old woman was wandering. There appears to be in the account rather the intermixture of several faiths, which might have met and contended or amalgamated at the time to which she alludes:—1. A primitive faith in a heavenly Lord or Creator. 2. The ancestor-worshipping faith, which confounds

Ubebe, who related the following, was a very old man, belonging to the Amantanja tribe. He had seen much. His people were scattered by the armies of Utshaka, and he showed four wounds, received at different times:—

Inkosi i ya buza kambe indaba yaobaba.

Aobaba ba be ti indaba yabo yendulo, be ti, "Unkulunkulu u kona o indoda, o pansi yena." Obaba ba be ti, "Inkosi i kona pezulu." Uma li leta, li duma, ba ti, "Inkosi i ya /loma, i ya leta. Lungisa ni." Be tsho kubo 'ma-

The chief[5] enquires then what our forefathers believed.

The primitive faith of our fathers was this, they said, "There is Unkulunkulu, who is a man,[6] who is of the earth." And they used to say, "There is a lord in heaven." When it hailed, and thundered, they said, "The lord is arming; he will cause it to hail. Put things in order."[7] They

the Creator with the First Man. 3. The Christian faith again directing the attention of the natives to a God, which is not anthropomorphic.

But she may intend to refer to the supposed ascent of Usenzangakona, the father of Utshaka, into heaven, which is recounted in the following izibongo, that is, flattering declamations by which the praises of the living or the dead are celebrated:—

Kwa ku izibongo zikasenzangakona, e bongwa abantu bake, be ti,

"Mntakajama, owa pota igoda la ya la fika ezulwini, lapa izituta zakwamageba zi nga yi 'kufika. Zo ba 'kukwela z' apuke amazwanyana."

There were lauds of Usenzangakona, by which he was lauded by his people; they said,

"Child of Ujama, who twisted a large rope which reached to heaven, where the Spirits of the Amageba will not arrive. They will again and again make fruitless efforts, and break their little toes."

Amageba ibizo elidala lamazulu. Li ti, amatunzi okumuka kwelanga; a ya geba ezintabeni. Amageba abakamageba, Unkulunkulu wakwazulu. Umageba u zala Ujama, a zale Usenzangakona, a zale Utshaka. Nomageba u kona Unkulunkulu wake, lapa tina si ng' aziko.

Amageba is an ancient name of the Amazulu. It means the shadows caused by the departing sun; they recline on the mountains. Amageba are the people of Umageba, the Unkulunkulu of the Amazulu. Umageba begat Ujama; he begat Usenzangakona; he begat Utshaka. And as regards Umageba, there is his unkulunkulu where we know not.

[5] The chief, that is, myself. A respectful mode of addressing the enquirer, as though the answer was being given to a third person.

[6] *Indoda*, that is, a male.

[7] That they may not be injured by the hail.

me, ku lungiswe impa*h*la zonke nezinkomo namabele.

Ku ti lapa inkosi i d*h*lalayo ngokuduma, ba ti uma ku kona ow esabayo, "W etuka ni, loku ku d*h*lala inkosi na? U tate ni yayo na?"

Kwa tiwa Unkulunkulu u te, a si be abantu, si lime ukud*h*la, si d*h*le. Kwa ti utshani bwa vezwa Unkulunkulu, wa ti, "A ku d*h*le izinkomo." Wa ti, "A ku tezwe izinkuni, ku be kona umlilo, ku vut' ukud*h*la." Wa ti Unkulunkulu, "A ku zalwane, ku be kona abalanda, ku zalwe, kw and' abantu em*h*labeni. Ku be kona amakosi amnyama, inkosi y aziwe ngabantu bayo, ukuba 'Inkosi le: ni butane nina nonke ni ye enkosini.'"

A si kw azi ukuvela kwake. Si zwa ku tiwa, "Abantu ba zalwa Unkulunkulu." Aobaba ba

said this to our mothers, and they set all things in order, cattle and corn.

And when the lord played by thundering they said, if there was any one afraid, "Why do you start, because the lord plays? What have you taken which belongs to him?"

It was said, Unkulunkulu said, "Let there be men, and let them cultivate food and eat." And the grass was created by Unkulunkulu, and he told the cattle to eat. He said, "Let firewood be fetched, that a fire may be kindled, and food be dressed." Unkulunkulu said, "Let there be marriage among men,[8] that there may be those who can intermarry, that children may be born and men increase on the earth." He said, "Let there be black chiefs; and the chief be known by his people, and it be said, 'That is the chief: assemble all of you and go to your chief.'"

We do not know the origin of Unkulunkulu. We hear it said, "Men are the children of Unkulunkulu." Our fathers used to

---

[8] *A ku zalwane.* Lit., Let children be begotten or born one with another. An allusion to a supposed period in which if blood relations did not marry there could be no marriage. The meaning really is,—Let brothers and sisters marry, that in the progress of time there may arise those who are sufficiently removed from close relationship, that there may be *abalanda,* that is, persons who may lawfully intermarry.

be ti, "Unkulunkulu lowo owa zala abantu cluhlangeni. Si nga m azi ke Uluhlanga uma wa e puma ngapi na; noma Unkulunkulu ba be puma ohlangeni lunye ini na. A s' azi ukuba Uhlanga umfazi ini, loku aobaba ba be ti si zalwa Unkulunkulu.

Sa si m buza Unkulunkulu kwobawo, si ti, "U pi Unkulunkulu e ni m tshoyo na?" Ba ti, "Ka se ko. Nohlanga futi," ba ti, "ka se ko." Ba ti aobawo, "Nati s' ezwa si tshelwa ukuti, sa zalwa Unkulunkulu nohlanga. Na kwobaba s' ezwa be tsho."

Unkulunkulu wa e mnyama, ngokuba si bona abantu bonke e si vela kubo bemnyama, nenwele zabo zimnyama. B' esoka ngokuba kwa tsho Unkulunkulu, wa ti, "A ba soke abantu, ba nga bi amakwenkwe." Unkulunkulu naye wa soka, ngokuba wa si tshela ukusoka.

say, "Unkulunkulu is he who begat men by Uthlanga.[9] We do not know whence Uthlanga came; or whether Unkulunkulu and Uthlanga both came from one Uthlanga or not. We do not know whether Uthlanga was a woman, for our fathers said we were begotten by Unkulunkulu.[10]

We used to ask our fathers about Unkulunkulu, saying, "Where is Unkulunkulu of whom you speak?" They said, "He is dead, and Uthlanga also is dead." Our fathers said, "We were told that we are the children[11] of Unkulunkulu and Uthlanga. And our fathers told us they were told."

Unkulunkulu was a black man, for we see that all the people from whom we sprang are black, and their hair is black. They circumcised because Unkulunkulu said, "Let men circumcise, that they may not be boys." And Unkulunkulu also circumcised, for he commanded us to circumcise.

[9] Here very distinctly Uthlanga is a proper name,—that of the first woman. But the origin of Uthlanga is not known; it is suggested that she came forth from Uthlanga together with Unkulunkulu —that is, an anterior Uthlanga.—Compare this with the legend above given, where it is said Umvelinqangi made an Uthlanga and begat children by her. See below, where it is said, "Uhlanga ka se ko," Uthlanga is dead; not, A lu se ko.

[10] This is a mode of asserting his belief that since the fathers said Unkulunkulu begat men, he could not do so without a wife, and that therefore Uthlanga was a woman.

[11] *Zala* is to beget and to give birth to: they were derived, viz., by generation from Unkulunkulu, and by birth from Uthlanga.

Umdabuko ng' azi o pezulu wodwa. Ba be ti abendulo, "Umdabuko u pezulu owona opilisayo abantu ; ngokuba abantu b' esuta, ba nga fi indhlala, ngoba inkosi i ba nika ukupila, ukuba ba hambe kahle emhlabatini, ba nga fi indhlala."

Uma l' omile, ku hlangana abanumuzana namakosi, ba ye enkosini emnyama ; ba ya kuluma, be tandaza wona umbete. Ukutandaza kwabo ukuba abanumuzana ba tshaye izinkabi ezimnyama, i nga bi ko emhlope. Zi nga hlatshwa ; b' enze ngemilomo ; ku hlatshwe i be nye, ezinye zi hlale. Kwa ku tiwa kukqala imvula i puma enkosini, nelanga li puma enkosini, nenyanga e kanyisa ngobumhlope, ku hlwile, abantu ba hambe be ng' apuki. Uma inyanga i nga se ko, ku tiwa, "Abantu a ba nga hambi, kumnyama ; ba ya 'kulimala."

As to the source[12] of being I know that only which is in heaven. The ancient men said, "The source of being is above,[13] which gives life to men ; for men are satisfied, and do not die of famine, for the lord gives them life, that they may live prosperously on the earth and not die of famine.

If it does not rain, the heads of villages and petty chiefs assemble and go to a black chief; they converse, and pray for rain. Their praying is this :—The heads of villages select some black oxen ;[14] there is not one white among them. They are not slaughtered ; they merely mention them ; one is killed, the others are left. It was said at first, the rain came from the lord, and that the sun came from him, and the moon which gives a white light during the night, that men may go and not be injured. If there is no moon, it is said, "Let not men go, it is dark ; they will injure themselves."

[12] *Umdabuko,* Source of Being,—local or personal,—the place in which man was created, or the person who created him. But if a place, it is possessed of a special potentiality. See Note 95, p. 50. But here the Umdabuko is called "the lord which gives them life."

[13] The argument is, since we see that life-giving influences,—the rain and sun,—come from heaven, we conclude that there too is the original source of life.

[14] It is supposed that black cattle are chosen because when it is about to rain the sky is overcast with dark clouds. When the ox is killed, its flesh is eaten in the house, and perfect silence is maintained till the whole is consumed, in token of humble submission to the lord of heaven, from whom, and not of the chief, the rain is asked. The bones are burnt outside the village. After eating the flesh in silence, they sing a song. The songs sung on such occasions consist merely of musical sounds, and are without words.

Uma izulu li be li tshayile izinkomo, ku be ku nga ḥlupekwa. Ku be ku tiwa, " Inkosi i ḥlabile ekudḥleni kwayo." Ku tiwa, " Okwenu ini na, loku ku ng' okwenkosi na ? I lambile ; i ya ziḥlabela." Uma umuzi u tshaywe unyazi, uma ku inkomo e bulewe, ku tiwa, " Ku za 'kuba inḥlanḥla kulo 'muzi." Uma umuntu e tshaywe, wa fa, ku tiwa, " U soliwe inkosi."

If lightning struck cattle, the people were not distressed.[15] It used to be said, " The lord has slaughtered for himself among his own food. Is it yours ? is it not the lord's ? He is hungry ; he kills for himself." If a village is struck with lightning, and a cow killed, it is said, "This village will be prosperous." If a man is struck and dies, it is said, " The lord has found fault with him."

UBEBE.

Having requested Umpengula to ascertain from Ubebe the meaning of Umdabuko more exactly, he made the following report :—

Ng' enze njengokutsho kwako ke, mfundisi, nga buza kubebe ukuti,

I HAVE done as you directed, Teacher, and asked of Ubebe what

---

[15] Contrast this with what Arbousset says of the superstition found among the Lighoyas :—

" When it thunders every one trembles ; if there are several together, one asks the other with uneasiness, ' Is there any one amongst us who devours the wealth of others ?' All then spit on the ground, saying, ' We do not devour the wealth of others.' If a thunderbolt strikes and kills one of them, no one complains, none weep ; instead of being grieved, all unite in saying that the Lord is delighted (that is to say, he has done right), with killing that man ; they say also that the thief eats thunderbolts, that is to say, does things which draw down upon men such judgments. There can be no doubt, they suppose, that the victim in such a case must have been guilty of some crime, of stealing most probably, a vice from which very few of the Bechuanas are exempt, and that it is on this account that fire from heaven has fallen upon him." *(Exploratory Tour in South Africa, p. 323.)*

Casalis says that, among the Basutos, " If any one is struck dead by lightning, no murmur is heard and tears are suppressed. ' The Lord has killed him,' they say ; ' he is, doubtless, rejoicing : let us be careful not to disturb his joy.' " *(The Basutos, p. 242.)*

"Bebe, lapa ku tiwa umdabuko wabantu, li ti ni leli 'zwi lokuti umdabuko na?" Kepa Ubebe wa ti, "Lapa si ti umdabuko, si kuluma lapa kwa vela abantu bonke kona, si ti ke umdabuko wabantu. Futi le inkosi e pezulu a ngi zwanga kwobaba be ti, "I nonina nomfazi." A ngi ku zwanga loko. Unkulunkulu yedwa e kwa tiwa wa veza abantu o/langeni ; sa ti, umdabuko u u/langa."

men meant by the word Umdabuko, when they say, "The Umdabuko of men." He replied, "When we say Umdabuko we speak of that[16] from which men sprang; and because they sprang from that, we say, 'The Umdabuko of men.' Further, as regards that lord who is above, I never heard our fathers say he had a mother or wife. I never heard such a thing. It is Unkulunkulu only of whom it was said he gave men origin by means of Uthlanga,[17] and so we said, the Umdabuko is Uthlanga."

I REQUESTED Umpengula to enquire of Unjan, of the Abambo tribe, a petty chief, who came to the village, what he knew about Unkulunkulu. He reported the following:—

WA ti ngoku m buza kwami ukuti, "Njan, u ti ni wena ngonkulunkulu lowo, e sa m tshoyo tina 'bantu abamnyama na?" wa ti, "Lo, e sa ti, w' enza konke na?" Nga ti mina, "Yebo. Ngi ya

WHEN I asked him, saying, "Unjan, what do you say about that Unkulunkulu, of whom we black men used to talk?" he replied, "Him who, we said, made all things?"[18] I replied, "Yes. I en-

---

[16] See Note 95, p. 50.

[17] *Or, out of Uthlanga;* "and so we said the Umdabuko is Uthlanga," either regarding Umdabuko as a female, or referring to that Uthlanga or Source of being from which Unkulunkulu himself and all things else sprang. But we are here, no doubt, to understand the latter, for above he states that the old men believed in an Umdabuko which is above, and which he calls, "the Lord which gives them life."

[18] Intimating that there are other Onkulunkulu about whom he might wish to enquire.

buza ukuze ng' azi loko oku isiminya imi*h*la yonke ngaye." Wa ti, "Ehe! A u boni ini ukuba Unkulunkulu, sa ti, w' enza konke e si ku bonayo ne si ku patayo konke?" Nga ti, "Ehe! Hambisa kambe. Ngi sa lalele lapa u za 'kuya 'kug*c*ina kona." Kepa wa ti, "O, noma kwa tshiwo kwa tiwa, w' enza konke; kepa mina ngi bona ukuti loku kwa tiwa umuntu omkulu wetu, umuntu njengati; ngokuba tina sa si nga kombi 'ndawo lapo e kona, kodwa kwa tiwa umuntu owa vela ku-k*q*ala kubantu bonke, o yena emkulu kwiti sonke, Umvelin*q*angi. Kanti ngi ya bona ukuti ngelizwi letu sa ti, Unkulunkulu w' enza konke, kepa a s' azi lap' a vela kona." Nga m buza nga ti, "Manje u pi na?" Wa ti, "O, ka se ko." Nga ti, "Wa ya ngapi na?" Wa ti, "Nati si be si buza, ku tiwe, 'Ka se ko.' Kepa ngaloko ku ya bonakala ukuti konke loko a kw enziwanga umuntu o nga se ko; kw' enziwa o se kona."

Kepa ngi buza kuye ngokuti, "Abafundisi bakwini a ba tsho ini ukuti le inkosi e pezulu i Unkulunkulu na?" Wa ti, "Hau!" quire that I might know what has always been the truth about him." He said, "Yes, yes! Do you not understand that we said Unkulunkulu made all things that we see or touch?" I said, "Yes! Just go on. I am listening for the conclusion." And he said, "Although it was said he made all things, yet for my part I see that it was said,[19] he was an old man of ours, a man like us; for we did not point to any place where he was, but said he was a man who came into being first of all other men, who was older than all of us, Umvelin*q*angi. So then I see that by our word we said Unkulunkulu made all things, but we know not whence he sprang." I asked, "Where is he now?" He said, "O, he is dead." I asked, "Where is he gone?" He replied, "We too used to ask, and it was answered, 'he is dead.' But by that it is evident that all things were not made by a man, who is now dead; they were made by one who now is."[20]

And when I enquired, saying, "Do not your teachers[21] tell you that the lord which is in heaven is Unkulunkulu?" he replied with a

---

[19] I see that it was *said* and nothing more; there was no truth in it.

[20] It is clear that this reasoning is the result of a certain amount of light. When once he had been induced to think, he said that the things around him could not, as the old men said, have had a mere human author, who came into being and passed away.

[21] This chief and his people live in the neighbourhood of the Roman Catholic Mission about fifteen miles from this place.

ngokwetuka, "Nakanye. A ngi zwanga be li tsho lelo 'lizwi; nokuba ba kulume ngalo nje a ngi ku zwanga. Kupela umfundisi yedwa e nga kuluma naye ngalo."

start, "Hau! by no means. I never heard such a word, neither did I ever hear them even mention the name. It is your teacher[22] alone with whom I have ever spoken about it."

The next day I asked him myself, when he made the following statement :—

Ba ti abendulo ba ti Unkulunkulu owa veza abantu, wa veza konke nezinkomo, konke nezilwane ezasend*h*le. Ba ti omdala umuntu owa veza lezo 'zindaba, e se ku tiwa ke umuntu omdala u inkosi, ku tiwa u inkosi e pezulu. Se si zwa ngani ukuti inkosi e pezulu e yona ey' enza konke. Abantu abadala ba be ti Unkulunkulu ukoko nje, umuntu omdala owa zala abantu, wa veza konke.

The ancients said that it was Unkulunkulu who gave origin to men, and every thing besides, both cattle and wild animals. They said it was an ancient man who gave origin to these things, of whom it is now said that ancient man is lord; it is said, he is the Lord which is above.[23] We have now heard from you that the Lord which is in heaven is he who made every thing. The old men said that Unkulunkulu was an ancestor and nothing more, an ancient man who begat men, and gave origin to all things.

───◆───

ULANGENI, umuntu omdala wasemak*x*oseni, kepa u sesikoleni, wa fika lapa kwiti. Nga ya kuye, ngi ya 'kubuza le 'ndaba kaukulunkulu, ngi bona omdala kakulu. Kepa ekungeneni kwami end*h*lini

ULANGENI, an old Ik*x*osa, but one living at a mission-station, paid us a visit. I went to him and enquired of him what he knew about Unkulunkulu, because I saw he was a very old man. When I entered the house where Ulangeni

---

[22] Some years ago whilst travelling I had had a conversation with him on the subject.

[23] This is rather obscure, but I prefer not to give a free translation. The meaning is, Our old men told us that it was an ancient man who created all things; but we hear from the missionaries that the heavenly Lord is he who created.

lapa e kona Ulangeni, nga m buza ngokuti, "Baba, ngi size ngale 'ndawo yokuti Utikxo, uma lelo 'gama kwa tiwa Utikxo o pi na? Noma li vele se ku fike abafundisi ini na?"

Kepa Ulangeni wa ti, "Kqa; leli 'gama lokuti Utikxo a si lo e si li zwa kumangisi; igama lakwiti elidala; ku be ku ti ngezikati zonke, uma ku timula umuntu a ti, 'Tikxo, u ngi bheke kade.'"

Kepa nga buza ngokuti, "Ni be ni ti tikxo nje, ni tsho ni na? Loku izidumbu zake na ni nga z' azi, na ni tsho ni na?" Wa ti, "Le 'ndaba yokuti tikxo indaba kwiti e be ku tiwa, uma li ya duma izulu, kw aziwe njalo ukuti a kona amandhla a ngapezulu; ku ngaloku kwa za kwa tiwa opezulu Utikxo. A ku tshiwongo kodwa ukuti u sendaweni etile pezulu;

was, I enquired of him, saying, "My father, help me in the matter of Utikxo, and tell me where Utikxo is said to be? And whether the word came into use after the arrival of the missionaries?"

And Ulangeni answered, "No; the word Utikxo is not a word we learnt of the English; it is an old word of our own. It used to be always said when a man sneezed, 'May Utikxo ever regard me with favour.'"[24]

Then I asked, "Since you merely used the word Utikxo, what did you mean? Since what is very truth about him you knew not, what did you mean?" He replied, "As regards the use of Utikxo, we used to say it when it thundered, and we thus knew that there is a power which is in heaven; and at length we adopted the custom of saying, Utikxo is he who is above all. But it was not said that he was in a certain place

[24] Just as among other people sneezing is associated with some superstitious feeling. In England and Germany old people will say, "God bless you," when a person sneezes. Among the Amazulu, if a child sneeze, it is regarded as a good sign; and if it be ill, they believe it will recover. On such an occasion they exclaim, "Tutuka," Grow. When a grown up person sneezes, he says, "Bakiti, ngi hambe kade," Spirits of our people, grant me a long life. As he believes that at the time of sneezing the Spirit of his house is in some especial proximity to him, he believes it is a time especially favourable to prayer, and that whatever he asks for will be given; hence he may say, "Bakwiti, inkomo," Spirits of our people, give me cattle; or, "Bakwiti, abantwana," Spirits of our people, give me children. Diviners among the natives are very apt to sneeze, which they regard as an indication of the presence of the Spirits; the diviner adores by saying, "Makosi," Lords, or Masters.

kwa ku tiwa lonke izulu u kulo lonke. A kw a*h*lukaniswanga."

Kepa nga ti, " Amalau a e ti ni wona ibizo lokubiza Udio ?" Wa ti, " Hau ! U tsho 'malau mani na ?" Nga ti, " Lawa 'malau abomvana." Wa ti, "Ngi y' ezwa. Kepa ba be pi labo 'bantu aba nga ze ba be notik*x*o na ? Angiti ba be *h*lala ezintabeni; ba tolwe Amabunu, nokuze ba be pakati kwabantu na ? A si lo igama lamalau ukuti tik*x*o. O-kwamalau kwa duka konke ngam*h*la be *h*langene namabunu. A si zwa 'luto lwawo."

I loko ke e nga ku zwa ngolangeni. Nga buza ke ngokuti, " Unkulunkulu ku m zwanga na ?" Kepa yena wa ti, " Uku mu zwa kwami Unkulunkulu, ngi mu zwe kakulu lapo ku bekwa amatshe pezu kwesivivane; umuntu a ti

in heaven; it was said he filled the whole heaven. No distinction of place was made."[25]

I asked, " By what name did the Hottentots call God ?" He said, " Hau ! what Hottentots do you mean ?"[26] I replied, " Those reddish Hottentots." He said, " I hear. But where were those people that they should use the word Utik*x*o ? Is it not the fact that they used to live in the mountains; and were taken into the households of the Dutch, and so came to live among the people ? Utik*x*o is not a Hottentot word. Every thing belonging to the Hottentots was thrown into confusion when they united with the Dutch. We have learnt nothing of them."

This, then, is what I heard of Ulangeni. So I enquired further, " Have you never heard of Unkulunkulu ?" He replied, " I have for the most part heard Unkulunkulu mentioned when stones are thrown on an isivivane;[27] when a

---

[25] It may be worth noting here that what the Amazulu say of the lord of heaven, for whom they have no name, the Amak*x*osa say of Utik*x*o.

[26] This is to be understood as expressing his utter contempt for the Hottentots, and unwillingness to admit that the Kafir could learn any thing from them. It cannot, however, be doubted that he is mistaken in supposing that they did not derive the word from the Hottentots.

[27] *Isivivane.*—Isivivane amatshe a *h*langaniselwa 'ndawo nye, 'enziwe ink*q*waba enkulu; ku po-

The isivivane consists of stones which are collected together in one place, and form a large heap;

J

lapa e ponsa itshe, a ti, 'Zizuku-lwane zikankulunkulu,' a dhlule." Nga ti ke, "E tsho mupi Unku- man throws a stone, he says, 'Generations of Unkulunkulu,' and passes on." So I said, "What nswe kona aba dhlulako kuso isivivane, amancane amatshe namakulu e ponswa kona, ku tiwa, "Sivivane saokoko, ngi ti ketshe-ketshe ukuhamba kalula."

UMPENGULA MBANDA.

those who pass by the isivivane cast stones on it; the stones which are thrown on it are both small and great; and it is said, "Isivivane of our ancestors, may I live without care."

The isivivane, then, is a heap of stones, the meaning of which the natives of these parts are unacquainted with. When they pass such a heap, they spit on a stone and throw it on the heap. Sometimes they salute it by saying, "Sa ku bona, bantwana bakasivivane," Good day, children of Usivivane; thus personifying Isivivane, and acting in correspondence with the Kæosa salutation to Unkulunkulu.—Sir James E. Alexander relates the following of the Namaquas:—"In the country there are occasionally found large heaps of stones on which had been thrown a few bushes; and if the Namaquas are asked what they are, they say that *Heije Eibib*, their Great Father, is below the heap; they do not know what he is like, or what he does; they only imagine that he also came from the East, and had plenty of sheep and goats; and when they add a stone or branch to the heap, they mutter, 'Give us plenty of cattle.' "—Among the Hottentots there are many such heaps, which they say are the graves of Heitsi Kabip, who, according to them, died several times and came to life again. *(Bleek. Hottentot Fables, p. 76.)*—Thus the Heitsi Eibip of the Hottentots appears to have some relation to the Unkulunkulu of the Kafirs.

Such heaps of stones are common in the South Sea Islands, and are there memorial heaps, as, it appears from the Scripture narrative, was that which Jacob raised (Gen. xxxi. 45—55); or they may have been raised over graves, as is still the custom among the Bedouins.

"The bearers of the corpse reached the newly dug grave at the head of the procession, and standing over it they slowly lowered the body, still rolled in its rough camel-hair shroud, into it, as the solemn chant suddenly ceased, and the silence which ensued seemed rendered deeper by the contrast. The corpse having been stretched out in its sandy couch, all those nearest the spot, with hands and feet, raked back the loose earth over the grave and closed it up. Ali and the other chieftain with him, each taking up a stone from the ground, now cast it in turn on the tomb, uttering, 'Allah yerdano,' God have mercy on him! Naif, silent and brooding, approached the spot, and with the same prayer cast his stone likewise over his brother's tomb, adding, 'The duty of revenging thee weighs upon me.'

"All the other members of the tribe present followed their chief's example, and pressed forward to pay their last tribute to the dead, a stone cast on the grave, and a muttered prayer for his peace;

lunkulu na?" Ukupendula kukalangeni, wa ti, "E tsho umuntu wokukqala kubo bonke abantu, owa vezwa Utikxo kukqala. Kepa abantu ba m bona. Utikxo wa sita kunkulunkulu, ka bonwanga umuntu; abantu ba bona yena Unkulunkulu, ba ti umenzi wako konke, Umvelinqangi, be tsho ngokuba lowo ow' enza Unkulunkulu be nga m bonanga. Ba ti ke u yena e Utikxo. I loko e ngi kw aziyo ngonkulunkulu."

Nga ti mina, " Ehe ! langeni. Ngi ya bona impela ukuba loko o ku tshoyo into nami e be ngi i tsho. Kodwa kuloko, loko 'kupendula kwako ku ukupendula kwomuntu o se punyelwe ilanga ; ngokuba u bona loko abaningi a ba bheki nakanye kuloko 'kubona kwako."

Wa ti, "Ku te ekufikeni kwamangisi kulo 'mhlaba kwiti, kwa kqala umfundisi o ku tiwa ibizo lake Uyegana. Wa fika wa fundisa abantu, nokukuluma kwake

Unkulunkulu does he mean?" Ulangeni said in reply, "He means the first man before all other men, who was created by Utikxo first. And men saw him. Utikxo was concealed by Unkulunkulu, and was seen by no one ; men saw Unkulunkulu, and said he was the creator of all things, Umvelinqangi ; they said thus because they did not see Him who made Unkulunkulu. And so they said Unkulunkulu was God.[28] This is what I know about Unkulunkulu."

I replied, " Yes, yes ! Ulangeni. I see clearly that what you say accords with what I said. But further, your answer is the answer of a man on whom the sun has risen ; for you see that which many do not regard in the least."

He said, " On the arrival of the English in this land of ours, the first who came was a missionary named Uyegana. On his arrival he taught the people, but they did

the multitudes crowding in succession round the spot, or spreading over the plain to find a stone to cast on the tomb in their turn. A high mound of loose stones rose fast over the grave, increasing in size every minute as men, women, and children continued swarming around it in turn, adding stone after stone to the funereal pile." (" Sketches of the Desert and Bedouin Life." *The Churchman's Companion. No. XII. December*, 1867, *p.* 524.)
Is our ceremony of throwing earth into the grave a relic of this ancient custom ?

[28] This is a very concise and simple explanation of the way in which the First Man came to be confounded with the Creator.

ku ng' aziwa uma u ti ni na, e lal' endhle, e nga lali ekaya; kepa uma e bona umuzi a ye kuwo; nakuba ukukuluma kwabantu e nga kw azi, a kwitize njalo kubantu, ba kohlwe uma u ti ni na. Wa za w' enyuka wa beka enhla; wa fumana abantu ababili—Ibunu nelau; wa buya nabo labo 'bantu, ba m kumushela. Sa kqala uku w' ezwa amazwi a wa tshoyo. Wa buza pakati kwetu ngokuti, 'Ni ti ni ngokwenza konke na?' Sa ti, 'Ow' enza konke, si ti Utikxo.' Kepa wa buza wa ti, 'U pi na?' Sa ti, 'U sezulwini.' Uyegana wa ti, 'Ehe. Ngi lete yena lowo ke pakati kwenu lapa.' Kepa kwa ku kona abantu ababili, be bakulu; omunye Unsikana, omunye Unxele. Ba kolwa bobabili. Unxele wa e hlala emzini wake. Unsikana wa hlangana noyegana, umfundisi. Laba 'bantu ba kqala ukubanga igama lokuti Utikxo. Unxele wa ti, ' Utikxo u pansi.' Unsikana wa nqaba, ngokuti, 'Hai! Nxele. Utikxo u pezulu. Ngi m bona e pezulu mina, lapa ku vela amandhla onke.' Ba pikisana ngaloko bobabili, wa za

not understand what he said; he used to sleep in the open air, and not in a house; but when he saw a village he went to it, and although he did not understand the people's language, he jabbered constantly to the people, and they could not understand what he said. At length he went up the country, and met with two men—a Dutchman and a Hottentot; he returned with them, and they interpreted for him. We began to understand his words. He made enquiries amongst us, asking, 'What do you say about the creation of all things?' We replied, 'We call him who made all things Utikxo.' And he enquired, 'Where is he?' We replied, 'In heaven.' Uyegana said, 'Very well. I bring that very one[29] to you of this country.' And there were two men, both men of consequence; one was named Unsikana, and the other Unxele. Both became believers. Unxele continued to live at his own village. Unsikana united with Uyegana, the missionary. These men began to dispute about the name Utikxo. Unxele said, 'Utikxo is beneath.' Unsikana denied, saying, 'No! Unxele. Utikxo is above. I see that he is above from whence power proceeds.'[30] The two disputed on that subject, until at length Unxe-

---

[29] That very one,—that is, all that relates to or concerns him.
[30] Compare this with Note 13, p. 59.

w' a/ilulwa Unxele, ngokuba wa
ti, 'E pansi,' e tsho Unkulunkulu
ngokuti, 'U pansi.' Kepa Unsikana wa ti, 'Hai! Utikxo u
sempakameni.' La za lelo 'gama
lokuti Utikxo la duma kakulu
ngokufika kwabafundisi. Ngokuba
tina sa si kuluma ngezulu lonke,
si ti, 'Ku kona Utikxo kulo lonke;' ku nga te ntsa ukukanya
kuleyo 'ndawo. Kepa lo 'nsikana
ukukolwa kwake ku ya mangalisa.
A si kw azi uma kwa ku njani na,
ngokuba ekwa/iluleni kwake U-
nxele, wa m kqambela ingoma
enkulu, wa ti 'Ekatikxo' lelo 'gama; na nam/ila nje li into enkulu
emakxoseni. Li ya baliswa nga-
mand/ila amaningi katikxo. Ku

le was overcome, for he said, 'He
is beneath,' meaning Unkulunkulu
when he said 'He is beneath.'
But Unsikana said, 'No! Utikxo
is in the high place.' At length
the word Utikxo was universally
accepted on the arrival of the missionaries. For we used to speak
of the whole heaven, saying,
'Utikxo dwells in the whole heaven;' but did not clearly understand what we meant. But the
faith of Unsikana is wonderful.
We do not understand what it was
like, for when he had refuted
Unxele, he composed a great hymn
for him, which he called 'The
Hymn of God;' and to this day
that hymn is a great treasure
among the Amakxosa. It cele-
brates the great power of God.[31]

[31] The following is the translation of the hymn alluded to given
by Appleyard, *Grammar, p.* 48 :—
Thou art the great God—He who is in heaven.
It is Thou, Thou Shield of Truth.
It is Thou, Thou Tower of Truth.
It is Thou, Thou Bush of Truth.
It is Thou, Thou who sittest in the highest.
Thou art the Creator of life, Thou madest the regions above.
The Creator who madest the heavens also.
The Maker of the stars and the Pleiades.
The shooting stars declare it unto us.
The Maker of the blind, of thine own will didst thou make them.
The Trumpet speaks,—for us it calls.
Thou art the Hunter who hunts for souls.
Thou art the Leader who goes before us.
Thou art the great Mantle which covers us.
Thou art He whose hands are with wounds.
Thou art He whose feet are with wounds.
Thou art He whose blood is a trickling stream—and why?
Thou art He whose blood was spilled for us.
For this great price we call.
For thine own place we call.

te lowo 'muntu o ku tiwa Unsikana w' enza ummangaliso ngam*h*la e fayo. W' emuka wa ya e*h*latini e nomfana wake. Wa ngena e*h*latini, wa funa umuti omkulu o ku tiwa umumbu ibizo lawo; wa u tola, wa u gaula, wa u n*q*uma; wa u linganisa naye, wa u baza, wa w enza umpongolo; wa funa nesivalo, e u baza, e zilinganisa pakati kwawo. Ku te uma u pele wa u twala, wa goduka nawo, wa *h*langanisa abantwana bake, wa ti, 'Bantabami, ni bona nje ngi gaule lo 'muti, ng' enzile ukuze ku ti uma se ngi file ni ngi fake kuwo, ni nga boni ubuncunu bami.' Nembala wa fa ngalezo 'zinsukwana."

U<small>MPENGULA</small> M<small>BANDA</small>.

And the man Unsikana did a wonderful thing at his death. He went with his son into the forest. When he entered the forest he sought for a large tree called the Umumbu; he found one and cut it down; he measured it by his own size; he carved it and made a box of it, and a cover for it, hollowing it so as to be equal to himself inside. When it was finished he carried it home; he assembled his children and said to them, 'My children, you see I have cut this tree, that when I am dead you may place me in it, and not look on my nakedness.' And in fact he died a few days after."

L<small>ELI</small> 'lizwi lokubiza Unkulunkulu e bizwa abantwanyana noma abafana ekwaluscni, u ya bizwa ngokuba ku tsho abadala. A ngi tsho ukuti a se be gugile, ngi tsho abakulileyo kunabanye. Ba ya tumela ukuti a ba ye 'ku m biza abantwana. Ngokuba ku nge ko namunye o ya 'kuti, " Ku ngani ukuba ni tanda ukud*h*lala ngesi*h*lobo sami na ? A n' azi ini uku-

As regards calling Unkulunkulu, when he is called by little children or by boys when they are herding cattle, he is called at the bidding of old people. I do not mean those who are really old, but those who are grown up more than others; they send children to go and call him. For there is no one who will say, " Why do you like to make sport with a relative of mine ?[32] Do you not know that

---

[32] A very common answer received from a native when asked who Unkulunkulu is, is, " Ukoko wetu," Our ancestor. But now, through the course of years, no one regards him as a relative; he is so far removed from all at present living by intervening generations.

ba kumina kubuhlungu na ?" Ku ngokuba indhlu yake Unkulunkulu e nga m enzela umunyu, a i se ko. Labo 'bantu bonke aba tumela abantwana ukuti a ba ye 'ku m biza, b' enza ngoku nga m nakakeli ngaluto. Loku 'kuhlekisa ngaye Unkulunkulu ku vela ngaloku. Ngokuba uma abantwana ba ya buza ukuti, " Unkulunkulu u ubani na ?" ba ti abadala, " Umvelinqangi ow' enza izinto zonke." Kepa ba buze ukuti, " Upi manje lapo e kona na ?" ba ti, " Wa fa ; a si sa l' azi izwe lapo a fela kona, neliba lake. I loku kodwa e si kw aziyo ukuti, lezi 'zinto zonke e si nazo sa zi nikwa u ye." Kepa ku nga bi ko 'nhloko yezwi eli veza ukuti, "Indhlu e sa lunge nonkulunkulu cyakwabani lo."

Ku ti uma ku landwa ukuma kwake Unkulunkulu, ku pelele etafeni nje, ku nga sondeli ngasezindhlini zokwelamana naye kulaba 'bantu aba se kona.

Ku njalo ke, u bona nje, ukubizwa kukankulunkulu ; ku nga ti u se inganekwane ; ka si yo inga-

it is painful to me ?" It is because the house of Unkulunkulu, which can feel pain for him, no longer exists. All the people who send children to go and call him, do so because they care nothing about him. That sport about Unkulunkulu springs from this. For if children ask who Unkulunkulu is, the old people answer, " Umvelinqangi, who made all things." But when they ask where is the place where he now is, they say, " He died, and we no longer know the place where he died, nor his grave. This only is what we know, that all these things which we have, he gave us." But there is no such conclusion as this come to, " The house which is descended from Unkulunkulu is the house of So-and-so."[33]

When the standing of Unkulunkulu is sought out, it terminates in the open plain, and makes no approach to houses which have followed him in succession till those men who now exist are reached.[34]

Such then, you see, is the calling of Unkulunkulu ; it is as though he was the subject of a

---

[33] That is, no one can trace up his ancestry to the First Man. Such a notion manifests the utter ignorance of the natives of the lapse of time since man was created.

[34] We know that Unkulunkulu was the first man, but if we were to attempt to give the names of his children we could not make up a genealogy, for we are at once lost, and cannot in any way connect him with people who are now left.

nekwane impela, ukuze a nge u inganekwane; ku ngokuba u umuntu wokukqala; ngapambili kwake ka ko omunye umuntu kutina 'bantu; u yena e sekukqaleni kwabantu; tina sonke si nganeno kwake. I ugaloko Unkulunkulu bonke abantwana ku tiwa a ba ye 'ku m biza. A ku tshiwo ukuti, "Si biza idhlozi na? Si li bizela ize? A s' azi ini ukuba li ya 'kutukutela, li si bulale na?" A ku ko loko 'kukcabanga okunjalo ngaye Unkulunkulu, ukuti u idhlozi. Kepa noma u idhlozi, ka ko o namandhla oku m pata lapa e hlabile inkomo; ngokuba ka namandhla okubalisa, njengaloko e nga balisa ngamadhlozi akubo a w' aziyo. Kubantu abamnyama igama likankulunkulu a li hlonipeki; ngokuba a ku se ko 'ndhlu yake. Se li njengegama lesalukazi esidala kakulu, si nge namandhla okuzenzela nokuncinyane, se si hlala lapo si hlezi kona kusasa li ze li tshone ilanga. Abantwana ba se be dhlala ngaso, ngokuba a si namandhla oku ba fumana noku ba tshaya; se si kuluma ngomlomo kodwa. Ku njalo ke negama leli likankulunkulu, ukuba abantwana bonke ku tiwa a ba ye 'ku m biza. U se isikohliso sabantwana.

mere nursery tale; he is not a fable indeed, though he may be like one; it is because he was the first man; before him there was not another man from whom we are derived; it is he who is the first among men; we stand this side of him. It is on that account that all children are told to go and call Unkulunkulu. They do not say, "Are we calling an Idhlozi? Do we call it for nothing? Do we not know that it will be angry and kill us?" There is no such thought as this about Unkulunkulu, that he is an Idhlozi. But if he is an Idhlozi, there is no one who can worship him when he kills a bullock; for he is not able to repeat his praisegiving names, as he can those of the Amadhlozi of his people which he knows. The name of Unkulunkulu has no respect paid to it among black men; for his house no longer exists. It is now like the name of a very old crone, which has no power to do even a little thing for herself, but sits continually where she sat in the morning till the sun sets. And the children make sport of her, for she cannot catch them and flog them, but only talk with her mouth. Just so is the name of Unkulunkulu when all the children are told to go and call him. He is now a means of making sport of children.

A ku tshiwo ko:lwa ukuba u ize. U umuntu impela; kodwa ku ya ko/liswa ngaye abantwana, ukuti a ba ye 'ku m biza. Ngokuba ku y' aziwa impela ukuti wa fa. Kodwa i loku oku bonakala ngako ukuba u isiko/liso sabantwana, ngokuba na lapo a fela kona a k' aziwa na abadala. Kodwa uma ku tunywa abantwana, ku tiwa a ba ye lapaya; noma u ngalapa eduze, na lapa e kona. Kepa abantwana ba bize ba bize kakulu kakulu, a nge sabele; ba buye ba ye 'kubika ukuti ka sabeli; ku tiwe, "A ni bize kakulu; memeza ni kakulu." Abantwana b' ezwe loku 'kutsho ngokuti, "A ku memezwe," ba memeze kakulu, a ze amazwi abo a tshe, ba hhotshoze; ba k*q*ale ukubona ukuti, " Si ya ko/liswa. Ini. ukuba Unkulunkulu a ng' ezwa ngamazwi a 'bukali e si memeze ngawo kukɋala ? Manje u sa ya 'kuzwa ngani, loku e se e tshile amazwi na ?" Kepa ngaloko, noma a tshile, a ba nako ukuyeka ukubiza. Ukupela kwokumemeza kwabo ukuba ku suke umkuiwana a ye 'bu ba biza, ukuti, " Sa ni buya." U tsho njalo ngokuba be se be kɋedile loko a be be tanda

But it is not said he is nothing. He is really a man; but children are made sport of through him, when they are told to go and call him. For it is well known that he died. But it is this which makes it clear that he is the means of making a sport of children, for even the place where he died is not known even to the old men. But when children are sent, they are told to go yonder; or they say that he is here near at hand, or that he is at this very place. And children call and call again and again; but he cannot answer. They return to report that he does not answer. The people say, "Shout aloud; call him with a loud voice." When the children hear it said that they are to shout aloud, they shout aloud until they are hoarse, and their voice is scarcely audible; and they begin to see that they are deceived, and ask, "How is it that Unkulunkulu does not hear shrill words with which we first shouted? Now, how can he any longer hear, since we are now hoarse?" But because they have been told to shout, even though they are hoarse they cannot leave off shouting. The end of their shouting is this:—One of the bigger boys goes to call them, saying, "Come back now." He says this because the people have now finished what they wished to

uku kw enza ngapandhle kwabantwana. Ba buya ke abantwana, ba ti, "K' esabeli." Ku tiwe, "O, u kude lapo e kona. A ku se 'kcala."

Ngaloko 'kumemeza a ba bongi Unkulunkulu ngako. Kodwa abantwana ngoku ng' azi kwabo ba memeza isiminya; ngokuba be ti, u za 'uvela. Kanti lab' aba ba tumileyo ba y' azi ukuti ka yi 'kuvela. Ngokuba kubo a nge tunywe o se bhekile ukuya 'kubiza Unkulunkulu; a nga ti uma ku tiwa, "Bani, hamba u ye 'kubiza Unkulunkulu," a nga ti ukupendula kwake, "Uma ni tanda ukwenza into yenu, noma ni tanda ukuba ni dhle ukudhla okutile kwenu e ni nga tandi ukuba ngi ku bone, noma ngi ku dhle; woti ni a ngi suke, ngi ye kwenye 'ndawo, ngi hlale kona, ni ze ni kqede loko kwenu; musa ukuti a ngi ye 'kubiza Unkulunkulu, njengabantwana laba aba ng' aziyo." Ku njalo ke abadala a ba tunywa.

Le 'ndaba kankulunkulu manje se si i bona ezincwadini, ukuti i ya sondela. Loku tina si be si ti, "Unkulunkulu umuntu wokuqala." A si m bonganga, noma do without the children. So the children return, and say, "He did not answer." The people reply, "O, he is a great way off. It is now no longer of consequence."

By this shouting they do not worship Unkulunkulu. But the children, through their ignorance, shout with sincerity, for they think he will appear. But those who send them know that he will not. For a person who is shrewd among them cannot be sent to go and call Unkulunkulu; if he is told to go and call Unkulunkulu, he may say in reply, "If you wish to do something in private; or if you wish to eat that food of yours, which you do not wish me to see, or eat, tell me to go away to some other place; don't tell me to go and call Unkulunkulu, like children who know nothing." So old people are not sent.

The account of Unkulunkulu we now see in books, that is, it is coming near to us, whilst we ourselves used to say, "Unkulunkulu is the first man."[35] We did not worship him, though we all sprang

---

[35] He means to say, that as regards the natives themselves, Unkulunkulu was something so far off that they never thought of him; but that now this old man is being brought forward by others as the object of a reverence which they never rendered to him.

sa vela kuye sonke. Si bonga Onkulunkulu betu e si b' aziyo; yena a si namandhla, ngokuba sonke ebuntwaneni si kohlisiwe ngaye, kwa tiwa a si ye 'ku m biza; sa biza, sa biza; nya ukuvela. Kepa manje uma umuntu e ti, a si bonge Unkulunkulu, laba Onkulunkulu betu e si ba bongayo si ya 'ku ba lahla kanjani ? si bonge e si kohlisiwe ngaye na ? Si nge vume. Ngokuba noma umuntu e qinisa ngokuti a si bonge Unkulunkulu, si ya 'kutunukala sonke, si ti, " Ku sa vuswa isikohliso e si kohliswe ngaso ebuntwaneni na ?" Ku tiwa, "Si kula nje, se si kohliwe ini ? Si s' azi ukuba si kohlisiwe kakulu ngaye." A ngi tsho ukuti si kohlisiwe ngokuti u ize; ngi ti, si kohlisiwe ngokutiwa, a si ye 'ku m biza, u ya 'kuvela; nokuba ku tiwa, a si m bonge, u ya 'ku si pa

from him. We worship our Onkulunkulu whom we know [by name]; we cannot worship him, for all of us in our childhood were deceived through him, when we were told to go and call him; we shouted and shouted; but he did not appear in the least. But now if a man tell us to worship Unkulunkulu, how shall we forsake these our own Onkulunkulu whom we do worship, and worship him by whom we have been deceived ? We cannot assent.[30] For if a man urge us to worship Unkulunkulu, the old sores of all of us will break out again, and we shall ask if the deception which was practised on us when young is brought up again. It is said, " Since we have grown up [in the presence of this deceit], have we now forgotten it ? We still know that we were much deceived through him. I do not mean that we were deceived because the people thought he was nothing; I mean, we were deceived by being told to go and call him and he would appear; and if we are told to worship him and he will give us so-and so and so-and-

---

[30] By this he means, that praying to Unkulunkulu, the first man, would prove just as great a deceit as children's calling to him; for as he could not appear to them, so he cannot hear our prayers, for he is but a man like ourselves, dead and buried long ago.

ukuti nokuti, noma ukupila, ku sa ku ba njengokukohliswa kwetu. UMPENGULA MBANDA.	so, or health, it will still be like our being deceived.[37]

INDABA yabantu abamnyama a ba i tsho kubelungu ngokuvela kwabo. Ku tiwa abantu abamnyama ba puma kukqala, lapa kwa datshukwa kona izizwe zonke ; kepa	THE account which black men give white men of their origin. It is said the black men came out first from the place whence all nations proceeded ;[38] but they did

[37] The native gives the following explanation of his words here :—

Ngi tanda ukuti ngaloku 'kubonga Unkulunkulu, uma si yekiswa Onkulunkulu betu e si ba bongayo, ku tiwe a si bonge lowo o kade a yekwa, si nge ze sa vuma, ngokuba naye u umuntu wokukqala, kepa na laba betu ba njengaye ; a si boni oku nga si sizayo ngaye ; ku se kunye nje.	I would say as regards the worship of Unkulunkulu, if we are made to leave our own Onkulunkulu, whom we worship, and are told to worship him whom we left long ago, we shall never assent ; for he too is a man—the first, and those which we call our people are men like him ; we do not see in what way he can help us ; they are all alike.

[38] We have already seen how prevalent is the tradition that man and all other things came out of the earth. The natives of these parts confess they do not know where this place is. But among other South African tribes, the tradition is associated with a certain locality. Thus the Basutos and Lighoyas point to a place which they call " Instuana-Tsatsi," which means the East. Arbousset says :—

" This spot is very celebrated amongst the Basutos and the Lighoyas, not only because the *litakus* of the tribes are there, but because of a certain mythos, in which they are told that their ancestors came originally from that place. There is there a cavern surrounded with marsh reeds and mud, whence they believe that they have all proceeded." *(Arbousset. Op. cit., p. 198.)*

And among the Baperis, " at the base of a small mountain which they call *Mole*, is a deep cavern called *Marimatle, fine bloods* or *pretty races*, because they maintain that men and the other animals came out of it ; and not only so, but that the souls return thither after death ; an opinion which reminds one of the old pagan doctrine of the infernal regions." *(Id., p. 255.)*

Campbell also gives us a similar account :—

" With respect to the origin of mankind, the old men had given him no information ; but there is a great hole in the Marootzee country out of which men first came, and their footmarks are still to be

bona a ba pumanga nanto 'ningi; kupela izinkomo namabele, oku ingcozana, nemikonto, namagejo okulima ngemikono, nokunye oku kona, umlilo wokubasa ukuze ba dhle ngawo, ukudhla okuluhlaza ku vutwe ngokupekwa; nebumba into a ba y' aziko, ukuba uma si bumba umhlaba, si w enze isitsha, si u yeke, w ome; lapo se w omile, si ye 'ku u tshisa ngomlilo, u be bomvu; s' azi ke ukuba noma se ku telwa amanzi, a u sa yi 'kubidhlika, ngokuba se u kqinisiwe; nokuhlakanipa oku lingene ukuzisiza, uma si lambile; nokukqikela isikati sokulima, ukuze si nga dhluli, si fe indhlala ngoku nga s' azi isikati esi fanele nesi nga fanele. Ukwazana kwetu kwa lingana ukuzisiza nje; a sa ba nako ukwazi okukulu.

not come out with many things; but only with a few cattle and a little corn, and assagais, and picks for digging with the arms, and some other things which they have; fire to kindle, that they might not eat raw food, but that which is cooked; and potters' earth is a thing which they know, to wit, if we temper earth, and make it a vessel, and leave it that it may dry; and when it is dry, burn it with fire, that it may be red; we know that although water be now poured into it, it will no longer fall to pieces, for it has now become strong; and wisdom which suffices to help ourselves when we are hungry, and to understand the time of digging, that it may not pass and we die of famine, through not knowing suitable and unsuitable times. Our little knowledge just sufficed for helping ourselves; we had no great knowledge.

Sa puma ke si pete loko oku lingene tina, si ti si nako konke, si hlakanipile, a ku ko 'luto e si nga lw aziko. Sa hlala, si zincoma ngokuti si nako konke.

So we came out possessed of what sufficed us, we thinking that we possessed all things, that we were wise, that there was nothing which we did not know. We lived boasting that we possessed all things.

seen there. One man came out of it long ago, but he went back, and is there yet. Morokey never saw the hole himself, but his uncle, who is dead, had seen it, and saw the footmarks very plain. The cattle also came from the same hole." *(Travels in South Africa. Campbell. Vol. I., p. 306.)*

Se ku ti namu*h*la, uma ku fike abelungu, ba fike nezin*q*ola, zi botshelwe izinkomo, b' embata ulwembu, be *h*lakanipile kakulu, b' enza izinto e si ti tina zi ng' e‑nziwe 'muntu, e si nga keabanganga ngazo nakanye, ukuba zi nga si siza. Inkomo sa si ng' azi ukuba i nemisebenzi eminingi; sa si ti, umsebenzi wenkomo ukuba i zale, si d*h*le amasi; inkabi si i *h*labe, si d*h*le inyama, ku be ukupela. Si nga w azi umsebenzi omunye wenkomo; e *h*latshiweyo si i pale isikumba sayo, s' enze amag*q*ila okuvata abesifazana nezipuku zokwambata, ku be ukupela ke umsebenzi wenkomo. Sa mangala si bona inkomo i botshelwe en*q*oleni, i twele impa*h*la, i dabula izwe, i ya kude, ku nge ko oku nge ko pakati kwen*q*ola; lapa ku kunyulwa kona, ku pume izinto zonke zalabo 'bantu; sa ti, "Ba fikile aomahambanend*h*lwane."³⁹ Ind*h*lwane si tsho in*q*ola.

Loko ke kwa si mangalisa impela. Sa bona ukuba, kanti tina abamnyama a si pumanga naluto nolulodwa; sa puma-ze; sa shiya

But now when the white men have come with wagons, oxen are yoked, they being clothed in fine linen, being very wise, and doing things which for our parts we thought could not be done by man; about which we did not think in the least, that they could help us. We did not know that the ox was useful for many purposes; we used to say, the purpose of the cow is, that it should have calves, and we eat milk; and of the ox that we should kill it and eat flesh, and that was all. We knew no other purpose of cattle. When one is killed we prepare its skin, and make women's clothes, and blankets; and that is the whole purpose of the ox. We wondered when we saw oxen yoked into a wagon, which had goods in it, and go through the country, and go to a distance, there being nothing that is not in the wagon; and when the oxen are loosened, there comes out all the property of those men; we said, "Those are come who go about with a house." By house we meant the wagon.

That, then, made us wonder exceedingly. We saw that, in fact, we black men came out without a single thing; we came out naked; we left every thing behind,

---

³⁹ The name given to snails, caddisworms, &c.

konke ngokuba sa puma kukqala. Kepa abelungu sa bona ukuba bona ba gogoda⁴⁰ uku*h*lakanipa ; ngokuba a ku ko 'luto olu s' a*h*lulayo tina be nga lw azi ; ba z' azi zonke e si nga z' aziyo ; sa bona ukuba tina sa puma ngamaputuputu ; kepa bona ba linda izinto zonke ukuba ba nga zi shiyi. Nembala ba puma nazo. Ngaloko ke si ya ba tusa, ngokuti, " I bona ba puma nezinto zonke etongweni elikulu ; i bona ba puma nobu*h*le bonke ; tina sa puma nobuula boku ng' azi 'luto." Manje se ku nga i kona si zalwako i bona, bona be fika nako konke. Se be si tshela konke, e nga si kw azi nati uma sa linda ; u loko si nga lindanga se s' abantwana kubo.

Ku ngaloko ke uku s' a*h*lula kwabo, a ba s' a*h*lulanga ngampi ; ba s' a*h*lula ngom*h*lalapansi—be *h*lezi, nati si *h*lezi ; s' a*h*lulwa imisebenzi yabo e si mangalisayo ; sa

because we came out first. But as for the white men, we saw that they scraped out the last bit of wisdom ; for there is every thing, which is too much for us, they know ; they know all things which we do not know ; we saw that we came out in a hurry ; but they waited for all things, that they might not leave any behind. So in truth they came out with them. Therefore we honour them, saying, " It is they who came out possessed of all things from the great Spirit ;⁴¹ it is they who came out possessed of all goodness ; we came out possessed with the folly of utter ignorance." Now it is as if they were becoming our fathers, for they come to us possessed of all things. Now they tell us all things, which we too might have known had we waited ; it is because we did not wait that we are now children in comparison of them.

Therefore, as to their victory over us, they were not victorious by armies ; they were victorious by sitting still—they sitting still and we too sitting still ; we were overcome by their works, which make us wonder, and say, " These

---

⁴⁰ *Ukugogoda*, to scrape out the very last portion of food, &c., left in a vessel. Hence, metonymically, to be very wise,—perfectly wise.

⁴¹ There is no doubt that *Itongo* is Spirit ; it is the general word employed to express spiritual power, and, I think, ought to be used instead of *umoya*.

ti, "Laba ab' enze nje, a ku fanele ukuba si keabange ngokulwa nabo," njengokuba imisebenzi yabo i ya s' a*h*lula, na ngezikali ba ya 'ku s' a*h*lula futi.

UMPENGULA MBANDA.

men who can do such things, it is not proper that we should think of contending with them," as, if because their works conquer us, they would conquer us also by weapons.

———————

ABELUNGU ba puma nokupelele etongweni elikulu.

Indaba yetongo elikulu eli tshiwo abantu abamnyama, ba ti, ekuveleni kwetu, tina 'bantu sa puma nezintwana ezi lingene ukuba si d*h*le si pile ngazo; uku*h*lakanipa kwa ba oku lingene ukuzisiza tina.

Ngaloko ke 'ku*h*lakanipa kwetu okuncinaue, si se sodwa tina abamnyama sa si nga tsho ukuti si nokuncinane; sa ti, si noku*h*lakanipa okukulu e sa piwako Unkulunkulu. Kepa manje se si ti kuncinane, ngokuba si bona uku*h*lakanipa okukulu kwabelungu oku sibekela ukwazana kwetu konke e sa si temba ngako.

Futi, sa si nga tsho ukuti, ba kona aba sala emuva ekudatshulweni kwezizwe. Sa si ti, sa puma kanye sonke. Si ya bona manje ukuti, "Ai; a si pumanga naluto olona sa abantu ngalo." Si

THE white men came out from a great Itongo with what is perfect.

As regards the great Itongo which is spoken of by black men, they say that we black men at our origin came out with little things, which were merely sufficient for us to obtain food and to live; our wisdom was enough to enable us to help ourselves.

As regards, then, that little wisdom, whilst we black men were by ourselves we used not to think we had little wisdom; we thought we had great wisdom, which Unkulunkulu gave us. But now we say it is little, because we see the great wisdom of the white men which overshadows all our little wisdom in which we used to trust.

Further, we used not to say that there were those who remained behind when the nations broke off. We used to say, we came out all together. But now we see it was not so, but that we did not come out with any thing which made us really men. We see that

bona ukuba abelungu bona ba sala ba zuza kakulu etongweni elikulu.

Lapa si ti itongo elikulu, kakulu a si tsho ngomuntu wakwiti ofileyo ukuti u 'litongo elikulu ; ngokuba a ku tshiwo futi ukuba leli 'tongo elikulu Unkulunkulu, e si ti wa dabula izizwe. Ilizwi lodwa eli kombako ukuba abelungu ba puma nako konke, ba kqedela okobuntu ; ba puma be hlubile, be nge njengati ; tina sa puma si se nolwebu, si nga hlubanga. Izinto zonke e sa puma nazo a si z' azanga kakulu uku zi kqonda. Ngaloko ke manje ilizwi lelo li kona lokuba abelungu ba puma nokupelele etongweni elikulu. Kodwa ngi nga l' azi uma leli 'tongo elikulu ku tshiwo Unkulunkulu ini ke ; kodwa ku be kona ukuba 'litongo elikulu ku nga tshiwo ukuba itongo lelo u yena Unkulunkulu, ngokuba naye ku tiwa wa vela ohlangeni ; a kw azeki kahle ke ukuba elona 'tongo i li pi na

the white men remained behind, and obtained very much from the great Itongo.

When we say the great Itongo, we do not speak of one of our dead, that he is a great Itongo. For it is not said that that great itongo is Unkulunkulu, who we say broke off the nations. It is only a word which points out that the white men came out with every thing, and possessed of every thing that was needed for manhood ; they came out perfect,[42] not like us who came out imperfect, not having cast off the skin of imperfection. And all those things with which we came out we did not know sufficiently to understand them. On that account the word has arisen that the white men came out with what is perfect from a great Itongo. But I do not know that that Itongo is said to be Unkulunkulu ; but it used not to be said that that Itongo was one with Unkulunkulu, for he too sprang from Uthlanga ; we cannot well understand whether

---

[42] The metaphor here is borrowed from the peeling off of the skin of a new born child, or the casting off of the skin by a snake, that it might be, as the natives think, more perfect. The white man cast off the skin of imperfection before leaving the source of being. The coloured man came out with the skin of imperfection still adhering to him, and it has not been cast off to this day.

kunonkulunkulu noklanga na. A
ku klanzekanga lapo.
    Umpengula Mbanda.

that Itongo is more likely to be Unkulunkulu, or Uthlanga.[43] That is by no means clear.[44]

[43] Pringle describes Makanna, the great Kafir prophet, as referring his mission to "Uthlanga, the Great Spirit:"—

"By his spirit-rousing eloquence, his pretended revelations from Heaven, and his confident predictions of complete success, provided they would implicitly follow his counsels, he persuaded the great majority of the Amakxosa clans, including some of Hinza's captains, to unite their forces for a simultaneous attack upon Graham's-town, the head-quarters of the British troops. He told them that he was sent by Uthlanga, the Great Spirit, to avenge their wrongs; that he had power to call up from the grave the spirits of their ancestors to assist them in battle against the English, whom they should drive, before they stopped, across the Zwartkops river and into the ocean; 'and then,' said the prophet, 'we will sit down and eat honey!' Ignorant of our vast resources, Makanna probably conceived that, this once effected, the contest was over for ever with the usurping Europeans." *(Narrative of a Residence in South Africa.* Pringle, p. 299.*)*

It would be interesting to know what were the exact words used by Makanna. Did he really use the words ascribed to him? or has Pringle paraphrased for him? However this may be, it is clear that Pringle had been led by his investigations among the Frontier Kafirs to conclude that their idea of God is to be found in the word Uthlanga.

Shaw also remarks:—

"Before Missionaries and other Europeans had intercourse with the Kaffirs, they seem to have had extremely vague and indistinct notions concerning the existence of God. The older Kaffirs used to speak of Umdali, the Creator or Maker of all things, and Uthlanga, which word seems to have been used to denote the source or place from which all living things came forth." *(Story of My Mission, p. 451.)*

There can be no doubt that whilst Uthlanga is used by some to mean a reed, which is supposed to have given origin to all things; and others speak of Uthlanga as the place from which all things came out, yet the majority give it a personal signification; and in tracing the tradition backwards, we rest at last in Uthlanga as the word which of all others has wrapped up in it the native idea of a Creator.

[44] This notion of successive egressions from the centre of creation, which is a new idea among the natives of this country, having arisen from a wish to explain the difference between themselves and us, has its counterpart among the native tribes of South America:—

"They believe that their good deities made the world, and that they first created the Indians in their caves, gave them the lance, the bow and arrows, and the stone-bowls, to fight and hunt with, and then turned them out to shift for themselves. They imagine that the dei-

The following account was obtained many years ago. It was in fact among some of the very first papers written at the dictation of natives. The native who gave it was an Izulu, who had just come as a refugee from Zululand. I laid it aside as useless because the first answers the man gave were absolutely contradictory to those I have recorded, which he gave when I began to write. But there is reason to think from statements made by other natives, which have been given above, that he was really speaking of two Onkulunkulu,—the first man, of whom he correctly affirmed that no one prayed to him, worshipped him, or offered him any honour, but to whom he refers the origin, at least the ordering, of things and customs; and of the Unkulunkulu of the Zulu nation, or of his own tribe, of whom he correctly affirmed afterwards that the Amazulu pray to and worship him :—

Unkulunkulu u ng' ubani na?	Who is Unkulunkulu?
Tina a s' azi Unkulunkulu. A ngi m azi Unkulunkulu. Ngi kombela pezulu, ngi ti, "Nanku Unkulunkulu."	We do not know Unkulunkulu. I do not know Unkulunkulu.[45] I point to heaven and say, "There is Unkulunkulu."[46]

ties of the Spaniards did the same by them; but that, instead of lances, bows, etc., they gave them guns and swords. They suppose that when the beasts, birds, and lesser animals were created, those of the more nimble kind came immediately out of their caves; but that the bulls and cows being the last, the Indians were so frightened at the sight of their horns, that they stopped up the entrance of their caves with great stones. This is the reason they give why they had no black cattle in their country till the Spaniards brought them over, who more wisely had let them out of the caves." *(Researches into the Early History of Mankind. Tylor, p. 313.)*

[45] In accordance with the answer invariably given by natives, when referring to Unkulunkulu, the first man.

[46] The native teacher thinks he must here refer to the legend of the ascent of Usenzangakona into heaven. Note 4, p. 55. This is quite possible; and that in the statements which follow he might be referring to supposed creative acts, which he ascribed to that chief. Compare Ukoto's statement, p. 50, with that of Ubapa's mother, p. 55, who sums up her faith with the statement, that "the whitemen are the lords who made all things."

Abantu ba m bonga Unkulunkulu na?

Yebo, ba m bonga. Si ya m tanda Unkulunkulu ngokuba si dhla amabele, si vube amasi; si hlabe inyama yetu, si dhle umbila wetu, si dhle imf' etu. Si ya m tanda Unkulunkulu, a ti, "Ma si tate abafazi ba be 'lishumi." Unkulunkulu si ya m tanda ngokub' a ti, "Ma si dhle inyama yetu." Yena Unkulunkulu w' ona ukub' a ti, "Ma si bulawe, si fe, si shiye inyama yetu." A ti yena, "Ma si fe, si nga se zi 'kuvuka." W' ona ke ukuba si fe ke si nga se zi 'kuvuka. Unkulunkulu muhle ngokuti, "Ma si kipe inkomo zetu, si tenge umfazi." Sa m tanda ke ngaloku, ngokuba si dhla amadumbi; sa m tanda ngokuba si dhla umhlaza. Sa m tanda ngokub' a ti, "Ma si puze utshwala betu." Si ya m tanda ngokuba a ti, "Ma si dhle inyamazane."

Abantu ba kuleka kunkulunkulu na?

Yebo, ba kuleka kuye, ba ti, "Mngane! Nkosi!"

Do the people worship Unkulunkulu?

Yes, they worship him. We love Unkulunkulu because we eat corn,[47] and mix it with amasi; and kill our cattle, and eat our maize, and our sweet cane. We love Unkulunkulu because he told us to take ten wives. We love Unkulunkulu because he told us to eat our meat. But Unkulunkulu erred when he said that we were to be killed, and die, and leave our meat. He said that we were to die and never rise again. He erred therefore when he allowed us to die and rise no more. Unkulunkulu is good because he told us to take our cattle and buy a wife. We love him on this account, because we eat amadumbi and umthlaza,[48] and because he told us to drink our beer. We love him because he told us to eat the flesh of game.

Do the people salute Unkulunkulu?

Yes, they salute him, saying, "O Friend! Chief!"[49]

---

[47] Compare what is said, p. 25. The worship of Unkulunkulu consists in rejoicing at what is supposed to be his gift, good or bad, and by casting on him and his ordinance the responsibility of their own evil doing.

[48] *Amadumbi*, edible tubers, a kind of arum, which the natives cultivate. *Umthlaza* is also an edible tuber.

[49] Or, Lord, or King.

Ba ya kcela into kuye na? Yebo. Ba ti, " Si pe imvula, nkosi, ku kule umbila wetu."	Do they ask him for any thing? Yes. They say, " Give us rain, O Chief, that our maize may grow."[50]
Abadala ba ti, " Wa be indoda Unkulunkulu, wa be nomfazi." A ngi l' azi igama na lomfazi. Abadala ba ti, " Wa e nomfazi, wa e zala abantwana." Unkulunkulu wa veza abantu ngokuzala.	The old men say that Unkulunkulu was a man, and had a wife. Neither do I know the name of his wife. The old men say that he had a wife, and that he had children. Unkulunkulu produced children by generation.

[50] This is the only instance I have met with in which even apparently a native has said that prayer is made to Unkulunkulu, the first man. On the contrary, every previous account implies the reverse. I cannot personally enquire of the native who related the above, but there can be little doubt that he was not alluding to Unkulunkulu, the first man; but to the head of the Zulu nation, or of his own family—Onkulunkulu which are admitted on all hands to be objects of worship and of prayer among the other Amatongo. Mr. Shooter, in his work on Natal, says :—

"The tradition of the Great-Great (Unkulunkulu) is not universally known among the people. War, change, and the worship of false deities have gradually darkened their minds and obscured their remembrance of the true God. Captain Gardiner states that the generality of the people were ignorant of it in his time." *(p. 160.)* See Note 3, p. 54. Captain Gardiner doubtless would find " the generality of the people " utterly ignorant of an Unkulunkulu in heaven, except as a part of their faith in such legends as that of the ascent of Usenzangakona. But I have never yet met with any native old or young, of Natal or Zululand, or from any part between Natal and the Cape, who was ignorant of the tradition of an Unkulunkulu who came out of the earth, the first man, who lived, gave laws to his children, and died.

Again, Mr. Shooter says :—

"There is a tribe in Natal which still worships the Great-Great (Unkulunkulu), though the recollection of him is very dim. When they kill the ox they say, ' Hear, Unkulunkulu, may it be always so.' "

This statement also appears to be the result of inaccurate investigation and misapprehension. I never met with a case, neither have I met with any native that has, in which Unkulunkulu is thus addressed. But the Onkulunkulu of houses or tribes are addressed, not by the name Unkulunkulu, but by their proper names, as Udumakade, Uzimase, &c. Instances of this worship of the Onkulunkulu have been already given. When we come to the "AMATONGO" we shall see more clearly what is really the nature of their worship, and that Unkulunkulu, the first man, is of necessity shut out.

Having had some conversation with Mr. Thomas Hancock on the meaning of Unkulunkulu, he summoned several old Amabakea living near him on the Umzimkulu; and we enquired the names of the fathers of generations, beginning from the present, and going backward. They gave the following:—

Ubaba	My father
Ubaba-mkulu	My grandfather
Ubaba-mkulu kababa-mkulu	My great-grandfather [lit., the grandfather of my grandfather]
Ukoko	My great-great-grandfather
Ukulu	My great-great-great-grandfather

They did not go further back, but were inclined to give the names of those who preceded. They said nothing about Unkulunkulu, until we mentioned the word, and asked who he was. They then threw their heads backward and said, "He was a long, long time ago, and begat many people."

Shortly after, Mr. Hancock sent one Usithlanu, an old Izulu, one of Utshaka's soldiers, with a note, in which he says:—"Since you were here I have questioned the bearer about Unkulunkulu, as also others. But unless I first give them the idea, they know very little or nothing about it but the name, and that he is one that has begotten a great number of children. He may be the fiftieth grandfather, or the five-hundreth."

I proceeded to enquire of Usithlanu by the aid of a native, directing him in the first place to ask Usithlanu to go backwards and tell me what the Amazulu call the fathers of generations, beginning with his own father. He answered:—

Owa zala ubaba ubaba-mkulu; owa zala ubaba-mkulu ukoko; owa zala ukoko unkulunkulwana; owa zala unkulunkulwana unkulunkulu.	The father of my father is ubaba-mkulu; his father is ukoko; the father of ukoko is unkulunkulwana;[51] the father of unkulunkulwana is unkulunkulu.

[51] This was the first time I had met with the word Unkulunku-

Here he stopped; but when I requested him to go on still reckoning backwards, he added:—

Owa zala unkulunkulu unkulunkulu o ngembili; owa zala unkulunkulu o ngembili[52] unkulunkulu o ngembili futi, Ud*h*lamini, U*h*lomo, Uhhadebe, Ungwana, Umashwabade.	The father of uukulunkulu is an anterior unkulunkulu; and the father of that anterior unkulunkulu a still anterior unkulunkulu, Udhlamini, Uthlomo, Uhhadebe, Ungwana, Umashwabade.

Beyond these he could not remember, but added, the five names here given are those by which they call their houses, that is, families, viz., their izibongo or surnames.

I then requested him to give me his own name, and the names of his father, grandfather, &c., as far back as he could remember, which he did as follows:—

Iwana in my intercourse with the natives. It is a diminutive, and means the lesser or inferior Unkulunkulu. But Captain Gardiner mentions it in the following extract:—

"It is agreed among the Zoolus, that their forefathers believed in the existence of an overruling spirit, whom they called Villenangi [Umvelinqangi] (literally the First Appearer), and who soon after created another heavenly being of great power, called Koolukoolwani, [Unkulunkulwana,] who once visited this earth, in order to publish the news (as they express it), as also to separate the sexes and colours among mankind. During the period he was below, two messages were sent to him from Villenangi, the first conveyed by a cameleon, announcing that men were not to die; the second, by a lizard, with a contrary decision. The lizard, having outrun the slow-paced cameleon, arrived first, and delivered his message before the latter made his appearance." *(p. 178.)*

In an earlier part of his journal, after an interview with Udingane, he says:—

"But what was God, and God's word, and the nature of the instruction I proposed, were subjects which he could not at all comprehend." *(p. 31.)*

[52] *Nyembili.*—Usithlanu has been living for many years among the Amabakca, and uses *ngembili* for the Zulu *ngapambili;* the Amalala say *nyak'embili.*

Usi*h*lanu	
Umantanda	Ubaba
Usigwak*q*a	Ubaba-mkulu
Umlotsha	Ukoko
Umselo	Unkulunkulwana
Ulinda	Unkulunkulu
Uvumandaba	Unkulunkulu o ngembili
Ud*h*lamini	ditto
U*h*lomo	ditto
Uhhadebe	ditto
Ungwana	ditto
Umashwabade	ditto

Izibongo zalabo bonke Ud*h*lamini nohhadebe nomtimkulu.	The surnames of all of them are Udhlamini, Uhhadebe, and Umtimkulu.[53]

Upon further enquiry it appeared that he did not mean that all the Onkulunkulu here mentioned were the heads of generations in regular retrogression, but that the last six were contemporary, and descended from one father. I asked him to go still further back, but he was unable; and added :—

Lapa si gcina kumtimkulu nongwana nomashwabade no*h*lomo, i bona aba dabula izizwe, amakosi.	We end with Umtimkulu and Ungwana and Umashwabade and Uthlomo, because they were the chiefs who divided the nations.

As he did not of his own accord go back to the first unkulunkulu, I asked him to tell me what, when he was a boy, he was told about the origin of man. He said :—

Ba ti, sa puma emanzini, em*h*langeni, elwand*h*le. Si zwe ku tiwa, "Wa vela umuntu wokuk*q*ala owa puma elu*h*langeni. Wa	They told us that we came out of the water, from a bed of reeds, by the sea. We heard it said, "There appeared the first man, who came out of a reed. He

---

[53] These three were great chiefs,—amakosi o*h*langa,—who left their names as izibongo of their respective tribes.

komba amabele e milile, wa ti, "Ka-nini.⁵⁴ Nank' amabele," e tsho Unkulunkulu wamandulo,⁵⁵ Ukqili. Ukqili kambe Unkulunkulu wokukqala owa puma emhlangeni, wa zala abantu.

Umuntu wokukqala u tiwa Unkulunkulu. Wa vela nomfazi; nabanye abantu ba vela emhlangeni emva kwake, abantu bonke bendulo. Yena owokukqala e mkulu kambe, yena a zala abantu. Si tsho tina 'bantu, si ti, "Ba zalwa nguye yena a vela kukqala."

Abantu bendulo a si b' azi ukuzalwa kwabo. Ba vela emhlangeni nje; naye Unkulunkulu wa vela

pointed to the growing corn and said, "Pluck. That is corn." This was said by the most ancient Unkulunkulu, Ukqili.⁵⁶ For Ukqili was the first Unkulunkulu who came out of the bed of reeds, and begat men.

The first man is called Unkulunkulu. He came out with a wife; and other men came out of the bed of reeds after him, all the primitive men. He the first was chief indeed, he who begat men. We say, "They were begotten by him who came out first."

We do not know that the primitive men were begotten. They came, as they were, out of the bed

---

⁵⁴ *Ka-nini*, Pluck, for Yika ni.

⁵⁵ *Wamandulo*.—The most ancient Unkulunkulu.

Ba kona abantu bendulo abaningi, kepa e si ti owamandulo o ngapambili kwalabo bendulo.

There are many ancients, but he whom we call owamandulo was before all the other ancients.

⁵⁶ *Ukqili*, ikqili made into a proper name. The-wise-one.

Ku tshiwo umuntu ow azi kakulu; ngaloko ke ngokuhlakanipa kwake a ku sa tshiwo ukuti ikqili, se ku tiwa Ukqili. Owokukqala ku tiwa Ukqili, ngokuba wa kw enza konke.

It means a man of exceeding knowledge; therefore on account of his wisdom he is not merely called in general terms wise, but by the proper name, "The-wise-one" (or Craftman). The first man is called Ukqili because he made all things.

Just as he is called *Umdali*, the breaker off, because he is supposed to have been the instrumental agent by which all things were broken off or separated from the source or place of being; and *Umenzi*, the maker, because he is supposed to have made all things, so the personal name *Ukqili* is applied to him to denote the wisdom manifested in the act of creation.

M

nje. A si m boni, si zwa nje ngoḣlanga. Si ti ke wa kqala, wa milisa umḣlaba, wa milisa intabake, amanzi, amabele, ukudḣla, inkomo, nako konke. Kwa puma konke nezinja nenkomo emanzini. Si ti kw' enziwa u yena, loku si te si vela kwa se ku kona konke loko.

Unkulunkulu wa puma eluḣlangeni e nomfazi; u tiwa nomfazi Unkulunkulu bobabili.

of reeds ;[57] and Unkulunkulu came out as he was. We do not see him, and hear only of Uthlanga.[58] So we say he was first; he made[59] the earth, and the mountains, the water, corn, food, cattle, and every thing. All things came out of the water, dogs and cattle. We say they were made by him, for when we came into being they were already all in existence.

Unkulunkulu came out of Uthlanga with a wife; she, as well as he, is called Unkulunkulu.

I asked him to trace back the female heads of generation, as he had already the male heads. He said:—

Owa ngi zala umame.

She who gave birth to me is umame.

Owa zala umame umakulu, noma ukulu.

She who gave birth to umame is umakulu or ukulu.

Owa zala umakulu ukoko wami.

She who gave birth to umakulu is my ukoko.

Owa zala ukoko wami ukulukulu.

She who gave birth to my ukoko is ukulukulu.

Owa zala ukulukulu unkulunkulu.

She who gave birth to ukulukulu is unkulunkulu.

[57] This notion appears to be frequently intimated in the legends of the origin of man,—that not only Unkulunkulu came out of the bed of reeds, but primitive men also (abantu bendulo). Unkulunkulu simply came out first; they followed with cattle, &c. The abantu bendulo therefore were not his offspring, but came out as they were from the same place as Unkulunkulu. An old Ikqwabi, in relating the legend, said that Unkulunkulu was a great man; he sat in a hole, somewhere near the Umtshezi, a river in Zululand, appearing with his body only above the ground, and thus sitting moulded all things. By this we are to understand that the Amakqwabi's traditional centre from which they sprang is on the Umtshezi.

[58] By Uthlanga meaning apparently the place from which Unkulunkulu and all other things came.

[59] Milisa, lit., caused to grow; but = bumba, enza.

Noma u indoda noma owesifazana, ku sa tiwa unkulunkulu naye nowesidoda. | Whether it is man or woman we say unkulunkulu, both of the female and of the male.

Thus, according to this native, the male and female heads of the fifth generation backwards are called Unkulunkulu. Thus:—

MALE:—
  Ubaba
  Ubaba-mkulu
  Ukoko ·
  Unkulunkulwana
  Unkulunkulu

FEMALE:—
  Umame
  Umakulu, or Ukulu
  Ukoko
  Ukulukulu[60]
  Unkulunkulu

I said to him, "Where now is the first unkulunkulu?" He replied:—

Okwetu sodwa tina, ku fa abancinane nabakulu, si muke ke isitunzi. Unkulunkulu wetu tina 'bantu u ye lo e si tandaza kuye ngenkomo zetu, si bonge, si ti, "Baba!" Si ti, "D*h*lamini! Hhadebe![63] Mutimkulu! Hlomo! | All we know is this, the young and the old die,[61] and the shade[62] departs. The Unkulunkulu of us black men is that one to whom we pray for our cattle, and worship, saying, "Father!" We say, "Udhlamini! Uhhadebe! Umutimkulu! Uthlomo! Let me ob-

[60] I had never before met with a native who thus separated Ukulukulu from Unkulunkulu. It is the reduplication of *ukulu* which is never, so far as I know, nasalised; and is equivalent to unkulunkulwana, the diminutive of unkulunkulu. Below we shall find another native making a similar distinction. But the majority of natives deny the correctness of this distinction.

[61] By this he means to say that Unkulunkulu no longer exists; that he has died like all others, young and old.

[62] *Isitunzi*, shade.—This is, doubtless, a word formerly used for the spirit of man, just as among the Greeks, Romans, &c. And scarcely any thing can more clearly prove the degradation which has fallen on the natives than their not understanding that isitunzi meant the spirit, and not merely the shadow cast by the body; for there now exists among them the strange belief that the dead body casts no shadow; and when they say, "Isitunzi si muke," The shade has departed, they do not mean that the soul has left its tenement, but that the body has ceased to cast a shadow.

[63] He said Uhhadebe was an Ithlubi, that is, one of the tribe of the Amathlubi.

Yebo, ngi tole, nkosi! ngi nga fi, ngi pile, ngi hambe kade." Abantu abadala ba m bona ebusuku.

tain what I wish, Lord! Let me not die, but live, and walk long on the earth."[64] Old people see him at night in their dreams.

I asked him if, when he was a boy in Zululand, the people ever said any thing about a heavenly lord. He replied:—

Mina si*h*lanu ngi ti, i b' i kona indaba yenkosi e pezulu, ngi tsho ngemvula, ngi tsho ngemitandazo yetu uma si keela imvula. A ku k*q*ali na kutshaka; na kwabendulo imitandazo yokukcela imvula ya i kona. Kepa Utshaka u fike wa d*h*lulisa eyake imitandazo. Wa mema abantu, umkand*h*lu omkulu, wa ba 'mnumuzana; wa buta inkabi ezimnyama nezimvu nezingcama ezimnyama; wa za 'utandaza; wa vuma ingoma, wa tandaza enkosini e pezulu; wa ti kokoko bake, a ba kulekele imvula enkosini pezulu. La na izulu. Ingoma:—

I, Usithlanu, for my part say there used to be something said about a heavenly lord, I mean as regards rain, and our prayers when we asked for rain. That did not begin even with Utshaka; even the primitive men used to pray for rain. But Utshaka came, and made his prayers greater than those who preceded him. He summoned the people, a great assembly, consisting of the chiefs of villages. He collected black[65] oxen, and sheep and black rams; and went to pray; he sang a song and prayed to the lord of heaven; and asked his forefathers to pray for rain to the lord of heaven. And it rained. This is the song:—

Ukuhlabelela—
  I ya wu; a wu; o ye i ye.
Ukuvuma—
  I ya wo.

One Part—
  I ya wu; a wu; o ye i ye.
Second Part, or Response—
  I ya wo.[66]

[64] Compare this with the account given p. 84, which it entirely corroborates; the Unkulunkulu of each tribe is the object of that tribe's veneration and worship. It may be as well also to note that, according to Burton, the Dahomans salute their king by crying, "Grandfather, grandfather."

[65] Black cattle are chosen because they wish black clouds, which usually pour down much rain, to cover the heavens.

[66] This song consists of musical sounds merely, but imperfectly represented by the above, without any meaning.

Lezo 'zinkomo ezomzimu; za butana 'ndawo nye. Ukuhlinzwa kwazo ku be ku tatwa imintsha yamantombazana, i binewe amalunga amakulu ezinkalweni; zi hlinzwe, zi tutwe ngabantu abanye abanciuyane, zi tutelwe endhlunkulu, ezindhlini zezalukazi, lapa ku nga yi 'kuya 'muntu. Ku ya 'kuze ku pume indoda enkulu e b' i zi hlinza nomuntu o be m bambela lap' o zi hlinzako; a zi hlahlelo kusasa, zi pekwe; zi pekwe ke 'ndawo nye ngembiza eziningi. Li muk' ilanga, a y opule ngezitebe, a u biza umpakati, a ti, a u kupuke umpakati. Ukukupuka umpakati u fike u pelele, i sa hlezi i nga dhliwa 'muntu; ba pelele b' ahluke ngezibaya ukuhlala; ba i nikwe kuhle inyama ezandhleni, ba i nikwe, be i pata, ba nga i yisi emlonyeni, ba ze ba pelele bonke, ba i yise bonke kanye emlonyeni.

Loku be kqala ba i hhubela ingoma be nga ka i dhli, ba vuma ke kakulu, ba vuma, kwa duma pansi. Ba y amukela ke emva kwokuhhuba, ba i yise kanye emlonyeni.

These cattle are the cattle of Umzimu;[67] they are collected into one place. When they are killed, the chief men gird themselves with the girdles of young girls; they are skinned and carried by other young persons and put in the chief village, in the huts of the old women, where no one enters. In the morning the great man who skinned them, and the man who helped him, go out, and divide them; and they are boiled together in many pots. When the sun is declining, they take them out and place them on feeding-mats, and tell the great men to come up. All the great men come up, the flesh not being touched by any one; all the people are made to sit down by their villages; they have the meat put in an orderly manner in their hands; they hold it without carrying it to their mouths, until all are given, and all carry it to their mouths at the same time.

They begin by singing the song before they eat; they sing it very loud, and the ground resounds with the noise of their feet. They take the meat after singing, and carry it all together to their mouths. If one has taken a long

---

[67] *Ezomzimu.* The cattle of Umzimu, that is, of the Itongo—especially dedicated to the Itongo. Captain Burton mentions a word very much like this, as being used for Ancestral Ghosts,—Muzimos,—among the people to the South-east of Dahome. *(Op. cit. Vol. II., p. 20.)*

Wa ti ow cpuze uku i kqeda, wa i beka pansi; wa ngeza wa hhuba, ukuba i pele emlonyeni.

time in eating the meat, he puts it on the ground, and sings again, when he has swallowed what is in his mouth.

During the conversation he remarked:—

Nina 'balungu na sala kweliku-lu itongo letu.

You white men remained behind with our great Itongo.[68]

I asked what he meant by "Itongo" here. Umpengula answered:—

Lapa e tsho itongo, ka kulumi ngomuntu o fileyo wa buya wa vuka; u kuluma ngesanda selizwe

When he says Itongo, he is not speaking of a man who has died and risen again; he is speaking of the up-bearer of the earth,[69] which

---

[68] Compare p. 80.

Lapa si ti, "Na sala." Futifuti ku tshiwo njalo abamnyama; lapa be bona abalungu ba kqedela bona ukuhlakanipa, ba ti ke bona, ba sala etongweni elikulu; tina a si hlalanga, sa puma, sa hamba si nge naluto. Tina si ti, ekwenziweni kwetu nani, nina na hlala, na kqedela ukuhlakanipa; tina sa puma ngokungati si ya 'ku ku tola lapa sa ya kona.

Here we say, "You remained." Black men frequently say this; when they see white men perfect in wisdom, they say they remained with the great Itongo, but we did not remain, but came out and went away without any thing. We say, at our creation together with you, you remained behind and perfected wisdom; we went out as though we should find it where we were going.

[69] *Isanda selizwe.*—*Isanda* is breadth which supports something upon it. Thus a table, bed, or sofa may be called an *isanda*. But here it means not only breadth supporting; but *the power underneath*, from which the support comes. The following was given as an explanation:—

Isanda selizwe ku tiwa inkosi, ngokuba a ku ko lapo i nge ko; y ande nezwe lonke; ngaloko ke ku tshiwo ku tiwa isanda sezwe. Njengaloku zi kona izanda eziningi zamabele; amabele a ya bekwa pezu kwesanda, ukuze amabele a nga boli ngokuhlala pansi, a hlale

The up-bearer of the earth is said to be the Lord, for there is no place where he is not; he is every where; he is therefore called the up-bearer of the earth. Just as there are many up-bearers of corn; the corn is put upon the up-bearer that it may not rot by lying on

es' emisa abantu nenkomo. Isanda umhlaba e si hamba ngawo; isanda somhlaba o si hamba ngaso e nga si nge ko uma si nge ko, e si kona ngaso.

supports men and cattle. The up-bearer is the earth by which we live; and there is the up-bearer of the earth by which we live, and without which we could not be, and by which we are.

He also related the following curious tradition:—

Indaba yetu yendulo. Kwa ke kwa ti kw' ehla izinto ezulwini pezulu. Yebo; za bonwa enzansi kwomuzi enkosini, kungwana; into zi nga zi mila uboya, zinhle,

One of our old traditions. It happened that some things came down from heaven. Yes; they were seen at the lower part of the chief Ungwana's village; they were as it were covered with hair; they were beautiful, and had the

pezulu. Ngaloko ke nendhlu futi yabantu y enzelwa isanda sezinti, ukuze upahla lu hlale pezu kwesanda, si paswe ukuze si nga wi.

the ground, but lie on a high place. For the same reason the native hut also has made for it an up-bearer of rods, that the roof may rest upon it, and be held up and not fall.

Inkosi ke ku tshiwo njalo ngayo ukuti i isanda sezwe, ngokuba izwe li paswa i yo.

In like manner, then, it is said the Lord is the up-bearer of the world, for the world is upheld by him.

E tsho na sala kwelitongo elikulu, u kuluma ngenkosi; ngokuba kwabantu abamnyama lapa be ti, "Umuntu u bhekwe itongo," a ba tsho ukuti lelo 'tongo umuntu otile; ngaloko leli 'gama lokuti itongo a li kulumi ngofileyo yedwa. Si ya bona izinhloko ezimbili, ngokuba abadala ba tsho ukuti, " Li kona itongo elikulu." Futi manje si y' ezwa futifuti ngale inkosi e si tshelwa ngayo. Abamnyama ba ya tsho ba ti, "Tongo elikulu likababa!" Omunye a buze ngokuti, " U tsho idhlozi na?" A ti, " Kqa. Ngi tsho itongo eli pezulu." Ngaloko ke itongo l' enziwa ukqobo olukulu.

When he says you remained with the great Itongo, he means the Lord; for among black men, when they say, " The Itongo looks on a man," they do not mean that the Itongo is a certain man; for the word Itongo is not used of a dead man only. We see it has two meanings, for the ancients said, "There is a great Itongo." And now we continually hear about that Lord which is mentioned to us. Black men say, " Great Itongo of my father!" And another asks, " Do you mean the ancestral spirit?" He replies, " No, I mean the great Itongo which is in heaven." So then the Itongo is made a great person.

zi 'mehlo a nga ti umuntu, zi milise kwomuntu. Kwa tiwa, "Izilwane, a zi bulawe." Kwa tiwa za zimbili. Za bulawa. Izwe la fa ke; inkosi y' emuka nomoya, ngokuba ku bulewe lezo 'zilo; nezindhlu z' emuka. S' ezwa ke wa fika Ugodongwana kajobe.

eyes and form of a man. It was said, "They are wild beasts; let them be killed." There were two. They were killed. The whole country died; the chief was carried away by the wind, because those animals were killed; and the houses were carried away. And we hear that there then began to reign Ugodongwana, the son of Ujobe.

Ugofana and Umyeni, two Amakuza, came to see me. I asked them to give me the names of the heads of generations on the female side. They agreed in the main, but Umyeni made Unkulunkulu the head of the fifth generation backwards, and Ugofana of the fourth; Umyeni inserting Ukulukulu as the fourth, like Usithlanu (see p. 91). I then asked them to give me the heads on the male side, in like manner. The result was as under:—

Ubaba	Umame
Ubaba-mkulu	Ukulu
Ukoko	Ukoko
Unkulunkulwana	Ukulukulu
Unkulunkulu	Unkulunkulu

I asked Ugofana what they said about the Unkulunkulu of all men. He said they knew nothing about him. They said he came out of a reed. He could not tell me any thing about that Unkulunkulu, nor any body else, for no one knew. All he could tell me was about his own Unkulunkulu, for said he, pointing to two others, "He has his; and he his; and I mine."

Owa dabuka Umdanga (Umdaka) wa zala Umsondo; Umsondo wa zala Uhlanguza; Uhlanguza wa zala Ujamo, owa zala mina.

Umdanga, who first broke off, begat Umsondo; Umsondo begat Uthlanguza; Uthlanguza begat Ujamo, who begat me.

I asked them what they meant by "Owa dabuka," Who first broke off. Umyeni replied, "Kuyise," From his father. And Ugofana, after a moment's thought, gave his name, "Kud*h*lad*h*la," From Udhladhla, the great ancestor of their house, who has given them their surname.

———•———

Two Amabakca, an old and young man, gave me the heads of generations as given above, p. 86.

"But," I said, "is there not another word, Ukulukulu or Unkulunkulu?"

They said, "He is further back (ngembili);" and went on to say that all who were heads of generations anterior to the okoko were called Ukulukulu, till they came to Umsondwo,[70]

owa vela kuk*q*ala, u lona ulu*h*langa lwabantu; u lona olwa dala abantu, ba dabuke kulo, olu Umsondwo owa dabuka wa dabula abantu, umdali, umdali welive.	who came out first; he is the uthlanga of men; he is that uthlanga who broke off men, they having been broken off from him. The uthlanga is Umsondwo, who broke off, and then broke off men, the umdali, the umdali of the earth.[71]

I asked them what they said about the Okulukulu. They replied:—

Aba ngembili kwokoko ba okulukulu bokoko njalonjalo, ba za ba yofika kumsondwo, owa vela kuk*q*ala, umdali welive.	They who are anterior to the okoko are the okulukulu of the okoko in continuous retrogression, till they reach Umsondwo, who first appeared, the umdali of the earth.

[70] Or, Unsondo, see p. 13.

[71] *Umdali* is the same as *Umdabuli*, from *ukudala*, the same as *ukudabula*. The creator, in the sense understood by the natives. (See Note 3, p. 1.)

I asked what they meant by Uthlanga. They answered :—

Uhlanga umuntu omdala owa dala izikci zonke nenkomo, nezinto, ne yonke impahla.	Uthlanga is an old man who made all things, both cattle and things, and all kinds of property.

Umdumo, an old man, one of Ukukulela's people, an Ikuza, being unwilling or unable to give me any account of the traditions of the people, I asked him to give me the names of the heads of generations backwards. He gave them thus :—

Owa ngi zala Upotshiyana, ubaba; owa zala Upotshiyana, Umzabani, ubaba-mkulu; owa zala Umzabani, Uhlomo, uyise kababamkulu; owa zala Uhlomo, Unsele, ukoko; owa zala Unsele, Usivunga, ukoko kababa-mkulu; owa zala Usivunga, Ulusibalukulu. Ulusibalukulu wa zalwa Udhlamini, ukulukulu owa dabula izizwe. Wa fika wa dabula Ubihla, inkosi; w' elekela Ukukulela nomaghaga.	He who begat me is Upotshiyana, my father; he who begat Upotshiyana is Umzabani, my grandfather; he who begat Umzabani is Uthlomo, the father of my grandfather; he who begat Uthlomo is Unsele, my ukoko; he who begat Unsele is Usivunga, the ukoko of my grandfather; he who begat Usivunga is Ulusibalukulu. Ulusibalukulu was begotten by Udhlamini, the ukulukulu who broke off the nations. When he came he broke off Ubithla, the chief; and afterwards Ukukulela and Umaghaga.

I asked him if there was not an Unkulunkulu. He replied, "Unkulunkulu and Ukulukulu is one."

I again asked him who was the first man. He answered :—

Udhlamini u yena owa dabuka kukqala, wa zala Ulusibalukulu, owa zala Usivunga.	Udhlamini is he who broke off first; he begat Ulusibalukulu, who begat Usivunga.

I again asked him still more pointedly, referring to their tradition of the origin of man. He replied :—

Udhlamini ibizo lowokukqala, e si ti Ukulukulu.	Udhlamini is the name of the first man, whom we call Ukulukulu.[72]

I asked, "Wa dabuka pi?" Where did he break off? He said:

Ku tiwa Udhlamini lowo wa dabuka entabeni, engome, isidabuko setu.	It is said that Udhlamini broke off from the mountain Ingome, the place of the origin[73] of our tribe.

I asked him what were the nations he broke off (izizwe owa zi dabula). He mentioned several, but I did not succeed in writing the names; but among them were those of which Ukukulela, Uisidoi, and Ufodo are chiefs. The isibongo or surname of these chiefs is Udhlamini, he being their common ancestor.

I OVERHEARD Uthlangabeza, one of Ukukulela's people, talking with some of the men of the village. He said Unkulunkulu and Ukukulu is one; and Umvelinqangi and Unkulunkulu is one; that all things came out of a mountain in the north; and that Uthlabati[74] is the name of that Unkulunkulu owa dabuka eluhlangeni,—who broke off from Uthlanga.

---

[72] Here we have a native distinctly stating that the founder of his tribe was the first man,—that is, he confounds the first Unkulunkulu with the founder of his own tribe, who, he asserts was the creator of all things, in the native sense of creation. Let the reader consider how easy it is entirely to mistake the meaning of such statements. And how unmistakeably it proves that the natives believe that the Unkulunkulu of all men was himself a man.

[73] Comp. Umdabuko, p. 50, Note 95.

[74] *Uthlabati*, that is, Earth-man, as Adam means "earthy" or "red earth."

APPENDIX.
ADDITIONAL NOTES.
Page 4, Note 11.

There is an interesting version of this legend given by Casalis as existing among the Basutos:—

" 'The Lord,' they say, 'in ages gone by, sent this message to men: Oh, men, you will die, but you will rise again. The messenger of the Lord was tardy in the performance of his mission, and a wicked being hastened to precede him, and proclaimed to men: The Lord saith, You will die, and you will die for ever. When the true messenger arrived, they would not listen to him, but replied, The first word is the first, the second is nothing.' In the legend the first messenger of the Lord is designated by the name of the Grey Lizard, and the other who supplanted him, by that of the Chameleon." *(The Basutos, p. 242.)*

The word here rendered by Casalis "Lord" is no doubt Morimo, the meaning of which see in the article on Utikxo.

Arbousset again gives another version "as current in South Africa," and which connects in a curious way the Hottentot legend with that of the natives of these parts:—

"The Lord *(Morena)* sent in the former times a grey lizard with his message to the world, 'Men die......they will be restored to life again.' The chameleon set out from his chief, and, arriving in haste, he said, 'Men die......they die for ever.' Then the grey lizard came and cried, 'The Lord has spoken, saying, Men die......they shall live again.' But men answered him, 'The first word is the first; that which is after is nothing.'" *(Op. cit., p. 342.)*

Campbell gives the following legend of the cause of death on the authority of a Mashow native:—

"Matoome was the first man, and had a younger brother of the same name, and a sister whose name was Matoomyan. She was the first who came out from the hole, and had orders respecting the cattle, and was appointed to superintend them; but her brother Matoome came out, and without leave went and led the cattle round the end of a mountain, which so enraged his sister, who possessed medicine for the preservation of life and health, that she returned to the hole, carrying with her the precious medicine; in consequence of which diseases and death came into the world, and prevail in it to this day." *(Op. cit. Vol. I., p. 306.)*

Page 65, Note 27.

The following extract from the Sire de Joinville's *Saint Louis, King of France*, is added as an interesting illustration of the existence of a custom similar to that of making the Isivivane:—

" He related to us yet another great marvel. While he was in their camp a knight of much means died, and they dug for him a broad and deep trench in the earth; and they seated him, very nobly attired, on a chair, and placed by his side the best horse and the best sergeant he had, both alive. The sergeant, before he was placed in the grave with his lord, went round to the King of the Comans, and the other men of quality, and while he was taking leave of them they threw into his scarf a large quantity of silver and gold, and said to him, 'When I come to the other world thou shalt return to me what I now entrust to thee.' And he replied, 'I will gladly do so.'

"The great King of the Comans confided to him a letter addressed to their first king, in which he informed him that this worthy man had led a good life and had served him faithfully, and begged him to reward him for his services. When this was done they placed him in the grave with his lord and the horse, both alive; then they threw over the trench boards closely fitted together, and the whole army ran to pick up stones and earth, so that before they slept they had erected a great mound over it, in remembrance of those who were interred."

THE following letter is republished from the *Natal Courier* to establish the fact that Ukulukulu is only a dialectic pronunciation of Unkulunkulu:—

To the Editor.

SIR,—You have thought the discussion of the meaning of Unkulunkulu worth a place in the *Courier*. Will you grant me space for a few more remarks?

I have, for some years, been perfectly satisfied with the accuracy of my views on this subject. Yet I have not discontinued my researches. Every fresh objection, and even every old objection repeated by a new objector, has led to new investigations; and every fresh investigation has led to a confirmation of my previous views, whilst it has at the same time extended them and made them more clear. This has been the case with A. B.'s objection, that I have confounded Unkulunkulu, the nasalized form, with Ukulukulu, the unnasalized word.

I have for a long time been aware of the use of the two words among the natives; and although I copied without comment Dr. Bleek's remark;—"perhaps the unnasalized form is at present more usual in the signification of a great-great-grandfather, or the first ancestor of a family or tribe;"—thinking he had authority for such a statement; it did not tally with my own experience, my impression being very decided, that the nasalized form is by far the most common, I having very seldom heard the unnasalized word used by natives. The reason of this is now obvious. My investigations have been conducted for the most part among the Amazulu: whilst the unnasalized form, Ukulukulu, is a tribal pronunciation. So far as I at present know, it is pronounced thus especially by the Amalala; but probably it is also in use among other tribes. The Amazulu, the Amakxosa, and the Amakuza use the nasalized form, Unkulunkulu.

It will perhaps help others to a

clear understanding of this matter, if I just detail some conversation on the subject with two sets of natives on two different occasions, since my last letter to the *Courier.*

There were three men working together. The eldest, Ungqeto, some time ago gave me Dumakade as the name of the Unkulunkulu of his house. This word Dumakade is his isibongo, and all members of his house can be addressed by it. I addressed him by the name, " Dumakade !" The other two smiled at my knowing his isibongo; and he, laughing, said—"I told you that name a year ago, and you remember it now."—I said—" Yes; you told me Dumakade was the name of the Unkulunkulu of your house." —He said—" Yes."

I turned to another, and said— " Usibamu, what is the name of yours ?"—He replied, without a moment's hesitation—" Ubaleni."

I turned to Utombo, and asked —" And of yours ?" He answered—" Ukwele."

Another native here joined us, and I asked him—" Ulwati, what is the name of the Unkulunkulu of your house ? "—He said— " Does he ask our isibongo ? "—I replied—" I said nothing of isibongo. I asked the name of your Unkulunkulu."—He answered— " Uzimande."

At a short distance there was a fifth man, Ugovana, working. I had asked him a few weeks ago if he knew anything of Unkulunkulu ; and he gave me the common version of the tradition of the origin of man. I went to him ; and he, having overheard us, said —" O, you were asking of that ! I thought you were asking me about the Unkulunkulu wabantu bonke (the Unkulunkulu of all men)."—I said—" Yes, I was,

when I asked you a short time since. But are there not many Onkulunkulu ?"—He said—" Yes. Ours is Umdaka."

Thus in the space of half an hour I have the names of five different Onkulunkulu given to me. And be it remembered that these Onkulunkulu are the objects of worship in their respective houses.

I observed, on another occasion, Umpengula, a native Christian, standing by the side of three heathen natives. Their names are Udingezi, Ubulawa, and Umkonto. They are all probably more than sixty years old. I called Umpengula and said—" They say I have confounded Unkulunkulu with Ukulukulu. What do you say ? "

He replied—" What do they mean ? Why, it is one word. The Amazulu say Unkulunkulu ; the Amalala say Ukulukulu."

I said—" I know. But what I want to ask is, whether you remember when Ukoto came, and I asked him about Unkulunkulu ?"

He said—" Yes. I remember quite well."

" He told me that their Unkulunkulu was Usenzangakona."

" Yes."

" Do you remember my asking him whether he did not mean Ukulukulu, and his answering, ' We (viz., Amazulu) say Unkulunkulu. But it is all one ? ' "

He said—" Yes. I remember."

" And you agree with him ? "

" Certainly."

I said—" Let us call Udingezi, and hear what he will say. Do you ask him, and I will be silent. Ask him what the heads of generations are called."

Udingezi came.

Umpengula put his question thus—" What is the name of your Ukulukulu (the unnasalized form) ? "

I was vexed with this, because I had not wished any thing to be suggested; and said—"No; ask him thus, What is the father of your father called, and so on backwards."

He began—"He who begat ubaba is ubaba-mkulu, or ukulu; he who begat ubaba-mkulu is ukoko; he who begat ukoko is unkulunkulu." Thus using the nasalized form, though the unnasalized word had been suggested. An *experimentum crucis* this!

We then went to Ubulawa and Umkonto, who were still sitting on the grass at a distance. They gave the heads of generations in the same way as Udingezi, viz., Ubaba, Ukulu, Ukoko, Unkulunkulu: each using the nasalized form.

I asked them what the Amalala called the head of the fourth generation back?

They thought for a little while, and Ubulawa answered—"Ukulukulu."

I said—"Then Unkulunkulu and Ukulukulu is one."

They replied—"Yes. The Amazulu say Unkulunkulu; the Amalala Ukulukulu."

I asked—"Are you Amazulu?"

They replied—"No; we are Amakuza."

I continued—"Well, you speak of one Unkulunkulu of all men. What was his name?"

They replied—"We do not know him. We know nothing about him."

I said—"I mean him who first came out of the bed of reeds, and brought out all things."

They replied they knew nothing about him.

We are not to understand this answer absolutely. Had I wished it, I could have got each of them to relate a version of the tradition.

I said—"But some of the Onkulunkulu have names?"

They replied—"Yes."

I asked—"What is the name of yours, Ubulawa?"

"Umpungulo."

"And of yours, Udingezi?"

"Ujikitshi."

"And of yours, Umkonto?"

"Usoni."

"Has the Unkulunkulu of the Amakuza tribe a name?"

"Yes; Uthlomo."

And Udingezi added, without my asking—"Udhlamiui is the name of him who divided the tribes."[75]

---

[75] We have met with this saying frequently in the previous pages. It has been understood to mean that *Unkulunkulu created the nations.* But it has no such meaning, and does not even allude to creation at all, as will be clear from the following explanation of the words:—

Ukudabula izizwe i loku ukwa-*h*lukanisa ind*h*lu etile netile, zi hamba ngokwa*h*lukana, zi zibusela. Ukudabuka ke loku; ngokuba a zi sa yi 'kubuyela emuva, se zi ya pambili njalo.

To divide (or break off) the nations is this, to separate house from house, that they may go in different directions, and have their own government. This, then, is division; for they will never again return to their first position, but separate further and further from each other.

Njengaloku ku tiwa ku kona ukudabuka kwegode m*h*la Udingane 'a*h*lukana nompande. Kwa

For instance, it is said there was a division of the rope when Udingane separated from Umpa-

From these conversations we conclude that there are many who are called Unkulunkulu:—
1. Great-great-grandfathers, of whom eight are here named.
2. The heads of tribes, of whom one is named.
3. The dividers of tribes, of whom one is named.
4. The Unkulunkulu of all men, whose name is unknown.

This last I have been accustomed to call, for the sake of distinction, Unkulunkulu the First, and the others, Secondary Onkulunkulu. Dr. Bleek feels the need of a distinctive epithet, and says, the Unkulunkulu *par excellence*.[76] We find a native making the distinction of his own accord, by saying the Unkulunkulu *of all men*. We have also the separate testimony of several natives that Ukulukulu is all one with Unkulunkulu, and that the former is a tribal pronunciation.

I think, Sir, that entirely independently of other materials in my possession, the position is fully established by what I have here written, that Unkulunkulu is, both on critical and religious grounds, an utterly unfit word with which to translate GOD. The error of supposing it to be, appears to me to have arisen from the fact that the natives ascribe in some sort the divine act of Creation to the first man. But I think I shall be able, at a future time, to show that their notions of creation are so widely opposed to ours, that most of the words they use to express it are unfit to be used for the purpose by the missionary, implying as they do a theory of creation utterly inadmissible in Christian theology, which is founded on the Word of God.　　　　H. C.

---

tiwa, "Umpande u dabukile kudingane, u se zihambela yedwa; nodingane u se yedwa." Nako ukudabuka.

Ukudabuka kwezizwe kukqala ukuba inkosi yo*h*langa y a*h*lukanise czind*h*lini zayo eziningi, i ti, "Bani, yaka ekutini, u pume lapa, u zimele." Na komunye, kubo bonke i tsho njalo.

I loko ke ukudabula izizwe; se be izizwe labo aba kitshiwe nemizi. Njengaloku Umahhaule u dabuke embo, nonjan, nomunyu, nongangezwe. Bonke labo ba puma kuzi*h*lan*h*lo, inkosi yabo enkulu.

nde. It was said, "Umpande has broken off from Udingane, and goes by himself; and Udingane too is by himself." That is to divide or break off.

The dividing (or breaking off) of the nations at first is this, that a primitive chief should make a division in his many houses, saying, "So-and-so, live in such a place. Depart from this place, and go and reign for yourself." He says the same to another, and to all his children.

This, then, is to divide (or break off) the nations. And those become nations who are taken out together with their villages. For example, Umahhaule broke off from the Abambo, and Unjan also, and Umunyu, and Ungangezwe. All these came from Uzithlanthlo, their great chief.

---

[76] Usithlanu calls him "Unkulunkulu wamandulo," The most ancient Unkulunkulu, see p. 89.

UTIKXO.

Utikxo, the word adopted for God by the early missionaries among the Kxosa or Frontier Kafirs, was not a word known to the natives of these parts, but was introduced by missionaries and others. And it is generally supposed that the word does not properly belong to the Kxosa or any other of the alliterative dialects spoken in South Africa;[1] but has been derived from the Hottentots. The word Utikxo has the nearest resemblance to the Tikxwoa of the Cape Hottentot dialect.

We cannot doubt that this is the word which Kolb means to express as the Hottentot name for God.[2] Having declared his undoubting conviction that the Hottentots generally "believe in a supreme Being, the Creator of heaven and earth, and of every thing in them; the arbiter of the world, through whose omnipotence all things live and move and have their being. And that he is endowed with unsearchable attributes and perfections," he goes on to say:—" The Hottentots call him Gounja Gounja or Gounja Ticquoa; that is, the God of all gods; and say he is a good man, who does nobody any hurt; and from whom none need be apprehensive of any; and that he dwells far above the moon."[3]

If the investigations of Moffat, Appleyard, Casalis, and others are correct, Kolb very much exaggerated the Hottentot notion respecting God, and substituted instead of what they really believed, the belief of a Christian man. Nothing is more easy than to enquire of heathen savages the character of their creed, and during the conversation to impart to them great truths and ideas which they never heard before, and presently

---

[1] Bleek. Comparative Grammar, p. 92, sec. 397.—Moffat. Missionary Labours, pp. 257, 258.—Appleyard. Kafir Grammar, p. 13.

[2] The Present State of the Cape of Good Hope, &c. Written originally in High German. By Peter Kolben, A.M. Done into English from the original, by Mr. Medley. Kolb's Work was published in German, Folio, 1729. I quote from the translation by Medley, 2 Vols. 8vo., published 1731.

[3] Id., Vol. I., p. 93.

to have these come back again as articles of their own original faith, when in reality they are but the echoes of one's own thoughts. But even here in Kolb's statement we have the idea, more clearly and distinctly enunciated by after investigators, that great, and mighty and good, as, according to him, the Hottentots might have regarded their Tikæwoa, they believed that he was but "a good man."

And further on Kolb tells us they also "worship an evil deity whom they look upon as the father of mischief, and source of all plagues. They call him Touquoa; and say he is a little, crabbed, inferior captain, whose malice against the Hottentots will seldom let him rest; and who never did, nor has it in his nature to do, any good to any body. They worship him therefore, say they, in order to sweeten him and to avert his malice."[4]

The two words—Ticquoa and Touquoa—here given for a good and evil deity, are remarkably alike; and it is not improbable that Kolb mistook two words, identical in meaning, and applied to one imaginary being, for the name of two beings, a good and evil one. If not, then we must suppose that since the time of Kolb a great corruption has taken place in the original creed of the Hottentots, and that the good and evil, which were formerly kept distinct and referred to different agents, have become confused, and are indiscriminately ascribed to one being.

Observing that Dr. Bleek speaks of Tikxwoa as being one with "Kolb's Tikquoa or touquoa," I supposed he might have more ample reason for thinking them identical than I had.[5] His reasons, however, are simply philological. I quote from his letter on the subject:—"By identifying this Toukquoa with Tikquoa, the name for God found in the vocabulary (where Cham-ouna is that for the devil, who is called in Nama Hottentot Kau-ap), I do not think I exceeded the probability. But it may yet be that Kolb meant a different word. However, considering it fully, I have not much doubt it is really the same word, identical with the Nama Tsuikxoap, which contain both the vowels in the first syllable of which the two renderings of Kolb give only each one."

I may add that whilst recently on a visit among the Griquas I met with several persons who were acquainted with the Hottentots, and understood their language. They told me that the

---

[4] Id., p. 104.
[5] Comparative Grammar, p. 92.

name they used for God was Tikqwa. They did not know any other name for an evil principle resembling it. They also understood the language of the Bushmen, and told me that their word for God was Ikqum'n; and that the meaning of the word was, "Father who is above."

Moffat quotes from Dr. Vanderkemp the following, which appears to justify the surmise that Kolb was mistaken in supposing the two words referred to two beings from not observing that he was dealing with a merely tribal difference of pronunciation:[6]—"A decisive proof of what I here say with respect to the national atheism of the Kafirs, is, that they have no word in their language to express the idea of Deity; the individuals just mentioned calling him 'Thiko, which is a corruption of a name by which God is called in the language of the Hottentots, literally signifying one *that induces pain*."[7]

But Moffat is equally decisive that the Hottentots and Namaquas are just as ignorant of God, and their language just as devoid of a word for God, as Dr. Vanderkemp and others have represented the Kafirs. Whilst pursuing his investigations among the inhabitants of Great Namaqualand, he says: —"I met with an ancient sorcerer or doctor, who stated that he had always understood that Tsui'kuap was a notable warrior, of great physical strength; that in a desperate struggle with another chieftain, he received a wound in the knee, but having vanquished his enemy, his name was lost in the mighty combat which rendered the nation independent; for no one could conquer the Tsui'kuap (wounded-knee). When I referred to the import of the word, one who inflicts pain or a sore knee, manifesting my surprise that they should give such a name to the Creator and Benefactor, he replied in a way that induced the belief that he applied the term to what we should call the devil, or to

---

[6] Dr. Bleek gives the following variations of the Hottentot name of God, which, not having the requisite characters, I shall spell in accordance with the principles laid down in the Preface to Vol. I. of *Zulu Nursery Tales*:—

"I add here the Hottentot name for God, which is *Tsuikqwap* (Schmelen's Tsoeikwap) or Tsuigxoap (Wallmann's Zuigxoap) in the Nama; and Tshukxoap in the Kgora dialect; Thuikxwe (Van der Kemp's Thuickwe) among the Eastern Hottentots; and Tikxwoa (Kolb's Tikqwoa or Toukqwoa) near the Cape." *(Comp. Gram., p. 92.)*

It will be seen that most of these words differ from each other more than the two words of Kolb.

[7] Moffat. Op. cit., p. 257.

death itself; adding that he thought death, or the power causing death, was very sore indeed."[8]

And then he asks:—"May not the Tsui'kuap of these people be like the Thlanga of the Kafirs, an ancient hero; or represent some power which they superstitiously dread, from its causing death or pain?"[9]

We see, then, that Moffat comes to a conclusion somewhat similar to that of Kolb, that there is an evil principle or being, feared by the Hottentots, and which has received the name of Tsui'kuap, which is equivalent to Utikxo. But he does not appear to have heard any thing of the good principle or being, of which Kolb speaks.

Again, Casalis expresses an equally decided opinion as to the "endemical atheism" of the inhabitants of South Africa generally. He says:—"The tribes had entirely lost the idea of a Creator. All the natives whom we have questioned on the subject have assured us that it never entered their heads that the earth and sky might be the work of an invisible being."[10]

Shaw also says:—"The Kafir nations cannot be said to possess any religion."[11] And again:—"Before Missionaries and other Europeans had intercourse with the Kafirs, they seem to have had extremely vague and indistinct notions of God. The older Kafirs used to speak of Umdali, the Creator or Maker of all things, and Uthlanga, which word seems to have been used to denote the source or place from which all living things came forth."[12]

A similar statement is made by Arbousset. He says:—"They have scarcely retained the idea of a Supreme Being. The more enlightened admit that there is a *Morena* in heaven, whom they call the *powerful master of things*, but the multitude deny that there is, and even this name of *morena* is the same as they give to the lowest of their chiefs. All the blacks whom I have known are atheists, but it would not be difficult to find amongst them some theists. Their atheism, however, does not prevent

---

[8] Moffat. Op. cit., p. 259.
[9] Id., p. 259.
[10] Casalis. The Basutos, p. 238.
[11] Story of My Mission, p. 444.
[12] Id., p. 451.—My reasons for thinking that these views require very considerable modification are given in another place.

their being extremely superstitious, or from rendering a kind of worship to their ancestors, whom they call *barimos*, or in the singular *morimo*."[13]

He says of the Mountain Bushmen's faith :—" They say that there is a *Kaang* or *Chief* in the sky, called also *Kue-Akeng-teng*, *the Man*, that is to say, the *Master of all things*. According to their expression, 'one does not see him with the eyes, but knows him with the heart.' He is to be worshipped in times of famine and before going to war, and that throughout the whole night, performing the dance of the *mokoma*."[14]

The same notion of malevolence is connected in the native mind among the Bechuanas with the word Morimo, which the Missionaries have adopted for God. The meaning of Morimo as given by Moffat,[15] and of Molimo as given by Casalis,[16] is, like that given to the Bushmen's Ikqum'n, " He that is in heaven." But, says Moffat, " Morimo, to those who knew any thing about it, had been represented as a malevolent *selo or thing*."[17] And again, " According to native testimony Morimo, as well as man, with all the different species of animals, came out of a cave or hole in the Bakone country."[18] " There is," says Casalis, " an obvious contradiction between the language and the received ideas."[19] —That is, I presume, Casalis supposes that the word Morimo or Molimo,—a heavenly one,—is a testimony preserved in the language of the people against their present infidelity and corruption of faith. And Archbishop Trench, in his work on " The Study of Words," has brought this word forward as a remarkable instance of the disappearing of an important word from a language, and with it " the disappearing as well of the great spiritual fact and truth whereof that word was once the vehicle and the guardian."[20]

But Dr. Bleek has made it more than probable that Moffat and Casalis are mistaken in the derivation and meaning of this word; and that Molimo has a sound by accident only similar to Moh'olimo —" one who is in heaven." He says :—" In other South African languages, different words are found indicating the idea of a supreme being; but in Se-tshuana at

---

[13] Op. cit., p. 69.
[15] Op. cit., p. 260.
[17] Op. cit., p. 261.
[19] Op. cit., p. 248.

[14] Op. cit., p. 363.
[16] Op. cit., p. 248.
[18] Id., p. 262.
[20] P. 18.

least the word for 'God' has a similar reference to their ancestor worship as the Zulu *Unkulunkulu*. Thus in Se-suto *Mo-limo* means God, and *me-limo* gods, but *mo-limo*, ancestral spirits, plur. *ba-limo*."[21]

This is a far more probable derivation. And when we remember that Morimo is supposed to have come out of the same hole that gave origin to man and beasts, as Unkulunkulu came out of the same bed of reeds ; and that in the native mind there is no connection of thought between a heavenly being and this Morimo, there can be little doubt of the correctness of the view taken by Dr. Bleek.

Further, it may be added in corroboration that although the Amazulu do not say Unkulunkulu is an Itongo,—an ancestral spirit ;—they say he was an Ukoko,—an ancestor: and not only does it appear that they suppose that at one time he was regarded as an Itongo, and was worshipped among other Amatongo by his own laud-giving names, but we find them incidentally giving intimations of a belief in a great Itongo from whom all things proceeded. Thus they are heard to say in explanation of the superiority of the white man to the coloured that the former remained longer with a great Itongo than the blacks, and therefore came into being more perfect, with better habits and accoutrements.[22]

This view brings the notions of different people of South Africa into a certain similarity and consistency. Whilst on the other view they are neither consistent with themselves nor with each other.

Appleyard gives a somewhat similar account to that of Moffat as to the meaning of Utikxo. He says:—"Tshoei'koap is the word from which the Kafirs have probably derived their Utixo, a term which they have invariably applied, like the Hottentots, to designate the Divine Being, since the introduction of Christianity. Its derivation is curious. It consists of two words which together mean 'the broken knee.' It is said to have been originally applied to a doctor or sorcerer of considerable notoriety and skill among the Hottentots or Namaquas, some generations back, in consequence of his having received some injury of the knee. Having been held in high repute for extraordinary powers during life, he continued to be invoked, even after death, as one who could relieve and protect ;[23] and hence, in process of

---

[21] Op. cit., p. 91.   [22] See p. 80.

[23] That is, strictly in accordance with the custom of an ancestor-worshipping people.

time, he became the nearest in idea to their first conceptions of God."[24]

If this account be correct, and there appears no reason whatever for doubting its accuracy, it is clear that the early Missionaries, in using the word Utikxo for God, adopted an isibongo, or laud-giving name, of some old brave.

To my mind nothing here found conveys the idea that the notion of divinity was ever in the uneducated native mind connected with Utikxo; much less that Utikxo ever meant God: on the contrary that it meant something very different from God; in some instances, at least, an evil spirit, which was worshipped just on the same grounds as the Yezidis worship Satan, "because he must be conciliated and reverenced; for as he now has the means of doing evil to mankind, so will he hereafter have the power of rewarding them."[25] And it appears to me to have been unwisely and improperly adopted by the early Missionaries; to be explained and excused only on the ground that at first the teachers and taught were unable freely to communicate ideas one to the other.

The term Molimo or Morimo appears equally improper. How very objectionable is it to use a word for God in teaching savages the doctrines of Christianity, to which they have a natural or rather educated repugnance, and of the Being whom it is meant to represent they can speak as a native chief spoke to Mr. Moffat: —"When we assured him that God (Morimo) was in the heavens, and that He did whatever He pleased, they blamed us for giving Him a high position beyond their reach; for they viewed their Morimo as a noxious reptile. 'Would that I could catch it, I would transfix it with my spear,' exclaimed S., a chief, whose judgment on other subjects would command attention."[26]

At the same time it is quite possible that the confusion of ideas between good and evil,—the association of the idea of evil with God,—which we here meet with, is a confusion of comparatively recent times; that originally there existed a defined belief in a good and an evil Being; but that the common multiform natural phenomena, which are constantly exhibiting the Creator's beneficence, were lost to these afflicted populations amidst phenomena of an ap-

---

[24] Grammar, p. 13.
[25] Layard's Nineveh. Vol. I., p. 298.
[26] Op. cit., p. 265.

parently opposite character, and especially amidst the sufferings and wants of their daily life; until created things spoke to them only of suffering, and fixed their attention on a pain-creating being, whom they feared more than reverenced, and whom if they worshipped, it was to deprecate wrath, rather than to express their faith in his love.

And may not the legend,—so bizarre and bald,—given by Dr. Bleek in the " Hottentot Tales "[27] of a contest between Heitsi Eibip and Gʠagʠorip be a confused tradition of some old faith, the fundamental principle of which was that of a contest between good and evil in nature; but which in process of time has been lost, and the good and the evil come to be confounded, and referred alike to one fabulous being.

According to Du Chaillu, we find even at the present time among the inhabitants of the Western coast of Africa the worship of a good and evil spirit. He says:—

"Aniambia enjoys the protection of two spirits of very great power, named Abambou and Mbuirri. The former is an evil spirit, the latter is beneficent. They are both worshipped; and their accommodations, so far as I was permitted to see, were exactly alike.

"Abambou is the devil of the Camma. He is a wicked mischievous spirit, who lives near graves and in burial grounds. He takes occasional walks through the country; and if he is angry at any one, has the power to cause sickness and death. In worshipping him they cry, 'Now are we well! Now are we satisfied! Now be our friend, and do not hurt us!'

"Mbuirri, whose house I next visited, is lodged and kept much as his rival. He is a good spirit, but has powers much the same as Abambou, so far as I could see. Being less wicked, he is less zealously worshipped."[28]

This coincides remarkably with Kolb's statement; and leads to a reasonable suspicion that his Touquoa,—probably only some local or tribal variation of the word now come down to the Kafirs as Utikxo,—and the Morimo of the Bechuanas and Basutos, is the same as the Abambou of the people of Aniambia. Yet what missionary would choose Abambou as the name for God, even though he should have ascribed to him, in addition to his own, the only "less wicked" attributes of Mbuirri?

Dr. Bleek's Hottentot legend just alluded to, begins with the

---

[27] P. 77.

[28] Op. cit., pp. 202, 203.

significant words, "At first there were two." And among the natives of these parts we have the two words Unembeza and Ugovana to express the good and evil hearts which are supposed to be contending within them. And they ascribe good and evil to the Amatongo which they worship, and worship more sedulously to avert evil than to acknowledge good.

Be this as it may, the impression so generally existing among those who have laboured long in South Africa of the "endemic atheism" of the different peoples, and the difficulty universally confessed of being able to determine whether the name, applied to some being to whom certain supreme acts are referred, is in the native mind any thing more than the name of their great forefather, or of some great hero-benefactor of times gone by, to whom with perfect consistency an ancestor-worshipping people would refer such acts, suggest that it would be both more wise and reverent, and more likely to be effectual in attempting to teach them a new faith, to introduce a new name,—a name not really newer to them than the idea of the supreme Being itself. I am myself persuaded that such a new name is very desirable, aye more, very necessary. For there is no name, whether Utikxo, or Morimo, or Unkulunkulu, which, without possessing any primary signification referring to divinity, has not much, both etymologically and traditionally, which is highly objectionable, and calculated to mislead the young convert. Bishop Colenso felt this on his first introduction to mission work. And I do not doubt that his impression was the result of devout and intelligent thought, which is not at all invalidated by a change of opinion, which led him to attempt to introduce an equally objectionable word for God, and to which exception has been justly taken by many on grounds similar to those which may be taken against Utikxo.

In connection with the word Utikxo, "the broken knee," the following interesting and curious corroboration of the idea that Utikxo is but the isibongo or laud-giving name of some ancient brave, is well worth considering. Among the Amazulu there is a word, clearly an isibongo, *U-gukqa-badele*, which means, He kneels and they get enough of it. And the following explanations appear to show the character and circumstances of the conflict from which he obtained the name:—

U-gukqa-ba-dele, umuntu o hla-nganyelwe abantu abaningi, be zitemba ubuningi, be ya 'ku m enza amehlo 'mnyama ngoku m hhakqa, a fe e nga bonisisi loko a nga kw enzako. Ku ti ngesikati sokulwa nabo, 'emi. Ku ti ba nga m hlaba, noma bo nga m hlabile, ba bone e ti kiti ngedolo, ba ti, "U ya wa; si m hlabile." Ba sondele kakulu, ku nga bi njengokuba be be sondele e s' emi, ku dhlulisise ukusondela kwabo kuye, e se wile, ngokuti, "E, manje ke, a si m kqede." Kepa ba ze ba dhlulwe isikati be nga m kqedi; e u yena yedwa o ba kqeda nganhlanye, be ng' azi uma ulukuni ngendawo enjani; ba ze ba ti, "Hau! sa za sa pela umuntu emunye na? A si m shiye."

Ba m shiye ke, e se kuyo leyo 'ndawo lapa be fike e kona. Ngaloko ke lapa se be mukile be m shiya be m bona, ba hambe be bheka, be m bona e sa gukqile, e ba lindile ukuti, kumbo ba ya 'utatela amandhla okubuya. Ku ti, ngoku nga buyi kwabo, 'esuke, a hambe.

Kanti ke ba delile, ukuti b' esuti, a ba sa m funi. U lowo ke

We apply the name U-gukqa-ba-dele to a man who has been surrounded by many others, who trust to their number, and expect to be able to confuse him by surrounding him, and so kill him before he can well see what to do; and perhaps they stab him, or without having stabbed him, they see him sink on his knee, and say, "He is falling; we have stabbed him." And they draw near to him, no longer now as when he was standing; they go quite close to him now he has fallen, saying, "Ah, now then, let us make an end of him." But a long time passes without their killing him; it is he alone who kills them, they not understanding in what way he is so difficult to kill; until at length they say, "Hau! are we then at length all killed by one man? Let us let him alone."

And so they leave him still in the same place where they first found him. So then when they have left, going away with their faces towards him, they go on looking back and see him still kneeling and watching them, for he thinks they may take heart and come back to him again. But when they do not return he arises and goes away.

They have had enough of it forsooth, that is, they are satisfied,

U-gukqa-ba-dele. Leli 'gama lokuti U-gukqa-ba-dele, a si lo igama lomuntu nje; igama e si li zwe li fika nabantu ekufikeni kwamabunu, e vela emakxoseni; a fika nabantu basemakxoseni; be funga be ti, "Tikxo o pezulu. Gukqa-badele." Kodwa lelo lokuti "gukqa" a li kqondeki ka/tle, uma la fika kanyekanye na, nelokuti "Tikxo" na. Sa li zwa ke ngamakxosa ukuba Utikxo inkosi e pezulu.

Ekukqaleni amakosi a e puma impi, a /tlasele nayo; kepa ku ti, ngokukalipa kwezita, z' enze ikcebo lazo lokuti, "Ukuze laba 'bantu si ba nqobe, a si bulale inkosi yabo le, ukuze ba pele amand/tla." Nembala ke ku ti ba nga i bulala inkosi, ba i kcite leyo 'mpi; ngokuba amakosi lawo a e puma ngokuti, "Kona abantu bami be ya 'kuba nesibindi, be bona ngi kona."

Kwa yekwa ke loko; a ku sa vamile; se ku kona kwezinye izizwe; kwazulu, a ku se njalo.

and do not go after him any more. Such a man, then, is called U-gukqa-ba-dele. It is not the name of a common person. It is a name which we heard from people when the Dutch first came from the Kxosa tribes; they brought some Kxosa people with them; when they took an oath, they said, "Tikxo who is above. Gukqa-ba-dele." But it is by no means clear whether the word "gukqa" (kneel) came at precisely the same time as the word Utikxo. We heard from the Amakxosa that Utikxo is the Lord who is above.[29]

At first chiefs used to go out with the army, and invade other people with it; but it happened through their shrewdness that the enemy devised a plan, saying, "In order that we may conquer these people, let us kill their king, that they may be discouraged." And in fact they might kill the king and scatter the army; for the kings used to go out, saying, "Then my people will be brave, when they see me there."

So the custom of accompanying the army was given up; it is no longer usual; it may still be among some nations; it is no longer the custom among the Amazulu.

---

[29] Compare the Bushman word, which is said to have a similar meaning, p. 64; and the dispute between the two Kxosa natives as to the use of Utikxo and Unkulunkulu, p. 68.

Kwazulu inkosi i bongwa ngokwenza kwabantu bayo, a ba kw enze eziteni; ba nqobe; a ku tshiwo ukuti, kw enze abantu bayo. Njengokuba, uma impi e namandhla ya vela ngenhla, enye i ngenzansi, i ti induna ehlakanipile, "O, indawo imbi; si ya 'utateka; a si mi kahle; gukqa ni ngamadolo, ni ba nqume amatumbu." Ngalelo 'keebo, uma ba nqoba ngalo, inkosi yabo i nga tiwa i U-gukqa-ba-dele, njengokungati kw enze yona; kanti kw enze abantu bayo ngesibindi sokukumbula inkosi yabo. Ku tshiwo njalo ke ukubizwa kwenkosi; njengaloku ku tiwa ukubongwa kwenkosi yakwazulu, ku tiwe, "Wena, wa dhla Ubani e be zalwa ng' Ubani; a kwa ba 'ndaba zaluto." I bongwa ke ngokwenza kwempi yayo. Lawo 'mandhla aw enziwa impi, i ye 'kutata izibongo zokuba ku bongwe inkosi ngazo. Ku njalo ke a ku bonakali ukuba kw enze yona ukqobo, noma kw enze abantu bayo na.

Among the Amazulu the chief is praised for the conduct of his people among the enemy; they conquer, and it is not said that the conquest was made by the king's people. For instance, if a powerful army appears on the high lands, and the other army is below, a wise officer says, "O, the place is bad; we shall be borne down; our position is bad; kneel, and stab them in the bowels." If they succeed by this stratagem, their chief may be called by the name U-gukqa-ba-dele, as though it was he who did it, when forsooth it was his people through the bravery which the recollection of their chief gave them. This is the manner, then, in which kings get names; as it is said when lauding the king of the Amazulu, "You who ate up So-and-so, the son of So-and-so; and it was nothing to you." So the chief is praised for the conduct of his army. The power which is exhibited by the army is the source from which the lauds of the chief are taken. So it is that it is not clear whether it was done by him in person or by his people.

Hence it appears certain that the word Utikxo is the laud-giving name of an ancient hero, and that it was given in consequence of some conflict in which he repulsed enemies more powerful from numbers than himself by the stratagem of kneeling, and so causing them to approach him under the impression that they could make an easy prey of him.

THE LORD OF HEAVEN.

In the previous pages we meet with frequent allusions to a lord above or heavenly lord. Thunder and lightning and aerial changes appear to be the only natural phenomena which have attracted the notice of the natives of this part of Africa, and led them to believe in a personal power above nature. Struck with terror by a thunder storm, they encourage each other by asserting that they have committed no crime against the powerful being in heaven who wields the lightning, and that he is not angry, but merely playing. But we shall be much mistaken if we hasten to conclude from this that because they speak of a heavenly lord, they have any conception of him which identifies him with God.

In almost every country there is some such notion of a heavenly being,—a relic possibly of heaven-worship; or it may be merely a natural suggestion of the human mind, springing up spontaneously among different peoples, and every where leading to a similar conclusion, that where there are such manifestations of power, there is also a personal cause.

There is the Indian Indra, called also "the lord of heaven;" the Zeus and Jupiter of the Greeks and Romans; the Esquimaux Pirksoma; the Mau or Ye-whe of Whydah; the So or Khevioso of Dahome; the Kaang or chief in the sky of the Bushmen; and the Thor of our own ancestors.

We have already seen that the Dahomans speak of thunder in the same way as the natives of these parts; they do not say it is the sign of an angry chief, but of a chief who is rejoicing or playing. Arbousset says that among the Bechuanas, "when it thunders every one trembles; if there are several together, one asks the other with uneasiness, 'Is there any one amongst us that devours the wealth of others?' All then spit on the ground, saying, 'We do not devour the wealth of others.' If a thunderbolt strikes and kills one of them, no one complains, none weep; instead of being grieved, all unite in saying that the lord is delighted, (that is to say, he has done right,) with killing that man." *(Op. cit., p. 323.)* In like manner among the natives of Natal, if the lightning kills their cattle, they neither complain nor mourn, but say, "The lord has taken his own." Neither do they cry the funeral wail over those who have been killed in this manner, lest, as they say, they should summon the lightning to kill them too. It is not lawful for them to touch the body of a person killed with lightning, until the doctor has come and applied medicines to the dead, and to the living of the village to which he belonged.— Among the Romans those struck with lightning were not buried, neither are they among the Dahomans; but they cut from the corpse lumps of flesh, which they chew without eating, crying to the passers by, "We sell you meat!—fine meat!—Come and buy!" *(Burton. Mission to the King of Dahome. Vol. II., p. 142.)*

The following statement by an intelligent, educated Christian native will show how utterly indistinct and undeveloped is their notion respecting a heavenly lord:—

Indaba ngenkosi yezulu a ku bonakali kakulu okona ku tshiwoyo ngayo. Ngokuba lapa izulu li tshaye kona, ku tiwa, "Inkosi i tukutele." Ku tshiwo ngokutshaya kwalo. A kw a*h*lukaniswa kakulu ukuti e yona 'nkosi i tshayayo i i pi, noma unyazi, noma unyazi lu amand*h*la ayo. Ku tshiwo ngonyazi ku tiwe, "Inkosi i tshayile." Kepa maningi amakosi a tshiwo abantu, nezilwane amakosi, in*h*latu nebubesi; kepa loko noma ku tshiwo ku ya bulawa; ku ya bonakala ukuti a ku lingani nenkosi yezulu.

It is by no means clear what is really said about the lord of heaven. For when the heaven [lightning] has struck any place, it is said, "The lord is angry." This is said because of the lightning stroke. It is not very clear which is the lord that strikes—whether it is the lightning, or whether the lightning is the lord's power. It is said of the lightning, "The lord has struck." But there are many who are called lords by men, and even beasts, as the boa and the lion; but although they are thus named, they are notwithstanding killed, that is, their being called lords is not the same as giving the name lord to the lord of heaven.

Ku kona inyoni yezulu; i ya bulawa nayo; y ehla ngesikati sokutshaya kwonyazi, i sale pansi; a ku tshiwo futi ukuti i yona i inkosi; a kw ahlukile kakulu ngenkosi ukuba i i pi kunonyazi kunayo e sezulwini. Si zwa ku tiwa ku kona abantu nje ezulwini na pansi kwomhlaba futi. Kulukuni ke ukwazi labo 'bantu aba ngapansi kwomhlaba ukuba ukuma kwabo ku njani na, na ngapezulu futi a b' aziwa uma ba njani nokuma kwabo. Izwi lodwa eli tshoyo ukuti ba kona.

There is a bird of heaven;[30] it too is killed; it comes down when the lightning strikes the earth, and remains on the ground; but neither is it said to be the lord; it is not very clear which is meant by lord, the lightning, or the lord which is in heaven. We hear it said there are men in heaven and under the earth. But it is hard to understand what is the condition of these underground men; neither do we know what is the condition of those who are above. All we know is that it is said they are there.

Among the Amazulu, when there is a thunder storm, they say:

Li ya duma, li ya na likamjokwane, likapunga nomageba; likagukqabadele.

The heaven of Umjokwane is thundering and raining, the heaven of Upunga and of Umageba; the heaven of Ugukqabadele.

The first three of these names are izibongo of the Amazulu, that is, of the royal family, the names of ancient chiefs. But Ugukqaba-

---

[30] "The bird of heaven" is a bird which is said to descend from the sky when it thunders, and to be found in the neighbourhood of the place where the lightning has struck. The heaven-doctors place a large vessel of amasi mixed with various medicines near a pool such as is frequently met with on the tops of hills; this is done to attract the lightning, that it may strike in that place. The doctor remains at hand watching, and when the lightning strikes the bird descends, and he rushes forward and kills it. It is said to have a red bill, red legs, and a short red tail like fire; its feathers are bright and dazzling, and it is very fat. The bird is boiled for the sake of the fat, which is mixed with other medicines and used by the heaven-doctors to puff on their bodies (pepeta) and to anoint their lightning-rods, that they may be able to act on the heavens without injury to themselves. The body is used for other purposes as medicine. A few years ago some peacocks' feathers were sold at a great price among the natives of Natal, being supposed to be the feathers of this bird.

dele is said to be a new name, invented for that Lord of heaven of whom the white man speaks to them. It means the Unconquerable (see p. 114). This is explained in the following account :—

Le 'ndaba yokuti, "Izulu likapunga nomageba nomjokwane," a ku vunywanga ukuba ku be kona into enkulu kunenkosi. Ubukulu bezulu kwa tiwa obukapunga, yena e inkosi enkulu yakwazulu; ngokuba u nga bona ngaloku ukuba into yokukukumeza umuntu a bizwe ngokutiwa nezulu elake.

Ku be ku ti uma ku kona um‑ /dola o vela pakati kwomuzi, w' enziwa inkosi. Njengaloku Utshaka wa ka wa fafaza igazi lenkomo esigod/dweni ebusuku, e ti i kona e ya 'kubona uma izinyanga zi kqinisile ini ngokunuka abantu. Kepa a zi nukanga ka/le; wa zi bulala zonke, kupela ya ba nye eya ti, "Kw enziwe izulu." Loko ke ukuti, " Ngi za 'kunuka izulu na?" Kupela ke; abantu b' azi ukuba u tsho izulu njalo, u tsho Utshaka; ngokuba nezulu ku tiwa elake. Loko a ku 'siminya; ukukuliswa kwenkosi nje. Ngokuba ku tshiwo ku tiwa, i ngangezintaba, ku tshiwo izintaba ezinkulu. Kepa ku be ku nge njalo, ngokuba uma

As regards the saying, "The heaven of Upunga and of Umageba and Umjokwane, it is not permitted that there should be any thing greater than the chief. The greatness of the heaven was said to belong to Upunga, who was a great Zulu chief; for you can see by this that it is merely something done for the purpose of exalting a man when it is said that the heaven too belongs to him.

It used to be said if any omen happened in a village, that it was occasioned by the chief. For instance, Utshaka once sprinkled the blood of a bullock in the royal house during the night, saying by that means he should know if the diviners were true when they pointed out offenders. But they did not divine rightly, and he killed them all but one, who said, "It was done by the heaven," and asked, if he could point out the heaven as the offender? That was all he said; and the people understood that by the heaven he meant Utshaka; for the heaven too was said to be his. This is not true; it is a mere exaltation of the chief. For they say he is as big as the mountains, meaning great mountains. But it is not so; for if he is standing or sitting at the foot of

e pansi kwaleyo 'ntaba, 'emi noma e hlezi, i nga m fihla, a nga bonakali. Ukukuliswa kwomuntu nje.

Futi, leli 'zwi lokuti Ugukqabadele, a si lo igama likatshaka noma Usenzangakona. Leli 'lizwi li vele lapa esilungwini; kwa tiwa igama lenkosi e pezulu. Ngokuba kukqala, lapa kwa fika Amabunu, kwa ba kona ukufunga ngokuti inyaniso, si fungiswa abalungu; ngokuba awakiti amakosi a ba w' azi noma umuntu u ti ni. Kwa ba kona nokuti, "Tikxo o pezulu;" nokuti, "Ngi funga inkosi e pezulu," nokufela umunwe ngamate a kombe pezulu a ti, "I nga ngi tabata, a ngi kw azi loko." Izwi lokuti Ugukqabadele, ku tshiwo inkosi e pezulu. Kepa ukugukqa isibonakaliso samandhla, ngokuba ku tiwa uma indoda i funa ukuba i zipase impela, i tate amandhla onke, i ya gukqa ngedolo, ukuze i nga suswa kuleyo 'ndawo; lowo 'muntu o lwa nayo u ya 'ku i shiya. I lona ke izwi lokuti "ba-dele," ukuti, ba m shiya lapo e gukqe kona.

the mountain it would hide him, and he could not be seen. It is the mere exaltation of a human being. Further, the word Ugukqabadele is not a name of Utshaka or Usenzangakona. It is a name which has arisen here among the English, as a name for the lord of heaven. For at first when the Dutch came, the white men used to make us swear to the truth of what we said; for they did not understand what a man said when he swore by our chiefs; so the oath was, "Utikxo o pezulu," God of heaven; or, "I swear by the Lord of heaven," and one spat on his finger and pointed towards heaven and said, "May He take me if I know this thing." The word Ugukqabadele means the Lord of heaven. And kneeling is a sign of strength; for it is said, if a man wish to make himself very firm, and avail himself of all his strength, he kneels, that he may not be moved from his place; and the man who is fighting with him will go away. That, then, is what is meant by "ba-dele," They pass on or have enough, that is, they leave him when he has knelt.

An old native, in expressing his gratitude for some act of kindness, said, pointing towards heaven, "Nkosi, elako ilanga," Sir, the sun is yours. On asking the meaning of this, I received the following explanation:—

Kwazulu kwa tatwa igama lozulu; uma li duma, kwa tiwa, "La duma izulu lenkosi." Ku nga tshiwo umninilo owa l' enzayo; ku tshiwo umuntu o inkosi nje; wa kuliswa ngokuti izulu elake. Abantu abaningi se be kuleka kwabanye ngokuti, "Wena wapakati, nezulu elako; konke okwako."

Be tsho ngokuba ngapambili kwabo be nga boni 'mumbe, kupela inkosi leyo, e yona i nga ti uma i tsho ngaleso 'sikati ukuti, "Ubani ka fe manje," nembala ku be njalo. Ba tsho ke ba ti, "Lowo 'muntu umninizulu; konke okwake." A kw anele kubo ukudumisa omkulu uma be ng' otulanga izulu li be pezu kwake; a ba kolwa; ba ya tanda ukutola ubukulu bonke, ba bu beke pezu kwalowo 'muntu.

Ku njalo ke ukukuleka kwabantu abamnyama; ngokuba inkosi i b' i nga tsho ukuti, "Ai; ni y' eduka; a si lo lami izulu nelanga; ku nomniniko; ngi mncinane mina." I b' i bheka ukuba ku

Among the Amazulu they use the name of heaven; and when it thunders they say, "The heaven of the chief thundered." They do not mean the owner of the heaven who made it, but a mere man who is a chief; he is exalted by saying the heaven is his. And many are now in the habit of making obeisance to others, saying, "Thou of the inner circle of greatness, the heaven is thine; all things are thine."

They say thus because they see no one else but the chief himself, who if he choose can command any particular person to die, and he will die at once. And so they say, "That man is the owner of heaven; and every thing is his." It does not suffice them to honour a great man, unless they place the heaven on his shoulders; they do not believe what they say; they merely wish to ascribe all greatness to him.

Such, then, is the reverence of black men; for the chief did not say, "No; you are ascribing to me what does not belong to me; the heaven and the sun are not mine; they have their own owner; for my part I am insignificant." He expected to have it said always

tiwe elayo njalo ; se be tsho njalo abakwiti kwabam*h*lope.

Ku kona indaba pakati kwabantu abamnyama. Ku ti ngosuku lapa ku puma impi ngalo, lokupela inkosi se i *h*langanise amabandh*l*a onke ayo, i kuluma nawo ; ngemva kwaloko kw enziwe ih*h*ubo eli vusa usikisiki lokuba izin*h*liziyo zi fudumale ngokunga impi i nga ba kona ngaleso 'sikati ; lokupela izulu li kewebile, li pendule ngomoya omubi, ku tiwe, "Izulu lenkosi li y' ezwa ukuba inkosi ibu*h*lungu." Ngaloko ke kwa k*q*iniswa ngokuti, "Izulu elenkosi," emakosini amakulu ; ngokuba lapa i *h*langanise impi yayo, nezulu li ya pendula, noma li be li sile.

that the heaven was his ; and now our people address white men in the same way.

It happens among black men when the chief calls out an army and he has collected all his bands, he addresses them, and then they sing a song which excites their passions, that their hearts burn with the desire of seeing their enemy ; and though the heaven is clear, it becomes clouded by a great wind which arises. And the people say, "The heaven of the chief feels that the chief is suffering." Therefore it was affirmed among great chiefs, that the heaven is the chief's ; for when he assembles his troops the heaven clouds over, although it had been quite bright.

ANOTHER native, named Ududula, who was a great courtier, whose highest notion of politeness was the highest hyperbole of praise, wished to borrow half-a-crown, which I had no wish to lend. At length he said, "Mfundisi, u ng' ubaba," Teacher, you are my father. I asked, "How ?" He replied, "Wa dabuka em*h*labeni, wa kula, wa ba ngaka ; mina be ngi ngaka nje," You broke off from the earth, and grew as big as this, (placing his hand six feet above the ground ;) but for my part I only grew as high as this, (placing his hand about a foot and a half from it.) By this he meant to say that I was not born like other men, but came out of the ground, like Unkulunkulu.[31]

---

[31] Arbousset appears to have noticed a similar custom. Yet his statement may have been made from not understanding the meaning of such phrases as "Iukosi yo*h*langa" (see Note 30, p. 14) :—" They

It appears, therefore, that in the native mind there is scarcely any notion of Deity, if any at all, wrapt up in their sayings about a heavenly chief. When it is applied to God, it is simply the result of teaching. Among themselves he is not regarded as the Creator, nor as the Preserver of men; but as a power, it may be nothing more than an earthly chief, still celebrated by name,—a relic of the king-worship of the Egyptians; another form merely of ancestor-worship.

A lad of the Waiau or Ajawa tribe, living on the Eastern coast of Lake Nyassa, informs me that among them the Rainbow is called Umlungu, that is, God; for Umlungu is the word they there use for the Supreme Being and supernatural powers. They also call the Supreme Being Lisoka, the Invisible, when they wish to distinguish him from the Rainbow.[32]—Among the Dahomans, the Rainbow is wor-

have no idol but he; it is before him, literally, that they prostrate themselves. He grants them permission to live, or he slaughters them according to his caprice. Can the devil really have whispered to the Zulu (the celestial) that he is a god? Be this as it may, many of the Matebeles, of the same people, believe, on the word of their princes, that the ancestors of these have sprung from the reeds of a fountain, instead of being born of a woman, as other men are." *(Op. cit., p. 231.)*—But the Amazulu are so called, not because they have arrogated to themselves the title of "Celestials," but from Uzulu, an ancient chief. He, however, may have obtained that name from the ascription to him of heavenly power. U-izulu, Thou art the heaven, became soon converted into the proper name, Uzulu.

[32] In Rowley's *Story of the Universities' Mission to Central Africa* we find the following account of the religion of the people in the neighbourhood of Lake Nyassa:—

"Both Manganja and Ajawa seemed to have a better idea of the Deity than most savage tribes. The Manganja called God, Pambi, or Mpambi; the Ajawa, Mulungu. Neither, as I have elsewhere said, looked upon Him as a God of wrath; indeed, they did not appear to assign any wrathful attribute to Him, nor did they in any way make Him the author of evil; they supposed evil to proceed from malevolent spirits—the Mfiti. We never, therefore, found them offering up human sacrifices in order to avert God's anger. If great danger, either famine or war, threatened them, they would assemble at an appointed place, and in an appointed way, offer up prayer to God to deliver them from the famine, or to give them the victory in the war. We saw instances of this. At Magomero, soon after the commencement of the first rainy season after we were in the land, there was a solemn assem-

shipped under the name of Danh, the heavenly snake. *(Burton. Op. cit., p. 148.)*

blage for prayer. The ground had been prepared, the seed sown; the rains came, the corn sprang up—all seemed as we desired it; and then the rains ceased: day by day, week by week, and no rain; the fierce sun seemed withering the young corn, famine appeared imminent. Chigunda assembled his people in the bush outside the village, then marched with them in procession to the appointed place for prayer; a plot of ground cleared and fenced in, and in the middle of which was a hut, called the prayer hut. The women attended as well as the men, and in the procession the women preceded the men. All entered the enclosure, the women sitting on one side of the hut, the men on the other; Chigunda sat some distance apart by himself. Then a woman named Mbudzi, the sister of Chigunda it was said, stood forth, and she acted as priestess. In one hand she had a small basket containing Indian corn meal, in the other a small earthen pot containing the native beer, pombi—the equivalent, doubtless, to the ancient offering of corn and wine. She went just into the hut, not so far but what she could be seen and heard. She put the basket and the pot down on either side of her. Then she took up a handful of the meal and dropped it on the floor, and in doing this called out in a high-pitched voice, 'Imva Mpambi! Adza mvula!' (Hear thou, O God, and send rain!) and the assembled people responded, clapping their hands softly, and intoning—they always intone their prayers—' Imva Mpambi!' (Hear thou, O God!) This was done again and again until the meal was expended, and then, after arranging it in the form of a sugar loaf, the beer was poured, as a libation, round about it. The supplications ceased, Mbudzi came out of the hut, fastened up the door, sat on the ground, threw herself on her back; all the people followed her example, and while in this position they clapped their hands and repeated their supplication for several minutes. This over, they stood up, clapped hands again, bowing themselves to the earth repeatedly while doing so; then marched to where Chigunda was sitting, and danced round about him like mad things. When the dance ceased, a large jar of water was brought and placed before the chief; first Mbudzi washed her hands, arms, and face; then water was poured over her by another woman; then all the women rushed forward with calabashes in their hands, and dipping them into the jar threw the water into the air with loud cries and wild gesticulations. And so the ceremonies ended."

NOTE.

SINCE writing Note 62, p. 91, on the Shade or Shadow of a man, I have found that many of the natives connect the shade with the spirit to a much greater extent than I supposed.

Their theory is not very consistent with itself nor very intelligible, neither is it easy to understand on what kind of observation it is founded. It is something of this kind. They say the shadow—that evidently cast by the body—is that which will ultimately become the *itongo* or spirit when the body dies. In order to ascertain if this was really the meaning, I asked, "Is the shadow which my body casts when I am walking, my spirit?" The reply was, "No; it is not your *itongo* or spirit,"—(evidently understanding me to mean by "my spirit" an ancestral guardian spirit watching over me, and not my own spirit) —"but it will be the *itongo* or ancestral spirit for your children when you are dead." It is said that the long shadow shortens as a man approaches his end, and contracts into a very little thing. When they see the shadow of a man thus contracting, they know he will die. The long shadow goes away when a man is dead; and it is that which is meant when it is said, "The shadow has departed." There is, however, a short shadow which remains with the corpse and is buried with it. The long shadow becomes an *itongo* or ancestral spirit.

In connection with this, the natives have another superstition. If a friend has gone out to battle, and they are anxious about him, they take his sleeping-mat and stand it upright in the sun. If it throws a long shadow, he is still living. If a short one, or none at all, he is dead!

PART II.

AMATONGO;
OR,
ANCESTOR WORSHIP.

AMATONGO;

OR,

ANCESTOR WORSHIP.

BA ti amatongo into a ba vela nayo kukqala ekuveleni kwabo. Ba vela se ku tiwa, "Ku kona amatongo;" kwa ba ukuba nabo b' azi ukuti ku kona amatongo. A ku 'nto a ba vela nje ba se be ya bona ukuti amatongo.

A si 'nto e velayo ngasemva kwokuvela kwabantu, uma ba wa bone ba ti, "Nank' amatongo." Izinkomo kambe za vela, ba zi bona, ba ti, "Nazi izinkomo," zi vela ngemva kwabo. Ku ya bonakala ukuba a si kulumi ngokuvela kwomuntu wokukqala; lapa

MEN say they possessed Amatongo as soon as they came into being.[1] When they came into being, men already spoke of there being Amatongo; and hence they too knew that they existed. It is not something which as soon as they were born they saw to be Amatongo.

It is not something which came into being immediately after men, which when they saw they said, "Those are Amatongo." They saw cattle indeed, which came into being, and said, "Those are cattle," they having come into being immediately[2] after themselves. It is evident that we are not speaking of the origin of the first

---

[1] Not at the time of the creation, but of their own birth. There is no one now who can remember when the Amatongo were first spoken of. As soon as he came to years capable of understanding, he heard others speak of the Amatongo, as they had heard others who were older than themselves.

[2] Note the distinction between *ngasemva* and *emva*.

B

si ti ukuvela kwabantu si kuluma ngemva kwake, ngokuba a kw aziwa ukuma kwowokukqala. Si tsho ke ukuti sa vela nawo tina 'ba vele se ku tshiwo ukuti amatongo, ku tshiwo abapambili.

Kwa tsho abokukqala bonke ke; kwa ba aba velayo ba se be vela se be ba tshela wona amatongo, ba w' azi ke ukuti a kona amatongo. Kw azise futi ukuti kona kukqala ba ti be vela nje, ba be vela kanye nezinyanga ezona za ba keansisela ukuti a kona. Ba ti ke, 'abiwa umuntu wokukqala, owa ti, "Ku kona amatongo a inyoka." Umuntu wokukqala Umvelinqangi, Unkulunkulu. 'Aziwa ke izizwe zonke. A kwa ba ko 'sizwe esa ti, "Tina 'basekutini ka li ko kwiti itongo."

Izizwe zonke za bonga amatongo, ngokuba kwa tsho Umveli-

man: when we say the origin of men we speak of those who came after him, for the standing of the first man is unknown. So we, who came into being when men who preceded us already spoke of there being Amatongo, say, "We came into being possessed of them."

All the first men, then, spoke of the Amatongo; and they told those who came into being after them, as soon as they came into being, that there are Amatongo. And further in the beginning, as soon as they came into being, they had doctors[3] who taught them that there are Amatongo. And so they said that the Amatongo were created[4] by the first man, who said, "There are Amatongo who are snakes." The first man is Umvelinqangi, Unkulunkulu. And thus all nations knew of the Amatongo. There was not a single nation which said, "We people of such a country have no Itongo."

All nations worshipped the Amatongo, because Umvelinqangi

---

[3] The izinyanga or doctors are thus represented as the appointed teachers of the people. They are, no doubt, the relic of an ancient priesthood.

[4] The native who relates this does not, he says, mean that when Unkulunkulu was speaking to primitive men, Amatongo were already in existence; but speaking of the future as already present, he appointed the spirits of the dead to be the protectors and helpers of the living:—that he said, "There are Amatongo," but the people looked around, but were unable to see them until death had deprived them of their parents, and then they addressed prayers to them, received visits from them in dreams, or in the form of snakes; and sacrificed to them.

nyangi, owa ba tshelako, wa ti, "Ni bona nje, into e ngi ni tshela yona; ngi ni tshela amatongo, ni bonge wona; ngi ni tshela izinyanga zokubula, ni bule kuzo, zi ni tshele uma umuntu e gula, e guliswa amatongo; zi ya 'ku li zwa ukuti u gula nje, u guliswa amatongo."

Zonke ke izizwe ke za se zi ti, noma be ya 'ku*h*lasela empini; noko i ba bulala, ba ti, abakubo labo abafileyo be bulewe impi, ba ti, "Li si fulatele elakwiti itongo." Ba ti, "Ini ukuba abantu ba ze ba pele bonke, impi ku nga buyi noyedwa na, nomuntu na?"

A ti um' e kona osindileyo, a ti, "Mina, ngi kyabuke, ngi sinda ke; ku be se ku tiwa nje, ma si pele sonke; kw ale umuntu wa ba munye; ngabe si te si kyedwa impi nje, yena owa be pi na? Ngi kyabuke, ngi sinda; ngi be ngi nga s' azi uma ngi za 'usinda, ngi bona abantu bonke bakwiti se be pelile."

commanded them to do so, saying, "You see, then,[5] I tell you about the Amatongo, that you may worship them. I tell you about divining Izinyanga,[6] that you may enquire of them, and they tell you when a man has been made ill by the Amatongo; they shall hear the Itongo declaring that he has been made ill by the Amatongo."

So all nations used to think when they were about to attack an army, that they should be assisted by the Itongo; and although they were killed by the army, the friends of those who were killed said, "The Itongo of our people has turned its back on us." They asked, "How is it that all our people have at length come to an end, and not one man come back from the army?"

If there is one who has escaped, he says, "As for me I escaped I know not how. The Amatongo had decreed that we should all die; one man[7] would not assent; when we were destroyed by the enemy, where was he I wonder? I escaped I know not how; I no longer expected to be saved, when I saw all our people destroyed."

---

[5] A mode of claiming attention, or commanding silence.

[6] *Izinyanga*.—It is, perhaps, better to retain the native word than to translate it by a word which does not fairly represent it. Inyanga, generally rendered *doctor*, means a man skilled in any particular matter = *magus*. Thus, an inyanga yokubula is a doctor or wise man of smiting, that is, with divining rods—a diviner. Inyanga yemiti, a doctor of medicines. Inyanga yensimbi, a smith, &c.

[7] That is, one man among the Amatongo—one of the Amatongo.

Ba ti ukukqala kwabo, ba ti, "Amadhlozi akwiti mabi! Ini ukuba umuzi u pelele empini wonke na ? Amadoda angaka na ! Impi ukupela na i kqedwe impi na! Kangaka a be fulatele, kw enze njani ? Into a be nga i tsho si zwe uma kw' enza njani na ? A ze a kqede umuzi na ? u pele wonke na ? Yena o kqabuke e sindisa ubani lo, u be ye ngapi na ? U be nga hambi ini pakati kwamanye amadhlozi na ?" Ba tsho njalo abakalayo.

Na labo abafayo empini se be ya 'kuba a wona amadhlozi futi.

Ba ti abasindileyo ab' amadhlozi akubo e ba bhekile, ba sinde, ba ti, "Si sindiswe amadhlozi akwiti." Ba fike ba buye, be vela empini, ba fike, ba wa gwazele izinkomo; ba bonge ukuba be ti a ba pilisile; ba zitele ngenyongo emzimbeni, be ti, "Ma kcakcambe, a be mhlope, a nga bi mnyama," ukuze a ba pilise ngolunye usuku futi. Ba bonge ku be kuhle.

Ku be ku kalwa ngalapa be file,

At first the people say, "The Amatongo of our people are good for nothing! Why has the whole village perished in the fight? So many men as there were! Our whole army destroyed by the enemy! How did it happen that they turned the back on so many? How is it that they never mentioned any thing to us that we might understand why they were angry? Have they at last destroyed the whole village? has it come utterly to an end? Where had the Itongo who saved So-and-so gone? Why was he not among the other Amatongo?" Those who weep for the dead say thus.

And those who died in the fight will now become Amatongo.

And those who escaped, whose national Amatongo looked on them and saved them, say, "We have been saved by the Amadhlozi of our people." When they come back from the army, they sacrifice cattle to the Amatongo; they return thanks because they think they have saved them; they pour the gall of the sacrifices on their bodies, saying, "Let the Amatongo be bright and white, and not dark, that they may save us on another occasion." They return thanks with glad hearts.

And there is funeral lamenta-

ku tiwe, idhlozi labo limnyama. Ba ze b' enzele ukuze ba ti noko nga inkosi yabo i ba pindelisa empini, i ti, ma ba hlasele, amadhlozi akubo a nga soli 'luto, ngokuba ba wa lungisile, ba wa kcakcambisa; se be ya 'kuti noko be fika kuyo impi se b' azi ukuti, "Umakazi loku sa wa lungisa amadhlozi, a ya 'kuti s' ona ngani na?" Lapa se be bona impi a ba ya 'kulwa nayo, ba kumbule amadhlozi, ba kcabang' izinto a ba z' enzayo, be wa kcola um' a be mahle; ba ku bone loko enhliziyweni zabo, b' az' ukuti, sa wa lungisa amadhlozi akwiti; noko si fa, ka si yi 'kutsho ukuti i kona into a wa be e i kalela.

Mbala ba tukutele ke, ba ti, "A ya 'kuba a si fulatele nje." Ngokuba uma be ya empini, ba ti, "Si hamba nawo amadhlozi akwiti," ba lwe ke nenye impi. A ti um' amadhlozi akubo emhlope, 'ale ukuba ba fe, ku be i bona be bulala abantu nganhlanye, ba bone ke ukuti si be si hambe namadhlozi

tion where they have lost their people; they say, their Idhlozi is dark. At length they sacrifice, that if perchance their chief lead them again to attack the enemy, the Amatongo of their people may have no cause of complaint, because they have made amends to them, and made them bright; and now when they reach the enemy they know what they have done, and say, "Can it be, since we have made amends to the Amadhlozi, that they will say we have wronged them by anything!" When they see the enemy with which they are about to fight, they remember the Amadhlozi, and think of what they have done for them, by sacrificing to them that they may be propitious; they see that in their hearts, and know that they have made amends to the Amadhlozi of their people, and that though they die they cannot say there is any thing of which the Amadhlozi have reason to complain.

So truly they are very brave, saying, "The Amatongo will turn their backs on us without cause." For when they go to the enemy they say, "The Amadhlozi of our people go with us;" and so they fight with the enemy. And if their Amadhlozi are white and do not allow them to die, and they kill on their side only, then they see that their Amadhlozi go with

akwiti. Ku ti kulabo abafileyo ba pike abaseleyo, ba ti, "A si namadhlozi. Ini uma si fe si pele na? Amadhlozi akwiti 'ahlulwe amadhlozi akwabanye abantu na?" Ngokuba be ti aba nga fanga, ba ti, "'Ahluliwe amadhlozi akwabani, 'ahlulwe akwiti."

Ku njalo ke kubantu abamnyama; a ba velanga nje ukuba be ti, "Amatongo ka wa ko." Ba vela se ku tiwa, "Amatongo a kona." Kodwa ke nati ke ka s' azi uma lowo 'muntu owa vela kuk*q*ala wa za wa ti nje, "Ku kona amatongo." U kona ini umuntu owa ke wa ti e hamba wa be inyoka na? Ngokuba nati si ya kohlwa lapo, uma Umvelin*q*angi wa za wa ti, idhlozi li inyoka nje, ngani. Loku umuntu e suka a fe nje e nge namsila; nati lapo ka si kolwa enyokeni; loku noma abantu be lele, u ti a nga pupa inyoka, a papame masinyane, 'etuke; a ti uma e pupa umuntu owa fayo, a kulume naye izindaba ekupupeni; inyoka umuntu e i pupa ka kalumi nayo izindaba, u y' etuka. Ngi ti mina, amadhlozi ka wa ko a nemisila. Umvelin*q*angi tina si ti w' eduka yena um' a t' abantu ba izinyoka. Ngokuba nabantu aba-

them. But on the part of those who are conquered, those who survive say, "We have no Amadhlozi. Why have we died utterly? Why have our Amadhlozi been conquered by the Amadhlozi of other people?" For those who have not died say, "The Amadhlozi of So-and-so have been conquered by the Amadhlozi of our tribe."

Thus it is with black men; they did not come into being when it was said, "There are no Amatongo." They came into being when it was already said, "There are Amatongo." But we do not know why the man which first came into being said, "There are Amatongo." Was there ever a man who whilst living said he was a snake? For we too do not understand why Umvelin*q*angi said, "The Idhlozi is a snake." For a man dies having no tail; and even we in that respect do not believe in a snake; for if a man is asleep, and dreams of a snake, he awakes immediately and starts; but if he dream of a dead man, he speaks with him of affairs in a dream; but if he dream of a snake, he does not talk with it; he starts. For my part, I say there are no Amadhlozi with tails. And we say Umvelin*q*angi made a mistake when he said, "People are snakes." For old men, when we ask why it

dala aba 'madoda si ti lapa si buzayo si ti, "Amadhlozi lawa ku tiwa a izinyoka nje ngani?" ba ti, "Ngoba kw amadhlozi." Si buze tina, si ti, "Ake ni si tshele abantu abafa be nemisila na?" Ba kohlwe lapa, ba nga si tsheli. Si ti ke, "O, ini ukuba ni nga si tsheli amadhlozi a izinyoka na?" Ba tsho njalo ke; ba kohlwa, ba nga si tsheli uma si zwe. Si y' ezwa uma be tsho amadhlozi enyokeni; ka si zwa uma inyoka i idhlozi.

is said that the Amadhlozi are snakes, say, "Because they are Amadhlozi." And we ask saying, "Just tell us if dead men have tails." They are puzzled there, and cannot tell us. And so we say, "O, how is it that you do not tell us whether the Amadhlozi are snakes?" So they repeat the same words; they are puzzled and do not tell us, that we may understand. We understand if they say, "The Amadhlozi are in snakes;" we do not understand if they say, "The snake is an Idhlozi."

Ukwaba equivalent to Create.

NJENGALOKO lapo inkosi ya tsho, ya ti, "A ku be kona ukukanya," kwa ba kona njengokutsho kwayo inkosi; si ti, "Kw' abiwa inkosi ukukanya." Ku njalo ke abantu ba ti, "'Abiwa amatongo Umvelinqangi." Ba ti futi, "Umuntu wokukqala w' aba amatongo, ukuti, wa wa veza." Ba ti, "Zonke izinto z' abiwa umuntu wokukqala, Unkulunkulu; z' enziwa uye;" ngokuba ku ya lingana ukwabiwa nokwenziwa.

Lapa tina ke, tina 'bantu si velayo, si ti, "Abantu abamnyama

JUST as when the Lord said, "Let there be light," and there was light in accordance with the word of the Lord; we say, "The light was created [abiwa] by the Lord." So the people say, "The Amatongo were created [abiwa] by Umvelinqangi." So they say, "The first man created [aba] the Amatongo, that is, he gave them being." They say, "All things were made by the first man, Unkulunkulu; they were made by him;" for ukwabiwa and ukwenziwa has one meaning.

We then, who come into being at the present time, now say,

ba la/zleka. Ini ukuba ba ti ka ba m azi Umvelinqangi na? Abantu abaziyo abafundisi; bona be kuluma ngemiteto yenkosi. Yona si i zwayo igama layo, nendodana yayo. Si ya ko/zlwa uma yena umuntu wokukqala wa be ubani; loku si zwa Unkulunkulu Umvelinqangi; si ng' azi uba yena Unkulunkulu lo wa zalwa ubani.

Loku abelungu ba fika nje nabafundisi, sa si li zwa igama lokuti, u kona Utikxo. Ku ya s' a/zlula okutshiwo abantu, uma ku nga bi ko umuntu o ti Unkulunkulu wa dabuka kukqala nje, umfazi wake kwa ku ubani, nendodana yake. Loku indodana katikxo si ya i zwa ngabafundisi ukuti Ujesu. Si y' a/zluleka; tina si ti ba la/zleka. Ini uma ba si tshele Unkulunkulu? Si zwe ukuti be ti wa dabula izizwe zonke ezimnyama; si nga i zwa indawo lap' e kona a zi dabulela kona.

Si ko/zlwe ke lapo kulabo 'bantu uma be ti s' enziwa Unkulunkulu, Umvelinqangi, (ukuti Umvelinqangi nje, ngokuba a vela kukqala

"Black men are mistaken. Why do they say that they do not know Umvelinqangi? The people who know are the missionaries, who speak of the commandments of the Lord. We hear His name, and that of His Son. We do not know who the first man was; this only we hear, that Unkulunkulu is one with Umvelinqangi; not knowing who was the father of Unkulunkulu.

But since the white men came and the missionaries we have heard it said that there is God. We cannot understand what the black men say, for there is no one who tells us that Unkulunkulu first came into being, and what was his wife's name, and that he had a son. But we hear the missionaries say that Jesus is the son of God. We do not understand what the black men say. We say, "They are mistaken. Why do they tell us about Unkulunkulu? We hear them say that he created all the black nations; but we do not hear of the place where he created them."

So we do not understand what these people mean, when they say we were made by Unkulunkulu, Umvelinqangi. He is called Umvelinqangi for no other reason but because he came into being first

ngapambili kwabantu.) Ba ti ke, "Wa memeza, wa ti, 'Ma ku vele abantu, ku vele izinto zonke, nezinja, nezinkomo, nezinteto, nemiti, notshani.'" Kepa ke si ng' eze s' azi ezinhliziyweni zetu uma si zwa be tsho njalo, be ti izinto z' enziwe Unkulunkulu; si nga u zwa umfula owa be zi dabulela kona izizwe a z' aba Unkulunkulu.

Si ti into e ize leyo kankulunkulu. B' eduka nobuula. A si i zwa into eyona y' enziwa Unkulunkulu. Tina si velayo si vela se be si tshela be ti s' enziwa Unkulunkulu. Si ti, "Into e ize. Ka i ko into yekqiniso lapo; ngoba a ba ko aba ti si y' azi lapa Unkulunkulu a dabulela kona abantu."

Si ti tina si zwa abelungu,—zona izindaba zenkosi zi sezincwadini. Si ti, "Nampa abakuluma ikqiniso, be ti, 'Inkosi i kona.'" Na manje inkosi i kona. Nati si ti si vela kwa ku tiwa i kona inkosi; i sezulwini, ukuti Utikxo. Indaba

immediately before men.[8] So they say, "He shouted saying, 'Let men come forth; let all things come forth,—both dogs and cattle, and grasshoppers, and trees and grass.'" But we could never understand in our hearts when we heard them say that all things were made by Unkulunkulu; and did not hear the name of the river where Unkulunkulu broke off the nations which he created [aba].

We say this matter about Unkulunkulu is a vain thing. They wandered with folly as a companion. We do not know a single thing that was created by Unkulunkulu. As soon as we were born they told us we were made by Unkulunkulu. We say, it is a vain thing. There is no truth in it; for there are none who say, they know the place where Unkulunkulu broke off the people.

We say we understand the white men,—the true accounts of the Lord which are in books. We say, "Behold the men who speak the truth, when they say, 'The Lord is.'" And even now the Lord is. And we too say that from our birth it was said, the Lord is; He is in heaven; that is,

---

[8] Note again the force of *nga* before *pambili*: *pambili*, before—any indefinite time before; *ngapambili*, just before, immediately or a short time before.

kankulunkulu a si y azi; a i kqondeki kahle; insumansumane nje. Loku noma be ti, Unkulunkulu wa tuma unwaba, wa ti, a lu yokuti ezizweni zabantu, lu yokuti, abantu ma ba nga fi; ba ti, kwa ti ngasemva kwonwaba wa tuma intulwa ngasemva kwonwaba, unwaba se lu hambile ukuya 'kuti, abantu ma ba nga fi; ya hamba ngasemuva intulo ukuya 'kuti, ma ba fe. Kwa za kwa fika intulo kukqala; ya fika, ya ti intulo, abantu ma ba fe. Kanti unwaba lu libele ubukwebezane, ya za ya buya intulwa; kanti unwaba olu tunywe ukukqala, ka lu ka fiki, lu libele ubukwebezane. Lu te se lu ya 'kufika kubantu, se lu fika lu ti, "Ku tiwa, abantu ma ba nga fi." Ba se be ti abantu, kqede lu memeze unwaba, lu tsho njalo, lu ti, "Abantu ma ba nga fi," b' ala abantu, ba ti, "Si bambe elentulo; se u kuluma ize wena; izwi e si li hambileyo, si bambe elentulo, yona i fike ya ti, 'Ku tiwa, Abantu ma ba fe.' Nant' igama e si li bambileyo. A si y azi leyo 'ndaba o i tshoyo, lunwaba." Tina ke si ti ke, mfundisi, si ti, izindaba zamanga; leyo 'ndaba i nge ko. Abantu b' enziwa inkosi. Unkulunkulu si ti wa kw azi ngani ukutuma izilwane ezihhukquzela ngesisu pansi, a ti i zona z' emuka za ya 'kukuluma kubantu indaba na? Si ti, ba kohlwa.

God. We do not understand the account of Unkulunkulu; it is not easily understood; it is a mere fable. For although they say, Unkulunkulu sent a chameleon to go and tell the nations of men that men were not to die; and that after the chameleon he sent a lizard to tell men that they were to die; and the lizard arrived first and said that men must die. The chameleon forsooth loitered at a bush of ubukwebezane, until the lizard came back again, and the chameleon which was sent first had not yet arrived, stopping to eat the ubukwebezane. And when it came to men it said, "Unkulunkulu says that men are not to die." And when the chameleon had made this proclamation, men refused to listen, and said, "We have received the word of the lizard; what you now say is vain; the word which we have received is that of the lizard, which came and said, 'Unkulunkulu says, Man must die.' That is the word which we have accepted. We do not understand the matter, Chameleon, of which you speak." We thus say, Teacher, that these are false accounts; the tale is not real. Men were made by the Lord. We ask how could Unkulunkulu send animals which creep on their bellies, to take a message to man? We say they are deceived.

A si y azi indawo lapo Umvelinqangi abantu a ba vezela kona, uma ba be kona nje. I ya s' a///ula nati le 'ndaba; nabadala abafayo ba fa be nga l' azi lelo 'zwe lapa Unkulunkulu a dabulela kona abantu uma ba be kona; nabadala abasala kwabafayo ka ba tsho ukuti, si ya l' azi lelo 'zwe lapa Unkulunkulu a dabulela abantu; nabo ba ya dinga nje ukuba nabo b' ezwe ngendaba ukuti, Unkulunkulu wa dabula izizwe. A b' ezwakali abanye Onkulunkulu balezo 'zizwe a nga dabulanga Unkulunkulu wakubo. Tina se si ti uma si ba buza si ti, "Ake ni si tshele Unkulunkulu, si zwe," ba ti, "Ka s' azi." Si ti, "N' ezwa kanjani na ukuti kwa ku kona Unkulunkulu na?" Ba ti, "S' ezwa ngabantu abadala aba ngapambili kwetu." Si ti, "Labo aba be ngapambili kwenu b' ezwa ngobani na?" Ba ti ke lapo, "Si ya ko///lwa; ka s' azi." Si ti, "Unkulunkulu wa be into e ize nje. Ini uma si ng' ezwa izindaba zake Unkulunkulu uku zi tshela zona izizwe a be z' enza Unkulunkulu na? Ku be i loku ni pika ngokuti kwa ku kona Unkulunkulu

We do not know the place where Umvelinqangi gave men being, that they might have life. Neither can we any more than our fathers understand this matter; and the ancients who are dead died without knowing the country where Unkulunkulu created men that they might have life; and the old people who are still living do not say they know the country where Unkulunkulu created men; and they too want to be told about the creation of the nations by Unkulunkulu. Other Onkulunkulu of those nations are not heard of, whom their own Unkulunkulu did not create.[9] And if we say to them, "Just tell us about Unkulunkulu, that we may understand," they reply, "We do not know." We say, "How did you hear that there was Unkulunkulu?" They reply, "We heard it of old men who were before us." We ask, "Of whom did those who were before you hear?" They say, "We cannot tell. We do not know." We say, "Unkulunkulu was a mere vanity. Why do you not understand the accounts of Unkulunkulu, which he told the nations which he made? Since you only assert continually that Unkulunkulu was, how can we understand

---

[9] He means that there is one supreme Unkulunkulu, from whom all other Onkulunkulu sprang.

njalo na? Si nga zi zwa izindaba zake na? Ka si kolwa."

UMPENGULA MBANDA.

ABANTU ba ti ku kona amadhlozi abo. Ba ya kolwa kuloko, ngokuba ka b'azi ukuba umuntu u ya ngapi ekufeni kwake. Ba fumana ukuti ukupenduka inyoka ngokucabanga kwabo. Ba ti umuntu u ya fa; ngemva kwaloku, uma e se file, a buye a penduke inyoka; ba ti ibizo lenyoka, ba ti, itongo; ba kuleka kulo ngoku li hlabisa izinkomo, ngokuba ba ti izinkomo futi ezalo, ba zi piwa ilo; futi ba ti, ba pila ngalo; ku ngaloko be li hlabisa izinkomo. Ba ti, uma be za 'ku li hlabisa, ba buyise izinkomo enhle, uma be se z' alukile; noma zi se sekaya, ba zi butela 'ndawo nye noma zintatu noma zine; ka ba zi buti zonke; ba leta lezo ezi neyakuhlatshiswa itongo, ba zi ngenise esibayeni; ba gakxe imvalo esangweni, be se be zi kqokqela. Umnikaziyo e se kuleka ematongweni, e ti, "Nansi inkomo yenu, nina 'bakwiti;" e se kuleka, e ba balisa oyise noniuakulu a se

what relates to him? We do not believe."

THE people say their Amadhlozi exist. They believe in that, for they do not know where men go when they die. When they thought of the matter they discovered that they turned into snakes. They say a man dies, and when he is dead, he turns into a snake; and they gave that snake the name of Itongo, and they worship it by sacrificing cattle, for they say the cattle too belong to it; it is it that gives them cattle; and they say it is by it they live; therefore they sacrifice cattle to it. When they are going to sacrifice, they bring home the cattle, if they have been driven out to pasture; or if they are still at home, they drive three or four together; they do not collect them all; they select those which are with the one they are about to sacrifice to the Itongo, and drive them into the pen; they close the gateway with poles, and then drive the cattle together in one place. The owner of the bullock having prayed to the Amatongo, saying, "There is your bullock, ye spirits of our people;" and as he prays naming grandfathers and grand-

ba fa, e ti, "Naku ukudhla kwenu; ngi ya kcela umzimba omnandi, ukuba ngi hambe kahle; nawe, banibani, u ngi pate kahle; nawe, banibani," e tsho njalo, e balisa ngabo bonke bakwabo a se ba fa. Emva kwaloko e be e se tata umkonto omunye o za 'ku i hlaba, e se nyonyoba, e se i gwaza emhlabankomo, ukuti eluhlangotini; i be se i kala, i ti, "Eh;" e be e se ti umniniyo, "Kala, nkomo yamadhlozi." E se pinda e balisa futi ngaloko, ngokuba e ti ba m nikela abakubo ukuba a hambe kahle ngaloko 'kukala kwenkomo. I be se i hlinzwa, se i pelile, umniniyo e be e se ka igazana elincinyane, e se sika umhlwehlwe futi, e se u tshisela ngasese negazana, e se li beke ngasese futi, e se tata impepo e se basa yona, e se beka umhlwehlwana pezu kwempepo, e ti, u pa abakubo usi olumnandi. Emva kwaloko ba be se be i dhla ke inyama. Ku pela.

mothers who are dead, saying, "There is your food; I pray for a healthy body, that I may live comfortably; and thou, So-and-so, treat me with mercy; and thou So-and-so," mentioning by name all of their family who are dead; and then the one who is going to kill the bullock takes an assagai and goes cautiously towards it, and stabs it in the place where the ox is usually stabbed, that is, in its side; and then the ox bellows, and the owner says, "Cry, ox of the Amadhlozi." And then he again mentions the Amatongo by name, because he thinks they have given him health, because of the cry of his ox. It is then skinned. When the skinning is completed, the owner takes a little blood, and cuts off a portion of the caul, and burns it in a secret place with the blood, which also he places in a secret place; and he takes incense and burns it, having placed the caul on the incense, thinking, he is giving the spirits of their people a sweet savour. After that they eat the flesh. That is the end.

Ku ti uma ku fe umuntu kubantu abamnyama a fulelwe ngamahlahla. Ku zinge ku hlolwa njalo umniniyo lowo 'muntu ofileyo. Noma

WHEN a man dies among black men the grave is covered over with branches. The person to whom the dead man belongs watches the grave continually. If

ku fe indodana uyise a linde njalo ihlahla, ukuze ku ti se be bona ukuba ihlahla li bunile ba dele, b' azi a ku ko 'luto olu nga m kipako, ngokuba u se bolile. Kepa uma e fumana inyoka ngapezulu, a tsho uma e se buyile lowo 'muntu o be yohlola, a ti, "O, ngi m fumene namhla nje e tamele ilanga ngapezulu kweliba."

Ngaloko ke uma e nga buyi ukuya ekaya, be nga m pupi, ku hlatshwe inkomo noma imbuzi, ku tiwe, u ya buyiswa enhle ukuba 'eze ekaya; ku ti uma be nga m pupi noma ku njalo, ba hlupeke ngokuti, "Lo 'muntu wa fa kanjani? a si m boni; itongo lake li mnyama." Ku yiwe enyangeni yobulawo uma ku umuntu womuzi

a son has died, his father watches the branches constantly, that when they see that the branches are rotten they may be satisfied, knowing that nothing can now disturb the remains, for they are rotten. And if he observe a snake on the grave, the man who went to look at the grave says on his return, "O, I have seen him to-day basking in the sun on the top of the grave."

So then if the snake does not come home, or if they do not dream of the dead, they sacrifice an ox or a goat, and it is said he is brought back from the open country to his home. And if they do not dream of him, though the snake has come home, they are troubled and ask, "How did this man die? we do not see him; his Itongo is dark." They go to a doctor of ubulawo,[10] if it is the chief man

---

[10] *Ubulawo*, A class of medicines, used for cleansing and brightening. Medicines used with the view of removing from the system something that causes dislike, and introducing into it something that will cause love.

There are two kinds used in each case—black ubulawo and white ubulawo; the black "washes," the white "wipes;" the black takes away the "blackness"—"the evil,"—which causes a man to be disliked; the white makes him "white"—causes him to be "bright "— gives him a "beauty,"—which causes him to become an object of love and admiration.

Both black and white ubulawo are roots of plants.

The black is first used. The roots are bruised, mixed with water, and "churned:" when a great deal of froth has been produced by the churning process, it is drunk and the body is washed with it. It is used for about a month. The first time of using it, the medicines are taken to some place where the aloe is abundant; there a large fire is kindled of aloe; and the medicine being prepared is drunk in large quantities; it is emetic, and the contents of the stomach are ejected

omkulu; ai, a ku tshiwo ngabantu kazana nje. Inyanga i fike i poḣle ubulawo, ku ḣlatshwe imbuzi, yona i nomsindo nokukala; imvu a i ḣlatshwa ngokuba ku tiwa itongo li ya 'kuba mnyama, ngokuba imvu i isiula, a i namsindo; a ku vamile ukuba ku ḣlatshiswe itongo ngemvu; itongo li ḣlatshiswa ngembuzi, yona ku ti umuntu e sa i ti kɛhu ngosungulo, i be se i bangalasa, ba tokoze ke kakulu, ba ti, "Kala, nkomo kabani, owa ti, wa ti, wa ti" (be tsho izenzo zake). Ba ti, "Si ti, Buya u ze 'kaya, si ku bone namḣla nje. Si ya ḣlu-

of a large village; but nothing is done as to the poor. The doctor comes and mixes ubulawo, and a goat is killed, it being an animal which makes a great noise and cries; but a sheep is not killed, because it is said it will cause the Itongo to be dark; for a sheep is foolish and makes no noise, and therefore it is not usual to sacrifice a sheep to the Itongo. The Itongo has a goat sacrificed to it; when a man pricks it with a needle, it at once makes a great noise; and so they rejoice greatly and say, "Cry, beast of So-and-so, who did such and such and such things" (mentioning the things he did). "We say, Come home again, that we may now see you. We are trou-

---

into the fire so as to quench it; the object being that the "badness," which is cast off, may be burnt up and utterly consumed. On subsequent occasions the contents of the stomach are ejected on pathways, that others may walk over it, and take away the "insila" or filth that is the cause of offence which has been cast out.

When the treatment by the black ubulawo has been continued for the proper period, the white is used much in the same way. The roots are bruised, mixed with water, and churned. If the man is using it because he has been rejected by some damsel, he adds to the medicine something belonging to her which has been worn next her skin, especially beads; whilst churning the medicines he praises the Amatongo, and prays for success. When the froth is produced and rises high above the mouth of the pot, he allows it to subside; and then takes some of the froth and puts it on his head and sprinkles it over his body; and then drinks the contents of the pot. It has an emetic effect. But the contents of the stomach are ejected in the cattle-pen. This place is selected because the white ubulawo is a "blessing."

The special circumstances under which such medicines are used are when a youth has been rejected; or when a man wishes to obtain a favour from a chief or great man; or when he has been summoned by the chief to answer a charge brought against him; or under the circumstances narrated in the text. But in the case of "bringing home" the Itongo, the white ubulawo only is used.

peka, uma si nge ze sa ku bona, si ti, u si sola ngani na? loku izinkomo ezako zi mi nje; uma u biza inyama, u nga tsho zi hlatshwe, ku ng' ali 'muntu."

bled if we never see you, and ask, why you are angry with us? for all the cattle are still yours; if you wish for meat, you can say so, and the cattle be slaughtered, without any one denying you."

Y elape ke inyanga leyo yobulawo, i bu pehle i m biza, bu bekwe emsamo. I tsho ukuti, "Ngi ti u za 'ku m bona namhla nje, u kulume naye; noma kade u nga m boni, namhla nje u ya 'uhlambuluka.

So the doctor of ubulawo practises his art; he mixes the ubulawo, calling the dead man by name, and puts the ubulawo in the upper part of the hut, and says, "I say, you will see him to-day, and talk with him; although you have not seen him for a long time, to-day he will be clear."

Ku njalo ke ukuyiswa kwesituta, si buyiswa ngenkomo na ngobulawo.

Such then is the means employed to bring back a ghost; it is brought back by sacrifice and ubulawo.

The people do not worship all Amatongo indifferently.

ABANTU abamnyama a ba kuleki ematongweni onke, abantu abafayo bakubo; kakulu ku kulekwa enhlokweni yalowo 'muzi kulabo 'bantwana balowo 'muzi; ngokuba abadala abafako a ba b' azi nezibongo zabo uma kwa ko obani na. Kepa uyise a ba m aziko u inhloko yokuba ba kqale ngaye, ba geine ngaye ekukulekeni, ngokuba ba ya m azi yena kakulu, na ngoku ba tanda kwake abantwana bake; ba ya kumbula uku ba pata kwake e se kona, ba linganise loko 'ku ba

BLACK people do not worship all Amatongo indifferently, that is, all the dead of their tribe. Speaking generally, the head of each house is worshipped by the children of that house; for they do not know the ancients who are dead, nor their laud-giving names, nor their names. But their father whom they knew is the head by whom they begin and end in their prayer, for they know him best, and his love for his children; they remember his kindness to them whilst he was living; they compare his

pata kwake e se kona, ba ku mise nokuti, "U sa 'ku si pata kanjalo noma e file. A s' azi uma u ya 'kubuye a bheke aobani ngapandhle kwetu na; 'kupela u ya 'kubheka tina."

Ku njalo ke noma be kuleka kwamaningi amatongo akubo, b' enza ugange olukulu lwoku ba vikela; kepa uyise u dhlulisisile ekupatweni kwamatongo amanye. Uyise u igugu kakulu kubantwana bake noma e nga se ko. Ku ti labo a se be kulile be m azisisa kakulu ukuba-mnene kwake nobukqawe bake. Ku ti uma ku kona ubuhlungu pakati kwomuzi, indodana enkulu i m bonge ngezibongo zake a zi zuza umhla e lwa empini, a wa weze ngamazibukwana onke; i m tetisa ngokuti, "Ku nga ze ku fe tina nje. U se u bheke 'bani? A si fe si pele, si bone uma u ya 'ungena pi na? U ya 'kudhla izintete; ku sa yi 'kubizwa 'ndawo uma u bulale owako umuzi."

treatment of them whilst he was living, support themselves by it, and say, "He will still treat us in the same way now he is dead. We do not know why he should regard others besides us; he will regard us only."

So it is then although they worship the many Amatongo of their tribe, making a great fence around them for their protection; yet their father is far before all others when they worship the Amatongo. Their father is a great treasure to them even when he is dead. And those of his children who are already grown up know him thoroughly, his gentleness, and his bravery. And if there is illness in the village, the oldest son lauds him with the laud-giving names which he gained when fighting with the enemy, and at the same time lauds all the other Amatongo; the son reproves the father, saying, "We for our parts may just die. Who are you looking after? Let us die all of us, that we may see into whose house you will enter.[11] You will eat grasshoppers; you will no longer be invited to go any where, if you destroy your own village."

---

[11] That is, they suggest to the Itongo, by whose ill-will or want of care they are afflicted, that if they should all die in consequence, and thus his worshippers come to an end, he would have none to worship him; and therefore for his own sake, as well as for theirs, he had better preserve his people, that there may be a village for him to enter, and meat of the sacrifices for him to eat.

Ngemva kwaloko ke ngoku m bonga kwabo, b' em' isibindi ngokuti, "U zwile ; u za 'kwelapa, izifo zi pume."

Ku njalo ke ukutemba kwabantwana etongweni eli uyise.

Futi uma ku kona inkosikazi yomuzi eyona i zala abantu, noma indoda i nga file, itongo layo li ya patwa kakulu indoda yayo nabantwana bonke. Leyo 'nkosikazi i itongo lokubonisa umuzi. Kepa kakulu uyise njalo o yena e inhloko yomuzi.

UMPENGULA MBANDA.

After that, because they have worshipped him, they take courage saying, "He has heard ; he will come and treat our diseases, and they will cease."

Such, then, is the faith which children have in the Itongo which is their father.

And if there is a chief wife of a village, who has given birth to children, and if her husband is not dead, her Itongo is much reverenced by her husband and all the children. And that chief wife becomes an Itongo which takes great care of the village. But it is the father especially that is the head of the village.

Ku tiwa ku kona itongo, inyoka. Ba pupe. Ba ti, ba nga pupa, a be se u ya gula ; a ti, " Ngi gula nje, ngi pupile." Ba buze abanye, ba ti, " U pupe ni na ?" A ti, " Ngi pupe umuntu." Uma kwa buba umfo wabo, a ti, " Ngi bone umfo wetu." Ba buze, ba ti, " U be e ti ni na ?" A ti, " Ngi m pupe e ngi tshaya, e ti, ' Kwa be u sa ng' azi na ukuti ngi kona na ?'" A ti, " Ngi m pendulile, nga ti, ' Uma ngi ya kw azi, nga u bona, ng' enze njani na ? Ngi ya kw a-

IT is said that there is the Itongo,[12] which is a snake. Men dream. A man dreams perhaps, and is then ill ; he says, " I am ill for no other reason than because I have dreamed." Others ask him what he has dreamed. He tells them he has dreamed of a man. If his brother has died, he says, " I have seen my brother." They ask what he said. He says, "I dreamed that he was beating me, and saying, ' How is it that you do no longer know that I am ?' I answered him, saying, ' When I do know you, what can I do that you may see I know you ? I know that you

---

[12] The *Itongo*,—a collective term meaning the inhabitants of the spirit-world, or abapansi.

zi, uma umfo wetu.' Wa ngi pendula, kqede ngi tsho njalo, wa ti, 'U ti una u hlaba inkomo, u nga ngi pati ini na?' Nga ti, 'Ngi ya ku pata, ngi ku bonge ngezibongo zako.' Nga ti, 'Ake u ngi tshele inkomo e ngi i hlaba, a nga ku pata. Loku nga i hlaba inkabi, nga ku pata; nga i hlaba inyumbakazi, nga ku pata.' Wa pendula, wa ti, 'Ngi ya i tanda inyama.' Nga m pikisa, nga ti, 'Kqa, mfo wetu, a ngi nankomo; u ya zi bona ini esibayeni na?' Wa ti, 'Neyodwa, ngi ya i biza.' U ti, nga ba se ngi ya papama, kwa se kubuhlungu esikaleni; nga ngi yati ma ngi pefumule, kw' ala; kwa nqamuka umoya; nga ngi yati ma ngi kulume, kw' ala; kwa nqamuka umoya."

Wa kqiuisela, ka vuma uku i hlaba inkomo. Wa gula kakulu. Wa ti, "Kona ngi gula nje, ngi ya si bona isifo esi ngi gulisayo." Ba ti abantu, "U si bona njalo, ku si lungisi na? Umuntu a ng' enza ngamabomu isifo esi mu gulisayo; e si bona, a tande ukuze a fe na? Lok' umhlaba, uma se u tukutelele umuntu, u ya mu tshonisa na?"

are my brother.' He answered me as soon as I said this, and asked, 'When you sacrifice a bullock, why do you not call upon me?' I replied, 'I do call on you, and laud you by your laud-giving names. Just tell me the bullock which I have killed without calling on you. For I killed an ox, I called on you; I killed a barren cow, I called on you.' He answered, saying, 'I wish for meat.' I refused him, saying, 'No, my brother, I have no bullock; do you see any in the cattle-pen?' He replied, 'Though there be but one, I demand it.' When I awoke I had a pain in my side; when I tried to breathe, I could not; my breath was short; when I tried to speak, I could not; my breath was short."

The man[13] was obstinate, and would not agree to kill a bullock. He was very ill. He said, "I am really ill, and I know the disease with which I am affected." The people said, "If you know it, why do you not get rid of it? Can a man purposely cause the disease which affects him; when he knows what it is, does he wish to die? For when the Itongo[14] is angry with a man, it destroys him."

---

[13] The narrator from this point appears to relate something he has actually known, and not any hypothetical case.

[14] *Umhlaba*, the earth, is a name given to the Amatongo, that is,

A ti, "Amanga, madoda; ngi njenje; ng' enziwa umuntu. Ngi ya m bona ebutongweni, ngi lele; u ti, ngokuba u tanda inyama, u ngi kwele ngamakcebo; u ti, ngi be ngi sa *h*laba inkomo, ngi nga mu pati. Ngi ya mangala ke mina, loku izinkomo ngi zi *h*laba kangaka; a ku ko inkomo e nga i *h*laba, a nga za nga m pata; zonke izinkomo e ngi zi *h*labayo, ngi ya mu pata; noma ngi *h*laba imbuzi, ngi ya m pata; ngi be ngi ya *h*laba imvu, ngi m pate. Ngi ti kodwa mina, u y' ona; a nga ti, uma e zibizela inyama, a ngi tshele nje, a ti, 'Mfo wetu, ngi tanda inyama.' A ti kumina, a ngi ze ngi nga m bonga. Mina ngi tukutele, ngi ti, u tanda uku ngi bulala nje."

He replied, "Not so, Sirs; I am thus ill; I have been made ill by a man. I see him in sleep, when I am lying down; because he wishes for meat, he has acted towards me with tricks, and says that when I kill cattle, I do not call on him. So I am much surprised for my part, for I have killed so many cattle, and there is not one that I killed without calling on him; I always called on him when I killed a bullock. And if I kill a goat, I call on him. And whenever I kill a sheep, I call on him. But I say, he is guilty of an offence; if he wished for meat, he might just tell me, saying, 'My brother, I wish for meat.' But he says to me that I never laud him. I am angry, and say he just wants to kill me."

---

the Abapansi, or Subterraneans. We find such expressions as these:—"U guliswa um*h*laba," The Itongo has made him ill. "U bizwa um*h*laba," He is summoned by the Itongo,—that is, he will die. "U petwe um*h*laba," He has been seized by the Itongo. "U tshaywe um*h*laba," He has been smitten by the Itongo. "U nom*h*laba,"—"U netongo," An Itongo has entered into him and is causing disease.

Umhlaba is said to be an *ukuhlonipa* word. The following words are also applied to the Ancestral Spirit:—Itongo, Id*h*lozi, Isituta. We also have Izinkomo zomzimu. Among the Amazulu, Umzimu is a word used only in this connection, and appears to be a collective term for the Amatongo. But on the Zambesi, Azimo or Bazimo is used for the good spirits of the departed. *(The Zambesi and its Tributaries. Livingstone, p. 520.)* Compare also Note above, p. 93. There is also another word, Unyanya, which is used in the same way as Itongo. Thus a man who has been fortunate says, "Ngi bhekwe Unyanya," I have been regarded by Unyanya. Among the Amalala, we meet with another word, Und*h*lalane, pl. Ond*h*lalane. Thus they say, "Und*h*lalane u ngi bhekile," Und*h*lalane has regarded me, that is, the Itongo. "Ond*h*lalane ba ngi bhekile," The Ond*h*lalane have regarded me.—These words are probably the names of some great ancestors, who, though now forgotten, were formerly especially remembered and worshipped for their great and good deeds whilst living.

Ba ti abantu aba m bonayo lapa e gulayo, ba ti, "Au! Lo 'muntu, u ti, u sa ku kqonda ini ukukuluma na? Si kuluma nawe nje ke; u pi na, kona nati ngapana si m buza na? Loku nati ku se u hlaba izinkomo; lapa u bonga, si kona u bonge, u m bonge, u m pate ngezibongo zake zobukqawe; nati si zwe. U ti, uma ku be, wena kabani na, uma ku be umfo wenu loua na, noma umuntu u fa kqede, a buye a vuke, nga si nga m buzi na, ukuti, 'U tsho ngani na?—loku Ubani u hleze e hlaba izinkomo izikati zonke, ku se e ku bonga, a ku bonge ngezibongo zako zobudoda; nati si zwe.'"

A ti "Ehe!" o gulayo; "a ti u gabe ngokuba e ti umfo wetu omkulu; ngokuba mina ngi muncinyane. Ngi ya mangala uma u ti, ma ngi kqede izinkomo nje. Yena wa fa e nge nazo ini na?"

Ba ti, "Au, umuntu wa fa, wena kabani. Tina si ti, uma si kuluma nawe nje, amehlo ako e sa

The people who see him when he is ill say, "Au! Do you mean to say that the man[15] still understands how to speak? We speak with you now; where is he, that we too might take him to task? For we too were present at all times when you slaughtered cattle; and when you lauded, you lauded him, and called upon him by the laud-giving names which he received for his bravery; and we heard. And, Son of So-and-so, if it could really be that that brother of yours, or any other man who is already dead, should rise again, could we not take him to task, and ask, 'Why do you say so?—since So-and-so is continually killing cattle, and lauds you with the laud-giving names which you received for your manliness; and we too heard.'"

The sick man replies, "Eh! My brother acts in this boastful way because he says he is oldest; for I am younger than he. I wonder when he tells me just to destroy all the cattle. Did he die and leave none behind?"[16]

They say, "Au, the man died, Son of So-and-so. For our parts we say, when we are really speaking with you, and your eyes are

---

[15] That is, he who is dead.
[16] "Did he die and leave no cattle behind?"—Since he did not sacrifice all his cattle to the Amatongo, but left some when he died, why should he be so unreasonable now he is an Itongo as to demand that I should sacrifice all mine?

bhekile nje,—tina si ti, lo 'muntu u nga u kuluma nje; noma u nembuzi, u m bonge. Kodwa si ti, u ne*h*lazo um' a be se u ya ku bulala, a nga ku tsheli ka*h*le, nawe u k*q*onde; u be u sa nga m pupa izikati zonke, u be se u za 'kugula na. Ipupo libi. Ini umfo wenu u b' u sa nga m bona u lele, u be se u ya gula na? Ku nani umuntu e pupe umfo wabo, a vuke umzimba umnandi, a tshele abantu a ba lauzele ukuti, ' Umzimba wami u polile, umnandi.' A ti, ' Ngi pup' umfo wetu e kuluma izindaba ezin*h*le kumina.' A ti, a nga fika izikati zonke kuwe, u fika ngempi, se u ya gula; se s' azi ukuti u gula nje ke, u ya 'kuba u pupe umfo wenu nje."

A ti, " Ehe, madoda, mina se ngi za 'ku mu nika inyama yake a i tandako; lokw e ti kumina ngi nga m pupa; u ya i pata inyama; u ya ngi bulala; ngi ti, ku nani uma a fike kumina ebusuku, ngi lele, a ngi tshele ka*h*le, a ti, ' Mfo wetu, ngi tanda ukuti,' si kulume nayo ka*h*le, ku bonakale ukuti ngi pupe umfo wetu? U y' ona, ku still really looking upon us,—we say, as regards that man, you should just speak quietly with him; and if you have a goat only, worship him with it. But we say it is a shame in him to come and kill you, without telling you properly, that you may understand. But you are dreaming of him constantly, and are then ill. It is a bad dream. Why do you constantly see your brother in your sleep, and become ill? It were well that a man should dream of his brother, and awake with his body in health, and tell the people his dream, saying, ' My body is now restored to health; it is without pain. I have dreamed of my brother, telling me pleasant news.' But now he comes to you at all times with hostile intent, and you are ill; and so we know that you are ill on that account, because you dream of your brother."

He says, " Eh, Sirs, I will now give him the flesh he loves; for he speaks to me when I dream of him; he demands flesh; he kills me; I say, what prevents him from coming to me by night when I am asleep, and telling me quietly, saying, ' My brother, I wish so-and-so,' that we may talk pleasantly with each other, and it be evident that I have dreamed of my brother? He wrongs me; daily I

ya sa ngi ya m pupa, ngi vuke ngi nenxeba; ngi ti, ka 'muntu; into e ya be ishinga, i tanda ukulwa nabantu. Kodwa, madoda, si be si da si zwa ni ti, 'Umuntu owa fa e ishinga eli nga kulumiswayo abantu, idhlozi lake li be lihle na?' Si be si da si zwa ni tsho njalo, ni ti u t' a nga fa, itongo lake li lunge, li be lihle. Kanti ku lunga umuntu owa be lunge kade. Umhlaumbe a ti nowa be lungile, a fike a be mubi uma e file; nowa be ishinga, a ti uma 'se file, a lunge, a be umuntu o 'tongo lihle. Ku ya fana loko kokobili. Si ya ni pikisa nina, nina ni ti umuntu owa fa e ishinga e nga kulunyiswa, a ti a nga fa, a be nedhlozi elihle. Tina si ti ku ya fana nje; nowa be lungile, u ya vuka a be uhlanya lapa 'se file; ka ku muki ngokulunga kwake um' e sa hamba ngapezulu; nohlanya lu fa kqede, lu lunge, lu be idhlozi elihle."

Ba ti, "Ehe, si ya ku vumela; u kqinisile. Ku ya fana kokobili."

A ti, " Ngi ti ke, umfo wetu u

dream of him, and then awake in suffering; I say, he is not a man; he was a thing which was a wretch, which liked to fight with people. But, Sirs, we have been accustomed to hear you say, 'As to a man who died being a wretch, one of a word and a blow, is the Idhlozi of such an one good?' We have been accustomed to hear you say thus, that when he is dead his Itongo becomes right and is good. But forsooth that man is good who had been good long before his death. Perhaps he too who was good becomes bad when he is dead; and he who was bad, when he is dead, is good, and becomes a good Itongo. Both are alike. We deny the truth of what you say, when you assert that a man who died being a wretch of a word and a blow, when he is dead, may have a good spirit. We maintain that the two things are alike; both he who was good will be a wrathful man when he is dead; it does not turn out in accordance with his righteousness which he had when he was still living on the earth: and the wretch when he is dead becomes righteous and becomes a good spirit."

They say, "Ehe, we agree with you; you speak the truth. The two things are alike."

He replies, "I say then, my

muke nobushinga bake una e sa hamba ngapezulu kwom*h*laba; noma e se file, id*h*lozi lake li fana naye e sa hamba ngapezulu, ngokuba yena u be nga kulumiswa. U be ti umuntu a nga kuluma naye, a tande ukuba a be se u ya lwa naye. Ku be ku nga fika ikcala; l' enziwe uye, a be se u ya lwa, a nga ku boni ukuti, ' Konje nje leli 'kcala l' enziwe umina; a ku fanele ukuba ngi lwe nabo laba 'bantu;' esuke a tande yena uku ba bulala abantu. Ned*h*lozi lake li njalo; libi; li ya tukutela; u ti uma 'se tukutele a lete izilwane. Kodwa mina ngi ya 'ku mu nika inyama yake a i funa kumina. Ngi lele ebutongweni, ngi ya vuka, e se ngi nike isifo emzimbeni wami. Ngi za 'ku mu nika. Uma ngi bone ke, ma ngi yeke, ngi pile, ngi ya 'ku zi *h*laba izinkomo kusasa; uma e nga ngi yekile, ngi ya 'ku zi yeka, ngi ya 'kuti, ' Ka si yena umfo wetu.' Uma ku uyena, ma ngi pile, ngi pefumule, ku yeke ukun*q*amuka umoya, njengaloku ngi n*q*amuka umoya nje."

brother has gone away with his wickedness which he exhibited whilst living on the earth; and though he is dead, his spirit resembles him whilst he was alive, for he was a man of a word and a blow. If a man spoke to him, he used to wish at once to fight with him; and then a dispute might arise; it was caused by him, and then he would fight, and did not see it nor say, ' So then the fault was committed by me; I ought not to fight with these people;' but he started up and wished to injure the people. And his spirit is like him; it is wicked; it is constantly angry; and when it is angry it sends animals.[17] But I will give him his flesh which he demands of me. I sleep, and when I awake find that he has affected my body with disease. I will give him; if I see that he leaves me and I am well, I will kill some cattle in the morning; if he does not leave me, I will have the cattle, and say, ' It is not my brother.' If it is he, let me get well and breathe, and my breath no longer cut me, as it cuts me at the present time."

---

[17] *A lete isilwane.*—Ukuleta isilwane, ngesinye isikati amatongo a zibonakalisa ngemi*h*lola, ku ngene isilwane; amagama ezilwane ku kona isalukazana nentulwa; nge-

They bring Animals.—As regards bringing animals, sometimes the Amatongo manifest themselves by signs, and animals enter the village; the names of the animals are isalukazana and other lizards;

Ba vuma ba ti, "Ehe, wena kabani na; ma ku se kusasa so u sindile, s' and' uma si bone uma ilona idhlozi lomfo wenu; uma ku sa u sa gula, a si yi 'kutsho ukuti

sinye isikati inyoka e nge si lo itongo; kumbe ku fike inyamazane ekaya; ku tatwe izibulo, ku yiwe enyangeni ngokwetuka ukuba ku bonwe into e umhlola; inyanga i tsho ukuti, "Loko e ni ku bonile Ubani, itongo lakwini. U ya zibonakalisa ngako. Bonga ni, ku muke."

A lete izilwane kwowakwabo ukuti ka fe, loku e nga vumi uku wa nika into etile a wa i bizayo; noma ku nge njalo e lungisa, o ng' oni nganto kuwo; ku ya vela ububi kuye lo 'muntu. A s' azi uma kw enza njani ukuti a ti pela umuntu o hlabisa njalonjalo amadhlozi, a banjwe inyoka, noma isilo, noma 'emuke namanzi, noma a kalakatele esiweni, noma a hlatshwe umuntu enkqineni, noma a hlatshwe inkomo; lezi 'zinto zi m velele. Uma e se file, abantu aba seleyo ba buzane omunye nomunye, ba ti, "Au, pela, ini ukuba Ubani a fe, loku ngensuku zonke si dhla inyama yezinkabi kuye, noma imbuzi, noma imvu, noma utshwala? Loko konke ku be kw enza ni na? Si be si nga ti tina u bonga Amadhlozi akubo na? Ini ukuba a fe pezu kwaloko na? O, kanti, nobongayo k' enzi 'luto; nongabongiyo u ya kolisa. Nga se ku yekwa nje."

They assent and say, "Yes, yes, Son of So-and so; if in the morning you are well, then we shall see that it is indeed the spirit of your brother; if in the morning you are still ill, we will not say it is sometimes a snake which is not an Itongo; perhaps an antelope comes to the house; the people then take divining-rods, and go to a diviner, being afraid because an omen has appeared; the diviner says, "That which ye have seen is So-and-so, the Itongo of your house. He reveals himself by it. Worship, that it may depart."

The Amatongo bring animals to some one belonging to the village that he may die, because he has not been willing to give them a certain thing which they demand; or on the contrary when he worships them, and has in nothing sinned against them; yet mischief befalls the man. We do not understand how it is that a man who constantly sacrifices to the Amadhlozi should be seized by a snake, or a leopard, or be carried away by a stream; or fall over a precipice, or be stabbed by a man in a hunt, or be gored by a bullock; these things happen to him. When he is dead, those who are living ask one another, saying, "Oh, then, how is it that So-and-so is dead, when we daily ate the flesh of bullocks at his house, or of goats or of sheep, or drank beer? What effect had all that? Did we not think he was worshipping the Amadhlozi of his people? How is it that he is dead notwithstanding? O, forsooth, the worshipper gains nothing by his worship; and the man who does not worship does well. Let it be left alone entirely."

uyena umfo wenu; si ya 'kuti, isifo nje."

La tshona ilanga, e sa ti kubuhlungu; kanti ukusongwa kwezinkomo wa ti, "Ngi pe ni ukudhla, ngi dhle." Ba buza abafazi bake, ba ti, "Ku njani na?" A ti, "Ni zwa ngi ti ni na?" Ba ti, "Si zwa u funa ukudhla."

A ti, "Amanga, banta bami; nami ngi zwa inhliziyo; ku nga ti ni nga ngi pa ukudhlana; ni nga ngi pi kakulu; ngi pe ni ingcozana; ke ngi zwe."

Ba mu pa abafazi bake, ba mu pa amasi. Wa ti, "Ni nga wa teli umkcaba kakulu; u tele ni u be muncinyane, ku be 'manzana, ku nga jii, ku tambe; ke ngi zwe uma ku sa 'uvuma uma kw ehle na sempinjeni na."

Ba mw enzela njengokutsho kwake; kwa ba 'manzi, ka kwa jia, kwa ba 'manzi. Ba mu nika, wa dhla. Kw' chla loko 'kudhla, ku be ku nga sa vumi uma a ku dhle. Ka z' a dhla kakulu; wa dhla ingcozana; wa nika abantwana bake. Wa ti, "Ake ni ng' enzele utshwala, ng' omile." Ba bu tata utshwala, ba mu nika. B' etemba abafazi bake enhliziyweni zabo, be bona indoda yabo i

your brother; we will say it is a simple disease."

When the sun went down he was still complaining of pain; but at the time of milking the cows he said, "Give me some food, that I may eat." His wives asked how the pain was. He replied, "What do you hear me say?" They said, "We hear you asking for food."

He replied, "I don't know, my children; even I[18] feel an inclination for food; it is as though you might give me a little; do not give me much; give me a little; let me just try."

So his wives gave him amasi. He said, "Do not put much crushed corn in it; put a little only, that it may be waterish, and not thick—that it may be soft; let me just try if the disease will now allow it to descend by the swallow."

They did for him as he asked; the food was fluid, not thick. They gave him and he ate. He was able to swallow, although he had been unable to eat. He did not eat much; he ate a little; he gave his children. He said, "Just give me some beer; I am thirsty." They took beer and gave him. His wives had confidence in their hearts when they saw their husband

---

[18] *Nami*, even I who have been so ill.

funda ukudhla; ba tokoza enhliziyweni zabo, loku be be se be hlezi be novalo ukuti, "Umakazi, ka ku dhli nje ukudhla, isifo sikulu?" Ba ba nokujabula enhliziyweni; ka ba pumisela emlonyeni, ba bhekana kodwa ngamehlo. Wa bu puza utshwala, wa kcela uguai, wa ti, "Banta bami, ngi shiyele ni noguai, ke ngi beme." Ba m shiyela, loku noguai e be e nga sa m bemi. Abafazi bake ba bhekana, ba mangala ukubona umuntu e se bema uguai, loku idhlozi li be li m vimbele na kuguai, e nga sa m bemi. Abafazi be pika enhliziyweni zabo, ukuti, "Elinjani idhlozi e se li m vimbele na kuguai na?" Ba be nokwesaba, be ti, "Isifo; a si lo itongo."

Wa m bema uguai, wa lala; u te uma a lale, bwa fika ubutongo, wa lala. U ti pakati kwamasuku wa fika umfo wabo, wa ti, "Mfo wetu, konje u tize izinkomo? u ya 'ku zi hlaba kusasa na?" Wa vuma oleleyo, wa ti, "Ehe, ngi ya 'ku i hlaba. Ini wena, mfo wetu, u ti kumina a ngi ze nga ku pata; zi be zonke izinkomo, ngi zi hlaba nje, ngi ku pate ngezibongo zako; ngokuba wa be u ikqawe, u hlabana?"

taking a mouthful of food; they rejoiced in their hearts, for they had been fearful, saying, "Is it then that the disease is great, since he does not eat?" They rejoiced in their hearts; they did not speak out their joy, but looked at each other only. He drank the beer, and asked for snuff, saying, "Give me some snuff too, my children; let me just take a little." They gave him some, for he had left off taking snuff too. His wives looked at each other, and wondered to see the man now taking snuff; for the Itongo had restrained him also from taking snuff. His wives had disputed in their hearts, saying, "What kind of an Itongo is this that restrains him even from snuff?" They were afraid, thinking it was disease and not an Itongo which was affecting him.

He took snuff, and lay down; and when he lay down, sleep came. And in the middle of the night his brother came and said, "So then, my brother, have you pointed out the cattle? will you kill-them in the morning?" The sleeper assented, saying, "Yes, yes, I will kill one. Why do you, my brother, say to me I never call on you, whilst whenever I kill cattle I call on you by your laud-giving names; for you were a brave, and stabbed in the conflict?"

Wa ti, "Ehe; ngi tsho ngakona, ngi funa inyama. Mina pela se nga fa, nga ku shiya nomuzi; wa ba nomuzi omkulu."

Wa ti, "Ehe, mfo wetu, wa ngi shiya nawo umuzi, wa ngi shiya nawo nje ke; wena wa fa, u zi kqedile ini izinkomo na?"

Wa ti, "Kqa, nga ngi nga zi kqedile."

A ti, "Po, wena kababa, u ti, mina ma ngi zi kqede ini na?"

A ti, "Kqa, a ngi tsho ukuti, zi kqede. Ngi ti, i kona ngi tanda uma umuzi wako u be mukulu."

Wa papama. Wa ti uma a papame, w' ezwa 'so sindile; ubuhlungu o be bu sesikaleni, se bu pelile. Wa papama, wa vuka, wa hlala; wa mu zamazisa umfazi, wa ti, "Mwabani, vuka, u kanyise eziko." Wa vuka umfazi, wa vutela, wa kcataz' uguai, wa bema; wa buza umfazi, wa ti, "Ku njani na?" Wa ti, "Au, ak' u tule; ngi papama, umzimba wami se u lula; kade ngi kuluma nomfo wetu; ngi papama, se ngi sindile nje." Wa m bema uguai ezimpumulweni zake, wa lala ubutongo. La pinda la fika futi lona lo 'mfo wabo, idhlozi. Wa fika wa ti, "Au, se ngi ku sindisile. Inkomo zi hlabe kusasa."

He replied, "Yes, yes, I say it with reason, when I wish for flesh. I indeed died, and left you with a village;[19] you had a large village."

He said, "Yes, yes, my brother, you left me with a village; but when you left me with it, and died, had you killed all the cattle?"

He replied, "No, I had not killed them all."

He said, "Well then, child of my father, do you tell me to destroy them all?"

He replied, "No, I do not tell you to destroy them all. But I tell you to kill, that your village may be great."

He awoke. When he awoke he felt that he was now well; the pain which was in his side being no longer there. He awoke, and sat up; he jogged his wife, and said, "So-and-so, awake, and light a fire." His wife awoke and blew up the fire; she poured snuff into her hand and took it, and asked him how he was. He replied, "Oh! just be quiet; on awaking my body was feeling light; I have been speaking with my brother; on awaking I was quite well." He took some snuff, and went to sleep. The Itongo of his brother came again. He came saying, "See, I have now cured you. Kill the cattle in the morning."

---

[19] *Nga ku shiya nomuzi*, I left you with a village, that is, I died, leaving you to inherit the property which I possessed.

Kwa sa kusasa wa vuka, wa ngena esibayeni. Loko be kona abafo wabo abanye abancinyane, wa ba biza, wa ngena esibayeni, nabo ba ngena abafo wabo esibayeni. Wa ti, "Ngi ni biza nje, se ngi sindile. Umfo wetu u t' u se ngi pilisile." Wa ti, "Kupula ni inkabi." Ba i kupula. Wa ti, "Kupula ni inyumbakazi leyo." Ba zi kupula zombili. Za fika pambi kwake enhla nesibaya, z' ema. Wa bonga, wa ti:—

"Ehe, yidhla ni, nina bakwiti. Idhloz' clihle, uma ku pile nezingane, imizimba i be mnandi! Ngi ti, ini wena ukuti u ng' umfo wetu, u da u ti u nga fika kumina ngi lele, ngi ku pupe, ngi be se ngi za 'kugula na? Idhlozi clihle eli fika kumuntu li kulume izindaba ezinhle. Indaba se ngi ya i kuluma, se ngi ya gula. Ezinjani izinkomo eziti zi dhliwa umninizo, zi be zi dhliwa ngokugula na? Ngi ti mina, Peza, ngi yeke uku ngi gulisa. Ngi ti, Fika kumina ngi lele, u ngi tshele indaba, u ti, 'Mfo wetu, ngi tanda ukuti.'—U ya fika kumina, u fika ngoku ngi bulala. Ku ya bonakala uma wa be umuntu o ishinga: u z' u be ishinga na ngapansi emhlabeni na?

In the morning he arose and went into the cattle-pen. But he had some younger brothers; he called them, and went into the pen, and his brothers went in with him. He said, "I just call you, for I am now well. My brother says he has now cured me." Then he told them to bring an ox. They brought it. He said, "Bring that barren cow." They brought them both. They both came to him to the upper part of the pen, and stood there. He prayed, saying:—

"Well then, eat, ye people of our house. Let a good Itongo be with us, that the very children may be well, and the people be in health! I ask, how is it that you, since you are my brother, come to me again and again in my sleep, and I dream of you, and am then sick? That Itongo is good which comes to a man and tells him good news. I am always complaining that I am constantly ill. What cattle are those which their owner devours, devouring them through being ill? I say, Cease; leave off making me ill. I say, Come to me when I am asleep, and tell me a matter, and say, My brother, I wish so-and-so.—You come to me, coming for the purpose of killing me. It is clear that you were a bad fellow when you were a man: are you still a bad fellow under the ground? I

Nga ngi nga ti mina, ku ya 'kuti itongo lako li fike ka/le kumina, li ngi tshele izindaba. Ini wena, u ng' umfo wetu omkulu wokulungisa umuzi, ku nga veli indaba embi ngapakati kwomuzi, ngoba mina ng' azi ukuti u ng' umnikaziwo ?"

U teta nazo ke, u ya bonga, e ti :—

"Nazi izinkomo e ngi ku nika zona—nansi inkabi ebomvu, nansi inyumbakazi encokazi. Zi /labe. Mina ngi ti, Indaba ngi tshele ka/le, ngi vuke umzimba wami umnandi. Ngi ti, A ba pelele bonke abakwiti, ba butane lapa kuwena, wena u tanda inyama."

A be se ti ke, "Zi gwaze ni." A u tate umkonto omunye umfo wabo, a be se i gwaza inyumbakazi, i we pansi. A i gwaze inkabi; zi bod/le zombili; a zi bulale, zi fe. A ti, "Zi /linze ni." Ba zi /linze ke; zi pele izikumba; ba i d/le ke esibayeni. Amadoda e butene onke e zokeela inyama; a w esuse ngezito; a d/le, 'esute, a bonge, a ti, "Si ya bonga, wena kabani. Si kulekela id/lozi eli/le. Uma si bone pela, uma, bala, id/lozi eligulisayo, si ya 'ubona ukuti, bala, i lona ishinga eli umfo

used not to think that your Itongo would come to me with kindness, and tell me good news. How is it that you come with evil, you, my eldest brother, who ought to bring good to the village, that no evil might come to it, for I know that you are its owner ?"

He says these words about the cattle, and returns thanks, saying :—

"There are the cattle which I offer you—there is a red ox, there is a red and white barren cow. Kill them. I say, Tell me a matter kindly, that on awaking my body may be free from pain. I say, Let all the Amatongo of the people of our house come here together to you, you who are fond of meat."

And then he says, "Stab them." One of his brothers takes an assagai, and stabs the barren cow; it falls down. He stabs the ox; both bellow; he kills them—they die. He tells them to skin them. So they skin them; the hides are taken off; they eat them in the cattle-pen. All the men assemble to ask for food; they take it away joint by joint; they eat and are satisfied, and give thanks, saying, "We thank you, Son of So-and-so. We pray that the Itongo may be propitious. When we see indeed that it is an Itongo which makes you ill, we shall see that that Itongo

wenu. Si be si ng' azi uma inyama si za 'ku i d/ila nawe ngokugula kwako okukulu kangaka. Si ya bona ukuti leli ishinga li ya ku bulala; se si y' etokoza ke ngokuba si ku bona u pilile."

UGUAISE MDUNGA.

is the wretch which is your brother. We did not know if we should eat meat with you through your very severe illness. We now see it is the wretch which is killing you; and so we now are glad because we see you are well."

The Amatongo are felt in the Shoulders.

AMAHLOMBE omuntu o inyanga indawo yokuzwa. Konke a ku zwayo ku vela kuleyo 'ndawo yama/ilombe. Ama/ilombe indawo yamatongo kubantu aba izinyanga. Uma umuntu o inyanga e bambelwa omunye u ya zonda; ngoku m pata lapo ku nga ti u m gwaza ngomkonto; u y' ezwa masinyane njengokungati ku kona isilonda. Nabanye aba nge 'nyanga a ba vumi ukubanjelwa ema/ilombe; ngokuba ba ti ku kona oku ba /ilupayo ngokubanjelwa. Futi uma umuntu 'emi emva kwenyanga i ya m susa masinyane ngokuti, "Suka, u ya ng' apula; njengokungati u /ilezi pezu kwami."

Lapa si ti, a li ko itongo kuyena emzimbeni, si kuluma ngokuba o be ku tshiwo, ku tiwa ku funwa amatongo, se kw enziwe; kepa ukufa ku ng' esuki; si ti ke, ka natongo; a li ko itongo kuye.

THE sensitive part with a doctor is his shoulders. Every thing he feels is in the situation of his shoulders. That is the place where black men feel the Amatongo. If a doctor is touched by another person he is in pain; if he touches him there it is as if he stabbed him with an assagai; he feels at once as though there was a sore place there. And others who are not doctors do not allow another to take hold of them by the shoulders; for they say it causes them pain to be laid hold of. And if a man stands behind a doctor he makes him go away directly, saying, "Get away, you are hurting me; it is as if you sat upon me."

When we say there is not an Itongo in his body, we say so because when that has been done which it was said the Amatongo wished, the disease remains; therefore we say, he has no Itongo; there is not an Itongo in him.

Laying the Itongo, or Spirit.

Ku ya bizwa inyanga uma ku kona umuntu o gulayo, kepa e katazwa umuntu emunye. Ku ti a nga m pupa lowo 'muntu owa fayo, umzimba wake u nga lungi; ku se e wa lauza lawo 'mapupo ngokuti, "Au, ngi ya hlupeka. Uma ku fika ubani ebusuku ngi lele, unzimba wami a u lungi. Ngi kohliwe ukuba ngi nga ze ng' enze njani."

Kepa uma nembala loko 'ku m pupa kwake se ku m gulisa, ku bizwe inyanga e za 'ku m vimba. I ti, " Bheka ke; a ko ti ngamhla u m pupayo, u tate lo 'muti, u u dhle; u tate netshe noma isikuni, u si fele ngalawo 'mate e u m pupe e semlonyeni ngokuhlanganisa amate na lo 'muti; u wa fele esikunini, noma itshe; u si jigijele nyovane u nga bheki. Uma u bheka a ya 'kubuya lawo 'mapupo." Nembala 'enze njalo.

I loko ke ukwelatshwa kwepupa. Uma ku dhlula, amapupa e buya futi, inyanga y enze okunye, i li vimbe lelo 'pupa lalowo 'muntu. Ku tatwe umuti o hlanganiswe neminye ngokwedukisa ukuba a nga be e sa m bona. A ye 'ku

A DOCTOR is summoned when a man is ill, he being troubled by one man.[20] He dreams perhaps of the dead man, and then has pain in his body; in the morning he tells others his dreams. He says, " O, I am troubled. When So-and-so comes to me by night, my body is in pain. I cannot tell what to do."

And if his dreaming makes him ill, they summon a doctor to come and close up the way against him. The doctor says to him, " Look; when you dream of him, take this medicine and chew it; then take a stone or a piece of firewood, and spit on it the spittle which is in your mouth when you dream of him, mixed with this medicine; spit it either on a piece of firewood or on a stone; and throw it behind your back without looking. If you look the dreams will recur." And he does so.

This is the way dreaming is treated. If the thing goes on, and the dreams come back again, the doctor adopts another plan of treatment, and closes the way against the man's dream. Several medicines are mixed together for the purpose of misleading the Itongo, that he may see it no more. He goes to a distance to shut him

---

[20] That is, one of the Amatongo.

m vimba kude, noma esidulini; loko a ku peteyo a ku fake kona, a goduke ke, a nga be e sa bheka ngemuva.

Ku njalo kubantu abamnyama. Ku tiwa, "Idhlozi eli katazayo uma li gulisa abantu ngoku li bona, li ya vinjwa." Kakulu lezi 'zinto zokuhlupa umuntu zi vela kwabesifazana aba felwe amadoda, ba ngenwe abafo wabo, kumbe abanye abantu. Kepa itongo lalo 'muntu o fileyo li ya landela njalo-njalo umfazi wake. Ku ti uma e se e miti, uma li fika itongo lake, a be se u ya gula, si ze si pume leso 'sisu; ku ze ku vele nokuba li vinjwe ngaloko 'kwenza kwalo.

Uma li m hlupa e kwenye indoda e ngu ngenwanga; uma lowo 'mfazi wa shiya abantwana baleyo 'ndoda efileyo, efileyo i ya m landa ngokuti kuye, "Abanta bami wa ba shiya kubani na? U zokwenza ni lapa na? Buyela kubanta bami. Uma u nga vumi, ngi za 'ku ku bulala." Li vinjwe masinyane kulowo 'muzi ngokuhlupa lowo 'wesifazana.

Kumbe elinye nembala a ze a buye kulowo 'mendo wake, a nga be e s' enda, a buyele ekaya, a ye 'kulonda abantwana. Ku tiwe wa buyiswa uyise wabantwana. Ku njalo ke ukuvimba itongo izinyanga.

UMPENGULA MBANDA.

up there, perhaps in an ant-heap; what he has in his hand he puts into the heap, and goes home, and he never sees it again.

Such is the custom with black men. It is said, "A troublesome spirit which appears to a man and makes him ill, is laid." These troublesome things occur most commonly in women who have lost their husbands, and are taken to wife by his brothers or by others. But the spirit of the dead husband follows the wife continually. If she is pregnant, and the spirit of her husband comes to her, and she is ill and miscarries; the Itongo is at length laid because it has acted thus.

If it trouble her when she has gone to another man without being as yet married; if she has left her husband's children behind, the dead husband follows her and asks, "With whom have you left my children? What are you going to do here? Go back to my children. If you do not assent I will kill you." The spirit is at once laid in that village because it harasses the woman.

Perhaps another spirit never leaves her until she returns to the village of her dead husband; she never marries again, but remains at home and takes care of her children. It is said the children's father brought her back again. This is how doctors lay a spirit.

The Amatongo reveal Medicines, &c., in dreams.

Ngesinye isikati kubantu abapata imiti ba y' a*h*lukanisa imiti yabo nemiti a ba i boniswa aba nga se ko. Njengaloku Undayeni u b' e kolise ukwazi imiti enjalo: ku tiwe kuye ebusuku, "Hamba, u ye endaweni etile, u fike u mbe umuti otile; lowo 'muti w elapa ukufa okutile." Undayeni wa e nemiti kakulu enjalo a i boniswa abakubo e lele. Leyo 'miti wa y a*h*lukanisa, nemiti a y aziyo na leyo 'miti a i boniswayo.

Futi a ku si ye yedwa kuloko. Baningi. Ngi be ngi ke ngi bone nobaba futi, Unkomid*h*lilale; lokupela u be inyanga enkulu yokwelapa izinkomo uma zi fa; futi e inyanga neyemiti. Ngi be ngi hamba naye uma e bizwa umuntu, ku fa izinkomo zake lowo 'muntu. Ngi zwe e se ngi tshela lapa si mba imiti, u ti, "Yimba lo 'muti; ngi u piwe ebusuku; kwa tiwa, ngi ya 'ku u *h*langanisa nemiti etile." Nembala ke kwa ba njalo;

Sometimes men who have medicines distinguish between their own medicines, and those they have been shown by the dead. For instance, Undayeni was frequently given the knowledge of such medicines: it used to be said to him in a dream, "Go to such a place, and when you get there dig up a certain medicine; that medicine is the remedy for a certain disease." Undayeni had very many such medicines, which he was shown by the spirits of his people whilst he slept. He made a distinction between the medicines he knew, and the medicines which were revealed to him.

And Undayeni was not alone in this respect. There are many like him. I have seen my father also, Unkomidhlilale;[21] for he was a great cattle doctor; and he also had many medicines for men. I used to go with him when he was called by any one whose cattle were ill. I heard him say as we were digging up medicines, "Dig up that; I had that revealed to me in a dream; I was told to mix it with certain other medicines." And so it was continually; there

---

[21] *U-nkom'-i-dhl'-i-lale*, The-bullock-which-eats-and-lies-down. Implying that as a bullock in abundant pastures eats and lies down, so he shall have abundance of food and freedom from care,—that he shall "dwell in a large pasture."

a ku pelanga loko 'kupupa imiti; wa ze wa ba nemiti eminingi. Ngako loko izinkomo uma zi fa u bo e zi siza, a z' elape, a zi uꞯumisela ilanga li be linye, a ti, "A zi nga wa puzi amanzi; a zo puza intelezi ku be ukupela." Nembala ku bekwa imbiza enkulu esibayeni, i gewale imiti namanzi; lapo amanzi e se kewebile, imiti i buyele ngapansi, zi puze ezinye; ezinye zi banjwe zi puziswe. Ku ti ngamhla e se zi nika amauzi, ku letwe leyo 'miti, ku yiwe emfuleni nayo, a fike a i tele emanzini, zi puze ngenzansi izinkomo.

U ke wa zi dhla izinkomo zabantu ngaloko 'kwelapa kwake. Wa duma wa ba inyanga. Uma za sinda lezo 'zinkomo, u se u puma nenkomo pakati kwazo. Uma e fika, ku kona e se zi lele pansi, a ti, "I nga fa le. Ngi ya 'kuba ng' ahlulekile." Nembala a zi vuse, a ngene pakati kwazo kusihlwa e pete isihlanti, e mumata amafuta, a si vutele isihlanti pakati kwezinkomo. Izinkomo z' etuke kakulu zi bona ilangabi elisabekayo e gijima nesibaya sonke a kꞯede; a ti, "Ku nga buyo ngi zwe, ku tiwa i kona inkomo e sale ya fa, ni nga be ni s' eza kumi; ku ya 'kuba ng' ahlulekile."

was no end of his dreaming of medicines, until he had a great many. Therefore he was useful to cattle when they were ill; he gave them physic; he ordered them for one day to drink no water, but only that into which he had put his medicines. And a large pot was put in the cattle-pen full of medicines and water; when the medicines had sunk to the bottom and the water was clear, some drank; others were drenched. When they were allowed to drink water, the medicines were taken to the river and put into the water, and the cattle drank lower down.

He obtained many cattle from people for doctoring their cattle. He became a celebrated doctor. If the cattle got well he had one given him. If when he came some were lying down, he said, "That one may die. [But if it die] I shall cure none of them." And so he roused them up, going into the midst of them in the evening, carrying in his hand a torch, pouring fat on it, and kindling it when in the midst of the cattle. The cattle were much frightened when they saw the great flame, as he ran through the whole cattle-pen; and he said, "If I hear that one of these cattle has died, never come to me again; I shall not be able to do anything."

Ngesinye isikati ku kona umuntu o hamba ngasese komunye e nga m boni; kepa omunye e ng' azi 'luto ngayo lowo 'muntu, e umngane wake. Kepa uma w' ezwa ebusuku ukuti, "Ubani lo u m onza umngane wako nje. A u boni ini ukuba u ya 'ku ku bulala na? U ti ku ngani uma u ti u ti?" (e tsho indaba,) nembala lowo 'muntu u ya 'ku i kumbula ukuti, "Hau. Nembala, uma ku njalo Ubani a nga ngi zonda ngendaba leyo." A kqalo ukupuma kuye ngoku m kxwaya. Kepa lelo 'pupa u ya 'ku li lauza, a ti, "Ngi ya mangala uma ngi bone Ubani e ngi bulala ngendaba etile." U se hambele kude naye. Noma lowo e ti, "Bani, manje wa hambela kude nami. Ini na? Si pambene ngani?" Kepa lowo u ya 'ku m pendula ngezwi loku m dukisa ngokuti, "O, wena kabani, kanti u ti nga ba ku kona indaba e ngi pambene nawe ngayo na? Kqa. A ku ko 'luto. Ngi libaziswa ukutinitini, kupela," e tsho izinbangcabangca nje.

U<small>MPENGULA</small> M<small>BANDA</small>.

Sometimes there is a man who is acting with a secret intention of injuring another without his suspecting it, and without his knowing any thing about him, he being his friend. But if he hears in a dream a voice saying to him, "So-and-so is pretending merely to be your friend. Do you not see that he will kill you? What do you think he means by saying such and such things?" (alluding to something he has said), he remembers it and exclaims, "Yes, surely. So-and-so may hate me on that account." And he begins to separate from him and to be on his guard. And he tells the dream and says, "I wonder that I have seen So-and-so killing me about such and such a matter." And he keeps at a distance from him. And if he says to him, "So-and-so, now you keep at a distance from me. What is it? What difference has arisen between us?" the other puts him off by saying, "O, Son of So-and-so, can you think there is any thing which has made me quarrel with you? No. There is nothing. I am occupied with such and such concerns. That is all," saying what is really mere subterfuge.

A man's Itongo resembles him in character.

Unjikiza kakcuba, Und*h*lebekazizwa, Unotshelwaczitshela, kwa ku ik*q*awe elikulu o namand*h*la kakulu, o nomzimba omkulu; ku isijak*q*aba sendoda o lukuni; e sukile o u dedele um*h*laba.

Kwa ti kwancolosi lapa a e konza kona, kwa fika Amazulu e ishumi o hamba e bulala lapa e tunyelwe kona. Kepa a nga yi ngomteto wenkosi; a zenzele pakati kwemizi lap' o nga tunyelwo kona, a pate kabi abantu, e d*h*la 'magula nokud*h*la ngokuti, " Loku si abantu bakomkulu, amapand*h*lo a ya 'kubaleka si sa vela nje. Ubani wasemapand*h*leni o ya 'kuya kwomkulu, a ye 'ku si mangalela na? Si ya 'kuzenzela nje, si diyo ngefusi letu." Nembala ke

Unjikiza, the son of Ukcuba, Undhlebekazizwa,[22] Unotshelwaczitshela,[23] was a celebrated brave, of great strength, and huge body; all his muscles were prominent and hard; and his head was high above the ground.[24]

It happened among the Amancolosi with whom he was living, that there came thè Amazulu going and killing wherever they were sent. But they did not act in accordance with the chief's law, but acted after their own heart in villages to which they had not been sent, treating the people cruelly, eating their milk and other food, saying, "Since we are the people of the chief, the rustics will fly as soon as they see us. Who among them will lay a charge against us before the chief? We will do just as we like, and set ourselves our own limit."[25] And

---

[22] *U-ndhlebe-ka-zi-zwa*, He-is-ears-which-hear-not, or The-ears-which-hear-not-man. Implying a man who refuses to listen to any counsel or explanation, but at once attempts to conclude a matter by fighting.

[23] *U-notskelwa-e-zi-tshela*, When-he-has-been-told-he-tells-the-news. That is, he pays no attention whatever to what is said to him, but at once gives his own account of the matter, and insists upon his own opinion.—These two names are izibongo given to him on account of his character.

[24] That is, he was very tall.

[25] This is a proverbial saying. "You shall set for yourself your own limit at my village,"—that is, you shall do just as you like.

'enza njalo, a z' a fika kwowakiti umuzi. A fika kwa 'besifazana bodwa, ku nge ko 'mlisa. A zenzela ekudhleni, a kalisa abantwana e b' amuka ukudhla, nabesifazana ba kala be ti, "Uma u kona Undhlebekazizwa nga ni ng' enzi nje. Yenza ni belu; u za 'ufika."

Nembala kwa ti ku 'sikati wa fika, w' ezwa umsindo wokukala e sesangweni. Wa tshaya ngewisa lake elikulu, e ti, "U lambile ke Unodhlolamazibuko. U za 'kwesuta ke namhla."

indeed they acted thus, until they came to our village. When they came, there were none there but women; there was not a single man there. They did as they liked with the food; they made the children cry by taking away what they were eating; and the women cried saying, "If Undhlebekazizwa were here, you would not do so. Go on then; he will be here presently."

And indeed after a time he came, and heard the noise of crying whilst he was at the gateway. He smote the ground with his huge club, saying, "Unothlolamazibuko is hungry.[20] It shall have its fill to-day."

---

[20] *U-nothlola-mazibuko.* The name of his club. It means, He-who-watches-the-fords, that is, to prevent an enemy crossing to do damage.—There is a terrible threat in his words.—It is common for braves among the natives to give names to their clubs, spears, &c. Thus, one calls his assagai which he uses for the purpose of getting food for his household *U-simbela-banta-bami,* He-digs-up-for-my-children. Another calls his *Imbubuzi,* The-groan-causer, because when it stabs men or cattle their groans are heard. *Igungehle,* the glutton, is the name of a club, because when used in fighting, the opponents are destroyed with as much rapidity as a glutton swallows his food. *U-silo-si-lambile,* the name of an assagai, meaning the-hungry-leopard, is so called because its owner attacks the enemy like a hungry leopard. *U-dhl'-ebusuku,* The-eater-in-the-dark; the name of a club, so called because it is used to destroy secretly and by stealth; the owner of it coming on his victims by night, or rushing on them from an ambush.

This custom of naming their choice weapons is met with among other people in olden times. Thus Arthur commenced his career of greatness by obtaining the miraculous sword Escalibore, which could
"Kerve steel, and yren, and al thing."
(Ellis's Specimens. Vol. I., p. 243.) He gave names also to his shield, sword, and spear. Thus:—"Over his shoulders he threw his shield called Priwen, on which a picture of holy Mary, mother of God, constantly recalled her to his memory. Girt with Caliburn, a

'Ezwa Amazulu; lokupela a ya m azi; kwa ti nya umsindo. A puma ngokunyiba, e baleka, 'emuka. Kwa ti kusa a e banjwa kwomunye umuzi ngokuhlupa kwawo; a botshwa, a yiswa emhumeni, a ngeniswa kona. Wa ti Undhlebekazizwa, " A ba tshiswe, ku gaulwe izinkuni." Ba ngena emhumeni, kwa fakwa izinkuni, kwa baswa umlilo, kwa bebezelwa ngamahhau, kwa ngeniswa umusi. Ba futelana, ba fa bonke. Ku ze ku be namhla nje a kw aziwa kwazulu ukuba ba ya ngapi na.

Kwa ti ke ekukcitekeni kwezwe li kcitwa Amazulu, kwa balekwa, kwa ngenwa emahlatini nezinkomo. A zi fumana zakwiti. Ya hlabana, y' ahlulwa yakwiti; kwa sala yena Undhlebekazizwa. A ti Amazulu, "Namhla ku namuhla! Si ya 'ubona ukuba u za 'u s' ahlula na. Loku kade u si hlupa, nxa si suke si hambele emapandhleni." Ba m hlaba ngemikonto kulelo 'hlati. Wa bulala amashumi ama-

The Amazulu heard; for they know him; the noise was at once hushed; and they went out stealthily and fled away. In the morning they were caught at another village because of the trouble they gave; they were bound and carried to a den and confined in it. Undhlebekazizwa told the people to fetch firewood and burn them. The people went into the cave and put down the firewood and lit a fire, and fanned it with their shields, and drove the smoke into the cave. They were unable to breathe, and all died. And it is not known to this day by the Amazulu what became of them.[27]

It happened when the land was desolated by the Amazulu, the people fled into the forests with their cattle. The Amazulu found ours. We fought with them, but our people were conquered; and Undhlebekazizwa alone remained. The Amazulu said, "To-day is to-day! We shall see if you will conquer us. For for a long time you have plagued us when we have gone to the outer districts." They stabbed him with their assagais in the forest. He

most excellent sword, and fabricated in the isle of Avalon, he graced his right hand with the lance named Ron. This was a long and broad spear, well contrived for slaughter." *(Id., p. 60.)*—Roland had his terrible sword Durindale. *(Id. Vol. II., p. 304.)* Otuel, the Saracen champion, had his sword Corrouge. *(Id., p. 317.)* Charlemagne had his good sword Joyeuse. *(Id., p. 346.)*

[27] That is, the matter was kept a secret, and the Amazulu did not know what had become of their soldiers.

bili. Wa ti, "Ngi bulale ni ke manje. Se ngi zendhlalele. Ngi za 'kulala pezu kwabantu." Ba m gwaza indawo zonke zomzimba. Kwa ba njengokumila kwomhlanga imikonto emzimbeni. Wa pela ke. I leyo ke indaba yake.

Isilo u be si bambisa kwengane nje e yedwa ehlatini; a hambe e kala njengengane, e gakqa ngamadolo. Isilo si fike kuye, si kwele, a si tate njengempukane, a si bulale.

U be sabeka. U be nge naluto lo 'muntu lu luhle e hlangane naye endhleleni, u be m bulala, a tate loko a ku tandayo. Ba jabula abaningi ngokufa kwake, ngokuba wa e hlupa kakulu; konke u be kw enza ngenhluzula; inyewe ya i nge ko. Ikcala li be li nga tetwa emzini wakwiti e se kona; u be li kqeda ngenduku. Li tetwe e nge ko; e kona kqa. Ku njalo ke.

Netongo lake libi. Ka patwa na namhla nje emzini wakwiti. Uma ku kona o m patayo, u tuliswa masinyane, ku tiwe, "Ka patwa lowo pakati kwomuzi. A nga u bubisa." U patwa ngamhla kw enziwe ukudhla kupela. Ka patwa ezindabeni.

Umpengula Mbanda.

killed twenty of them. He then said, "Kill me now. I have now spread out a mat for myself to lie on. I shall lie on men." They stabbed him in every part of his body. Their spears stuck in him as thick as reeds in a morass. So he died. This is his history.

He would lay hold of a leopard by himself in the forest, as though it was a mere child; he would go along crying like a child, crawling on his knees. The leopard would leap on him, and he seize it as though it was a fly and kill it.

He was much dreaded. Every one who had any thing pretty whom he met with in the way, he would kill and take what he liked. Many were glad at his death, for he gave much trouble, and did every thing in an arbitrary way; he had no patience. No matter was discussed in our village when he was there; he would bring it to a conclusion with a stick. It was discussed when he was absent, but not when he was at home.

And his Itongo is wicked. His name is never mentioned to this day in our village. If any one mentions him, he is at once silenced, and told not to mention his name in the village, for he might destroy it. He is mentioned only when any cattle are killed. He is not mentioned at other times.[28]

---

[28] This modern Samson has all the characteristics of the cham-

A Doctor of Medicine deceived by the Itongo.

Ku te ngezinsukwana ezi dhlulileyo, kwa ku kona umuntu emakuzeni; w ake enhlavini ngakusigwili kamsengana. Lowo 'muntu u inyanga yemiti. W' esuka kumahaule ngeminyaka edhlulileyo; u yena Omahaule nomazwana nofaku ba pambana ngaye, ukuze ba kcitane nje. Umahaule wa m kxotsha; kepa Umazwana nofaku ba m pikela, ngokuba umukwe kamazwana; igama lake Unqanqaza. Wa fika ke lapa emakuzeni kusigwili, w' aka.

Naku ku ti ngamhla ku vela ukufa okukulu kwembo, se ku ngene kwasigwili, kwa susa abantu ababili. Usigwili e nga ka bi nakeala, wa fika ke Unqanqaza e pete umuti; wa ti kusigwili, "Sigwili, ngi za lapa nje kuwe, ngi letwa itongo; li ti, a ngi zoku kw elapa." Usigwili lowo isidukwane lapa emakuzeni, kubo inkosana kwambanjwa, mukulu kutoi lo kwabakambanjwa.

A LITTLE while ago there was a man among the Amakuza; he lived on the Iuthlavini near Usigwili, the son of Umsengana. He was a doctor of medicine. Some years ago he left Umahaule; it is he on account of whom Umahaule quarrelled with Umazwana and Ufaku, until they separated one from the other. Umahaule drove him away, and they defended him, for he is Umazwana's father-in-law; his name is Unqanqaza. So he came here among the Amakuza, and lived with Usigwili.

At the time when severe epidemic dysentery prevailed, and attacked the household of Usigwili, it carried off two people. Whilst Usigwili was as yet free from disease, Unqanqaza came to him with medicines, and said to him, "Usigwili, I come to you because the Itongo told me to come and treat you." That Usigwili is a great man here among the Amakuza; among his own people, the house of Umbanjwa,[29] he is a petty chief, the elder brother of Utoi among the descendants of Umbanjwa.

---

pions of old legends. It is difficult to conceive such a description as is here given to refer to a man of a generation just passed away. He was the uncle of the narrator.

[29] Umbanjwa, the Unkulunkulu of that family.

Usigwili nayo wa y azi indaba yetongo, wa kolwa; ka buzanga ukuti, "Ku ngani uma itongo li ze kuwe, nganqaza, li nga tsheli mina ukuba ngi za 'ugula, ngi fanele ng' elatshwe masinyane uwe?" Ka buza 'luto ngaleso 'sikati ngovalo lokuba nembala idhlozi li kqinisile; loku impi naku se i ngene emzini wami ukufa.

Wa vumela pezulu ukuti, "Yebo, yelapa." Lokupela lo 'muntu u y' etembeka ngobunyanga bake. Wa kohlwa ukuba kumahaule u kxotshwe ngokutakata: ngoku m pikela kwabo kwa fipaza ukukcabanga kwake ngaloko 'kutukwa kwake. Wa u puza ke umuti lowo. Wa ti, "Ngi ku puzise wona nje; u ya 'upuma ngendhlela e ngapansi, a u z' ukubuya ngengapezulu; u ya 'kuya ngengapansi." Kepa umuti wa pambana nokutsho kwake. Wa hamba ngendhlela zombili nengapansi; wa kqinisa kuzo zombili; wa tsho ngapezulu na ngapansi; kwa kqina kwa ti nkqi loko 'kuhamba kwawo.

Se be twal' amehlo, ba ti, "Nganqaza, lungisa; umuntu wa

Usigwili too knew what the Itongo had said,[30] and believed; and so did not ask, "How is it that the Itongo comes to you, Unqanqaza, without telling me that I am about to be ill, and it is proper that I at once put myself under your care?" He asked no question at the time because he was afraid that the Itongo had spoken the truth, and said, "See, death has come like an army into my village."

He assented at once, saying, "Yes, take me under your care." For the man is trusted much for his knowledge of disease. He forgot that he was driven from Umahaule's tribe for sorcery: because he had been defended by Umazwana and Ufaku, he had no thought of the bad name which he had had. So he drank the medicine. Unqanqaza said, "I give you this medicine; it will act as an aperient, not as an emetic." But the medicine did not act in accordance with his word. It acted both as a purge and an emetic in an excessive degree.

The people now began to stare, and said, "Unqanqaza, correct the effects of your medicine; is the man dead whilst you are looking

---

[30] He knew because he too had dreamed a dream similar to that of Unqanqaza.

fa na?" Kepa u se ko/iliwe noku u buyisa umuti wake, u s' a/ilulcka; u se putuzela; ka sa k*y*ondi a kw enzayo. Umuti lowo se u ukufa; u se u funa ukutabata isidumbu.

Se ku mangelwe ngaloko 'kwenza kukan*q*an*q*aza. Nam/ila leso 'situko sokuti u umtakati si ya kula kubo bonke, ukuti, " Nembala, ubani o nga ti ku nga gulwa e nga biziwe, a zibize na? Umtakati impela."

Ku se njalo ke. A kw aziwa uma i za 'uzala 'nkonyana ni na.
UMPENGULA MBANDA.

at him?"[31] But he was now unable to regulate the action of his medicine; he was quite beaten; and acted without reason, no longer knowing what to do. The medicine became poison, and now wished to take away the dead body.[32]

People began to wonder at what Un*q*an*q*aza had done. And now the word which pronounced him a sorcerer is heard every where, and people say, "Who ever went to a man who was not ill, without being called by him, of his own accord to treat him for disease? He is indeed a sorcerer."

Thus the matter stands at present. We do not know what the result will be.[33]

How the Amatongo are worshipped.

ITONGO kakulu li vama ukuzibonakalisa kwalo li ngena ngomuntu, li m bambe endaweni etile yomzimba, a be se u ya gula. Kepa ku tiwe, "Bani, u njenje, u nani na?"

THE Itongo for the most part when it reveals itself enters a village through some individual living there, and seizes on some part of his body, and so he is ill. And his friends ask him, "So-and-so, since you are in such a state, what is the matter with you?" He

---

[31] "Umuntu wa fa na?"—We cannot render this literally. The saying casts the responsibility of death, if it takes place, on Un*q*an*q*aza.

[32] Medicine is here personified. The medicine is now Death; and is working for the purpose of getting a corpse.

[33] Lit., It is not yet known what calf the cow will bring forth. A proverbial saying.—This account was given to me in 1865. Usigwili died. And Un*q*an*q*aza died soon after, probably privately murdered.

A ti, "O, namhla nje a ngi tokozi, ngi vuka umzimba wami u shiyene; ku zonde kakulu kuleyo 'ndawo." A bonakale noma e zikqinisa ukuti, "Kqa, lo 'muntu, noma e zikqinisa, u ya fa; si ya m bona."

Kepa ngoku nga peli masinyane loko 'kufa, ku ze ku yiwe enyangeni yokubula. I fike inyanga, i ku tsho loko a gula iko. Kanti naye lowo 'muntu o gulayo ka tshongo 'luto ngaloko 'kufa; ngokuba ku vama ukuba labo 'bantu, noma be pupile, kwa sa umzimba ubuhlungu, a ba tandi ukuveza indaba bona; ngokuba kubantu abamnyama ukuhlaba izinkomo kw ande kakulu, kwa tiwa zi bizwa idhlozi; kepa ku buye ku tiwe kwomunye, "Hai! loku ku s' and' ukuhlatshwa, idhlozi eli ti ni

replies, "O, to-day I am not happy, having woke with my body well in one part and unwell in another;[34] it is very painful in this place." And it is clear that he is ill, though he makes the best of it, and they say, "No, the man, though he makes the best of it, is ill; we see that he is not well."

And because the disease does not cease at once they at length go to the diviner. The diviner comes and tells them the cause of the illness. But the sick man himself had said nothing about his illness; for it is generally the case that such people, although they have dreamed and in the morning awoke in pain, do not like to talk about it themselves; for among black men slaughtering cattle has become much more common than formerly, on the ground that the Idhlozi has demanded them; but they make reply to one who says so, "No! since a bullock has just been slaughtered, what does the Itongo say?[35] O, people are

---

[34] "Umzimba wami u shiyene."—Lit., My body has left itself,—is affected differently in different parts. "Amasimu a ya shiyana," The fields are not all ripe at the same time. "Obani ba shiyene," Those men have gone one farther than the other.

[35] "Idhlozi eli ti ni na?"—This Zulu idiom, which places the relative in the interrogative sentence, implies what cannot be expressed in a translation, that the person who asks the question does not believe that the Idhlozi has said any thing.—Idhlozi li ti ni na? is a simple enquiry for information.—Again, a person may say, Abantu a ba ka pelele, The people have not yet all arrived. If a man replies, O pi na o nge ko? Who is absent? it is understood at once that he sees that all are present; and the person who asserted that they were not

leli? O, abantu se be tanda inyama nje, umuntu a ti, 'Ngi pupe idhlozi,' kanti w enzela ukuze a dhle inyama." Kepa loko ku nga tshiwo obala, ku tshiwo ngasese. Ku ngaloko ke abantu be nga sa tsho ukuti, "Ngi gula nje, ngi pupe idhlozi." Se be yeka, ngokuti, "O, lo zi kona izinyanga ezi ya 'kutsho na loko e ngi ku bonileyo." Noma e buzwa ku tiwa, "Ku bonanga 'luto ekulaleni kwako na?" Kepa a landule. Kanti w' ahluleka ukuti itongo li biza inkomo, a ti, a ku nga pumi emlonyeni wake loko. A ku pume enyangeni.

Ngokuba itongo a li bambi umninimuzi yedwa; li bamba nabantu nje bomuzi. Kepa umuntu nje, e nge si ye umninimuzi, ka namandhla okuti, "Ku tiwa abapansi, 'A ku hlatshwe.'" Umninimuzi yedwa o nga yi 'kuvuma, uma ku banjwe yena ngesifo, ukuti a ku yiwe enyangeni; u ya 'kuti yena, noma ku patwa inyanga, a landule, a ti, "Ai! Ngi zwile. Hlaba ni inkomo etile; ngi za 'ululama." Ngokuba yena izinkomo ezake nomuzi owake; kubantwana bake a

now very fond of meat, and a man says he has dreamed of the Idhlozi, and forsooth he says so because he would eat meat." But this is not said openly, but secretly. Therefore a man no longer says, "I am ill. I have dreamed of the Idhlozi." They have left off saying so, and a man says, "O, since there are diviners who will say what I have seen," [why should I say any thing?] And even though they ask him, "Have you not seen something in your sleep?" he denies. For he is unable to say that the Itongo demands a bullock, determining not to mention such a thing; but to let the diviner mention it.

For the Itongo does not choose the head of a village only, but also common people. But a mere man who is not the head of a village is not able to say, "The Amatongo command a bullock to be slaughtered." It is the head of the village alone who, if he is seized by disease, will not allow them to go to the diviner; if a diviner is mentioned, he will refuse, saying, "No! I have heard. Kill such and such a bullock, and I shall get well." For the cattle and the village are his; there are none among his children who can

---

all there looks again, and says, Nembala, So they are. If he says, Umu pi na? or Aba pi na? the other mentions the person or persons not yet come.

ba namandhla okuzigabisa ngokuti a ku hlatshwe inkomo etile ezinkomeni zikayise, ngokuti i bizwe itongo. Ai; nowesifazana ka namandhla; noma e bonisiwe, ka yi 'kutsho; noma e se gula kakulu, ka yi 'kutsho 'luto ngenkomo; kupela u gabe ngenyanga yodwa.

Ku ti ke uma se ku yiwe enyangeni, inyanga i ku tsho konke loko a ku bonayo lowo 'muntu. Uma se ku buyiwe, ba m tetise lowo 'muntu ngokuti, "Ku ngani ukuba loku ukufa wa ku bona, si ku buza kangaka, u nga ze wa si tshela na? Wa w esaba ni? Kw' enza wena ini, lo kw' enza abapansi nje na?" A ti, "Nga ngi ti, 'Yizwa ni ngenyanga.'" A ku vume loko 'kutsho kwenyanga, a ti, "O, eh; i tsho konke e nga ku bonayo."

I hlatshwe ke inkomo. Ku tiwe lapa i nga ka hlatshwa, a pume umninimuzi, a ngene esibayeni e pete impepo. Uma ku inkomo e isidanda, a i pulule ngempepo njalo emhlana, a ti, "Yeti, nina 'basekutini," (lelo 'zwi lokuti yeti, izwi leli lokuti abantu a ba lalele loko oku za 'utshiwo ngaleso 'sikuleko e ku kulekwa ngaso ematongweni;

take upon themselves to say, "Let such and such a bullock among the cattle of my father be killed, for the Itongo has demanded it." No; neither can a woman; even though the Itongo has made it most evident to her, she will not say any thing about it; even though she is very ill, she will not say any thing about a bullock; she trusts only to the diviner.

When they have gone to the diviner, he will tell them every thing which the man has seen. When they come back again, they scold the man, saying, "Why, when you knew the disease, and we asked you so much, did you not tell us? What were you afraid of? Did you make yourself ill? was it not the Amatongo only?" He replies, "I said, 'Hear the diviner.'" And he assents to what the diviner has said, saying, "Yes, yes; he says all that I saw."

And so the bullock is killed. Before it is killed, the head of the village goes into the cattle-pen, carrying incense in his hand. If the bullock is tame, he gently rubs it again and again with incense on the back, and says, "All hail, Spirits of our tribe" (the word "All hail" tells all the people to listen to what is about to be said in the prayer which is made to the

nembala ke ku tule, ku ti nya ekaya, ku nga bi ko umsindo wokukuluma; ku kulume yena lowo 'muntu yedwa; abantu be lalele, e kuluma namadhlozi, e ti,) "Kuhle ini, abantu be njengani nje, ukuba ni zinge ni ti lapa nga ni keela ukudhla; kepa ni zinge ni fika ngokufa ngezikati zonke na? Kuhle loku na? Ai! A ni boni ke namhla ni hlazekile, ni nukiwe inyanga? Loku ku fanele ukuba uma ni biza ukudhla, a ngi yi 'kunqaba. Nako ke ukudhla kwenu. Bizana ni nonke nina 'bakwiti. A ngi zi 'kutsho ukuti, 'Bani, nank' ukudhla kwako,' ngokuba ni nomona. Kodwa wena, 'bani, o gulisa lo 'muntu, mema bonke, ni ze 'kudhla loku 'kudhla. Uma ku uwena ngi za 'ubona pela ngalo 'muntu e ku tiwa u patwe uwe. A ng' azi ke loko e u ku bizayo. Se ngi ku nikile. Ka sinde lo 'muntu. Ni hlangane nonke, nina 'basekutini, e na ti na ti" (e tsho e ba weza ngamazibuko e bala ubukqawe babo uma be sa hamba).

Amatongo; and truly they are silent—not a sound is heard, nor the least talking; the chief man only speaks, and the people listen whilst he is speaking to the Amatongo, saying) "Is it proper that people like you should habitually, instead of asking for food in a proper manner,—should habitually come to us at all times in the form of sickness? Is that proper? No! Do you not then see that you are disgraced this day, having been smelt out by the diviner? For it is proper if you demand food, that I should not refuse it. There then is your food. All yo spirits of our tribe, summon one another. I am not going to say, 'So-and-so, there is thy food,' for you are jealous.[36] But thou, So-and-so, who art making this man ill, call all the spirits; come all of you to eat this food. If it is you I shall then see by the recovery of this man whom, it is said, you have made ill. I now no longer know what you can demand. I have already given you what you ask. Let the man get well. Come together all of you of such-and-such a people, which did so-and-so and so-and-so" (that is, he lauds them by recounting the mighty actions which they did whilst living). He is very earnest,

---

[36] So other heathens represent their gods as jealous. The Iliad is but a history of the results of the jealousy of two goddesses.

A tukutele ngokuti, "So ngi ya mangala nawe, 'bani, o te wa ti, u se u zinge u fikisa kwesela; lapa u sa hamba kwa ku nge njalo; wa u kw enza konke obala. A ku pele uku ngi nyenyela. Hamba ni obala, ngi ni bone; loko e ni ku bizayo a ngi yi 'kunqaba nako; ngokuba nga ku piwa ini konke— izinkomo nabantwana namabele. Nesalukazi sakiti ni si bize, si ze 'kudhla; nengane eya fayo, a i ze 'kudhla; si jabule."

Nako ke ukubonga kwabantu, be bonga idhlozi; i hlatshwe ke.

Ba ba hlanganisa ngoku ba biza, ngokuba abanye a ba sa b' azi amagama abo; kepa bona aba ngapansi ba ya b' azi bonke, ba sa ba siza, a ba ba yeki; kepa ngaloko aba ngapezulu ba ti, "Woza ni nonke, ni zokudhla." Ngokuba kukqala kwa ku bizwa abantu ab' aziwayo; kepa ngaloko 'kwenza kwa bangwa ukufa, kwa ba kukulu; ku yiwe enyangeni ukuti,

saying, "I now greatly wonder that you too, So-and-so, who used to do such-and-such mighty things, now continually come as a thief; whilst you were still living it was not so; you used to do every thing openly. Let this coming to me stealthily be at an end. Go openly, that I may see you, for that which you ask for I will not refuse; for you gave it all to me, —the cattle, the children, and the corn. And thou, old woman[37] of our tribe, we call you to come and eat; and the infant which is dead, let it come and eat; that we may rejoice."

Such, then, is the worship with which they worship the Itongo; and so the bullock is killed.

They unite all the Amatongo in one invitation, for some of them they no longer know by name; but the dead know all of the living, and continually help them and do not forsake them; and on that account the living say, "Come, all of you, and eat." For at first those who were known were called by name; but by doing so they summoned disease, and it was very great; and they went to the diviner, saying, "Hau! what

---

[37] The old woman and the infant are mentioned in conclusion because he wishes to include all. The old woman and the infant are

"Hau! ini pela, loku si hlabe lukulu[38] lungaka lwetu inkabi, si nga toli isikala sokupefumula na? Se ku ini?" Kepa inyanga i tsho, umuntu o nga patwanga aba nga m aziyo, isalukazi noma ingane; labo aba solayo. Kwa vela ke ukungaketi; se ku hlanganiswa bonke.

Nako ke ukubonga kwabantu, be bonga idhlozi; i hlatshwe ke. Ku ti uma a i gwaze omunye, i kale i ti be, a be e se pinda ukubonga, e ti, "Kala, nkomo yakwetu, ngokuba kwa ti, kwa ti," e balisa amatongo akubo. I we.

Ku ti uma i hlinhlwe, i botshoswe, ku be se ku tatwa umhlwehlwe kancinyane nodengezi nelahle lomlilo nempepo, se ku yiwa endhlini lapa ku gulwayo kona; noma endhlini enkulu, lapa ku tiwa amatongo a hlala kona; ngokuba pela ku njalo, ku tiwa itongo li hlala endhlini enkulu. Ku

is the meaning then of this, that we have killed so great an ox of our tribe, and yet cannot get any breathing time? What is the meaning of this?" And the diviner tells them, there is a man whom they have not worshipped, whom they do not know, an old woman or an infant; it is they who find fault. And thus arose the custom of making no distinction; and all are now invited together.

Such then is the manner in which people worship the Amatongo; and then the bullock is killed. And if when another appointed for the purpose stabs it, the bullock cries,[39] the head of the village again worships, saying, "Cry, bullock of our people," and he then recounts the valorous deeds of the dead, mentioning the names of the Amatongo of their tribe. The bullock drops.

When it is skinned, it is laid open and a small piece of the caul is taken and a sherd, and a live coal, and incense, and they go with it into the house of the sick man; or into the chief house of the village where it is said the Amatongo dwell; for it is said that the Itongo lives in the great house. And the smoke arises in

---

[38] That is, *uluto*, something.

[39] If the bullock cries it is considered a good omen, and the man is expected to get well. But if it makes no noise they doubt whether the sacrifice is accepted and expect death.

x

tunyiswe ke, ku be se ku nuka ulwasu endhlini.

Inyongo i se i telwa ulowo 'muntu o gulayo. U ya i tela, u ya teta. (A ngi tsho ukutukutela; ukuteta ngesinye isikati ku tshiwo ukubonga.) Ku telwe ke abantu bonke balo 'muzi; abanye ba i tela ezinyaweni, abanye ba i tele ekanda, abanye ba i puze.

Ku njalo ke indaba yamadhlozi. Ku ti umswani u falakahlwe ezindhlini zonke, ukuze ba dhle. Ku be se ku ukupela ke. Se ku dhliwa inyama.

Se ku bhekwa ukusinda kulo 'muntu. Uma e nga sindi, ku ya 'kuhlatshwa enye, a ze a zi kqede lowo 'muntu. Kanti u nesinye isifo. Kepa noma ku njalo, ku kona isiminya esi tolwayo emadhlozini; ngokuba abamnyama ba kqinisile ukuti, a kona, a ya ba siza. Ngokuba ukutsho kwabo ukuti a ya ba siza, a ba tsho ngamazwi ezinyanga zabo a ba bulayo kuzo; ba tsho a ba ku bona. Noma be lele ku fike umuntu owa fayo, a kulume nomuntu, a ti, "Bani, kulo 'muzi kuhle ku be ukuti nokuti," e tsho indaba e za

the house, and there is the odour of the burnt caul.

Then the sick man pours the gall on his body. He pours it on himself, and talks. (I do not mean he is angry, for sometimes ukuteta means to return thanks.) And all the people of the village have the gall poured on them; some pour it on their feet, some on their heads, others drink it.

Such then is the account of the Amatongo. The contents of the bullock's stomach are sprinkled in all the houses, that the Amatongo may eat. And that is the end of it; and then the flesh is eaten.

After that they look for the recovery of the man. If he does not get well, another bullock will be killed, until he kills all he has. And forsooth he has some other disease not occasioned by the Amatongo. But notwithstanding, sometimes what is said about the Amadhlozi turns out to be true; for black men steadily affirm that the Amatongo exist and help them. For when they say that the Amatongo help them, they do not say so from what diviners have said, but from what they have themselves seen. For instance, when they are asleep, a dead man appears, and talks with one of them, and says, "So-and-so, it is well that such and such be done in this village," telling him

'uvela. Njengaloku ku be ku tiwa kwabamnyama, "A ku gaywe utshwala obukulu;" nembala bu gaywe, ku tiwe, "Ku tsho idhlozi, li ti, 'Ngi za 'ku ni pa amabele.'" Uma se be wa zuzile ngalo 'nyaka, ba ya 'ku wa bonga; futi ekupeleni kwonyaka ba wa bonge lawo 'mabele e kwa tiwa b' eza 'ku wa piwa. I loko ke oku ba fipazayo, ukuti, "Kanti ba ya kuluma nati, si kw enze loko, si pile na? Ba bize inkomo etile ngomuntu o gulayo, a pile na?"

something that will happen. For instance, black men used to be commanded to make a great deal of beer; and so they made it, and said, "The Idhlozi says, 'I will give you corn.'" If they obtain it that year they bless the Amatongo; and at the end of the year[40] they return thanks for the corn, which they were promised. It is this which blinds them, and they say, "But do they not speak with us, and we do what they tell us to do and obtain health? Do they not demand a certain bullock of a man, and he gives it and gets well?"

The mode of slaughtering a Bullock.

Lapo ku hlatshiwe, umnininkomo u misa umuntu ukuze a bheke, kona inkomo yake i nga yi 'kwenakala; ku be i lowo o kipa isito, a si shiyele ukuze a kqedele emuva isikeubi a si kipe, a fake kweyake imbiza. Ku ti kwabakipa izito, u lowo njalo o kipa isito a si shiyele ukuze ngemva a zi kipele izikeubi, a zi fake embizeni. Labo abakipayo izito ku ya bizwa kakulu kubo inyama aba seziko; ba ya

When an ox is slaughtered, the owner of it appoints some one to watch lest it should be spoilt; and each one who cuts off a leg leaves a portion of it behind, that he may afterwards take the piece of flesh thus left, and put it in his own pot. For among those who separate the legs from the carcase, each one leaves portions still attached to the carcase, that he may afterwards cut them off and put them in his own pot. Those who are sitting round the fire ask for meat of those especially who cut off the legs; as they cut them

---

[40] That is, at the end of harvest.

kipa, ba ya ponsa njalo izikcubana, ba ya dhla, ba ya kala, be kala nemitamo emlonyeni, be ti, "Sa tsha." U lowo njalo u pete umkonto wake, u dhlela pezulu, i ze i botshoswe ngapakati.

Loku kunjalonjalo kwohlinzayo, u lowo u pete imbiza yake, ukuze a ke ububende. Ku ti uma i tiwe kqeke, ku vele ububende, ku be se ku suka umuntu a be munye, o za 'ukelela ezimbizeni zonke, a zing' e ka ngendebe, e tela kuleyo na kuleyo, be zinge be dedelana, zi ze zi gcwale izimbiza. Ku ti ku bo kona amagugu okuhlinza; a buye imbiza yake i gewele, inyama e i hlome na ngezinti e nga ngenanga embizeni. A fike endhlini yake, abantwana bake ba i dhle, i ba dake njengaloko kungati ku hlabe yena.

I tutwe ke, i siwe endhlini, i bekelelwe emsamo 'ndawo nye; i nga pekwa ngalelo 'langa; ku dhliwe ububende ngalelo 'langa; ku ti ku sa i be i hlahlelwa, se i za 'upekwa; ku kitshwa nemilenze, nemihlubulo noma insonyama; ku

off they throw continually small pieces of flesh to them, and they shout even with their mouths full, "We are burnt."[41] And each one has his assagai and eats standing, until the bullock is opened.

And each one that skins the bullock has his own pot, that he may pour the blood into it. When the carcase is completely opened, one arises to dip out the blood into all the pots; he dips it out with a cup and pours it into each vessel, the people giving way for each other until all the pots are full. The person who skins the bullock has the power of purloining; and he goes home with his pot full; and meat too stuck on rods which is not put into the pots. He enters his house, and his children eat, and it more than suffices them, just as though he had himself killed an ox of his own.

The meat is carried into the house and placed at the upper end in one place; it is not cooked on the day it is killed, but the blood is eaten; on the following morning it is cut up when it is going to be cooked; they separate the legs and the ribs,[42] and the

---

[41] *We are scorched or burnt.*—Meaning by this they are standing before a fire with nothing between them and the flame. They wish for meat to put on the fire.

[42] The *umthlubulo* is that portion of the ribs which is left after cutting away the breast or brisket, and includes the flesh down to the hip. The flesh of the flank which forms a part of the *umthlubulo* is called *itebe*.

hlinhliswa ab' clama' nayo. Ngokuba ku njalo kubantu abamnyama: omkulu w etulelwa insonyama; o ngapansi a hlinhliswe umhlubulo, noma umkono; umlenze u nikwe induna.

Ku ti uma i vutwe, lokupela i dhliwa lapa ilanga li kqala ukupenduka, loku ku njalonjalo ku kandene kulowo 'muzi abantu bemizi yonke yaleso 'sizwe abaseduze, nakwamanye amabandhla 'akelene nalabo 'bantu. Ku ti uma se i za 'kwepulwa, bonke abantu ba ye esibayeni ngapakati, lokupela inkomo kubantu abamnyama a i dhlelwa endhlini, i dhlelwa kona esibayeni njalo, ukuze ku bonakale nodhlayo nongadhliyo. A y epule ke ngezitebe ngezitebe, i tutwe i ngeniswe esibayeni, i bekwe 'ndawo nye ukuba y abiwe; a y ahlukanise njengokuma kwamabandhla; izinsizwa zi be nesitebe sazo, namakehla namadoda amakulu; kw abelwe nabezizwe. Ku ti uma ku kona noma emunye o vela kwamanye amabandhla o nge si ye walapo, isitebe sake si be sodwa, ku tiwe, "Nansi yasekutini." A bonge naye, a tate abantu balapo ukuze a dhle nabo.

insonyama;[43] and give to those who are of their house. For this is the custom with black men: the insonyama is taken to the eldest; the ribs are given to the next, or the shoulder; and the leg is given to the officer.

When the meat is cooked, for it is eaten when the sun is declining, men belonging to all the villages of the tribe, and strangers who are neighbours, press together to the village. When the meat is about to be taken from the pots, all the people go into the cattle-pen, for among black men cattle are not eaten indoors, but always in the cattle-pen, that those who are eating, and those who are not, may be seen. The chief of the village takes out the meat and puts it on the various feeding-mats, and it is carried into the cattle-pen, and put in one place, that it may be distributed; he distributes it in accordance with the positions of the assembly; the young men have their mats; those with headrings, and the chief men, have theirs; and strangers have theirs. And if there be only one who belongs to another people, his feeding-mat is by itself, and they say to him, "Here is the meat of such a place." He thanks them, and takes people belonging to the place that he may eat with them.

---

[43] The *insonyama* is the superficial layer of flesh from the hip to the ear, including the pectoral muscles.

Ku ti uma ba dhle bonke, abanye ba kqede kukqala, b' esuke kwesabo isitebe, b' elekela aba sa dhlako, ba ti, " O, a si n' elekele; si ya bona ukuba ni ya hlupeka."

Ku ti uma i pele i ti du, ba nga kqali ba valelise; ku landwe umhluzi, nobubende obu buya bu pume emva kwenyama, obu salako.

Ku ti uma ku pele konke loku, 'esuke umnimuzana, nomunyo umuntu o pete isitebe, 'enyuke kancane, a ti, " Tula ni, ni ti nya." Nembala ku ti nya. A ti, " Ehe; nina 'bakwiti, e na ti na ti, ngi ya kuleka, ngi kuleka ubuhle ngemva kwalo 'nkomo yakwetu. Ngi ti, ku nge ti, lokupela izinkomo lezi zi kona nje, ngi zi piwa inina. Kepa uma ni biza ukudhla kumina e ni ngi pa kona, a ku fanele ini ukuba ngi ni pe kona na? Ngi kuleka izinkomo, ukuba zi gewale kulesi 'sibaya. Ngi kulekela amabele, ku ngene abantu abaningi kulo 'muzi wenu, ba kxokozele, ba dumise nina. Ngi keela nenzalo, ukuba lo 'muzi u keume, ukuze igama lenu li nga peli." A kqede ke.

When all have eaten, and some have finished before the rest, they join themselves with those who are still eating, and say, " O, let us join with you; we see you are in trouble."

When it is all eaten they do not begin to take leave; but the broth, and the blood which is still uneaten, are brought out after the meat.

When all is finished, the head man and another man who carries a feeding-mat go a little towards the head of the cattle-pen, and the head man says, " Be perfectly silent." And the assembly becomes very silent. He says, " Yes, yes; our people, who did such and such noble acts, I pray to you—I pray for prosperity, after having sacrificed this bullock of yours. I say, I cannot refuse to give you food, for these cattle which are here you gave me. And if you ask food of me which you have given me, is it not proper that I should give it to you? I pray for cattle, that they may fill this pen. I pray for corn, that many people may come to this village of yours, and make a noise, and glorify you. I ask also for children, that this village may have a large population, and that your name may never come to an end." So he finishes.

Ba valelise ke bonke basemizini, ba pume, ba goduke. Lokupela uma ku inala kw enziwe notshwala obukulu. Ku ti eyamanina inyama i be yodwa ; ku ya *h*laka-zeka amaband*h*la e ti nya, ku *h*langana amanina, 'epula eyawo. Nemizi e seduze i bizane ukuza 'kud*h*la inyama kulowo 'muzi. I pele ke. Ba goduke bonke.

So all strangers take leave, and go home. And if it is a time of plenty, much beer is also made. And the meat of the women is by itself; when the men have departed and the place is still, the women come together and take out their meat. And neighbouring villages send messages one to another to come and eat meat at the village. So it is all eaten, and they go home.

Laying the Spirit of Divination.

INDABA ngokuvinjwa kwomuntu o netongo lokubula, uma e ng' azi ukuba u pupa amapupa a k*r*onde pi ; u zinge e pupa njalo izinyoka eziningi zi m tandela umzimba wonke e semanzini, e sesizibeni ; u ya puma u se sindwa izinyoka : e wela nomfula u gewele. U ze umzimba wake w enyele, e ng' azi ukuba lawo 'mapupa emi*h*la yonke a komba ni na.

THE account of barring the way against a spirit of divination which visits a man when he does not understand the meaning of his dreams ; he dreams continually of many snakes encircling his whole body whilst he is in a pool of water ; he quits the water heavy with snakes : or he dreams he is crossing a flooded river. At length his body is relaxed, he not knowing what is the meaning of those daily dreams.

A ze a gule ; ku be kona noku-d*h*la a ziliswa kona, e tshelwa e lele, ukuti, " Ukud*h*la okutile u nga ku d*h*li." Nembala a ku yeke. Uma e ku d*h*la ngenkani, umzimba u nga tokozi. A ze a ku yeke ngokuti, " Ngi petwe."

At length he becomes ill; and there is certain food he is obliged to abstain from, being told in his sleep not to eat such and such food. So he no longer eats that food. If he eat it from opposition, his health suffers. At length he leaves it alone, saying, "A spirit has visited me."

Uma e tanda ukuba inyanga, a ye enyangeni yokubula; i m pehlele ubulawo obumhlope, i m kenkeambise, ukuze amapupa a kanye, a nga bi lufifi.

Uma e nga tandi, nabakubo be nga tandi, ku funwe imvu yoku m vimba, nonyanga e nge si yo yokubula, inyanga enkulu yoku m vimba. Ku ti ngamhla e pupile kakulu amatongo, e m twesa ubunyanga, i bizwe inyanga, i ze nemiti emnyama, ku hlatshwe imvu, ku tatwe umswani wayo, ku kandwe imiti emnyama, a puziswe; a hlanzele esitsheni, ku fakwe umswani wemvu; ku yiswe loko emhumeni o nga neti nakanye, ku mbelwe pansi, ku vinjwe ngomhlaba; umuntu a nga bheki ngemuva a z' a fike 'kaya, e nga bhekanga emuva. I loko ke ukuvinjwa kwetongo. Ku ti noma li fika kuye ngobusuku, li nga be li sa kanya, ku be mnyama, a nga be e

If he wishes to be a diviner, he goes to a diviner; the diviner prepares for him white ubulawo,[44] and makes him white, that his dreams may be clear, and no longer uncertain.

If he does not wish to be a diviner, nor his friends, they take a sheep for the purpose of barring the way of the spirit, and a doctor who is not a diviner is consulted —a doctor of celebrity—for the purpose of barring the way. When he has dreamed a great deal of the spirits, and they initiate him into the knowledge proper to doctors, the doctor is called, and comes with black medicines;[45] a sheep is killed, and the contents of the paunch are taken, and the black medicines bruised, and the man is made to drink them; he throws the contents of his stomach into a vessel, and the contents of the sheep's stomach are added to them; this is taken to a cave into which no rain enters; it is buried there in the earth, and closed up with soil; and the doctor does not look behind him till he gets home. This, then, is the method of barring the way against a spirit. And though it come to him by night, it is no longer distinctly visible, but obscure, and the man

---

[44] See Note above, p. 142.

[45] Black medicines, that is, medicines which have the power of rendering the Itongo dark or indistinct.

sa bonisisa ka*hl*e njengokuk*q*ala, li muke ke, a zi d*hl*e zonke izid*hl*o, a nga zili 'luto.

Kepa kwabanye u vinjwa, ku ye ngako; kwabanye a ku yi ngako; ku y' a*hl*uleka, lo 'muntu a fe ngokubangwa amatongo nabahambayo; a fe masinyane. I loko ke e ngi ku zwayo.

no longer sees it distinctly as at first; and so it departs, and he eats all kinds of food, and abstains from nothing.

And with some the way is barred successfully; with others without success; it is tried to no purpose, and the man dies through being claimed at the same time by the Amatongo and by living men, and dies very soon. This, then, is what I have heard.

The subject of the following narrative was a convert of some eleven or twelve years' standing. He has always manifested great uncertainty of character and a very impressible nervous system, and for many years has had from time to time subjective apparitions, and been in the habit of dreaming strange, life-like dreams. One day he suddenly left the mission station. The following account was obtained from a native who was sent to enquire of him at the village where he was living. I have had an opportunity of seeing him since the underneath was given me. He has many symptoms of hysteria, appears fully to believe in his feelings; and yet at the same time to be practising deceit on others, and probably too on himself.

INDABA yokugula kukajames, u gula ukufa oku nga k*q*ondeki kubantu aba amakolwa; ngokuba ku ti noma umuntu ku nga u y' etasa, ku ti a nga ya eskoleni, ku pele loko ngokuzing' czwa izwi lenkosi. Baningi aba be njalo, se kwa pela. Kepa ngayo umuntu omdala kangaka, ku ya mangalisa ukuba a

The account of the illness of James, which is not intelligible among Christians; for although a person may appear to be affected with those symptoms which precede the power of divination, yet when he goes to a mission station all that ceases through continually hearing the word of God. There are many who were so affected, but are now so no longer. But as regards him who is now so old, it is marvellous

Y

kqalwe ile 'nto njengokungati u ya fika emzini wamakolwa.

Nga fika si nopaulu, si hamba ngoku m zuma ukuti, "Ka nga si zwa, ka nga si boni ; ka kqabuke si ngena nje endhlini e nga ka zilungisi, si bone ukuma kwake uma e nga boni 'muntu ukuba u se njani na."

Sa fika e lelc, 'embete izingubo ezimbili—enye imnyama, enye impofu, se i guga. Wa si bona, wa lala, wa tula. Nga m vusa, nga ti, "Vuka." Wa zibinya, e ti, "Ake w enze kahle ; ngi za 'uvuka. Ngi pangise ni ! Ngi pangise ni ! Kw enze njani ekaya na ?" Kwa za kwa ba isikati e nga vuki.

Wa vuka ke, wa si bingelela. Sa vuma. Nga m buza ukuti, "U njani, james, na ?" Wa ti, "Ngi ya gula kakulu." Nga ti, "U nani na ?" Wa ti, "Ngi nokufa e ngi nga kw azi." Nga ti, "Ngi landise konke." Wa kqala ngokuti:

"O, nembala, u kqinisile. Uma ku buza umfana nje, ngi be ngi nga yi 'kutsho 'luto nakanye.

that he should begin to be so affected, as though he had only just come to a Christian village.

I and Paul reached the place where he is, going with the intention of taking him by surprise, saying to each other, "Do not let him hear or see us ; let him first see us when we are already in the hut, before he puts himself to rights, that we may see what he does now when no man is looking at him."

When we came he was lying down covered with two blankets —one black, the other grey and old. When he saw us he remained lying and was silent. I aroused him, saying, "Arouse." He writhed himself and said, "Just have patience. I am about to arise. Make haste and tell me ! Make haste and tell me ! What has happened at home ?" But it was a long time before he arose.

At length he arose and saluted us ; and we saluted him. I asked him, saying, "James, how are you ?" He said, "I am very ill." I said, "What is the matter with you ?" He said, "I have a disease with which I am not acquainted." I said, "Tell me all about it." He began by saying :

"O, truly, you are right. If it were a mere boy who asked, I would not say a single word. But

Kepa lok' u buza wena, a ngi zi 'kushiya 'luto. Kukqala nga ng' e-saba, ngi ti, 'Ku za 'utiwa ni?' Kepa namhla loku loku 'kufa se ku ng' ahlukanisile nani, ngi nge fihle 'luto.

"Kade loku 'kufa kwa ngi kqa-la, ngi nga ka pumi na sekaya lapaya, ukubuyela endhlini le entsha yami; kwa ngi kqala ngi se pakati kwomuzi. Nabakama-pontshi laba ba ya kw azi. Kepa kwa buya kwa pela. Ukwenza kwako kukqala ngokukupuka emi-nweni na semizwanini, ku kupuke ngemikono na ngemilenze; ku gi-jima ku ti saka nomzimba wonke; kw enyuke, ku ze pezulu nomzi-mba, ku fike ku me emahlombe, kw enze umsiti ku be nzima ka-kulu lapa; ku nga ti ngi twele into e sindayo.

"Kepa manje a ku se loko ko-dwa; ngokuba manje se zi kona izinto e ngi zi bonayo ngesikati sokulala. Ekupumeni kwami ekaya, ngi pume se ngi kqambe ama-gama amatatu, ngi nga w' azi uku-ba a vela pi na; ngi zwe igama, se ngi li hlabelele nje, ngi li kqede lonke, ngi nga li fundanga.

"Kepa into e ngi hlupa kakulu manje, ukuba izwe leli lonke a ku ko e ngi nga l' aziyo; ngi li kqeda

since it is you who ask, I will tell you everything. At first I was afraid, and said, 'What will men say?' But now since this disease has separated me from you, I can make no concealment.

"Long ago this disease began, even before I quitted the house on the other side of the river to go to my new house; it began whilst I still lived in the village. And the family of Umapontshi know it. But it passed off again. It first began by creeping up from my fingers and toes; it then crept up my arms and thighs; it ran and spread itself over the whole body, until it reached the upper part of the body, and stopped in my shoulders, and caused a sensation of oppression, and there was a great weight here on my shoulders; it was as if I was carrying a heavy weight.

"But now it is not that only; but now there are things which I see when I lie down. When I left home I had composed three songs, without knowing whence they came; I heard the song, and then just sang it, and sang the whole of it without having ever learnt it.

"But that which troubles me most now is, that there is not a single place in the whole country which I do not know; I go over

lonke ebusuku ngi lele; a ng' azi lapa ngi ng' aziyo uma u pi na.

"Ngi bona nezindhlovu nezimpisi, nezingonyama nezingwe nezinyoka, nemifula i gcwala. Konke loku ku hlangana kumi, ku za 'u ngi bulala. Amasuku onke, a ku ko 'langa ngi ke ngi lale ngi nga bonanga.

"Futi, ngi bone se ngi ndiza, ngi nga sa nyateli pansi lapa."

Nga buza ukuti, "Loku se ku njalo, inkosi yako u sa i kumbula njena na?"

Wa ti, "Kqa. Se ku ukufa loko. Uma ngi linga ukuti, 'A ngi tandaze,' ku nga ti ngi biza ukufa konke ukuba ku ngi bulale masinyane. Indaba yenkosi se i kitshiwe kumi ilesi 'sifo. Se ku fulatele sona kupela."

Nga ti, "U ya kumbula indaba yepupa elidala lako na?"

Wa ti, "U tsho lemikumbu na?"

Nga ti, "Yebo."

Wa ti, "Au! A ngi kohlwa

it all by night in my sleep; there is not a single place the exact situation of which I do not know.

"I see also elephants and hyenas, and lions, and leopards, and snakes, and full rivers. All these things come near to me to kill me. Not a single day passes without my seeing such things in my sleep.

"Again, I see that I am flying, no longer treading on this earth."

I asked him, "Since it is thus with you, do you still remember your Lord?"

He said, "No. To do so is death to me. If I try, saying, 'Let me pray,' it is as if I summoned all kinds of death to come and kill me at once. The Lord's tidings are plucked out of me by this disease. It alone has now the dominion over me."

I said, "Do you remember that old dream[46] of yours?"

He said, "Do you speak of that of the boats?"

I said, "Yes."

He replied, "Oh! I do not

---

[46] This dream was recorded at the time. He dreamt that he was crossing a river with Umpengula in a boat. When they were in the middle of the river, without any apparent cause, the bottom of the boat opened and let him through, and, after struggling for a time in the water, he found himself on a sandbank in the midst of the stream, and saw Umpengula on the other side, he having reached without difficulty the place of their destination. All this time he seemed to himself as one dead, though not deprived of sensation—that is, he thought he had died. He found himself surrounded by huge dogs, which appeared ready to devour him, and many black people, among whom he observed his own mother, who expressed her wonder at finding him among them.—This is just one of those prophetic dreams

ilo. Ngi li bona kahle namhla nje ukuba umkumbu 'lukolo lwami o se lu tshonile namuhla. Nezinja lezo e nga zi bona zi ya ngi dhla namhla nje."

Nga ti, "Kepa uma inkosi yako se isita kuwe, u ya 'kusinda ngobani na?"

Wa ti, "Kqa. Se ngi file kupela. A ngi tsho ukuba ngi sa 'uba umuntu wokuba ku ngene ukuma okutsha e ngi nga ku kqondi nakanye. A ng' azi ukuba ngi ini. Bheka, ngokuba ngi umuntu o tanda abantwana bami kakulu. Kepa namhla nje a ngi sa b' azi noma ba kona ini. Into enkulu i lesi 'sifo kupela."

Wa ti, "Manje se ngi ke ngi pume ebusuku, ngi yalelwe umuti, ku tiwe, u sendaweni etile ; a ngi ye 'ku u mba. Ngi pume, ngi fike kona, ngi nga u boni, ngi zule nje, ngi ze ngi buye. Se ku njalo manje kumi.

forget it. I see clearly now that the boat is my faith, which has now sunk into the water. And the dogs which I saw are now devouring me."

I said, "But if your Lord is now your enemy, who will save you?"

He replied, "No. I am now dead altogether. I do not think that I am still a man who can enter into a new position, which I do not in the least understand.[47] I do not know what I am. Attend, for I am a man who loves my children dearly. But now I do not care whether they are alive or not. The great thing is this disease alone."

He continued, "And now I begin to go out by night, having an internal intimation about medicine ;[48] it is said, 'The medicine is in such a place ; go and dig it up.' I go out and reach the place, but do not find the medicine ;[49] I merely walk up and down, and at length return. This is my present state.

---

which is suggested to a man by his own thoughts and wishes, and which help on its own fulfilment by placing before his mind during sleep a distinct tableau of the future such as whilst awake he would be afraid to form for himself.

[47] That is, he no longer understands the Christian faith, and does not believe it can again enter him ; or that he can change again.

[48] Lit., Having had a charge given me respecting a medicine, or plant possessed of medical properties. The charge, of course, being supposed to be given by the Itongo.

[49] It is said to be thus with those who are about to be diviners ; they are often deceived before they learn to comprehend the voices of the Itongo by which they are called.

"Ziningi izinto e ku nga ti ngi ya zi bona, ngi fike kona ngi nga zi boni. Ku ze kwa ti ngolunye usuku ekusoni kakulu, kwa tiwa, a ngi ye 'kumba umuti. Nga hamba, nga fika kona, a nga u bona; nga buya. Ngi te ngi fika ekaya, kwa ku tiwa, 'U shiyele ni umuti na? i wona lowo o ke wa u bona. Hamba, u ye 'ku u mba.' Nga za nga hamba, nga fika nga u mba. Nga buya nga u laḥla, ngokuba ngi ng' azi ukuba ngi za 'kwenza ni ngawo. Omunye kwa tiwa, a ngi ye 'ku u mba esiḥlutankungu. Ng' ala; na namḥla nje a ngi yanga.

"Kepa into enkulu inyama; ku tiwa njalonjalo, 'A ku ḥlatshwe.' Ku nga ti ngi nga dḥla inyama imiḥla yonke. Ku funa inyama loku 'kufa; kepa a ngi vumi.

"Ngi ḥlutshwa izinja; ku nga ti lapa ngi kona inja i nge tshaywe; ngi y' esaba kakulu. Nenyanga yokubula ku nga ti ngi nge i bone; ku nga fika yona, ngi ya fa masinyane, ngi we pansi, ngi fe. I loko ke oku ngi ḥlupayo. Manje a ngi sa tandi 'muntu. Inḥliziyo yami a i sa ba tandi aba-

"There are many things which I seem to see, but when I go to them I cannot see them. At length it happened one day very early in the morning, I was told to go and dig up some medicine. I went to the place, but did not see the medicine, and came back again. When I reached home, it was said, 'Why have you left the medicine? it is that which you saw. Go and dig it up.' At length I went to the place and dug it up. Again I threw it away, for I did not know what to do with it. I was told to go and dig up another medicine on the Isithlutankungu. I refused, and I have not been to this day.

"But the great thing is meat; it is said constantly, 'Let a bullock be killed.'[50] It is as though I could eat meat daily. This disease longs for meat; but I will not kill cattle.

"I am harassed by the dogs; it is as if where I am the dogs must not be beaten; I am greatly afraid of the noise. And it is as though I could not look on a diviner; he may come, I am at once in a dying state, and fall down and die. It is this, then, that troubles me. And now I no longer love any one. My heart no longer loves

---

[50] Not that he likes meat; he eats only a small quantity; but it is the custom with such people to ask to have sacrifices continually made to the Amatongo. It is therefore common when these symptoms first manifest themselves to seek means for laying the Itongo, lest the frequent sacrifices demanded should impoverish them.

ntu. Ku nga ti ngi nga *h*lala lapa ku te nya, ku ng' czwakali umsindo nakanye. A ng' azi uma u ti a ngi buye nje, ngi ya 'ku*h*lala pi, loku insimbi kwiti i kala futifuti. A ngi *h*langani nomsindo onjalo; ngi y' esaba kakulu. A ngi yi 'ku*h*lala. Ngi ya 'kukitshwa insimbi."

Kwa ba njalo ke sa kuluma ngokubuya, ngi ti, " Buya, uma u gulela lapa, umkako e nga ku boni, ka tsho ukuba u y' elatshwa nakanye. Kuyena u m shiyile nje, ukuba ku ya 'kuti um*h*la ku fike uyise a m tate, a hambe naye. U y' azi nawe ukuba abafazi betu ba ya kuluma, noma ku nga guli 'muntu, ba si tshele ukuti, ' Uma indoda i *h*lubuka, i buyela ngapand*h*le, i donswa ubumnandi bakona, kona mina, ngokuba a ngi b' azi ubumnandi bakona, se ng' a*h*lukana nayo masinyane, ngi nge fe ngokufa komunye umuntu e zibulala ngamabomu.' A ngi ti u y' azi ukuba ba tsho njalo abafazi betu na ?"

Wa vuma, wa ti, "Yebo. Uhannah u fikile lapa ngensuku ezi d*h*lulile. Wa ti, a ngi kipe loku 'kufa; uma ku nga pumi, si ya 'kwa*h*lukana. Nga m pendula ngokuti, ' Ukukipa ukufa ukwenza

men. It is as though I could stay where it is perfectly still—where there is not the least sound. When you tell me to return, I do not know where I could stay, for the bell of our village sounds again and again. I do not like such a sound as that; I am much afraid. I shall not stay. I shall be driven away by the bell."

And then we spoke of his return, I saying, " Come home, if you are ill here; your wife, not seeing you, does not suppose at all that you are under medical treatment. To her way of thinking, you have merely forsaken her; therefore when her father comes he will come and take her away with him. You know yourself that our wives talk, and although a man is not sick, they tell us that if a husband rebels and returns to heathen life, attracted by its pleasant things, yet his wife, because she does not know any pleasant things of heathen life, will at once separate from him, and not die with the death with which another wilfully kills himself. Do you not know that our wives say thus?"

He assented and said, "Yes. Hannah came here some days ago. She told me to get rid of this disease. And if I did not get rid of it, we should separate. I answered her and asked, ' What is meant

njani na? Ngi ya ku tanda ini na? Kw' enziwa imi ini na? O, a ngi kw azi ukukitshwa kwokufa. Umniniko o gula iko.' S' a/lukana ke. Nami ngi za 'kubuya ngalelo 'zwi lokuti, 'Uma ku nga pumi, si za 'kwa/lukana.' Se ngi za 'ubuya, nayo umkami a zibonele loko oku nga kipa loku 'kufa. Ngi nge tsho usuku. Ni ya 'ubona ngi fika nje. Umzimba wami ubu/lungu, ngokuba ngalobu 'busuku e ni fika ngabo ngi ni bonile ni za kumi, ni abelungu. Wa ngi bulala umlungu; wa ngena lapa, wa ngi tshaya emlenzeni lo ow' apukayo, wa w apula. Ng' esuka, nga m tela ngomlota. Ngi gula iloko ke. Ngi y' a/luleka uku ni tshela usuku.

"A ngi guli imi/la yonke. Ngolunye usuku ngi ya tokoza nje, kakulu ngesonto. Ku ti ngalo, noma ngi nga sa l' azi, ngi ya pila kakulu. Se ng' azi ngomzimba ukuba isonto nam/la nje. Ku njalo ke ukufa kwami.

"Hamba ni. Ke ngi ni pelezele; ngi za 'kubuya lapa ngapezulu."

Nembala ke sa hamba nje nayo. Kodwa u se hamba-ze, u se binca imintsha. Nga ka nga u bona umuntsha wake, isitobo esimnyama.

by getting rid of it? Am I fond of it? Did I produce it? O, I do not know how the disease can be got rid of. The disease is master of the sick man.' And so we separated. And I am now about to return home for that saying of hers, 'If the disease does not cease we shall separate.' I will now come back, that my wife may see for herself that which can get rid of the disease. I cannot fix the day. You will see me when I come. My body is in pain, for on the night before you came I saw you coming to me, but you were white men. A white man hurt me; he came in here and struck me on the thigh which was broken, and broke it again. I arose and threw ashes over him.[51] I am ill from that then. I cannot tell you the day.

"I am not ill every day. Some days I am quite well, especially on Sunday. On Sunday, although I no longer know it is Sunday, I am very well. I now know by my body that it is Sunday. Such then is my disease.

"Go. I will accompany you; I will come back from the top of the hill."

So then we went with him. But he now goes naked, and wears the umuntsha. I just caught sight of his umuntsha; the hinder part was black.

---

[51] That is, in a dream.

Futi nga buza ngokuti, "Ku ngani ukuba u pume ekaya ngokunyenyela umfundisi, o inyanga yezifo zonke, u nga m tshelanga na?"

Wa ti, "A ngi m tshelanga ngokuba ng' esaba, nga ti, 'Uma ngi m tshela, u za 'kuti ngi ya *h*lanya, a ngi bambe, a ngi yise emgungund*h*lovu, ngi *h*lale kona isikati eside.' Ng' esaba loko ke, ngi nga m tshelanga nje ngokuti, ' O, loku u*h*lanya l' ona izinto zabantu, mina a ng' oni 'luto, ngi ya zigulela nje;—O, k*q*a, a ngi nga m tsheli. Kumbe ngi ya 'kupila uma ngi zifunele izinyanga. A ngi hambe.' Nga hamba ke. Nga hamba ngaloko ke.

Sa hamba ke, s' a*h*lukana naye eu*h*la kwomuzi, e hamba e nga kæugi; umlenze a w omile; u lingana nomunye nje. Kodwa ekwe*h*leni ku ya bonakala ukuba lo 'muntu wa limala. Kodwa ekwenyukeni u hambisa kwabantu nje bouke.

Ukud*h*la a ku d*h*layo kutatu kupela—inyama, izinsipo ku gaywe umkeuku; uma ku nge ko a d*h*le imifino yasen*h*le. Nako ukud*h*la a pila ngako. Amasi ka wa faki nakanye; u ya zondana nawo.

Further, I asked him, "Why did you leave home unknown to our Teacher, who is a doctor of all diseases, without telling him?"

He replied, "I did not tell him, for I was afraid, and said, 'If I tell him, he will say I am mad, and seize me and send me to Pietermaritzburg, and I shall stay there a long time.' I feared that then, and did not tell him, thinking, ' O, since a mad man destroys people's property, and I do no harm, but my sickness is an injury to myself only;—O, no, let me not tell him. It may be I shall get well if I find doctors for myself. Let me go.' So I went away."

So we left, and separated from him at a place above the village. He walked without limping; his thigh has not dried up, it is of the same length as the other. But when he is going down hill, it is evident that he is a man who has been injured. But when he goes up hill, he looks like all other men.

There are only three kinds of food that he eats—meat, and the dregs of beer mixed with boiled maize; if these cannot be had he eats wild herbs. That is the food on which he lives. He does not put amasi into his mouth by any means; he dislikes it, and it disagrees with him.

z

Futi, ngolunye usuku ebusuku wa tshelwa ukuti, "Vuka, u tshone ngalapa emfuleni, u za 'kufumana inyamazane i sem*hlonhl*weni i banjiwe; hamba, u ye 'ku i tata." U ti, "Nga vuka ke. Kwa ti lapa se ngi hambile umfo wetu wa ngi landela, Umankamane." Wa ponsa ngetshe, wa tshaya in*hl*aba. W' etuka Ujames, wa baleka, wa buyela kuye, wa m tetisa ngokuti, "W enze ni ukuba u ng' etuse lapa ngi za 'kutata inyamazane yami na?" Kwa ku pela ke, kwa pela loko o be ku m k*q*uba ukuba a yotata inyamazane. Ba goduka nje ke, ku nga se ko 'luto.

Ku tiwa abakubo, lu*hl*obo olubutataka kakulu, lu ba izinyanga. Ku kona ababili abafo wabo bakwazulu ba izinyanga. Ujames wa ngi tshela, wa ti, "Kwa fika Uheber lapa, e vela kwazulu; wa ngi tshela ukuti, 'Abafo wenu kwazulu le se be izinyanga, Ubani nobani.'" U ti ke Ujames ke, "Nanko ke umuutu owa ngi bangela ukufa loku. Wa ti e sa tsho nje nga tshaywa uvalo olwesabekayo. A ngi m pendulanga; nga tula nje. Se ngi *hl*abekile, ngokuba e kuluma indaba ey' enzekayo kumina; kodwa ngi nga kulumi ngayo, ngi ng' azi ukuba isifo sini na. Yena wa ng' azisa, ku ze ku be nam*hl*a nje.

Again, once at night he was told to awake and go down to the river, and he would find an antelope caught in a Euphorbia tree; and to go and take it. "So," said he, "I awoke. When I had set out, my brother, Umankamane, followed me." He threw a stone and struck an aloe. James was frightened, and ran back to him and chided him, saying, "Why did you frighten me when I was about to lay hold on my antelope." That was the end of it, and he was not again told by any thing to go and fetch the antelope. They went home, there being nothing there.

James's people say they are of a family who are very sensitive, and become doctors. There are two of his brothers in Zululand who are doctors. James told me, saying, "Heber came to us on his arrival from Zululand; he told me that my brothers in Zululand are now doctors, So-and-so and So-and-so." And so James said, "He then is the man who brought this disease on me. Whilst he was telling me I was seized with a fearful dread. I did not answer him, but remained silent. I am now ill because he spoke of what I myself was experiencing; but I did not speak of it, for I did not know what disease it was. He made me understand; and I understand it to this day."

AMATONGO.

Ku tiwa uyise kajames, Ukokela, wa e umuntu o inceku yenkosi yakwazulu. Kepa wa banjwa iso lesi 'sifo sokwetasa. Inkosi ya tukutela uma i zwe loko. Ya mu d/la izinkomo zonke zake. Wa /lala nje. Nanko ke umuti owona w' elapa Ukokela. Kwa pela.

Abanye ba izinyanga na lapa esilungwini. Odade wabo ba y' etasa njalo; baningi aba nalesi 'sifo esi kujames. Abanye ba ya vinjwa, ku pele. Abanye ku ze ku zipelele nje, ku katale, ku m yeke. Omunye, ka si ye wakubo, ngi mu zwile lapa kujojo; intombi yasembo kanoponya; ku tiwa naye u be tasa, 'enza njengojames njalo. Kepa w' elatshwa izinyanga eziningi. Z' a/luleka, e se hamba ezintabeni, e nga sa /lali ekaya; umfazi. Wa za w' elatshwa Ujojo kamanzezulu; wa m a/lula. Wa /laba izimbuzi ezimbili — imvu nembuzi; imbuzi im/lope, imvu imnyama. Wa m elapa ngazo; emnyama ey' enza ukuba itongo li be mnyama, li nga kanyi; em/lope ey' enza ukuba itongo li be m/lope, li kanye, li m bonise ka/le.

It is said that James's father, Ukokela, was the steward of the Zulu king. But he was seized with the disease which precedes the power to divine. The king was angry when he heard it. He ate up all his cattle. That was the medicine which cured Ukokela. That was the end of it.

Others are doctors here in the country of the English. His sisters have the initiatory symptoms; there are many who have James's disease. Some have the Itongo laid. With others the disease ceases of its own accord; it is tired, and leaves them. Another, not one of James's relatives, I heard Ujojo mention her; she was a girl of the Abambo, the daughter of Unoponya; it is said, she was affected, and did as James does. But she was treated by many doctors. They could not cure her; she still went to the mountains, and did not stay at home; she was a married woman. At length she was treated by Ujojo, the son of Umanzezulu; he cured her. He killed two goats—or, rather, a sheep and a goat; the goat was white, the sheep black. He treated her with them; the black sheep made the Itongo indistinct, and no longer bright; the white goat made the Itongo white and bright, that it might make her see clear-

Wa m vimba ke, wa m godusa, wa m hlalis' ekaya. U se umuntu nje manje. Nami ngi ke nga m bona. Kwa tiwa, kade e hamba ezintabeni. Kepa manje ka sa bonakali ukuba u ke wa hamba.

Izinyanga zokubula zi ti ku-james, naye u ya tasa, u za 'kuba inyanga. Kodwa ka ng' elatshwa ngemiti emnyama yoku m vimba; u ya 'kufa; ka yekwe nje. Nga-loko ke abakubo se be kohliwe into a ba za 'ku y enza, loku ku tiwa, u ya 'kufa. Se be buka nje. Izwi lezinyanga li umteto kubo; ba nge li dhlule nakanye.

UMPENGULA MBANDA.

ly.[52] So he laid the Itongo, and she went home; he caused her to live at home. And she is now a human being. It is said, for a long time she lived in the mountains. But it is now no longer apparent that she ever did so.

The diviners tell James that he too is beginning, and will soon be a doctor. But they say he must not be treated with black medicines to lay the Itongo, for he will die; he must be just left alone. His friends therefore do not know what to do, since it is said, he will die. They merely look on. The diviners' word is their law; they can on no account go beyond it.

How to distinguish Snakes which are Amatongo from common Snakes.

UKUPENDUKA kwabantu be penduka izinyoka, lezo 'nyoka a ba ba i zo a ziningi, zi ketiwe, zi y' aziwa, —ukuti, imamba emnyama, nen-yandezulu e imamba eluhlaza; amakosi lawo ke. Abantu um-

THE snakes into which men turn are not many; they are distinct and well known. They are the black Imamba, and the green Imamba, which is called Inyande-zulu. Chiefs turn into these.

---

[52] This, as it is told in the text, is not clear. It appears that the doctor pursued two systems of treatment, with opposite objects. And this was really the case. He first tried the "darkening" system, by using together with the black sheep other medicines possessed of a darkening power; but not succeeding, he tried the opposite system— the "brightening" plan, that is, he acted subtlely, making the Itongo bright and clear, and willing to come near the patient, and then by suddenly again resorting to the "darkening" system, he made the Itongo dark for ever, and so "the spirit was laid," and has never appeared since.

hlwazi, amakosikazi ke lawo. Enye ubulube ukuti inkwakwa, nomzingandhlu, kupela kwezinyoka ezi abantu.

Kepa ukubonwa kwazo uma zi abantu, zi bonwa ekungeneni kwazo endhlini; a zi vami ukungena ngomnyango. Kumbe zi ngena ku nge ko 'muntu, z' enyuke zi y' emsamo, zi hlale kona, zi zibute. I nga li dhli isele nempuku, i hlale nje, i ze i bonwe umuntu, a bize abanye; i ng' etuki ukubaleka, i ze i shiywe nje. Abanye ba ti, "A i bulawe." Abanye ba ti, "Umuntu lo?"

Uma i nenxeba ohlangotini, a vele ow' azi ubanibani wakona owafayo, a tsho ukuti, "Ubani lo. A ni li boni inxeba leli ohlangotini na?" I yekwe ke. Ku lalwe.

Ku ti ebusuku umninimuzi a pupe ipupo ukuti, "Ni se ni funa uku ngi bulala nje? Se ni kohliwe ini imina na? Nga ti, ngi zokeela ukudhla; na ngi bulala na? Ngi Ubani."

Ku so kusasa e wa lauza lawo 'mapupo, a ti, "A ku neencezwe ukuxe itongo li nga tukuteli, li si bulale." Ku funwe inkomo, noma

Common people turn into the Umthlwazi, and chieftainesses. Another snake is called Ubulube or Inkwakwa, and another Umzingandhlu; common people turn into these only.

These snakes are known to be human beings when they enter a hut; they do not usually enter by the doorway. Perhaps they enter when no one is there, and go to the upper part of the hut, and stay there coiled up. A snake of this kind does not eat frogs or mice; it remains quiet, until some one sees it and calls others; it is not afraid so as to run away, and it is left alone. Some say, "Let it be killed." Others say, "What, kill a man?"

If the snake has a scar on the side, someone, who knew a certain dead man of that place who also had such a scar, comes forward and says, "It is So-and-so. Do you not see the scar on his side?" It is left alone, and they go to sleep.

During the night the chief of the village dreams, and the dead man says to him, "Do you now wish to kill me? Do you already forget me? I thought I would come and ask for food; and do you kill me? I am So-and-so."

In the morning he tells his dreams, and says, "Let a sin-offering be sacrificed, lest the Itongo be angry and kill us." They fetch a bullock or goat; and pray

imbuzi, ku bongwe, ku dhliwe. Ku kqabukwe i nga se ko. Se i te nya.

Inyoka nje i ngena endhlini, i talaze, y esab' abantu; i bulawe, ngoba i y' aziwa ukuba umlalandhle.

Futi i y' aziwa na ngokqobo lwayo nje, ukuba isilwane, i bulawe noma i nga talazi, ngokuba a i si yo imamba e ku tiwa umuntu, nenyandezulu i y' aziwa ukuba umuntu. Z' ahlukene ezi abantu nezi nge 'bantu ngombala wazo. Njengebululu nevuzamanzi nenhlangwana nemamba empofu, neluhlaza i namabala, zi y' aziwa lezo ukuba imilalandhle. A kw enzeki ukuba i be umuntu ngesinye isikati; a zi penduki; zi imilalandhle njalo. Nezi abantu zi abantu njalo; zi bonwa kqede, ku tiwe abantu; nembala zi kulume ngamapupo; noma zi nga kulumi, kw aziwe ukuba umuntu.

Ukwaziwa kwazo lezo ezi abantu z' aziwa ngokujwayela ekaya, na ngokungadhli izimpuku, nokungetuki umsindo wabantu; zi bonwe njalo i ng' etuki isitunzi somuntu, i ng' esabeki kubantu, ku nga bi

and eat the flesh. They look, and the snake is no longer there. It has now entirely disappeared.

A mere snake, when it comes into a hut, looks from side to side, and is afraid of men; and it is killed because it is known to be a wild snake.

A snake is also known by its mere appearance to be an animal, even though it does not look from side to side, because it is neither an Imamba[53] that is a man, nor the Inyandezulu,[54] which is known to be a man. Those which are men and those which are not, are distinguished by their colour. The Puffadder, the Ivuzamanzi, the Inthlangwana, and the grey and spotted Imamba, are known to be mere beasts. It is impossible for them to be ever men; they never become men; they are always beasts. And those which are men are always men; as soon as they are seen they are known to be men; and truly they speak in dreams; and even if they do not, it is known that they are men.

Those which are men are known by their frequenting huts, and by their not eating mice, and by their not being frightened at the noise of men; they are always observed not to be afraid of the shadow of a man; neither does a snake that is an Itongo excite fear in men,

---

[53] That is, the black imamba.
[54] Or green imamba. There is besides a spotted green, and grey

ko nesitunzi endhlini sokuba ku kona isilwane, ku pole nje, ku zwakale ukuba ku fike umninimuzi. Ekuboneni kwabantu ku nga ti ngoku i bona nje i ya kuluma ukuti, "Ni ng' esabi. Umina." Ba tola 'mandhla njalo ukuhlangana nayo.

Uma i bulewe umuntu o ng' aziyo, i buye i vuke, i fike nazo izinduku lezo e b' i bulawa ngazo, zi semzimbeni imivimbo; i kulume ngepupo, i sola ukupatwa kabi kwayo. Ku ncencezwe emva kwaloko. I loko ke e z' aziwa ngako izinyoka.

Ku ti owa e nesikei emzimbeni, a bonwe ngaso; nekcide li bouwe ngeso enyokeni; nengozi i bonwe ngayo; nonyonga lu bonwe ngako. Zi bonwa ngaloko ke, ngokuba abantu imvamo ba vame ukuba nezikei, izinyoka zabo zi njalo. Aba nge nazikei ba ya kuluma. Noma ku bonwa ukuba itongo, kodwa e uge nasikei, ku tiwe, "Umuntu lo;" kodwa a si m azi. A zivezo ngokukuluma. Z' aziwa ngaloko ke.

Futi, uma inyoka e itongo i lala

and there is no feeling of alarm as though there was a wild beast in the house; but there is a happy feeling, and it is felt that the chief of the village has come. When men see it, it is as though it said as they look at it, "Be not afraid. It is I." So they are able at all times to associate with it.

If it has been killed by someone who is ignorant, it comes to life again, and has the marks of the rod on its body by which it was killed; and complains in a dream of the treatment it has received. And after that a sin-offering is sacrificed. This, then, is how snakes are distinguished.

He who had a scar is recognised by that; and he who had but one eye is recognised by the snake into which he has turned having one eye also; and another is recognised by the marks of injuries; and a lame man is known by the lameness of the snake. That is how they are known, for men usually have some marks, and the snakes into which they turn have similar marks. The man who had no mark speaks in dreams. And if it is seen that it is an Itongo, but it has no mark, it is said to be a man, but we do not know who it is. He reveals himself by speaking. This is how they are known.

Again, if a snake which is an

ngom*h*lana, i bekise isisu pezulu, ku y' esabeka, ku tiwa inkulu indaba e za 'uvela—noma, ku za 'ububa umuzi. Ku keolwe, ku yiwe enyangeni yokubula, i ku lande loko okwenziwa itongo ngako; ku lungiswa.

Uma i tandela isitsha, i y' ala ukuba si tabatwe, ku ze ku funwe into, ku tetwe, i suke.

Futi, uma inyoka e itongo i ngena ngen*h*luzula, kw aziwe ukuba itongo lomuntu owa e ihhatanga e sa pila. U sa hamba ngako ukwenza kwake. Ku lungiswe ngento.

I loko ke e ngi kw aziyo ngamatongo.

UMPENGULA MBANDA.

Itongo lies on its back, with its belly upwards, it is a cause of alarm, and it is said something of consequence is about to happen,— or, the village is about to be destroyed. The people sacrifice and pray, and go to a diviner, and he tells them why the Itongo has done as it has. They do as they are directed.

If a snake coils around a vessel and will not allow any one to take it, the people bring a sacrifice and worship, and it goes away.

And if a snake which is an Itongo enters a house rapidly,[55] it is known to be the Itongo of a man who was a liar whilst he lived. And he is still a liar. They sacrifice something to such an Itongo.

This is what I know about the Amatongo.

Men turn into many kinds of Animals.

Ku tiwa abantu ba penduka izilwane eziningi. Omunye ku tiwa u ba umnyovu; omunye a be isalukazana; nomunye imamba; nomunye inyandezulu; imvamo ba

It is said that men turn into many kinds of animals. It is said that one becomes a wasp; another an isalukazana;[56] another an imamba;[57] another an inyandezulu;[58] but the greater number turn into

---

[55] Rapidly, or rather, without any shame,—arbitrarily, as one that has a right to do as he likes, whose will is his law.

[56] *Isalukazana,* a kind of lizard.

[57] *Imamba,* a poisonous snake.

[58] *Inyandezulu,* a poisonous snake, the green imamba.

penduka umhlwazi oluhlaza nonsundu. Leyo 'mihlwazi yombili umuntu a nga ze a vume, a ti, "Yebo, abantu laba," e tsho ngokuba i nga twali 'mehlo njengalezo 'zilwanyana ezine. A w esabi umhlwazi umuntu, u hamba kahle; uma umuntu e u bona u lele, ku ze ku fike abaningi ba u bone; noma be u vusa, u ti siki, u me.

Ngaloko ke ku tiwa, u itongo, ngokuba a u bonanga u luma 'muntu; isilwane e si nge nalulaka kuzo zonke. Oluhlaza nonsundu i ya fana ngokuba-mnene.

Kepa ezinye, noma ku tiwa zi amatongo, kepa a zi jwayeleki emehlweni, ngokuba lu uhlobo lwezilwane ezi lumako. A i bonakali imamba yasenhle neyasekaya ngombala; umbala wayo munye, amehlo ayo manye; neyasenhle ukubheka kwayo kunye—ukubheka kwempi okwesabisa umuntu; a nga melwa isibindi ukuti, "Itongo. Ngi nga sondela kuyo." Ai; u tsho e kude e nga sondeli. Kodwa

the umthlwazi,[59] which may be green or brown. As regards the two kinds of umthlwazi, a person may allow that they are men, because they do not stare fiercely like the other four. The umthlwazi is not afraid of a man, it moves slowly; if a person sees it lying, it remains quiet until many come and look at it; and if they arouse it, it moves slightly, and again remains quiet.

Therefore it is said to be an Itongo, for it never bites any one; it is a beast which is less fierce than all others. The green and brown kinds resemble each other in gentleness.

And the others, although they are called Amatongo, yet the eyes do not get accustomed to them,[60] for they belong to a kind of animal which bites. The imamba which frequents open places, and those which frequent houses, are not distinguishable by colour; their colour is the same, their eyes are alike; and when they are in an open place, their stare is of the same character—the stare of an enemy, which makes one afraid; and a man does not pluck up courage by saying, "This snake is an Itongo. I can approach it." No; he says it is an Itongo when he is at a distance from it, without

---

[59] *Umhlwazi*, a harmless snake.
[60] They do not become common in the eyes, that is, so as to be approached familiarly,—the eyes do not get accustomed to them.

emhlwazini si tsho, si sondela kuwo.

Kakulu imamba ku tiwa amakosi; kepa izalukazana ku tiwa abafazi abadala; umhlwazi ku tiwa abantu. Umnyovu a ku tshiwo ngokubonakalako, ukuti u itongo, ngokuba u vela emntwini; ku nga u itongo ngokutunywa; i ilo ngokubonwa kwawo ke, ku tiwe, u itongo; ngokuba ku tiwa ngawo, ku nga u isitunywa.

approaching near to it. But we say the umthlwazi is an Itongo, and go up to it.

But the imamba is said especially to be chiefs; the isalukazana, old women; and the umthlwazi, common people. As regards the wasp, it is not clear that it is an Itongo, because it appears to a man; it is as it were an Itongo because it is sent; it is an Itongo through being seen, and so it is said to be an Itongo; for people say of it, it resembles something that has been sent.

The order in which the Amatongo are worshipped.

Ku ya bizwa amatongo onke ngetongo lokukqala el' aziwayo. Li bizwe njengaloku isizwe, ku tiwa, esakwabani; esetu ku tiwa samapepete. Isibongo ku tiwa Gwala, umuntu wokukqala, ukuti, unkulunkulu wamapepete. Uyena e inhloko yesizwe sonke; si kuleka ngaye. Ku ti uma ku hlatshwe, ku tiwe, "Nina'bakwagwala, pelela ni nonke, ni ze 'kudhla. Naku 'kudhla kwenu."

Kepa manje ngokuba ku kona izinyanga, a ku sa kqalwa ngaloko; ngokuba kwabafayo u y' aziwa oyena e ngeniso isifo; w' aziwa

ALL the Amatongo are called upon by the name of the first Itongo who is known. It is called just as a nation is called after a certain person; ours is the nation of the Amapepete. The family name is Gwala, the first man, that is, the Unkulunkulu of the Amapepete. It is he who is the head of the whole nation; we pray by his name. And when we sacrifice we say, "Ye people of Gwala, come all of you to eat. Behold your food."

But now since there are diviners we no longer begin in this way; for it is known who among the dead has caused disease; he is

ngokubula ezinyangeni, ukuba, "Ubani lowo u gula nje, u bulawa Ubani lowo wakini. Ni ya m a-zi; u ti, ku ngani ukuba ku ti lapa ni pete ukud*h*la ni nga m kumbuli na?" Ngaloko ke ku ya bizwa yena kuk*q*ala, ku tiwe, "Bani kabani," e bongwa ngezi-bongo zake; ku ze ku fikwe na kuyise, a ngeniswe naye kule 'n-daba yokufa; ku ze ku fikwe kwo-wokupela; se ku ya gciuwa ke uma ku tiwa, "Nina 'bakwagwala, owa ti wa ti" (ku balwa izibongo zake), "pelela ni nonke."

Ku njalo ke ukwa*h*lukanisa amatongo. 'A*h*lukaniswa ngokuba u ba munye ematongweni o yena e veza isifo. Abanye ba nga tsho 'luto. Ku bizwe yena ke kuk*q*ala, njengokuba e kala ngokuti, "Ku ngani ukuba ngi nga be ngi sa patwa na?" Ku njalo ke.

Njengaloku kwiti, kwa ka kwa gula ubabekazi; kwa tiwa ezinya-ngeni, "U bulawa umfo wabo, ngokuti, 'Kulo 'muzi, noma ku petwe ukud*h*la, a ngi sa kunjulwa;' e tsho, ngokuti, 'Ku ngani ukuba ku nga k*q*alwa ngaye ukubizwa ematongweni onke na?'"

Amatongo a sa *h*lupa abantu ngaloko. Ilelo li ya banga njalo, known by enquiring of the di-viners; they tell us, "Since So-and-so is ill, he is made ill by So-and-so, one of your people. You know him; he says, how is it that when you have food you forget him?" Therefore he is called upon first, and it is said, "So-and-so, son of So-and-so," he being lauded by his laud-giving names; then they proceed to his father, and he too is mentioned in con-nection with the disease; and so in time they come to the last; and so there is an end, when it is said, "Ye people of Gwala, who did so and so" (his great deeds being mentioned), "come all of you."

Such then is the distinction be-tween Amatongo. They are dis-tinguished, because it is one among them which causes the dis-ease. The others say nothing. So he is called upon first, as though he complained saying, "How is it that my name is no longer men-tioned?" That is how it is.

Just as with us, our uncle was ill; the diviners said, "He is made ill by his brother, because he says, 'In that village when they have food, I am no longer remem-bered;' and he asks, 'How is it that you do not begin with him when you call on the Amatongo?'"

The Amatongo continually trou-ble men on that account. Each

ukuze onke a be nezinkomo zawo, noma e patwa onke. Kepa otile u kumbula ngokuti, "Mina, a ba bonanga be ngi pata kukqala uku ngi hlabela inkomo etile; ngi za 'uziveza ngokufa."

I njalo ke indaba yokwahlukanisa amatongo.
UMPENGULA MBANDA.

one of them constantly puts in a claim, that each may have his own cattle [sacrificed for him individually], though the names of all be called upon. And a certain one remembers they never worship him first by killing for him a certain cow; and he says, "I will reveal myself by disease."

This then is the word about making a distinction between the Amatongo.

Tale of an Imamba.

INDABA yemamba e itongo lakwiti emapepeteni. Inkosi yakona Umaziya. Leyo 'nkosi ya penduka imamba ekupumeni emzimbeni wobuntu. Ya bulawa embo. Kwa ti ekukcitekeni kwezwe lakwazulu, abantu ba tanda ukuza lapa esilungwini. Kepa yona ya se i file. Indodana yayo Umyeka owa sala esikundhleni sikayise, nomfo wabo Umgwaduyana wa fa yena, wa shiya amadodana amabili, enye Umadikane, enye encane, Ubafako.

Kepa ngaleso 'sikati sokukciteka kwezwe, lowo 'mfana wa e nesilonda esibi etangeni; kepa se ku

THE account of the Imamba which is the Itongo of our people among the Amapepete. The chief of that nation was Umaziya.[61] That chief became an Imamba when he went out of his human body. He was killed by the Abambo. When the people were scattered from the country of the Amazulu, they wished to come here to the English. But he had been dead for some time. It was his son, Umyeka, who remained in his father's place, and his brother too, Umgwaduyana, died, and left two sons, one named Umadikane, and the younger one, Ubafako.

But at the time of the scattering of the people the lad Ubafako had a bad sore on his thigh; they

---

[61] *Umaziya.*—The z pronounced like z in azure.

hanjiwe enhle, ku punyiwe emakaya, e gula kakulu ileso 'silonda; se kw elatshiwe ngemiti; kepa imiti i nga namateli, si be loku si biba njalo. Ku ze kwa ti ngolunye usuku, ku hleziwe emadokodweni okubaleka, kwa ngena imamba; loku umntwana u lele, abantu ba ngqazuka, b' etuka be bona isilwane si ngena endhlini; kepa a i ba nakanga nokwetuka nje, kupela ya pikelela ukwenyuka i ye kumntwana; unina e se kala e ti, "Inyoka i ya 'kudhla umntwana."

Kepa kwa se kw aziwa ukuba inkosi le; kepa a ba melwanga 'sibindi, ngokuba se i nomunye umzimba, a ba nga jwayelani nawo—umzimba wezilwane. Ya fika, ya beka umlomo esilondeni, kwa ba isikatshana i tulisile, y' esuka, ya puma.

Ku ti ngemva kwaloko kwa yiwa ezinyangeni, ukuba ku zwakale ukuba lo 'mhlola ongaka wemamba ini na. Kepa za ti zona izinyanga, "Inkosi yakwini leyo; i zokwelapa umntwana wendodana yayo."

Nembala ke kwa hlaliwa; isilonda sa buya, sa za sa pola.

were then living in the open country and had quitted their homes, when he was ill with that sore; and it had been already treated with medicines; but the medicines would not adhere, and the sore increased continually. At length it happened one day, as they were living in the temporary booths erected in their flight, an Imamba entered; the child was asleep; the people started up and were frightened when they saw the beast enter the house; but it neither took any notice of them nor was in the least afraid, but pressed onward to go up to the child; the mother now cried out, "The snake will kill the child."

But it was already known that it was the chief; but they had not any courage on that account, for he had now a different body, to which they were not accustomed, —the body of a beast. It reached the child and placed its mouth on the sore, and remained still a little while, and then departed and went out of the house.

After that they went to the diviners, that they might hear what was the meaning of so great an omen. But the doctors said, "It is your chief; he comes to heal the child of his son."

So the people waited in patience; and the sore contracted, and at length healed.

Ku be ku ti lapa ku hanjwa, ku ziwa, lapa ku hanjiwe, nayo i bonwe lapa ku welwa emazibukweni; i be i wela ngenzansi njalo; kwa za kwa fikwa lapa emkambatini, lapa ya sala kona ngesikati sokweh́la kwendodana, Umyeka, e ya enanda, e balekela Amabunu.

Kepa inkosi leyo y' ala, ya ti, "A ngi yi 'kuza ezweni lolwandh́le. Ngi za 'kuh́lala lapa, ngi zidh́lele izintete nje." Nembala ke kwa ba njalo. Kwa za kwa gula Umyeka kakulu, e pupa ku tiwa, "Wa m shiyela ni uyih́lo? U ya ba biza; u ti, a ba buye." Kepa a ba vumanga ngokwesaba umlanjwana wamabunu, ngokuba kwa dh́liwa izinkomo zawo Umyeka.

Kwa ba njalo ke, ku ze kwa kupuka omunye ubabekazi omkulu, e ya kubaba, ow' elamana no zala tina. W' esuka lowo 'baba, e dedela ubabekazi, wa buyela

And it used constantly to happen, when they were travelling towards this country, when they had set out, the Imamba too was seen where they crossed at the fords of rivers; it used to cross lower down constantly; until they reached Table Mountain, where it still was when his son, Umyeka, went down to the Inanda, flying from the Dutch.

But the chief[62] refused, saying, "I will not go to a country by the sea. I shall stay here, and eat grasshoppers."[63] And so indeed it was. At length Umyeka was very ill, and it was said to him in a dream, "Why did you forsake your father?[64] He is calling the people; let them return." But they would not agree, fearing their feud with the Dutch, for Umyeka had stolen their cattle.[65]

So it was until our eldest uncle went up to our father,[66] who was younger than our own father. Our father departed, leaving our eldest uncle, and returned

---

[62] That is, the imamba,—the dead chief.

[63] It is to be understood that this was said to the son in a dream.

[64] That is, forsake the place where his Itongo revealed itself.

[65] It is supposed by the narrator that this tribe stole at least a thousand head of cattle from the Dutch.

[66] Both the Ubabakazi, eldest uncle, and the Ubaba, father, were uncles. There were three brothers. The eldest is here called Ubabakazi; the second, the father, was dead; the youngest, here called father, had charge of the family of the second.

enxiweni elikulu lenkosi yakwiti. Kodwa wa bhekana nalo ; ka ngenanga kulo ; kwa linywa nje kulo. Ku ze kwa ti ngolunye usuku ubaba e lele wa pupa inkosi leyo i kuluma naye. Lokupela ngaleso 'sikati kwa ku sobusika, amanzi e banda kakulu, ya ti, "Ngqokqwane, kuhle ukuba u ng' enzele ikqamuka ezibukweni, ngi wele ngalo, ngi z' ekaya ; ngokuba ngi ya godola amakaza, ngi bandwa na amanzi futi."

Nembala ng' ezwa ubaba e se ngi biza, e ti, "Mntanami, woza, si ye lapaya ezibukweni eli ya enxiweni lasemzimvubu, umuzi wenkosi, si yokwenzela inkosi kona ikqamuka lokuwela." Nembala ke sa gaula iminga kakulu nemisenge, sa i nqumisa kabili emfuleni, sa tela umhlaba ngapezulu.

Ku ngezinsukwana lezo, lokupela nga ngi umfana wezinkomo o vala isango, nga libala kakulu ukuya 'uvala, kwa za kwa hlwa ; ngi te se ngi ya, nga ngi ya, se ku dhlule isikati sokuvala. Nga i bona ngi sa ya njeya into e kwebezela emivalweni. Kepa a ngi nakanga ukuba ini. Nga ya ngamandhla, ngi tanda ukuvala masi-

to the old site of our chief's great kraal. But he was on the other side of the stream to it ; he did not build on the old site, but dug there only. Until on a certain day our father whilst asleep dreamt the chief was talking with him. And as at that time it was winter, and the water was very cold, he said to him, "Unggqokqwane, it would be well for you to make a bridge for me, that I may cross on it and come home ; for I am cold, and the water makes me colder still."

And truly I heard my father calling me and saying, "My child, come, let us go yonder to the ford which leads to the old site of Umzimvubu, the village of the chief, and make there a bridge for the chief to cross over." And truly we cut down many mimosa trees and elephant trees, and laid them across the stream, and poured earth on the top of them.

A few days after, for I was then the herd-boy who closed the cattle pen, I put off for a long time going to close it, until it was dark ; and did not set out to do it until the usual time had passed. As I was going, I saw yonder something glistening on the poles with which the gateway was closed. But I did not trouble myself as to what it was. I went in a hurry, wishing to close the gateway at once,

nyane, ngokuba nga shiya endhlini ku za 'udhliwa amasi. Ngaloko ke nga tanda ukuvala masinyane. Kepa nga tata lowo 'muvalo; wa sinda, ng' ahluleka; na komunye kwa ba njalo; ya ng' ahlula imivalo. Nga kqala ukubhekisisa ukuba namhla nje imivalo i ngi sinda ngani, loku imivalo emidala nje na? Nga bhekisisa, kanti inyoka enkulu e lele pezu kwemivalo. Nga kala. Kwa punywa ekaya, kwa buzwa ini na? Nga ti, "Nansi inyoka."

Ubaba wa fika masinyane, wa bhekisisa, wa ti, "Yeka ukuvala." Nga buza, nga ti, "Ini le na?" Wa ti, "Inkosi." Nga ti, "Inyoka le na?" Wa ti, "Yebo."

Sa buyela endhlini. Ku te ku sa wa e si tshela, e ti, "Inkosi i ti, 'Ku ngani ukuba ni ng' etuke?' A ngi ti ya tsho ya ti, a kw enziwe indhlela, i za 'kuza na?'"

Kwa ba se ku ya bongwa ke ubaba, e bonga inyoka leyo ngezibongo zayo inkosi i sa hamba; be bonga nomamemkulu o zala ubaba. Ngokuba kwiti ku njalo. Itongo li hlala kumuntu omkulu, li kulume nayo; noma ku bongwa ekaya,

for I left them about to eat amasi in the house. Therefore I wished to close the gateway at once. But I took the first pole; it was heavy, I could not raise it; and it was the same with another; the poles were too heavy for me. I began to examine intently into the cause why the poles were too heavy, since they were old poles. I looked intently, and forsooth it was a great snake which was lying on them. I shouted. They came out of the house, and asked what it was. I replied, "Here is a snake."

My father came immediately, and looked intently, and said, "Do not close the gateway." I enquired, "What is it?" He said, "It is the chief." I said, "What, this snake?" He said, "Yes."

We returned to the house. In the morning he told us, saying, "The chief asks why you were afraid of him. Did he not tell us to make a bridge, that he might cross?"

Then my father gave praises, praising the snake with the laud-giving names which the chief had whilst living; praising in concert with our grandmother, the mother of my father. For such is the custom with us. The Itongo dwells with the great man, and speaks with him; and when worship is

ku bonga indoda enkulu nesalukazi esidala es' aziyo abantu a se ba fa.

Kwa ba njalo ke; kwa za kwa kupuka umuzi wenkosi omunye, w' eza lapa si kona. Loku ku ze kwa fika Ungoza, wa si kipa ngczwi likasomseu. Sa kciteka, sa ya ezindaweni eziningi. Nanso ke into e nga i bonako. I leyo ke.

Kwa ti ngemva kwaloko ya kupuka inkosi, Umyeka. Ku tiwa, "A ku yiwe enziweni, ku yiwe 'kubiza inkosi, uyise wenkosi; ngokuba kwa tiwa, umuzi u buba nje, ngokuba inkosi i nga vumanga ukweńla." Nembala ke kwa fikwa nenkomokazi, ikolokazi, ntambama; se ku ńlanganiswa izikulu zonke zamadoda namakeńla. Kw' enziwa igama likayise lomkosi, uku m vusa uku m kumbuza ukuba, "Nembala ba ya ńlupeka abantwana bami, ngokuba ngi ngeko kubo." I leli ke igama ela ńlatshelelwa, lokuti :—

"Limel' u ńlole amazimw[67] etu asesiwandiye.

chief man, and the oldest old woman, who knew those who are dead, who worship.

Under these circumstances, one of the chief's kraal at length came up to where we were living; and we lived together till Ungoza came and turned us out by the direction of Usomsou. We were scattered, and went to other places. That, then, is a thing which I saw.

After that Umyeka, the chief, came up. The people said, "Let us go to the old dwelling to call the chief, the present chief's father; for the village is perishing because the chief did not consent to go down to the coast." So then they brought a duncoloured cow in the afternoon; and all the chief men, both old and young, were assembled. They sang a song of their father which used to be sung on great festivals, to arouse him to the recollection that his children were truly in trouble because he was not among them. This is the song which was sung :—

"Dig for[68] the chief, and watch our gardens which are at Isiwandiye.[69]

---

[67] Amazimu *for* amasimu ; the z being used for s to give weight to the sound ; the u changed into w before the vowel in the following word.

[68] *Limel'*—dig for, not known for whom, but probably, as here translated, the chief.

[69] *Asesiwandiye*—Isiwandiye *for* Isiwandile. The name of a place, as if of a place where there were many gardens.

"Amanga lawo. Limel' u hlole amazimw etu asesiwandiye. Amanga lawo. Asesiwandiye, I-i-i-zi—asesiwandiye. Amanga lawo." Kw' enziwa umkumbu omkulu ngapandhle kwenxiwa. Kwa gujwa, loku se ku pelele abafazi notshwala nezintombi. Kwa za kwa kcitekwa, se li tshona, izulu se li na; kwa yiwa ekaya emzini wakwiti, lokupela utshwala bu y' esabeka ubuningi; kwa dhliwa ke utshwala nenyama, kwa kcwaywa umkcwayo.

Ku te ku se njalo kwa puma omunye o ikehla; ku tiwa Umahlati ibizo lake; u t' e buya wa e tsho ukuba "Inkosi se i fikile, si kcwaya nje. Nansi lapa se i butene kona pezu kwendhlu." Kwa boboswa indhlu pezulu, ukuze i buke umkcwayo. Kwa kcwaywa kwa za kwa nga ku nga sa ngokujabula okukulu, ukuba ku tiwa, "Idhlozi lakwiti li hlangene nati namuhla; umuzi u za 'kuma." Kwa ba njalo ke. Ukupela ke kwendaba leyo.

"Those words are naught.[70] Dig for the chief, and watch our gardens which are at Isiwandiye. Those words are naught. Which are at Isiwandiye, I-i-i-zi[71]—which are at Isiwandiye. Those words are naught." A large circle was formed outside the old site. They danced. There were there also all the women with beer, and the damsels. At length they separated when the sun was going down and it was raining, and they went home to our village, for the abundance of beer was fearful; so they consumed beer and meat, and sang hut-songs.[72]

In the midst of these doings, one of the young men, named Umathlati, went out; on his return he said, "The chief has come, even whilst we are singing. There he is, coiled up on the house." A hole was made in the house, that he might look on at the singing. They sang until it was near morning, rejoicing exceedingly because it was said, "The Idhlozi of our people has now united with us; our village will stand." Thus then it was. That is the end of the tale.

---

[70] *Those words are naught*,—that is, we object to dig at Isiwandile.

[71] *I-i-i-zi.*—Z in zi pronounced as in azure. This chorus is used for the purpose of emphatically asserting the subject of the song.

[72] The *umkcwayo* is a song which is sung in the hut, the singers sitting, and accompanying the song with regulated motions of the body.

Kepa lapa ya i hlala kona leyo 'nyoka, i b' i hlala otangweni esibayeni; kumbe na sendhlini cukulu; ngokuba ku be ku tiwa izinyoka eziningi pakati kwomuzi kwaleyo 'ndhlu enkulu, ku tiwa amanxusa enkosi, a hamba neukosi; ku tshiwo abantu aba fa nayo. Ngemva kwaloko ke ya nyamalala ekufikeni kwomuzi wenkosi; a ya be i sa vama ukubonwa lapo, i bonwe ngesinye isikati, ku be ukupela.

Imamba itongo lendhlu 'nkulu; abantu nje a ba penduki imamba, ba penduka imihlwazi, inyoka cluhlaza, imhlope ngapansi, ikanjana layo lincane. Ukuma kwayo, i bheka umuntu, a i bhekisi kwesilwane es' esaba ukubulawa, i bheka kahle nje; ku nga butana abantu abaningi kuwo umhlwazi. Kepa noma umuntu e u tinta ngento u nga baleki, u gudhluka nje. Umhlwazi isidanda esikulu ezinyokeni; endhlini u hamb' indhlu yonke, a w esabi 'ndawo, na pezulu u ya bonakala, na sezingutsheni u hlale; umuntu a tate kahle ingubo yake, a u shiye pansi, u ng' enzi 'luto. Ku tiwa u itongo.

UMPENGULA MBANDA.

And the place where the snake stayed was in the fence of the cattle-pen; and it may be even in the great house; and it was said that the many snakes which were in the village belonging to the great house, were the chief's attendants which accompanied him; they were said to be the men who were killed at the same time as the chief. After that he disappeared on the arrival of the chief's kraal; and was no longer seen frequently at our kraal, but only occasionally.

The imamba is the Itongo of the great house; the common people do not become izimamba, they become imithlazi; this snake is green and white on its belly, and has a very small head. Its custom is, when looking at a man, not to look like an animal which fears to be killed; it looks without alarm; and many people may gather around an umthlazi. And even if a man touches it with a stick, it does not run away, but just moves. The umthlwazi is much tamer than other snakes; it moves about the whole house, and fears nothing, and it is seen in the roof, and it remains among the garments; and a man takes up his garment gently and leaves the snake on the ground, and it does nothing. It is said to be an Itongo.

Removing from one country to another.

Ku ti uma ku za 'usukwa ku yiwe kwelinye izwe, uma ku bonwa ukuba itongo a ba li boni kulo 'muzi omutsha, la sal' emuva, ku gaulwe ihlahla lompafa, kumbe ku yiwe nenkomo, ku ye 'kuhlatshwa kona enxiweni, ku bongwe, li bizwe, kw enziwe amahhubo a e hhuba ngawo e sa hamba; loko isibonakaliso soku m kalela, ukuvusa umunyu, ngokuti, "Nembala, abanta bami ba nesizungu uma be nga ngi boni." Ku hholwe ihlahla lapa se ku hanjwa, ku yiwe nalo lapa ku yiwe kona. Kumbe i landele; kumbe y ale ngamazwi e nga tandi ngawo ukuya kuleyo 'ndawo, i kuluma nendodana ngepupa; kumbe nomuntu omdala walo 'muzi; noma inkosikazi endala.

When we are about to go to another country, if the people do not see the Itongo at the new village, it having staid behind, a branch of umpafa is cut, and perhaps they take a bullock with them, and go to sacrifice it at the old site; they give thanks, and call on the Itongo, and sing those songs which he used to sing whilst living; this is a sign of weeping for him, to excite pity, so that he may say, "Truly, my children are lonely because they do not see me." And the branch is dragged when they set out, and they go with it to the new village. Perhaps the snake follows; perhaps it refuses, giving reasons why it does not wish to go to that place, speaking to the eldest son in a dream; or it may be to an old man of the village; or the old queen.

Royal Attendants.

Amanxusa abantu benkosi njengezinceku, aba hamba nayo; ku ti noma se i file inkosi, kakulu uma i bulawa, i bulawa namanxusa, ukuze a i lungisele pambili, nokudhla a i funele. Kakulu kiti ku

Amanxusa are people of a chief like servants, who go about in company with him; and even when the chief is dead, and especially if he has been killed together with his Amanxusa, they go with him, that they may prepare things before hand, and get food for him. It was especially the

be ku ti endulo, uma ku fe inkosi, i nga fi yodwa; lokupela be be tshiswa abantu kukqala; se i file inkosi, ngam/la i pum' ekaya, se i ya 'ula/ilwa, ku /lonywe izi/langu, ku vunulwe kakulu imvunulo yempi. Ku ti uma ku fikwe endaweni lapa inkosi i za 'utshiswa kona, ku gaulwe izinkuni eziningi; loku neziukabi zi kona futi, ku ti inkabi yayo e d/lala umkosi ngayo i /latshwe nayo, kunye nayo, i fe njengayo. Ku ti uma umlilo u vuta, i fakwe; ku be se ku ketwa izinceku zayo, zi i landele; ku landwe izikulu, zi tatwe ngaziuye. Ku tiwe, "Ubani u fanele a hambe nenkosi." Ku ti lapa umlilo u kqala ukulota, ku tiwe, "Kwezela, 'bani." A ti lapa e ti u /langanisa izikuni, ba m fake kona; zonke izikulu ku hambe ku tatwe ngabanye ezind/lini ezinkulu zomdeni naba nge 'mdeni; ku fe abantu abaningi ngalelo 'langa. Nanko ke aman*x*usa.

Ku be se ku ti uma inkosi i file ba tubelise abantwana babo; abanye ngokuti, "Ngi y' azi ukuba uma ngi vumela ukuba umntanami

case with us at first, when a chief died, he did not die alone; for at first the bodies of the dead were burnt, and when a chief died, and they went from their home to dispose of the remains, they took shields and adorned themselves with their military ornaments; and when they came to the place where the remains of the chief were to be burnt, they cut down much firewood; and as there were oxen there too, the chief ox with which he made royal festivals was killed with him, that it might die with him. When the fire was kindled, the chief was put in; and then his servants were chosen, and put into the fire after the chief; the great men followed, they were taken one by one. They said, "So-and-so is fit to go with the chief." When the fire began to sink down, they said, "Put the fire together, So-and-so." And when he was putting the firewood together, they cast him in; they went and took all the great men one by one from the chief houses of the chief's brothers, and from those who were not his brothers. Many people were killed on that day. Such then are the Amanxusa.

When a chief dies the people conceal their children; some saying, "I know that if I let my

a ye lapa ku fele inkosi kona, ka sa yi 'kubuya." Ba vame uku ba tubelisa. Nokugula futi abanye ba zigulise, ba bikwe kakulu, ku tiwe, "Ubani a si ko nako ukufa."

I ti uma i tshe i ti du, ku be se ku tatwa umlota wonke, u ye u telwe esizibeni.

Amanxusa abantu aba be konza Utshaka. Ku ti emva kwokufa kwake zonke izikulu zake eza zi m konza, za ti uba zi fe za hlangana naye ukuya 'u m konza. Ku tiwa ku kona izinyoka eziningi; lezo 'nyoka ku tiwa amanxusa; zi kona kwazulu; ku ti lapa ku bonwa Utshaka, nazo zi be zi kona; ngokuba ku tiwa u imamba enkulu; u ya bonwa ngezikati zonke e landelwa izinyoka; ku tiwe amanxusa ake. Ngesinye isikati ku tiwa wa ka wa bonwa e lwa nodingane, lapa se be file bobabili; ba lwa isikati eside; kwa za kwa puma impi eningi ukuya 'ku ku bona loko 'kulwa. Ku tiwa Umpande wa tanda ukwelamulela Utshaka, a bulale Udingane, ngokuba wa e tanda uku m bulala; wa sinda ngondhlela.

Amanxusa a hlala endhlini en-

child go to the place where the king has died, he will never come back again." So they usually conceal them. Others too feign sickness, and cause the report of their sickness to be spread abroad in all directions; they say, "So-and-so is very ill indeed."

When the chief is entirely consumed, they take the ashes and throw them into a pool of the river.

Amanxusa are men who used to wait upon Utshaka. And after his death all the great men who used to wait on him, when they died, joined him that they might wait on him. It is said there are many snakes among the Amazulu; these snakes are Amanxusa; when Utshaka is seen, then too are seen the snakes; for it is said he is a large imamba; he is seen continually, followed by snakes; and they are all said to be Amanxusa. It is said that he was once seen fighting with Udingane, when both were dead; they fought a long time, until at length a very great number went out to see the fight. It is said Umpande wished to help Utshaka and kill Udingane, because Udingane had wished to kill Umpande, but Undhlela[73] saved him.

The Amanxusa remain in the

---

[73] An officer under Udingane.

kulu kwabo kankosi kwiti emapepeteni. Amanzusa a be hlala endhlini kasokane, umuntu omkulu. Owesifazana ngolunye usuku a ti, "Ngi ya hlupeka. Ngesinye isikati ngi kohlwa nokubeka izitsha nje, ngi vinjelwa izinyoka." Aba z' aziyo lezo 'nyoka ba ti, "Amanzusa enkosi; abantu aba be hamba nayo inkosi."

UMPENGULA MBANDA.

chief house of our chief among the Amapepete. The Amanzusa used to remain in Usokane's[74] house, a great man. One day a woman said, "I am troubled. I am sometimes unable even to put down a vessel, there being always snakes in the way." Those who knew them said, "They are Amanzusa of the chief; people who were living with the chief before he died."

Izalukazana.

ISALUKAZANA ku tiwa itongo lomuntu wesifazana owa e se gugile.

Ku kona indaba ngesalukazana, isilwanyana esi fana nentulwa; kepa si nge si yo; si uhlobo lwesibankhwa; kepa isibankhwa sibutshelezi, sinsundu ngapezulu, ngapansi ku nga simhlope. Kepa leso 'salukazana sibana, si ihhambana kakulu; a si tandeki; kepa si lulana, si tshetsha ukusuka masinyane. Kepa a si vami ukubaleka, si vama ukukcatsha. Ku ti uma umuntu e si bona ngalapa, si be se si ti bande ngalapaya. Uma u ya ngakona, si pambane nawe. Uma u si bone kukqala, sa tshetsha ukwebanda. Uma u kombisa umuntu, u ti, "Isilwanyana ngi si bone lapa," se si te site ngalapaya. A nga ti, "A si

THE lizard is said to be the Itongo of an old woman.

There is a tale about the isalukazana, an animal which resembles the intulwa; but it is not an intulwa; it is a kind of isibankhwa; but the isibankhwa is smooth, and purple on its back, and whitish on its belly. But the isalukazana is rather ugly, and very rough; it is not liked; and it is active, and runs away quickly. But it does not commonly run away, but hides itself. And if a man sees it on this side of any thing, it at once goes round to the opposite side. If you see it first, it makes haste to go round to the other side. If you point it out to another, saying, "I saw an animal here," it is already hidden on the other side. He may say, "Let us look;" but

---

[74] A very old man, who had grown up with Umaziya, the king.

bheko;" kepa si bone isitunzi somuntu si vela, si penduke, si pambane naso. A nga ze a ku pikise, a ti, "Ku njani ukuba umdala kangaka u kqamba 'manga na?" A ze a be isiula lowo o be si bonile, ngokuba emva ka sa si boni. Ba nga ze ba si bone uma b' aẖlukana, omunye 'eme, omunye a zungeze umuti; ba si bone ke; lapa si balekela omunye, si vele ngakomunye.

Ku ti uma si funwa endẖlini, si te kcatsha otingweni, noma u sensikeni; omdala a si bone kumbe, a nga tsho 'luto, a nga tandi ukwandisa indaba; ngokuba ku tiwa mubi umuntu emdala a bone into e njengomẖlola. U ẖlup' abantu; ba ya 'kutshaywa izinvalo, ba ẖlale be kcabanga ngaleyo 'nto e boniweko. Ku ti uma ku vela umkuba omubi pakati kwomuzi, leso 'salukazana si nga yekile ukubonakala kuleyo 'ndawo, ku tiwe i sona si bika ukufa. A i zeke ke indaba lo owa si bonako, a ti, "Kunsuku ngi bona isalukazana kamabani. Nga ngi ti, a ku yi 'kuvela 'luto; nga i fiẖla leyo 'ndaba. Kepa loku naku se ku vele umkuba, kuẖle kw aziwe."

Abanye ba ti, "A ku yobulwa." Abanye ba ti, "Ku sa funwa ni? loku naku umẖlola se u vele nje

it sees the shadow of the man as soon as it appears, and turns back in the opposite direction. Until he disputes, saying, "How is it that one so old as you tells lies?" And the one who saw it appears foolish, for he no longer sees it. They may see it if they separate, and one stands still, and the other goes round the tree; for so they see it; when it runs away from one of them, it appears to the other.

If it is seen in the house, it hides itself among the wattles, or it may be on the post of the house; perhaps an old person sees it, but says nothing, not wishing to make much of the affair; for they say an old person is wicked if he see a thing which is like an omen. He troubles the people; they will be smitten with fear, and continue to think of that which has been seen. If something bad happens in the village, the isalukazana is seen continually in the same place, and it is said to prognosticate death. Then he who saw it says, "For some days I have seen an isalukazana in So-and-so's hut. I said nothing will come of it; and hid what I had seen. But now since the evil has come, it is proper that it should be known."

Some say, "Let us go to the diviner." Others say, "What do we want? See, there is the omen

na ? Kuhle ku funwe into uma i kona, leso 'salukazana si kxotshwe si muke." Nembala ke ku hlatshwe imbuzi, noma itole.

Ku tiwa isalukazana ukubizwa kwalezo 'zilwanyazana. A ku tshiwo itongo lendoda nelabantwana; ku tiwa itongo lomuntu wesifazana owa e se gugile. Futi a ku tshiwo ukuti ubani igama lake. Isalukazana njalo ukubizwa kwaso; a s' aziwa uma isalukazana esi unobani igama laso.

Kepa lezo 'zalukazana kubantu abamnyama zi ya zondeka; a zi fani netongo eli inyoka; ngokuba lapa be bona isalukazana, ba ya hlupeka ngokwazi ukuba isalukazana si 'muva-mubi,—umuva waso a u muhle. Ku ti ku nga vela sona, ku be kona umkuhlane omningi pakati kwomuzi, u vame ukututa abantu. Ku be se ku tiwa umuva wesalukazana lowo; noma umuntu wa gwazwa impi, ku be ku ke kwa bonwa isalukazana endhlini yakwake. Ku be se ku tshiwo njalo, ku tiwa umuva waso.

Kepa ku te uba nati si i zwe leyo 'ndaba, si kule ng' ezwa umamemkulu, o zala ubaba, e kuluma ngazo izalukazana, lapa mina ngi zi tshaya esibayeni ngamatshe.

come of its own accord. It is proper to get something if there is such a thing, to send away the isalukazana." And so they sacrifice a goat or a calf.

These animals are called isalukazana [little old women]. It is not said to be the Itongo of a man or of a child; but the Itongo of some old woman. Neither is it called by the name of any particular person. It is merely called isalukazana; it is not known who the isalukazana is.

But these lizards are hateful to black men; they are not like the Itongo which is a snake; for when they see an isalukazana, they are troubled because they know that it is an omen of future evil,—that evil comes in its train. Perhaps it appears, and then much fever occurs in the village, which carries off many people. And that is said to be in the train of the isalukazana; or a man is stabbed in battle, after an isalukazana has been seen in his house. And so that too is said to be something which has come in the train of the isalukazana.

But we heard this tale from our grandmother, our father's mother; she told us about these lizards when I killed some in the cattle-pen with stones. For they are

Ngokuba izilwanyana ezi tanda kakulu izigcagi ngenkati yobusika. Ku ti ukupuma kwelanga u si fumane si te ne otini ukunamatela, s' ota ilanga. Ngaloko ke uku si bulala kwami nga m tshela ukulu, nga ti, "Ngi bulele lapa esibayeni izibankhwana ezi ihhambana." Ukulu a ngi tetise ngokuti, "Izalukazana lezo abaninimuzi; a zi bulawa; zi y' esatshwa." Kepa si bone ku isilwane nje isibili sasen*h*le; si goduswe ngemilomo ukuletwa ekaya. Kepa a ku banga 'keala ngesikati soku zi bulala kwami; kepa amadoda, lapa be zi bona, ba *h*lale se be bheke indaba e za 'uvela.

Ku ti uma zi bonwa futifuti, ku vele isifo, ku *h*latshwe nenkomo uma i kona, ku tiwe, "A zi d*h*le, zi goduke. Zi funa ni ekaya lapa na? Ini ukuba zi be impi yokubulala umuzi? A zi goduke. Naku ukud*h*la kwenu. Yid*h*la ni, ni hambe." Kepa noma ku tshiwo njalo, a zi muki; ku se si zi bona lapa zi be zi kona izolo. Kodwa abadala a b' esabi ngemva kwokukeola, ngokuba ba ti, "A si se nakeala, loku se si keolile."

animals which are very fond of the sunshine during winter. When the sun rises you can find them sticking to a post, basking in the sun. So then when I killed them I told grandmother, saying, "I have killed some little rough lizards in the cattle-pen." Grandmother reproved me, saying, "Those lizards are chiefs of the village; they are not killed; they are reverenced." But we saw it was a mere wild animal; it became domestic from being called an Itongo by the people. But no evil consequences arose when I killed them; but when the men saw them, they constantly looked out for some evil to arise.

If they are frequently seen, and disease arises, a bullock is sacrificed if there is one, and the people say, "Eat, and go home. What do you want here? Why are you an enemy come to destroy the village? Go home. Here is food for you. Eat and depart." But though they say thus, they do not depart; on the following day we still see them where they were the day before. But the old people are not afraid afterwards, for they say, "We are no longer guilty of aught, for we have paid a ransom."

Crying at the Holes from which Medicines have been dug.

Isiмo sabantu abamnyama aba izinyanga, lapa inyanga i mba umuti, i mba i bonga itongo kona lapo, ukuti, "Nansi inkomo, nina 'bakwiti. Lo 'muti ngi u mba nje, ngi temba nina, ukuba ni u nike amandhla, u kipe ukufa kulo 'muntu o gulayo, ukuze ngi nconywe ezizweni ukuba ngi inyanga ngani, 'bakwiti."

Ngaloko ke umuti u u mba ngenhliziyo emhlope, e bheke ukuba ku sinde lowo 'muntu. Kepa uma 'elapile, labo 'bantu ba linga uku mu dhla ngobukqili, nokuti, "O, a si ti kuye, umuti wako nga u dhla, a ngi zuzanga 'sikala sokupumula. Kwa ba ngi dhle amabele nje." Ngokuba loko kubantu abamnyama ku vamile ukufihla amandhla omuti; ba ingcozana aba dumisa imiti. Ngalobo 'bukqili se kwa za kwa funwa izinsaba emakcaleni. Inyanga i ti, "Wena, 'bani, u ye u ngi bekele indhlebe. Nank' umuti wami. Ngi ya 'ku ku vuza. Ngi y' azi ukuba ba ya 'ku u fihla, ba ti, a w enzanga 'luto, b' enqena ukukoka inkomo. Ngaloko ke ngi misa wena, ukuze u ngi bhekele."

It is a custom with black doctors, for a doctor when digging up medicines, to dig worshipping the Itongo at the place where he is digging; he says, "Here is a bullock I may gain, ye people of ours. I dig up this medicine trusting in you, that you will give it power to take away the disease from the sick man, that I may become celebrated among the nations, as a great doctor, by your power, ye people of ours."

He digs up the medicine, then, with a pure heart, expecting the man to get well. But when he has applied his medicines, the people try to eat him up by craft, and say, "Let us tell him that I took his medicine, but gained no relief. It was as though I had taken nothing but corn." For it is common among black men to conceal the power of medicines; they are but few who praise them. In consequence of this craft there came to be appointed secret spies. The doctor says to a man, "So-and-so, do you go and listen for me. There is my medicine. I know that the people will conceal its efficacy, and say it was useless, for they are slow in giving me a bullock. I therefore appoint you to look out for me."

Nembala ke, lapa e s' elapile, a *h*lomele ukuzwa indaba yenkubele yake, ukuti u za 'kuzwa uma se ku njani na. Ku be i loku e tsho njalo, ngokuti, "O, wena kabani, ngi sa gula; a ngi k' ezwa 'ndawo emnandi, nomuti wako lowo kwa ba ngi d*h*le amabele nje." A ma-ngale umniniwo ow aziyo ukwenza kwawo ngapakati kumuntu, 'ezwe umuntu e landula nokukipa ububi ngapakati, a ti, "K*q*a; kwa puma amanzi nje." Kepa in*h*lomeli yake i mu tshele ukuti, "Umuti wako wa sobenza kulo 'muntu; ba ya ku ko*h*lisa; u se hamba emaja-dwini na sematshwaleni; u se si-ndile. Kepa inkomo i be lukuni ukupuma; ku kule ukugula kuno-kupila."

Inyanga i ze i tsho ukuti, "Ba-ni, loku u ti wena a u yi 'ku ngi nika inkomo, se ngi za 'kuya 'ku-mbulula amagodi e ng' emba imiti yoku kw elapa kuwo; ngi kale kuwo. Ku kona oku ya 'uvela kuwe, uma nga u ngi d*h*la inkomo yami ngamakeebo. U ze u nga tsho ukuba ngi umtakati. Sa u *h*lala nenkomo leyo. A ngi sa i funi."

Uma nembala e m ko*h*lisa, 'ale, a ti, "O, wena kabani, mina a ngi

So then when he has treated the patient, he waits to hear what happens, that he may know how he is. And when he hears him say, " O, Son of So-and-so, I am still ill; as yet I am in pain all over; and as to that medicine of yours, it was as if I had only eaten corn." So the owner of the medicine wonders who understands its action in the human body, when he hears the man denying that it even brought any thing away, saying, "No; there came away nothing but water." But his spy tells him that his medicine worked well in the man; that the people deceive him, and the man now goes to wedding-dances and to beer-drinkings; that he is quite well. But it is hard for him to give a bullock; he makes more of the disease which remains than of the health which has been restored.

At length the doctor says, "So-and-so, since you refuse to give me a bullock, I shall now remember the holes where I dug up the medicine which has cured you; and cry there. Something will happen to you, if you eat my bul-lock deceitfully. Do not say I am a sorcerer. Keep the bullock. I no longer wish to have it."

If he is really deceiving him, he refuses, saying, "O, Son of So-

tsho ukuba se w aḥlulekile ; ngi ti mina u inyanga yami, noma umuti wako nga u dḥla, a nga bona 'luto ; kepa umzimba ku nga ti u nga ba owomuntu, uma u naka u ngi funel' imiti. Inkomo yako u mina. U ti wena, uma ngi sindile njalo, ngi nga zifiḥla kanjani na? Musa ukuti u za 'ukala emagodini. Wo ba se u ya ngi bulala uma w enze njalo. Ng' elape nje. Inkomo yako se i kona."

Uma e nga vumelani nenyanga, nembala ke iuyanga i vuke ekuseni ngenḥliziyo ebuḥlungu kakulu ngokuzwa ngaofakazi ukuba lo 'muntu u m sizile ; kep' a nga vumi yena ukuba u siziwe. A ye ke emagodini, e ya 'ku wa panda, e kala izinyembezi, e kuluma ngokuḥlupeka kwake, e kuluma namatongo akubo, ukuba, "Ku ngani ukuba ni dḥliwe umuntu, kanti ngi m elape, wa sinda na? A ku bonakale okonakona. Inkomo yami i nge dḥliwe umuntu o hamba ngezinyawo ; a kwaḥluke imiti yami ; a i nga bi ize nje. Ngi kuluma nani nina, kw eyenu. Ng' elapa ngani. Kumnandi ini uma ni dḥliwa izinkomo na?"

Lapo ke u tsho njalo e kala.

and-so, for my part I do not say the disease has beaten you ; I say you are my doctor, although I took your medicine without feeling any effects from it ; yet it feels as if my body was about to be that of a man, if you persevere in getting medicines for me. I am your bullock. How do you think, if I get well, I can hide myself? Do not talk about crying at the holes where you dug up the medicines. You will kill me if you do so. Just doctor me. Your bullock is ready for you."

If he does not agree with him, the doctor awakes in the morning with his heart much pained because he hears from witnesses that he has really helped the man ; but he will not allow that he has been helped. So he goes to the holes where he dug up the medicines, and scrapes away the earth and sheds tears, and tells the Amatongo of his trouble, saying, "Why are you eaten up by a man whom I have cured? Let the truth appear. Let not my bullock be eaten by a living man ; let the power of my medicines be evident, and not be a mere vain thing. I tell you, the medicines were yours. I cured him by your power. Is it pleasant to have your cattle eaten?"

He says this weeping. For it

Ngokuba ku tiwa, amagodi uma e mbululwa ku kalwa, lowo 'muntu ka yi 'kulunga, uma nembala e fihla amandhla emiti; u ya 'kufa. Ku njalo ke. Kwiti ku y' esabeka ukuba inyanga i yokala emagodini; ngaloko ku tiwa, ku bang' ukufa loko 'kwenza njalo kwenyanga. I loko ke ukukala emagodini.

is said if the holes where the medicines were dug up be opened, and the doctor weeps there, the man will be ill and die, if he has really concealed the power of the medicines. Thus it is. With us it is a fearful thing that the doctor should go to the holes to cry; and it is said if he does so he calls down death on the patient. This, then, is what is meant by crying at the holes.

Sneezing.

UKUTIMULA kubantu abamnyama ku tiwa ku isibonakaliso senhlanhla yokuba umuntu u se nokupila. U ya bonga ngemva kwokutimula, a ti, "Nina 'bakwiti, ukuhamba okuhle ngi zuze e ngi ku sweleyo. Ni ngi bheke." Isikati sokutimula isikumbuzo sokuba umuntu a pate itongo lakubo masinyane, ngokuti, "I lona eli ngi pa loku 'kutimula, ukuze ngi li bone ngako ukuba li se nami."

Ku ti uma umuntu e gula e nga timuli, ku ya buzwa ku tiwe ab' ezo'u m bona, "U ke a timule nje na?" be buzela ukuze b' eme isibindi sokuba ukufa loko ku ya 'ubuye ku dhlule. Uma e nga timuli ba kununde ngokuti ukufa kukulu. Ku njalo ke.

AMONG black men sneezing is said to be a lucky sign that a person will now be restored to health. He returns thanks after sneezing, saying, "Ye people of ours, I have gained that prosperity which I wanted. Continue to look on me with favour." Sneezing reminds a man that he should name the Itongo of his people without delay, because it is the Itongo which causes him to sneeze, that he may perceive by sneezing that the Itongo is with him.

If a man is ill and does not sneeze, those who come to see him ask whether he has sneezed or not. They ask that they may take heart and believe that the disease will pass away. If he has not sneezed, they murmur, saying, "The disease is great."

Nengane uma i timula, kuyo ke ku tiwa, "Tutuka!" ku tshiwo ukuhambela pambili enhlanhleni njalo. Ku isibonakaliso sokupila kwomuntu, nesokupatwa itongo.

Ku njalo ke ukutimula kubantu abamnyama ku vusa amandhla okuba umuntu a kumbule ukuba itongo li ngene, li kumina. A bonge ngokutokoza okukulu, e nga ngabazi ngako loko.

Lapa umuntu e ti "Makosi" ekutimuleni, ka tandi ukuti, "Ba-ni wakiti," ngokuba e ng' azi ukuba u mu pi o yena e mu pe loku 'kupila na; ku ngaloko ke u ya hlanganisa ngokuti, "Makosi, ni nga ngi fulateli." Uma e ti, "Baba," lowo u ya kuluma, kumbe wa timula ngesikati uyise e s' and' ukububa, inhliziyo i nga ka kohlwa u ye; u tsho ke ukuti, "Baba, u ngi bheke, ngi be nenhlanhla kuloko e ngi nge nako."

Noma unina, a tsho njalo, uku-ti, "Mame, u nga ngi fulateli." Futi ku tiwa, "Bobaba," e hlanganisa amatongo akubo onke, abafo baoyise, a se ba fa; a ti, "Bobaba, ni ngi bheke, ni nga ngi fulateli." Noma ku nge si bo aoyisekazi ngesibili, kepa loku se

And if a child sneezes, it is said to it, "Grow!" meaning by this that it should continually advance in prosperity. It is a sign of a man's health, and that the Itongo is with him.

So then sneezing among black men gives a man strength to remember that the Itongo has entered into him and abides with him. And he returns thanks with great joy, having no doubt about it.

When a man, on sneezing, says, "Chiefs," it is because he does not like to say, "So-and-so of our people," because he does not know who it is of the Amatongo who has bestowed on him the benefit; therefore he puts them all together and says, "Chiefs, do not turn your back on me." When he says, "My father," the man who speaks sneezes, perhaps, shortly after his father's death, and his heart does not yet forget him; and so he says, "Father, look upon me, that I may be blessed in such matters as at present I have not."

Or if his mother has lately died he says in like manner, "My mother, do not turn thy back on me." He says, "My fathers," uniting in one all the Amatongo of his people, the brothers of his fathers who are dead; and so he says, "Fathers, look upon me, and do not turn your back on me." And though they may not be in reality his

be file, se be abalondolozi, u ti, "Bobaba," ngaloko.

Amakxosa a ti, "Tikxo wakowetu, ngi bheke, u be nami njalo, ngi hambe ngenhlanhla." A kwazeki uma ku nga ka tshiwo ukuti Utikxo u yena e itongo lawo Amakxosa, a e ti ni na. Manje amakolwa lapa e timula a wa sa tsho ukuti "Baba" etongweni; a se ti, "Mlondolozi, u ngi bheke," noma "Menzi wezulu nomhlaba." Ku gukqulwe ke njalo loko o be ku kona.

father's brothers, yet since they are dead they are now preservers, and therefore he says, "My fathers."

The Amakxosa say, "Utikxo of our people, look upon me, and be ever with me, that I may live in prosperity." It is not known what they used to say before they used the word Utikxo, who is the Itongo of the Amakxosa.[75] And now among the Amakxosa believers when they sneeze no longer say to the Itongo "Father," but, "Preserver, look upon me," or, "Creator of heaven and earth." Thus a change has taken place.

Ukutimula kubantu abamnyama ba ku biza ngegama lokuti, "Ngi sa pilile. Idhlozi li nami; li fikile kumi. A ngi tshetshe ngi bonge kulo, ngokuba i lo eli ti, 'A ngi timule.' Ngemva kwokutimula ngi ya 'kubona izinto e ngi fanele ukubonga ngazo kwabakwiti, ukuti, ' Nina 'basekutini, e na ti na ti, ngi keela kuni ukuba ngi zuze izinkomo nabantwana nabafazi, ngi zale kubo, ukuze igama lenu li

When a man among black men sneezes, he says, "I am now blessed. The Idhlozi is with me; it has come to me. Let me hasten and praise it, for it is it which causes me to sneeze. As I have sneezed, I will see the things for which it is proper for me to praise the spirits of the dead belonging to our family, and say, 'Ye of such a place, which did such and such great actions, I ask of you that I may get cattle and children and wives, and have children by them, that your name may not

---

[75] Utikxo is supposed to be a word not originally used by the nations who speak the alliterative class of language; but to be derived from the Hottentot Tikqwa. It is now, however, used by the Amakxosa generally, whether Christian or not. But it is not known when the word was first introduced among them, or what have been the causes of its being universally adopted.

nga siteki; ku hlale ku tiwe, U kwabani lapaya. Ngokuba uma ngi nge nanzalo, a ku yi 'kutshiwo ukuti, U kwabani lapaya. Uma ngi ngedwa, mhlaumbe ngi ya 'kuhlala emhlabeni; lapa ngi nge nanzalo, ukufa kwami li ya 'kupela igama lami; ni ya 'kuzwa se ni dhla izintete; ngokuba ngaleso 'sikati sokufa kwami u ya 'kuba u se u wile umuzi, a ni 'kungena 'ndawo; ni ya 'kufa amakaza ezintabeni. Amanye amadhlozi a ya busisa abantu bawo. Nami ngi ti, Ngi pe ni kakulu; ni nga ngi kohli. Ku ini ukuba n' ahlulwe i mi, ngi ngedwa na? Uma si ba ningi, nga ku njani na?'"

perish, but it may still be said, That is the village of So-and-so yonder. For if I have no children, it will not be said, That is the village of So-and-so yonder. If I am alone, it may be I shall live long on the earth; if I have no children, at my death my name will come to an end; and you will be in trouble when you have to eat grasshoppers; for at the time of my death my village will come to an end, and you will have no place into which you can enter; you will die[76] of cold on the mountains. Other Amadhlozi bless their people. And I too say, Give me abundantly; do not forget me. Why are you unable to give me, I being alone? If we were many, how would it be?'"

Vows to Sacrifice to the Amatongo.

UMA ku gula umuntu, kepa ku nge ko isikati soku i hlaba inkomo, ngokuba a ku yiwanga enyangeni, ku tiwa umninimntwana ematongweni, "Uma ku i nina, 'bakwiti

IF a person is ill, and there is not time to sacrifice an ox, for they have not been to a diviner, the father of the child addresses the Amatongo thus:—"If it is you,

---

[76] He does not speak of the actual death of the Amatongo; for the people believe that the Amatongo do not die, but of their suffering from cold. In another place we read of killing an imamba which was the Itongo of Udingane. Under such circumstances the people say, "I pind' i vuke," It comes to life again. And they say it is the same identical snake which rises to life again, for if it has been killed by any particular wound, it will have the mark of the wound on its body.

ab' enza nje, ngi beka; nansi inkomo etile; ka sinde Ubani, ni i dhle." Noma e nga tsho "ukubeka" kakulu, a ti, "Ngi misa inkomo; nansi; ka sinde." Uma i nge ko inkomo, u ya kala uyise ngokuti, "Po, uma ni funa inyama, ku njani ukuba ni nga m pilisi, ngi hambe ngi i tate inkomo na, ngi ni hlabele, ni dhle? Ngi ya 'kubona kanjani uma e nga vuki na ukuba i nina?" A nga tsho ukuti, "Ngi ni misela ukuya 'kulanda inkomo," ukuti ke, "Ngi linde ni; ngi ya 'ku ni funela, ngi fike nenkomo yenu."

people of our house, who are doing this, I make a vow; behold there is such and such a bullock; let the child get well, that you may eat." Or he may not say "devote," but, "I set apart a bullock; there it is. Let the child get well." Or if he does not possess a bullock, the father cries, saying, "If you wish for food, why do you not cure my child, that I may go and get you a bullock, and kill it for you, that you may eat? How shall I know that it is you, if the child does not get well?" Or he may say, "I vow to you to go and fetch you a bullock," that is, "Wait for me; I am going to find you a bullock, and will bring it home for you."

It may be worth while to note the curious coincidence of thought among the Amazulu regarding the Amatongo or Abapansi, and that of the Scotch and Irish regarding the fairies or "good people."

For instance, the "good people" of the Irish have ascribed to them in many respects the same motives and actions as the Amatongo. They call the living to join them, that is, by death; they cause disease which common doctors cannot understand, nor cure; they have their feelings, interests, partialities, and antipathies, and contend with each other about the living. The common people call them their friends or people, which is equivalent to the term *abakubo* given to the Amatongo. They reveal themselves in the form of the dead, and it appears to be supposed that the dead become "good people," as the dead among the Amazulu become Amatongo: and in the funeral processions of the "good people," which some have professed to see, are recognised the forms of those who have just died; as Umkatshana saw his relatives among the Abapansi.[77] And the power of holding communion with the "good people" is consequent on an illness, just as the power to divine among the natives of this country.[78]

So also in the Highland Tales, a boy who had been carried away by the fairies, on his return to his home speaks of them as "our folks," which is equivalent to *abakwetu*, applied to the Amatongo.[79] And among the Highlanders they are called "the good people," "the folk." They are also said to "live underground," and are therefore Abapansi, or Subterraneans.[80]

They are also, like the Abapansi, called ancestors. Thus "the Red Book of Clanrannald is said not to have been dug up, but to have been found *on* the moss. It seemed as if the ancestors sent it."[81]

---

[77] See Nursery Tales of the Zulus, p. 317.
[78] See Croker's Fairy Legends, especially "The Confessions of Tom Bourke," p. 46.
[79] Campbell. Vol. II., p. 56.
[80] Id., p. 65, 66.
[81] Id., Vol. II., p. 106.

DREAMS, &c.

DREAMS, subjective apparitions, and similar psychical phenomena are in the native mind so intimately wrapped up with the Amatongo, that this is the proper place for considering their views on such matters, without which their views on the Amatongo would be incomplete.

The Amatongo make revelations by Dreams.

UMA u lele wa pupa umuntu o nga m azelele ukuba a nga kw enza kabi ; kepa ku ti ebusuku u lele, u bone e ku gwaza ngoku ku zuma, e nga ku gwazi obala, e ku d*h*la imfi*h*lo, uma se u vuka, u ya mangala kakulu, u ti, " Wau ! Kanti Ubani lo, ngi ti, umuntu omu*h*le nje, kanti u ya ngi zonda na?" U ti, "Ngi ya'li bonga itongo lakwiti eli veze lo 'muntu kumina, ngi nga m azi. Manje ngi nga m azi, loku itongo se li m tikisile. Wa fika e ngi bulala, ngi nga lw azi uluto lwake e ngi lu d*h*lile." U *h*lale, u m *h*lakanipile lowo 'muntu ngokuti, " Leli 'pupo a li tsho 'manga ; i kona indaba e ngi nga y aziyo, e kulo 'muntu."

Futi uma u lele u pupe isilwane si ku zingela, si funa uku ku bulala, ku ti uma u vuke, u mangale u ti, " Hau ! Ku njani loku, uma ngi pupe isilo si ngi zingela ?" Ku ti uma ku ya 'uzingelwa kusasa,

IF during sleep you dream of a man whom you do not thoroughly know to be of such a character that he may do you an injury ; yet if in your sleep you dream that he suddenly stabs you, not openly, but by stealth, when you awake you are much amazed and say, " Oh ! Forsooth I thought such a one a really good man. And does he hate me ? I thank the Itongo of our people which has revealed the man to me, that I may know him. Now I know him, for the Itongo has caused him to approach me. And he came to kill me. I do not know in what respect I have injured him." And you continue on your guard against the man, believing that the dream does not lie, but that there is something in the man with which you are not acquainted.

Again, if in your sleep you dream of a beast pursuing you and trying to kill you, when you wake you wonder and say, " How is this that I should dream of a wild beast pursuing me ?" And if in the morning they are going to

noma izilo noma izinyamazane, u hambe w azi ukuba "Ngi sengozini;" w azi ukuba "Lesi 'silo si letwe itongo, ukuze ng' azi ukuba uma ngi nga bheki, ngi nga fa." Uma u ya enk*q*ineni, u ye se u *h*lakanipile. Kumbe u nga yi, ngokuti, "Isalakutshelwa si zwa ngomopo." U ti, "A ngi *h*lale." U *h*lale, u zilondolozile, ngokuti, "Ngi sa funa kupi, loku itongo se li ngi tshelile, ukuba ngi ya empini?"

Futi, uma u lele ubutongo, u pupe u buyela kwabakini, uma w' a*h*lukana nabo isikati se si side; u bone be *h*lezi kabi, aobani naobani; u vuka umzimba u mude; w azi ukuba "Itongo eli ngi yise kulabo bakwiti, ukuze ngi bone lobo 'bubi a ba nabo; uma ngi ya kona, i kona indaba e ngi nga i fumana kona yoku*h*lala kabi." U *h*lale u beke ind*h*lebe, u *h*lomele ukuti, "Ngi ya 'kuzwa indaba, uma ku kona umuntu." Nembala ku ti ku nga fika umuntu wangakona, u buze in*h*lalo yabakini. Uma e ku tshela uku*h*lala kubi, u

hunt, whether wild beasts or game, you go knowing that you are in jeopardy; you know that the Itongo brought the beast to you, that you might know that if you do not take care you may die. If you go to the hunt, you are on your guard. Perhaps you do not go, saying, "Isalakutshelwa hears through trouble.[82] Let me stay at home." And you stay at home and take care of yourself, saying, "What do I want further, when the Itongo has already told me that I am going into danger?"[83]

Again, if during sleep you dream of returning to your people from whom you separated a long time ago; and see that So-and-so and So-and-so are unhappy; and when you wake your body is unstrung;[84] you know that the Itongo has taken you to your people that you might see the trouble in which they are; and that if you go to them you will find out the cause of their unhappiness. And you continue listening and expecting to hear news if any one comes. And truly a man may come from the neighbourhood, and you ask after the welfare of your people. If he tells you they are in bad circumstances, you say, "O, I mere-

---

[82] *Is'-ala-'kutshelwa*, He who when told refuses to listen, hears in the time of trouble. A proverbial saying. Another form is, *Ihlonga-'ndhlebe li zwa ngomopo*, He who is without an ear hears in the time of trouble.

[83] *Empini*, lit., to an army, or enemy.

[84] *Umzimba u mude*, your body is long, that is, relaxed, unstrung.

ti, "O, ngi buza kodwa. Se ng' e-zwa ngepupo." Futi, uma umuntu e file, kanti ku kona o m hlekako ngaloko 'kufa, e nga m kaleli, noma e se file u ya buya a buze komunye o sa pilile, a ti, "Ubani lo u ngi hleka ngokufa, ngokuba yena e nga yi 'kufa ini na ?" Kw a-ziwe ngepupo ukuba Ubani lo kanti u ya hleka. Ku tiwe loli 'zwi li fike nesitunzi sake o fileko.

Futi, kubantu abamnyama, ku ti ngesikati sokuvama kwempi, abantu abaningi ba sinde itongo; li fika ngepupo; kumbe pakati kwobusuku umuntu a pupe e vu-swa Ubani, umuntu wakubo owa fako; a ti, "Bani, vuka, u tate abantwana bako nezinkomo, u pume. I ya ngena impi lapa." Ku ti ngokudelela, e ti, "Ipupo nje," a lale. Li pinde li fike li ti, "Vuka." Ubutongo bu ze bu be bubi. A kqale ukubona ukuba indaba le. Kumbe a t' e ti sululu, i be i vimbezela, 'ezwe se ku kala abantu. A bonge kakulu itongo lakubo.

Ukufika kwalo 'muntu ka fiki e inyoka, nesitunzi nje; ku fike

ly ask. I have already heard the news in my dream." And if one dies, and there is one who laughs at his death and does not mourn for him, and if the dead man return again and enquire of another who is still living, saying, "Does So-and-so laugh at my death because he will not die ?" it is known by the dream that the other laughs. It is said the shade of the dead comes with the message.

Further, among black men, when enemies are numerous, many people are saved by the Itongo; it comes in a dream; perhaps in the middle of the night a man dreams that one of his people who is dead wakes him, saying, "So-and-so, awake, and take your children and cattle, and go away. An enemy is coming into this village." And through despising it and thinking it a mere dream, he goes to sleep. And the Itongo comes again and says, "Awake." And at length he cannot sleep well. And he begins to see there is something real in the dream. Perhaps just as he has got out of the way the enemy surrounds the village, and he hears the people crying. He then returns hearty thanks to the Itongo of his people.

When a dead man comes he does not come in the form of a

yena ukqobo lwake nje, ngokungati ka fanga, a kulume nomuntu wakubo; na lowo e nga tsho ukuti umuntu owa fayo, a ze a bone uma e se papama ukuti, "Kanti ngi ti Ubani u sa hamba nje; kanti ku fike isitunzi sake." Ku ti uma wa fa izinto zake zi semzimbeni nokubuya u buya e se nazo; lezo 'zinto z' aziwa.

Futi ku kona kwabamnyama inyoka i ngena end*h*lini; i bonwe, ku bizwane, ku tiwe, "Nansi inyoka." Abantu ba ti budubudu ukuya 'u i bona leyo 'nyoka, uma i nga baleki. Ba ti, "Uma eyasend*h*le, nga i baleka i bona abantu. Kepa loku a i baleki, eyasekaya." Abanye ba ti, "Isilwane; a i bulawe." Ku pikiswane; omunye a i bulale, i la*h*lwe ngapand*h*le. Ku lalwe. Ipupo li fike; lo 'muntu owa fayo, li ti, "Ku ngani ukuba ni ngi bulale, ni ngi bona na? U mina lowo e ni m bulele. Ngi Ubani." A vuke lowo 'muntu, a wa lauze lawo 'mapupo. Ku mangalwe. Ku ngaloko ke ku tiwa inyoka i itongo. Ku tshiwo ngokuba ku tsho wona e ti, "U mina leyo 'nyoka e ni i boniloko."

snake, nor as a mere shade; but he comes in very person, just as if he was not dead, and talks with the man of his tribe; and he does not think it is the dead man until he sees on awaking, and says, "Truly I thought that So-and-so was still living; and forsooth it is his shade which has come to me." And when he returns he has the same clothes on as those in which he died, and the clothes are known.

Sometimes among black men a snake enters the house; when it is seen they call one another, saying, "There is a snake." All the people hurry to look at the snake if it does not run away. They say if it were a wild snake[85] it would run away when it sees men. But as it does not run away, it is a tame snake.[86] Others say, "It is a beast; let it be killed." They dispute, and one kills it and throws it away. They go to sleep, and a dream comes, and the dead man says, "How is it that you kill me when you see me? It is me whom you have killed. I am So-and-so." The man awakes, and tells his dreams, and the people wonder. It is on this account, then, that they say that the Itongo is a snake. They say so because the dead man tells them in dreams that he is the snake which they have seen.

---

[85] *Eyasend*h*le*, a wild snake, that is, not an Itongo.
[86] *Eyasekaya*, a home snake, that is, an Itongo.

Ecstasy and Dreams.

Isiyezi si njengokuba umuntu wa fa kancinyane. U ya vuka u se bona izinto a nga zi boni uma e nge nasiyezi.

Undayeni umuntu o be hlakanipile o be tsho ukuti, "Ngi namandhla okubona oku ngalapaya," noko e nge ko lapo. U ya ku bona ngesinye isikati oku ngalapaya, a tsho kubantu ukuti, "U kona umuntu, u y' eza ngale 'ndhlela," noma isihlobo sake, noma umuntu nje.

Ngesinye isikati ezweni lakwiti ku be ku zingelwa izinyati. Uma e lele ebusuku, u ya 'kuvuka kusasa, a si tshele, a ti, "Madoda, uma si ya 'kuzingela izinyati namhla nje, i kona into enhle e ya 'kuvela ekuhambeni kwetu. Ngi fumene izinyati ebusuku, si zi zingela; za ba izinkomo nje." Li pela lapo lelo 'pupo eli njalo. Izinyati si fike kuzo, zi be njengezinkomo njalo njengokutsho kwake; si zi bulale, si nga bi namdwa nomuncinyane nje.

Ngesinye ke isikati, uma ku kona ukuzingela, abantu be be hlangene ngokuti, "Madoda, ngosuku olutile ku fanele ukuba ke si yozingela izinyati emfuleni otile."

Ecstasy is a state in which a man becomes slightly insensible. He is awake, but still sees things, which he would not see if he were not in a state of ecstasy.

Undayeni was a clever man, who used to say he was able to see things afar off from him. He would sometimes see what was going on on the other side of a hill, and tell the people, saying, "There is a man coming by that path," whether it was a friend, or a stranger.[87]

Sometimes in our country they hunted buffalo. If he had slept at night, he would awake in the morning and tell us, saying, "Sirs, if we go to hunt buffaloes to-day, we shall be lucky. I saw some buffaloes during the night; we were hunting them; they were just like cattle." That was all such dreams made known to us. When we found the buffaloes, they were just like cattle, as he had told us; we killed them, and did not get so much as a scratch.

On another occasion, if there was a hunt, the men having already agreed, saying, "Sirs, on such a day it is well for us to go and hunt buffaloes by such a river."

---

[87] That is, in the ecstatic state he could see that some one was coming, but could not see whether it was an acquaintance, or a stranger.

Ba vumelane. Ku se kusasa ba puma, ba hamba. Ku ti ekuhambeni a tsho, a ti, "Madoda, kodwa ngi bonile ekulaleni kwami, noko si ya 'uzingela, a no zingela ngobudoda. Izinyati, ngi ti, zi nolaka." Mbala, ku be njalo eku zi fumaneni kwabo; noma zi nga bulalanga 'muntu, zi vame uku ba ponsa noma izinja. Ba ya ya kuzo se be hlakanipile ngokupupa kwake; ba ya 'kuvika futifuti.

Sa m bona ukuti, noko e nge si inyanga, kodwa ukupupa kwake kuhle. Futi wa e indoda e kalipayo, e nesibindi; uma inyati i ya 'kumisa obala, lapo ku nge ko 'muti wokukwela umuntu, yena a ti, "Kwela ni emitini nina. Ngi za 'kuya, ngi ye 'kuyoka ukuze i ze kunina, si i bulale." Kodwa abantu b' ahluleke, ukuti, "U za 'kuyoka e nga hambi pezulu, e nge najubane nje? U ya 'kwenza njani na? U ya 'kubaleka kanjani na?" Noko a hambe a ye kuyo, a i qale ngomkonto, a i hlabe, a baleke a ye kona lapo be kona abantu, a kwele emtini; uma ku kona abantu aba nemikonto, ba i hlabe, i ze i fe.

They would agree, and when the morning arrived set out on their journey. As they were setting out he would say to them, "Sirs, but I have seen in my sleep, although we are going to hunt, do you hunt like men. For I say the buffaloes are full of rage." And truly it was so when they came up with them; although they did not kill any one, they tossed the men or dogs continually. But they went to the hunt made cautious by his dream; and escaped again and again by dodging.

We noticed that although he was not an inyanga, yet his dreams were good. He was besides a brave man and courageous; if there were a buffalo in an open spot, where was no tree upon which a man could climb, he would say to the people, "Do you climb into the trees. I will go and draw him towards you, that we may kill him." But the people could not see that, but said, "How will he draw the buffalo towards us, for he cannot fly, and is not able to run fast? What will he do? How will he escape?" But he went to the buffalo, and began the attack by stabbing it, and then ran away to where the people were, and climbed into a tree; and if there were any men who had assagais, they killed it.

Abantu ba be ti ngaye, u inyanga, noko e nga buli; u tsho okubonakalayo; ngokuba izinyanga, noko zi bula, ngesinye isikati zi tsho okungabonakaliyo. Wa e intwesi futi yamazwi, ngokuba amazwi ake a e bonakala.

Kwa tiwa, amad*h*lozi akubo nakoninalume—akoninalume a tanda uku m enza inyanga, akubo a wa tandanga. Ngemva kwaloko ka be sa ba nako ukubula njengezinyanga; kodwa yena wa kuluma nje ngomlomo, ka bula. Kodwa ukwenza kwake kwa ku fana nenyanga, e nge si yo noko; ngokuba u be e zamula futifuti, a timule njalonjalo; loko ke okwezinyanga ezi bulayo; noko e nga buli, wa e pakati kwaleyo 'ndawo yokubula nokungabuli.

Indaba e ngi i kumbulayo enye kandayeni. Kwa ti si s' ake emgeni; kwa ku kona idwala li nengobozi, lapo ku ma amanzi kona; kepa sonke tina si 'batsha lawo 'manzi e isibuko setu, lapo si zibuka kona. Ku te ngolunye usuku wa si buza, e vuka ebutongweni, wa ti, "I kona ini indawo edwaleni, lapo ni zibuka kona na?" Sa ti, "Ku kona ni kona na?" Wa ti, "Ai. Ngi ya buza, ngo-

The people used to say of him, that he was a diviner though he did not divine; for he said what was true; and diviners sometimes say what is not true. He was also an eloquent man, for what he said came to pass.

It was said, the Amatongo of his own people and the Amatongo of his maternal uncle disagreed. Those of the maternal uncle wished to make him a diviner; those of his own people did not wish it. After that he was unable to divine like a diviner; but said what was true without divination. But his habits were those of a diviner, though he was not one; for he used to yawn and sneeze continually; and this is done by diviners; although he did not divine, he was midway between divining and not divining.

There is another thing which I remember of Undayeni. We were living on the Umgeni; there was in the neighbourhood a rock, in which was a hollow, where water stood; and that water was the looking glass in which all we younger ones used to look at ourselves. One day on awaking from sleep he asked us, saying, "Is there a place in the rock which you gaze in as a looking glass?" We replied, "What harm is there in that?" He replied, "No. I merely ask because I have seen

kuba ngi bonile e ngi ku bonileyo ebusuku." Sa vuma, sa ti, "I kona." Wa ti, "Ngi ti, kuleyo 'ndawo ni nga be ni sa ya kona. U kona umuntu o kade e ni bona ukuba se n' ejwayele kuleyo 'ndawo ukuzibuka. Kepa u fake ububi kuleyo 'ndawo. I yeke ni leyo 'ndawo." Kepa ngokuba nembala kwa ku umuntu e si m azi, ukuti u kuluma isiminya, a si pikanga, sa vuma, sa i yeka leyo 'ndawo. Loko ke ka ku bonanga esiyezini, wa ku bona e lele.

Ngokuba na sendabeni, uma ku kona umuntu o nekcala, kepa Undayeni uma e ti, "Bani, indaba i ya 'ku ku la/la." Nembala lowo 'muntu, uma e m azi, a ku sa swelekile kuye ukuba a ye emakcaleni; u se e fanele ukuti a zilungisele ka/le kulo 'muntu, ku nga yiwa emakcaleni.

U be njalo ke ukuhamba kwake. I loko ke e ngi ku kumbulayo ukwenza kwake.

Kepa ngesiyezi a be e bona ngaso, u be umuntu kakulu o nga tandi uku/lala pakati kweningi labantu; u be tanda ukuzi/lalela yedwa, ngokuba u be umuntu kakulu e si ti u kuluma isiminya.

what I have seen during the night." Then we told him that there was such a place. He replied, "I tell you never to go to that place again. There is some one who for some time has seen that you are accustomed to look at yourselves there. And he has put bad medicine[88] into the hollow. Leave the place." And because he was a man whom we knew, we saw that he spoke the truth, and did not refuse to obey, but left the place. This he did not see in an ecstatic state, but during sleep.

And even in disputes, if there was any one who was in fault, and Undayeni said to him, "So-and-so, you will lose the case,"—if the man knew Undayeni he would no longer want to go into court, but was now ready to act rightly to the other without going into court.

Such then was the character of Undayeni. This is what I remember of his acts.

And as regards the ecstasy into which he fell, he was a man who did not like to sit in the midst of many people; but liked to sit alone, for he was a man who, we said, spoke the truth.[89] I do not

---

[88] *Ububi*, that is, some medicinal substance, capable of making any one who looked into the water hateful to others. See "Superstitious Use of Medicines."—Among the Highland Tales there is mentioned a magic basin which made a person beautiful when he washed in it. *(Campbell. Vol. I., p. 97.)*

[89] He sat alone that he might become ecstatic, and in that state see what he could not see in his ordinary condition.

A ngi tsho ukuti u be nga hlali nakanye pakati kwabantu, kodwa u be nga vami.

Njengaloku pakati kwabantu abamnyama indaba zamapupo ku tiwa a y aziwa ukuma kwawo. Ngokuba amanye amapupo a ya vela njengokungati ku njalo, kanti a ku njalo; amanye a kombise indaba e za 'kwenzeka. Ngokuba ku kona pakati kwabantu abamnyama ukuti, uma umuntu e lele wa bona iketo elikulu, ku sinwa; uma ku gula umuntu, a ku tshiwo ukuti si y' etemba ukuti u ya 'kusinda; masinyane kulowo 'muntu o bone ku sinwa, u y' esaba kakulu, a hlale e se beka indhlebe; uma ku umuntu o nge si ye walapo ku gulwayo, e beka indhlebe, ngokuti u za 'kuzwa isililo. Kepa noma ku nge si yo leyo 'mini ukuba ku kalwe, ku y' esabeka, a ku tembeki loko 'kupupa.

Kepa ukupupa okutembekayo kubantu abamnyama, uma umuntu o gulayo ku putshwe e se e file, e se e ya 'kulahlwa egodini, ba bone nokugqitshwa kwake, nokukalelwa kwake konke, nokulahlwa kwezinto zake ku pele ngaleso 'sikati sobusuku. Ku tiwa ke ngaloko, "Ngokuba si m pupela ukufa, ka yi 'kufa."

mean that he never sat amidst other people, but he did not usually do so.

In like manner among black men the real meaning of dreams is not known. For some dreams have every appearance of reality, but they are not true; others point out something which is about to happen. For among black men it is supposed that if a man dream of a great assembly, where they are dancing, if there is any one ill, we have no confidence that he will get well; but immediately the man who dreamt of the dance is much alarmed, and if he is not a man of the same village as that where the man is ill, he continually listens, expecting to hear the funeral wail. And although the wail is not heard on the same day, he is still fearful and without confidence.

But a dream which produces confidence among black men, when any one is ill, is one in which they dream that someone is dead and about to be buried, and that they see the earth poured into the grave, and hear the funeral lamentation for him, and see the destruction[90] of all his things during the night. They say of such a dream, "Because we have dreamt of his death he will not die."

---

[90] Some of the dead man's personal property—as his assagais, his blanket, and dress—is buried with him, and some is burnt.

A s' azi ke uma loko kw enza ngani. Lokupela njengokuma kwokupila nokufa ku be ku fanele ukuba o za 'kufa nembala a fe, uma e gula e putshwa ; a ti o za 'kupila a pile, uma ku putshwa e pila. Nembala loko ngi ku bonile kokobili. Ijadu ngi li bonile, umuntu wa fa ; futi ukufa ngi ku bonile ngomuntu o be gula, kepa wa pila. Njengokuba ekuguleni kwomfundisi wetu ngonyaka owa d*h*lulayo, nga m pupa e se e file, e fele emgungund*h*lovu. Kepa ka la*h*lwanga emalibeni, wa la*h*lwa pakati kwend*h*lu em*h*lope ngapakati ; kepa ku gewele abantu abaningi abafayo, e se lele ngapezulu kwalabo 'bantu ; ikanda lake li bheke empumalanga, izinwele zi fi*h*le ame*h*lo. Loko nga ku bona ngi lele. Ekuvukeni kwami a ngi *h*lalelanga, ukuti, " A ngi bheke ukuba nembala incwadi e za 'kufika ; i za 'kufika, i ti, ' O, se ku njalo, u file.' " A ngi *h*lalelanga loko ; nga vuka nje, nga bona se ku njalo ; nga kala masinyane ngabo lobo 'busuku ; ng' esaba nokuba incwadi i fike, ngokuti i za 'kutsho loko. Kwa nga i ng' epuza ukufika. Nga *h*lala ngi zije-

We do not understand how this happens. For as regards living and dying, it would appear proper that he who is about to die should die, if when he is ill people dream he is dead ; and he who is about to live should live, if people dream that he is well. But in truth I have seen both. I have dreamt of a wedding-dance, and the man died ; again, I have dreamt of the death of a sick man, but he got well. For example, when some years ago our Teacher was ill, I dreamt that he was dead, and that he had died at Pietermaritzburg. But he was not buried in a grave, but was placed in the middle of a house which was white inside ; and it was full of dead men, and he was placed on the top of the dead men ; his head was directed towards the east, and his hair covered his eyes. This I saw in my sleep. When I awoke, I waited, saying, " Let me look out for the letter which will come shortly ; it will come and say, ' O, it is so, he is dead.' " I did not wait for that, but saw it was already really true, and at once wept during the rest of the night ; I was afraid for a letter to come, thinking it would tell us of his death. I longed that it might be a long time before it arrived. My eyes remained full of tears

jana ngaloko 'kupupa. Kepa ekufikeni kwenewadi a kwa ba njalo. Ng' ezwa ilizwi lokuti, " U ti, a ku kupuke ingola, u m hlangabeze." Nga ti, "O, nembala ukupupa ukufa a ku bonisisi ukufa."

A ngi ka kqedi ukuti se ku isiminya loko; ngokuba kwabanye ba bona ukufa, nembala ku be i ko; nokupila ngesinye isikati ku be ukupila. Kepa nami a ngi tsho ukuti ukupupa ku hamba ngaloko oku bonwayo umuntu; ngesinye isikati ngi nga pupa into, nembala i ya 'kuba njalo njengokuba ngi i bonile. Kepa kakulu ngi ya kuluma ngokufa kwomuntu ogulayo nokupila, ukuti, a ku hambi ngendhlela e be ku fanele ukuhamba ngayo; ku ya pambanisa.

Abantu ba ti, amapupo asehlobo a tsho isiminya; kepa a ba tsho ukuti, a tsho isiminya kanyekanye; kodwa ba ti, ehlobo a ku vamile ukuba amapupo a geje. Kodwa ba ti, ubusika bubi, bu fika namaongoongo, ukuti, amapupo amaningi kakulu a nga kqondekiyo kahle. Kepa ngaloko a ku tshiwo ukuti, ubusika bu pupisa kahle, noma umuntu e pupile amapupo, uma e wa lauzela omunye, lowo u ti masinyane, "O, 'bani, amaongoongo obusika lawo,"

because of the dream. But when the letter came it was not so. But I heard it said, "Our Teacher has sent for the waggon to go to Pietermaritzburg, to fetch him." So I said, " O, truly, to dream of death does not show that death will take place."

I have not yet come to a certain conclusion that this is true; for some dream of death, and death occurs; and sometimes of health, and the person lives. And I do not say that a dream turns out to be true; sometimes I dream of something, and in fact the thing happens as I have dreamed. But I speak especially of the death or life of one who is ill, that the event turns out different from what it ought to, and goes by contraries.

People say, summer dreams are true; but they do not say they are always true; but they say that summer dreams do not usually miss the mark. But they say the winter is bad, and produces confused imaginations, that is, very many unintelligible dreams. And therefore it is said that winter causes bad dreams, and if a man has dreamed and tells another, he will at once answer him, saying, " O, So-and-so, that is nothing but the confused imaginations caused by the winter." He says thus

DREAMS, ETC.

e tsho ngokuba e ti, a ku ko 'n*h*lamvu pakati kwawo. Njengaloku i*hl*obo ku tiwa, a li nazo izindaba eziningi zamanga. Kepa uma se ku fike ubusika, abantu ba ya k*q*ala ukuba nevuso, ngokuti, bu za 'kufika ke ubusika namafukufuku amaningi, ukuti amanga.

Ipupo e ku tiwa li vela etongweni, uma li fika ngezwi likabani o nga se ko, ukuti, "Ini uma ku ng' enziwa ukuti nokuti na?" Njengaloku kubantu abamnyama, uma u zuze amabele kakulu, ngesinye isikati ku ti ekulaleni kumninimuzi a pupe, ku tiwa, "Ini ukuba u piwe ukud*h*la okungaka, u nga bongi na?" Kepa masinyane uma e se e vukile ka ngabazi ukuti loli 'pupo li tsho 'kud*h*la kuni? U ya bona nje ukuti, "O, nembala!" A be e se ti emzini wake, "A kw enziwe utshwala; ku ya 'ku*h*latshwa." A be ke e se bonga ngaloko 'kud*h*la a kw enzileyo. Noma e zuze izinkomo, 'enze njalo futi.

Kwa ti ngesikati lapa Amazulu a ya empini, emuva kwaloko kwa *h*latshwa umkosi ukuti, "Zi mi

because there is no sense in the dream. In like manner it is said there is not much that is false in the dreams of summer. But when the winter comes the people begin to be afraid that the winter will bring much rubbish, that is, false dreams.

A dream which is said to be sent by the Itongo, is one which comes with a message from the dead, enquiring why such and such a thing is not done. For example, among black men, if one has an abundant harvest sometimes the head of the village dreams that it is said to him, "How is it, when you have been given so much food, that you do not give thanks?" And as soon as he wakes he has no doubt as to what food the dream means. But he perceives at once that the dream speaks to the point. And he immediately commands his people to make beer, for he is about to sacrifice. So he praises the Amatongo for the food which they have given him. And if he has gained many cattle he does the same.

It happened once when the Amazulu had gone out to battle,[91] the word was passed among the people telling them that the cattle were standing without guard at

---

[91] To fight with the Dutch in the time of Udingane.

zodwa edhlokweni." Kepa bonke abantu b' esukela pezulu, ukuti b' eza 'utola izinkomo. Kw' esuka namakægu e pete izindondolo; kepa lolo 'lusinga olu njalo lwa za lwa susa nobaba. Lokupela ya fika ntambama leyo 'ndaba, wa ti komame, "Ngi gayele ni isinkwa, ngi ze ngi dhle endhleleni." Kepa ekulaleni kwake, kwa fika ilizwi, la ti, "U nga yi lapo ku yiwako; a ku yi 'kubuya namunye." Nembala ekuseni, ngokuba kwa ku ihlazo uma indoda i ti, " Mina a ngi yi," kepa wa ti, " O, mina, 'bakwiti, ngi lele ngi zilungisele ukuhamba; kepa manje ku se umlenze wami w ala; se ngi ya kænga." Nembala wa zikæugisa.

Ba hamba be ti, ba za 'kutitiliza; kanti ukufa ku ya 'kutitiliza bona. O, kwa fika wa ba munye, Usihhile; e fika, be m dabule ikanda ekealeni kweudhlebe ngomkonto; o ti, "Ni bona mina nje ukupela." Loko kwa kqiniseka kubaba, ukuti, "Nembala ngi vusiwe ngepupo." Kepa wa li lauza lelo 'pupo emveni ukuti, " Nami be ngi ya, kepa ngi bone loko ebusuku."

Idhlokwe.[92] And all the people started up, thinking they should get cattle; and even old men went out, leaning on their staves; and at length our father was carried away by the infection. And as the news came in the afternoon, he said to our mothers, "Make me some bread, that I may eat on the journey." But whilst he was asleep a voice came to him, saying, "Do not go where the others are going; not one will come back again." So in the morning, as it was a shame to a man to say he was not going, he said, "O, for my part, neighbours, when I lay down I had got ready to go; but now my leg prevents me; I have become lame." In fact he pretended to be lame.

They set out thinking they should gain very many cattle; and forsooth death made a very great gain of them. O, one only came back, whose name was Usichile; he came with an assagai wound by his ear. He said, "You see me only." That was a confirmation to my father that he had been truly warned by the dream. And after that he told the dream, saying, "I too was going, but I saw what has happened in a dream."

---

[92] *Idhlokwe*, a secure place, where there was abundant pasture and forest, where the cattle could feed in concealment.

Futi ngcpupo uma ku hlaselwa, umuntu wa lala, wa pupa e gwaza umuntu kukqala, a m bulale, ekuvukeni kwake u y' enyela ngokuti, "Hau! ku njani loku, uma ngi pupe ngi bulala umuntu? Kqa. La 'mapupo a ya pambanisa. Ku ya 'kufa mina." A hambe ngokuhlakanipa—a nga hambi pambili, a hambe emuva; i hlangane kqede, anduba a ngene, impi se i 'mehlo 'mnyama, a gwaze umuntu. A nga kohlwa i lelo 'pupo, a zing' e l' azi njalo.

UMPENGULA MBANDA.

Again, if when making an incursion into another country one has dreamt that he stabbed a man first and killed him, he murmurs saying, " Oh, how is it that I have dreamt that I killed a man? No. The dream goes by contraries. It is I who shall be killed." So he goes cautiously—does not go in front, but behind the others; but when the two armies have joined battle, then he enters into the engagement, when the enemy is confused, and stabs someone. He does not forget the dream, but bears it constantly in mind.

Uguaise's Dream.

INHLIZIYO yami imbi. Ngi kwel' o[93] ubutongo obubi. Nga pupa isililo, ku kala abantu be bauingi. Ya ba mbi inhliziyo yami, ngokuba ngi pupe izinto eziningi! Nga pupa nomjadu, abantu abaningi abasinayo.

Inhliziyo yami ya keabanga ukuba umjadu u ipupo elibi. Uma u pupa umjadu, ku ba ka ku lungile; ku ba u kona umuntu ofileyo; umjadu u isililo; uma u pupa abantu be sina, libi lelo 'pupo.

My heart is heavy. I have had a bad dream. I dreamt of a funeral lamentation; many people were weeping. How heavy my heart is because I have dreamt of many things! I dreamt also of a wedding-dance; many people were dancing.

I thought in my heart, a wedding is a bad dream. If you dream of a wedding, there is something not right; there is someone who has died; the wedding is a sign of lamentation; if you dream of men dancing, it is a bad dream.

---

[93] A similar form of expression occurs in the following sentence —Nga se ngi zwa isililo, se ku kalwa ukuti, "Maye! wa m gwaz' o!" It occurs not unfrequently in songs.

Kepa nga vuka kusasa, nga ba tshela abantu, nga ti, "Inhliziyo yami imbi. Nga pupa umjadu, nga pupa isililo." Ba ti abantu, "Into embi o i pupileyo. Umjadu isililo. Loku wa shiya ekaya ku gulwa, isililo si ipupo elihle; lelo 'pupo lesililo a li nakcula; lihle, lo 'pupe isililo; ipupo elibi elomjadu. Ba ti futi, "Nalo lomjadu ngesinye isikati uma u ba u pupa, ize nje; ku ba nosuku nje, li ti lona elibi ipupo li kqamb' amanga nje."

Nga ti mina, "Nga ka nga u pupa umjadu. Ani[94] a ku lungile ekaya. Anti[94] umkwekazi wami u bubile."

Ngi be ngi s' and' ukupupa wona umjadu, kwa fika umuntu, nga tshaywa uvalo. Uma ngi sa m bona lo 'muntu, nga puma endhlini yokupeka, nga m bingelela, nga ti, "Sa ku bona." Nga ti, "Kona ngi ku bingelela nje, ngi ku bone kqede, nga tshaywa uvalo; kwa nga ti i kona indaba o za 'ku ngi tshela." Ngoba ngi m bone kqede, nga tshaywa uvalo. Wa ti, "O, kuloko, uvalo lokutshaya ngakona. Ekaya le ku kona in-

And I woke in the morning and told the people, saying, "My heart is heavy. I have dreamt of a wedding-dance, and of a funeral lamentation." The people said, "You have dreamt of a bad thing. A wedding-dance is a sign that there will be a funeral lamentation. Since when you left home there was someone ill, the funeral lamentation is a good dream; the dream of a wedding is of no consequence; your dream of a funeral lamentation is good; the dream of a wedding is bad." They further said, "And sometimes if you frequently dream of a wedding, it is nothing; or if you dream of it once only, it is not a sign that can be depended on."

I said, "Some time ago I dreamt of a wedding. When I awoke I said, 'It is not right at home. My mother-in-law is dead.'"

Immediately after I had dreamt of the wedding, a man came, and I was alarmed. As soon as I saw him I went out of the cooking house, and saluted him, and said, "Although I thus salute you, as soon as I saw you I felt alarmed; it felt as if there was something you have come to tell me." For as soon as I saw him I felt alarmed. He said, "O, you felt alarm with reason. There is bad news

---

[94] Dialectic for *kanti*.

daba embi. Umkwekazi wako u bubilo." Nga ti mina, "U bube isifo si ni na?" Wa ti, "Wa bika empinjeni; wa ti, 'Kubu*h*lungu lapa.'" Wa ti, "Ka banga nalusuku; usuku s' ezwa se ku kalwa isililo nje. Sa dinga uma ku fe mupi umuntu. Sa buza tina ukuti, 'Ini na? Ku kalwa nje, kw enze njani na?' 'Ku bube umkwekazi kaguaise.' Sa buza ukuti, ' U be nani na? Loku na kutangi si be si naye na, e nga guli na?' 'Au, a s' azi, nati si y' etuka nje. Nati si zwa ngaso isililo nje.' 'Au, ku tiwa ukufa kuni na?' 'Au, wa bika empinjeni; wa ti, Kubu*h*lungu umpimbo; wa ti, Wa kwelwa in*h*loko; wa ba se u ya fa.'"

Abantu ba mangala umuntu ukufa e nga gulanga. Kwa ba kona abantu, ba ti, "A ku yiwe ezinyangeni, ku yozwakala lesi 'sifo esi m bulala umuntu e nga gulanga."

Kwa yiwa ezinyangeni. Izinyanga za fika za ti, "U bulewe umuntu. Lowo 'muntu umkulu o m buleleyo; u n*x*anele ukuk*q*eda lowo 'muzi; umuntu omkulu, umunumuzana."

Ngi ti ke, "Ngi pupe nam*h*la nje, nga tshaywa uvalo. In*h*liziyo at your home. Your mother-in-law is dead." I said, "Of what disease did she die?" He said, "She complained of pain in her throat. And on that very day we heard the funeral lamentation. We could not tell who had died. But asked, 'What is it?' Since there is lamentation, what has happened?' They said, ' Uguaise's mother-in-law is dead.' We asked, 'What was the disease? For only the day before yesterday we were with her, and she was not ill?' They answered, ' O, we do not know, and we too are startled. We too hear only by the lamentation.' We said, ' O, what disease is it said to be?' They said, 'She complained of pain in her windpipe. Then her head was affected, and she died.'"

The man wondered at death when the person was not ill. And some said, "Let us go to the diviners, that we may hear what the disease is which kills a man without his having been ill."

They went to the diviners. The diviners said, "She has been killed by someone. He who has killed her is a great man; he wishes to destroy the village; he is a great man, a captain of villages."

So I say, "I have dreamt to-day, and am alarmed. My heart

ya kumbula lawo 'mapupo a ng' e-
uza ngapambili; inhliziyo yami ya
ti, ' Umakazi leli 'pupo lomjadu li
ngi hlonze nje, uma kulungile nje
na ekaya na? Loku nga shiya ku
gula umfazi wami, ku gul' umame.
Ini nkuba ngi pupe ipupo e nga li
pupa kukqala, kwa bonakala na?"

Ba pendula ba ti abakwiti Om-
pengula, ba ti, " O, libi ipupo lomjadu. Inhliziyo yako imbi ngakona; ipupo lomjadu li fana ne-
pupo lokuba ku gula umuntu.
Uma u m pupa e gula kakulu, u
nga m pupa e kulupele, e fak' i-
zinto zake zonke ezinhle, impahla
yake; lo 'muntu u ba u file; ka
sindi. Umuntu um' e gula, ku
ba kuhle u m pupe e file, e kalelwa
isililo; lo 'muntu ke u ya 'usinda;
a ka yi 'kufa."

O tsho njalo kumina, ku pendula
Umpengula; wa ti, " Ehe, guaise,
kodwa i 'kuba u pupe umjadu, umjadu u 'pupo 'libi." A ti Uklas,
" O, loko, guaise, elinye ipupo li
se li ti lona; ipupo umuntu u li
pupe ngesinye isikati, u pupe nje,
ku nga veli 'luto."

A ti Umpengula, " Ehe, u kqi-
remembers the dreams which I
formerly dreamt; and my heart
asks, ' Can it be, since this dream
of a wedding comes to me again,
that it is not right at my home?
For when I left my home, my wife
and mother were ill. Why have
I dreamt a dream which I dreamt
formerly and it came true?' "

Our people, Umpengula and the
rest, answered me, saying, "The
dream of a wedding is a bad sign.
Your heart is heavy with reason;
to dream of a wedding is like
dreaming that a man is ill. If
you dream of him when he is very
ill, you may dream that he is fat,
and decked in his fine things; and
that man is dead; he does not get
well. When a man is ill, it is
well to dream he is dead, and that
they are weeping for him; then
that man will get well; he will
not die."

It was Umpengula who answered me thus; and he said, "Yes,
yes, Uguaise, but since you have
dreamed of a wedding-dance, a
wedding-dance is a bad dream."
And Uklass answered, "O, as to
that, Uguaise, one dream will turn
out to be a bad omen; and a man
may dream the same dream another time, and it turn out to be
but a dream, and nothing come of
it."

Umpengula answered, "Yes,

nisilo, klas, ku ba njalo ngesinye isikati ; umuntu u pupa nje omunye, ku nga veli 'luto." Wa ti Umpengula, " Nami, guaise, nga ka nga li pupa nami ipupo. Ku gula Undayeni. E gula, nga pupa e vunule impa*h*la yake, wa binca umuntsha wake wezinsimba, e fake amatshob' ake ; nga pupa ku ketwa. Nga vuka kusasa nami, guaise, nga vuka in*h*liziyo yami imbi. Nga ba lauzela abantu, nga ti ngi *h*lezi nje, ngi bhekile, nga bona ku ti kcatsha izinyembezi eme*h*lweni ami. Nga ti mina, " Uma u file Undayeni—' Ngi te ngi sa ku gcina loko,—lo ngi sesilungwini, ngi ya sebenza,—ngi te, ' Ngi za 'uguk*q*ula ame*h*lo emzileni,' nga m bona umfana ; owakwiti lo 'mfana. Nga ti mina, ' O, u file Undayeni. Lo 'mfana u se zoku ngi bikela.' U te e sa fika, nga ti mina, ' Kona, mfana, u fika nje, ngi ti, u file Undayeni.' Wa ti umfana, ' Ehe, ngi fike nje, ngi zokubikela wena ukuti u file Undayeni.' Nga ti mina, ' Nami be se ngi bonile njalo ke.' "

A i se vi mbi in*h*liziyo yami. I ya kuluma kodwa, i ti, uma nga ku kona indaba, ngapana ngi bona ku fike umuntu o za 'ku ngi tshela. In*h*liziyo yami i bona lona leli 'zwi eli tshiwo amadoda akwiti ; nami se ngi ya bona ukuti, uma ku kona

yes, you say truly, Uklass, it is so sometimes ; a man dreams merely of another, and nothing comes of it. And I too, Uguaise, once dreamt a dream. Undayeni was ill. During his illness I dreamt I saw him dressed in his best attire, with his umuntsha of wild cat's skins, and having put on his tails ; I dreamt there was a dance. I awoke in the morning, Uguaise, with my heart depressed. I told the people my dream, and remained waiting, my eyes filling with tears. I said, ' If Undayeni is dead—' As I was saying those words,—for I was working with the white men,—I said, ' I will turn my eyes towards the road,' and I saw a lad coming ; it was a lad belonging to us. I said, ' O, Undayeni is dead. The lad is coming to tell us.' As soon as he came I said to him, ' Lad, you have come because Undayeni is dead.' The boy said, ' Yes, yes ; I come merely for the purpose of telling you that Undayeni is dead.' I replied, ' I too had already seen that it was so.' "

My heart is no longer heavy. But it says if there is any thing the matter, I shall see someone coming to tell me. My heart sees that what the men of the place say is true ; and I too now see that if

indaba, ngapana si fika isigijimi kumina ukuza 'u ngi bikela. Kodwa ngi sa bhekisisile, inhliziyo yami i ya 'udela kqede ku kqubeke izinsuku ngasemuva kwokupupa kwami. Ng' and' ukuba ngi ti, "Ai, a ku 'ndaba. Ubutongo kodwa bu ngi kwele ngamaongoongo."

Uguaise.

there is any thing the matter I shall see a messenger coming to tell me. But I am still in deep expectation, and my heart will be satisfied when many days have passed after the dream. Then I shall say, "No, there is nothing the matter. But sleep has filled my mind with mere senseless images."

Subjective Apparitions.

Kwa ti ngalezo 'nto ezi izilo ezi bonwa umuntu lapa e ti u ye 'kukuleka ngasese, nami nga ku bona loko futifuti. Lapa ngi ti ngi ya kqala nje ukugukqa, kumbe ilizwi lokukqala e ngi li tshoyo ngi ya li tsho, se ku kona okunye o se ku kqala ukusondela; njengokuti, "Manje u wa valile amehlo, ka sa yi 'ku ngi bona; a ngi sondele, ngi m lume, noma ngi m bambe, noma ngi m gwaze." Uma ngi ti ngi ya kqinisela, ng' ala ukuvuka, O, masinyane kwa fika umsindo omningi wokukqeda isibindi, nokuba ku be kona ukuti, "Ku kqinisile. Okwokukqala ku be kuncinane; manje se ku fike okukulu oku za 'ku ngi bulala."

Lezo 'zinto zi njalonjalo ukufika kwazo, zi fika ngazinye; ku fike inyoka i namehlo amakulu, i nokwesabeka, ukuba lapo ngi gukqe

As regards those wild animals which a man sees when he is going to pray in secret, I too have seen them again and again. When I was beginning to kneel, or when I was saying the first word perhaps, there was something beginning to approach me; as though it said, "Now he has closed his eyes, and will no longer see me; let me draw near and bite him, or lay hold of him, or stab him." If I steadily refused to arise, O, at once there came a great noise which took away all my courage, and led me to say, "This is something real. The first was a little thing; now there is coming a great thing to kill me."

When these things come to any one they always come separately; there comes a snake with great eyes and very fearful; so that

kona, ngi nga be ngi sa kqinisela, ngi ya 'kuvuka.

Uma ku nge si yo, ku fika isilo si hamba ngokunyenya ukuze si ngi bambe, loku ngi nga boni, ngi bheke pansi, ngi ti ngi ya kuleka enkosini. Kepa ukukuleka kwami ku nga be ku sa kqina; ngi kqale ukukuleka kancinane ngapakati, ng' enza izikau, ukuze indhlebe yami i nga bi ekukulekeni kodwa, i be na sekulaleleni ukukqwabaza kwesilo si hamba ngoku ngi zuma. Uma se ngi bona ngokuba pela ku njalo, ku ti uma ngi bone ukuti, "O, manje sa kqala ukulunga ukuze si ngi bambe," ngi vuke lapo.

Futi uma ku nge si so isilo, umuntu o ngi zondayo, u pete umkonto, umude, 'enzela ukuze a ngi gwaze, ngi fele kuleso 'sikundhla; naye u hamba ngokunyonyoba, ukuze ngi nga mu zwa.

Lokupela ku njalonjalo, ku ngokuba uma umuntu e ya ngapandhle u be e nga kuleki ngenhliziyo, kodwa u be kuluma a pumisele; kepa ke ku ngaloko lezo 'zilo e be zi ngi bona zi be zi ngi bona ngokuzwa ukuvungazela; kepa zi sondele. Nalowo 'muntu ngi ya m bona uma e se pakamisa ingalo ukuze a ngi gwaze; ngi ya bona noma e se e linga uku ngi gwaza impela.

when I have knelt, I could not remain firm, but rose up again.

If it was not a snake, a leopard would come on stealthily to lay hold of me, for I could not see, but was looking on the ground, intending to pray to the Lord. But my prayer was no longer steady; I began to pray a little in my heart, praying and stopping that my ear may not only listen to my prayer, but also to the crackling made by the leopard as it came to seize me. When I saw that it was something real, and that the leopard was preparing itself to seize me, I arose.

And if it was not a leopard, it would be a man who hated me, with a long assagai in his hand, approaching to kill me, that I may die in that place; and he too went stealthily, that I might not hear him.

For under these circumstances a man who went out to pray would not pray with the heart only, but speak aloud; therefore those animals saw me because they heard the murmuring of my voice; and drew near. And I saw the man when he raised his arm to stab me, or when he really tried to thrust the assagai into my body.

Lokupela ku njalonjalo ngi ya kuleka, a ngi sa kuleki nganhliziyo 'nye, se ngi kuleka ngamaputuputu, ngi tanda ukuba ngi buke masinyane kuleyo 'ndawo, ngokuba ngi ya bulawa.

A ti uma lowo 'muntu e se ngi gwaza, ngi vuke, nalelo 'lizwi e be ngi kuluma ngalo li nga ka peli; se li pumile lona, kepa ngi nga ka li kqedi, li nqamuke kabili. Ngi vuke ukuze ngi sinde. Ukuvuka kwami ngi vuke ngokwetuka, ngi kqalaze ngalapo lowo 'muntu e vele ngakona, ngi nga m boni.

Ku nga be ku sa ba ko ukuba ngi buyele ekukulekeni, ngi kqedele loko e be ngi tanda uku ku tsho. Hai! Se ku pelile; a ngi sa ku boni ngaleso 'sibelu esi ngi tusileyo. O, kwa za kw' anela. Ku i loko njalo ekukulekeni. Ngi ya vuka se ngi jambile, ngokuba ng' etuswe amanga, nga kolwa. Kepa nga za nga ku bona loko, ukuti, ku amanga, nokuba kw' enziwa ngokuba ngi be ngi puma ku se luvivi, ngi ba shiye be sa lele, ng' enzela ukuti, kona ngi ya 'kuba nesikati sokuzikulekela enkosini; ngokuba uma ngi puma se ku silo, nabo se be pumile ukuya 'kwenza imisebenzana yabo, noma ukuya ngapandhle; ba be se be

When I prayed under such circumstances I no longer prayed with singleness of heart, but in a hurry, wishing to look without delay to the place from which the danger threatened me, for I was in danger.

And when the man was now stabbing me, I would arise, the sentence which I was uttering being unfinished; it was already begun but not ended, but cut in two. I arose that I might escape. When I arose I arose with a start, and looked to the place whence the man came; but did not see him.

It was no longer possible for me to return to my prayers and finish what I had begun to say. No! There was now an end of it, and I could no longer say what I wanted for the false alarm which had frightened me. O, this was repeated again and again. It happened continually in my prayers. I arose ashamed because I had been frightened by fantacy, and believed in it. But at length I saw that it was fantacy, and that it happened because I went out before it was light, leaving the people still asleep, doing so because I should then have time to pray for myself to the Lord; for if I went out while it was day, they too would have gone out to do their daily work, and would hear,

ngi zwa, ba hlebelane ngami ukuti, "O, lo 'muntu u se u ya kolwa; ngi m zwile e kuleka; kuhle ukuba a ti lapo e kuleka kona, si hambe, si ye 'ku m vusa, noma si m tshaye, ukuze a nga be e sa pinda lezo 'zinto."

Ezi izilo nga zi bona ngokupuma ku se mnyama, ku nga ka kanyi ukusa. Kepa ukuze ngi bone ukuti a ku 'siminya nga bona ngokuba ku ze amasuku a ze 'anele ku njalonjalo, nga ze nga zi dela, ukuti, "Au, ku ya 'kusiza ini ukuba ngi ti lapa ngi kuleka ngi vuswe izilwanyana ezi ngi dhlayo, kanti a zi ko? loku ngi nga zuzi nje loko e ngi ku vukela enkosini, ngi vinjelwa izilo e ngi zi bonayo. Ake ngi kqinisele ngi ze ngi zwe se zi ngi bamba impela, ngi pikelele ukukuleka njalo."

Nembala nga ti ngi sa gukqa, sa fika isilwanyana esi inyoka ukwenza okwemisuku. Nga ti, "Ai! Namhla a ngi zwe ngomzimba ukuti se si ngi bambile." Ng' ahlula lapo. Kwa fika isilo esikulu. Nga ti na kuso, "A ngi zwe ngomzimba." Ng' ahlula. Kwa fika umuntu 'eza e gijima ukuze a ngi nqume masinyane. Loku ngi s' eisile isilo, naye nga ti, "Ngi ya

and whisper about me one to another, saying, "O, that man is now a believer; I heard him praying; it is well for us to go to the place where he prays, and arouse him, or beat him, that he may not repeat such things."

The animals I saw because I went out whilst it was still dark, before the day had fully dawned. But at last I saw that it was not real because they appeared continually for many days, until I despised them, saying, "O, of what use will it be if when I pray I am made to arise from my knees by beasts which devour me, when forsooth they are not real? for I cannot get that for which I awake early to pray to the Lord, being prevented by the beasts which I see. Just let me strengthen myself until I feel them really seizing me, and persevere in prayer without ceasing."

And indeed when I was kneeling there came a snake to do as on other days. I said, "No! To-day let me feel by my body that it has already seized me." Then I conquered. There came a huge leopard. I said also to it, "Let me feel by my body." I conquered. There came a man, running to stab me at once. Since I had despised the leopard, I said too of the man, "Let me feel by my

'kuzwa ngomzimba." Nga m aḣlula. Nga goduka ngi kqalabile, ukuti, "O, kanti ngi vinjelwe amauga."

Nga ti 'ngi pinda ukwenza njalo, a kwa be ku sa vama uku ng' esabisa. Kwa ya kwa pela, kwa ya kwa ti nya, ku ze ku be namḣla nje, a ku se ko. Abaningi ba vinjelwa i loko; lapo be ti ba ya kqala nje ukukuleka, ba bone lezo 'zilwane ezi za 'ku ba dḣla, ba vuke masinyane, ba goduke, a nga be e sa tsho umuntu ukuti, "Ngi ya 'kupinda ngi ye kuleyo 'ndawo;" a se ti, "Ngomso kuḣle ngi ye ngalapa, ngi bone uma ku ya 'kuba njalo na." Ku be njalo; a ḣlale e se saba omunye. Ku njalo kwabanye. Kepa kwabaningi ku amanga njalo; ngokuba omunye uma e se vinjelwe, u ze a zibike ngokuti, "Au, ngi ya mangala kambe, ngokuba ngi ya kqutshwa ukuba ngi kuleke enkosini. Kepa ngi nga ka ti leke nokuti leke nje, O, nasi isilwane, nenyoka, nomuntu; loku ku fikela uku ngi bulala, se ngi vuka, ngi vinjelwe i lezo 'zinto." A miswe isibindi u lowo okwa ka kw' enza njalo kuye; a ti, "A ku 'luto loko; noma u bona into enjalo, u nga buki; kuḣle

body." I conquered him. I went home having ascended a rock of safety, saying, "O, forsooth I have been hindered by fantasies."

I did so again, and the things no longer continued to frighten me. And at last they ceased altogether, and have not returned to the present day. Many are hindered by such things; when they merely begin to pray, they see these beasts which come to devour them, and they at once start and go up, and no one thinks of going to the same place again; but a man says, "To-morrow it will be well for me to go to such a place, and see if the same thing will happen again." It does happen again; and he is afraid ever after. Thus it happens with some. But with the generality these things are known to be fantasies; for if a man is hindered by them, he tells some one else, saying, "O, I wonder, for I am impelled to pray to the Lord. But before I begin to open my mouth, lo, there is a beast, a snake, or a man; these come to kill me, and I start up and am hindered by these things." He is encouraged by the other to whom the same thing has happened; he says, "It is nothing; though you do see such things, do not look; it is proper

ukuba u kqinisele; u ya 'ugoduka; a ku yi 'kud*h*liwa impela njengokungati u za 'kud*h*liwa." Nembala ku be njalo; a buye e se e ncoma ukuti, "O, kanti ngi ko*h*liswa amanga, 'bani."

UMPENGULA MBANDA.

to be firm; you will go home uninjured; you will not be really devoured as it appears to you that you will be." And so it turns out; and he tells his friend, "O, So-and-so, forsooth I was deceived by fantasies."

KWA ti ngesikati sokulungiselwa kwami ukubapatiswa, nga ngi zinge ngi tandaza njalo ugezikati zonke ngasese. Ng' enza njalo ngoba ku ti lapo ngi tandazayo ku be njengokuba ya ngi bona impela inkosi. Ngi y' esuka lapo, in*h*liziyo yami i kcakcambile kakulu. Ng' enza njalo ngoba ngi bona ukuti, "Ku nga ba ku*h*le ukuba ngi kolwe kuyo inkosi, ngi be umntwana wayo nami." Kepa ku ti ngesinye isikati la ngi tandazayo ngi bone ku fika isilwane esibi, ku nga ti si ya 'ku ngi limaza. Ng' etuke, ngi shiye ukutandaza; kanti ka ngi boni 'luto. Kwa ba njalo ngezikati ezibili. Kwa ti ngesobutatu nga kqinisela, nga ti, "Ake ngi bone uma si za 'ku ngi limaza ini na?" Nga kqinisela, nga za nga kqoda ukutandaza. Ka nga be ngi sa bona 'luto uma se ngi kqedile. Nga balisa ngaloko, nga ti, "Ku ini loku?" Kepa nga se ngi zwile ngapambili ngamakolwa ukuti, "Uma umuntu e tandaza yedwa, u ya fikelwa izinto ezimbi

IT happened when I was being instructed for baptism, I used habitually to pray at all times in secret. I did so because when I prayed it was as if I really saw the Lord; and I went away from prayer with my heart very white indeed. I did so because I saw that it would be well for me too to believe in the Lord, and to become His child. But once when I was praying I saw a venomous beast coming to me as though it was about to injure me. I started up and left off praying. But forsooth I saw nothing. This happened twice; but on the third time I strengthened myself and said, "Let me just see if it will injure me or no." I strengthened myself till I had ended my prayer. And I saw nothing when I had finished. I doubted about it, and asked what it meant. But I had already heard from believers that when a man prayed alone, venomous creatures came to him when

uma zi kqutshwa Usatan." Nga bona ngaloko ukuti, "Ngi lingwa Usatan nje." Kepa ku zinge kw enza njalo njalo ngezikati zonke. Kwa za kwa ti ngemva kwesibindi sami, nga bona ukuti, "Ku ize nje." Kwa fika ngamandhla ukukanya okukulu; nga buya nga ti, uma ngi bona ukukanya okugeweleyo kumina, ngi buye ngi zisole ngi ti, "Ku ini ukuba ngi zinge ng' etuka into e ize nje na?" Kepa nga kqinisa ngamandhla enkosi, ngi bona ukuti, "Inkosi i nami ngezikati zonke." Emva kwaloko uma ngi tandaza ngi bona ukuti, "Inkosi i kona; ku nga ti ngi ng' andiza ngi ye kona ngokujabula okukeikeimayo enhliziyweni yami." Kwa ba njalo ke. Kepa a ngi tsho ukuti ngi wa kqeda onke amagama amanye e nga ngi wa bona ngaleso 'sikati, kwa za kwa fika isikati sokubapatizwa kwami.

USETEMBA DHLADHLA.

they were urged on by Satan. I saw by that that I was merely tempted by Satan. But this continued without cessation, until I took courage, and saw that it was nothing. And then there came with power a great light to me; and when I found myself full of light, I reproved myself for being continually startled by nothing. But I strengthened myself with the strength of the Lord, and saw that He was with me always. After that when I prayed I saw that the Lord is, and it was as if I could fly away to Him for the joy which overflowed my heart. So it was. But I do not say that I have mentioned every thing that I saw at that time before the time came for me to be baptised.[95]

---

[95] The reader will see repeated in these narratives the experiences of St. Antony, Hilarion, and other early saints.

INKOSAZANA.[96]

THE following superstition as regards the Inkosazana appears to be the relic of some old worship; and is therefore properly considered in this place.

INDABA ngenkosazana eya vela mhla ku vela abantu emhlabeni.

A i vami ukubonwa ngamehlo. Si zwa ku tiwa y' aziwa abendulo. A ku ko namunye kwaba se kona owa ke wa i bona. Ku tiwa inyamazanyana encane, i ngangekqakqa, i nemitshwana emhlotshana nemnyama; ngolunye uhlangoti ku mile umhlanga namahlati notshani; ngolunye umuntu. I mile kanjalo ke.

Ku ti uma i hlangana nomuntu i zifihle, i kulume naye e nga i boni, 'ezwe izwi nje lokuti, "Fulatela; u nga ngi bheki, ngokuba ngi hamba-ze." I tsho ngokuba ngemuva isinqe sayo si bomvu beje. Nembala ke umuntu a nga be e sa bheka, a kolwe ukuba "I

THE account of the Inkosazana who came out on the same day that men came out of the earth. She is not commonly seen. We hear it said the primitive men knew her. No one existing at the present time ever saw her. She is said to be a very little animal, as large as a polecat, and is marked with little white and black stripes; on one side there grows a bed of reeds, a forest, and grass;[97] the other side is that of a man. Such is her form.

If she meet with a man she conceals herself and speaks with him without his seeing her; he hears only a voice saying to him, "Turn your back; do not look on me, for I am naked." Saying thus because her buttocks are red like fire. And so the man no longer looks in that direction, but believes that

---

[96] *Inkosazana*, Princess, or Little Chieftainess.

[97] Not, says the native who gives the narrative, to be understood literally; but that there was something growing on her like a bed of reeds, a forest, and grass. But compare Ugungqu-kubantwana, *Zulu Nursery Tales*, p. 176; and Usilosimapundu, p. 184.

yo inkosazana e ngi za ngi zwa indaba yayo. I yo ke le." A fulatele ngokwesaba ukuba ku tiwa uma umuntu e i bonile, wa bhekana nayo, ka lungi, u ya fa masinyane.

I hamba nobu lwabantwana abaningi aba landela ngemuva, aba fana nayo.

Ku ti ngesinye isikati uma umuntu e i funyene ensimini i ti kuye, "Nonyaka u za 'kutola ukudhla; nakuba u kade u nendhlala, a u sa yi 'kuba nayo manje."

Futi i yona e veza imikuba eminingi pakati kwabantu abamnyama. I ti abantwana a ba kitshwe emabeleni, ba nga nceli; noma be bancane kakulu ba kitshwe masinyane ngezwi layo, ngokwesaba ukuti uma be nga kitshwa ku ya 'kuvela umkuba omubi kubantwana wokuba ba fe.

Y enza imiteto enjalo ke; imiteto yayo y enziwe, a i delelwa; ngokuba ku tiwa, "Ku tsho inkosazana." Nenkosi e busayo a i tsho ukuti insumansumane; izwi lenkosazana li ngapezulu kwelenkosi.

Lelo 'zwi lokuti a ku kitshwe abantwana, a i kulumi kubantu abaningi; i kuluma kumuntu e

it is indeed the Inkosazana about whom he has heard; and turns his back from fear, because it is said that if a man look on her face to face, he will be ill and very soon die.[98]

She goes followed by a large troop of children which resemble her.

Sometimes if a man meet with her in his garden she says to him, "This year you shall have food; although for a long time there has been famine, it shall be so no longer."

Besides it is she who introduces many fashions among black men. She orders the children to be weaned; and although they are very young, they are at once weaned in obedience to her commands, for they are afraid if they do not wean them they will be seized with some disease and die.

She makes such laws as these; and her laws are obeyed and not despised; for they say, "The Inkosazana has said." And the reigning chief does not say it is a fable; the word of the Inkosazana is greater than the chief's.

When she orders the children to be weaned she does not speak to many people; she speaks but to

---

[98] It may be interesting to compare this superstition with the following passages:—Exodus xxxiii. 20; Genesis xxxii. 30; Judges vi. 22, xiii. 22, 23.

munye, noma u sendhle a hlangana nayo; noma u sokaya, i fike ngobusuku kumuntu o tandwa i yona, i kulume naye; a landise ke izwi lelo; nomhlaba wonke w esaba uku li fihla, ngokuba a nga fa; a li fihlwa izwi layo. Na manje ku se kona loko.

Ngesinye isikati ku tiwa, a ku gaywe utshwala, bu yo'utelwa entabeni. Bu gaywe izizwe zonke, ku be i leyo 'nkosi nesizwe sayo; bu telwe entabeni, nesinye s' enze njalo, ku kitshwe ikcala.

Njengaloku ku be ku kona umuntu lapa emlazi, ku tiwa Ubobobo ibizo lake; u lowo ke umuntu o be 'enza imikuba yokuhlupa abantu ngokuti, "Inkosazana i ti, 'A ku gaywe utshwala, bu kcitwe ezintabeni; ku kitshwe abantwana emabeleni; izintombi a zi gane kwabatsha, z' ale abadala.'" A buy' a ti ngomunye unyaka, "Izintombi ngi zi nika amakxegu, z' ale abatsha."

Nemiteto eminingi i banjwe yonke, i menyezelwe ezweni lonke; i dume kakulu indaba kabobobo a

one man, sometimes meeting with him in the fields, sometimes at his home, coming by night to the man she loves and telling him; and he repeats her word to the people; and every one is afraid to hide her word, for he may die; her word is not kept secret. And this exists to the present time.

Sometimes she orders much beer to be made and poured out on the mountain. And all the tribes make beer, each chief and his tribe; the beer is poured on the mountain; and they thus free themselves from blame.

For example, there used to be a man in this country, living on the Umlazi, named Ubobobo;[99] he was a man who troubled people much by appointing customs by asserting that the Inkosazana had spoken to him, and said, "Let much beer be made and poured on the mountains; let the children be weaned; let the damsels marry young men, and reject the old." Another year he would say, "She says, 'I give the damsels to the old men; let them reject the young.'"

And many other such commands were all observed, and were published throughout the land; and whatever Ubobobo was told by the Inkosazana was rumoured in

---

' This man has only lately died. I saw him once. He appeared to b mad.

i tata kuyo inkosazana. I leyo ke indaba e ngi y aziyo.

A ku tshiwo ukuti i itongo, ngokuba i ya zikulumela nabantu. A ngi zwanga ukuba ku ya kcelwa ukuti nokuti kuyo, ngokuba a i hlali nabantu, i hlala ehlatini, y elanywe umuntu e be zihambele nje, a buye nczwi layo.

all directions. This is what I know about it.

It is not said that she is an Itongo (spirit), for she speaks with men of her own accord. I never heard that they pray to her for any thing, for she does not dwell with men, but in the forest, and is unexpectedly met by a man, who has gone out about his own affairs, and he brings back her message.

PART III.

IZINYANGA ZOKUBULA;

OR,

DIVINERS.

IZINYANGA ZOKUBULA;

OR,

DIVINERS.

The Initiation of a Diviner.

UKUMA kwomuntu o za 'kuba inyanga i loku, ukuba kukqala u nga umuntu o kqinileyo emzimbeni; kepa ekuhambeni kwesikati a kqale ngokutetema, e nga guli umzimba wake, u tetema kakulu. A kqale ngokuketa ukudhla, a zile okunye ukudhla, a ti, "Ukudhla okutile ni nga ngi pi kona; ku ya ngi bulala umzimba uma ngi ku dhlile." A zinge e puma ekudhleni, e keta ukudhla a ku tandayo, nako a nga ku kqinisi; a zinge e zibikabika. Futi e tsho nokuti, "Ngi pupe ngi muka namanzi." E pupa izinto eziningi, umzimba u

THE condition of a man who is about to be an inyanga[1] is this: At first he is apparently robust; but in process of time he begins to be delicate, not having any real disease, but being very delicate. He begins to be particular about food, and abstains from some kinds, and requests his friends not to give him that food, because it makes him ill. He habitually avoids certain kinds of food, choosing what he likes, and he does not eat much of that; and he is continually complaining of pains in different parts of his body. And he tells them that he has dreamt that he was being carried away by a river. He dreams of many things, and his body is muddled[2]

---

[1] See note 6, p. 131.

[2] *Dungeka.*—*Ukudunga* is to stir up mud in water, so as to make the water turbid, or muddy; and is hence applied by metaphor to

dungeke, a be indhlu yamapupo. Ku be i loko e pupa njalo izinto eziningi, e vuka, e ti, "Namhla nje umzimba wami u dungekile; ngi pupe ngi bulawa abantu abaningi; nga kqabuka, ngi sinda nje. Naku se ngi vuka, umzimba se u shiyene, u nga se wonke." A ze lowo 'muntu a gule kakulu, ku bulwe ezinyangeni.

Izinyanga kukqala zi nga tshetshi ukungena masinyane ukubona ukuba lo 'muntu u za 'kuba nenhloko ebutakataka. Ezinyangeni ku be lukuni ukubona isiminya; zi zinge zi buda, zi tsho oku nge ko, ku ze ku pele izinkomo ngokutsho kwezinyanga, zi ti, idhlozi lakubo li biz' inkomo, li ti, a li piwe ukudhla.

Nembala loko 'kutsho kwezinyanga abantu ba ku vumele pezulu, ngokuti zi y' azi zona. Ku ze ku pele konke kwalo 'muntu, e gula njalo; ku ze ku kohlwe uku-

and he becomes a house of dreams.[3] And he dreams constantly of many things, and on awaking says to his friends, "My body is muddled to-day; I dreamt many men were killing me; I escaped I know not how. And on waking one part of my body felt different from other parts; it was no longer alike all over." At last the man is very ill, and they go to the diviners to enquire.

The diviners do not at once see that he is about to have a soft head.[4] It is difficult for them to see the truth; they continually talk nonsense, and make false statements, until all the man's cattle are devoured at their command, they saying that the spirit of his people demands cattle, that it may eat food.

So the people readily assent to the diviners' word, thinking that they know. At length all the man's property is expended, he being still ill; and they no longer

---

confusion or muddling of mind by trouble,—disturbance of a family or a village by contention and quarrelling, and, as above, to general derangement of the body from disease. (Compare MUDDLE, *Wedgwood's Dictionary of English Etymology.*) From this word we have the compounds *Idungamuzi*, A stirrer up of strife in a village, or Village-muddler; and *Idungandhlu*, A stirrer up of strife in a house, or House-muddler.

[3] *A house of dreams*, meaning that he dreams constantly; that dreams take up their abode with him. Many dreams are supposed to be caused or sent by the Amatongo, but not all.

[4] *A soft head*, that is, impressible. Diviners are said to have *soft* heads.

ba ku za 'kwenziwa njani, loko izinkomo se zi pelile, nezihlobo zake zi m size ngento e swelekayo.

Ku ti ngelikade ku vela inyanga, i zi pikise zonke izinyanga, i ti, "Ngi y' azi ukuba ni za kumi lapa nje, se n' ahlulekile ; a ni se nasibindi sokuti i kona inyanga e nga ni sizako. Kepa mina, 'bangane bami, ngi bona ukuti abangane bami ba lahlekile. A ba i dhlanga impepo. A ba tasanga kahle. Ini ukuba b' ahlulwe, ukufa ku sobala? Ngi ti mina lezo 'nyanga zi ni hlupile. Loku 'kufa a ku funi ukuba kw elatshwe ngegazi. Lo 'muntu a ngi boni okunye, 'kupela ngi bona ukuti u nomhlaba. A ku ko 'kunye. U hanjwa umhlaba. U ya hanjwa lo 'muntu abakwini. B' ahluke kabili ; aba-

know what to do, for he has no more cattle, and his friends help him in such things as he needs.

At length an inyanga comes and says that all the others are wrong. He says, "I know that you come here to me because you have been unable to do any thing for the man, and have no longer the heart to believe that any inyanga can help you. But, my friends, I see that my friends, the other izinyanga, have gone astray. They have not eaten impepo.[5] They were not initiated in a proper way. Why have they been mistaken, when the disease is evident? For my part, I tell you the izinyanga have troubled you. The disease does not require to be treated with blood.[6] As for the man, I see nothing else but that he is possessed by the Itongo.[7] There is nothing else. He is possessed by an Itongo. Your people[8] move in him. They are divided into two

---

[5] *Impepo* is of two kinds—white and black.

The *black* is first used as an emetic to remove all badness and causes of dimness from the system.

The *white* is burnt as incense when sacrificing to the Amatongo ; izinyanga use it as an emetic to prevent the return of dimness of the inner sight after the use of the black impepo ; they also eat it; and place it under their heads at night, that they may have clear, truthful dreams. They believe that by the use of this medicine they are enabled to divine with accuracy. Hence to have "eaten impepo" means to be a trustworthy diviner.

[6] *Treated with blood*, that is, of sacrifices.

[7] *Umhlaba*, i. e., the Itongo. See p. 147, note 14.

[8] *Your people move in him*, that is, the Amatongo. See p. 226. Or, he is possessed by your people.

nye ba ti, 'Kqa, a si tandi ukuba umntwana wetu 'oniwe. A si ku funi.' Ngaloko ke kungako e nga sindi nje. Uma ni m vimba, ni ya 'kuba ni ya m bulala. Ngokuba ka sa yi 'kuba inyanga; futi ka sa yi 'kubuyela ebuntwini; u ya 'kuba i loku e nje. Uma e nga sa guli, u se ya 'kutetema njalo, a be isiula, a nga kqondi 'luto. Ngi ti mina ni ya 'ku m bulala ngemiti. Yeka ni nje, ni bheke impeto lapa ukufa ku bhekisa kona. A ni boni ini ukuba ku ti ngamhla e nga i dhlanga imiti, a ke a funde nomfino na? Mu yeke ni ngemiti. Ka yi 'kufa ngokugula, ngokuba u ya 'kupiwa ubuhle."

Nembala ke a gule lo 'muntu iminyaka emibili, e nga sindi; kumbe i dhlule kuloko, e gula. A pume endhlini izinsukwana, abantu ba kqale ukuti, "U za 'usinda." Kqa, a buyele endhlini. Ku zinge ku ba njalonjalo a ze a hlutuke izinwele. Kepa umzimba wake u be lututuva, a nga tandi amafuta. Abantu ba mangale ngokuhamba

parties; some say, 'No, we do not wish that our child should be injured. We do not wish it.' It is for that reason and no other that he does not get well. If you bar the way against the Itongo, you will be killing him. For he will not be an inyanga; neither will he ever be a man again; he will be what he is now. If he is not ill, he will be delicate, and become a fool, and be unable to understand any thing. I tell you you will kill him by using medicines. Just leave him alone, and look to the end to which the disease points. Do you not see that on the day he has not taken medicine, he just takes a mouthful of food?[9] Do not give him any more medicines. He will not die of the sickness, for he will have what is good[10] given to him."

So the man may be ill two years without getting better; perhaps even longer than that. He may leave the house for a few days, and the people begin to think he will get well. But no, he is confined to the house again. This continues until his hair falls off. And his body is dry and scurfy; and he does not like to anoint himself. People wonder at the progress of the disease.

---

[9] When he takes medicines, he eats nothing, and is worse than usual. When he leaves off medicines he is better, and takes a little food.

[10] *What is good*, viz., the power to divine.

kwaleso 'sifo. Kodwa in*h*loko i k*q*ale ukubonakala into e ku nga ti i za 'kuba yona. A bonakale ngokuzamula futifuti, na ngokuti*m*ula futifuti. Abantu ba ti, "K*q*a! Nembala lo 'muntu ku nga u za 'kuhanjwa um*h*laba." A bonakale na ngokutanda uguai kakulu; a nga bi nasikati eside uguai e nga m bemanga. Abantu ba k*q*ale ukubona ukuti u nikelwe ubu*h*le.

Ku ti ngemva kwaloku a gule, a ke a k*q*uleke, a telwe ngamanzi, ku tulatule isikatshana. E zinge e kala izinyembezi, e pumisela ku ze ku be kanye, ku ti pakati kwobusuku, lap' abantu be tatekile ubutongo, 'ezwakale, a vuse abantu bonke ngoku*h*labelela; u se k*q*ambe igama, abantu ba vuke abesifazana nabamadoda, ba ye kuye, ba ye 'ku m vumisa lelo 'gama a li *h*labelelayo.

Lokupela ku njalonjalo, ku be se ku bonwa ngokusa; se ku lu-

But his head begins to give signs of what is about to happen. He shows that he is about to be a diviner by yawning[11] again and again, and by sneezing again and again. And men say, "No! Truly it seems as though this man was about to be possessed by a spirit." This is also apparent from his being very fond of snuff; not allowing any long time to pass without taking some. And people begin to see that he has had what is good given to him.

After that he is ill; he has slight convulsions, and has water poured on him, and they cease for a time. He habitually sheds tears, at first slight, and at last he weeps aloud, and in the middle of the night, when the people are asleep, he is heard making a noise, and wakes the people by singing; he has composed a song, and men and women awake and go to sing in concert with him.

In this state of things they daily expect his death;[12] he is now

---

[11] Yawning is considered a sign of approaching inspiration by the Itongo.—In the Icelandic Legends we find a remarkable power ascribed to yawning. The female troll who had assumed the likeness of a beautiful queen betrays her secret by saying, "When I yawn a little yawn, I am a neat and tiny maiden; when I yawn a half-yawn, then I am as a half-troll; when I yawn a whole yawn, then am I as a whole troll." *(Legends of Iceland. Powell and Magnusson. 2nd Series, p. 448.)*

[12] Lit., It is now seen by the morning, viz., that he is still alive. They retire to rest doubtful whether they shall find him still living at daybreak.

ngelelene amatambo; ku se ku
tiwa eli ngomso ilanga a li yi 'ku
m shiya. Ba mangale abantu,
b' ezwa e *h*laba igama, ba m tshayele ke. Ba k*q*ale ukuma isibindi
ngokuti, "Yebo ke; manje si ya
i bona in*h*loko."

Ngaloko ke ngaleso 'sikati uma
e se tasa, abantu balowo 'muzi ba
*h*lupeke ngoku nga lali 'butongo;
ngokuba umuntu ow etasayo u ya
*h*lupa kakulu, ngokuba ka lali, u
ya sebenza kakulu ngen*h*loko;
ukulala kwake u ti *h*lwati nje, u
ya vuka u se vuka namagama
amaningi; nemizi e seduze nowa-
kubo i puma kona ebusuku, i zwe
ukuba izwi lake se li pezulu, ba ye
'ku m vumela. Kumbe a *h*labelele
ku ze ku se, ku nga lalwanga.
Abantu bomuzi be m tshayela
izand*h*la zi ze zi be 'bu*h*lungu.
Lapo ke u se lingisa kweselesele
pakati kwend*h*lu; ind*h*lu se inci-
nane ukuk*x*ok*x*oma, 'esuka 'ek*q*a
e *h*labelela, e vevezela, e lingisa
kwom*h*langa u pakati kwamanzi,
a juluke a be 'manzi.

Zi d*h*liwe ke izinkomo ngaleso
'sikati. Ku *h*langabezwa lobo
'bu*h*le, ku keakeambiswa id*h*lozi,
ukuba li m kanyise kakulu. Ku

but skin and bones, and they think
that to-morrow's sun will not leave
him alive. The people wonder
when they hear him singing, and
they strike their hands in concert.
They then begin to take courage,
saying, "Yes; now we see that it
is the head."[13]

Therefore whilst he is under-
going this initiation the people of
the village are troubled by want
of sleep; for a man who is beginning to be an inyanga causes great
trouble, for he does not sleep, but
works constantly with his brain;
his sleep is merely by snatches,
and he wakes up singing many
songs; and people who are near
quit their villages by night when
they hear him singing aloud, and
go to sing in concert. Perhaps he
sings till the morning, no one
having slept. The people of the
village smite their hands in concert till they are sore. And then
he leaps about the house like a
frog; and the house becomes too
small for him, and he goes out,
leaping and singing, and shaking
like a reed in the water, and drip-
ping with perspiration.

At that time many cattle are
eaten. The people encourage his
becoming an inyanga; they employ means for making the Itongo
white, that it may make his
divination very clear. At length

---

[13] Lit., We see the head, viz., that it is affected in that way
which is followed by the power to divine.

ze ku be kona enye inyanga endala ey aziwayo. Ku ti ebusuku e lele a yalelwe, ku tiwe, "Hamba u ye kubani, u ye a ku pe*hl*ele ubulawo boku*hl*anza, ukuze w etase kanyekanye." Nembala a ti nya amasukwana, e yile kuleyo 'nyanga, e ye 'kupe*hl*elwa ubulawo ; u ya buya u se omunye, u se *hl*ambulukile, u se inyanga ke.

Ku ti uma e za 'kuba nemilozi, ku zinge ku ba kona izwi lokuti kuye, "Wena ku z' ukukuluma nabantu ; abantu b' eza 'kutshelwa i ti konke ab' eza ngako." A zinge e wa lauza lawo 'mapupo, e ti, "Ba kona abantu aba ngi tshela ebusuku, ba ti, b' eza 'uzikulumela bona nabantu ab' ezo'u bula." Nembala ku ze ku ye ngako loko ; e sa bula yena, ku be kanye ku n*g*amuke ; labo 'bantu aba kuluma ngemilozi 'ezwe se be kuluma kuye, a ba pendule naye njengomuntu nje ; a ba kulumise naye ngoku ba buza ; uma e nga

another ancient inyanga of celebrity is pointed out to him.[14] At night whilst asleep he is commanded by the Itongo, who says to him, "Go to So-and-so ; go to him, and he will churn for you emetic-ubulawo,[15] that you may be an inyanga altogether." Then he is quiet for a few days, having gone to the inyanga to have ubulawo churned for him ; and he comes back quite another man, being now cleansed and an inyanga indeed.

And if he is to have familiar spirits, there is continually a voice saying to him, "You will not speak with the people ; they will be told by us every thing they come to enquire about." And he continually tells the people his dreams, saying, "There are people[16] who tell me at night that they will speak for themselves to those who come to enquire." At last all this turns out to be true ; when he has begun to divine, at length his power entirely ceases, and he hears the spirits who speak by whistlings[17] speaking to him, and he answers them as he would answer a man ; and he causes them to speak by asking them questions ; if he does not under-

---

[14] That is, by the Itongo in a dream.
[15] *Ubulawo.*—See p. 142, note 10.
[16] *People*, viz., the dead, the Amatongo.
[17] The supposed voice of the familiar spirits is always in a shrill, whistling tone ; hence they are called *imilozi*.

ku kqondi loko a ba ku tshoyo, bona ba m kqondise konke a ba ku bonayo. Imilozi a i kqali ngokubula imiḣlola yabantu ; i kqala ngokukuluma nomuntu wayo, i m azise loko oku za 'kuba i ko, anduba i bulele abantu izindaba zonke.

Nako ke e ngi kw aziyo ngemilozi na ngezinyanga.

Ku ti uma umuntu lowo o guliswa umḣlaba, abakubo aba hambayo be nga tandi ukuba a bule, ba bize inyanga enkulu yokwelapa, i m vimbe, ukuze a nga buli. Kepa lo 'muntu noma e nga sa buli, ka lungi ; u ḣlala e isiguli ngezikati zonke. Nako ke e ngi kw aziyo. Kepa noma e nga sa buli, ngokuḣlakanipa u fana nenyanga yokubula njengondayeni. Yena, abakubo be nga tandanga nkuba a bule, ba ti, " Kqa ; a si tandi ukuba indoda engaka, e namandḣla angaka, i be into nje e se i ḣlala ekaya, i nga se namsebenzi, ku ukupela ukubula kodwa." Ba m vimba ke. Kwa se ku ḣlala kuye isibonakaliso sokuti, " Lo 'muntu, uma wa e inyanga, wa e za 'kuba ubandubandu, ukuti inyangisisa."

stand what they say, they make him understand every thing they see. The familiar spirits do not begin by explaining omens which occur among the people ; they begin by speaking with him whose familiars they are, and making him acquainted with what is about to happen, and then he divines for the people.

This then is what I know of familiar spirits and diviners.

If the relatives of the man who has been made ill by the Itongo do not wish him to become a diviner, they call a great doctor to treat him, to lay the spirit, that he may not divine. But although the man no longer divines, he is not well ; he continues to be always out of health. This is what I know. But although he no longer divines, as regards wisdom he is like a diviner. For instance, there was Undayeni. His friends did not wish him to become a diviner ; they said, " No ; we do not wish so fine and powerful a man to become a mere thing which stays at home, and does no work, but only divines." So they laid the spirit. But there still remained in him signs which caused the people to say, " If that man had been a diviner, he would have been a very great man, a first-class diviner."

Leyo 'milozi, a u bi munye umlozi o kulumako; ibandhla eliningi nje labantu; namazwi a wa fani; omunye u nelake nomunye njalo; elalowo 'muntu a ba ngene kuye izwi lake li lodwa. Futi ngokuba naye u ya buza kuyo ujengabanye abantu, naye u ya bula kuyo. Uma i nga tsho 'luto, k' azi loko oku ya 'utshiwo i yo; a nge ba tshele abantu ab' ezo'ubula, ukuti, ni za 'kutshelwa ukuti nokuti. Ai. Okwake ukwamukela into leyo e fike nabantu ab' ezo'ubula 'kupela. Naye u ya buzana nayo, ba kulumisane.

Ku ti uma ab' ezo'ubula be fika kulo 'muntu e nemilozi ba kuleke, a tsho kubo ukuti, " O, ni fika nje ngi ngedwa. Ku mukiwe izolo. A ng' azi lapa ku yiwe kona." Ba hlale ke abantu labo. Ekufikeni kwayo i ya 'kuzwakala ngokubingelela labo 'bantu, i ti, " Sa ni bona ke." Ba ti, " Si bona nina, 'makosi." Naye lowo o hamba nayo a buze ukuba, " Ni ya fika na?" I vume. Ngaloko ke kulukuni ukukqonda kitina ukuba ku inkohliso, lapa si zwa amazwi amaningi a kuluma nomuntu o nayo, naye e kuluma.

As to the familiar spirits, it is not one only that speaks; they are very many; and their voices are not alike; one has his voice, and another his; and the voice of the man into whom they enter is different from theirs. He too enquires of them as other people do; and he too seeks divination of them. If they do not speak, he does not know what they will say; he cannot tell those who come for divination what they will be told. No. It is his place to take what those who come to enquire bring, and nothing more. And the man and the familiar spirits ask questions of each other and converse.

When those who come to seek divination salute him, he replies, " O, you have come when I am alone. The spirits departed yesterday. I do not know where they are gone." So the people wait. When they come they are heard saluting them, saying, " Good day." They reply, " Good day to you, masters." And the man who lives with them also asks them saying, " Are you coming?" They say, they are. It is therefore difficult to understand that it is a deception, when we hear many voices speaking with the man who has familiar spirits, and him too speaking with them.

The way in which a person begins to be a Diviner.

Uhlabo lu bonakala ngokwenza isibobo; u ti umuntu, "Kubuhlungu esikaleni, pansi kwesipanga, ohlangotini, enyameni. Lw enza isibobo; lu pumele ngapakati kwomzimba izindawo zombili."

Ba buze abantu, ba ti, "Leso 'sifo isifo sini na? loku lu fana nohlabo nje."

A ti, "Ehe; nami ngi ti i lo uhlabo; i lo lolu olu pumela esikaleni somzimba, lw ale ukuba ngi pefumule, lw ale ukuba ngi lale pansi."

Lu ze lw ahlulwe inyanga e lw aziyo umuti walo. Ngokuba abamnyama ba ti ukxulo; ba ti, lw enziwa umhlaba. Lo 'muntu o

Uthlabo[18] is known by causing a sensation of perforation[19] of the side; and the man says, "I have pain under the armpit, beneath the shoulder-blade, in my side, in the flesh. It causes the feeling as if there was a hole there; the pain passes through my body to each side."

The men ask, "What is this disease? for it resembles nothing but uthlabo."

He replies, "Yes, yes; I too say it is uthlabo; it is that which comes out[20] from the side of my body and will not let me breathe, neither will it let me lie down."

At length the doctor who knows the medicines for uthlabo cures it. But black people call it also ukxulo,[21] and say it is caused by the Itongo.[22] And when a

---

[18] *Uhlabo*, the name of a disease, from *ukuhlaba*, to stab, because it is attended with a stabbing pain or *stitch* in the side. It is applied either to pleurodynia or pleurisy.

[19] *Isibobo*, A hole,—that is, the patient feels as though a hole had been made in his side with a sharp instrument. The same sensation that we call a "stitch in the side."

[20] He speaks of the disease as though it was a knife, or something of that kind; he personifies it.

[21] *Ukxulo.*—The same as *uhlabo*, from *ukukxula*, to stab.

[22] We may compare the following faith in evil Nats, which seem to hold very much the same position in the East as the Amatongo among the Amazulu:—

"The Nats or Dewatas play a conspicuous part in the affairs of this world. Their seats are in the six lower heavens, forming, with the abode of man and the four states of punishment, the eleven seats of passions. But they often quit their respective places, and interfere

tandwa ukɀulo izikati zonke, ku se lu m bambe njalo izikati zonke, kubantu abamnyama ku tiwa, u ya hanjwa um*h*laba ; amatongo a hamba kuyena emzimbeni. Lu ti uma lw epuza ukupela emzimbeni, ku ze ku yokubulwa czinyangeni. Zi tik' izinyanga, zi ti, " U nom-*h*laba. U nabakubo abafayo." Zi ti uma zi ti, " Kwa ku kona umuntu kubo owa be e inyanga ; naye u hanjwa njalo emzimbeni ; ku

man is constantly affected[23] by uthlabo, black men say the Itongo is walking in him ; Amatongo are walking in his body. If the disease lasts a long time, they at length go to enquire of diviners. They come and say, " He is affected by the Itongo. He is affected by his people who are dead.[24] There was one of them who was an inyanga ; and this man has the Itongo in his body ; his people

---

with the chief events that take place among men. Hence we see them ever attentive in ministering to all the wants of the future Budha. Besides, they are made to watch over trees, forests, villages, towns, cities, fountains, rivers, &c. These are the good and benevolent Nats. This world is also supposed to be peopled with wicked Nats, whose nature is ever prone to the evil. A good deal of the worship of Budhists consists in superstitious ceremonies and offerings made for propitiating the wicked Nats, and obtaining favours and temporal advantages from the good ones. Such a worship is universal, and fully countenanced by the Talapoins, though in opposition with the real doctrines of genuine Budhism. All kinds of misfortunes are attributed to the malignant interference of the evil Nats. In case of severe illness that has resisted the skill of native medical art, the physician gravely tells the patient and his relatives that it is useless to have recourse any longer to medicines, but a conjuror must be sent for, to drive out the malignant spirit who is the author of the complaint. Meanwhile directions are given for the erection of a shed, where offerings intended for the inimical Nat are deposited. A female relative of the patient begins dancing to the sound of musical instruments. The dance goes on at first in rather a quiet manner, but it gradually grows more animated, until it reaches the acme of animal phrenzy. At that moment the bodily strength of the dancing lady becomes exhausted ; she drops on the ground in a state of apparent faintness. She is then approached by the conjuror, who asks her if the invisible foe has relinquished his hold over the diseased. Having been answered in the affirmative, he bids the physician to give medicines to the patient, assuring him that his remedies will now act beneficially for restoring the health of the sick, since their action will meet no further opposition from the wicked Nat." *(The Life or Legend of Gaudama, the Budha of the Burmese. P. Bigandet, p.* 71. Comp. also p. 537.*)*

[23] *Tandwa*, lit., loved.

[24] That is, the Amatongo.

funwa abakubo a z' a be nenhloko ebutakataka, a bule, e tasile."

Zi ti izinyanga ezi bulayo, "Ni nga be ni sa mu nika imiti. A ni boni ini, lapa ni mu funela imiti yohlabo, lu nga vumi ukupela na? Ni ti ni nga mu puzisa umuti, ku be i kona ni mu bangelayo na? Mu yeke ni ngemiti. Lo 'muntu u ya hanjwa abakubo. Ba tanda uma a pupe."

Ku ti uma kwa ku kona umuntu owa fayo, owa be inyanga, ba m bize ngegama, e bizwa izinyanga ezi yokubula, zi ti, "U hanjwa Ubani lowo; o yena e ti, m' a be inyanga. U hanjwa umuntu owa be e inyanga enkulu." Ku tsho izinyanga ezi yokubula. Zi ti, "Lowo 'muntu owa be inyanga, o hamba kuye emzimbeni, wa be inyanga neyokumbulula. Ya be i mbulula." Zi ti izinyanga, "Naye wish him to have a soft head,[25] and become a diviner, when he has been initiated."

The diviners say, "Do not give him any more medicines. Do you not see when you get uthlabo-medicines for him, the disease does not cease? When you give him medicine, do you not thereby increase the disease? Leave him alone. His people are in him. They wish him to dream."

And if one of his people who is dead was an inyanga, the diviners who come to divine call him by name, and say, "So-and-so is in him; it is he who says he is to be an inyanga. It is a great inyanga that possesses him." That is what the diviners say. They say, "The man who was an inyanga, who is walking in his body, was also an inyanga who could dig up poisons.[26] He used to dig them up. And since he who used to

---

[25] To have a soft or impressible head, that is, to be an inyanga.

[26] *Ukumbulula.*—Sorcerers are supposed to destroy their victims by taking some portion of their bodies, as hair or nails; or something that has been worn next their person, as a piece of an old garment, and adding to it certain medicines, which is then buried in some secret place. They are at once the subjects of disease, and suffer and die. The power alluded to above is that of discovering and digging up this poison. Very similar to the practice of sorcerers amongst ourselves, who used to make an image of wax or clay of the person they wished to kill, and treat it with poisons, &c., and every thing done to the image was felt by their victim.

The following account is given among Danish Traditions:—

"In a certain house everything went perversely; for which reason the inhabitants sent to a well-known wise woman. She came and went about the house both within and without. At last she stood

lokw e hanjwa u ye lowo 'muntu owa be e mbulula ubuti babatakati a ba bulala ngabo abanye abantu, naye k*q*ed' 'etase, a m etasise, u ya 'kuba ned*h*lozi elim*h*lope, naye u ya 'kumbulula nayo, njengalowo wakubo Ubani, owa be e inyanga, e mbulula; u za 'kumbulula naye. Mu yeke ni ngemiti." Zi ti izinyanga o ku bulwa kuzona, zi ti zona, " Imiti i la*h*le ni ; ni nga be ni sa mu nika; se ni ya 'ku m bulala, uma ni ti ni mu nika imiti. Ni ti i yona i ya 'ku m sindisa. Ka i yi 'ku mu sindisa. W' enziwa ngamabomu. Lo 'muntu dig up the poison of the sorcerers by which they destroyed others has taken possession of this man, he too as soon as he has been initiated will have a white Itongo,[27] and will dig up poisons as So-and-so, one of his people, used to do. Leave him alone as regards medicines. Throw away medicines, and give him no more; you will kill him if you do. You think they will cure him. They will not cure him. He is purposely thus affected. The Amatongo wish

---

still before a large stone, which lay just without the dwelling. 'This,' said she, 'should be rolled away.' But all that they could do with levers and other means was to no purpose : the stone would not move. At length the wise woman herself hobbled up to the stone, and scarcely had she touched it before it moved from its old station. Beneath was found a silken purse filled with the claws of cocks and eagles, human hair and nails. ' Put it into the fire together with a good bundle of pea-straw, that it may catch quickly,' said the old woman ; and no sooner was this said than done. But the moment the fire began to take effect it began to howl and hiss as if the very house were ready to fall, and people who stood out in the fields hard by plainly saw a witch sally forth on her broomstick from the mouth of the oven. At the same moment the old woman died, who, it was supposed, had bewitched the house, and all the sorcery was at an end." *(Northern Mythology. Benjamin Thorpe. Vol. II., p. 189.)*

[27] That is, an Itongo who shall influence for good, and enable him to see *clearly* and help others. They also speak of an Itongo elimnyama, a dark or black Itongo, that is, one that is jealous, and when he visits any one causes disease and suffering without giving any reason for his doing so. It is said, " Li lwe li tulile," that is, It fights in silence,—contends with people without telling them what to do to pacify it. They suppose that sorcerers are aided by the Amatongo of their house to practise sorcery with skill and effect ; but such Amatongo are not said to be black or dark, but white, because they reveal with clearness their will to their devotee.

ku tandwa um' a be inyanga emhlope. Tula ni, ni bone uma k' ezi 'kuyalelwa na ebusuku e lele? Ni ya 'ku m bona e se fika nje kusasa, ni nga m bonanga ukupuma kwake, e yalelwe imiti a yoku i mba entabeni, e mbe ubulawo bokuhlanza, a bu pehle, bu be nengwebu, a bu puze, a hlanze ngabo, 'etase. Ku ti ngesinye isikati a yalelwe impepo, a yoku i ka emhlangeni."

Ba mu tume ukuhlaba inyama, ngokuba abantu abafayo ba tanda inyama kakulu kumuntu a se be tanda uku m enza um' a be inyanga. U ya zi hlaba, e ba hlabela abakubo abafayo. Zi ya ngena ezinye. U ya zi hlaba njalo; zi ya ngena futi ezinye, zi vela ekwelapeni kwake, na sekubuleni kwake, nezokumbulula izinkomo. Uma abantu be buba, be bulawa abatakati, i muke i yokumbulula, i hlanzise abantu aba dhliswayo abatakati.

him to become a white[28] inyanga. Be quiet, and see if the Amatongo do not give him commands at night in his sleep. You will see him come home in the morning, not having seen him go out, having had medicines revealed to him which he will go to the mountains to dig up; you will see he has dug up cleansing-ubulawo, and he will churn it and make it froth and drink it, and cleanse himself by it, and so begin to be an inyanga. And at other times he will be commanded to fetch impepo, which he will go to the marsh to pluck."

The Amatongo tell him to kill cattle, for the dead are very fond of demanding flesh of one whom they wish to make an inyanga. He slaughters them for his people who are dead. And others enter his kraal.[29] He slaughters constantly, and others again come in in their place, the cattle being derived from his treatment of disease, and from divining, and digging up poisons. When men are perishing, being destroyed by sorcerers, he goes and digs up the poisons, and purifies those whom the sorcerers are poisoning.

---

[28] As we speak of "white witches;" an inyanga who shall see clearly, and use his power for good purposes.

[29] By sacrificing to the Amatongo he obtains their blessing; they enable him to treat disease and to divine successfully; and thus he obtains many cattle, which enter his kraal instead of those he has sacrificed.

Uma umuntu e gula, e guliswa amadhlozi, u ya haiya. Amatongo a m kqambise igama, ku butane abantu basekaya, ba mu tshayele igama a li kqambelwe itongo,— lokwetasa,—lobunyanga.

Abanye abantu ba pike, ba ti, "Kqabo. Lo 'muntu u ya hlanya nje. Ka nalo itongo." Ba ti abanye, "O, u netongo; u se inyanga."
Ba ti abanye, "Kqa; u uhlanya. Ni ka ni mu tukusele na, loku ni ti u inyanga?"

Ba ti, "Kqa; a si ka mu tukuseli."
Ba ti, "Se ni mu bona ngani, ni bone u inyanga na?"
Ba ti, "Si m bona ngokuyalelwa imiti a yoku i mba."

Ba ti, "O, u uhlanya nje. Ngapana si be si ya vuma uma u inyanga uma ku be ni ya mu tukusela, lezo 'zinto e be ni mu tukusele zona u ya zi gila. Anti ni si tshel' ize, ukuti u inyanga, loku a ni ka mu tukuseli."

Ba ti uma ba kulume, ba tsho njalo, be pikisana ngoku mu tuku-

When the Amatongo make a man ill, he cries "Hai, hai, hai."[30] They cause him to compose songs, and the people of his home assemble and beat time to the song the Amatongo have caused him to compose,—the song of initiation, —a song of professional skill.

Some dispute and say, "No. The fellow is merely mad. There is no Itongo in him." Others say, "O, there is an Itongo in him; he is already an inyanga."
The others say, "No; he is mad. Have you ever hidden things for him to discover by his inner sight, since you say he is an inyanga?"

They say, "No; we have not done that."
They ask, "How then do you know he is an inyanga?"
They say, "We know it because he is told about medicines, which he goes to dig up."

They reply, "O! he is a mere madman. We might allow that he is an inyanga if you had concealed things for him to find, and he had discovered what you had concealed. But you tell us what is of no import, as you have not done this."

As they are talking thus and disputing about concealing things

---

[30] *Haiya*, To cry as the diviner; a continual repetition of Hai, hai, hai.

sela, ku ti ebusuku, ekulaleni kwake, a pupe e m tshela lowo 'muntu wakubo owa fayo, o yena o mw etasisayo um' a be inyanga, a mu tshel' a ti, "Be be pikisana, be ti, ku vi u inyanga wena."

A buze o tasiswayo, a ti, "Ba ti, a ngi vi ngi inyanga ngani na?"

A ti, "Ba ti, ku vi u inyanga; ba ti, u uhlanya nje; ba ti, u ya tukuselwa na, loku ku tiwa u inyanga na?"

A buz' a ti, "Ngi tshele, ku tsho obani na?"

A ti, "Ku be ku pikisana obani nobani."

A ti, "Wena u ti b' enz' amanga ini uma be tsho njalo na?"

A ti, "Tula. Loku be tsho njalo, mina ngi ti, u za 'kuba inyanga ey ahlula izinyanga zonke, ba dele bonke abantu lapa emhlabeni, ukuti u inyanga enkulu, ba kw azi."

A ti yena ow etasiswayo, a ti, "Mina ngi ti ba keinisile uma be ti, ng' uhlanya. Mbala a ba bonanga be ngi tukusela."

A ti lowo 'muntu owa be inya-

for him to find, at night when he is asleep he dreams that the man of his people who is dead, and who is causing him to begin to be an inyanga, tells him saying, "They were disputing with each other, saying you are not an inyanga."

He who is beginning to be an inyanga asks, "Why do they say I am not an inyanga?"

He replies, "They say you are not an inyanga, but a mere mad man; and ask if they have hidden things for you to discover, since the others say you are an inyanga."

He says, "Tell me who they are who say so."

He replies, "So-and-so and So-and-so were disputing."

The man asks, "Do you say they lie when they say so?"

He replies, "Be quiet. Because they say so, I say you shall be a greater inyanga than all others, and all men in the world shall be satisfied that you are a great inyanga, and they shall know you."

The man who is beginning to be an inyanga says, "For my part I say they speak the truth when they say I am mad. Truly they have never hidden anything for me to find."

Then the man who was an in-

nga, o yena o m etasisayo, a ti, "Tula ke. Ngi za 'ku ku yisa kona ekuseni. U vele entabeni; u nga ba zumi; u vele entabeni e sesita, u haize; u z' u ti ukuhaiza kwako entabeni e sesita, ba ku zwe. Ba ya 'kuti uma u haiza k*q*ede, ba ng' ezwa; u pumele entabeni e sobala; u nga veli kakulu; u vele k*q*ede, u haize, u b' ezwise kodwa. Ba ti uma b' ezwe ukuti u wena, u buye, u tshone, u buyele entabeni e sesita. Ngi ti ke, ba ya 'kubona, ba ya 'kuzwa, ukuti be be ku pete wena, umuntu o inyanga, o tasisiweyo; ba ya 'kwazi ngaloko a ba be pikisana ngako, be ti, u u*h*lanya, a u si yo inyanga."

Mbala, w' enza ngaloko. Wa haiza entabeni e sesita; ka ba mu zwa kakulu; b' ezwa ku zinge ku ti, Nkene, nkene, nkene, nkene, nkene, nkene. 'Ezwe omunye umuntu, a ti, "U nga ti ku kona umuntu o nga t' u ti u ya *h*labelela." Ba ti abanye, "A si zwa; tina si zwa ku nkeneza nje."

A bone lowo o inyanga li fike itongo kuye, li m tshele, li ti, yanga, he who is initiating him, says, "Just be quiet. I will take you to them in the morning. And do you appear on a hill; do not come upon them suddenly; but appear on a hill which is concealed, and cry 'Hai, hai, hai;' cry thus on the hill which is concealed, that they may hear. When you cry 'Hai, hai, hai,' if they do not hear, then go on to a hill which is open; do not expose yourself much; as soon as you expose yourself, cry 'Hai, hai, hai,' so that they may just hear. When they hear that it is you, go down again from the hill, and return to the one which is concealed. So I say they will see and understand that they have spoken of a man who is beginning to be a doctor; they shall know by that, that when they said you were a mad man and not an inyanga they were mistaken."

So he does so. He cries "Hai, hai, hai," on a hill which is hidden; they do not hear him distinctly; they hear only a continual sound of Nkene, nkene, nkene, nkene.[31] One of them says, "It sounds as though there was some one singing." Others say, "We do not hear. We hear only an echo."

The Itongo comes to him and tells him that they cannot hear,

---

[31] *Nkene*, from *ukunkeneza*, to echo.

"Amanga; ka b' ezwa; a ku pumele ingcozana entabeni e sobala, u za 'ubuya u tshone kule 'ntaba e sesita."

Mbala w' esuka ngokutsho kwetongo, wa pumela entabeni e sobala, wa haiza; ba mu zwa bonke ukuti Ubani. "Konje, 'madoda," (lapa se be pikisana futi, kqede ba mu zwe ukuti u yena,) "konje, 'madoda, u za ngayo leyo 'ndaba e sa si pikisana ngayo, si ti, u u*h*lanya na?"

Ba ti, "O, ni sa buza ni na? U za ngayo, uma nga nembala na kuluma ukuti, ka v' e inyanga,[33] u u*h*lanya."

A ti umuntu omkulu wakona, lapa ekaya kulowo 'muzi, lapa i ya kona inyanga, e ti, "Nami ngi ya tsho ukuti u u*h*lanya. Ake ni tate izinto, ni yoku zi tukusa, si bone uma u ya 'ku zi kipa na."

Ba zi tate izinto, ubu*h*lalu, ba yoku bu tukusa; abanye ba tukuse amageja; abanye ba tukuse imikonto; abanye ba tukuse amasongo; abanye ba tukuse izinduku zabo; abanye ba tukuse imintsha yabo; abanye ba tukuse izipand*h*la zabo; abanye ba tukuse izimkamba zabo; abanye ba tukuse izimbenge; ba ti, "Ake si bone ke uma u za 'kufika, a zi kipe lezi 'zinto, a zi

and bids him go out a little on the open hill, and then return again to the hill which is hidden.

So he departs at the word of the Itongo, and goes out to the open hill, and cries "Hai, hai, hai;" and they all hear that it is he. They are again disputing about him, and as soon as they hear that it is he, they say, "Can it be, sirs, that he comes about the matter we were disputing about, saying, he is mad?"

Others[32] say, "O, why do you ask? He comes on that account, if indeed you said he was not an inyanga, but a madman."

The great man of the village to which the inyanga is approaching, says, "I too say he is mad. Just take things and go and hide them, that we may see if he can find them."

They take things; one takes beads, and goes and hides them; others take picks, and go and hide them; others hide assagais; others bracelets; others hide their sticks, others their kilts, others their ornaments, others their pots; others hide baskets, and say, "Just let us see if he will find all these

---

[32] That is, who were not present at the former discussion.

[33] *Ka v' e inyanga*, i. e., *ku vi e inyanga*, Isilala for *ka si yo inyanga*; and above, *ku vi u inyanga* for *a u si yo inyanga*.

kqede na." Abanye ba tukuse
izikwebu zombila; abanye ba tukuse izikwebu zamabele; abanye
ba tukuse izikwebu zemfe ; abanye
ba tukuse izikwebu zikajiba ; abanye ba tukuse amakamu opoko.

Ba ti abanye, " O, kona uma i
kipa, ka se i ya 'kuza i katale na ?
Ini ukuba ni i tukusele izinto zi be
ziningi kangaka na?"

Ba ti, " Yebo pela, si bone pela
ukuti inyanga."

Ba ti, " Ake ni nqamule ; izinto
ziningi e ni zi fiħlileyo."

Ba buye ba buyele ekaya, ba
ħlale. Li m tshele itongo entabeni
e ngaseyi; loku kade li m tshela,
li ti, " Yenza kaħle ; ba sa tukusa ;
u nga kqal' u vele. Ba funa ukuti,
lapa se u zi kipa izinto, ba funa
ukuti u be u zi bona. U tule, ba
tukuse, ba kqedele kona, b' eza 'ku
ku dela ukuti u inyanga." Li tsho
ke idħlozi, li m tshele, li ti, " Ba
tukusile manje, se be buyile, ba
sekaya. Ku fanele ke u ye ke
ekaya lalabo 'bantu aba tukusayo,
aba ti i uħlanya, ka si yo inyanga."

Ya pumela ke entabeni e sobala,
ya ti i ya ekaya, ya se i gijima, i
landelwa abakubo abantu aba be i
funa, ngokuba i pume ebusuku ;

things or not." Others hide cobs
of maize ; others the ears of amabele, or sweet cane, or of ujiba, or
the heads of upoko.

Some say, "O, if he find all
these things, will he not be tired?
Why have you hidden so many?"

They say, "We hide so many
that we may see that he is really
an inyanga."

They reply, "Stop now; you
have hidden very many things."

They return home, and wait.
Then the Itongo tells him on the
concealed hill ; for it had already
said to him, "Keep quiet; they
are now hiding things; do not
begin to appear. They wish to
say when you find the things that
you saw when they hid them. Be
quiet, that they may hide all the
things ; then they will be satisfied
that you are an inyanga." Now
the Itongo tells him, " They have
now hidden the things, and gone
home. It is proper for you now
to go to the home of the people
who say you are mad and not an
inyanga."

So he comes out on the open
mountain, and runs towards their
home, being pursued by his own
people who are seeking him, for he
went out during the night, and

ka ba i zwa lapo i pumile ekuseni, uma ku 'luvivi, ku 'mpondo zankomo. Ya fika ekaya labo; ba fika nabakubo, yona inyanga a be be i funa, se be i tolile. Ya fika, ya sina; ba i tshayela lapa se i sina; kw' esuka naba kona aba i tukuseleyo, ba tshaya nabo; ya sina, ba i tshayela kakulu.

they did not hear when he went out very early in the morning, when it was still dark, when the horns of the cattle were beginning to be just visible.[34] He reaches their home, and his own people who were looking for him, and have now found him, come with him. On his arrival he dances; and as he dances they strike hands in unison; and the people of the place who have hidden things for him to find, also start up and strike hands; he dances, and they smite their hands earnestly.

Ya ba tshela, ya ti, "Kouje ni ti ni ngi tukusele na?"

He says to them, "Have you then hid things for me to find?"

Ba pika, ba ti, "Kqa; a si ku tukuselanga."

They deny, saying, "No; we have not hidden things for you to find."

Ya ti, "Ni ngi tukusele."

He says, "You have."

Ba pika, ba ti, "Amanga; a si ku tukuselanga."

They deny, saying, "It is not true; we have not."

Ya ti, "Ngi nge zi gibe na?"

He says, "Am I not able to find[35] them?"

Ba ti, "Kqa; u nge zi gibe. Si be si ku tukusele ini?"

They say, "No; you cannot. Have we hidden then things for you to find?"

Ya ti, "Ni ngi tukusele."

He says, "You have."

Ba pika, ba ti, a ba zi tukusanga. Ya pika, ya ti, ba zi tukusile.

They deny, declaring that they have not done so. But he asserts that they have.

Ba ti uma ba kqinise ngokupika

When they persist in their de-

---

[34] *Ku 'mpondo zankomo,* It is the horns of a bullock; a saying to express the earliest dawn, when the horns of the cattle are just becoming visible.

[35] Lit., Take out, viz., from the place of concealment.

kwabo, y' esuka, ya zinikina. Y' esuka, ya bu giba ubu*h*lalu ; ya wa giba amageja; ya i giba imintsha; ya wa giba amasongo ; ya zi giba izikwebu zombila ; ya zi giba· izikwebu zamabele ; ya zi giba izikwebu zikajiba ; ya zi giba izikwebu zemfe; ya wa giba amakamu opoko; ya zi giba zonke izinto a be be zi tukusile. Ba i bona ukuti inyanga enkulu, i zi gibile zonke izinto a be be zi tukusile.

Ya buya ya buyela ekaya k*q*ede i zi gibe izinto zonke, i zi k*q*ede, ku nga sali 'luto end*h*le lapo be yokutukusa kona. I ti ukufika ekaya, ukubuya kwayo la i be i yokugiba kona emfuleni, i fike, se i katele ; a i tshele amatongo ukuti, " Kona u katele nje, a u z' ukulala lapa ; si za 'nhamba nawe, si goduke, si y' ekaya." Ku tsho amatongo, e tshele inyanga i se i katele ukukipa izinto.

Ba ti aba hamba nayo bakubo konyanga, ba ti, " Yitsho ni pela uma ka si yo inyanga na ? "

I ti yona, " Ngi zi gibile izinto zonke e kade ni zi tukusa, ngi zi k*q*edile zonke ; a ku ko 'luto olu sele end*h*le; izinto zonke zi lapa ekaya. Ngi ze nje ngi yalelwe kunina, ngokuba nina kumina ni ti kumina a ngi si yo inyanga ; ni ti, ngi u*h*lanya ; ni ti, abakwiti ba ka ba ngi tukusela na." Ya ti,

nial, he starts up, shaking his head. He goes and finds the beads ; he finds the picks, and the kilts, and the bracelets ; he finds the cobs of maize, and the ears of the amabele and ujiba and of upoko ; he finds all the things they have hidden. They see he is a great inyanga when he has found all the things they have concealed.

He goes home again as soon as he has found all the things, and not one thing remains outside where they had hidden it. On his return to their home from the river whither he had gone to find what was hidden, he is tired, and the Amatongo say to him, " Although you are tired, you will not sleep here ; we will go home with you." This is what the Amatongo say to the inyanga when he is tired with finding the things.

The inyanga's people who accompany him say, " Just tell us if he is not an inyanga ? "

And he says, " I have found all the things which you hid ; there is nothing left outside ; all things are here in the house. I was commanded to come to you, for you said I was not an inyanga, but a madman, and asked if my people had hidden things for me to find.

"Ake ni ngi tshele lezo 'ndaba, uma ngi zi tshelwa ubani na? lezo 'zindaba e na ni zi kuluma na? Ni ti kumina, ngi uhlanya. Na ni ti nina ni kuluma nje. Ni ti, ka b' ezwa ini na abapansi na? Na ti ni kuluma, ba be ni zwa. Nga lala pansi, kanti ba ngi tshela njo ukuma ni ti, ka ngi inyanga yaluto, ngi into e uhlanya nje."

Ba i kunga. Kwa ba o vela nobuhlalu, wa i nika; kwa ba o vela nembuzi, wa i nika; kwa ba o vela nomkonto, wa i nika; kwa ba o vela nesinda, wa i nika; kwa ba o vela nokeu lobuhlalu, wa i kunga; wa ti umunumuzana wa i nika inkomo; zonke izikulu ezinye za veza izimbuzi, za i kunga, ngokuba i be i zile ekaya, i yalelwe amatongo.

UGUAISE.

Just say who told me the things about which you were speaking. You said I was mad. You thought you were just speaking. Do you think the Amatongo[36] do not hear? As you were speaking, they were listening. And when I was asleep they told me that I was a worthless inyanga, a mere thing."

Then the people make him presents. One comes with beads and gives him; another brings a goat; another an assagai; another a bracelet; another brings an ornament made of beads, and gives him. The chief of the village gives him a bullock; and all the chief men give him goats, because he had come to their village at the bidding of the Amatongo.

The Doctor of Divination, the Isanusi, Ibuda, or Umungoma.

I YONA inyanga isanusi, ibuda,

THE doctor is called Isanusi,[37] or Ibuda,[38] or Inyanga of divina-

---

[36] *Abapansi*, Subterraneans, that is, the Amatongo.

[37] *Isanusi*, a diviner; etymology of the word unknown.

[38] *Ibuda*, a diviner; but for the most part an epithet of contempt, and used pretty much in the same way and spirit as Ahab's servant applied the term "mad fellow" to the young prophet that anointed Jehu. (2 Kings ix. 11.) It is derived from *ukubuda*, to talk recklessly, or not to the point; also to dream falsely.

It is interesting to note that in Abyssinia we meet with the word *Bouda*, applied to a character more resembling the Abatakati or Wizards of these parts. To the *Bouda* is attributed remarkable power of doing evil; he invariably selects for his victims "those possessed of youth and talent, beauty and wit, on whom to work his evil

inyanga yokubula, umungoma; ngokuba ba ti uma be bula, ba ti, "Si ya vuma, mngoma." Zi zodwa izinyanga zokwelapa; ngokuba tion,[99] or Umungoma;[40] for when people are enquiring of a diviner, they say, "True, Umungoma." Doctors who treat disease are dif-

deeds." His powers are varied. "At one time he will enslave the objects of his malice; at another, he will subject them to nameless torments; and not unfrequently his vengeance will even compass their death." The *Bouda*, or an evil spirit called by the same name, and acting with him, takes possession of others, giving rise to an attack known under the name of "Bouda symptoms," which present the characteristics of intense hysteria, bordering on insanity. Together with the *Bouda* there is, of course, the exorcist, who has unusual powers, and, like the *inyanga yokubula* or diviner among the Amazulu, points out those who are *Boudas*, that is, Abatakati. An exorcist will suddenly make his appearance "amongst a convivial party of friends, and pronounce the mystical word *Bouda*. The uncouth appearance and sepulchral voice of the exorcist everywhere produce the deepest sensation, and young and old, men and women, gladly part with some article to get rid of his hated and feared presence. If, as sometimes happens, one or two less superstitious individuals object to these wicked exactions, the exorcist has a right to compel every one present to smell an abominable concoction of foul herbs and decayed bones, which he carries in his pouch; those who unflinchingly inhale the offensive scent are declared innocent, and those who have no such strong olfactory nerves are declared *Boudas*, and shunned as allies of the Evil One." It was the custom formerly to execute hundreds of suspected *Boudas*. *(Wanderings among the Falashas in Abyssinia. By Rev. Henry A. Stern, p. 152—161.)*

[39] *Inyanga yokubula.*—*Inyanga* is one possessed of some particular skill or knowledge, as that of a smith, or carpenter; or of medicine: —*inyanga yemiti*, one skilled in medicine, a doctor of medicine; it is applied to especial departments—*inyanga yezilonda*, a sore-doctor; *inyanga yomzimba-mubi*, an abscess-doctor, &c. *Inyanga yokubula* is a person skilled in divination. He is so called from the custom of using branches of trees to *smite* the ground with during the consultation. These rods are called *izibulo*, because they are used to smite *(bula)* the ground with; hence *ukubula* comes to mean to *consult* a diviner by means of *rods*, that is, by smiting the ground; and to divine or reveal what is asked. This beating of the ground appears to have two objects: first, to be a means of expressing assent or otherwise on the part of those who are enquiring; second, to excite them and throw them off their guard. By these means the diviner knows when he is following a right clue; and is able to keep their attention from himself. It is also quite possible that it may also produce an exalted or mesmeric condition of mind in the diviner.

[40] *Umungoma*, a diviner, but an epithet of respect. Etymology unknown.

inyanga yokwelapa uma i namandhla ekwelaponi; nezokubula zi ya i nuka leyo 'nyanga e pata imiti e sizayo. Zi ti 'zokubula, "Ni ya 'kuya kubani, umuntu e si m bonayo woku s' ahlula leso 'sifo." Bala ke ba ye kona kuleyo 'nyanga yemiti e nukwe ezokubula. A t' uma e gula i sona leso 'sifo esi tshiwo izinyanga zokubula, a sinde i leyo 'miti yaleyo 'nyanga e zi i uukileyo.

Ku ze ku ti uma i be i s' elapa leyo 'nyanga yemiti lowo 'muntu o gulayo, ka ba nako ukupila, i ti leyo 'nyanga yemiti, "Si ya ng' ahlula lesi 'sifo. Kona inyanga zi ngi nukile nje, ake ni ye 'kuzwa futi kwamanye amabuda; kona umhlaumbe nga ba li kona ibuda eli ya 'uza li ni tshele umuti e ngi nga mu sindisa ngawo."

Bala ke ba vume, ba ti, "O, u kqinisile. Ku fanele um' ake si yokuzwa kwamanye amabuda; umhlaumbe li nga ze li be kona eli ya 'ku u tsho umuti o nga m sindisa ngawo." Ba hambe ke ba ye emabudeni, uma b' ezwe a ya 'kulandelana na.

Uma be fikile kulo ibuda, be ya 'kubula kulo, ka ba tsho ukuti

ferent from those who divine; for a man is a doctor of disease if he is able to treat disease; and diviners point out the doctor of medicine who is successful. They tell those who enquire of them to go to a certain doctor whom they know to have successfully treated the disease from which their friend is suffering. And so they go to the doctor of medicine that has been pointed out by the diviners. And if he has the disease which the diviners say he has, he will be cured by the medicines of the doctor that they point out.

But if the doctor of medicine treats the sick man and he does not get well, he says, "This disease masters me. Since the diviners did nothing more than send you to me, just go and hear what other diviners say; then perhaps some diviner will tell you the medicine with which I can cure this man."

So they assent, saying, "O, you say truly. It is proper for us to go to hear what other diviners may say; perhaps we shall find one who will tell us the medicine with which you can cure him." So they go to other diviners to hear whether they will all give the same advice.

When they come to the diviner, they do not say to him, "We are

ebudeni, ukuti, "Si zokubula." Ba ya fika nje, ba kuleke, ba ti, "Ehe, mngan'! Indab' ezin*h*le!" Li b' ezwe ke ibuda ukuti b' ezokubula. Ba *h*lale ke, nalo li *h*lale, li ba bingelele, li ti, "Sa ni bona." Ba ti, "Yebo, mugan'."

Li ti, "Hau, yeka! Laba 'bantu ba fika end*h*laleni; a si yo nend*h*lala kwiti lapa, inkulu; si lambile; nokud*h*lana o be ku kona se si ku k*q*ede izolo. A s' azi uma umfino wokud*h*la ni ya 'kutola pi."

Ba ti, "O, 'mngane, si be si nge ku tole noku ku tola; si lambe kakulu: ku be ku nge vele ukud*h*la. Tina uma be si tola nezinkobe, si be si ya 'kuti si tolile. Si be si nga sa funi nokud*h*la loko oku kalelwa u wena, 'mngane; tina se si funa nezinkobe nje; si y' ezwa wena ukuti u kalela ukud*h*la kwamanzi."

Li ti ke, "O, ba funele ni, ni ba pekele isijingi, ni ba pekele nombak*q*anga." Ba ba pekele ke abafazi.

Ku ti ku sa pekiwe ukud*h*la kwabo, li be se li keataza ugnai, se li bema kona end*h*lini, li be se li

come to enquire." They merely go and salute him, saying, "Yes, yes, dear sir! Good news!"[41] Thus the diviner understands that they have come to enquire. So they sit still, and the diviner sits, and salutes them, saying, "Good day." They reply, "Yes, yes, dear sir."

He says, "O, let be! These people have come in a time of dearth; we have no food ready; we are hungry; and the beer which we had, we finished yesterday. We cannot tell where you can get any food."

They reply, "O, sir, we cannot get much food; we are very hungry: food cannot be obtained. For our parts, if we get boiled maize, we shall say we have got food. We were not wishing for that food you are calling for, sir; we for our parts are wishing for nothing but boiled maize; we understand that you are calling for beer."

He says, "O, get them some food; cook them some porridge; cook for them very thick porridge." So his wives cook for them.

When their food has been cooked, he pours some snuff into his hand, and takes it there in the

---

[41] That is, we ask you to tell us good news, with which we may return home with gladdened hearts.

hlasimula, se li zamula, li be se li puma li ya ngapandhle esihlahleni, se li tuma umuntu e ya 'ku ba biza. A ba bize umuntu, ba hambe ba ye kulona esihlahleni, ba fike ke kulona ibuda.

Li ti, "Yika ni izibulo." B' esuke, ba zi ke izibulo, ba buye, ba hlale pansi. Li be se li kipa isidhlelo salo, li be se li kcataza, li beme ; nabo ba kcataze kwezabo izidhlelo, ba beme.

Ba ti lapa be bemako, li be se li ti, "Tshaya ni." Ba ti, "Yizwa!" Abanye ba ti, "Si ya vuma!"

Li ti, "Ni ze ngesifo."

Ba li tshayele.
Li ti, "Si kumuntu."

Ba tshaye.
Li ti, "Umuntu omkulu." Li ti, "Na ka na ya kwomunye umngane wami."
Ba tshaye kakulu.

Li ti, "Tshaya ni, ngi zwe uma lowo 'mngane wami e na ni ye kuyena ni yokubula, uma wa fika wa ti ni na."
Ba tshaye.
Li ti, "Nanku umngane wami a fika wa si tsho isifo kulowo 'muntu."

house ; he shudders and yawns, and then goes out of doors to a clump of trees and sends a man to call them. The man calls them, and they go to the clump of trees to the diviner.

He tells them to pluck rods for beating the ground. They go and pluck the rods, and return and sit down. He takes out his snuffbox, pours snuff into his hand and takes it ; and they do the same.

When they have taken snuff, he tells them to smite the ground. Some say, "Hear!" Others say, "True!"

He says, "You are come to enquire about sickness."

They smite the ground for him.
He says, "It is a human being that is ill."

They smite the ground.
He says, "It is a great man. You have already been to another friend of mine."

They smite the ground vehemently.

He says, "Smite the ground, that I may understand what that friend of mine to whom you went seeking divination said to you."

They smite the ground.
He says, "There is my friend[42] who told the disease by which he is affected."

---

[42] That is, he gazes into space with a kind of ecstatic stare, as though he really saw or had a vision of the other diviner.

Ba tshaye kakulu, ba ti, "Si ya vuma."

Li ti, "Lowo 'mngane wami u kona umuntu owa m nukayo; inyanga; ka si yo inyanga yokubula; inyanga yamayeza."

Ba tshaye lapo kakulu.

Li ti, "Ngi buze ni. Ni nga ngi yeki."

Ba ti, "A si namand/la oku ku buza; ngokuba u kuluma zona izindaba. Ibuda li buzwa li nga kulumi zona izin/lamvu zokufa."

Li ti ke, "Tshaya ni futi, ngi zwe lowo 'mngane wami uma wa ti a nga m siza e m pe 'yeza lini na?"

Ba tshaye, ba ti, "Si ti, 'mungoma, a ku s' a/lukanisele lapo iyeza e lona li ya 'ku m siza; loku u m bonile lowo 'muntu owa nukwa umngane wako, si ya 'kuzwa ngawe neyeza eli ya 'ku m siza."

Li ti, "Ngi za 'ku ni tshela. Ba ya tsho abakwiti, ba ti, b' eza 'ku ni tshela."

Ba ti, "Si y' etokoza kona loku, 'mungoma, uma ba kcakcambe aba kwini, ba /langane kanye naba-

They smite the ground vehemently, and say, "Right."

He says, "There is someone to whom that friend of mine sent you; he is a doctor, not a divining doctor; he is a doctor of medicine."

Upon that they smite the ground vehemently.

He says, "Do you question me. Do not leave me."

They say, "We cannot question you. For you speak the very facts themselves. We put to the question a man that talks at random, and does not mention the very nature of the disease."

Then he says, "Smite the ground again, that I may understand what medicine my friend told him to give to cure him."

They smite the ground, and say to him, "Diviner, tell us at once the medicine that will cure him; for since you have seen the man to whom your friend directed us, we shall hear from you the medicine too that will cure him."

He says, "I am about to tell you. Our people[43] say, they will tell you."

They say, "We are glad, diviner, that your people are white,[44] and unite with our peo-

---

[43] *Our people*, that is, the Amatongo or ancestral spirits belonging to our house or tribe. As below, the enquirers speak of their people, that is, the ancestral spirits belonging to their house or tribe.

[44] *White,*—clearly seen by you, and so giving a clear revelation.

kwiti, ku lunge. Ngokuba tina ka si sa tsho ukuti u ya 'kusinda. Ngokuba inyanga eya nukwa umugane wako, s' etemba ezin*h*liziyweni zetu, sa jabula, sa ti, "Loku ku tsho ibuda, li si tshela inyanga yoku m siza, u se ya 'kusizeka, a pile.' Sa ya kuleyo 'nyanga e tshiwo umngane wako; sa bona nanku ukufa ku d*h*lule, ku bhekise pambili; sa k*q*ala ukumangala, ukuti, 'Yeka!' Loku si be se s' etemba, si mi 'sibindi, si ti, 'M*h*laumbe u ya 'kupila, loku se ku tsho ibuda, li tsho njalo.'" Ba ti, "Se si wa tsho nje lawo 'mazwi, ngokuba kuk*q*ala e kulunywe u we; wa u bona uma sa ka sa ya kwelinye ibuda. Uma lawo 'mazwi u be u nga wa tshongo ukuti, sa ka sa ya kwelinye ibuda, si be si nga yi 'ku wa kuluma; se si wa kuluma ngokuba nawe u se u wa bonile."

Li ti, "Tshaya ni, ngi ni tshele umuti o ya 'ku m siza, a pile."

Ba tshaye lapo, be tshaya kakulu.

Li ti, "Lowo o ya 'ku m siza, ngi ya 'ku ni tshela mi-

ple, that the case may turn out well. For we have no more hope that he will recover. For as regards the doctor whom your friend pointed out, we trusted in our hearts, saying, 'Since the diviner has told us the doctor that can cure him, he will now be cured, and get well.' We went to the doctor whom your friend mentioned; but lo, we saw the disease passing onward, tending to get worse and worse, and began to wonder, saying, 'Let be!' For we were trustful and of good courage, saying, 'Perhaps he will get well, for the diviner says so.'" They go on, "We have just said these words, because you said them first; you saw that we had already been to another diviner. If you had not said we had already gone to another diviner, we should not have said them; we say them because you already said them."

He says, "Smite the ground, that I may tell you the medicine that will cure him."

They then smite the ground vehemently.

He says, "For my part I tell you that the medicine that will cure him is inyamazane.[45]

---

[45] *Inyamazane*, Large animals, which are supposed to have been used by some one to produce the disease from which he is suffering. These are the *Inhluzele*, the Harte-beest. That this has been used with other medicines as a poison is known by bloody micturition and

na, inyamazane. U nomsizi." | The man has umsizi."[40]

other symptoms. The *Indhlovu*, Elephant, which is known to have been used by excessive borborygmus. The *Isambane*, or Ant-bear, by pain in the hip-joint, as though the femur were dislocated; possibly, sciatica. When a man is suffering from such symptoms it is said, *U nenyamazane*, He has a disease occasioned by a wild animal; or the disease may be distinguished,—*U nenhluzele*, *U nendhlovu*, *U nesambane*, He has harte-beest, that is, the disease occasioned by it; He has elephant; He has ant-bear,—that is, the diseases occasioned by them. To cure these diseases the natives act on the homœopathic principle, and administer the wild beast that is supposed to have occasioned the disease, with other medicines.

[40] *He has Umsizi.*—*Umsizi* is a disease occurring among the Amalala, and said not to be known to the Amazulu or Amakxosa. It is supposed to arise from the administration of medicine, in this way. A man is suspicious of his wife's fidelity. He goes to a doctor of celebrity,—an umsizi-doctor,—and obtains of him medicine, which he takes himself without his wife's knowledge, and by cohabiting with her once conveys to her the seed of disease. And if any one is guilty of illicit intercourse with her after this, he will have umsizi; the wife all the time remaining quite free from disease. The symptoms of umsizi are intense darkening of the skin, and contraction of the tendons with excessive pain; severe pain in a finger or a toe, from which it shifts to different parts of the body, especially the joints.

Umsizi is also the *medicine* used for treating the disease. It consists of various substances,—plants, their roots, bark, and seeds; animals, their flesh, skin, tendons, entrails, bones, and excrements; and stones.

These substances are partially charred, not reduced to ashes, so as to destroy their virtue, but sufficiently to admit of their being powdered.

The medicine is used for the most part endermically by rubbing it into scarifications. It is also mixed with other medicines to make an *izembe*.

Umsizi ozwakalayo, Umsizi which is felt.—This term is applied to the medicine used to make a man sensitive to the existence of that state in the woman which can produce the disease called umsizi. It is also applied to that condition of body which renders him thus sensitive. *Umsizi ozwakalayo* is a kind of umsizi, which the doctor supplies to a person to be used as a trial medicine. It is rubbed into scarifications made on the back of the left hand. If his wife or another woman whom he approaches is in that state which is capable of conveying to him the disease called umsizi, when he places his hand on her thigh, the hand is at once affected by spasmodic contraction of the fingers. And he abstains from her until she has undergone a course of treatment.

Or it is rubbed in on either side of the Tendo Achillis; and the

Ba tshaye lapo, ba ti, "Si ya 'kuzwa ngawe, 'mungoma. Tina ka si s' azi; se si ko/*h*/liwe nje; se si 'ziula; a ku se ko uku/*h*/lakanipa kutina. Na lawo 'mazwi o wa tshoyo, u ti u ya 'ku si tshela iyeza eli ya 'ku m sindisa, ezin/*h*/liziyweni zetu ka si sa tsho ukuti na lelo 'yeza o za 'ku li tsho ukuba li ya 'ku m pilisa. Tina se si ti ukufa se ku ya 'ku m tumba. Ka si s' emi nesibindi, ngokuba ukufa ku lapo nje; ka s' azi, ngokuba se ku m tshayisa itwabi.

Li ti, "Tshaya ni ke; tshaya ni ke kona lapo etwabini, ngi ni tshele."

Ba tshaye.
Li ti, "Itwabi, ka ku 'nto loko. Ngi ya 'ku ni nika umuti wetwabi, li ya 'kupela."

Ba ti, "Si ya tokoza, 'mungoma; ngaleyo 'ndawo o i tshoyo. I kuba si ng' azi kodwa. Zonke izinyanga zi /*h*/leze zi tsho njalo; a d/*h*/lule umuntu, a fe. Nina 'zinyanga a ni sa si misi 'sibindi. Zi /*h*/leze zi tsho njalo zonke. Se si za si tokoze lapa si bona umuntu e se

They then smite the ground, and say, "We will hear from you, diviner. For our parts we know nothing; now we can do nothing; now we are fools; there is no longer any wisdom in us. And as for the words you say, promising to tell us the medicine which will cure him, in our hearts we no longer say that even the medicine you mention will cure him. We now say that death will carry him away captive. We have no more courage, for the disease is there; we do not understand, for he is now affected with hiccup."

He says, "Smite the ground then; smite the ground then at that point of hiccup, that I may tell you."

They smite.

He says, "The hiccup is nothing. I will give him medicine for hiccup, and it will cease."

They say, "We are glad, diviner, for what you say. But we do not know. It is customary for all doctors to say so; and yet the man gets worse, and dies. You doctors no longer inspire us with courage. It is customary for them all to speak thus. And we now rejoice when we see a man already

---

man touches her with his foot or toe. If she can affect him with umsizi, the leg at once is affected with spasm.

It is from the dread of this disease that a man will not marry a widow until she has been subjected to medical treatment to remove all possibility of her communicating it.

pilile ; s' and' ukuba si tsho ukuti, 'Inyanga,' uma si bona umuntu e sinda. Uma ukufa ku bhekise pambili nje, a si vi si tsho ukuti i bulile. Si ti, 'I dukile. I lahlekile.' Uma e pilile umuntu, si ti, 'I bulile ;' si i babaze kakulu, si ti, 'I ya bula.' Kanti ke si tsho ke ngokuba umuntu e sindile."

Li ti, "Tshaya ni, ngi ni tshele."
Ba tshaye.
Li ti, "Itwabi lelo a li 'luto. Ba y' al' abakwiti, ba ti, ' Itwabi ize.' Ba ti, ba za 'u ni tshela umuti o ya 'ku m pilisa. Ba ya m pikisa umngane wami e na ya 'kubula kuye ; ba ti, ka bonanga e u nuka umuti woku m siza ; wa nuka inyanga nje yokwelapa ; ka tshongo ukuti u ya 'kusizwa umuti wokuti."

Ba tshaye lapo.
Li ti, " Tshaya ni kakulu."

Ba tshaye.

Li ti, " Ka bonanga e tsho ukuti u ya 'kusizwa umuti wokuti. Ngi za 'ku ni tshela ke umuti woku m siza, a pile ; ni buyo ezinye-

in health ; and then we say, 'He is a diviner,' when we see the man getting well. If the disease increases, we do not say the inyanga has divined. We say, 'He has wandered. He is lost.' If a man has got well, we say, 'The diviner has divined ;' and we praise him much, saying, 'He is one who divines.' Forsooth we say so because the man has got well."

He says, "Smite the ground, that I may tell you."
They smite the ground.
He says, "The hiccup is nothing. Our people say it is not dangerous ; they say, the hiccup is nothing. They say they will tell you a medicine that will cure him. They find fault with my friend to whom you went seeking divination ; they say, he did not see what medicine would cure him ; he merely pointed out a doctor to treat him, and did not mention the medicine which would cure him."

Then they smite the ground.
He says, "Smite the ground vehemently."
They do so.
He says, "He never named the medicine which would cure him. So I am going to tell you the medicine which will restore him to health ; and you leave off the

mbeziui e be se ni nazo, ni ti, u se file."

Ba ti, " Mungoma, si ya 'kuzwa ngawe; si bula nje; si nezinyembezi; izinyembezi zi kutina; si lapa nje, ka s' azi emuva—uma ngaleli 'langa lanamuhla si ya 'ku m fumana e se kona nje na."

Li ti, " Tshaya ni. Ni ya 'ku m fumana e kona." Li ti, " Tshaya ni, ngi ni tshele umuntu ow elapayo, o ya 'ku m siza, o ya 'kufika a m sindise ngalona lelo 'langa o ya 'kufika ngalo."

Ba tshaye.
Li ti, " Ngi ti, yiya ni enyangeni etile, yasekutini. I ya 'ku ni pa iyeza lomsizi. I fike i m pe ikambi, i m puzise lona, a li puze. Y' and' ukuba i mu geabe, i m

tears you have been shedding,[47] thinking he was already dead."

They reply, " Diviner, we will hear what you say; we merely beat the ground ;[48] we weep ; tears are our portion ;[49] whilst we are here, we do not know what will happen—whether during this day's sun we shall find him still living."

He says, " Smite the ground. You will find him still alive. Smite the ground, that I may tell you of a man who treats disease, who will do him good, who will come to him, and cure him on the very day he comes."

They smite the ground.

He says, " I say, go to such and such a doctor, of such and such a place. He will give you umsizimedicine. And he will himself come and give him an expressed juice[50] to drink, and he will drink it. After that he will scarify him,[51] and give him medicine.[52]

---

[47] Lit., Come back from the tears you have been shedding.

[48] That is, We are enquirers only. We know nothing.

[49] Lit., We have tears; tears are with us.

[50] *Ikambi* is the name given to a large class of medicines, the expressed juices of which are used. The green plant is bruised, and a little water added, and then squeezed. The juice may be squeezed into the mouth, or eyes, ears, &c.

[51] Medicines are rubbed into the scarifications.

[52] *Ukuncindisa* is a peculiar way of administering a medicine. The medicine is powdered, and placed in a pot or sherd over the fire ; when it is hot the dregs of beer are squeezed into it, or the contents of a stomach of a goat or bullock, or whey is sprinkled on it. It froths up on the addition of the fluid, and the patient dips his fingers into the hot mixture, and conveys it to his mouth rapidly and eats it ; and at the same time applies it to those parts of the body which are in pain. Medicine thus prepared is called *izembe*.

DIVINERS. 291

ncindise. U ya 'kusinda ngalelo 'langa i ze nekambi. Ngi za 'ku ni nika wona owetwabi, ni ze ni m puzise wona, u m bambezele ku ze ku fike yona leyo 'nyanga e ngi ni tshela yona. I ya 'ku m siza."

Li ba pe ke umuti wetwabi woku m bambezela.

Ba goduke ke, ba ye kona ekaya lalo ibuda, ba ye 'kudhla ukudhla a ba ku pekelweyo. Ba fike ke, ba ngene endhlini, ba nikwe ke ukudhla; ba dhle, ba dhle ke, b' esute, ku pele ukulamba loko a be be lambe ngako. Ba buze, ba ti, "Ku hlwile?" Ba ti abanye, "O, se ku hlwile." Li ti ibuda e kade li ba bulele, "O, lala ni, ni ze ni hambe kusasa."

B' ale, ba ti, "O, atshi, 'mungoma; ku fanele uma si hambe; loku naku u si nikile umuti; si tanda uma si fike kona ebusuku, noma si fika ku sa; a ku yi 'kuba 'kcala; s' enze uma a fike a puze umuti."

Li vume ke ibuda, li ti, "O, bala, ni kqinisile. Kodwa uma ni fike nalo leli 'yeza lami, na leyo 'nyanga uma i kude nje, yo za i fike li ya 'ku m bambezela lona.

He will get well on the day the doctor comes with the expressed juice. I will give you hiccup-medicine; and do you give it him; it will keep him alive[53] until the doctor whom I have mentioned to you comes. He will cure him."

So he gives them hiccup-medicine to keep him alive.

Then they go back to the diviner's house to eat the food which has been cooked for them. They enter the house, and the people give them food; they eat and are satisfied, and their hunger ceases. They enquire if it is dark. Some say that it is now dark. The diviner who has just divined for them says, "O, sleep here, and go in the morning."

They refuse, saying, "O, on no account, diviner; we must go; for, see, you have given us medicine; we wish that the man should drink this medicine whether we reach home in the night, or whether we reach home in the morning; it will not matter; we wish him to take this medicine."

So the diviner agrees, saying, "Surely, you are right. But if you reach him with this medicine of mine, and the doctor is ever so far away, until he comes it will keep him alive. Further, as to

---

[53] *Ukubambezela* means to bring the disease to a stand *(ukumisa)*, that it may not increase till the doctor can come with powerful remedies. Medicines given with this object are called *izibambezelo*.

Unganti ngalo, noma ngi fike nalo, umuntu e se vuswa pansi, e nga zivukeli, ngi nga m puzisa lona, u ya 'kuvuka, noma e be e nga sa vuki."

Ba hambe ke kona ebusuku, ba fike, ba fike lapo ku sayo. Ba fumanise abantu be butanele kona kuyena end/lini lap' e gulela kona. Ba fike ba u kame lowo 'muti a ba fika nawo wetwabi, ba u kamele esitsheni, e sa kwelwe i lona njalo itwabi. Ba m puzise. Wa puza, wa ti uma a u puze, la m tshaya futi itwabi; wa /lakanipa. B' esab' abantu end/lini, ba ti, "Mbala, ka se yalela njena na?"

Ba bhekana end/lini, ba buza kulaba aba fikayo nawo umuti, ba ti laba, "Au, lo 'muntu wa /lakanipa! U njani lo 'muti wenyanga na?"

Ba ti, "O, inyanga, si fika nawo nje lo 'muti; li si nike wona ibuda, la ti, i kona u ya 'ku m bambezela ku ze ku fike inyanga yokwelapa. Li te, ka sa yi 'kufa si nga ze si fike nawo lo 'muti, kwo za ku fike inyanga eli i tshiloyo."

this medicine, even if I come to a man so ill as to be raised by others, he being unable to raise himself, and make him drink this medicine, he will raise himself, even though before he could not do so."

They set out at once by night, and reach their home in the morning. They find the people assembled in the sick man's hut. They squeeze out for him the hiccup-medicine, they have brought, into a cup, he being still affected with hiccup. They make him drink it. When he has drunk it, he is seized with hiccup again, and he becomes sensible.[54] The people in the hut are alarmed, and say, "Truly, is he not now just about to die?"[55]

Those in the house look at each other, and enquire of those who have brought the medicine, saying, "O, how the man has lighted up! What kind of medicine is that of the doctor's?"

They say, "O, as to the doctor, we merely bring the medicine; the diviner gave it to us, and said it would keep him alive till the doctor came to treat the disease. He said he would not die if we reached home with this medicine, until the doctor came whom he named."

---

[54] *Wa hlakanipa,* He becomes sensible, sharp. Applied to what is sometimes called by us "lighting up before death."

[55] *Ukuyalela* is to manifest the signs which precede immediate dissolution. The man is sometimes conscious of his approaching end, and calls his wives and children around him, and says farewell.

Wa hlakanipa kodwa, ka z' a fa. B' emi 'sibindi njengokutsho kwalo ibuda. Ba lala kanye; kwa ti kusasa ba ti, "O, che, ibuda li nuke inyanga yokwelapa yasekutini. Li te u nomsizi; leyo 'nyanga i ya 'kufika nekambi lokuma a li puze; kw' and' ukuba i m ncindise, i m geabe. Se si ya hamba nje si ye kuleyo 'nyanga."

B' etokoza, ba ti, "Si y' etokoza; kuhle ukuba ni hambe. Bala, i loku ni m puzise umuti wetwabi ka banga nalo namhla nje ngalobu ubusuku. Se si ya bona ukuti ni be ni ye ebudeni eli kulumayo, eli kw aziyo ukufa, ni fike nawo lo 'muti. Se si mi 'sibindi. Se si bona amohlo ake e hlakanipile."

Ba hambe ke, ba ye kuleyo 'nyanga e nukwe i leli 'buda. Ba nga be be sa ya kweyakukqala, ngokuba nayo ya i landa, ya ti, "Mina ng' ahlulekile; ini uma ibuda li nga tsho umuti e ngi ya 'ku m sindisa ngawo na?"

Ba ya ba fika ke kuleyo 'nyanga. Ba fike, ba kuleke, ba ti, " E, 'mngan'." Ba ngene endhlini, ba ba bingelele, ba ti, " Sa ni bo-

But he lights up only, and does not die. They take courage from what the diviner said. They stay one night, and on the following morning say, " O, yes, the diviner pointed out a doctor of such a place to come and treat him. He said he has umsizi, and that the doctor will bring medicine for him to drink; then he will give another medicine, and scarify him. So now we will go to that doctor."

They rejoice and say, " We are glad; it is well for you to go. Truly, since you gave him the hiccup-medicine he has not had the hiccup all night. We now see that you went to a diviner who speaks[56] truth, and knows the disease; you have brought the right medicine. We now have confidence. We now see that his eyes are bright."

So they go to the doctor which the diviner has pointed out. They do not go any more to the first doctor, for he told them he could not do any thing for the sick man, and asked why the diviner had not mentioned the medicine with which he might cure the patient.

They reach the doctor's. When they reach him, they make obeisance, saying, " Eh, dear sir." They go into the house; they salute them, saying, " Good day,"

---

[56] Lit., A diviner who speaks, that is, does not rave and talk nonsense.

na." Ba vume, ba ti, "Yebo, 'makosi." Ba ti, "Ni vela pi na?"

Ba ti, "Si vela kwiti."
"Ni hambela pi na?"
"Si hambele kona lapa."
"Ini e ni i babele lapa na?"

Ba ti, "O, 'makosi, si ze enyangeni yokwelapa. Si ya gulelwa."

Ba ti, "I kona ini po kwiti lapa na inyanga yokwelapa na?"

Ba ti, "O, 'makosi, ni ngu si tshela lapa i kona inyanga yokwelapa; si ye kuyona."

Ba *h*leka end*h*lini.

Ba ti, "O, 'makosi, musa ni uku si *h*leka. Si ya *h*lupeka."

Ba ti, "Ni *h*lutshwa ini na?"

Ba ti, "O, si *h*lutshwa isifo. Si ya gulelwa."

Ba buze, ba ti, "Ni ze lapa nje, ni zwe ku tiwa inyanga i kona ini lapa na?"

Ba ti, "Ehe; si zwile ukuti i kona."

Ba ti, "Na i zwa ngobani na?"

Ba ti, "Au, 'makosi, si nge ze sa fi*h*la nokufi*h*la. Ngokuba si ze lapa nje, sa si ye ebudeni, le 'nd*h*lela si i tshengiswe, nokuba i kona lapa inyanga. Sa si ng' azi; ngokuba sa si ye kwelinye ibuda;

and they return the salutation, saying, "Yes, sirs." They say, "Whence do you come?"

They say, "From our home."
"Where are you going?"
"We have come to this place."[57]
"What business have you here?"

They say, "O, sirs, we are come to the doctor. One of our people is ill."

They say, "Is there then any doctor here?"

They reply, "O, sirs, you can tell us where the doctor is; we have come to him."

Those in the house laugh.

The others say, "O, sirs, do not laugh at us. We are in trouble."

They say, "What troubles you?"

They say, "O, we are troubled by disease. One of our people is ill."

They ask, "As you have come here, have you heard that there is a doctor here?"

They say, "Yes; we have heard that there is one here."

They say, "Who told you?"

They reply, "O, sirs, we cannot make a great secret of it. For we have come here because we went to a diviner, and he showed us the path, and told us there was a doctor here. We did not know it; for we had gone to another diviner, and

---

[57] Viz., We are going no further.

la fika la nuka enye inyanga, la ti, i yona i ya 'ku m siza; sa ya kuleyo 'nyanga, ya b' i s' elapa, y' ahluleka. Ya za ya ti leyo 'nyanga, 'Ng' ahlulekile; lelo 'buda e na ni bula kulona l' ona ukuma li nga ni tsheli umuti owona ngi ya 'ku m siza ngawo.'" Ba ti, "Sa i vumela leyo 'nyanga yokwelapa; sa ya ke kwelinye ibuda. La fika lu si nukela, la ti, inyanga e nga m sizayo i kwini lapa. Ni si bona, si fika nje, 'makosi."

Ba ti, "O, aha; u kona, tina, lapa umuntu owelapayo."

Ba ti, "Si tshenise ni ke uma u mu pi na?"

Ba ti, "Nanku."

Wa ti, "Ehe, i mina. Yitsho ni, ngi zwe into eyona ni ze ngayo kumina lapa."

Ba ti, "Ai, 'nkosi; si ze ngaso isifo. Ngokuba si letwe ibuda lapa kuwe."

I ti inyanga, "Lona lelo 'buda, ni ti uma ni li buzayo, la ti, ngi ya 'ku m siza ngamuti muni na?"

Ba ti, "Si li buzile; la ti, u ya 'ku m siza ngomuti; ikambi umuti o ya 'ku m siza ngawo. La ti, u nomsizi; u ya 'ku m siza ngekambi lo 'msizi."

Ya ti, "Ni ze nanto ni na?"

he pointed out another doctor, who, he said, would cure the sick man; we went to that doctor, and he treated him, but could do nothing. At length he told us he could do nothing, and that the diviner of whom we had enquired erred, because he did not name the medicine with which he could cure the patient. So we agreed with that doctor, and went to another diviner. On our arrival, he told us that there was a doctor here who could cure the sick man. And now you see us, sirs; we have come."

They say, "O, yes, yes; there is a man here who treats disease."

They say, "Tell us where he is."

They say, "There he is."

And he says, "Yes, yes, it is I. Tell me why you have come here to me."

They say, "We come, sir, on account of sickness. For the diviner sent us here to you."

The doctor says, "Did the diviner, when you asked him, tell you with what medicine I could cure him?"

They say, "We asked him, and he told us the medicine with which you could cure him. He said he had umsizi, and that you could cure him with umsizi-medicine."

He says, "What have you brought for me?"[53]

---

[53] The doctor demands first *ugxha*, that is, the stick which he

Ba ti, "Nkosi, ka si ze naluto. Uma u m sizile, u ya 'kuziketela ekaya izinkomo o zi tandayo."

Ya ti, "Ni zoku ngi kipa ngani ekaya lapa na?"

Ba ti, "Nkosi, si zoku ku kipa. Into yoku ku kipa i sekaya—imbuzi."

Ya ti, "Ni be ni ng' eza 'ku ngi tata ngembuzi na, lo 'muntu o ngi ya 'ku m siza njalo na?"

Ba ti, "O, 'mngane, u nga zikatazi ngokukuluma; nenkomo i sekaya yoku ku tata. Si tsho, kona ibuda li tshilo nje, si ti tina ku za wa m siza, ngokuba u ya gula kakulu."

Ya ti, "Mina ngi ya 'ku m siza, loku ku tsho ibuda, la ti, woza ni kumina." I buze kubona, i ti, "I te leyo 'nyanga, ngi ya 'ku m siza ngamuti muni na?"

Ba ti, "O, 'mngane, i te, u ya 'ku m siza ngekambi; kw' and' ukuba u m ncindise, u m gcabe.

They say, "Sir, we have not brought any thing. When you have cured him, you shall pick out for yourself the cattle you like at our home."

He says, "What will you give me to cause me to quit my hut?"

They say, "Sir, we will give you something to cause you to quit the hut; it is at home—a goat."

He says, "Is it possible that you come to take me away with a goat, to go to a man whom I am going to cure?"

They say, "O, dear sir, do not trouble yourself with talking; there is also a bullock at home to take you away. We say that as we have only the diviner's word, you will never cure him; for he is very ill."

He says, "I shall cure him, because the diviner told you to come to me." And asks, "What medicine did the diviner say I could cure him with?"

They reply, "O, dear sir, he said you would cure him by giving him an expressed juice; and then you would give him another medicine, and scarify him. And that

---

uses to dig up medicines. This he does by asking, "Ni zoku ngi kipa ngani ekaya lapa na?" With what are you going to take me out of my house? viz., that I may go and dig up medicine. The *ugxha* is generally a goat, or perhaps a calf. He then demands an *umkonto* or assagai, saying, "Imiti i za 'kutukululwa ngani?" With what can the medicines be undone? They give him an assagai, which remains his property. If the man gets well, he is given one or more cattle. If he is paid liberally, the *ugxha* and *umkonto* are given to the boy that carries his medicines, or helps him to dig them up.

I te, u ya 'kupila ngalona lelo 'langa o fika ngalo, ukutsho kwebuda."

Ya ti leyo 'nyanga, "Hamba ni ke, ni goduke ; ngi ya 'kuza ngomhl' omunye."

B' ala, ba ti, "Hau, mngane, a si hambe nawe ; u nga sali."

Ya za ya vuma, ya ti, "Ai ke, se ngi za 'uhamba nani."

Ya hamba ke nabo, se i li pete ikambi nemiti yoku m ncindisa neyoku m gcaba. Ba ya ba fika nayo ekaya. Ya fika, ya m puzisa, wa u puza ; ya m ncindisa, ya m gcaba. Ya funa imbuzi, ya i hlaba, ya m ncindisa ngayo. Ya funa inkomo futi, ya m ncindisa ngayo.

Ba m bona ukuti, i za 'ku m ahlula. Wa hlakanipa, wa i dhla inyama yembuzi neyenkomo. Ba buza, ba ti, "Ku njani lapa kubuhlungu kona na ?"

Wa ti, "O, tula ni, madoda ; ngi sa lalelisile. Ngi ya 'kuzwa

he would get well on the very day you go to him. That is what the diviner said."

He says, "Go home then, and I will come the day after to-morrow."

They object, saying, "O, dear sir, go with us ; do not stay behind."

And at length he assents, saying, "Well, then, I will go with you."

So he goes with them, taking with him plants to express their juice for him, and other medicines, and medicines to rub into the scarifications. At length they reach their home with the doctor. On his arrival he makes the man drink the expressed juice, and then gives him other medicine and scarifies him. He asks for a goat, and kills it, and makes medicine with it, and gives it to him. He asks also for a bullock, and makes medicine with it, and gives him.

The people see that he will cure him.[59] He becomes strong, and eats the flesh of the goat and the bullock. They ask, "How is the pain now ?"

He replies, "O, be silent, sirs ; I am still earnestly looking out for it. I shall feel whether it is still

---

[59] Lit., Overcome him, that is, the disease from which he is suffering,—overcome the sick man by getting rid of his sickness.

ngomuso, kwand' ukuba ngi ni tshele. Ubutongo tina ngi bu lalile. Ngi ya 'kutsho ngomuso, madoda, ukuti inyanga lo 'muntu."

Bala, kwa *h*lwa, ka sa fika leso 'sifo. Wa lala ubutongo. Kwa sa kusasa ba buza, ba ti, "Ku njani na ?"

Wa ti, "O, madoda, se ngi ya 'kupila."

Ya tsho ke inyanga, "Se ngi m pilisile. Veza ni inkomo zami. Ngi ya hamba kusasa; ngi ya tanda ukuma ngi zi bone, ku se ngi zi k*q*ube. Ngi ti, ka ngi lale ngi zi bonile."

Ba ti, "O, yebo, mngane; u k*q*inisile. Se si ya m bona umuntu wako, ukuti u inkubele."

Ba m bouisa ke izinkomo zake; ba tshaya inkomazana i pete itokazi, ba tshaya umtantikazi—za ba ntatu.

Ba ti, "Yitsho ke, nyanga; si ti, nanzi inkomo zako."

Ya ti, "Ngi ya bonga; ngi ya zi bonga lezi 'nkomo. Ng' esule ni ame*h*lo ke kodwa."

there to-morrow, and then tell you. I have indeed had some sleep. I will tell you to-morrow, sirs, whether that man is a doctor or not."

Indeed, night comes, and there is no return of the pain. He sleeps. In the morning they ask him how he is.

He says, "O, sirs, I shall now get well."

The doctor then says, "I have now cured him. Show me my cattle. I am going in the morning; I wish to see them, and in the morning drive them home. I say, let me see them before I lie down."

They say, "O, yes, dear sir; you are right. We now see that your patient is nearly well."

So they shew him his cattle; they point out a young cow with a heifer by her side, and a calf of a year old—three altogether.

They say, "Say what you think, doctor; we say, there are your cattle."

He says, "I thank you for the cattle. But give me something to wipe my eyes with."[60]

---

[60] " Give me something to wipe my eyes with." Lit., Wipe my eyes for me. A proverbial saying, meaning that he is not wholly satisfied; that his eyes are not yet quite free from dust, so that he is unable to see clearly the cattle they have given him. The natives have another saying when purchasing cattle. When they have agreed about the price, the purchaser says, " Veza ni amasondo," Bring out the hoofs. Very much like, " Give me a luck-penny." The person who has sold will then give a small basket of corn.

Ba m nika ke imbuzi. Ya i ḣlaba imbuzi, ya twala inyongo. Ya ti, "Se ngi ni shiya nemiti, ukuze ni m potule. Se ngi kqedile mina, ku pela."

So they give him a goat. He kills the goat, and places the gall-bladder in his hair. He says, "I shall leave medicines with you, that you may wash him with them. I have now entirely finished for my part."

The Diviner mistaken.

Ku tiwa ukutasa kwenyanga i kqala ngokugula; ku tiwa u guliswa amadḣlozi; i b' i s' i ḣlatshiswa izimbuzi; emva kwaloko i twale izinyongo eziningi. Isibonakalo sokuba umuntu u inyanga uma e nezinyongo eziningi. I be se i tasa.

Ukutasa kwayo i hamba i ḣlanya i y' esizibeni, i kewile pansi, i funa izinyoka; i zi tole, i zi bambe, i pume nazo, i zinqwambe ngazo zi s' ezwa, ukuba abantu ba bone ukuba inyanga mpela. Emva kwaloko ba kqale uku i linga ngezinto eziningi, ukuba ba bone ukuba u ya 'kuba inyanga e bula kaḣle ini na. Ba be se be fika, inyanga i be se i b' ezwa se be i tshela ukuba b' eze kuyo; i be se i ti, "Tshaya ni, ngi zwe ukuba ni ze

It is said a man begins to be a diviner by being ill; it is said he is made ill by the Amatongo; and he has many goats killed for him; and when they have been killed he carries the gall-bladders in his hair. It is a sign that a man is becoming a diviner if he wears many gall-bladders. After that he begins to be a diviner.

On his initiation, he goes like one mad to a pool, and dives into it, seeking for snakes; having found them, he seizes them and comes out of the water with them, and entwines them still living about his body, that the people may see that he is indeed a diviner.[61] After that they begin to try him in many ways, to see whether he will become a trustworthy diviner. They then go to him, and the diviner hears them say they have come to divine; and he tells them to smite the ground, that he may understand why

---

[61] See the account of Ukanzi at the end of this article.

ngani na?"—Ba be se be tshaya, be ti, "Yizwa."—I be se i ti, "Ni ze ngokuti."—Be se be tshaya,—I ti, "Ni ze ngokuti ngokuti;" i be se i ba tshela ukwenza kwaleyo 'nto a b' eze ngayo; se i ba tshela imigidi e vela ngalowo 'muntu a b' eze ngaye. Ba be se be i nika umvuzo uma be bona ukuba i bule ngezinto a ba zi zwayo, ba be se be muka; se be fika ekaya, se b' enza imigidi a ba i zwileyo ngenyanga. M*h*laumbe ku be se kw enzeka ngawo amazwi enyanga; m*h*laumbe ku ng' enzeki; ba bone ukuba a kw enzekile ngamazwi aleyo 'nyanga, ba be se be ya kwenye; m*h*laumbe kw enzeke ngamazwi aleyo 'nyanga. I loko ke e ngi ku zwayo.

Kwa ti emgungund*h*lovu kwa la*h*leka inkomo kajoje, umlungu wami. Sa i funa, ka sa ze sa i bona. Sa se si ti kujoje, ka si nike u*h*lamvu, si ye 'kubula, ngokuba sa se si *h*lupekile ukufuna, si ng' azi lapo si za 'kufunela ngakona. Wa se si nika u*h*lamvu, se si hamba si ya enyangeni ey ake ngasembubu. Sa se si fika, sa i fumana i *h*lezi esibayeni; sa se si

they have come. And they smite the ground and cry, "Hear."—And he then says, "You have come for such and such a matter."—And then they smite the ground.—He then says, "You have come for so and so;" and he proceeds to tell them what has taken place as regards that about which they have come; and he tells them what the man about whom they have come has done. They then reward him if they see that he has divined about matters which they understand; and depart; and when they reach home they do as the diviner tells them. Perhaps it turns out in accordance with what the diviner has said; perhaps it does not so turn out; when they see that it has not turned out in accordance with his word, they go to another diviner; and perhaps what he says comes to pass. That is what I have heard.

Once at Pietermaritzburg a heifer belonging to Mr. G., my white master, was lost. We looked for it, but could not find it. We then asked Mr. G. to give us a shilling, that we might enquire of a diviner, for we were now troubled with looking for it, and did not know where to look for it any further. He gave us a shilling, and we went to a diviner who lives near the Zwartkop. On our arrival we found him sitting in the

kuleka, sa ti, "E, mngane;" sa hlala pansi.

Ba si bingelela, sa vuma.

Ba ti abakonyanga, "Ni vela pi na?"

Sa ti, "Si vela emgungundhlovu, si babele lapa enyangeni."

Ba ti, "Ni babele ni lapa na?"

Sa ti, "Si ze ngendaba zetu, ku lahlekile izinkomo." Sa se si keela uguai; se be si shiyela, se si bema. Emva kwaloko se i ti, "Puma ni, si ye lapaya ngapandhle kwomuzi."

Se i puma, se si landela ngasemva. Se i fika, se i ti, "Tshaya ni, ngi zwe, bangane bami, ukuba ngi zwe ukuba ni ze ngani."

Sa tshaya, si tshaya ngezandhla, sa ti, "Yizwa."
Ya ti, "Ni ya hlupeka."
Sa ti, "Yizwa."
Ya ti, "Ake ngi zwe ukuba inkomo ni na?"

Sa tshaya.
Ya ti, "Inkomokazi."
Sa tshaya.
Ya ti, "Ai; inkabi."
Sa tshaya.

cattle-pen; and we saluted, saying, "Eh, dear sir," and sat down.

They saluted us, and we replied.

The diviner's people asked us whence we came.

We told them we came from Pietermaritzburg, and had come to enquire of the diviner.

They said, "Why have you come here?"

We told them we had come on our own account, some cattle[62] having been lost. We then asked for snuff, and they gave us some and we took it; and after that the diviner said, "Let us go yonder outside the village."

He went out, and we followed him. He said to us, "Strike the ground, that I may understand, my friends, what is the reason that you have come to me."

We smote our hands together, and said, "Hear."
He said, "You are in trouble."
We said, "Hear."
He said, "Let me just understand what kind of a bullock it is?"

We smote our hands together.
He said, "It is a cow."
We smote our hands.
He said, "No; it is an ox."
We smote our hands.

---

[62] They say "some cattle," although it was but one that was missing, that they may not give the diviner too much knowledge. They leave him to discover the deception; and if he does not, but proceeds to speak as though many cattle were lost, they know he does not understand divination.

Ya ti, "Ai; a si yo inkabi."
Sa tshaya.
Ya ti, "Ni ya hlupeka, bafana."

Sa tshaya.
Ya ti, "Kodwa inkomo kade ya lahleka."
Kodwa ya tsho ikqiniso lapo.
Sa tshaya.
Ya ti, "Ake ngi zwe ukuba y' ebiwa abantu ini na."
Sa tshaya.
Ya ti, "Ai, a i biwanga abantu; kodwa i kona."
Sa tshaya.
Ya ti, "Inye."
Kodwa ya tsho ikqiniso futi lapo.
Sa tshaya.
Ya ti, "Ake ngi zwe ukuba i 'mbal' u njani na?"
Sa tshaya.
Ya ti, "Incokazi."

Kodwa ya i kqagela lapo, a i tshongo ikqiniso lapo.
Sa tshaya.
Ya ti, "Ai; isitole; a si ka zekwa."
Sa tshaya.
Kodwa lapo ya tsho ikqiniso futi.
Ya ti, "Ke ngi zwe ukuba mbala le 'nkomo i se kona nje na."
Sa tshaya.
Ya ti, "Ai, a i ko le 'nkomo."

He said, "No; it is not an ox."
We smote our hands.
He said, "You are in trouble, lads."
We smote our hands.
He said, "But the cow was lost a long time ago."
And there he spoke truly.
We smote our hands.
He said, "Just let me understand if it was stolen by any one."
We smote our hands.
He said, "No, it was not stolen by men; but it is still living."
We smote our hands.
He said, "It is one that is lost."
And there too he spoke the truth.
We smote with our hands.
He said, "Let me just understand of what colour it is."
We smote with our hands.
He said, "It is a red and white cow."
But there he made a guess, and did not speak truly.
We smote our hands.
He said, "No; it is a heifer; it is not yet in calf."
We smote our hands.
And there too he spoke truly.

He said, "Let me understand if the heifer is still living or not."
We smote our hands.
He said, "No, the heifer is dead."

Sa tshaya.
Ya ti, " Ai, i kona."
Ya ti, "Ake ngi zwe ukuba i pi na."
Sa tshaya.
Ya ti, " I se/tlanzeni."

Sa tshaya.
Ya ti, " Ake ngi zwe ukuba i ngapi kwe/tlanze na."

Sa tshaya.
Ya ti, " I senzansi nomsunduze."
Sa tshaya.
Ya ti, "Ake ngi zwe ukuba i sa hamba njc na."
Sa tshaya.
Ya ti, " I sa hamba, i d/tla umtolo nomunga. Hamba ni, ni ye 'kufunela kona; ni ya 'ku i tola lapo."
Sa ti si zwa ukuba i si tshelile indawo, loku kade si nga y azi indawo e si nga funela kuyo.

Sa i nika u/tlamvu. Sa hamba, sa ya emgungund/tlovu. Sa fika kujoje, sa m tshela amazwi enyanga, si ti, "I te i sen/tlanzeni, a si yofunela kona enzansi nomsunduze."

Wa ti, a si hambe si yokufuna lapo ku tsho inyanga. Sa hamba sa ya 'kufuna, s' eusa umsunduze.

We smote our hands.
He said, " No, it is still living."
He said, " Let me just understand where it is."
We smote our hands.
He said, " It is in the mimosa thorn-country."
We smote our hands.
He said, " Just let me understand in what part of the thorn-country it is."
We smote our hands.
He said, " It has gone down the Umsunduze."
We smote our hands.
He said, " Just let me understand if it is still living."
We smote our hands.
He said, " It is still living, and eating umtolo and umunga.[63] Go and look for it there, and you will find it."
We thought we understood that he had now told us the place, for for some time we had not known where to go to look for it.

Then we gave him the shilling, and returned to Pietermaritzburg. When we came to Mr. G. we told him that the diviner said it was in the thorn-country, and that we were to go and look for it down the Umsunduze.

He told us to go and look for it in the place mentioned by the diviner. We went to look for it, going down the Umsunduze. As

---

[63] *Umtolo* and *umunga*, mimosa trees.

Si hambo si funa, si kqonde ohlanzeni lapo i tsho kona. Sa ya sa fika ngakutomas, sa funa ngalapo; sa i swela, ngokuba ihlanze la li likulu. Sa hamba si buza imizi yonke e sehlanzeni. Ba ti, a ba y azi; abanye bo ti, a si yo 'kufunela kutomas, umlungu o dhla izinkomo ezilahlekileyo zabantu. Kodwa tina s' esaba ukuya lapo kutomas, ngokuba ku 'mlungu o nolaka, e ti a nga bona abantu a nga b' aziyo be hamba ezweni lake a be se ba tshaya. Sa se si buya si nga yanga kutomas, sa ya ekaya emgungundhlovu; sa fika sa ti kujoje, a si i bonanga; si i swele ngalapo ku tsho inyanga. Wa se ti, "A se ni hlala." Sa se si hlala; sokuba ku pela ke.

USETEMBA DHLADHLA.

we went along we looked for it, going towards the thorn-country which he had pointed out. At length we got as far as T.'s, and sought for it in that neighbourhood; we could not find it, for the thorns were very thick. As we went we enquired at all the native villages in the thorn-country. The people said they knew nothing about it; and others told us to go to T., the white man who ate up the cattle of the people that were lost.[64] But we were afraid to go to him, for he is a passionate white man who beats any coloured men whom he does not know if he see them passing through his land. So we went back to Pietermaritzburg without going to T.; and told Mr. G. that we had not found the heifer at the place pointed out by the diviner. So he told us to give up the search. We did so, and that was the end of it.

---

[64] That is, if any cattle strayed into his land he took possession of them.

The Account of Ukanzi.

THE following narrative gives an interesting and striking instance of the power a bold man may possess even over venomous snakes. The snakes caught by the diviners and hung in festoons about their bodies, are probably charmed in some such manner as here related of Ukanzi. It is quite possible that both possessed medicines which are either offensive or pleasing to snakes, by which they caused them to be afraid or gentle. But it is not necessary to suppose that Ukanzi used any such medicines; the mere daring and yet cautious coolness with which he approached the snake is quite sufficient to explain why it became so cowed before him. But how are we to explain his insusceptibility to the snake poison? Why did the poisoned fangs broken off and remaining in his lips produce no symptoms? It is likely that he was naturally insusceptible to the influence of such animal poisons, just as others possess a natural intense susceptibility to it, so that the sting of a bee has in them been followed by fatal consequences. This is much more likely, than that he possessed any powerful remedies by the use of which he rendered the snake poison innocuous. The son inherited the same insusceptibility. Of course all statements as to the invariable efficacy of some particular remedy possessed by savages, must be received with great caution; and if subjected to rigid enquiry would probably prove not to be founded in well-observed facts.

INDABA kakanzi kanjoko yobunyanga bake ngesi/clungu.

Umuntu o mangalisayo kakulu ngobunyanga bake. A ku ko 'muntu ezweni lakiti o njengaye ngokun<i>q</i>oba isi/clungu sezinyoka; yena u ng' umuntu o tembekayo kanyekanye ngesi/clungu.

Ku ti uma umuntu e d/cliwe inyoka enjani nenjani, ka tsho

THE account of Ukanzi, the son of Unjoko, and of his knowledge of snake-poison.

He is a man who causes us to wonder much at his knowledge. There is no one in our country like him who can render inert the poison of snakes; he is a man trusted to the uttermost in cases of snake-bites.

If any one is bitten by any kind of snake, he does not say he

ukuti, "Isihlungu saleyo 'nyoka a ngi naso." Kqa; ku pela yena u ya tokoza nguzo zonke izinyoka; ka vinjelwa 'luto kuzo. Uma ku tiwa u dhliwe inyoka enkulu etile umuntu, a tate isihlungu soku y a-hlula.

Futifuti u zinge 'ahlukanisa isihlungu senyama yenyoka nesihlungu sezibilini, si hambe sodwa, si nga hlangani nesomzimba.

Isibonakaliso sake sokuba u inyanga ukuba izinyoka e zi bamba kuye zi njengezimpuku nje. Nga ka nga m bona ngamehlo ami, a ngi zwanga 'ndaba. Wa bamba inyoka enkulu, umdhlambila, imamba yesiwa, si zingela izinyamazane. Sa fika pansi kwesiwa, si inkqina, kanti imamba i pezulu emtini y ota ilanga. Sa i bona i gewele emtini, empofu umbala wayo; i 'mehlo a 'zinjonjo; i bheka umuntu kw esabeke.

Sa m biza, sa ti, "Nansi inyamazane yako!" W' eza e gijima, wa fika wa ti, "I pi?" Sa komba, wa i bona. Wa beka izikali pansi, wa kwela emtini, wa ya kuyo. Nga ti ngenhliziyo, "Ngi

does not possess the remedy[65] for that kind of snake-poison. No; for his part he is only gladdened by all kinds of snakes; nothing prevents his curing the bite of any of them. If a man is said to have been bitten by some deadly snake, he at once selects the proper remedy.

And he continually separates the remedy for the poison which is in the body, and that which is in the viscera, and keeps them distinct.

A proof that he is a doctor is that the snakes which he catches are to him no more than mice. I once saw this with my own eyes, and did not merely hear it by report. He caught a great snake called Umdhlambila, the rock imamba, when we were hunting. When we, the hunting party, came under a precipice, there was a snake in a tree basking in the sun. We saw it occupying the whole tree; it was of a grey colour; its eyes were piercing; it was fearful when it looked at any one.

We called him, saying, "Here is your game!" He came running and asking where it was. We pointed it out, and he saw it. He laid his weapons on the ground, and climbed the tree and went to it. I said in my heart, "I shall now see.

---

[65] Note that *isihlungu* is used both for the snake-poison and its remedy.

za 'uke ngi bone. Loku ka pete | For since he has not taken a stick,
'nduku, ukuba ugongolo olungaka | what will he do to this snake
u za 'u lw enza njani na? A lu | which is as large as a post?[66]
z' 'u mu d*h*la ini?" Wa faka isa- | Will it not devour him?"[67] He

[66] Lit., To so great a post, or trunk, as this.

[67] The following account is taken from the *St. James's Magazine*:

"In the course of a country ramble, some Europeans fell in with a company of Eisowys bound for Tangier. A halt was called under a spreading fig-tree, at the foot of which ran a delightful little stream. The snake-basket was emptied out on the ground, and the performance was carried on much in the way just described. While the operator was washing his wounds, and spitting out blood enough to discolour the stream, some one suggested that it was all a sham, and that the snakes had not poison enough among them to kill a sparrow. On this being interpreted to the proprietor, who was by this time up to his knees in the water, trying to wash away the traces of his last experiment, he very considerately offered to place his basket at the disposal of any one who might be inclined to take his first lesson in snake-charming. There was a pause; for it was suddenly remembered that a luckless Portuguese had once tried the experiment, and had to suffer the loss of one of his arms by amputation, as a memorial of his temerity. Meanwhile the snakes were indulging themselves in a merry wriggle on the grass, and nobody was sufficiently devoted to the interests of science to disturb their sports. There the matter would have ended, but for a happy thought. 'Fetch a fowl,' cried one of the Europeans, and away scampered a native servant to buy one. By way of improving the time a lean-flanked Eisowy, who had hitherto contemplated what was going on with a sulky air, roused himself up and declared his readiness to eat a snake for a suitable consideration. The offer was sensational, and the required amount was subscribed, on condition that he should eat a snake to be chosen by the Europeans. Bang went the tambourine louder than ever, and up jumped the Eisowy, incumbered with nothing heavier than his skin and drawers, and looking hungry enough to eat the snakes, basket and all. Long and anxious was the consultation of the Europeans, as to which was the nastiest and most venomous of the snakes. The Leffa, which had bitten the man so badly, was to be reserved for an experiment on the fowl; so the choice fell on a speckly monster of most alarming vitality. No sooner was the selection proclaimed, than the operator seized him by the tail, which he instantly thrust into his mouth with the manifest intention of making a hearty meal. Before it was possible to rush forward and stop the disgusting exhibition, the Eisowy had drawn in himself so much in earnest about his work, that he had drawn in several inches of the reptile, chewing away violently at the unsavoury morsel. There was no standing such a loathsome sight, so one of his companions was hastily bribed to snatch the writhing serpent from his hands. It was impossible to make him comprehend that the exhi-

ndhla emlonyeni, wa si hlanhlata; | put his hand in his mouth and gently bit it all over; he took it bition was not agreeable. He evidently thought that there was some mistake about the snake, and to show that he was equal to the emergency, he most obligingly proposed that another selection should be made, and, on this being declined, he undertook, for a further consideration, to find a wild one, and eat him on the spot. Somewhat chagrined at the signs of disapprobation with which his suggestion was received, and thinking that he was in duty bound to do something for his money, he produced an iron skewer, and thrust it through his cheek, making it appear on the other side of his face. This was an evident relief to his feelings, for he drew out the skewer, wiped it on the grass, and squatted on his haunches with the air of a public benefactor. The truth is, that the habits of these men are so temperate, and they have so little spare flesh on their bones, that there is nothing for inflammation to fasten on. It is likely enough that if the spectators had not had enough of this sensational kind of exhibition, another famished-looking Eisowy would have made good his promise to eat a handful of nails or broken glass, at the option of the company. The capacity of these men for eating seems to be limited by none of the laws which regulate the appetites of ordinary mortals."

The same power is also found among the Chinese:—

" Behind a counter is seen an itinerant doctor, dilating on the virtues of an antidote against the bite of serpents; one of his coadjutors is actually putting the head of the *cobra capella*, or hooded snake, into his mouth, while a less intrepid, but equally useful assistant, is exchanging the miraculous drug for *cash* or *tseen*. The great impostor himself, mounted on a stool, his head protected by a conical hat of split bamboo, a vestment of thick, coarse, compact cloth enclosing his arms, and a similar covering being secured around his waist by a silken girdle, holds a serpent in one hand, and the antidote to its venomous bite in the other;

'Thus is he doubly arm'd with death and life:
The bane and antidote are both before him.'

So perfect is the education of this mischievous reptile, that it essays to bite its owner, and submits to disappointment with the appearance of reluctance. Having proved that this particular enemy of mankind still retains its propensity to injury in the most entire manner, and requires to be guarded against with caution, the doctor takes a medicated ball from one of the packets with which the counter is strewn, and, when the snake renews its attempts, presents the ball to it, upon which it instantly recoils, and endeavours to escape from his grasp. Should this demonstration be insufficient, the efficacy of the charm is still more convincingly established by merely rubbing the forehead, cheek, hand, or any other unprotected part with the antidote, and presenting it to the reptile, which appears to retreat with the same dislike and precipitation as when the entire ball was shown to it."
(China, in a Series of Views, &c. By Thomas Allom, Esq., and the Rev. G. N. Wright, M.A. Vol. II., p. 14.)

wa si kipa, wa s' clulela kuyo; y' etuka, y' emis' ikanda, ya tshoba i funa ukubaleka. Kepa isand*h*la sake sa ba loku si i landela njalo emtini, i buye. Ngi ti, i za 'ugalela en*h*loko, a tambe, i ng' enzi 'luto ; a buye a pakamise isand*h*la ; ya za ya tamba, ya beka in*h*loko esand*h*leni, i nga i beki ngakulwa, i se i beka ngokuzetula kanyekanye esand*h*leni sake, se i zila*h*la ukuba 'enze a ku tandayo. Wa i bamba in*h*loko, wa i faka emlonyeni, wa i *h*lofoza ngamazinyo ; amazinyo ayo 'apukela emlonyeni wake ; wa wa kumula lapa e se i bulele, a kwa ba 'ndaba zaluto ; kwa nga ti u kumula ameva nje ; ka d*h*la 'muti ukuze ku pele isi*h*lungu ; kwa ukupela.

Sa mangala si pansi, sa ti, "Ukanzi umtakati." Wa i donsa, wa zisonga ngayo, w' e*h*la nayo. Wa funa utshani, wa i bopa ngabo, wa goduka nayo, e ti, "Se ngi i bulele mina inyamazane ; se ngi ya 'ku i lungisa ekaya." Nembala, wa i twala, wa hamba nayo.

Nendodana yako Ugidinga i

out and extended it towards the snake; it started and raised its head, and turned in every direction, wishing to escape. But his hand followed it constantly wherever it went on the tree. When I thought it would strike him on his head, he withdrew himself and it did nothing ; and then raised his hand again ; at length it became gentle, and laid its head in his hand, not placing it there in a hostile manner, but laying its head with all gentleness in his hand, and letting him do what he liked with it. He seized its head, and put it in his mouth, and chewed it ; the snake's teeth broke in his mouth ; he picked out the teeth when he had killed the snake, and nothing happened ; it was as if he picked out thorns merely ; he took no medicine to counteract the poison ; he merely picked out the teeth.

We who were standing on the ground wondered, and said Ukanzi was a sorcerer. He drew the snake towards himself, and twisted it round his body, and came down with it. He got some grass and tied the snake up in it, and went home with it, saying, "For my part I have now killed my game ; I shall prepare it at home." So he carried it away.

And his son Ugidinga resembles

njalo nayo, i ujengoyise ngokubamba izinyoka. Se ya funda kuyise. Wa fika nayo ekaya, wa y ebula, wa y a*h*lukanisa isikumba nenyama, wa i kewiya; wa y osa ukuze i nga boli, y ome; a i peke nemiti yesi*h*lungu. In*h*liziyo i hambe yodwa; umzimba u hambe wodwa; u nezi*h*lungu zibili—si sodwa sen*h*liziyo, si sodwa somzimba.

Ku ti uma umuntu e d*h*liwe inyoka e hamba nokanzi, a m pe imputshana a i kote ngolimi, a ti, "Ku pela ke. Se ngi ku sizile." Lo 'muntu a hambe 'esaba, e nga kolwa ukuba u siziwe, ngokuba e nga boni umuti omningi nokwelapa okuningi. A ze a bone e k*q*eda izwe nje be hamba ku nge ko 'ndaba, ku nga bi ko nokuvuvuka, ku nga ti ka lunywanga, w' enz' amanga nje. Ku njalo ke ukwenza kwake.

Kepa lobo 'bunyanga bake a b' aziwa ukuba w' enza njani ukwa*h*lula izinyoka kanje. Kodwa kwa tiwa wa zelapa kuk*q*ala ngemiti emikulu; ngokuba noma inyoka i ngena emgodini u i bamba

his father in his power of catching snakes, he having learnt of his father. When he reached home with the snake, he skinned it, and separated the skin and the flesh, and selected different portions of the body; he roasted it that it might not decay, but dry; he boiled it with other snake-poison remedies. The heart was set aside by itself; and the body by itself; and he had thus two remedies—that obtained from the heart, and that from the body.

If a man walking with Ukanzi were bitten by a snake, he would give him a little powder to lick with his tongue, and say, "That is all. I have now cured you." The man would go on in fear, not believing that he was cured, for he had not seen much medicine, or much treatment. But at length he saw when they had gone a great distance and nothing happened, and there was no swelling, and it was as if his being bitten at all was a mistake. Such, then, was how he acted.

But as to his knowledge, no one knew by what means he cured all kinds of snake-bites in this manner. But it was said he first treated himself with powerful medicines; for even if a snake ran into a hole he would catch it by

ngomsila, i penduke, i m lume ; i be i lungile kuye, a i bambe ngen-hloko, a i bulale ngoku i faka emlonyeni, a nga zelapi nakanye ngaloko 'kulunywa, ku be u dhliwe impuku nje.

the tail, and it would turn round and bite him ; it was no matter to him, but he would catch it by the head and kill it by placing it in his mouth, and adopted no treatment whatever for the bite any more than if he had been bitten by a mouse.

Consulting the Diviner.

UMA umuntu e gula, ba ye kuso isanusi, ba ye 'kubula. Si ti, " U nokufa." Umhlaumbe si ti, " U bulawa umuntu o 'mtakati." Abantu ba ya goduka, se be m azi umuntu o takatayo.

Kodwa abanye ba pike, ba ti, " Kqa ! Inyanga i namanga ; ka takati." Kodwa abanye ba ti, " I kqinisile." A z' a ku zwe ukuti inyanga i m nukile. A tukutele, 'emuke kuleyo 'ndawo, a ye 'kukonza kwabanye abantu. Kodwa abantu ba ya kolwa kuzo izindaba zesanusi. Kodwa abanye a ba kolwa.

Uma ku gula umuntu, ba ya 'kubula esanusini. Si ti, " Umuntu u bulawa idhlozi. Ma ba dhle inkomo ; umuntu u ya 'kusinda uma ba i dhle inkomo." Ba i dhle inkomo. Ba bonge amatongo, ba i hlabe.

Ba ti se be i dhlile ba i kqede

IF a man is ill, the people go to a diviner, to enquire of him. He says the man is suffering from disease. Or perhaps he says, he is injured by some one who is a sorcerer. They go home, now knowing the man who practises sorcery.

But others dispute, saying, " No ! The diviner lies ; that man is not a sorcerer." Others say, he speaks the truth. At length the man hears that the diviner has pointed him out as a sorcerer. He is angry, and leaves the place, and goes to be a dependent among other people. But the people believe in what the diviner says. But others do not believe.

If a man is ill, they go to enquire of the diviner. He says, " The man is made ill by the Idhlozi. Let them eat an ox ; the man will get well if they eat an ox." They eat an ox. They worship the Amatongo, and kill it.

When they have eaten all the

inyama yayo, umuntu a nga sindi, a gule njalo, a ze a fe, ba ti abanye, "Inyanga i kqamb' amanga." Abanye ba ti, "U bizwe amatongo; inyanga a i namandhla okwahlula amatongo."

A ti, e se file, ba ye 'kubula enyangeni. I ti inyanga kubona, "U bizwe amadhlozi; a ya tanda uma a fe, a ye 'kuhlala nawo." Noko abantu a ba yeki ukubula enyangeni. Ngesinye isikati ba ti inyanga i kqinisile; ngesinye isikati ba ti i namanga. Ngokuba ku ti uma ku gula umuntu ba ye 'kubula enyangeni; i ti inyanga, uma ba hlabe inkomo umuntu u ya 'kusinda. Ba i hlabe inkomo, a sinde umuntu; ba se be kolwa izwi lenyanga; kanti umuntu u be za 'kusinda kade. Kodwa bona abantu ba kolwe ukuti, u sindiswe amatongo.

Uma umuntu e gula, a bizelwe izinyanga; zi m elape, a ti e se sindile, izinyanga zi bize izinkomo, zi ti, ka koke, ngokuba zi m sindisile; a koke; ku ti e se kokile, a gule futi, a ye kuyona inyanga a i kokeleyo; i m elape, i nga kw ahluli ukufa; i ti, y ahlulekile. A ti umuntu o gulayo, " A i buye inkomo yami, ngi ye kwezinye

flesh and the man does not get well, but is constantly ill until he dies, some say, "The diviner lies." Others say, " He was called by the Amatongo; a diviner cannot conquer the Amatongo."

When he is dead, they go to enquire of the diviner. He says, "He has been called by the Amatongo; they wish him to die, and go and live with them." And yet people do not cease to enquire of the diviner. Sometimes they say, the diviner is true; sometimes they say, he is false. For when a man is ill they will enquire of a diviner; and the diviner says, if they kill an ox the man will get well. They kill an ox, and the man gets well; and then they believe in the diviner's word; and yet forsooth the man would have got well after a time. But the people believe he has been saved by the Amatongo.

When a man is ill, they call doctors to see him; they treat him, and when he gets well they demand cattle, telling him he must pay because they have cured him; he pays; and after he has paid, he is ill again, and goes to the same doctor whom he has paid; he treats him, but does not remove the disease; and tells him, it masters him. And the sick man asks his ox to be sent back, that he may go to other doctors. They

izinyanga." Ba yo kwezinyo izinyanga; zi m elape; umhlaumbe zi kw ahlule ukufa; i ti inyanga yokukqala i zonde, ngokuti u sindiswe i yona, ba i kokele ey elape 'muva.

Lapo inyanga y elapa umuntu o gulayo, i fik' i hlabe inkomo, i nqume imisipa ezitweni zenkomo; ku ti i se i nqumile, i i hlanganise nemiti, i i gayinge, i tshe, y ome. I ti, se y omile, ba i gaye, a geatshwe umuntu o gulayo, a telwe ngenyongo, ukuze ku fike amatongo, a ze 'ku m bona, a m kote, ukuze a sinde.

Ba ti abantu ba ya bula enyangeni uma i ba tshele. Ba ya hamba nje enyangeni; ba fike kuyona, ba nga kulumi ukuti, "Si ze ngendaba etile." Ba ya tula. Kodwa i ba tshele, i ti, "Ni ze ngendaba." Ba vuma ngokutshaya. Uma be tshaya kakulu, b' ezwa inyanga i tsho izindaba a ba z' aziyo, a ba ze ngazo. Uma i tsho izindaba a ba nga z' aziyo, ba tshaye kancinyane. Uma i tsho izindaba ezi kona, ba tshaye kakulu.

go to others; they treat him; perhaps they cure the disease; then the first doctor feels hurt, and says that the sick man was cured by him, but they have paid the man that gave him physic last.

When a doctor treats a sick person, he kills an ox, and cuts away the tendons of the legs, and mixes them with medicines, and chars them, till they are dry. When they are dry they are powdered, and the sick man is scarified, and the medicines are rubbed into the scarifications; and the gall is poured on him, that the Amatongo may come and see him and lick him, that he may get well.

Men go to the diviner that he may tell them what they wish to know. They merely go to him, and on their arrival do not tell him for what purpose they have come. They are silent. But he tells them they have come on some matter of importance. They assent by striking the ground. If they strike vehemently, they do so because they hear the diviner mention things which they know and about which they have come to him. If he mentions things unknown to them, they strike the ground slightly. If he mentions the very things they know, they strike vehemently.

Uma ku la*h*lekile uto nenkomo, ba ye 'kubula enyangeni, i ba tshele ukuti, 'ma be ye 'kufuna endaweni ba ya 'ku i tola. Ba ye 'kufuna lapo inyanga i tsho kona, ba i tole. Ba ti uma be nga i tolanga, ba ti, "Inyanga i namanga; a i kw azi ukubula." Ba ye kwenye a ba i zwayo abantu ukuti, i bul' ik*q*iniso; ba ye kuyo, i ba tshele, ba ya 'kufuna lapo. Um*h*laumbe ba i tola into, ba kolwa i yona inyanga, ba ti, i k*q*inisile.

If any thing is lost, an ox for instance, they go to a diviner, and he tells them that if they look for it in a certain place they will find it. They go to the place he mentions, and find it. But if they do not find it where he says, they say, the diviner is false; he does not know how to divine. They then go to another, who is known to divine truly; he tells them, and they go and seek there. If they find it, they believe in that diviner, and say, he is a true diviner.

To bar the way against the Amatongo and against disease supposed to be occasioned by them.

UKU m vimba kwayo inyanga | WHEN a doctor bars the way[68] for

---

[68] *Ukuvimba* is to stop, to put a stopper in a bottle. The natives say, *U'ku m vimba umuntu*, To stop a man, as though there was some opening by which the Itongo had access. Or *U'kuvimba itongo*, or *U'ku m vimba itongo*, or *U'kuvimbela umuntu*,—all of which various modes of expressing the same thing may be translated by our phrase, "to lay a ghost or spirit."

In Jón Arnason's *Icelandic Legends*, translated by Powell and Magnússon, we find numerous allusions to ghosts and methods of laying them. One Ketill, having found the corpse of an old woman lying in the road, passed by without paying the least attention to it. The next night and every night after, the old woman visited him in his dreams, assuming a horrible and threatening aspect, and hounding him on to an untimely grave. *(P.* 159.*)* A man lays the ghost of his deceased friend by pouring a keg of brandy on his grave to moisten his "dry old bones," of which the ghost complained. *(P.* 160.*)* "The boy who did not know what fear was" has a stand-up fight with a giant-goblin, whom he manages to detain till "the first ray of dawn," which striking the goblin's eyes, he sinks into the ground in two pieces, and is for ever prevented from rising again by two crosses driven into the places where the two parts disappeared. *(P.* 165.*)* Some are laid by extorting a promise from them not to appear again. "The deacon of Myrká" haunts his betrothed, as the ghosts of the Amazulu do their wives, and all means for laying the spirit having failed, even the reading of psalms by the priest, they send for a man

umuntu o nesidhlalo, ku funwa imiti etile ey aziwayo, ku fikwe, ku tatwe kuye igazi, li tatwe, li yiswe esidulini esilukuni, esi ya 'kubuya s' akiwe izilwanyazane ; a si bobose lowo 'muntu o inyanga, a fake kuso umuti o negazi lomuntu o gulayo, a vimbe ngetshe, a shiye, a nga be e sa bheka emuva a ze a fike ekaya. Loku 'kufa ku tiwa ku vinjiwe ; a ku sa yi 'kubuya futi.

Uma si vimba ngeselesele lomfula, li ya banjwa, ku ziwo nalo ekaya ; umuntu e geatshiwe lapo

a man who has isidhlalo,[69] he takes certain known medicines with him to the sick man, and takes some of his blood and goes to a hard ant-hill which the ants will repair again if broken down ; he makes a hole in it, and places in it the medicine with the blood of the sick man, and closes up the hole with a stone, and leaves the place without looking back[70] till he gets home. So it is said the disease is barred out, and will never return again.

When we bar the way with a frog of the river, we catch a frog, and take it home ; when the patient has been scarified over the

---

skilled in witchcraft, who seizes the deacon's ghost, uttering potent spells, and forces him beneath a stone, and there he lies to this day. *(P. 177.)* Grímur lays the very substantial ghost of Skeljúngur by fastening him to a rock ; and when the ghost went away with it, cut off his head and burnt him, and cast the ashes into a well. *(P. 199.)*

Another plan of getting rid of goblins is to outwit them by setting them about some task which is impossible to be fulfilled, as spinning ropes of sand.—Hothershall Hall, near Ribchester, is said to have been troubled by the nightly visits of a goblin ; but the goblin " is understood to have been 'laid' under the roots of a large laurel tree at the end of the house, and will not be able to molest the family so long as the tree exists. It is a common opinion in that part of the country that the roots have to be moistened with milk on certain occasions, in order to prolong its existence, and also to preserve the power of the spell under which the goblin is laid. None but the Roman Catholic priesthood are supposed to have the power of 'laying an evil spirit,' and hence they have always the honour to be cited in our local legends." *(Lancashire Folk-lore. John Harland, F.S.A., and T. T. Wilkinson, F.R.A.S., p. 57.)*

[60] *Isidhlalo*, a disease supposed to be caused by the Itongo.

[70] Here again we have a superstition analagous with what we find in our own country. To charm warts away, a piece of flesh is stolen and rubbed on the warts, and then buried ; or a number of pebbles, corresponding with the number of warts, is placed in a bag, which is thrown over the back. But in neither case will the charm work if the person " looks back till he gets home."

e pela kona kakulu, ku kiwe igazi lakona, ku funzwe isele, li buyiselwe endaweni yalo; li patwe kahle, li nga fi. U viujiwe ke.

Ku ti uma umfazi e bujelwe indoda, ipupa li m kataze kakulu owesifazana, lapa e lele indoda yake i buye i z' end*h*lini, a i bone njengokungati i sa hamba ngemi*h*la yonke, ku be njalo a ze a zakce owesifazana ngokuti, "Ngi ya *h*lupeka uyise kabani; ka ngi dedeli; kunga ka fanga; ngi ba nayc njalo, a nyamalale ngi vuka. Umzimba se u ze w enakala; u ya kuluma ngabantwana na ngemfuyo yake na ngezindatshana eziningi." Ngaloko ke ku ze ku funwe umuntu ow azi uku m vimba. A m nike umuti, a ti, "Nang' umuti. Ku ya 'kuti uma u m pupile, u vuke, u d*h*lafune wona; amate u nga wa kciti lawo o pupe u lele; u nga feli amate; u fele lapa, ukuze lelo 'pupa si li vimbe."

most painful spot, the blood is taken from that place, and is placed in the frog's mouth, and it is carried back to its place; it is handled gently, lest it should die. So the disease is barred out from the man.

Again, if a woman has lost her husband, and she is troubled excessively by a dream, and when she is asleep her husband comes home again, and she sees him daily just as if he was alive, and so she at last wastes away, and says, "I am troubled by the father of So-and-so;[71] he does not leave me; it is as though he was not dead; at night I am always with him, and he vanishes when I awake. At length my bodily health is deranged; he speaks about his children, and his property, and about many little matters." Therefore at last they find a man who knows how to bar out that dream for her. He gives her medicine, and says, "There is medicine. When you dream of him and awake, chew it; do not waste the spittle which collects in your mouth whilst dreaming; do not spit it on the ground, but on this medicine, that we may be able to bar out the dream."

---

[71] The woman must respect *(hlonipa)* her husband's name; she does not call him by name, but as here, when addressing him or speaking of him, says, "Father of So-and-so," mentioning one of his children by name.

Nembala ke i fike inyanga, i buze uku m pupa; a vume. I buze ukuba "W enzile njengokutsho kwami?" a vume owesifazana. I buze ukuti, "Lowo 'muti e ngi ku nike wona, ukuze u d*h*lafune, u fele amate lawo e u pupe u se nawo emlonyeni, u wa fela kuwona na?" a vume. I ti, "Leti ke; hamba, si ye nawe lapa ngi ya 'ku m vimbela kona."

Lelo 'pupa i l' elape ngemiti e banga ubumnyama; i nga l' elapi ngemiti em*h*lope; i l' elape ngemiti emnyama; ngokuba pakati kwetu, tina 'bantu abamnyama, si ti, ku kona ubulawo obumnyama nobum*h*lope; ngaloko ke inyanga i m pe*h*lela obumnyama, ngokuba ipupa li ya m kataza.

I hambe naye ke ukuya 'ku m vimba endaweni etile; kumbo i mu vimbe esigak*q*eni senkomfe. Si boboswe ekcaleni, kw enziwe imbotshana, ku fakwe lowo 'muti o *h*langaniswe namate epupa, ku valwe ke ngesivimbo; ku mbiwe pansi, i buye i fakwe kwesinye isigodi, ku g*q*itshwe ukuze i mile.

A be se u y' esuka ke naye, a ti, "Bheka ke, u nga ze wa ba u sa bheka emuva; u se u bheko

Then the doctor comes and asks if she has dreamt of her husband; she says she has. He asks if she has done what he told her; the woman says she has. He asks whether she has spit on the medicine he gave her to chew, the spittle which collected in her mouth whilst dreaming; she says she has. He says, "Bring it to me then; and let us go together to the place where I will shut him in."

The doctor treats the dream with medicines which cause darkness; he does not treat it with white medicines; for among us black men we say there are black and white ubulawo; therefore the doctor churns for the woman black ubulawo, because the dream troubles her.

So he goes with her to a certain place, to lay the Itongo; perhaps he shuts it up in a bulb of inkomfe.[72] The bulb has a little hole made in its side, and the medicine mixed with the dream-spittle is placed in the hole, and it is closed with a stopper; the bulb is dug up, and placed in another hole, and the earth rammed down around it, that it may grow.

He then leaves the place with the woman, saying to her, "Take care that on no account you look back; but look before you con-

---

[72] *Inkomfe*, a bulbous plant, the leaves of which contain a strong fibre, and are used for weaving ropes.

318   DIVINERS.

pambili njalo, u z' u fike ekaya. Ngi ti a li sa yi 'kubuya nakanye, ukuz' u ngi dele ukuba ngi inyanya. U ya 'ku ngi dela nam*h*la uje. Uma li pinda, u ngi tshele masinyane."

Nembala ke lelo 'pupa, uma l' elatshwe inyanga ey azi ukuvimba, li pele. Ku ti noma e m pupa ku nga bi impikelelwana yamalanga; a m pupe ngam*h*la e pupako njalo, ku nga naki loko njengokuk*q*ala. Ku buzwe ke eduze nalawo 'masuku ukuti, "Se ku njani manje na?" A ti, "Ai ke. A ngi ka boni 'luto. Kumbe ku y' eza." Ba ti abantu, "U be ke 'enze isikati ini e nga fiki na?" A landule owesifazana, a ti, "Ku be ku ngu bi ko nasinye isikati. Ngi sa *h*lomela ukuba isiminya ini na."

A m a*hh*lule njalo ngalelo 'pupa; a ze a tsho owesifazana ukuti, "O! Ubani u inyanga. Naku manje mina a ngi sa m azi uyise kanobani. W' emuka njalo kumina."

Ku njalo ke ukuvinjwa kwamapupo.

stantly, till you get home. I say the dream will never return to you, that you may be satisfied that I am a doctor. You will be satisfied of that this day. If it returns, you may tell me at once."

And truly the dream, if treated by a doctor who knows how to bar the way against dreams, ceases. And even if the woman dreams of her husband, the dream does not come with daily importunity; she may dream of him occasionally only, but not constantly as at first. The people ask her for a few days after how she is. She replies, "No. I have seen nothing since. Perhaps it will come again." They say, "Formerly was there ever a time when he did not come?" The woman says, "There was not. There used not to be even one day when he did not come. I am still waiting to know whether he is really barred from returning."

The doctor prevails over the dead man as regards that dream; at length the woman says, "O! So-and-so is a doctor. See, now I no longer know any thing of So-and-so's father. He has departed from me for ever."

Such then is the mode in which dreams are stopped.[73]

---

[73] See p. 142, where it is stated that means are employed to cause dreams of the departed. This is called *ukubanga ipupo*, to cause a dream by medicines or medical charms. This system has many ramifications, and will be again alluded to at the end of the volume.

Umwahleni, the Diviner.

Kwa ku kona inyanga enkulu pakati kwetu e kwa tiwa Umwa-*h*leni. Ku be ku ti uma ku za umuntu ebusuku o takatayo, u ya 'kuvuka pakati kwobusuku, a m k*x*otshe lowo 'muntu; kumbe a m tetise e nga ka pumi end*h*lini, a ti, "Baui, buya, buyela emzini wako. Loko o kw enzayo ngi ya ku bona." A m k*x*otshe pakati kwobusuku. Ku be ku inyanga yakwiti edumileyo kakulu.

Ku be ku ti ngesinye 'isikati a pume lapa ku za 'kusa, a ye emfuleni, a fike a ngene esizibeni; u ya puma, u se puma, e zigcobe ngomdaka ebusweni; u y' eza ekaya, intamo yake i gcwele imamba e zwayo. A i bambe, a i tandele entanyeni, noma a y enze ikcele lake; u ya fika ekaya, u y' esabeka; a bute abantu bomuzi b' ezoku*h*labela amagam' ake.

Inyanga umuntu olula kakulu; u ze a k*q*ede ind*h*lu 'ek*q*a njalo njengenyoni, e suka e *h*lala. Kepa lawo 'magama amagama e ku tiwa u wa nikwa abapansi; amagama ake 'a*h*lukene namagama etu; a k*q*ambele abesifazana uku-

There was a great inyanga among our people, whose name was Umwathleni. If a sorcerer came by night, he would awake in the middle of the night and drive the man away; perhaps he would scold him before quitting the hut, saying, "So-and-so, go back to your own village. I see what you are doing." And he would drive him away in the middle of the night. He was a very celebrated inyanga of our people.

Sometimes he would go out when it was about to dawn, and proceed to the river, and go into a pool, and would come out having his face smeared with white earth, and go home having his neck entirely circled with a living imamba. He would catch it and twist it round his neck, or wear it as a fillet; when he reached home he was fearful to look at; and he would call the people of the village to come and sing the songs he had composed.

He was a very active doctor; he hopped about the whole house like a bird, starting from one place and pitching in another. And the songs were said to be songs which the Amatongo gave him; his songs were different from ours; he composed a first part for the

hlabelela; ngemva 'enze isivumo; abesifazana ba m tshayelé, a vume yedwa endhlini, 'enza imikuba eminingi.

Kepa lezi 'zinyanga zamanje ku tiwa a zi sa fani nezinyanga zesikati esidhlulileyo; ngokuba Umwahleni lowo, ukuze ku bonwe ukuti u inyanga, kwa ti ngamhla e ngenayo ebunyangeni wa fihlelwa izinto eziningi. Lezo 'zinto ezifihlwayo, noma ezinkulu, noma ezincinane, zi ya 'kukebisa inyanga. Umwahleni w' enziwa njalo ke, e lingwa ngobunyanga bake, ukuze kw aziwe ukuba u inyanga impela. Ekufikeni kwake wa fika e 'mikqambokqambo, ukuti ukuvunula na ngodaka olumhlope. Wa fika ekaya, loku abantu se be fihlile izinto zonke, ba zi fihle ezindaweni ezinqabileyo endhle na sekaya njalo, ukuze ke lezo 'zinto a zi kipe. O, wa fana nohlanya e ngena ekaya. Loku se ku miwe amakqongokqongo, ukuti izikxuku zabantu ab' eza 'kubona ummangaliso. Wa hamba ngejubane, e ya 'kukipa leyo 'nto efihlwayo, a i beke obala. A ngene na sendhlini, a i kipe. A tshone na

women; and then a second part; the women smote their hands and sang the first part for him, and he sang the response alone indoors, playing many pranks.

But the izinganga of the present time are said no longer to resemble those of former times; for this Umwathleni, in order that men might see that he was an inyanga, had many things concealed for him to find on the day he was formally declared to be an inyanga. All the things which are hidden, whether great or small, become the property of the inyanga. The people then acted thus with Umwathleni, and tested his skill as an inyanga, that it might be known that he was an inyanga indeed. When he came to find the things which were concealed, he had his body ornamented and daubed with white clay. When he reached his home, the people had already hidden all kinds of things in very obscure places, both out of doors and in the houses, for him to find. O, he resembled a mad man entering the house. Already many crowds of people were assembled, who had come to see the wonder. He went rapidly and took out of the place of concealment whatever was hidden, and placed it before the people. He entered the house, and took out whatever was hidden there. He went down to the

semfuleni, a i kipe. Lezo 'nto zonke kwa ba 'zake, ukuze a dume, ku tiwe, "Inyanga Umwa*h*leni." Ngokuba ku njalo pakati kwabantu abamnyama, inyanga i ya fi*h*lelwa, ukuze i bonwe. Umwa*h*leni lowo w' enziwa njalo. Kepa kwezamanje a ku sa bonakali uma izinyanga impela; se si ti, "A zi i d*h*langa impepo;" si zi biza ngokuti amabuda, ukuti, izinto ezi nga tsho 'luto.

Uma ku tiwa, "Inyanga a i d*h*langa impepo," ku kulunywa ngento e yona; i ukwazi impela. Uma umuntu wa d*h*la impepo e d*h*liwa izinyanga ezik*q*inisileyo, noma e ti wa d*h*la yona impela, ku tiwa, "K*q*a, a i si yo leyo 'mpepo e d*h*liwa izinyanga; wa d*h*la imbe." Kepa uma ku tshiwo njalo, ukuti, "Ka d*h*langa impepo," ku tshiwo ngokuba ukubula kwake ku nga fani nokubula kwenyanga impela. Impepo kakulu i loko 'kukcakcamba oku senyangeni; i ng' a*h*luleki; into en*q*abileyo i i bona masinyane. Si tsho ke ukuti, "Le

river, and took out whatever was hidden there. All these things became his, that he might be celebrated, and people say, "Umwathleni is a diviner." For it is the custom among black men to conceal things for a diviner to find, that he may be seen to be a diviner. So this was done for Umwathleni. But among diviners of the present time there is no longer any clear evidence that they are diviners; and we now say, they have not eaten impepo, and we call them amabuda, that is, things which do not speak the truth.

When we say, "A diviner has not eaten impepo," we speak of reality; impepo means true knowledge. If any one has eaten the impepo which is eaten by real diviners, or if he says he has really eaten it, we say, "No, it is not the impepo which diviners eat; he ate another kind." But when it is said he has not eaten impepo, we mean that his divination does not resemble the divination of real diviners. Impepo means especially that clearness of perception[74] which a diviner possesses; nothing is too hard for him; but he sees a difficult thing at once. So we say of such a diviner, "He has eaten impepo."

---

[74] *Kcakcambisa*, to make white; applied metaphorically, to whiten or make clear the perceptions. See note 5, p. 261.

'nyanga ya i d*h*la impepo." I leyo ke e tshiwoyo abantu benyanga.

I yona le 'mpepo e si i bonayo; kodwa leyo 'mpepo e si i tshoko, a si tsho ukuti umuntu a nga i d*h*la ngokuba ku tiwa i kcakcambisa izinyanga, naye a be se u ba inyanga. K*q*a; i nge m enze i yodwa ukuba inyanga, ku nge ko oku ngapakati oku nga *h*langana nempepo, ku m kcakcambise.

Impepo imbili. I yodwa impepo em*h*lope; kuleyo 'mpepo em*h*lope si ya kolwa kuyo kakulu; kepa impepo emnyama a si kolwa kuyo nakanye; indaba zayo ku tiwa zimnyama. Ngokuti ku ti noma umuntu e pupa umuntu a nga m tandi uku m bona njalonjalo, a d*h*le yona emnyama, a m k*æ*otshe ngayo, ukuze noma e fika, a nga m bonisisi, a nga m k*q*ondi. Noma ku *h*latshwe, a ku tatwa impepo emnyama, ku tatwa em*h*lope njalo. Ku ti kumadoda amakulu, noma kwabancinane, u nga i fumana njalo i kona emik*q*ulwini yamakcansi, ukuze a pupe ka*h*le.

It is this which the diviner's people say.

This is the impepo which we see; but as regards the impepo of which we are speaking, we do not say that a man may eat it because it is said to impart to diviners clear inner sight, and so become a diviner himself. No; it cannot make him a diviner by itself, if there is nothing within him which can unite with the impepo and make him clearsighted.

There are two kinds of impepo. White impepo has its own peculiarities; we believe especially in white impepo; but we do not believe at all in the black impepo;[75] that which arises after eating it is dark. For example, if a man dreams continually of a man he does not wish to see, he eats the black impepo, and drives him away by it, that should he come again he may not see him distinctly, nor understand who it is. Or when we sacrifice we do not take the black impepo, but always the white. And one always finds the white impepo in the folds of the sleeping mats of old and young, that they may have distinct dreams.

---

[75] That is, in its power to produce distinct or clear vision.

Divining with Sticks and Bones.

INDABA zenyanga zokubula, ukukqala kwazo ukungena endabeni yokubula. A kw aziwa 'muntu ukuba lo 'muntu u ya 'kubula. I kqala ngokuhlupeka ukugula; ku nge u za 'upila, kauti kqa. I lapo ke lapo si ti inyanga ukutasa kwazo kunye nokwenyanga yemilozi nokwenyanga yokubula; kw ahlukene ngemikuba, ngokuba inyanga yemilozi a i njengenyanga yokubula.

Inyanga yokubula yona, lapa i bulela abantu, nayo i beka kubantu ikqiniso e li zuzile ebantwini. Uma ngaloko 'kwenza kwenyanga si buta yonke indaba, si ya 'kuti, aba bulayo abantu; ngokuba inyanga a i kqali limbe izwi eli ng' aziwa ab' eza 'kubula.

Ku nga ku kona ubukqili obukulu enyangeni, ngokuba lapa i bulako i ti, "Tshaya ni, ngi zwe uma ni ze ngani." Ba tshaye abantu.

I ti, "Into inye e ni ze ngayo." Ba ti kqoto ukutshaya. I linge ukukqinisela kuloko e ku tshoyo, i ti, "Tshaya ni." Ba pinde ba kqotoze njengokukqala.

THE account of diviners when they begin to enter on divination. No one knows that a man will be a diviner. He begins by being affected with sickness; it appears about to cease, but it does not. It is in this respect at the commencement that diviners, and those that have familiar spirits, are alike; they differ in their mode of divination, for the diviner with familiar spirits does not resemble another diviner.

When a diviner divines for people, even he tells back to the people the truth which he first took from them. If as regards that which is done by the diviner we put all together, we shall say, it is the people who divine; for the diviner does not begin with any thing that he has not heard from the people who come to divine.

There appears to be great cunning in the diviner, for when he divines he says, "Smite the ground, that I may understand why you have come." The people strike the ground.

He says, "There is one thing only about which you have come." They strike gently. He tries to establish that which he says, and tells them to strike the ground. But they again strike gently as at

I pume kuloko e b' i ku tsho, i bone ukuti, "Kqa, ba ya pika; ngi y' eduka." I hambe se i hlanhlata i ze i fike lapo b' aziyo.

I ti i sa tsho nje, ukuti, "Loku ni ze ngokuti okutile nje, a ni tshayi ngani?" lapo ke ba tshaye ba i nike izibulo, ngokuti, "U b' u kona." Lapo ke i se i za 'uhamba ngokukqotomezela, i landa lowo 'mkondo wesiminya, i linge ukwenza umlunge wesiminya. Kokunye ba i vumele; kokunye ba i pikise ngokutshaya kancinane; ba zinge be i kalima ekudukeni kwayo ngokutshaya kancinane; i ze i bone ukuti, "Kqa; indaba le yaloku 'kufa i suka kuyo leyo 'ndawo e ngi ke nga i pata kukqala; i zinge i tatela emazwini akukqala a ba i vumela kahle, i zinge i hamba ngakuwo, i ze i fumane isiminya ngokubuza ngokuhlanhlata i ze i ngene endabeni i ti gudu.

Lapo ke i se i za 'kukqala ukutsho naba nga kw aziyo, ngokwazi ukuti, "Se be ya 'ukolwa, noma

first. And he leaves that which he was saying, and perceives that they do not assent, and that he is going astray. Then he goes on nibbling till he hits upon something they know.

When he says, "As you came on such an account and nothing else, why do you not strike the ground?" then they smite and freely use the divining sticks, saying thus to him, "You hit the mark there." Now then he will proceed carefully, following that footprint of truth, and trying to make it into a continuous track.[76] They assent to some things; to others they object by striking gently; they continually turn him back from his wandering by striking gently; at last he perceives that the real importance of the disease starts from that point which he just touched on at first; and he continually starts from the first words to which they gave their assent, and continually goes near them, till he finds out the truth by asking and nibbling until he is on the right track.

Having succeeded thus far, he now begins to speak also about things with which they are not acquainted, knowing that they will now believe in the things he

---

[76] Like a man who has lost his cattle, having found a footprint he will return again and again to it, till he succeeds in connecting it with others, and thus form a continuous track, which leads him to the lost property.

be nga kw azi loku e ngi ku tshoyo; kodwa ngamakqiniso akukqala a ba sa yi 'kulahla 'luto lwala 'mazwi, ngokuba ngi b' esutise kukqala; konke loku se be ya 'kuti isiminya." Ku njalo ke ukuhamba kwezinyanga zokubula.

Si ti i ya tshelwa, ngokuba i ya zibuza nayo ezindhlebeni zabantu ngoku i pikisa lapo i tsho kona; i ze i ti, " Ake ngi zwe uma loku 'kufa ukufa kuni," i pendupenduka i bheka ngalapa na ngalapa. Ku ya bonakala ukuba i ya funa, i lahlekelwe; kepa ukufumana kwayo, uma ku ng' aziwa ab' eza 'ubula, ku ya lahlwa. Si ti ngaloko nazo zi ya tshelwa. Ngokuba ba kona abantu aba ng' aziyo ukubula uma kw enziwa njani; ku ti ngokuvela kwokufa ku tunywe umuntu, kanti ka bonanga e ya 'kubula enyangeni; k' azi noma kw enziwa njani; ku ti noma 'azi a sole ngenhliziyo ngokuti, " O, uma ngi za 'ubula enyangeni ey aziyo, ngi fumane i njengami; i be i yona i funa ukuba ngi i tshele isiminya; a ku ko 'nyanga. Kanti inyanga ku fanele i kulume izindaba e ngi z' aziyo ne ngi nga z' aziyo; i yeke ukuhlanhlata nje njengomuntu o ng' aziyo."

says, though they are not acquainted with them; but because he has satisfied them by the truths he spoke at first, they will not despise any of his words; but every thing he says will be true in their eyes. Such is the method of diviners.

We say he is told, because he too asks of himself in the hearing of the people, denying the correctness of what he himself has said; and says, "Just let me see what the disease is," turning about continually and looking hither and thither. It is evident that he is seeking, and that the thing is lost to him; and as to his finding it, if those who come to enquire do not know, it is not found at all. Therefore we say the diviners too are told. For there are those who do not know how divination is managed; and when disease occurs one is sent who forsooth never went to enquire of a diviner before; and does not know how it is managed; and even if he does know he murmurs in his heart, saying, "O, when I go to a diviner who knows, I find him just like myself; and he too wants me to tell him the truth; there is no such thing as a diviner. A diviner, forsooth, ought to tell me things which I know and which I do not know; and not nibble at the affair like a man who knows nothing."

Ngaloko ke lowo 'muntu o hla-kanipile a ti enhliziyweni yake, "Kqa, ngi ya bona izinyanga lezi zi ya tshelwa. Ngokwazo a z' azi 'luto. Ku ngani ukuba zi hla-nhlate endaweni yokutsho isiminya na?"

Nembala ke lowo 'muntu ngam-hla e ya 'ubula, u ti, "Mina, ngi ya 'kuba umuntu o ng' azi 'luto. Nawe, bani, kuhle ukuba lap' i-nyanga i ti, 'Tshaya ni,' si tshaye kakulu kuko konke nasemangeni, si kqiuise. Si ya 'upikiswa i yona tina, si be tina si ti amakqiniso onke; lokupela tina a s' azi 'luto, si ze 'kubuza kowaziyo."

Nembala ke ku nga bi ko a ba ku pikayo. Ukutshaya kwabo ba buduzele kuko konke, i ze i dide-ke, i ze i buze ukuti, "Hau, ba-ngane bami, na ka na bula njena na?"

Ba ti, "O, kakulu, nkosi. Ku bula tina."

I buze i ti, "Kuzo zonke izi-nyanga n' enze njena?"

Ba ti, "Yebo, ngokuba pela tina namanga a si w' azi, namakqi-niso a si w' azi. Ku ya 'uketa inyanga kuko konke loko."

The wise man then says in his heart, "No, I see that these di-viners are told. By themselves they know nothing. Why do they nibble at the affair instead of tell-ing the truth at once?"

So then such a man when he goes to enquire says, "For my part I shall be a man who knows nothing. And you too, So-and-so, it is well when the diviner tells us to smite, for us to smite vehe-mently at every thing, even when he does not speak truly. We will be set right by him; we will say that every thing is true that the diviner says. For we do not know any thing; we are going to enquire of one who knows."

And so they dispute nothing the diviner says. They smite in assent to every thing, till the di-viner is confused, and at length asks them, saying, "O, my friends, did you ever smite in this manner when enquiring of a diviner be-fore?"

They say, "O, sir, again and again. We are they who enquire."

He asks, "Have you acted thus with all diviners?"

They say, "Yes, for as to us truly we neither know what is false nor what is true. The di-viner will distinguish in all such matters."

I hlale, i pumule, i beme, i nikine inhloko, i ti, "Kqa, bangane bami ; a ni buli kahle. Inyanga isitupa. Ini ukuba ngi tsho loko ni tshaye kakulu, ku nga bi ko e ni ku pikayo na ? "

Ba ti, " O, pela tina, nkosi, si be si ng' eza kuwe, uma ku kona e si kw aziyo. A si zi lapa kuwe nje, ukuze si zwe okonakona uma i ku pi na ? "
I ti, " Kqa. A n' azi nina. Tina 'zinyanga si ya tshelwa. Uma abantu be bulisa kwenu nje, a s' azi 'luto."

He remains silent, takes snuff, and shakes his head, and says, "No, my friends ; you do not smite properly. The diviner is the thumb.[77] Why do you smite the ground vehemently whatever I say, there being nothing which you dispute ? "

They reply, " O, truly, sir ; we should not have come to you if we had known any one thing. Have we not come to you to hear from you what is the very truth ? "
He says, " No. You do not understand. We diviners are told. If people smite as you smite, we know nothing."

---

[77] *A doctor of the thumb*, or *thumb-doctor*,—so called because he cannot proceed without the assistance of those who enquire, which they give either by silence or striking the ground gently with the *izibulo* or divining-rods, when he is not correct ; or by assenting by saying " Hear " or " True," and by striking the ground violently, and by *pointing to the diviner in a peculiar way with the thumb*, when he is correct.

The diviners are separated into four classes :—
1.—*Thumb-doctors*, in whom no great confidence is placed.
2.—Diviners who have eaten *impepo*, that is, who possess a real gift of divination, and who are able to divine without any help from the enquirers.
3.—Those who use *bones* or *sticks* in divination. The bones are called simply *amatambo*, and are obtained from various wild animals. The doctors who employ them are called *bone-diviners*. The sticks used are about a foot long, and are called *omabukula-izinti*, or in the singular, *umabukula-izinti*, which is a compound word : *ukuti bukula* is to lie down gently and comfortably,—*uma*, when ; " When the sticks lie down gently," that is, the diviner receives intimation by the mode in which the sticks act. Such a diviner is called a *stick-diviner*. The natives place much confidence in these doctors.
4.—Those who have *familiar spirits*. The people have much confidence also in these, especially because they are not able to comprehend the source of the voices which appear to come from invisible beings. It is supposed that this mode of divination is of modern origin.

Ku njalo ke ukuma kwezinyanga zokubula. Si nga ngabaza ngazo; a zi fani nemilozi; zona zi ya tshelwa, ngokuba zi tata amazwi kubantu.

Njengaloku Ujan wa ka wa ya 'ubula enyangeni, ku gula udade wabo. Wa bula ke, e funa ukwazi ukuba u guliswa ini na. Kepa ukutshaya kwake wa buduzela, ngokuti, "Mina a ng' azi 'luto. Inyanga e ya 'u ng' ahlukanisela oku i ko."

Inyanga ya m sola ngokuti, "Mngane wami, imbala wa ka wa bula nje na?"

Kepa wa vuma yena ngokuti, "O, u mina pela obulayo, ngokuba umuzi wakwiti u melwe u mina. A ku ko 'ndoda enye; kupela u mina nje."

Inyanga ya ti, "Ngi ya bona. A u kw azi ukubula." Ya za y' enza ikeebo kumuntu wayo, ya ti, "Lo 'muntu k' azi nakanye ukubula. Hamba, u ke u m buze,

Such is the position of diviners. We may entertain doubts about them; they are not like those who have familiar spirits; they are told, for they take the words from the people who come to enquire.

John, for example, went to enquire of a diviner when his sister was ill, wishing to know what was the cause of her illness. But when he smote the ground he smote mechanically, assenting to every thing the diviner said; for he said to himself, "For my part I know nothing. It is the diviner that shall point out to me the real facts of the case."

The diviner reproved him, saying, "Surely, my friend, did you ever enquire of a diviner in this way before?"

John replied in the affirmative, saying, "O, it is I indeed who enquire,[78] for I am now the responsible head of our village; there is no other man in it; there is no one but me."

The diviner said, "I see. You do not know how to enquire of a diviner." At length he devised a plan with one of his own people, saying, "This man has not the least notion of divination. Just go and ask him, that he may tell

---

[78] The head of the village alone enquires of the diviner, either in person or by his representatives. Great men send messengers to the diviner, and do not go in person.

a ku tshele into e yona 'eze ngayo, ukuze u ngi tshayele kahle wena."

Nembala ke lowo 'muntu wa ti kujan, "Inyanga i ti, a u kw azi ukubula. Tshela mina indaba o ze ngayo. U ya 'ubona ukuze si i tshayele kakulu lapa i tsho kona ; uma i nga tsho kona, si nga i tshayeli kakulu."

Ujan wa ti ukupendula kwake kulo 'muntu, " O, a ngi kw azi mina loko o ku tshoyo. Mina ngi ze enyangeni nje ukupela ukuza 'kuzwa ukufa. A ngi zile ukuba ngi buye ngi kulume ngokufa kuwe. Ngi za 'kuzwa enyangeni mina, uma ukufa kuni."

W' ala njalo ; wa buyela lo 'muntu kuyo ; ya ti inyanga, " Ka sondele ke, si zwe."

Nembala Ujan wa buya wa tshaya kakulu, wa i vumela kuko konke e ku tshoyo. Ya za ya penduka isiula, ya ti, " O, mngane wami, ngi ya bona impela ukuba a u kw azi ukubula."

I tsho ngokuba Ujan ku nge ko lapa e vuma kakulu, na lapa e vuma kancinane, i bone ukuti lapa

you why he has come, that you may smite the ground for me in a proper manner."

So indeed the man said to John, " The diviner says you do not know how to divine. Tell me the cause of your coming. You will see that we smite the ground for him vehemently when he speaks to the point ; and if he does not speak to the point, we do not smite much."

John said in answer, " For my part I do not understand what you say. I have merely come to the diviner for no other purpose than to hear of him the nature of a disease. I did not come to talk with you about it. For my part I shall hear from the diviner what the disease is."

So he refused to tell him ; and the man went back to the diviner ; he said, " Let him come to me again, that we may hear."

So John again smote the ground vehemently, and thus expressed his assent to every thing the diviner said. Until he became quite foolish, and said, " O, my friend, I see indeed that you do not know how to enquire of a diviner."

He said this because there was no point where John assented very much, nor where he assented slightly, that he might see by his

u vuma kancinane nje a ngi hlabile kona, lapa 'azi kona. Uma ngi hlaba lapa 'aziyo, u ya 'utshaya kakulu; kodwa uma ng' egeja, u ya 'utshaya kancinane. Ya yeka ukubula, ya ti, "Kqa, mngane wami, a ngi bonanga ngi m bona umuntu o bulisa kwako nje." Y' ahluleka.

Wa ti Ujan, "O, mngane ke, loku u nga ku boni ukufa, sa u leta uhlamvu lwami, ngi ziyele kwenye inyanga."

Nembala ke leyo 'nyanga ya m nika uhlamvu lolo. Igama layo Umngom'-u-ng'-umuntu.

W' emuka ke, wa ya kunomantshintshi, o bula ngezinti. Ku tiwa igama lazo Umabukula. Ukubula kwazo ku ya mangalisa.

Wa fika ke Ujan kuzo. Umninizo wa zi tata, wa zi beka pansi; wa dhlafuna umuti, wa zi lumula, ukuze zi mu tshele kahle indaba eyonayona. Ukubula kwazo a zi fani nenyanga yokubula. Ngokuba zona zi ya buzwa ngomlomo. Wa zi buza ke Unomantshintshi, wa ti, "Ngi tshele ni kambe uma loku 'kufa kukumuntu

assenting slightly that he had not hit the mark. He expected if he hit the mark John would smite the ground vehemently; but if he missed it he would strike gently. So he left off divining, and said, "No, my friend, I never met with a man who enquired like you." He could do nothing.

John said, "O then, my friend, as you do not see the nature of the disease, now give me back my shilling, that I may betake myself to another diviner."

So the diviner gave him back the shilling. His name was Umngom'-u-ng'-umuntu.[79]

John then went to Unomantshintshi, one who divined by means of pieces of stick. The name of these pieces of stick is Umabukula. The mode of divining by them is remarkable.

So John came to the sticks. Their owner took them and laid them on the ground; he chewed some medicine, and puffed it over them, that they might tell him truly the very facts of the case. Divination by these sticks does not resemble that by a diviner. For the owner of them enquires of them. Unomantshintshi asked them, saying, "Tell me, how old

---

[79] *Umngom'-u-ng'-umuntu*, a name apparently given because whilst professing to divine he manifested no skill in divination. It means, "The diviner who is a man," that is, a common man, without any special endowments.

o ngakanani na?" Za tsho ke. Ngokuba ukukuluma kwazo a zi namlomo; uma z' ala, ukukuluma zi wa masinyane; uma zi kuluma isiminya, zi y' esuka, zi kɀume kakulu, zi fike kulo 'muntu o ze 'kubula kuzo. Za m tshela ke Ujan ukufa kukadade wabo, za i landa iminonjana yonke ey' aziwayo Ujan. Wa vuma ke, wa lu shiya u*h*lamvu kuzo, wa ti, "Ngi funa loku ke, ukuba inyanga i ngi tshele e ngi kw aziyo, i nga buzanga 'luto kumina. Ngi ya kw azi ukuba i bulile ngoku ngi tshela imi*hl*on*h*lo yokufa e ngi kw aziyo."

Ukukuluma kwazo ukuba ku ti uma ku buzwa ukufa lapa ku bambe kona, zi kɀume masinyane, zi bambe indawo lapa ukufa ku m bambe kona. Uma ku m bambe esiswini, zi bambe isisu so ze 'kubula. Uma ku sekanda, zi kwele ekanda. Zi wa k*q*ede onke amalungu omzimba lapa ku bambe kona isifo. Noma ku buzwa inyanga e nga m sizako lo 'muntu uma i ngapi na, zi ti ukukɀuma kwazo zi lale ngalapa inyanga i ngakona. Umninizo uma nembala 'azi ukuba

is the person who is ill?" And they said. But as they have no mouth they speak thus:—If they say no, they fall suddenly; if they say yes, they arise and jump about very much, and leap on the person who has come to enquire. In this way they told John the character of his sister's illness, and traced out every little ramification of it which was known to John. So John assented, and left his shilling with the sticks, and said, "This is what I want, that the diviner should tell me things which I know without having asked me any question. I shall know that he has divined by his telling me the symptoms of the disease which are known to me."

Their mode of speaking is this: —If it is asked where the disease has seized the patient, the sticks jump up at once and fix themselves on the place where the sick man is affected. If it has affected the abdomen, they fix themselves on the abdomen of the man who has come to enquire. If the head, they leap upon his head. They go over every joint of the body that is affected by the disease. Or if they are asked where the doctor is who can cure the sick man, they leap up and lie down in the direction of the place where the doctor lives. If the owner of them knows for certain the name of a

ubani o inyanga ngakuleso 'sizwe, a i pate ngegama layo kuzo; uma ku i yona, zi vuke masinyane, zi kæukæume ngoku m bamba umninizo; 'azi ke ukuba zi ya vuma.

Abantu abaningi ba kolwa kumabukula kunenyanga yokubula. Kodwa a ku vamile ukuba ku be kona umabukula kubantu abaningi. E ngi m aziyo ukuba o naye u yena Unomantshintshi lowo, nokaukau. Nampo e ngi b' aziyo. Omunye Undangezi, indoda ebomvu yakwand/lovu, lapa kwa ku bula kona ubabekazi ngesikati ngi se umfana, a buye nendaba eziningi ezi tshiwo umabukula. Ujan owa ka wa bula kumabukula, wa i landa yonke indaba yokufa kukadade wabo. Nembala e tsho ukufa lapa kwa kqala kona, na lapa ba be hambe kona. Wa kolwa ka/le, wa goduka e delile.

I njalo ke indaba ngomabukula nendaba yenyanga yokubula. Z' a-/lukene; a zi /langani.

Ukubula kwamatambo, lawo 'matambo awezilo zonke; ku kona nelend/lovu, ku kona nelebubesi, izilo zonke ezinkulu ezidumileko.

doctor who lives among the tribe to which the sticks point, he mentions the name to them; if it is he they mean, they jump up and down and fix themselves on their owner; and he knows thereby that they assent.

Many believe in the Umabukula more than in the diviner. But there are not many who have the Umabukula. Those whom I know who have them are that same Unomantshintshi and Ukaukau. These I know. There is a third, Undangezi, a red man of the house of Undhlovu, of whom my uncle used to enquire when I was a lad, and came back with many things which the Umabukula had said. The Umabukula of which John enquired gave him an exact account of his sister's illness, saying truly where the disease began, and where they had gone to enquire as to its nature. He believed fully, and went home satisfied.

This, then, is the account of the Umabukula and of the diviner. They differ from each other; they are not the same.

As regards divination by bones, the bones of all kinds of wild beasts are used; there is that of the elephant, and that of the lion, and the bones of all great and well known wild beasts.

Inyanga yamatambo, uma ku fike umuntu 'eza 'kubula, umniniwo u y' esuka, a kumule isikwama lapa amatambo e *h*lala kona, a d*h*lafune umtshana, a wa lumule; a be se u ya wa tulula, a kete obani nobani, izilwane a za'obula ngazo; a lingane izand*h*la zozibili; a wa tate, a wa *h*langanise, a wa tele pansi; a we amatambo onke. Kepa indaba yawo a i bonakali e tshiwo amatambo kumuntu o ze 'kubula; uma e nga w' ejwayele ka boni 'luto, k' azi noma ini ke le na.

Umniniwo a wa *h*lele ka*h*le onke. Elinye eku wa ponseni kwake li kwele pezu kwelinye, a buze ukuti,—uma ku ind*h*lovu nempisi,—a ti, " Ind*h*lovu le i ti ni nempisi?" A m tshele ke ngemva, ngoku wa *h*lela kwake a ti, " Amatambo a tsho ukuti nokuti; amatambo ngi wa bona e tsho loko."

Lowo 'muntu a vume, a ti, " Yebo; amatambo a tsho into e ngi ze ngazo lapa."

Umniniwo ngemva kwaloko a tsho kulowo 'muntu, a ti, " Ake u wa tate wena ngokwako, u buze kuwo uma leyo 'ndaba i njalo nje ngani na."

A wa ponse pansi umniniwo, a wa *h*lele ka*h*le ngemva kwaloko, a

The diviner by bones, when any one comes to him to enquire, unfastens the bag in which the bones are kept, chews some little medicine, and puffs on them; he then pours them out, and picks out the bones of certain animals with which he is about to divine; they fill both his hands; he brings them all together and throws them on the ground; all the bones fall. But what the bones say is not clear to the man who comes to enquire; if he is not accustomed to them he sees nothing, and does not know what it means.

The owner of the bones manages them all properly. When one in falling rests an another—if for instance it is the bone of an elephant and of the hyena—he says, " What does the elephant and hyena say?" And afterwards by his management of the bones, he tells the enquirer that the bones say so and so; that he sees that the bones say this and that.

And the man replies, " Yes; the bones mention that for which I came here."

Then the owner of the bones says to the man, " Just take them yourself, and ask them why it is so."

He throws them down, and the owner then manages them pro-

m tshele indaba e tshiwo amatambo, a ti, "U bona leli 'tambo li mi ngaloku nje; li tsho indaba etile emzini wako. Leli li tsho ukuti ukuba u fanele w enze ukuti." Li tsho konke loku lowo 'muntu a kw aziyo.

Ku ti ngokwejwayela kwomuntu ukubula kuwo amatambo, naye a wa *h*lele ka*h*le; ngoku wa *h*lela loko ku vela indaba, naye a zibonele. I ya m tshela nje inyanga, i se i landela yena, u se bonile ngokwake loko oku tshiwo amatambo. Ku njalo ke ukubula kwamatambo.

Nami nga ka nga ya ematanjeni. Kwa ku kona imbuzi kamjijane, umfo wetu omunye, i se i namasukwana i zuza, kepa sa mangala ukuba i nga zali. Sa hamba naye ukuya enyangeni, umfo kamatula, o bula ngamatambo. Sa fika, sa kuleka ngokuti, "E, mngane, indaba zako!" Sa goduka ke, si ya ekaya emzini wake. Wa tata umtshana, wa u d*h*lafuna, wa lumula isikwama lapa ku *h*lala amatambo; wa wa *h*liki*h*la, wa wa

perly, and tells him what the bones say; he says, "You see this bone standing in this manner; it speaks of a certain matter in your village. This says you must do so-and-so." They say every thing the man knows.

And a person by accustoming himself to divine with bones, himself manages them properly; from that proper management the matter is made evident, and he sees for himself. The diviner just points it out to him, and then follows him, when he has already seen by himself what the bones say. Such then is the mode of divining by bones.

I myself once went to enquire of the bones. There was a goat of Umjijane, one of my brothers, which had been yeaning for some days, and we wondered why it did not give birth to its young. We went to a diviner, the brother of Umatula, who divined with bones. On coming to him we made obeisance, saying, "Eh, friend, your affairs!"[80] We went home with him to his village. He took a little medicine and chewed it, and puffed on his bag in which the bones were kept; he rubbed them,

---

[80] A mode of informing the diviner that they come to divine; and expressing a wish that he will divine for them favourably. Chiefs are sometimes addressed in this way when a man is about to ask a favour.

tela pansi; wa wa hlela, wa ti, "O, imbuzi le i ti ni? Nauka amazinyane amabili—elinye limhlope, elinye, nanti, limpunga. A ti ni?"

Sa ti tina, "A s' azi, mngane. Ku ya 'kuzwa amatambo."

Wa ti, "Le imbuzi, egambukazi, i ya zala. Kepa ku nga ti a i zele. Kepa ni ti ni? Ni ti, imbuzi i ya hlupeka. O, ngi ti mina, uma ngi bona amatambo e kuluma nje, ngi bona ukuba amazinyane lawa a se ngapandhle. Amatambo a ti, 'Itongo lakwini, mjijane, li ti, ku ze u nga li pata. A ku ko 'keala. Li ti li ku sizile kakulu. Kukulu ukufa oku telwa abatakati kulowo 'muzi wakini. Nga se ku milile; kw' ala amatongo akwini. Imbuzi leyo i banjwe ngamabomu.' Amatambo a ti, 'Ni ya 'ufika i zele amazinyane amabili. U ze u fike, u bonge ekaya.' Amatambo a tsho njalo."

Sa m nika imali, sa goduka, ngi nga kolwa ukuba ku indaba loko, ngokuba amatambo a wa kulumanga. Kepa ngi zwe umu-

and poured them out on the ground; he managed them, and said, "O, what does the goat mean? There are two kids—one white, and the other, there it is, it is grey. What do they mean?" We replied, "We do not know, friend. We will be told by the bones."

He said, "This goat, which is a female black goat, is yeaning. But it is as though she had not yet yeaned. But what do you say? You say, the goat is in trouble. O, I say for my part when I see the bones speaking thus, I see that the young ones are now born. The bones say, 'The Itongo of your house, Umjijane, says, you never worship it. There is nothing the matter. It says it has helped you very much. The disease which sorcerers have poured upon your village is great. It would have taken effect, but the Amatongo of your house would not allow it. The goat has been made ill wilfully by sorcerers.' The bones say, 'When you reach home the goat will have given birth to two kids. When you reach home, return thanks to the Amatongo.' This is what the bones say."

We gave him money and went home, I not believing that there was any truth in it, for the bones did not speak. But I had heard

ntu e wa kulumela. Sa fika eka-ya, sa fumana imbuzi leyo se i mi emnyango namazinyane amabili—eliuye lim*h*lope, eliuye limpunga. Nga dela masinyane. Kwa *h*latshwa, kwa bongwa.

a man speaking for them. When we reached home we found the goat now standing at the doorway with two kids—one white and the other grey. I was at once satisfied. We sacrificed and returned thanks to the Amatongo.

Magical Practices.[81]

UMLINGO ku tiwa u vela ezinyangeni. Uma inyanga i tate imbiza, i tele amanzi pakati kwayo; se i k*q*ale ngokwelapa kuk*q*ala. Kodwa loko 'kwelapa a ngi kw azi ukuba kw enziwa njani na. I be se i basela imbiza, i nga ze ya bila. I base umlilo kakulu.

Futi i tate umkonto noma usu-

It is said that doctors are the authors of magical practices. As when a doctor takes a pot and pours water into it; and then begins to medicate it. But I do not understand the medication, how it is done. He then kindles a fire under the pot, but it does not boil.[82] He kindles a very great fire.

Or he may take an assagai or a

---

[81] Some of the following examples appear to be instances of legerdemain,—mere tricks.

[82] "The heroes of the Finne," in one of their wanderings, fell in with " a great wild savage of a giant," who, after enquiring the news, arose, and " put a cauldron on the fire, and a stag of a deer in it.

" ' Sit,' said he, ' and burn (fuel) beneath that cauldron, but unless the deer be cooked when I awake, you shall have but what you can take off his head, and by all you have ever seen do not take out the head.'

"They were tormented by hunger, and they did not know what they should do. They saw a little shaggy man coming down from the mountain. ' Ye are in extremity,' said he, himself; ' why are ye not tasting what is in the cauldron ? '

"'We are not,' said they ; 'fear will not let us.'

"They took the lid out of the end of the cauldron, when they thought it was boiled, and so it was that there was frozen ice came upon it." *(Popular Tales of the West Highlands. J. F. Campbell. Vol. III., p. 299.)*—See also below the charge brought against Udumisa for preventing the pot boiling.

ngulo, i beke noma ukamba pezu kwosungulo, lu nga za lwa wa. Ku tiwa umlingo lowo.

Nga ka nga bona nami. Ku fakwe amatambo entanjeni. Ku tiwa umabukula loko. Nga bona inyanga i w' enze njalo ke amatambo: i wa fake entanjeni, y eza kwiti, i zokubulela ubaba. Ya k*q*ala, ya tshanela pansi, ya lungisa ibala elibanzi; ya wa pata ezand*h*loni, ya wa k*x*ukuza, i wa bonga ngamagama, ya ti, "Ngi za ke ngi zwe ke, bu*h*luza-bonungu! mabala-maji!" Ya wa falaga*h*la pansi, a bekelela udwendwe, 'emi em*h*labeni, a komba kuyo esinyeni. Ya se i wa *h*lazulela ukuti, "Amatambo a ti, isifo si sesinyeni." Ba se b' azi ngaloku ukuti umsizi, isifo esi *h*lala esinyeni.

Ku tiwa futi umlingo ukuba inkosi uma i ya 'kulwa nenye,

needle, and place even a large pot on it, and it does not fall. That is called an umlingo, or magical practice.

I myself once saw this. A doctor had a lot of bones hung on a string. They are called Umabukula. I saw the doctor act thus with the bones: he had hung them on a string, and came to our village to divine for my father. He first swept the ground, and prepared a broad space; he then took the bones in his hands, shook them violently, and praised them by name, saying, "I come that I may hear, Buthluza-bonungu! Mabala-maji!"[83] He then scattered them on the ground; they formed a line, standing up on the ground, and pointing to his bladder. He then interpreted for them, saying, "The bones say the disease is in the bladder." They knew by that that the disease was umsizi, a disease which is seated in the bladder.

It is called also an umlingo if, when a chief is about to fight

---

[83] *Buhluza-bonungu! mabala-maji!*—These words are *izibongo* or praise-giving names, by which the doctor addresses the bone which is taken from the porcupine. Each bone has its *isibongo*, one or more. *Ukubuhluza*, to stab into the abdomen. *Bonungu* is from *Inungu*, a porcupine, and is equivalent to Porcupine-men. These bones are derived from the Abasutu. *Maji* is a Sutu word, meaning apparently many. *Mabala-maji*, many colours, referring to the various colours of the quills.

izinyanga zayo z' enze izita kuyo ukuba zi nga bonisisi ngokwenza umnyama pakati kwazo.

with another chief, his doctors cause a darkness to spread among his enemies, so that they are unable to see clearly.[84]

Other modes of divining.

Ku kona kubantu abamnyama into e ukubula ngapakati kwomuntu. Ku ti uma ku la*h*leke into e igugu, i funwe masinyane ukuze i tolwe; ku ti ngokwepuza uku i tola, ku be i lo'wo a k*q*ale ukubula ngapakati, e se funa ukuba 'ezwe le 'nto lapa i kona; loku ngamo*h*lo e s' a*h*lulekile, 'ezwe ngapakati kwake ukukomba kokuti, "Le 'nto uma u tshona endaweni etile, i kona, u za 'u i fumana;" ku ze ku pele ukuti, "U za 'u i fumana." A ze'a i bone, e se sondele kuyo; e nga ka k*q*ali ukusuka, a i bonisise impela, ku pele ukungabaza. Ngaloku 'kubona, ku nga ti ka sa i boni ngokwongapakati, u se i bona isidumbu sayo, nendawo lapa i kona; 'esuke ngokutshetsha e se ya kona; uma indawo i sitile, a hambe ngokuziponsa, ku nga ti ku kona oku m k*q*uba, ukuba a hambise kwomoya ngokutshetsha. Nembala leyo 'nto a i fumane, uma ku ng' enze ngokuk*q*andela kwekanda nje. Uma kw enze

There is among black men a something which is divination within them. When any thing valuable is lost, they look for it at once; when they cannot find it, each one begins to practise this inner divination, trying to feel where the thing is; for not being able to see it, he feels internally a pointing, which tells him if he will go down to such a place, it is there, and he will find it; at length it says he will find it; at length he sees it, and himself approaching it; before he begins to move from where he is, he sees it very clearly indeed, and there is an end of doubt. That sight is so clear that it is as though it was not an inner sight, but as if he saw the very thing itself and the place where it is; so he quickly arises and goes to the place; if it is a hidden place, he throws himself into it, as though there was something that impelled him to go as swiftly as the wind. And in fact he finds the thing, if he has not acted by mere headguessing. If it has been done by

---

[84] Compare 2 Kings vi. 17—20.

ngokubula okonakona, a i bone
impela. Kepa uma kw enze ngokuk*q*andela ngekanda nje nokwazi
ngokuti, "Loku endaweni etile
netile ngi nga yanga, se ngi fune
zonke indawo, k*q*a, ngi ya i bona
i sekutini," loko ku vama ukwe-
geja, a ku zinge ku tshaya kona.

real inner divination, he really
sees it. But if it is done by mere
head-guessing, and knowledge that
he has not gone to such a place
and such a place, and that therefore it must be in such another
place, he generally misses the
mark.

UMA izinkomo zi la*hl*ekile, ku
ng' aziwa lapa zi kona, ku tolwa
isilwanyazane, igama laso isipungumangati, si buze kuso ngokuti,
"Sipungumangati, inkomo zi pi
na?" Si petwe ngesand*hl*a, si
miswe in*hl*oko e geijile i bheke
pezulu; uma si komba kwenye
'ndawo si kombe ngen*hl*oko, ku
bonakale lapa si komba kona, si
ya 'kuyeka ukukombakomba okuningi kwaso, si bhekisise lapa si
k*q*inisa ukukomba ngakona; kumbe si zi tole; kumbe si nga zi
toli.

WHEN cattle are lost, and it is not
known where they are, a little
animal whose name is Isipungumangati[85] is found, and we ask it,
saying, "Mantis, where are the
cattle?" We hold it in our hand,
and place it with its pointed head
looking upwards; if it points in
another direction with its head,
and it is clear in what direction it
points, we shall pay no attention
to the various directions in which
it points, but look earnestly to the
place where it points its head steadily; and perhaps we find them
there; and perhaps we do not.

---

[85] The Mantis, or Hottentot God. There is also a bird called
Isipungumangati, which boys use for the same purpose. If the cattle
are lost, and they see this bird sitting on a tree, they ask it where the
cattle are; and go in the direction in which it points with its head.
It is about the size of a crow, and has a crest.

Chiefs divine.

Ukuhamba kwenkosi yo*h*langa kubantu abamnyama, i *h*langanisela kuyo izinyanga ezinkulu zoku i misa, ukuze i be inkosi impela; i nga bi inkosi ngokuzalwa kodwa nje, i be inkosi ngokwengezezela ubukosi ngokubiza izinyanga ezi nemiti emikulu nemilingo emikulu; zi i mise izinyanga lezo.

Ku fike leyo, y enze, y enze, i tsho amag*q*ino ayo. Nenye y enze njalo; y enze, i ti, "Mina, ukuze u ng' azi ukuba ngi inyanga, ku*h*le ukuba u kipe impi, ngi sa ku pete nje, ukuze u ngi k*q*onde. Nampu ubulawo. Ubani, uma u bu pe*h*la esitundwini sako, u m bize, u bone

As to the custom of a chief of a primitive stock of kings among black men, he calls to him celebrated diviners to place him in the chieftainship, that he may be really a chief; and not be one by descent merely, but by adding a chieftainly character by calling doctors who possess medicines and charms; and these doctors place him in the chieftainship.[86]

One comes and performs many ceremonies, telling the chief the power of his medicines. Another does the same; he performs ceremonies, and says, "For my part, in order that you may know that I am a doctor, it would be well for you to levy an army to attack another chief, whilst I am treating you with my medicines, that you may understand me. There is ubulawo. If you churn it in your vessel,[87] and call So-and-so, you

---

[86] Here the *izinyanga* stand out very clearly as a priesthood, whose duty it was to "consecrate" the chiefs. They, however, did it with charms and sorcery. When a chief has obtained from the diviners all their medicines and information as to the mode of using the *isitundu*, it is said that he often orders them to be killed, lest they should use their sorcery against himself.

[87] The *isitundu* is a narrow-mouthed vessel, made of a grass called *umsingizane* or of *izingqondo-zelala*, the fibres of the vegetable ivory; the grass or fibres are twisted into a small cord, which is sewn together into the proper form by the fibres of the *ilala*. It is sufficiently compact to hold water.

ke ukuba ku yi 'ku m nquma nge-sikatshana esi nge ngakanani na. Ku*h*le u linge ngalolu 'suku, ugi se kona nje."

Nembala ke leso 'situndu senkosi si k*q*alwe i zo inyanga. Uku si pe*h*la i pe*h*le, i m bize lowo o inkosi, o pambene nenkosi leyo, i bonga namakosi amadala a nga se ko. Bu ti uma bu suke bu pupume, loku inyanga le i m biza ngamand*h*la, i tsho ukuti, "Bheka ke, wena kabani, u ze u ngi buze. Ngi ti, ngaleli 'langa eli sen*h*loko se u mu n*q*umile. Uma ku kona umkonto, ngi be ngi za 'ku ku tshela." Leyo 'nyanga e k*q*ondisa inkosi leyo ukupatwa kwesitundu, nokubhekisisa ukwenza kwobulawo obu pe*h*lwayo ukwenza kwabo, ukuze indaba i i bone kona ngokubheka.

Nembala ke i k*q*ede loko, inyanga i ti, " U ze u ngi buze. Uma ku nga se njengokutsho kwami, ngi ya 'ku i la*h*la yonke imiti, ngi nga bi 'nyanga."

I i kupe ke inyanga impi, ukuze i hambe nayo; i i zungeze, i tshise may see whether you will not cut him off in a very little time. It is well for you to begin this very day, whilst I am here."

Truly then the vessel of the chief is first used by the doctors. When he churns[88] it, he calls the chief who is the enemy of his chief; and lauds ancient chiefs who are now dead. If the ubulawo froths up, the doctor shouts his name aloud, and says to his chief, "Behold, thou son of So-and-so, hereafter thou mayst take me to task. I say, on the very day when you go out against him you will destroy him. If there were any danger I would tell you." And the doctor tells the chief how to use the vessel, and to consider thoroughly the action of the ubulawo which is churned, that he may see what will happen by looking into the vessel.[89]

When he has finished his instruction the doctor says, "You can take me to task. If it does not turn out in accordance with what I say, I will cast away my medicines, and be no longer a doctor."

So the doctor leads out an army that he may go with it; he goes round about it and burns his

---

[88] Churns it, that is, twists round and round by means of a stick the contents of the vessel, consisting of sundry plants steeped in water.

[89] This appears to be similar to the divination by looking into a cup or vessel or crystal, still practised in North Africa and other places. Compare what is said of Joseph's cup, Gen. xliv. 5.

umuti wayo, i tsho ukuti, "Nemikonto yabo i ya 'uvama ukudhlula uje kinina." I i pelezele ke, i ye, i buye entabeni, i goduke, i ze enkosini.

Ku ti uma leyo 'nkosi e hlaselwako ku kona kwayo o se ku tutiwe, ngesikati sokupuma kwempi inkosi i hlale pezu kwenkata, ku fakwe kuyo, i nga zamazami. Loko 'kwenza njalo i ti, "Ngi ya m toma; se ngi m nyatele; u se ngapansi kwami. Ngo ka ngi zwe uma u ya 'usinda ngendawo enjani na."

Si njalo ke isitundu senkosi; isitundu inyanga yokubula kwenkosi. Ngokuba inkosi uma ku kona lapa i tukutelele ngakona, i ya kuso, i zinge i pehla; futi i keinsa yena lowo e m zondayo; i keinse li nga ka pumi ilanga ngokwenza njalo, i toma lowo e m zondayo.

Y enze njalo inkosi ngesitundu sayo; indaba e za 'kwenza i vama uku i tsho, ku nga k' enzeki, i ti, "Ku ya 'kuba ukuti nokuti; ni ze ni ti ni ti." Ku njalo ke ku ti uma impi i puma, abantu ba bheke izwi eli za 'uvela enkosini loku ba tembisa, ukuze b' ezwe noma ba

medicines, and says, "Even their assagais shall constantly miss you." He goes a little way with it, and returns from the top of the hill, and then returns to the chief.

And if they already have any thing belonging to the chief that is attacked, when the army is led forth, the chief sits without moving on a circlet made of medicines within which that which belongs to the other is placed. Whilst he does this he says, "I am overcoming him; I am now treading him down; he is now under me. I do not know by what way he will escape."[90]

Such then is the vessel of the chief; his vessel is a diviner to him. For if there is any place about which the chief is angry, he goes to his vessel, and churns it continually; and spits in the direction of the person he hates; he spits before sunrise at the time of churning his vessel; and subdues the man he hates.

A chief does thus with his vessel; and he generally mentions what he is about to do before it is done, saying, "Such and such will happen; and you will do so and so." And so it is when an army is led out, the men look for a word to come from the chief to give them courage, that they may know what kind of people it is to whom

---

[90] Lit., I shall just hear by what kind of a way he will escape.

ya kubantu abanjani na. Loko ku nga ku y' aziwa ngapambili.

Kepa ku njalo, ngokuba futifuti inkosi i zinge i tsho ukuti, "Impi a ni yi 'kufumana. Ngi ti, Ubani se ngi m bulele. Se ngi m bona lapa futifuti. Ni ya 'utata izinkomo nje. A ku ko 'luto, abafazi nje."

Lelo 'zwi lenkosi li ya tembisa empini yayo; i y' azi ukuba, "Si hamba nje; inkosi se i ku bone konke oku ya 'kwenzeka, loko e ku bona esitundwini sayo." A njalo amakosi; a pata isitundu, a bula ngaso.

Njengaloku isoka eli nobulawo obubukali, ku ti lapa li bu pe*h*la, li bize intombi kabani, li bu pe*h*la; ubulawo bu lukuzele, l' azi ukuba "Se ngi i n*q*obile." Li tate izinto zayo, li zi fake okambeni, li i pe*h*le, ukuze in*h*liziyo yayo i li bheke. Ku njalo ke ukupe*h*la umuntu, e pe*h*lwa inkosi.

Ku ti njengamaduna amakulu; ku ti uma li mukile enkosini yalo, inkosi i tsho ukuti, "Ubani, noma e mukile, u za 'kubuya, 'eze lapa. Se ngi *h*lezi pezu kwake. A ng' azi ukuba u ya 'u ngi shiya ngen-

they are going. And it is as though they knew this beforehand.

But it is so, because again and again the chief is accustomed to say, "You will not see any army. I say, I have already killed So-and-so. I have seen him here again and again. You will only take the cattle. There are no men, but mere women."

The word of the chief gives confidence to his troops; they say, "We are going only; the chief has already seen all that will happen, in his vessel." Such then are chiefs; they use a vessel for divination.

In like manner also a young man that has powerful ubulawo, when he churns it, calls on the name of the daughter of such an one, churning it at the same time; if the ubulawo froths up, he knows that he has prevailed over her. He takes some things belonging to her and places them in a pot, and thus churns her, that her heart may regard him. It is the same as the churning of a man who is churned by a chief.

It is the same as regards petty chiefs; if one has gone away from his chief, the chief says, "Although So-and-so has departed, he will come back again. I am now sitting upon him. I do not know by what way he will go away from

dawo enjani na." Ku njalo ke ukuhamba kwamakosi ngesitundu.

Inkosi i ya *h*lupeka, i be nevuso, i zakee, uma i pe*h*la isitundu, si nga ze sa vuma ukuhamba ka*h*le. I ya *h*lupeka kakulu ; ku nge se i za 'kufa, i za 'kubulawa enye inkosi ; a i k*q*ini uma isitundu si nga i tembisi. Ku njalo ke inkosi itemba layo, li sesitundwini sayo.

Isitundu lesi, ku fakwa imiti e ubulawo, i kandiwe, ku telwe amanzi, ku zinge ku pe*h*lwa inkosi. I leso ke isitundu. A si so isitundu uma ku nge ko loko oku fakwa kuso. Uma leso 'situndu sa la*h*leka, indaba enkulu enkosini. Ku ya 'kuba uku*h*lupeka, nabantu ba fe abaningi ngemva kwaleso 'situndu ; uma si nga bonakali, izinyanga zi nuke abantu abaningi, ku fe abaningi. Ku kandane izinyanga zokumisa inkosi isibindi ngoku y elapa, na ngamazwi oku i k*q*inisa, ku ze ku pele ukwesaba, uma i bona nembala i sa pila.

me." Such then is the conduct of a chief with a vessel.

A chief is troubled, and is afraid, and gets thin, if, when he churns his vessel, it no longer gives propitious indications. He is greatly troubled ; it is as though he was about to die, or about to be killed by another chief; he has no strength if his vessel does not give him confidence. Such then is the confidence of a chief with which he trusts in his vessel.

Various kinds of ubulawo having been bruised, they are placed in the vessel, and water is poured on them, and the chief churns them continually. And this is what we mean by a chief's vessel. It is not a divining vessel if nothing is placed in it. If such a vessel is lost, it is a great matter with the chief. There will be much trouble, and many men die after the loss of the vessel ; if it is not found, the diviners point out many men, and many are killed. The doctors crowd together to produce courage in the chief by their medicines and by words of encouragement, until his fear ceases when he sees that he continues to live.

The Chief's Vessel.

Kwazulu inkosi yakona i ya lumba enye inkosi, be nga ka lwi nayo. Ku tatwa izinto zakona zi ze kuleyo 'nkosi, i geze ngezintelezi, ukuze i nqobe leyo 'nkosi lapa be kqala ukulwa. Kanti kade y' ahlulwa ngokutatelwa izinto.

Futi uma izinkomo zi baleka, zi balekela impi, ku tatwe ubulongwe nomkondo wazo, ku yiswe enkosini, ukuze i zi pehle, i hlale pezu kwazo. Ku tiwa, "Inkosi se i hlezi pezu kwazo; se i zi dhlile; si ya 'ku zi fumana." Lapa be zi fumanako, ba tsho ukuti, "Inyanga yenkosi inyanga impela."

Ubulongwe nomkondo ku fakwe esitundwini; kw enziwe inkata, zi

A chief among the Amazulu practises magic[91] on another chief before fighting with him. Something belonging to that chief is taken, and the other washes himself with intelezi,[92] in order that he may overcome the other when they begin to fight. And forsooth the one was conquered long ago by having his things taken and practised upon by magic.

And if the cattle fly from an enemy, their dung, and the earth which retains the marks of their footprints, are taken to the chief, that he may churn them and sit upon them. And the men say, "The chief is now sitting upon them; he has already eaten them up; we shall find them." And when they have found them they say, "The doctor of the chief is a doctor indeed."

The dung and earth which retains the mark of the footprints are placed in the chief's vessel; a circlet is made with medicines,[93]

---

[91] *Ukulumba* and *ukuhlunga* are to practise a peculiar kind of sorcery by means of medicines. See below, at the end of the volume.

[92] *Intelezi*, various kinds of plants, &c., used as charms, and believed to possess magical powers.

[93] The plants used to make a circlet of this kind are *umabope, usangume, umatshwilitshwili, omfingo*, &c.; they are supposed to have some especial power—to restrain a man from running away, to force him to come back, to take away his courage or his strength, his judgment, &c.

songwe; isitundu si bekwe pezu kwayo, ku hlalwe. Loko ke 'kwenza okunjalo, inkosi i ya tsho ukuti, "Se ngi ba ngobile. Lezo 'nkomo se zi lapa; se ngi hlezi pezu kwazo. A ng' azi ke uma zi za 'usinda ngendawo enjani na."

Isitundu imbonge e tungiwe kahle ngelala; i be 'nkulu, umlomo wayo u be umcinane. Ku tiwa isitundu ngokuba umlomo u lingan' isandhla. Leyo 'nto i hlala imisebenzi yokwazi kwenkosi. Ku ti uma i tanda ukubulala Ubani o inkosi, i tate izinto zake, i zi fake kona, i m hlunge, ukuze i m bulale e nga se namandhla.

Ku ti lapa inkosi se i tatela enye, i i pehle esitundwini sayo; i i biza masinyane; lapa i i biza, i bheke kakulu ukwenza kobulawo, i tsho ukuti, "Kodwa ngi ti mina noma ubani ngi ya m nquma ikanda; kepa ngi ti umkonto ni ya 'ku u fumana. Ngi ya bona ukuba u mi ngobudoda. Ngi bona

in which portions of them are wrapped up; the chief's vessel is placed on the circlet, and they then wait. When he has done this, the chief says, "I have now conquered them. Those cattle are now here; I am now sitting upon them. I do not know in what way they will escape."

The isitundu is a vessel which is well sewn with palmetto fibres; it is large, but its mouth is small. It is said to be an isitundu because its mouth is just large enough to admit the hand. All the knowledge of the chief is in this vessel.[94] If he wishes to kill another chief, he takes something belonging to that chief, and puts it in the vessel, and practises magic on it, that he may kill him when he has no power left.

When a chief has taken another chief,[95] he churns him in his vessel; and at once calls him; when he calls him he inspects carefully the mode in which the ubulawo acts, and says, "But I say that although I am cutting off the head of So-and-so; yet I say you will meet with an army. I see that he stands firm by his manliness.

---

[94] This is a free, but really literal rendering, as in the following sentence:—*Ilau lomfundisi li hlala izincwadi zake zonke*, The private room of the missionary contains all his books; or, All the missionary's books are in his private room.

[95] That is, something belonging to the chief; by taking and churning that, he says he takes and churns the chief.

DIVINERS. 347

esitundwini sami lapa ngi m pe-
hlako; ngi ya bona ukuba ubulawo bulukuni lapa ngi m bizako.
Kodwa ngi ti ngi ya 'ku m nquma
ikanda. Kepa a no ba kqinisa;
ba ya tshisa, ba umlilo."

I tsho noma be ya 'ku zi dhla
be ng' ezwanga ubuhlungu, i ti,
"Ngi ti, ni ya 'u zi dhla li puma
ilanga; li ya 'kuti li ti patsha, ni
be se ni m ahlulile. Kade ngi m
nqobile. Ngi ya bona esitundwini
sami. Ngi ti, ngomso kusasa inkomo zi ya 'kufika lapa, ezi za
'ubika."

Ngaloko ke impi i hambe i nesibindi sokuti, "A ku ko impi.
Inkosi Ubani se i m bopile. Si
ya 'ugwaza amabekce nje a nge
namkuba."

I see this in my vessel when I am
churning him; I see that the ubulawo is hard[96] when I call him.
But I say I shall cut off his head.
But do you fight with determina-
tion; they burn; they are a fire."[97]

He also tells them if they will
eat the cattle without any loss to
themselves, saying, "I say, you
will eat up the cattle when the
sun rises; whilst it is still rising
you will already have overcome
him. I have already overcome
him. I see it in my vessel. I
say the cattle will come here to-
morrow morning, to report that
you have conquered."

Therefore the army goes out
courageously, saying, "There is
no enemy with which we shall
have to fight. Our chief has already bound So-and-so. We shall
stab mere water-melons,[98] which
are unable to resist."

---

[96] The ubulawo is hard, that is, does not give out readily the signs which indicate a favourable issue.

[97] That is, when you fight with them, it will be like handling fire, and unless you fight well you will get burnt by the enemy.

[98] They are soft, and easily overcome,—mere women.

Divining by Familiar Spirits.

Kwa ti ngesikati sokugula kukamamekazi, umkababa, ubaba w' emuka wa ya emaʰlatini ukufuna inyanga yokumbulula e kwa bulawa ngabo. Abantu ba m yalela inyanga yemilozi, ba ti, "Yiya kumancele o ya 'ku ku siza." Wa fika kuye, wa ti, "Mngane, u bona nje ngi fika kuwe, ng' aʰlulekile kuzo zonke izinyanga; ngi ti, umʰlaumbe wena u nga ngi siza kunezinye izinyanga. Ngi funa ukuhamba nawe kusasa." Wa vuma Umancele.

Kwa sa kusasa izulu li buyisile,

When my aunt was ill, the wife of my father by adoption,[99] my father went to the forest-country to find a doctor to dig up the poison which was killing her. The people directed him to a doctor with familiar spirits,[1] saying, "Go to Umancele; it is he who will help you." When he came to him he said, "My friend, you see I come to you, for I have got no good from all the other doctors; I think that perhaps you can help me more than they. I wish you to go with me in the morning." Umancele assented.

In the morning there was a

---

[99] Not the man's own father, but his uncle, his father's brother, who on the death of the real father took possession of the wife and family of the deceased, becoming the husband of the wife and father of the children, and is therefore called father simply, in accordance with native custom.

[1] This, perhaps, is the best rendering we can give to the words, *Inyanga yemilozi*. The *imilozi* are supposed to be *amatongo* or spirits of the dead, who wait on a particular diviner, and speak in a low whistling tone, so as to be heard by those who come to enquire. They are called *imilozi* from this mode of speaking; *umlozi* is the whistling sound made by the mouth, short of a full whistle. The natives do not call them by any term equivalent to "familiar," but they say they are "*Amatongo a hamba nomuntu*,"—Spirits who live with a man. The wild cat and baboon are said to be *amanxusa*—attendants, i. e. familiars—of the *abatakati* or wizards; and as we shall see below, they are supposed to have power to bewitch various animals, as dogs, cattle, or snakes, and to send them on a message of malice to injure those they hate. These are of the same character as "the Sending" which we read of in Icelandic legends. They also use the *imikovu*, that is, little people whom they have raised from the dead by incantations and magic; and who may also be called *familiars*.

wa hlala izinsuku eziuingi; l' enza umvumbi, be nge nakuhamba. Kwa ti ngamhla li sayo ba puma. Sa bona be fika, si nga sa lw azi usuku a ba ya 'kufika ngalo.

Ekufikeni kwabo, ba tshelwa bonke abantu e sa s' ake nabo ukuti i fikile imilozi. Kwa butana abantu bonke endhlini kamantshayo, o gulayo. Ukugula kwake, wa e nga guli enyameni; u be gula ngokubujelwa abantwana. Ku ti abantu aba ngenayo ukuza 'kubingelela inyanga, si ng' azi kahle ukuba u nemilozi impela, kodwa s' azi ukuti u nemilozi ngokuzwa ngabantu, si nga bonanga ngawetu amehlo.

Si ngene ukubingelela, abanye ba i bingelela; abanye, ku ti, be nga ka i bingeleli, b' ezwe se ku tsho yona, i ti, "Sa ku bona, bani," i m biza ngegama lake. 'Etuke, a ti, "Au! ku tsho pi loku? Ngi be ngi bingelela Umancele lo na."

Kwa sa kusasa, kwa pumelwa ngapandhle esangweni lomuzi ukuya 'kubula inyanga. Umancele wa ti, "O, nkomidhlilale, (igama

change of weather, and he staid at Umancele's house many days; there was very heavy rain, so that they could not set out. On the first fine day, they set out. We saw them on their arrival, not knowing the day on which they would come.

When they came, all the people that lived with us were told that the familiar spirits had come. All the people collected in the house of Umantshayo, the sick person. Her sickness was not that she was in suffering; she was sick because all her children died. We who went in to salute the doctor did not know for certain that he had familiar spirits, but we heard it said by other people that he had; we had seen nothing with our own eyes.

When we had gone in to salute, some saluted the familiar spirits; but others before they saluted heard the spirits saluting them, saying, "Good day, So-and-so," calling the person by his name. He started, and exclaimed, "O! whence does the voice come? I was saluting Umancele yonder."

In the morning they all went out to the gateway of the village to enquire of the diviner. But Umancele said, "O, Unkomidhlilale,[2] (my father's name which was

---

[2] *U-nkom'-i-dhl'-i-lale*, The-bullock-which-eats-and-lies-down. Implying that he lives in the midst of abundance.

likababa a li kqanjwa imilozi,) a ng' azi mina uku ku tshela izwi noma li linye lokuti nokuti. A kona amakosi a ya 'ku ku pendula."

Bala a pendula, a ti, "Nkomidhlilale, si nge bule u nga si kokelanga 'luto. A u boni ngani ukuba si ze 'ku ku siza? Koka inkomo, ukuze si ku kanyisele izinto o wa bulawa ngazo."

A sa bona umuntu o kulumayo nonkomidhlilale; s' ezwa izwi nje li tsho li ti, "Funa inkomo." Sa kqalaza ukuti, "Au, Umancele umlomo wake u tulile nje. Ku kuluma pi loko na?" Sa bhekana sonke omunye nomunye.

Unkomidhlilale wa ngena ngapakati ukufuna inkomo, wa i tshaya, wa ti, "Nansi ke, makosi, inkomo yenu. Mbala uma ni tsho ni ti nina ni ze 'u ngi vusa, ngi nge nqabe nenkomo, noko zi nga se ko; za pelela ezinyangeni; ngi ni nika yona eya salayo kuzo." Ya bonga imilozi, ya ti, "Kuhle. Si ya i'bonga inkomo yako." Wa hlala pansi ubaba.

Ya kuluma imilozi, ya ti, "Nkomidhlilale, u ya gulelwa umfazi wako. U se mutsha. U

given him by the spirits,) for my part I cannot give you a single word, one way or the other.[3] There are masters[4] who will answer you."

And they did answer, saying, "Unkomidhlilale, we cannot divine unless you pay us. Do you not see that we have come to help you? Give us a bullock, that we may show you the things which are killing you."

We did not see any one speaking with Unkomidhlilale; we merely heard a word telling him to get a bullock. We looked round, saying, "O, Umancele's mouth is quite still. Whence does the voice come?" We all stared one at the other.

Unkomidhlilale went into the cattle-pen to look for a bullock, and, selecting one, said, "Here is your bullock, my masters. Truly if you are come to give me life again, I cannot refuse a bullock, even though there are none left; they have all gone to the doctors; I give one which was left." The spirits returned thanks, and said, "It is well. We thank you for the bullock." My father sat down.

The spirits spoke, saying, "Unkomidhlilale, it is your wife who is sick. She is still young. You

---

[3] Almost precisely the words with which Balaam answered Balak, Numb. xxii. 38.

[4] Masters,—the *imilozi*.

ya mangala ukuti, 'Ini? Loku lo 'mfazi ngi mu tete kuyise e intombazana; wa fika lapa kumi, wa zala umntwana wentombi; ngemva kwake kw' ala ukuzala; wa zalela pansi. Kw enze njani na?' Kepa tina si za 'ku ku tshelā ō kw enza ugako loko kumkako. Wena u ya funa, u ti, 'Umkami w ekqe pi?' Kepa k' ekqanga 'ndawo; ukufa ku m fikele ekaya, ni d/la utshwala. Umuntu owa m bulalayo. Umkako wa fa ngobu/le. Wa ti e pumela pand/le ukuya 'kutunda, kanti lowo 'muntu u m /lomele; wa ti 'esuka, wa e fika, wa tabata igade lomtondo wake, wa li songa endaweni yake, wa ti en/liziyweni yake, 'Ku njani ke? Loku e ng' ala, e nga vumi ukuba a be umkami, ngi za 'ku m sweziscla, ukuti, ngi za 'kubulala inzalo yake, a /lupeke naye njengami.'"

Loku okwa tshiwo imilozi ukuti kwa ba njalo, wa tabata imbozisa,

are astonished and say, 'What is this? For I took this wife from her father when she was still a little girl; she came here to me, and gave birth to a female child; after that she could not have children; she gave birth for the ground.[5] How has this happened?' But we are about to tell you how this happens to your wife. You ask where your wife walked over poison.[6] But she has no where walked over poison; the disease came to your house when you were drinking beer. It is a man who injured her. Your wife died[7] for her beauty. She went out to make water, but the man was watching her; and when she went back, he took the earth which was saturated with her urine, and wrapped it up, and said in his heart, 'How now then does the matter stand? Since she refused me and would not be my wife, I will bereave her, that is, I will kill her children, that she too may be troubled as well as me.'"

The spirits said he did thus:—
He took poisonous plants[8] and

---

[5] That is, for burial. None lived.

[6] The natives believe that the wizard has power to place poisons in the path of a person he wishes to injure, and that by merely passing over it the victim will be affected with whatever disease the wizard desires; and further, no one besides the devoted victim will suffer by passing over it. This is called *ukubeka ubuti*, to lay poison; and the person affected is said *ukwekqa ubuti*, to leap over or pass over poison.

[7] *Died;* her disease is called death.

[8] *Imbozisa*, a general term applied to certain medicines capable

ukuti umdhlebe nembuya nezinto ezinye ezibulalayo, wa zi hlanganisa negade lomtondo wake, wa tunga izingcaba, wa zi mbela eziko ngapansi kwomlilo, ukuze ku ti ngesikati lapa owesifazana e piswa umtondo, a ti lapa e ti ka tunde, ku be buhlungu esinyeni, ku tshise. Wa m bulala ngaloko. Bala ngemva kwaloko wa be 'ya tata isisu, sa dhlula. Kepa tina 'milozi si namandhla ukuya 'ku ku mbulula loko. Si nga ya si ku tabate, si buye nako, ni ku bone ngamehlo enu. A si namandhla okuti, 'Hamba, u ye enyangeni ngokwelapa, i bozise loko.' Z' ahluleka zonke. Ku ya 'kuya tina 'milozi. Si ya 'kuhamba ngomso. Namhla nje si katele. Si se za 'upumula."

bound them up with the earth impregnated with her urine, and made little bags of skin, in which he placed the mixture, and buried them under the fireplace of his own hut, that when the woman had a call of nature and went to make water, she might have a burning in her bladder. He injured her by these means. After that indeed she became pregnant, but miscarried.[9] The spirits continued, "But we spirits can go and dig up the mixture. We can go and take it and bring it here, and show it to you. We cannot advise you to go to a doctor for the sake of obtaining his advice, that he may cause that which is injuring you to rot. The doctors can do nothing. We spirits will go. We will go to-morrow. To-day we are tired. We are now going to rest."

Kwa vela nabanye aba bulawa kanye naye, ba ti, "Nati, makosi, ni y' azi ukuba sa s' ake 'ndawo nye, s' aleka kulowo 'muntu."

Others came forward who had been injured at the same time with her, and said, "You know, masters, that we lived together, and were hated by that man."

---

of causing a slough—escharotics—from *ukubozisa*, to cause to rot. But here they are not supposed to be applied to the body, or to produce any escharotic effect, but to be mixed with the urine of the victim, and to be thus capable of causing her offspring to perish. Two medicines are here mentioned—*umdhlebe* and *imbuya*; not the common *imbuya*, generally called wild spinach, but a larger plant possessed of poisonous qualities.

[9] *Sa dhlula*, i. e. *isisu*, the word *isisu* being applied to the abdomen, to the womb, and to that which is conceived. "The offspring passed away." The natives use the same form of a man dying,—"*U se dhlulile*," He has now passed away—he is dead.

Ya ti imilozi kundayeni, "Si y' azi ukuti wena u indodana kankomidhlilale. Wa bulawa nawe ngobuhle bomfazi wako; a ku tandwanga ukuba a zekwe u we umubi kangaka; kepa wena wa m zeka ngamandhla ako—ngokuba wa b' u nezinkomo ezinhle, za tandeka kuyise wentombi, wa ku nika yona; kepa kulowo 'muntu kwa ba isizondo kuye ukuti, 'Ini ukuba intombi inhle kangaka Ujadu a i nike umfokazana e mubi kangaka na?' Wa ti, 'Ngi za 'ku m bulala, ngi m shiyise yona; si bone ukuba e file a ngi yi 'ku i zeka na.' Wa bulawa ngaloko wena. Kepa amadhlozi akwini a wa vumi ukuba u fe, a ti, 'Ku ng' enzeke ukuba umntwana wetu a bulawe ngobuhle bomfazi wake. Sa mu nika izinkomo ukuba a zeke, nati si dume ngoku m pata kahle.' Kodwa ke, ndayeni, noko u hamba ngosuku lwanamuhla, u ya bulawa, namadhlozi a wa sizi 'luto, ngokuba u ku naanele njalo ukuze a buye nesidumbu sako. Si za 'kuya 'ku ku mbulula loko

The spirits said to Undayeni, "We know that you are Unkomidhlilale's son. You too are injured on account of your wife's beauty; it was not liked that she should marry one so ugly as you are; but you took her to wife because you were powerful—because you had so many beautiful cattle, which were an object of admiration to the maiden's father, and so he gave her to you; and that excited hatred in the other's heart, and he said, 'How is it that Ujadu has given so beautiful a damsel to so ugly a beggar as that? I will kill him, and force him to leave her; and when he is dead we shall see whether I shall marry her or not.' You were made ill on that account. But the spirits[10] of your people would not allow you to be killed, but said, 'It cannot be permitted that our child should be killed on account of the beauty of his wife. We gave him cattle that he might marry, and we be honoured for treating him well.' But notwithstanding that, Undayeni, although you are living now, you are being killed, and the ancestral spirits give you no help, for that sorcerer is constantly longing to bring home your corpse.[11] We are going to dig up that by which you are in-

---

[10] Amadhlozi or Amatongo.
[11] That is, to kill you; and like a warrior return with the spoil—the dead body of the conquered.

owa bulawa ngako, u ku bone ngameh̀lo."

Kwa ti kusasa ya tsho imilozi, ya ti, "Si pe ni ukudh̀la, s' encame, si hambe." Kwa funwa ukudh̀la, kwa letwa utshwala bu ngokamba, lwa bekwa kumancele; wa puza ke nabantu bake, kwa pela. Ya bonga, ya ti, "Si ya bonga ke; se si hamba, si hamba nabakwini—Ukcubá nobutongwane nabo bonke bakwini. A si tsho ukuti loko si ya 'ku ku tata obala; si ya 'kulwa nabakona; kodwa si ya 'ku b' ah̀lula, si buye nako loko. Sala ni kah̀le ke." Ya hamba.

Sa sala tina nomancele nabantu bake, si mangele si ti, "I za 'kuba 'ndaba ni lena na?" Y' emuka amasuku amatatu. Umancele wa sala nati. Sa buza kuye ukuti, "I ya 'kufika nini na?" Wa ti, "Na ngomso i nga fika, uma pambili ku nge lukuni, i b' ah̀lulile. Kodwa a ng' azi nami usuku lwokufika kwayo, ngokuba a ba ngi tshelanga usuku a ba ya 'kubuya

jured, and you shall see it with your own eyes."

On the following morning the spirits said, "Give us some food, that we may eat and set out." The people fetched food, and beer in a pot, and placed it before Umancele; he and his people ate and drank it all. The spirits returned thanks and said, "We thank you; we are now going; we are going with the spirits of your people—with Ukcuba and Ubutongwane and all the people of your house.[12] We do not say that we shall take that which is killing you without difficulty; we shall fight with the spirits of that place; but we shall conquer them; and bring back what we are going for. So good bye."[13] They went.

We, Umancele and his people remained, we wondering and asking, "How will this matter turn out?" The spirits went away for three days. Umancele remained with us. We asked him when the spirits would come back again. He replied, "They may come perhaps to-morrow if they do not find it a difficult work where they are gone, and they conquer them. But I do not myself know the day of their return, for they did not tell me, for they go to an enemy.

---

[12] Viz., the dead,—the Amatongo.
[13] Compare this contest between the contending factions of the Amatongo with the battle of the good people, given in "The Confessions of Tom Bourke," *Croker's Fairy Legends.*

ngalo, ngokuba ba ya eziteni. Si ya 'kubona ngoba se be fika nje."

Si buze tina, si ti, "Uma be fikile si ya 'kubona ngani na?" A ti Umancele, "Ni ya 'kuzwa izwi labo; noma ni banga umsindo, ni kuluma ngamandhla, ba ya 'kuti, 'Tula ni; si fikile.' Noma ni ng' ezwa, lowo o pakamisa umsindo ba ya 'ku m biza ngegama lake, ba ti, 'Tula, bani. A u zwa ini na?' Ku ya 'kuba njalo ke ukufika kwabo."

Umancele wa be e pakati kwetu njengomuntu wasemizini, e nga fani nenyanga; wa dhla, wa puza nabantu bake.

Kwa ti ngolwesine ntambama kwa fika wa munye umlozi; s' ezwa u se u ti, "Ngi fikile." Wa buza Umancele, wa ti, "Ubani na?" Wa ti, "Ng' Ubani," u tsho igama lawo. Wa buza futi Umancele, wa ti, "Au, bani, bonke ba pi na?" Wa ti, "Au, si ya hlupeka. Ba sele; ba ya fa abantu; ba ya si gwaza; a ba vumi ukuba si mbulule; kodwa nati si namadoda akwiti a ya lwa nabo. Ngi ze 'ukeela ukudhla. Si lambile. Ngi ya buyela. A ngi z' 'ulala lapa."

We shall know only by their arrival."

When we asked how we should know when they arrived, Umancele said, "You will hear them speak; and if you are making a great noise and talking aloud, they will say, 'Be quiet; we are come.' And if you do not hear, they will call him by name who is making the noise, and say, 'Be quiet, you So-and-so. Do you not hear?' Thus it will be when they come."

Umancele was amongst us like a stranger, not like a doctor; he and his people ate and drank.

On the fourth day in the afternoon one spirit came, and we heard it saying, "I have come." Umancele asked, "Who are you?" It replied, "I am So-and-so," giving the name of the spirit. Umancele again enquired, saying, "O, So-and-so, where are all the rest?" It replied, "O, we are troubled. They remain behind; the people are dying;[14] the enemy is stabbing us; they will not let us dig up the poison; but we too have our men, and they are fighting with them. I have come to ask for food. We are hungry. I am going back. I shall not sleep here."

---

[11] It is supposed that the Amatongo, or the dead, can die again. Here we have allusions to their being killed in battle, and of their being carried away by the river. See above, p. 225, note 76.

Kwa funwa ukudhla, kwa bekwa kumancele, noma isikafu, noma utshwala. Wa dhla Umancele, wa kqeda. Umlozi wa bonga, wa ti, "Sala ni kuhle." Wa buza Umancele, wa ti, "Ni ya 'kubuya nini na?" Wa ti, "A ng' azi, ngokuba abantu ba katele; u loku sa fika, amasuku omatatu sa lwa njalo ku ze ku be namuhla. Umhlaumbe na ngomuso si nga fika. A ng' azi; si ya 'kubona pambili." W' emuka.

Sa lala lwesihlanu. Kwa ti ngomso emini, sa ti si hlezi, si ng' azi 'luto, s' ezwa se i tsho emsamo, i ti, "Tula ni umsindo; se si fikile; kodwa a si fiki sonke; abanye b' emuke namanzi."

Wa buza Umancele, wa ti, "Obani na?"

Ya ti, "Ubutongwane. Ka vumi ukuwela; w' esaba amanzi. Kodwa nezinto e be si ye 'ku zi tata, a zi pelele; zi mukile futi namanzi; ku muke ingcaba kabani, e nokuti nokuti yake; nekabani y' emuka njalo; kodwa ezinye zi kona; ekabani nobani bonke aba takatelwayo, si fika nazo."

The people fetched food and placed it before Umancele, both solid food and beer. He ate it all. The spirit returned thanks, and said, "Good bye." Umancele asked when they would come back. It said, "I do not know, for the people are tired; from the time we got there, all three days, we have been constantly fighting till to-day. Perhaps we may come to-morrow. I cannot say; we shall see by and bye." It departed.

We retired to rest on the fifth day. On the morrow at noon, as we were sitting unconscious of any thing, we heard the spirits speaking at the upper part of the house, saying, "Cease your noise; we are come; but we are not all here; some have been carried away by the river."

Umancele asked who they were.

They replied, "Ubutongwane. He would not cross; he was afraid of the water. But all the things which we went to fetch, are not here; they too were carried away by the water; the little bag of So-and-so, the one with such and such things in it, has been carried away; and that of So-and-so; but other things are here; the bag of So-and-so, and of So-and-so, and of all the others who are poisoned, we bring with us."

Tina s' ezwa se ku tiwa, "I fikile imilozi," ku nyenyezwa aomame. Sa buza, sa ti, "I fike nini na?" Ba ti, "I fike emini nje. Kepa i ti, uyi*h*lo u mukile namanzi, nezinto ezinye zi muke namanzi." Sa puma ukuti, "Ake si ye 'kuzwa nati." Sa ngena end*h*lini, sa *h*lala; s' ezwa bala ku njalo, i kuluma imilozi. Sa funa ukuba i kuluma pi. Sa bheka emlonyeni kamancele; a sa bona 'kukuluma. Sa ko*h*lwa uma ku tsho pi loko na.

I ti, "Si fike sonke." I k*x*ok*x*a impi yayo uku*h*labana kwayo. I ti, "Sa b' a*h*lula. Ukuze si b' a*h*lule, sa b' enzela ingomane ugomlilo; sa b' a*h*lula. Sa *h*lala, si linda umlilo, ukuze u keime, si mbulule izinto lezi e si fika nazo; kwa ba njalo sa zi mbulula, si fika nazo zonke. Ni ya 'ku zi bona kusasa, ukuti nokuti njalo."

Kwa sa kusasa, kwa ti emini kwa kitshwa izinto zonke end*h*lini, kwa sindwa, ukuze izibi zonke zi pume; y' oma ind*h*lu; kwa butwa abantu baleyo 'mizi yakwiti ukuza

We heard our mothers whispering that the spirits had come. We asked when they came. They said, "Just now, at noon. But they say, your father has been carried away by the river, and some of the things also." We went out, saying, "Just let us go and hear too." We went into the house and sat down; and truly we heard it was so; the spirits were speaking. We tried to discover where the voice came from. We looked earnestly at Umancele's mouth; we did not see him speaking. We could not understand where the voice was.

The spirits said, "We have all come." They related all the acts of the army. They said, "We conquered them. In order that we might conquer them, we made an attack with fire; and so conquered them. We remained watching the fire, that when it had gone out we might dig up the things which we have brought; so we dug them up, and have brought them all. You will see them in the morning, every one of them."

On the following day at noon, every thing was taken out of the house, and the floor was smeared with cowdung, that all dust might be taken away; the floor dried; and all the people of our villages[15]

---

[15] There were three villages situated near each other, and the inhabitants of all of them came together.

'kubona izinto ezi fikileyo. Kwa ketwa abadala, amadoda nesifazana, aba za 'kungena endhlini; kwa ti abancane besifazana nabalisa abancane ba hlungwa; a ba ngena, ba sala ngapandhle. Kwa tiwa, abancane a ba nako ukungena lapa; a ku fanele ukuba ba boniswe izinto zobulima obubi.

Kwa ti be sa kuluma, ya ti imilozi, "Hlela ni, ni hlale kahle, ni tule umsindo, ni ti nya." Bala kwa ba njalo, ba tula, ba ti nya. Ya tsho imilozi, ya ti, "Kqapela ni oku wayo." Ba hlala ngokukqapela. B' ezwa kw ehla into pezulu, i njengento i ponswe umuntu, i ti geitshi. Kwa ba kuningi kw enze njalo ukuwa kwako, kwa za kwa pelela. Kwa ti se ku pelile, ya tsho ukuti, "Ku bute ni; ku pelele manje." Ba ku buta. Ku ti a ba nga ku boniyo, b' ezwe se u tsho umlozi, u ti, "Bheka ni okunye; nako ngotingo olutile, nokunye kwolutile." Ba ku buta konke.

Ya tsho, ya ti, "Ku pelele ke manje. Hamba ni, ni ye emfuleni, emadwaleni, ni ku hlakazele kona; ni ya 'kubona kona izinto

were collected to see the things which had come. The old people, men and women, were chosen to go into the house. The young people, female and male, were separated; they did not go in, but remained outside. They said young people could not go in; it was not proper for them to see the things of wicked sorcery.

As they were still speaking, the spirits said, "Arrange yourselves properly, and be quite quiet." And truly they were absolutely silent. The spirits said, "Look about you for that which falls." They waited and watched. They heard something fall from above, like a thing thrown by some one; it fell with a sound. Many things fell in this way, until all had fallen. When all had fallen, the spirits said, "Collect them; all are now here." They collected them. When there was any thing they did not see, they heard a spirit saying, "See, there is something else; there it is near such a wattle; and there is another by such a wattle."[10] They collected every thing.

The spirits said, "You now have every thing. Go to the rocks in the river, and spread them abroad there; you will there see

---

[10] The English reader may require to be reminded that the native hut is made of wattles, covered with grass.

e na bo ni zi funa; ingcaba kabani, nanso etile, nekabani etile." Ya z' ahlukanisa zonke izingcaba ngabaninizo.

Ya ti, "Hamba ni ke, ni keite emanzini uma se ni bonile, ku muke namanzi. Ni ya 'kupila; no be e felwa u ya 'kupila; nogulayo u ya 'kutokoza, ukuze n' azi ukuba si izinyanga impela."

Bala b' emuka, ba hlakazela emanzini; abanye ba fumana ubuhlalu bwabo; abanye ba fumana umhlaba u botshiwe; nabanye ba fumana izidwaba zabo; nabanye ba fumana iziziba zabo; bonke ba fumana okwabo njalo; ba ku lahla emanzini, kw' emuka. Ba geza izandhla nemizimba, be ti, "Si nge goduke nepunga lamanyala."

Ba fika ekaya, sa buza kwomame ngokunyenyeza ukuti, "Ni zi fumene izinto zonke zetu na?" Ba ti, "Au, impela. Si ya kolwa ukuba ba izinyanga. Se si ku bonile; nokuti kukabani, e sa si ku bona ku nga ka lahleki; zonke izinto e si z' aziyo sa zi bona. Si y' etemba ukuba si za 'kusinda manje."

the things which you have been looking for; So-and-so's little bag, and such and such a thing you will see; and that thing of So-and-so." They distinguished all the little bags according to the persons to whom they belonged.

They said, "Go then, and cast them into the water when you have seen them, that they may be carried away by it. You will get well; and she whose children died will get well; and he who is sick will rejoice, that you may know that we are indeed diviners."

So they went and spread them out by the water; some found their beads; some found earth bound up; others found pieces of their old tattered garments; others their rags; all found something belonging to them; they threw them into the water, and they were carried away. They washed their hands and bodies, saying, "We cannot go home with the stench of this filth upon us."

When they came home we asked our mothers in whispers if they had found all our things. They replied, "Yes, surely. We believe that they are diviners. We have seen the things; there was that of So-and-so which we used to see before it was lost; we saw every thing which we knew. We now believe that we shall get well."

Kwa ti ngangomuso Umancelo wa nikwa inkomo yake. Wa valelisa, wa goduka. Sa bonga, sa ti, "Hamba ni ka*h*le ke, makosi. Si bonile ubunyanga benu. Kodwa se si ya 'kuk*q*apela ukupila kodwa." B' emuka.

Sa sala si bhekile. Wa si tata isisu Umantshayo; za pela izinyanga zokubeleta; wa beleta; ingane ya *h*lala amasuku ama*h*lanu, ya *h*labeka, ya tsho ngapansi na ngapezulu, ya d*h*lula. Sa buyela emuva, sa ti, "Au! loku ku tiwe si mbululiwe, ku vela pi loku na? Hau! si za 'uk*q*apela ngemuva; uma si bona ku ba nje, si ya 'udela, si ti, nokumbululwa a ku sizi 'luto. Si ya *h*lupeka."

Wa *h*lala isikati eside; wa tabata isisu; za pela izinyanga zake; wa beleta; ya *h*lala ingane amasuku a nge mangaki; kwa ba njalo ya tsho ngapansi na ngapezulu, ya d*h*lula.

Sa ti, "Hau! okona 'ku i ko i ku pi! Loku se si bona ku se si kale. Inkomo yetu sa i delela ni? I ku pi na, loku si nga sa boni umntwana njena na?" Sa ti, "O, imilozi i ya si ko*h*lisa. A i tabatanga ukufa e sa bulawa ngako.

On the morrow Umancelo was given his bullock. He took his leave and went home. We gave thanks, saying, "Go in prosperity, our masters. We have seen your skill. But we are now looking out for our recovery." They departed.

We remained in expectation. Umantshayo became pregnant; her months were ended; she gave birth to a child; after five days it was attacked with violent sickness and diarrhœa; it died. We lost heart again, and said, "O! since it was said the poison which was killing us has been dug up, whence comes this? O! we shall look back again; when we see that it is thus, we shall be satisfied, and say that even digging up the poison is of no use. We are in trouble."

She remained a long time; she became pregnant; her months were ended; she gave birth to a child; it lived a few days; again it was seized with the same disease, and died.

We said, "O! what is the real truth in this matter? For we see that we are still weeping. Why did we give our bullock? Where is the truth of the matter, since even now we see no child born to live? O, the spirits are deceiving us. They did not take away the poison which was killing us. They

I si tungele okwayo, ukuza 'kutabata inkomo yetu. A si ku boni ukumbululwa kwetu ; si fela pezu kwako. Ku ze ku be namuhla, u ya felwa Umantshayo."

Nondayeni ka tolanga 'sikala sokupumula ; kwa ba i loku wa gula, wa za wa fa, ku nge ko 'nyanga nanye e m sizayo, z' ahluleka zonke. W' eza wa dhlala ngomkababa lo o nge nanyanga ; z' ahluleka zonke. Nabo bakondayeni ba kala ngakukala kunye nati.

Umpengula Mbanda.

sewed up to deceive us their own things in the bags, that they might come and take our bullock. We do not see that they dug up the poison for us; we are dying notwithstanding. And to this day the children of Umantshayo die."

And Undayeni did not get the least rest; he was always ill, and at last died; not a single doctor helped him; all were unsuccessful. And he trifled with my father's wife, who had no doctor who could cure her; all failed. And the people of Undayeni had the same cause of complaint that we had.

Another account.

Nga ka nga ya kuwo umlozi, ngi ya 'kubula umfana wakwetu, e gula, e nesifo, e kquleka. Sa mangala nobaba nomfo wetu naomame uma isifo sini lesi, loku e kade e nge naso lesi 'sifo. Si ya si kqabuka esokuba si zwiwe. Sa hamba, sa fika kuwo umlozi. Sa kuleka, sa ti, "E, mngane; indab' ezinhle." Sa hlala. Ya ti, "Sa ni bona." Sa vuma, sa ti, "Yebo." Ya kcataz' uguai, ya bema, ya zamula, ya zelula, ya

I once went to a person with a familiar spirit to enquire respecting a boy of ours who had convulsions. My father and brother and mothers and I wondered what was the nature of the disease, since it was a new thing. We saw at first sight that it was something about which we must enquire of the diviner. We set out and went to the person with a familiar spirit. We made obeisance, saying, "Eh, friend; we come to you for good news." We waited. The doctor said, "Good day." We replied, saying, "Yes." She poured out some snuff, and took it; she then yawned and stretched, and also

hlasimula futi, ya ti, "Ka ba ka fiki aba bulayo."

Sa hlala isikati eside, sa za nati sa keataz' uguai, sa boma; si te lapa se si kohliwe, s' ezwa ukufika kwayo imilozi; ya ti ya si bingelela, ya ti, "Sa ni bona." Sa kqalaza endhlini ukuba i tsho pi.

Ya ti, "Ni kqalaza ni, loku si ya ni bingelela nje, si ti, 'Sa ni bona?'"

Sa ti, "Si kqalaza ukuba si nga ni boni lapa ni kona."

Ya ti ke, "Si lapa. A ni namandhla oku si bona. Ni ya 'kusizwa ngokushumayela nje."

Izwi layo li vela kuyo, li nga tuti elomuntwanyana omncinyane, a li namandhla okukuluma kakulu, ngokuba li kuluma pezulu ezintingweni.

Sa ti, "Yebo."

Ya ti, "Ni ze ngendaba."

Wa ti umnikaziyo, "Ba tshayele ni; nampo be ni tshela, be ti, ni ze ngendaba."

Sa tshaya ke.

Ya ti, "Indaba inkulu e ni ze ngayo; umhlola u kumuntu."

Sa i tshayela, sa buza, sa ti, "U

shuddered, and said, "They who divine are not yet here."

We remained a long time, and at length we too took some snuff; when we were no longer thinking of the reason of our coming, we heard that the spirits were come; they saluted us, saying, "Good day." We looked about the house to see where the voice came from.

The spirits said, "Why are you looking about, for we merely salute you?"

We said, "We look about because we cannot see where you are."

They said, "Here we are. You cannot see us. You will be helped by what we say only."

The voice was like that of a very little child; it cannot speak aloud, for it speaks above, among the wattles of the hut.

We replied to the salutation.

The spirits said, "You have come to enquire about something."

The person whose familiars they were said, "Strike the ground for them; see, they say you came to enquire about something."

So we struck the ground.

They said, "That about which you have come is a great matter; the omen has appeared in a man."

We struck the ground, and asked, saying, "How big is the

kumuntu o ngakanani na wona lowo 'mhlola na?"

Ya ti, "U kumuntu omncinyane."

Sa tshaya kakulu lapo, uma si zwa ukuti ya hlaba kona.

Ya ti, "Ngi ti, umhlola njalo isifo."

Sa tshaya kakulu.

Ya ti, "Si semzimbeni kulowo 'muntu omncinyane." Ya ti, "A ngi zwe uma umuntu muni?" Ya ti, "Umfana."

Sa i vumela kakulu.

Ya ti, "Ka k' alusi. U se muncinyane."

Sa tshaya kakulu.

Ya ti, "Kodwa ni ya mangala, ni mangaliswa umkuba o kuye emzimbeni." Ya ti, "Tshaya ni, ngi zwe uma lo 'mkuba o semzimbeni kulowo 'mfana omncinyane nje, uma umkuba muni na."

Sa tshaya kakulu, sa ti, "Si ya 'kuzwa ngawe, lok' u m bonile wena ukuti umfana muncinyane."

Ya ti, "Naku; ngi m bona, e nga ti a nga kquleka bo."

Sa tshaya kakulu lapo.

man in whom the omen has appeared?"

They replied, "It is a young person."

We struck the ground vehemently there, when we perceived that she[17] had hit the mark.

They said, "I say the omen is a disease."

We smote the ground vehemently.

They said, "It is disease in the body of that young person." They said, "Let me see what that person is? It is a boy."

We assented strongly.

They said, "He does not yet herd. He is still small."

We smote violently on the ground.

They said, "But you wonder at what has occurred to him." They said, "Strike the ground, that I may see what that is which has occurred to the body of the little boy."

We struck the ground vehemently, and said, "We will hear from you, for you have seen that it is a little boy."

They said, "There he is; I see him; it is as though he had convulsions."

Upon that we smote the ground vehemently.

---

[17] The woman with the familiar spirits. The divination of the spirits is spoken of as something done by the woman, without whom they do not divine.

Ya ti, " Ukukqulcka i 'kwonze njani? Ngi buze ni."

Sa ti, "A si nako ukubuza. Ngokuba naku ni y' azi; se ni si tshelile nina ngapambili. Loku u ngapane u ti, a si ku buze nje, a u yi ngayo indhlela; loku si zwa u ya ngayo nje, si nga ze si buze ni na?"

Ya ti, "Ngi ti pela, ngi buze ni; ungabe ngi y' eduka."

Sa ti, "Kqa; ka w eduki; u ya ngayo indhlela e si i bonayo nati."

Ya ti, " Lowo 'mfana ku kqale lap' e ti, 'esuke, a hambe. U se mncane kakulu, a ni ku bonanga loku 'kufa—lapa e se ingane encane; wa za wa kqala ukuhleka, e nga ka bi naso leso 'sifo; wa za wa hlala, e nga ka bi naso; wa za wa kasa, e nga ka bi naso; wa za w' esuka w' ema, e nga ka bi naso leso 'sifo; u te lapa e se lu susa unyawo uma a keatule, sa fika leso 'sifo. Uku si bona kwenu leso 'sifo, ni si bone si fika ngoku m bulala nje; wa fela ezandhleni zikanina; unina wa m tela ngamauzi, e se yalule amehlo; unina

They said, "What kind of convulsions are they? Enquire of me."

We said, "We have nothing to ask about. For behold you know; you have already first told us. For it is proper that you should tell us to ask, if you were not going the right way; but as we perceive that you are going the right way, what have we to ask of you?"

They replied, "I tell you to ask, for perhaps I am going wrong."

We said, " No; you are not going wrong; you are going by the way which we ourselves see."

They said, "The disease began in the child when he began to walk. When he was very young, you did not see the disease—when he was a little infant; at length when he began to laugh, the disease had not yet appeared; at length he began to sit up, it not having yet appeared; at length he began to go on all fours, it not having yet appeared; at length he began to stand before he was affected by it; when he began to lift his foot from the ground to toddle, the disease came upon him. When you saw the disease, you saw it without expecting anything of the kind; he died in his mother's arms; his mother poured water on him when he was turning up his eyes; she uttered a great

wa kala kakulu, n' etuka, na gijima, na ya endhlini; ni te ni fika
endhlini, na fika e se vukile. Wa
ti unina, 'Ni ngi zwa ngi kala
nje, u file umntanami. A ni mu
boni emanzi? Kade ngi mu tele
ngamanzi, nokuma a ze a vuke
nje.'" Ya ti imilozi, "Ngi ni
tshele loko ke; ngi pikise ni uma
ka si kona loko e ngi ku tshoyo
na."

Sa ti, "Si nge ze sa ku pikisa;
si ku tshelile na kukqala, sa ti, u
hamba ugayo indhlela."

Ya ti, "Leso 'sifo si fana nesifo
somuntu esi isitutwane. Nina ni
ze lapa nje, ni ti, ka ni zwe uma
leso 'sifo esi kumntwana, lesi 'sifo
sini esi fana nesitutwane lesi, uma
isifo sini."

Sa ti, "Ehe, u kqinisile; si
tanda ukuti ma si zwe kuwena,
mlozi; wena u ya 'ku si tshela
nesifo nokuti isifo sokuti, si ze
s' azi ukukqonda uma lesi 'sifo
isifo sokuti; ngokuba se si si tshe-
lwe u we; u si tshele nemiti yoku
s' elapa, uma si ya 'kwenza njani
na."

Ya ti, "Ngi za 'ku ni tshela
isifo. Nina ni novalo olukulu
ngokuba ni ti, lo 'mntwana u nesitutwane; ngokuba isitutwane
umuntu waso ka lungi; u zitshisa
na semulilweni. Mina 'ngi za 'ku
ni tshela, ngi ni kqondise ukwenza
kwaleso 'sifo. Ake ni tshaye, ugi

cry, you started, and ran into the
house; when you entered he had
again come to life. The mother
said, 'You heard me cry; my
child was dead. Do you not see
he is wet? I poured water over
him for some time, and therefore
he has come to life again.'" The
spirits continued, "I have now
told you this; deny if what I say
is not true."

We replied, "We can in no
way dispute what you say; we
have told you already that you
were going by the right path."

The spirits said, "This disease
resembles convulsions. You have
come to me to know what is this
disease which is like convulsions."

We said, "Just so, you say
truly; we wish to hear from you,
spirit; you will tell us the disease
and its nature, that we may at
length understand of what nature
it is; for you have already told us
the name of the disease; tell us
also the medicines with which we
shall treat it."

They replied, "I will tell you
the disease. You are greatly
alarmed because you say the child
has convulsions; and a child with
convulsions is not safe; he burns
himself in the fire. I shall tell
you what caused this disease. Just
smite on the ground, boys, that I

zwe uma lo 'mntwana i 'kupela kwake ini kuyise, bafana, na?"

Sa ti, "Ehe; i 'kupela kwake."

Ya ti, "Tshaya ni, ngi zwe nina, uma ni bula nje, ni ini naye na, nalowo 'mfana na, o gulayo na."

Sa tshaya kakulu.

Ya ti, "Lowo 'mfana umfo wenu." Ya ti, "Tshaya ni, ngi zwe uma umfo wenu kayihlo wenu ngempela na." Ya ti, "Amanga. Ka si ye okayihlo wenu ngempela. Ba y' elamana kodwa oyihlo. Umfo wenu, ngokub' oyihlo b' elamana."

Sa tshaya kakulu.

Ya ti, "Tshaya ni, ngi zwe uma umupi omkulu kwoyihlo bobabili. Ngi ti uyihlo wenu, bafana, ka se ko, wa fa. Tshaya ni, ngi zwe uma wa fela pi." Ya ti, "Nanku; ngi m bona; a fel' endhle uyihlo wenu, bafana. Wa gwazwa ngomkonto. Wa gwazwa isipi 'sizwe nje?"

Sa tshaya kakulu.

Ya ti, "Wa gwazwa amazulu nganeno kwotukela; lap' a fela kona uyihlo, bafana. Lona uyihlokazi ngokwelamana noyihlo; yena uyihlo omkulu."

may understand if the child is the only son of his father."

We said, "Yes; he is his only son."

They said, "Smite the ground, that I may understand what relation you are to the child, since you come here to enquire."

We smote vehemently on the ground.

They said, "The boy is your brother. Smite the ground, that I may see if he is really your brother born of your own father, or not. Not so. He is not really the son of your father. Your fathers are brothers. He is your brother, because your fathers were brothers."

We smote the ground violently.

They said, "Smite, that I may understand which is the older of the two fathers. I say, boys, your own father is dead. Smite, that I may understand where he died. There he is; I see him; he died, boys, in the open country. He was stabbed with an assagai. By what tribe was he stabbed?"

We smote the ground vehemently.

They said, "He was stabbed by the Amazulu on this side the Utukela; that is where your father died, boys. The father of that child is your uncle, because he was your father's brother; he was the elder of the two."

Ya ti, "A ngi ni tshele ukufa ke kaloku oku kumfana lowo. Kodwa isifo sake si fana nesitutwane; kodwa ka si so sona. Nina se ni y' esaba kakulu, ngokuba ni ti isitutwane. Mina ngi za 'ku ni tshela ke, ngokuba ni nga sa yi 'kupinda ni m bone e k*r*uleka. Ngi za 'ku ni yalela into e ni ya 'ufika, ni y enze. Na ka na m *h*labela nje? A ni bonanga ni m *h*labela."

Ya ti, "Ake ngi zwe uma n' ake pi, lapa n' ake kona. Ni ka*h*longwa, isizwe e ni kusona. Ke ngi zwe nina isizalo sakwini ni abapi na. Ni abasemadungeni." Ya ti, "Ke ngi zwe kona emadungeni, uma ni se lapa nje ka*h*longwa, emadungeni n' esuswa ini kwini uma ni ze ni ze ka*h*longwa nje." Ya ti, "N' ek*x*abana nabakwini, n' eza ke kwa*h*longwa lapa." Ya ti, "Tshaya ni, ngi zwe uma se ni w akile nje umuzi wakwini na?"

Sa tshaya.

Ya ti, "A ni ka w aki. N' ake ngapakati kwomunye umuzi; a ni ka w aki owakwini umuzi entabeni. Umfana lowo leso 'sifo si m velela ngapakati kwalowo 'muzi." Ya ti, "Tshaya ni, ngi zwe yena lowo 'muntu e n' aka naye emzini wake uma ni ini naye na."

Sa tshaya.

They said, "Let me now tell you the disease which has attacked the boy. His disease is like convulsions; but it is not convulsions. And you are greatly alarmed because you think it is convulsions. But I shall tell you, for you will not again see him have a fit. I shall tell you what to do when you get home. Did you ever sacrifice for him? You have never sacrificed for him."

They said, "Let me just see where you live. You live among the Amathlongwa; that is the tribe where you live. Let me just see where you were born. You belong to the Amadunga. Just let me see, since you are here among the Amathlongwa, why you were separated from the Amadunga to come here. You quarrelled with your own people, and so came here to the Amathlongwa. Smite the ground, that I may see if you have built your own village."

We smote the ground.

They said, "You have not yet built it. You live in the village of another; you have not yet built your own village on the hill. As for the boy, the disease attacked him in the village where you now are. Smite the ground, that I may see what relation the man with whom you live is to you."

We smote the ground.

Ya ti, " Umitshana wenu e n' ake kuye." Ya ti, "A ngi boni 'luto ngapakati kwomuzi womitshana wenu ; u lungile nje ; a ngi boni indaba ezimbi ngapakati kwawo ; ngi u bona umuhle nje ; ni dhla ni kcimele, ngoba ni nga soli 'luto." Ya ti, " Uto e ngi za 'ku ni tshela lona, ngi za 'ku ni tshela itongo. Ka si ko isitutwane kulowo 'mntwana." Ya ti, " Ngi ti mina u netongo."

Sa mangala ukuba imilozi si nga i boni, si zinge si i zwa i kuluma ezintingweni, i kuluma izindaba eziningi si nga i boni.

Ya ti, " Ngi nuka itongo lakwini. Ni ya 'ufika, ni tate imbuzi. Nansi impongo ; ngi i bona."

Sa ti, " Ni i bona ngani na ? "
Ya ti, " Tula ni, ngi za 'ku ni tshela, ngi ni delise umbala wayo. Umbala wayo imhlope. Nanso i s' and' ukufika, i vele ngapetsheya kwelovo emanzimtoti. Se i impongo enkulu. Ni ya 'kuhlaba yona, ni m tele ngenyongo. Ni ti ukusuka ni ye 'ku m kelela umuti o ikambi lomhlaba." Ya ti, " Ngi bona idhlozi lelo ; li ti, ma ku pume umuzi wakwini, u b' eutabeni. Angiti li ya buza idhlozi, li ti, ' Umuzi u b' u kade u ngapakati kwomunye ini na ? ' Li

They said, " He is your cousin on the mother's side. I see nothing wrong in the village of your cousin ; he is good ; I see no practising of sorcery there ; I see that the village is clear ; you eat with your eyes shut, for you have nothing to complain of. What I shall tell you is this, it is the ancestral spirits that are doing this. It is not convulsions the child has. For my part I say he is affected by the ancestral spirits."

We wondered that we should continually hear the spirits which we could not see, speaking in the wattles, and telling us many things without our seeing them.

The spirits said, " I point out your ancestral spirits. When you reach home you shall take a goat. There it is, a he goat ; I see it.

We said, " How do you see it ? "
They said, " Be silent, I will tell you, and satisfy you as to its colour. It is white. That is it which has just come from the other side of the Ilovo from the Amanzimtoti. It is now a large he goat. You shall sacrifice it, and pour its gall on the boy. You will go and pluck for him Itongo-medicine. I see that Itongo ; it says that your village is to be removed from its present place, and built on the hill. Does not the Itongo ask, ' Why has the village staid so long in the midst of another ? '

bulala umfana lowo nje, li ti, 'A ku pume umuzi.' Impongo leyo emhlope ni ya 'ku i hlabela unyokokulu, o yena 'ala naye umfana lowo um' a fe, ngokuba yena uyihlomkulu u be tshele ukuba a m bulale, a fe, a lahlwe ngokukayihlomkulu. Ngi ya ni tshela loko ke uma ni dele. Ngi ni tshela, ukuze ku ti loku 'kufa ku nga buyela, ni ze ni ze kumina, ni zoku i tata imali yenu. Mina ngi ti, ngi ni tshela nje ukuba leso 'sifo s' enziwa idhlozi, ngokuba li ti, ' A ku pume umuzi.' "

Ya tsho kitina, ya ti, " Se ngi ni bulele; leti ni imali yami ke."

Sa i veza imali.

Ya ti ke kumnikaziyo, ya ti, " Tabata ke; nansi imali."

Ya ti, " Ngi i tata nje imali yenu le. Ni ya 'kubuya, ni zoku i tabata, si nga buyela leso 'sifo. Ngi ti, a si sa yi 'kubuyela."

Umnikaziyo wa hlala pakati kwendhlu ngesikati sasemini lapa si bula; ngokuba ka i namandhla okuhamba yodwa uma i ya 'kubula; ku hamba umnikaziyo. Ngokuba uma i ya tanda uma i hambe, i ya m tshela umnikaziyo, i ti, " Hamba, si hambe, si y' en-

It injures the lad, saying, ' Let the village remove from this place.' The he goat you will sacrifice to your grandmother; it is she who refuses to allow the child to die, for your grandfather had been earnest to kill him, that he might die and be buried in accordance with his wish. I tell you this to satisfy you. I tell you that if the disease returns, you may come back to me and take your money. I tell you that this disease is caused by the ancestral spirit, because it wishes that your village should remove."

The spirits said, " Now I have divined for you; so give me my money."

We took out the money.

Then they said to her whose familiars they were, " Take it; there is the money."

They added, "I just take this money of yours. You will come and take it again if the disease returns. I say, it will never return again."

The woman with the familiar spirits sat in the midst of the house, at the time of full daylight, when we enquired of her; for the spirits cannot go alone when they are going to divine; their possessor goes with them. For if they wish to go they tell their possessor, saying to her, " Let us go to such a

daweni etile," lapa i tanda uma i ye kona. Umnikaziyo ka namandhla okukuluma; u zing' e kuluma kancinane, ngokuba naye u ya i buza, a ti, " Bobani, ni tsho njalo, ni kqinisile uku ba tshela kwenu laba 'bantu aba zokubula kumina?" Ukupendula kwayo, ya vuma yona, ya ti, " Si kqinisile, si zek' indaba e kqinisileyo, nabo aba zokubula ba ya 'ku i bona le 'ndaba." A ti, " Wo ba tshela ni ikqiniso. Mina ba ya 'kuza kumina lapa, uma b' eza 'kutabata imali yabo; uma kanti ni ba tshela amanga, ngi ya 'ku ba nika imali. Uma ni nga ba tshelanga isiminya, ngi ya 'ku ba nika." I vume, i ti, " U z' u ba nike. Tina si kuluma isiminya; a si wa kulumi amanga."

Wa y amukela imali umnikaziyo imilozi.

Ya ti kutina, ya ti, " Hamba ni kuhle ke." Sa mangala uma i ti, a si hambe kahle, si nga i boni. Ya ti, " Wo si konzela ni kubantu bakwini bonke ekaya." Sa vuma, sa ti, " Yebo ke."

Ya ti, " Ni fike, n' enze ngakona loko e ngi ku tshiloyo."

Sa ti, " Ehe; si ya 'kwenza ngako kona e ni ku tshiloyo."

place," wherever they wish to go. The possessor of them cannot speak;[18] she usually says little, for she too enquires of the spirits, and says, " So-and-so, when you say so, do you tell the people who come to enquire of you, the truth?" In reply they say, they do tell the truth, and those who come to enquire will see it. She says, " Tell them the truth. They will come to me here if they come to take back their money; and if you tell them falsehoods, I shall give them back their money again. If you do not tell them the truth, I shall give it back to them." The spirits assent, saying, " You may give it back. For our parts we speak truly; we tell no lies."

So the possessor of the spirits took the money.

The spirits said to us, " Go in peace." We wondered when they bid us go in peace, without our seeing them. They told us to give their services to all our people at home. We said we would.

They said, " When you get home, do exactly what I have told you."

We replied, " Yes; we will do all you have told us to do."

---

[18] That is, divine. Those diviners who divine by means of the *imilozi* generally speak in a low muttering tone; and they sometimes have peculiar closed eyes. They " peep and mutter," reminding us of Isaiah viii. 19.

Sa hamba ke, sa fik' ekaya. Sa fika, umfana e se *h*lakanipile. Sa se si kuluma naye, si kuluma, w' eza ubaba end*h*lini; sa ti, "O, baba, i 'kuba si ng' azi inyanga. Si be si ti, 'U bulile umlozi,' ngokuzwa kwetu ezind*h*lebeni. I bule imilozi; ya ku kuluma konke—nokuzalwa kwetu, nokwelamana kwetu, nokuba lona e si kuyena umitshana wetu; ya ku k*q*eda konke. Umfana lo i te ka nakcala. I te si y' esaba, si ti u nesitutwane; tina sa vuma, sa ti, 'Ehe; si ti u nesitutwane.' Ya pika inyanga, ya ti, 'Ka naso; u ned*h*lozi. Id*h*lozi li ti, a ku pume umuzi.' Ya nuka impongo em*h*lope, i ti, ku ya 'ku*h*latshelwa yena, ku pume umuzi ke; ya ti, si ya 'ku mu kelela ikambi lom*h*laba, i *h*latshwe impongo leyo. I tize, ku nga buyela loku 'kufa, ya ti, a si ze si zoku i tabata imali yetu."

Wa ti ubaba, "O, i bulile, kanye nomitshana wetu. Si ya i zwa ukuti i bulile." Wa ti ubaba, "Ini po uma ba nga ngi tsheli ngi

So we went home. On our arrival we found the child better. As we were speaking with him, our father came into the house, and we said, "O father, we never had such confidence in a doctor. When we heard we said, 'The spirit has divined.' The spirits divined; they told us all things—our birth, and the order of our birth, and that he with whom we live is our cousin; they told us every thing. They said the boy has nothing the matter with him that will kill him. They said we are alarmed, thinking he has convulsions; and we assented, saying, 'Yes, yes; we think he has convulsions.' The diviner denied, saying, 'No; he has not convulsions; he is possessed by a spirit. The spirit says that your village must be moved.' The spirits pointed out a white goat, and directed that it should be sacrificed for the child, and the village be moved; and they ordered us to pluck for him Itongo-medicine, and sacrifice the goat. They said, if the disease returned, we were to go and take back our money."

Our father said, "O, they have divined, both as regards the disease and our relations with our cousin. We see they have divined. Why did not our ancestral spirits tell me in a dream that there

lelo a kona be ku funayo, ba vela ngokuba se b' eza 'kubulala umntwana njena na? Ku nani uma ba fike ngi lelo ba ngi tshele na into a ba i solayo, ba vela ukuba se be bulala umntwana njena, ba nga be be sa ngi tshela na? Abantu abafayo laba ba iziula! Ba vela ngokuba se ba bulala umntwana njena, be nga sa ngi tshelanga na?" Wa ti, "Hamba ni, no i tata impongo, bafana."

S' emuka, sa ya 'ku i tata impongo endhlini. Ya hlatshwa ke, wa telwa lo 'mfana ngenyongo. Umitshana wetu wa ya 'ku li ka ikambi; wa li kamela esitsheni, wa m puzisa lona, wa si lahla isitsha ngapandhle kwomuzi. Ya dhliwa imbuzi.

Kwa tiwa, sa ti ukubonga kwetu, "Uma si bona uma i lona idhlozi, si ya 'ubona um' a pile, a nga b' e sa gula; si ti umlozi w' enz' amanga um' e sa gula. Si ya 'ubona ngokupila; s' and' uma si ti, i kqinisile imilozi. A s' azi uma ni bulala umntwana nje. Abadala ba nani uma ni gulise bona? Idhlozi lihle eli putshwayo, was something which they wanted, instead of revealing themselves by coming to kill the child in this way? What prevented them from telling me in a dream what they complained about, instead of revealing themselves by coming to kill the child in this way, without saying any thing to me first? These dead men are fools! Why have they revealed themselves by killing the child in this way, without telling me? Go and fetch the goat, boys."

We went to fetch the goat from the house. We killed it, and poured the gall over the boy. Our cousin went to pluck the Itongo-medicine; he squeezed the juice into a cup, and gave it to the boy to drink, and left the cup outside the kraal.[19] The goat was eaten.

We worshipped the ancestral spirits, saying, "We shall see that the child is possessed by a spirit by his getting well, and not getting ill again; we shall say the spirit has lied if he is still ill. We shall see by his recovery; and shall then say, the spirits have told the truth. We do not understand why you have killed such a child as this. What prevents you from making old people ill? That is a good spirit which appears in dreams, and tells what it wants."

---

[10] It is a very common practice with native doctors to destroy the vessel which has been used to administer medicines.

li kuluma izindaba." Kw' enziwa njalo ukubonga kwetu.

Wa ti ubaba, " Se ngi ya 'upuma nomuzi kusasa, se u ya 'kuma entabeni. Ini ngi ti ngi be ngi hlezi kahle, ungani pela ngi sa dingile? Li kona inxiwa; ngi be ngi za 'ku li bheka kahle. Se ngi za 'ku u puma ke; li pole inxiwa, li be lihle, a nga be e sa gula umfana lo wami. A nga gula, ngi ya 'kuti a si lo idhlozi; nemilozi ngi ya 'ku i pikisa, ngi ti, a i bulanga kahle." Wa tsho njalo ke ubaba. Wa ti, " Inxiwa ngi ya 'ku li funa kusasa; si ze si hambe, mitshana wami, si yoku li funa inxiwa, si li hlole, loku ngi ti ngi sa dingile; ba be se be ngi bulala."

Ba hamba ke nomitshana wake kusasa, ba ya 'ku li hlola. Ba fika ezweni emahlongwa umfula, ba li hlola, ba li bheka, ba ti, "Lihle; ku fanele uma s' ake lapa, ngokub' amanzi a seduze." Ba buya, ba buyela ekaya.

Kwa ti kusasa sa tata izimbazo, sa ya 'kugaula. Sa gaula ke, wa ba se u y' esuka umuzi, u ya puma ngapakati kwowomitshana wetu;

Such were the words with which we addressed the spirits.

Our father said, " I shall now quit this place with my village in the morning, and put it in a place by itself. Why, when I thought I was living in peace, am I still obliged to be a wanderer? There is a site of an old village; I will examine it well. I shall now remove the village; may the new place be healthy and good, and this boy of mine be no longer ill. If he is still ill, I shall say he is not possessed with a spirit; and I will quarrel with the spirits, and say they have not divined properly." Our father said thus. He said, " I will look at the new site in the morning; let us go together, my cousin, and look at the new site, and inspect it well, for I say I am still a wanderer; for the ancestral spirits have killed me for staying here."

So he and his cousin went in the morning to inspect the site. They went to a place on the river Umathlongwa, and thoroughly inspected it and thought it good, and that it was a proper place for us to build on, for there was water near. They returned home.

In the morning we took our axes, and went to cut wattles and poles for the village. When we had finished cutting, the people of our village left that of our cousin

sa ba se si ya w aka, si ya u kqeda. Umfana ka pindanga a gule. Kwa ba njengokutsho kwomlozi owa ti, ' Ka yi 'kupinda a gule ;' ka gulanga. Wa za wa kula, wa kubela esibayeni, w' alusa amatole ; wa za wa buya wa puma ematoleni nezimbuzi, wa buya wa kw alusa konke, kanye namatole nezimbuzi nezimvu nezinkomo. Wa za wa ba indoda. Igama lake Umpini. Se ku indoda, u kutele. Ngonyaka o za 'uvela u za 'kusenga.

Umkaukazi igama lomnikaziyo, owesifazana. A si yo indoda, umfazi. Wa s' azi ngokukuleka, se si fikile kuye ; ngokuba nati sa tshelwa abanye abantu aba ka ba ya 'kubula kuyena, ba ti, u ya bula kakulu. W ake emtwalume enzansi, elwandhle, kude nati. Ku lalwa kanye endhleleni, ku ya sa ku ya fikwa.

Uguaise.

and went to it, and then we completed it. The boy was not ill any more. It turned out in accordance with the word of the spirit ; he was not ill again. At length he took out the calves at milking time, and herded the calves ; at length he not only herded the calves and goats, but all the cattle—calves, goats, sheep, and cows. And at length he grew to be a man. His name is Umpini. He is now a diligent man. Next year he will milk the cows.

The name of the woman with the familiar spirits is Umkaukazi. It was not a man, but a woman. She saw us for the first time when we saluted her on our arrival ; for we too had been told by others that she was a great diviner. She lived on the Umtwalume by the sea, at a distance from us. It is a day and a half's journey from this.[20]

---

[20] The Hebrew Ovoth, according to Gesenius, was "a soothsayer who evoked the manes of the dead by incantations and magical songs in order to give answers as to future and doubtful things." The demon or familiar spirit spoke in a half-whisper, half-whistling voice ; and the Septuagint render the word by "ventriloquist," just as those who have witnessed divination by the *imilozi* have been disposed to attribute the phenomenon to ventriloquism.

Among the Polynesians the ancestral spirits are believed to speak to those who enquire of them with a similar mysterious voice, which there too is ascribed to ventriloquism. (See *Westminster Review*, No. XLII., April 1862, p. 313.)

HEAVEN-DOCTORS, &c.

Heaven-herds.[21]   *Rain-doctors.*

Isikqoto a s' a*h*lukene kakulu nonyazi; si ti kokubili ku impi yenkosi e si tshaywa ngayo lapa

We do not make a great distinction between hail and lightning; we say, each is an army of the lord who smites us in this world.

---

[21] *Heaven-herds;* or Sky-herds.

Abalusi bezulu ku tiwa b' alusa izulu, ngokuba ku ti ngesikati sokuh*l*oma kwalo ba bone masinyane ukuba izulu nam*hl*a nje libi, li pumile ekutuleni, li pumela ukwenza kabi; ku fudumale in*hl*iziyo zabalusi, ba nga be be sa ncibilika, nokud*hl*a ku ng' c*h*li, ba ngenwe ivuso, ku nga ti ku za impi yoku ba bulala. Ku ze ku ti gidi isibindi lapa se li fikile. Ba pume, ba li k*q*ok*q*e, be linga uku li buyisela emuva lapa li pume kona; b' ale amatshe ukuba a we, ngokwazi ukuba a ya 'kuk*q*eda uku*hl*a notshani nemiti. Ngaloko ke ba abalusi bokwalusa, ukuze izulu li nga fo*hl*i, li zenzele ezintweni. A ba kalimi imvula, i lungile yona; ba kalima unyazi nesikqoto; ba kalima kulowo 'muzi lapa b' emi kona unyazi.

Heaven-herds are said to herd the heaven, because when it is overcast, they at once see that the heaven is bad, and has ceased to be calm, and has gone out to do evil; and the hearts of the herds are kindled; they are no longer happy, are unable to swallow any food, and are struck with fear, as though an enemy was coming to kill them. At last they become brave when the lightning begins to flash. They quit their huts and drive it away, trying to make it return to whence it came; they forbid the hailstones to fall, because they know that they will destroy the food, the grass, and the trees. They are therefore herds who herd the heaven, that it may not break out and do its will on the property of people. They do not turn back the rain, for it is good; they turn back the lightning and the hail; they turn back the lightning from the village where they live.

emhlabeni. S' ahlukene kodwa ngokwenza kwaso; unyazi lu nokwenza kwalo; kepa isikqoto ku y' ezwakala lapo si vela ngakona; ngokuba ngemva kwodumo olukulu ku zwakala umsindo omkulu ezulwini u hhubisa kwezinkobe se zi tsha. Kepa aba izinyanga zokwalusa, uma ku zwakala loko, ba ya puma masinyane, si s' ezwakala kude, ba kqala ukuba ba base esolweni, b' enzela ukuti noma li nga ka fiki eduze, li s' ezwakala kude, a li ti li fika eduze li be se li dumele, nokukuza ku size. Ngokuba uma inyanga lapo izulu li duma a ya kqala i pume, ya hlala endhlini kwa za kwa fika izulu, noma i puma uma se li fikile, a i se namandhla okunqoba isikqoto leso; ngokuba kulukuni uku si buyisela emuva uma se si fikile.

Zi ti ngokuhlomela kwazo, zi li zwa li sa ndindizela, nazo zi kqale ukuzilungisa, ukuze zi nga kohliseki. Ngokuba isikqoto leso, uma

We distinguish them, however, by the effect of the hail, which is different from that of the lightning; and the hail is heard in the direction from which it is coming; for after great thunder there is heard a great sound in the sky, which resembles the singing of maize in a pot when the water has boiled away. And the doctors, who are herds of the sky, when they hear that, go out at once, whilst the sound of the hail is still afar off, and begin to light a fire in the isolo;[22] they do this before it has come near, whilst it is still audible at a distance, that when it comes near it may have lost its power, and chiding[23] be sufficient. For if when it thunders the doctor does not at once go out, but stays indoors till the hail comes, even should he go out when it has come, he has no longer power to overcome the hail; for it is difficult to make it turn back again when once it has come.

As regards their preparing for the contest, when they hear the sky rumbling, they too begin to get themselves ready, that they may not be conquered. For as to

---

[22] *Isolo* is a fireplace outside the kraal, but near it, where medicines capable of influencing the heaven—heaven-medicines—are burnt.

[23] That is, by burning the heaven-medicines whilst the hail is still distant, they diminish its power, so that when it comes, if it should be able to come at all, it may be unable to do any harm; but may be readily made to obey the doctor's command to depart.

inyanga i nga zili ukudhla, ku tiwa uma amatshe e i tshaya kakulu i seduze engozini ; ku tiwa amatshe lawo a bonakalisa ukuti a i se namandhla okumelana nonyazi. I ya 'kuswela ukuba i buye i hlanziswe ngakumbe, ukuze i be nesibindi. Ngokuba uma i bona ekwaluseni kwayo i nga tobi noma isikqoto noma unyazi, loko kokobili, a i sa melwa 'sibindi, i se i y' esaba ; noma i bona unyazi lu vimba amehlo ayo i y' esaba, i fise ukungena endhlini.

I loko ke abantu abamnyama a ba kuluma ngako ukuti, ku kona amandhla kubantu abamnyama ; ngokuba be ti ulaka olu vela ezulwini lonke, ba ya lw azi uku lu keima, lawo amandhla amabili, unyazi nesikqoto. A ngi tsho ukuti nezulu uku li nisa ba ya kw azi ; kepa ba tsho bona ukuti ba ya kw azi.

Kodwa kakulu i loku oku b' enza amehlo amnyama, ngokuba a

the hail, if a doctor has not fasted, it is said if the hail-stones strike him much he is near to danger ; and it is said that the hail-stones make it manifest that he has no longer any power to contend with the lightning.[24] And he will require to be again purified a second time, that he may have courage. For if whilst herding[25] he observes that he cannot subject either the hail or the lightning, he has no longer any courage, but is afraid ; and even if he see the lightning dazzle his eyes, he is afraid, and wishes to go indoors.

It is this then about which black men speak, when they say that black men have power ; for they say that they know how to quell the wrath which comes from the whole heaven, that is, the two powers, lightning and hail. I do not say they know also how to make the sky rain ; but they say they know.

But it is especially this which darkens their eyes, for they do not

---

[24] *Ukumelana nezulu,—ukumelana nonyazi,—*to counteract the heaven or the lightning,—is an expression we shall often meet with. I point out, without being able to say whether there is any similarity in meaning, a passage—Ps. lxxiii. 9—" They set their mouth against the heaven," which we shall best render by, *Ba melana ngomlomo wabo nezulu.* No doubt the heaven in the Hebrew Scriptures is often synonymous with God ; in other places it is spoken of as an object of idol-adoration. There were sorcerers, diviners, and those with familiar spirits known to the Hebrews ; there might also have been rain-doctors and sky-doctors.

[25] That is, whilst endeavouring to turn back the storm.

ba tsho ukuti, lu kona olunye ulaka ngapand*h*le kwalolu a se be lu funele imiti yoku lw a*h*lula.

Isik*q*oto lesi ke izinyanga ezindaweni zonke; noma ku kona inkosi esizweni esitile, abantu a ba tsho ngamabele ukuti, "Amabele lawo si wa d*h*la ngenkosi le;" ba ti, "La 'mabele si wa d*h*la ngokabani; ngokuba li ya ti li futuzele, si nga s' azi ukuba li ya 'kubuyela kwenye indawo, a ti a nga kwitshiza, 'enze konke, si me 'sibindi."

Nank' ukuduma; uma izulu li ya duma, li nga leti 'matshe, li k*q*ube unyazi, a ba i beki inyanga yesik*q*oto, ba beka inyanga yonyazi, ukuba i pume, i memeze; b' eme 'sibindi uma umalusi 'alusile pand*h*le. Kepa uma e nge ko lowo 'malusi, ku kitshwa nengubo yake, i bekwe pand*h*le. Y enziwe uku nga ti uk*q*obo lwake.

I loko ke ukwenza kwezinyanga ezalusayo izulu. Ngokuba uma izulu li ya duma, li k*q*inisile, inyanga i ya k*q*ala ukunyakama,

say there is any other wrath but that, for which they have already found medicines, which are capable of subduing it.

The hail then has its doctors in all places; and though there is a chief in a certain nation, the people do not say, "We have corn to eat through the power of the chief;" but they say, "We have corn to eat through the son of So-and-so; for when the sky rolls cloud upon cloud, and we do not know that it will go back to another place, he can work diligently and do all that is necessary, and we have no more any fear."

There is thunder; if it[26] thunders without hailing, but hurls lightning, they do not appoint an inyanga of hail to herd, but an inyanga of lightning to go out and shout; and take courage when there is a heaven-herd herding outside the house. But if the herd is not at home, they take his blanket, and put it outside. The blanket is made, as it were, the herd himself.

This then is what those izinyanga do who herd the heaven. For if it thunders excessively, the inyanga begins to frown, that he

---

[26] *It—izulu*, throughout spoken of as though it was a person, possessed of intelligence. The literal translation of the sentence is: There is thunder; if the heaven thunders, without bringing hailstones, but urges on the lightning.

ukuba i *k*lwe nayo njengezulu li *k*loma. Uma abantu bakona end*h*lini, noma i nga ka pumi, uma abantu be kuluma ngokuxxokozela, i ya ba tiba ngokuti, "Tula ni, ni ti nya." Ngokuba i ti mayo in*h*liziyo yayo i se i futuzele, njengaloko nalo li za ugamand*h*la; a i be i sa tanda ukuba ku kulume omunye umuntu, 'kupela i yo yodwa e kulumayo ngokumemeza. Futi uma u hamba nayo end*h*leleni, izulu la ni kandanisa ni se kude nemizi, noma u be u hamba pambi, yona i semuva, i ya 'kutsho kuwe ukuti, "D*h*lula, u hambe pambili;" yona i hambe emuva kude nawe; ngokuba i ti uma u hamba emuva kwayo u ya 'kuzuza ingozi, ngokuba izulu li ti u ya i bulala. Inyanga i ku d*h*lulise ukuhamba pambili ni ze ni fike ekaya.

Ku njalo loko 'kwenza kwezulu nezinyanga; ngokuba abantu abamnyama ba ya kolwa kuloko 'kukuza izulu nokutiba isik*g*oto. Lezo 'zinto zombili a ba kcabangi ngazo ukuti noma be ti ba ya z' azi, ba ziko*h*lisa; ba ti bona ku isi-

too may be dark as the heaven when it is covered with clouds. If the people of the house, whether he has gone out or not, speak very loudly, he silences them, saying, "Be still altogether." For his heart too is gathering clouds, as the heaven when it is coming quickly; and he no longer wishes that any one else should speak, but himself only by shouting. And if you go with him on a journey, and it suddenly thunders whilst you are at a distance from any village, and you are going first and he following, he will say to you, "Go on in front;" and he will follow at some distance from you; for he says if you go behind him you will meet with an accident, for the heaven will think you are killing him.[27] And he makes you go on in front till you reach home.

Such then is the action of the heaven and of the inyanga; for black men believe in that scolding of the heaven, and that silencing of the hail. They do not imagine that when they say they know these things, they deceive themselves; they say that it is true

---

[27] From this it is clear that we are not to regard the heaven-herd as an opponent of the heaven; but as a priest to whom is entrusted the power of prevailing mediation. He is under the protection of the heaven; and his enemies, real or supposed, are liable to be destroyed by it, whilst he is safe so long as he is observant of the laws of his office. Heathen have sometimes asked me to pray for rain because I am one whose office it is "ukumelana nenkosi," to contend with God. Compare Gen. xxxii. 24—28. And see below, where the heaven avenges the death of the rain-doctor.

minya loko ukuba inyanga yokwalusa i namandhla okumelana nonyazi nesikqoto; ngokuba ba ti labo 'bantu, uma si buza tina, "Si ng' azi ukuba loko 'kwenza ba kw enza ngesibindi a ba si tate pi ukumelana nezulu na."

Ba ti, ku ti uma li za 'kuhloma, noma amafu e nga ka bonakali ukuba li za 'kuduma kabuhlungu, inhliziyo yenyanga i be se i zwile ngokuti ku kona ukufudumala ngapakati, umuntu u vuswa ukutukutela; lapa izulu li ya kqala ukuhloma nje, naye a hlwe njengalo. Ngokuba be ti bona, se ba li gcaba, ba li dhla. Uku li dhla loku ba tsho ngokuba li dhla inkomo, kepa lezo 'zinkomo i ya

that the heaven-herd[28] is able to contend with the lightning and hail; for these people say, if we ask them, that they do not understand where they get the courage with which they contend with the heaven.

They say that when the heaven is about to be clouded,[29] and before the clouds appear or it is evident that it is about to thunder excessively, the inyanga's heart already feels, for there is heat within him, and he is excited by anger; when the sky just begins to be clouded, he too becomes dark like it. For the doctors say they scarify with the heaven,[30] and eat it. To eat the heaven is this, for the heaven eats cattle, and the

---

[28] Or sky-doctor, heaven meaning the sky, which is not supposed to be very high above the earth.

[29] Lit., about to arm.

[30] I have translated literally here, but it will be scarcely intelligible to the English reader without explanation. The natives say 'they scarify with the heaven, that is, make scarifications and rub in medicines, and eat it. The heaven is here used for those substances in which it, or its power or virtue, is supposed to be. A bullock struck with lightning is supposed to have the heaven, or power of the heaven, in it; so the thunderbolt which comes from heaven; and the fabulous bird which is supposed to descend in a thunder storm. Therefore when they say they scarify with the heaven, they mean that the doctors make scarifications in their own bodies and rub in medicines mixed with the flesh of a bullock struck with lightning, or with the thunderbolt, or with the flesh of the *inyoni-yezulu*, the lightning-bird. And "eating the heaven" means in like manner eating those things in which the heaven, or its power or virtue, is supposed to be. By this practice they are brought into sympathy with the heaven,—feel with it, know when it is going to thunder, and are able to counteract it. Here again we see the homœopathic principle coming out in their therapeutics, as we do in so many other instances; *similia similibus*,—lightning by lightning.

tatwa inyama yazo, i bekwe ode-ngezini, inyanga i i d/ɦle ngoku i ucinda, i pitikezwe nemiti yayo; ngokuba ku ti lapo li /ɦlabe kona pansi, izinyanga zi ti u kona umsuka o salela pansi, kepa lowo 'msuka ku tiwa inyela; ba ya li mba ba ze ba li fumane, ba sebenze ngalo; ba tsho ke nkuti, isibindi leso a ba naso sokumelana nezulu i lelo 'nyela eli funyanwa lapo izulu li /ɦlabe kona. Kakulu nenyoni leyo e ku tiwa eyezulu;

doctor takes the flesh of such cattle, and places it in a sherd, and the doctor eats it whilst hot,[31] mixed with his medicines; for where the lightning strikes the ground, the doctors say there is something resembling the shank of an assagai,[32] which remains in the earth, and this thing is called a thunderbolt; they dig till they find it,[33] and use it as a heaven-medicine; and so they say that the courage which they possess of contending with the heaven is that thunderbolt, which is found where the lightning has struck. Especially the bird also which is called the lightning-bird,[34] they

---

[31] *Ukuncinda*, makes an *izembe*, and eats it, see p. 290, note 52.

[32] *Umsuka* is the shank of an assagai, or of a native pick, or any thing of that kind.

[33] It is said that the doctors are directed to the place where the thunderbolt is by watching during a storm, and, going to the place where they suppose they saw the lightning strike, they find a heap of jelly-like substance over the spot where the bolt entered, and digging find it.

[34] In the legends of the American Indians we meet with accounts of Thunder-birds, or Cloud-birds. "They frequently explain the thunder as the sound of the cloud-bird flapping his wings, and the lightning as the fire that flashes from his tracks, like the sparks which the buffalo scatters when he scours over the stony plain." A metaphor which probably arose from personifying the clouds, and supposing that motion meant life, and where there was a voice there must be a living being to utter it; like the Maruts or Storm-gods of the Hindoo. The metaphor may have been a simple metaphor at first, to become at last to the minds of the masses a truth expressing a fact of nature. *(Brinton's Myths of the New World, p. 102—104.)*—A Dahcotah thus explains the theory of thunder:—"Thunder is a large bird, flying through the air; its bright tracks are seen in the heavens, before you hear the clapping of its wings. But it is the young ones that do the mischief. The parent bird would not hurt a Dahcotah. Long ago a thunder-bird fell from the heavens; and our fathers saw it as it

ngokuba i yona umngomo leyo 'nyoni emitini yonke. Uma inyanga i nge nayo leyo 'nyoni, inyanga kodwa, i nge melwe 'sibindi njengaleyo e nayo, eya i d*h*layo. Ngokuba leyo 'nyoni izinyanga zi gaba ngaleyo 'nyoni; ngokuba i namafuta; ku tiwa amafuta i wona e inyanga i siza ngawo kakulu, noma ku kona umuntu owa futwa izulu, la m shiya; kepa la m shiya nokukulu ukwesaba. Uma li ya duma ka melwa 'sibindi, u ya *h*lupeka njalonjalo; ka *h*lupeki en*h*liziyweni kodwa; ku ya bonakala uku*h*lupeka kwake ngokuba u ya nyakaza njalonjalo end*h*lini, e swele indawo lapo nga e zifaka kona. Kepa inyanga leyo uma ya bizwa ukuba i ze 'ku m nika lona izulu, uma se li duma ngenuva u ya tsho, a ti, "Inyanga ya ng' clapa; a ngi s' esabi."

say that that is the most powerful among all lightning-medicines. If a doctor does not possess it, but is a doctor only, he cannot have courage as that doctor can who possesses the lightning-bird, and who has eaten it. For doctors make their boast of this bird; for it is fat, and it is said to be the fat especially with which the doctors treat those who are struck, when one has been slightly struck and then left; but has been left full of dread. If it thunders he has no courage, and is much troubled at all times; he is not troubled mentally only; it is evident that he is troubled, for he continually moves about in the house, and seeks a place where he may hide himself. But if the doctor has been summoned to come and give him heaven-medicine,[35] then after that if it thunders he says, "The doctor has given me medicine; I am no longer afraid."

---

lay not far from the Little Crow's village." *(Dahcotah; or, Life and Legends of the Sioux. By Mrs. Mary Eastman, p.* 191.) See also the legend of Unktahe and the Thunder-bird. Cloudy-Sky, during one of his earthly sojournings, had allied himself with the thunder-birds to fight against the spirits of the waters, and with his own hand killed the son of Unktahe, the God of rivers. For this he was doomed to death on his fourth appearance on earth as a great medicine-man. *(Id., p.* 213, *&c.)*—Catlin relates that some Indians led him to "The Thunder's nest," where it is supposed the thunder-bird, a very small bird indeed, hatches its eggs, and the thunder is supposed to come out of the egg. *(Life among the Indians, p.* 166.)—Jupiter's Eagle probably has some connection with such legends.

[35] Lit., the very heaven, meaning thereby, the fat of the lightning-bird, or its flesh, or portion of a thunder-bolt.

Ngokuba leyo 'nyoni, baningi aba i bonileyo ngamehlo. Kepa kakulu izinyanga nabantu aba i bone ngesikati sokuduma kwezulu, ukuba unyazi lu tshaye pansi; i ya sala. Uma u kona umuntu eduze naleyo 'ndawo, u ya i bona ezinkungwini pansi, a ye 'ku i bulala. Uma e se i bulele, a kqale ukubalisa ngokuti, "Umakazi ngi ya 'kuhamba nje na, loku ngi bulele le inyoni e ngi nga i bonanga? A si yo nje le inyoni e ku tshiwo ukuti, i kona inyoni yezulu e hamba nonyazi?" U ya balisa ngokuba e i bona ukuma kwayo ku nga fani nokwezinyoni a kade e zi bona; a bone ku kodwa okwayo, ngokuba i ya bazizela izimpape zayo. Umuntu a nga ti ibomvu; a bone ukuti, "Ai; iluhlaza." Kepa uma e bhekisisile a nga ti, "Kqa, i pakati kwaloko, ngi ku bona." Kepa mina ngi lu bonile upape lwayo uma ngi se semsunduzi; ngokuba ngi be ngi swele njalonjalo ukubona lowo 'mbala wenyoni; kepa nga za nga lu bona upape lwayo. Lowo 'muntu owa

But as regards that bird, there are many who have seen it with their eyes. And especially doctors, and those persons who have seen it when it thunders and the lightning strikes the ground; the bird remains where the ground was struck. If there is any one near that place, he sees it in the fog on the ground, and goes and kills it. When he has killed it, he begins to be in doubt, saying, "Can it be that I shall continue to live as I have hitherto, seeing that I have killed this bird, which I never saw before? Is it not really that bird which it is said exists, the lightning-bird which goes with the lightning?" He is in doubt because he sees that its characteristics are not like those of birds which he has known for a long time; he sees that it is quite peculiar, for its feathers glisten. A man may think that it is red; again he sees that it is not so, it is green. But if he looks earnestly he may say, "No, it is something between the two colours, as I am looking at it." And I myself once saw a feather of this bird whilst I was living on the Umsunduzi; for I had wished for a long time to see the colour of the bird; and at length I saw one of its feathers. The man to whom it belonged

e lu pete wa lu kumula esikwameni sako; nga bona nembala, nga tsho ukuti, "Hau! olwenyoni esabekayo." Wa ngi bonisa netambo layo; la fana netambo li fakwe umtanjana omuncinyane wegazi nomtshwana o hlangana nompofana; nga bona imitshwe eminingi etanjeni layo, nga ti, "Nembala." I loko ke e nga ku zwa ngaleyo 'ndaba. Kwa pela ngaloko ke, e nga zibonela kona ngawami amehlo.

Izinyanga zokwalusa si kuluma ngomfanekiso, ngokuba umuntu owalusa izinkomo u nezikali negqokwe lemvula. Sa tata lelo 'gama lomalusi wezinkomo, si biza omelana nonyazi, ngokuba uma e lu tiba u ya memeza njengomfana wezinkomo; yena uma e ngena esibayeni nezikali zake, a tule nje, zi nge pume izinkomo; kepa ngokuhlohla ikwelo, izinkomo zi y' ezwa ukuba u ti nga z' aluka, ukuti a zi pume esibayeni. Na lowo 'malusi owalusa unyazi w enza njengalowo wezinkomo; w enza njalo ke ngokuhlohla ikwelo; a ti, "Tshui-i-i. Hamba, u ye le; u ng' ezi lapa." A pinde njalonjalo.

Lezo 'zinyanga zi tsho ukuti zi y' ezwana nezulu. I loku ukutsho

took it out of his bag; and truly I saw it, and said, "Indeed it is the feather of a dreadful bird." He also showed me one of its bones; it was like a bone in which are many little blood-vessels and many little grey lines; I saw many lines in the bone, and said, "Truly." This then is what I have heard on this matter, and that was confirmed by what I saw for myself with my own eyes.

When we say herding-doctors, we speak metaphorically, for a man who herds cattle has weapons and his rain-shield.[36] We take the name of a herder of cattle, and give it to one who counteracts the lightning, for when he keeps it back he shouts as a boy who is herding cattle; if he goes into the cattle-pen with his weapons and is silent, the cattle cannot go out; but by whistling the cattle understand that he tells them to go to the pastures, that is, to go out of the pen. And the herd that herds the lightning does the same as the herder of the cattle; he does as he does by whistling; he says, "Tshui-i-i. Depart, and go yonder; do not come here." He repeats this again and again.

Such doctors as these say they have a common feeling with the heaven. They say this because

---

[36] A small shield which is used as an umbrella to ward off rain and hail.

kwazo, ukuba ngesinye isikati ku tiwa inyanga etile i ya li tumela kwenye uku i linga, i bone uma inyanga e k*q*inileyo na. Kodwa a i i lingi eya miselwa i yo; i linga izinyanga ezinye e nga zi k*q*ondi uma za miselwa kanjani na; ngokuba i loku e i bona ngako ukuba inyanga impela, ngoku i buyisela lona, nayo i k*q*ale ukuputuzela ukungena end*hl*ini ukuzilungisa.

sometimes it is said a certain doctor sends the lightning[37] to another doctor to try him whether he is a powerful doctor or not. He does not try the doctor who appointed him; he tries others whose appointment he does not understand;[38] for it is this by which he sees that another is a doctor indeed, by his sending back to him the lightning, and he too begins to bustle about and to enter his house to set himself in order.[39]

---

[37] Lit., the heaven, or sky.

[38] Here again we have apparently an intimation that the *izinyanga* were priests—not self-appointed, but commissioned by others who preceded them. But there appears also to have been dissidents—those whose commission was not known. Man is the same every where.

[39] We find similar trials of skill among sorcerers of other countries. It is said a German sorcerer was called to see if he could not "extinguish" our far-famed sorcerer Roger Bacon. He raised a spirit which he ordered to carry off Roger Bacon. But Roger was too strong for the German, and the raised spirit, instead of taking away Roger as commanded, carried off his own master.—In like manner "the priest Eirikur" having snatched by his sorcery from the hands of "the good folk of Sída" a murderer who was condemned to lose his head,—a not very priestly act, it may be,—they "hired a man from the West firths who dabbled in magic to send a great cat to slay Eirikur." Eirikur's magic and prophetic power could not protect him from this cat. The sender worked,—the "sending" was sent,—and unlooked-for rushed upon its victim; and Eirikur was saved, not by magic and inner sight, but by "quickness" and help of a pupil in sorcery. And "Puss," that is, the "sending," soon lay dead upon the ground. Eirikur had triumphed. But triumph is nothing without revenge. He must teach the people that Eirikur—priest and sorcerer, strange but not uncommon combination—must not be trifled with. So he "despatched a sending to the man in the West firths, and put an end to him almost as quickly as to his goblin-cat." *(Icelandic Legends, p. 262.)*

Kwa ti ngesikati esadhlulayo ukuhambela kwami kwiti, nga fika nga lala; kwa ti ku sa, ntambama izulu la hloma, la ba libi kakulu, ngesikati umbila u kahlela. Nga ngi hlezi emnyango, li duma kakulu; nomne wetu u inyanga, wa ngena endhlini e gijima, w' etula ihau lake nezikqu zake, wa puma. Li ti uma li tsho ngamandhla, naye wa tsho ngamandhla ukumemeza nokuhlohla ikwelo. Nga buza kumame, nga ti, "Lo 'muntu w enza ni na?" Wa ti, "Musa ukukuluma, loko uma ku nje a ku be ku sa kulunywa. Umalusi." Nga tula ke. Kepa la w' chlisa amatshe amaningi. Nga ti u za 'kufa, ngokuba ng' ezwa ukutshaya kwawo chawini lake; kwa nga ku keitekele umbila. Kepa noko wa bangeka, ka ngenanga endhlini. Na ngonyazi l' enze njalo; ka z' a ngena la za la sa.

Ku te kusasa ng' ezwa ku tiwa emzini kababekazi enzansi, enyameni, Umahlati u te u ya puma, izinyanga ezinkulu zi nga ka pumi; wa memeza kanye, e ti,

It happened in times past when I visited my people, on my arrival I lay down; on the following day in the afternoon the sky became overcast, and was very dark indeed; at the time when the maize was blossoming. I was sitting at the doorway whilst it was thundering excessively; and my brother who is a doctor entered the house, running, and took down his shield and his string of medicines, and went out. When it thundered aloud, he too shouted aloud, and whistled. I asked my mother what the man was doing. She replied, "Do not speak, for when it is like this no one any longer speaks. He is a heaven-herd." So I was silent. And the heaven cast down many hail-stones. And I thought he would die, for I heard them striking on his shield; it was as though maize had been thrown on him. But although he was resisted very much, he did not enter the house. And as regards the lightning, in like manner the heaven resisted him; but he did not enter the house until it was bright again.

In the morning I heard it said that at my uncle's village, at Inyama, down the river, one Umathlati said he would go out before the great doctors went out; he shouted aloud, saying, "Depart,

"Muka, u ye le." Kwa ti swiswi emzimbeni, wa ngena nyovane end*h*lini. Wa pinda nomunye, wa ti u ya memeza, la m vimba umlomo. Ngaleyo 'mini la u fulatela lowo 'muzi; wa ba owalo, la zenzela. Ba *h*lala ngezind*h*lu; la wa k*q*eda amabele, la wa ti nya.

Kepa nga ti uma ngi ku zwe loko, nga ti, "Kanti inyanga enjengaleyo i y' a*h*luleka na? Si ya 'kud*h*la ni nonyaka, loku z' a*h*lulekile ngokwalusa na?"
Kwa tiwa, "A ba zilanga. B' a*h*lulekile nje."

and go yonder." But the hail smote loudly on his body, and he came into the house backwards. Another went out, and when he shouted, the heaven stopped his mouth. On that day the heaven turned its back[40] on the village; it was entirely in its power, and it did its will. They remained in their houses; it entirely destroyed the corn.

When I heard this I said, "Forsooth is such a doctor as that conquered? What shall we eat this year, since they have been unable to herd?"
They replied, "They did not fast.[41] They are therefore conquered."

---

[40] It is well to note this use of *fulatela*; to turn the back on an enemy means to have conquered him utterly.

[41] Here we find fasting—abstinence from food and labour—one of the conditions of successful performance of the duties of an office. There is this saying among the natives, "*Umzimba ow esutuyo njalonjalo u nge bone kuhle oku-imfihlo*," The continually stuffed body cannot see secret things. And they have no faith in a *fat* diviner—do not believe that he can divine. Their diviners fast often, and are worn out by fastings, sometimes of several days' duration, when they become partially or wholly ecstatic, and see visions, &c. This is very instructive, and throws light on the results of fasting among those who suppose themselves to be the objects of a divine revelation.

It is curious how universally a system of fasting prevails amongst different peoples, being regarded as a merit, or as a means of preparation for a work, or for the reception of a revelation from a superior power, or as an expression of self-contrition, or as a means of producing a high order of spirituality. It would be interesting to trace this custom to its root, but this is not the place for such a subject. We may, however, refer to some instances among the Polynesians, where neglect of fasting by others is supposed to have seriously interfered with the work of some great man :—

"Maui then left his brothers with their canoe, and returned to the village; but before he went he said to them, 'After I am gone, be

Loku 'kuzila oku tshiwoyo ngomuntu owalusayo, ku tiwa inyanga eya mu misayo i ti, " Ka muse	As regards this fasting which is spoken of a man that herds the sky, it is said that the doctor who appoints him says, " Let him not

courageous and patient; do not eat food until I return, and do not let our fish be cut up, but rather leave it until I have carried an offering to the gods from this great haul of fish, and until I have found a priest, that fitting prayers and sacrifices may be offered to the god, and the necessary rites be completed in order. We shall thus all be purified. I will then return, and we can cut up this fish in safety, and it shall be fairly portioned out to this one, and to that one, and to that other; and on my arrival you shall each have your due share of it, and return to your homes joyfully; and what we leave behind us will keep good, and that which we take away with us, returning, will be good too.'

" Maui had hardly gone, after saying all this to them, than his brothers trampled under their feet the words they had heard him speak. They began at once to eat food, and to cut up the fish. When they did this, Maui had not yet arrived at the sacred place, in the presence of the god; had he previously reached the sacred place, the heart of the deity would have been appeased with the offering of a portion of the fish which had been caught by his disciples, and all the male and female deities would have partaken of their portions of the sacrifice. Alas! alas! those foolish, thoughtless brothers of his cut up the fish, and behold the gods turned with wrath upon them, on account of the fish which they had thus cut up without having made a fitting sacrifice. Then, indeed, the fish began to toss about his head from side to side, and to lash his tail, and the fins upon his back, and his lower jaw. Ah! ah! well done Tangaroa, it springs about on shore as briskly as if it was in the water.

" That is the reason that this island is now so rough and uneven—that here stands a mountain—that there lies a plain—that here descends a vale—that there rises a cliff. If the brothers of Maui had not acted so deceitfully, the huge fish would have lain flat and smooth, and would have remained as a model for the rest of the earth, for the present generation of men. This, which has just been recounted, is the second evil which took place after the separation of Heaven from Earth." *(Polynesian Mythology. By Sir George Grey. Pp. 43—45.)*

So when the powerful magician Ngatoro-i-rangi wished to ascend to the snow covered top of Mount Tongariro he said to his companions, " Remember now, do not you, who I am going to leave behind, taste food from the time I leave you until I return, when we will all feast together." Then he began to ascend the mountain, but he had not quite got to the summit when those he had left behind began to eat food, and he therefore found the greatest difficulty in reaching the summit of the mountain, and the hero nearly perished in the attempt. *(Id., p. 156.)*

ukudhla uma e piwa utshwala bu isikope." Futi, "Ka muse ukudhla imifino e nga shwamanga." Futi, "Ka muse ukukcapuna eziko, uma izinkobe zi nga k' epulwa." Futi, "Ka muse ukudhla inyama, uma inkomo i nga ka boboswa." Futi, "Ka muse ukudhla izindumba uma e nga zi nikwanga." I loko ukuzila ukudhla okutshiwoyo izinyanga. Noma e lambile, wa fumana abantu be dhla utshwala, uma bu nga se gcwaliswe, a nga ti ukuti, "Mina kambe ni y' azi ukuba ngi y' alusa."

Umuntu wemvula nga m bona ebuncinyaneni bami uma ngi ngangongangamana; ibizo lake ku tiwa Umkqackana. Wa be inyanga enkulu na kwazulu yokunisa drink if he is given beer in a cup that is not full." And, "Let him not eat herbs before the feast of firstfruits."[42] And, "Let him not take a handful of boiled maize from the fireplace, if the maize has not been taken from the pot." And, "Let him not eat the flesh of a bullock until it has been opened." And, "Let him not eat izindumba if he has not been given them." This is the fasting which the doctors speak of. And if a man is hungry and come to men who are drinking[43] beer, if the vessel is not full, he would say, "For my part indeed you know that I herd the heaven."

When I was young, about the size of Ungangamana, I saw a rain-man;[44] his name was Umkqackana. He was a great doctor even among the Amazulu,[45] skil-

[42] At the period of the year when the new food is ripe, varying with different places, the chief summons all his people to a festival, (which is called *ukudhlala umkosi;*) all the people make beer, which they take with them to the chief's village; at the chief's village, too, much beer is made. When the people are assembled the chief has oxen killed by his soldiers, and there is a great feast of one day with singing and dancing. This is called *ukushwama*, and the people return to their homes and begin to eat the new produce. If any one is known to eat new food before this festival he is regarded as an *umtakati*, and is killed, or has all his cattle taken away.

[43] The natives speak of beer as food,—and of eating it, and appeasing hunger by it. They also call snuff food, and speak of eating it.

[44] I translate literally, a rain-man or man of rain, a rain-doctor, one capable of causing rain or drought.

[45] Lit., In the house, country, or nation of Uzulu; that is, of the traditional founder or unkulunkulu of the Zulu nation.

imvula. Kepa kwazulu wa e nge vele kakulu enkosini ; ngokuba amakosi akwazulu a e nga vumi ukuba umuntu kazana nje ku tiwe u pata izulu ; ngokuba izulu kwa ku tiwa elenkosi yakona kupela. Ngaloko ke wa fi/tleka. Kepa e nga yekile uku li nisa ngasese. Wa za wa wela, ngokuba w' ezwa ku tiwa, " Izinyanga zonke zezulu a zi bulawe." W' ek*q*a, wa fika lapa esilungwini ; wa fika e nga pete 'luto, e hamba nje. Kepa kw' azisa ukuba u fika nje, u fikele kwabakubo aba m aziyo.

Wa tolwa inkosi yakwamad/tla- la ; nati e ya i si tolile ; ibizo layo ku tiwa Unjeje kasehhele. Kepa wa /tlala isikatshana, la ba li balele kakulu izulu. Ba k*q*ala abantu bakubo ukunyenyeza ngaye enkosini, ukuti, " Lowo 'muntu u m bona nje ; uma u keela kuye imvula, u nga ku keonisela.

ful in producing rain. But among the Amazulu he did not show himself much to the chief; for the chiefs of the house of Uzulu used not to allow a mere inferior[46] to be even said to have power over the heaven; for it was said that the heaven belonged only to the chief of that place. Umk*q*aekana therefore remained hidden. But he did not cease to produce rain in secret. At length he crossed to this side the Utukela, for he heard that Utshaka had said, " Let all the heaven-doctors be killed." He escaped, and came among the English ; he came here without any property, by himself alone.[47] He came without any thing, because he came to his own relations.

He became a dependent of the chief of the Amadhlala ; it is the same to whom we were subject ; his name was Unjeje, the son of Usechele. And when he had staid a short time, the heaven became very hot and dry.[48] His own people began to whisper about him to the chief, saying, " You see that man ; if you ask him, he can cause the rain to drop for you.

---

[46] *Uzana*, dim. of *ize*, nothing ; *izana*, a little nothing, that is, something less than nothing itself. *Uzana*, a proper name, meaning *The-less-than-nothing-man*. All men of low degree are called *abantwana bakazana*, Children of Uzana,—this hypothetical man of naught.

[47] Lit., Just walking, that is, without any incumbrances of property or cattle.

[48] There was long continued drought and hot weather.

Inyanga enkulu pezu kwazo zonke izinyanga."

Kepa loko kwa hamba kancinyane, kwa za kwa pumela obala; s' ezwa sonke ukuba Umk*q*ackana u inyanga yemvula. Inkosi i keelile kuye ukuti, ka ke enze, i bone uma ku isiminya loko na. Kepa—ngokuba ngalesi 'sikati izulu la li balela—ng' ezwa ku tiwa, " U ti, 'A ba li bheke ngosuku lokuti; li ya 'kuna.'"

Kepa w' emuka wa ya e*hl*atini, e ya 'kulungisa izinto zake; wa zing' e hamba njalo, kwa za kwa fika leyo 'mini. Kwa ti ngam*hl*a li nayo, kwa tiwa, " Nembala u inyanga!" Kwa ba njalo ke njalonjalo. Wa piwa izinkomo, wa keeba masinyane.

Kepa ngemva kwalo 'nyaka izulu la ba lukuni ukuna. Ba m *hl*upa kakulu. Loko 'ku m *hl*upa nami nga m bona, nga m hhaukela, ngokuba ngi bona amadoda e fika na sebusuku e tshaya ngamawisa emnyango wend*hl*u yake, a m kipe, a ti, ka pume, a koke izinkomo zawo a m nika zona, ngokuba izulu a li sa ni. B' enza njalonjalo. Kepa a *hl*upeke kakulu, ngokuba ngesinye isikati a fike ekuseni, a m kipe; a baleke, a m jigijele

He is a great doctor above all other doctors."

And this was first spoken of a little, and at last openly; and we all heard that Umk*q*ackana was a rain-doctor. The chief asked him just to set to work, that he might see if it were true or not. And— for at that time the heaven was hot and dry—I heard it said, " Umk*q*ackana says, 'Let the people look at the heaven at such a time; it will rain.'"

And he went away into the forest to get his things ready; he went there continually, until the day he had mentioned came. And when it rained, the people said, " Truly, he is a doctor!" And it was always thus. He was given cattle, and very quickly became rich.

And after that year the heaven was hard, and it did not rain. The people persecuted him exceedingly. When he was persecuted I saw him and pitied him, for I saw men come even by night and smite his doorway with clubs, and take him out of his house, telling him to come out and give them back their cattle which they had given him, because the heaven no longer yielded rain. They did this constantly. And he was greatly troubled, for sometimes they came in the morning and took him out of his house; he fled, and they

ngamawisa; a baleke, a tshone ehlatini, li ze li tshone, e nga dhlanga, 'esaba ukuza ekaya; ngokuba ba be ti ba ya 'ku m bulala impela, uma imvula i nga ni. Kepa loko be ku tsho ngekeebo labo, ukuti i kona e za 'kwenza masinyane, ngokuba e ti, "Loku ngi za 'kufa na." Kepa izulu nga ku bona li ya na ngesinye isikati emkatini wokusebenza kwake.

Ku te ngomunye unyaka, uma ba bone ukuba izulu li ya tanda ukubulala amabele, ba m zonda kakulu. Ngaleso 'sikati nga ngi nga se ko. Nga se ngi lapa kwiti, emapepeteni. Ng' ezwa ku tiwa izulu li na nje kakulu, li gqiba Umkqackana u file. Ku tiwa ba m bulele ngobuti; a ba m bulele ngoku m gwaza. Ng' ezwa loko ke; kwa tiwa, ba ya hlupeka labo 'bantu, ngokuba amasimu abo a ya kukuleka imvula. I loko ke e nga ku zwayo ngenyanga yemvula.

Kwa ti ngolunye usuku umfana wake, (o yena e be tandwa kakulu uyise, igama lake Unqeto; uma e ya ehlatini uyise u be hamba naye; ngokuba e ti u m tanda ngoba e tumeka; ngokuba uma umuntu e nisa izulu u swele umntwana ukuba a tume yena njalo, a nge nqabe

threw clubs at him; he ran away down into the bush, until the sun set, without eating, being afraid to go home; for they said they would really kill him, if it did not rain. But they said that through their subtlety, thinking that he would do what they wished at once, because he expected them to kill him. And I saw that it sometimes rained whilst he was working.

And on another year, when they saw that the heaven wished to destroy the corn, they hated him exceedingly. I was not there at that time. I was with my own people, the Amapepete. I heard it said that it rained excessively, that it might cover the dead body of Umkqackana with earth. It is said they poisoned him, and did not stab him. I heard it said that those people were troubled, for their gardens were carried away by a flood. This then is what I heard of this rain-doctor.

One day his son, (the one that was most dear to his father, named Unqeto, who went with his father to the forest when he went there; for he said he loved him because he could send him where he wished;[49] for if a man is causing it to rain, he requires a child, that he may send him constantly without refusing in the least, that the hea-

---

[49] Lit., *Send-able,*—ready to go on a mission.

nakanye, ukuze izulu li tambe,)— wa tsho ngemva kwokuncenga, wa ti, "Woza ni, ngi ye 'ku ni bonisa lapo ubaba e beka kona izinto zake zezulu." Sa hamba emini, s' alusile ngakona. Sa fumana empandwini ku kona izitsha zi sibekelwe, nebakza lokupe*h*la ; wa si bonisa loko 'kwenza kukayise, nemifunzana e botshwe ngenkon*h*lwane ; wa si bonisa nokupe*h*la kukayise. Kepa sa ku bona loko, s' esaba, a sa tanda ukungena, sa baleka njeya, ngokuti li funa izulu li si tabate uma si pata imiti yenyanga. Sa m shiya pakati, sa baleka, sa ya ezinkomeni.

Ku pela ke leyo 'ndaba e nga i bonayo.

UMPENGULA MBANDA.

ven may be yielding,)—this son said to me, after I had earnestly besought him, " Come, and I will show you where my father placed his things with which he treated the heaven." We went at noon, having herded our cattle near the place. Under an overjutting rock we found covered vessels, and a churning stick ; he showed us what his father did, and little bundles of medicine bound with inkonthlwane ;[50] he showed us also how his father churned. But when we saw that we were afraid, and did not wish to go in, but ran away, thinking perhaps the lightning would strike us if we touched the medicines of the doctor. We left them under the rock, and ran away to the cattle.

This is the end of what I saw.

The Sky, Sun, Moon, and Stars.

IZULU e si li bonayo leli elilu*h*laza si ti idwala, li ye la *h*langanisa

THE blue heaven which we see we suppose is a rock,[51] and that it

---

[50] *Inkonthlwane*, a small tree whose bark is white, and used to tie up bundles.

[51] The notion that the heaven is a solid body or roof over this world is very common, probably universal, among primitive peoples. The Hebrews spoke of it as a firmament, that is, a beaten out solid expanse, which was "strong as a molten looking glass." Job. xxxvii. 18. It was supposed to support a celestial reservoir of waters, and to have doors, open lattices, and windows, through which rain, hail, and dew descend. It also supported the heavenly bodies ; and is spoken

umhlaba, umhlaba u pakati kwezulu, izulu li gcinile ngapandhle kwomhlaba; si ti a u se ko umhlaba ngale kwezulu.

Nabantu e si ti ba kona ngale kwezulu, a s' azi ukuba ba kulo idwala ini, noma ku kona indawana e umhlaba ngale; a si kw azi loko. Into e si y aziyo inye nje ukuti ba kona. Ngaloko ke si ti ku kona indawo yabo, njengeyetu le.

Ilanga lona nalo si ti a li ko ngale; ngokuba uma li ngale nga si nga li boni; nga li sitile, njengalabo 'bantu aba ngale, e si nga ba boniyo. Lona li nganeno, ngoba si li bona kahlekahle lonke; a ku site nendawana nje yalo.

encircles the earth, the earth being inside the heaven, and the heaven ending outside the earth; and we suppose there is no other earth on the other side of the heaven.

And the men[52] who, we suppose, are on the other side of the heaven, we do not know whether they are on the rock, or whether there is some little place which is earth on the other side; we do not know that. The one thing which we know is this, that these heavenly men exist. Therefore we say there is a place for them, as this place is for us.

And the sun we do not say is on the other side of the heaven; for if it were on the other side we should not be able to see it; it would be hidden like the men who are on the other side whom we do not see. The sun is on this side, for we see the whole of it thoroughly; not even one little spot of it is concealed.

---

of as a floor on which the throne of God rests. Ezek. i. 26. The Greeks had similar ideas, and applied the terms brazen and iron to the sky. The Latin coelum is a hollow place, or cave scooped out of solid space. *(Smith's Dictionary of the Bible.* FIRMAMENT.*)* The Arabs believed in numerous heavens one above the other, a belief which St. Paul entertained, and which is common to the Hindus, and to the Polynesians. Among the Chinese there is a myth, in which Puanku or Eldest-Antiquity is represented as having spent 18,000 years in moulding chaos, and chiseling out a space that was to contain him. And it is through openings made by his mighty hand that the sun, moon, and stars appear; not as the Amazulu think, shining on this side of the blue rock. (See *Nursery Tales of the Zulus.* Vol. *I., p.* 152. The Heaven-Country.) See some amusing diagrams by Cosmas-Indicopleustes, made on the supposed revealed cosmogony of the Bible. *(Types of Mankind.* Nott and Gliddon, *p.* 569.*)*

[52] See *Nursery Tales of the Zulus.* Vol. *I., p.* 316. Appendix.

Nenyanga futi nayo i nganeno njengelanga, nezinkanyezi futi zi nganeno nazo,—kokutatu loko. Namafu a nganeno; nemvula si ti i nganeno, i nela lo 'mhlaba; ngokuba uma i ngale nga i nga fiki lapa, ngokuba si ti izulu li idwala.

Ilanga ukuhamba kwalo indhlela zalo zimbili kupela nje; emini indhlela yalo li hamba ezulwini; ngokuhlwa indhlela yalo li ngena elwandhle, emanzini, li hamba ngawo li ze li pume endaweni yokupuma yakusasa.

Ilanga ukuhamba kwalo endhleleni yalo yokubusika, i yodwa; ngokuba li ya li hambela njalo li ze li geine endaweni etile, noma intaba, noma isihlahla; a li dhluli kulezo 'ndawo zombili; li pume endhlini yalo yobusika; ukupuma kwalo li buyele endaweni yehlobo. Si ti ngokupuma kwalo endaweni yobusika li landa ihlobo, li ze li geine ngentaba noma umuti; li buye li landa ubusika njalo. Zi kona izindhlu zalo lapa si ti, "Manje ilanga li ngenile endhlini;" si tsho ngokuba li ma izinsukwana kuleyo 'ndawo; uma li

And the moon too, like the sun, is on this side; and the stars too are on this side,—all three. And the clouds are on this side; and rain we say is on this side, which descends on this world; for if the rain were on the other side it could not come here to us, for we suppose that the heaven is a rock.

The sun in its course has only two paths; by day it travels by a path in the heaven; at night it enters by a path which goes into the sea, into the water; it passes through the water, until it again comes out at the place where it rises[53] in the morning.

As regards the path of the sun, its winter path is different from its summer path; for it travels northward till it reaches a certain place—a mountain or a forest, [where it rises and sets,] and it does not pass beyond these two places; it comes out of its winter house; when it comes out it goes southward to its summer place. We say that when it quits its winter place it is fetching the summer, until it reaches a certain mountain or tree; and then it turns northward again, fetching the winter, in constant succession. These are its houses, where we say it enters; we say so, for it stays in its winter house a few days;

---

[53] We see here the reason of the rising of the sun being expressed by *ukupuma*, to come out, because it is supposed to come out of the water.

puma s' azi ke nkuba li bu geinile ubusika, se li landa iḣlobo; nembala li ye li hambela ku ze ku ti ukukula kweḣlobo li ngene endḣlini yaseḣlobo izinsukwana, li pume njalo.

Inyanga ukutwasa kwayo si ti i twasile inyanga ngokuba si i bona entshonalanga. Kwa ku tiwa inyanga i fa nya; kanti a ku njalo; i dḣliwa izinsuku, i ye i ncipa, i ze i be ngangozipo uje emeḣlweni; lapo ke se i tatwa ilanga; li i funana empumalanga, li hambe nayo, li ze li i shiye entshonalanga, i bonwe lapa ku kqala ukuti zibe ukuḣlwa, ku tiwe i twasile inyanga; i ye i kula; i ze i fulatele enzansi, si ti inyanga se i bheka enzansi, i ye i ḣlangane ukutshona kwelanga, i ze i selwe; i buye i ncipe futi, i ze i fe.

Izinkanyezi a si tsho ukuba zi ya hamba njengelanga nenyanga; zi mi njalo zona. Kodwa zi kona izinkanyezi ezi hambayo, ezi fayo futi njengenyanga.

and when it quits that place we know that it has ended the winter and is now fetching the summer; and indeed it travels southward, until, when the summer has grown, it enters the summer house a few days, and then quits it again, in constant succession.

As to the renewal of the moon, we say it is new moon because we see it in the west. It used to be said the moon dies utterly; but it is not so; the days devour it,[54] and it goes on diminishing until to appearance it is as thin as a man's nail; and then it is taken by the sun; the sun finds it in the east and travels with it, until he leaves it in the west, and it can be seen when the twilight begins, and we say it is new moon; and it goes on growing until it is full. At last it has it back to the east,[55] and we say the moon is rising more and more eastward, and at last it is full ;[56] it rises when the sun sets; and at last the sun rises before the moon sets; and it again wanes, until it dies.

We do not say the stars travel like the sun and moon; they are fixed continually. But there are stars which travel, and which die like the moon.

---

[54] How easily a mythical personification may arise from such a metaphor as this.

[55] *Enzansi* here meaning by the sea, which is, Eastward.

[56] *Dilingana* is also used to express full moon. *Inyanga se i dilingene*, The moon is now full.

Isikcelankobe ngesinye isikati si ya nyamalala, si bonakale ngesinye isikati.

Futi isilimela si ya fa, si nga bonakali. Ebusika a si ko, ku ze ku ti lapa ubusika se bu pela si kqale ukubonakala si sinye—inkanyezi; si be zitatu; si ye si kula si ze si be isikxukwana, si dandalaze obala lapa se ku za 'kusa. Si tsho ke ukuti isilimela si twasile, nonyaka u twasile; ku linywe ke.

Ikwezi li ma endaweni yalo njalo; lona l' andulela ukusa nelanga; ku bonwa ngalo ukuba ku ya sa manje; ubusuku bu dhlulile, li pumile ikwezi, nomtakati a finyele lapa e ya kona, ngokuti, "Uma ngi hamba kancane ngi za 'kuselwa, ngi ya 'kufika ekaya ku sile." Nenhloli i finyele ku nga puma ikwezi; y azi ukuba se ku sile. I njalo ke leyo 'nkanyezi.

Indosa inkanyezi e puma ngapambili kwekwezi ukuhamba kwo-

Isikcelankobe[57] (the evening star) is sometimes invisible, sometimes seen.

And Isilimela[58] (the Pleiades) dies, and is not seen. It is not seen in winter; and at last, when the winter is coming to an end, it begins to appear—one of its stars first, and then three, until going on increasing it becomes a cluster of stars, and is perfectly clear when the sun is about to rise. And we say Isilimela is renewed, and the year is renewed, and so we begin to dig.

Ikwezi (the morning star) keeps its place constantly; it precedes the morning and the sun; and by its rising we see that the morning is coming; the night has passed, the morning star has arisen, and the sorcerer turns back rapidly from the place where he is going, because he says, "If I go slowly, the light will rise on me, and I shall reach home when it is light." And the spy rapidly turns back; when the morning star rises he knows that it is now morning. Such then is this star.

Indosa is a star which arises before the morning star, when night

---

[57] *Isikcelankobe*, also called *Isipekankobe.—Isi-kcela-nkobe : Izinkobe* is boiled maize; *ukukcela*, to ask. The star which appears when men are asking for boiled maize,—their evening meal.—*Isi-peka-nkobe : ukupeka*, to boil. When the maize is boiling for the evening meal.

[58] *Isilimela*, The digging-for-[stars.] Because when the Pleiades appear the people begin to dig. *Isilimela se si ba landile abalimi*, The Pleiades have now fetched the diggers.

kuhlwa; ku ti noma abantu be libele be hlezi be dhla utshwala, noma ukudhla kwomtimba, ba nga bona indosa i pumile, ngokuba yona i ba bomvu, ba ti, "A si lale; se ku hlwile." Ku lalwe ke. Umuntu ka tsho ukuti, "Loku ku pume indosa a ngi sa yi 'kulala;" u ya 'kulala a z' a kohlwe. Indosa ku sa i pezulu kakulu, li pume ke ikwezi.

is advanced; and if men have staid drinking beer, or eating the meat at a wedding feast, if they see Indosa arisen, for it arises red, they say, "Let us lie down; it is now night." And so they lie down. A man does not say, "Since Indosa has arisen I shall not now lie down;" he will lie down for a long time.[59] In the morning Indosa is very high in the heaven, and the morning star risen.

The Sun, Moon, and Stars.

UKUMA kwelanga ngokutsho kwabantu, ku tiwa ilanga li inkosi enyangeni na sezinkanyezini; ngokuba uma li pumile zi ya fipala zombili inyanga nezinkanyezi, ku kanye lona lodwa, li ze li tshone, and' uba zi kanye zona.

Ku tiwa ukuhamba kwalo li ya hamba impela ezulwini, li ze li ngene elwandhle; li buyele empumalanga lapa li puma kona. Ku tiwa li hamba emanzini. Lapa li puma kona ekuseni ku kona isigakqa esikulu; ku tiwa leso 'sigakqa unina walo; si ya li pelezela lapa se li za 'upuma, si li shiye ekupumeni kwalo, si buyele elwandhle. Si bomvu njengomlilo. I loko ke e ngi kw aziyo ngelanga.

As regards the position of the sun, in the opinion of the people he is chief above the moon and stars; for when he has arisen both moon and stars become dim, and he alone shines, until he sets, and then they shine.

As regards his motion, it is said he really travels in the heaven, until it goes into the sea, and returns to the east from whence he arose. It is said he travels in the water. Where he arises in the morning there is a great ball; this ball is called the sun's mother; it accompanies him when he is about to rise, and leaves him on his arising, and goes back into the sea. It is as red as fire. This then is what I know about the sun.

---

[59] Lit., until he forgets, that is, is in a deep sleep.

Ngenyanga kwa tiwa kuk*q*ala i ya fa, ku pinde ku vele enye inyanga. Kepa kwa za kwa bonwa ukuba k*q*a; kanti a i fi, inye njalo njengelanga. Kodwa ukufa kwayo ukuba i ncipa, i d*h*liwa izinsuku, i ze i site elangeni, i sitwa imisebe yalo, i nga b' i sa bonakala. I tatwe ilanga, li hambe nayo izinsukwana, i pinde i shiywe, i bonakale ekutshoneni kwalo. Izing*q*apeli za za za bona ngokuk*q*apela kwazo, zi ti, "Ku ng*a*ni ukuba inyanga ku tiwe i file, loku i sita elangeni nje na?" Ku ti emini lapa izulu li bukeka, nelanga li nga sa *h*labi kakulu ame*h*lo ngemisebe, i bonwe ngoku*h*lala emtunzini omkulu; umuntu a bheke pezulu, a k*q*apelisise eduze nelanga, a yeke ukubheka um*h*laba, 'enyusele ame*h*lo pezulu, ku ze ku pele ukukanya oku ka*o*pa ame*h*lo, 'ejwayele ukubona eduze nalo, nezulu li kewebe ka*h*le eme*h*lweni, li nga wa vimbeli, i ya bonwa ekealeni kwelanga, noma li ya 'ku i shiya ekutshoneni kwalo, noma li ya 'kutshona nalo. O i bonileyo a bize omunye, a ti, "Inyanga a i

As regards the moon, it was said at first the moon dies, and another moon comes into being. But at length it was seen that it is not so; that the moon does not die, but is one like the sun. But its death is that it diminishes, being eaten by the days, until it hides itself in the sun, that is, in its rays, and is then no longer visible. It is taken by the sun, and he goes with it a few days, and then leaves it again, and the moon is seen when the sun sets. Observers at length saw by their observation, and said, "Why is it said that the moon is dead, when it is merely hiding itself in the sun?" And during the day when the sky can be looked at, and the sun no longer pierces the eyes much with his rays, the moon is seen by a man standing in a deep shade, and looking upwards, and fixing his eyes intently on a spot near the sun and ceasing to look on the earth, and raising his eyes to the sky, until the light which pierces the eyes ceases, when the eyes are accustomed to look at a spot near the sun, and the sky is clear to the eyesight, and the sun no longer forces him to close his eyes, the moon is seen at the edge of the sun, whether the sun will leave it when he sets, or set with it. He who sees it calls another,

file, njengokuba ku tiwa i ya fa; nansi. Bheka pezulu. W ake umkanya, u kcimisise ame*h*lo, u jwayele elangeni, u za 'ku i bona." Nembala a fune, a fune, a ze a i bone, a ti, "Nembala i li*h*lwe inisebe."

Kwa bonwa nezinkanyezi emini; nami loko nga ku bona. S' ake embava. Emini enkulu nami ngi pika, ngi ti, "Inyanga i ya fa impela." Kwa ti s' alusile lapa ilanga se li pezulu kakulu; si *h*lezi emtunzini, si lele ngemi*h*lana, si keambalele, si bheke pezulu. Umfo wetu wa ti kumi, "U ya i bona inyanga. Nansiya, i namatele ekcaleni kwelanga." Nga m pikisa. Wa ti, "K*q*ingisisa; u za 'ku i bona." Nembala nga tulis' ame*h*lo, nga bheka elangeni na sekcaleni kwalo, ame*h*lo a *h*langana nayo. Nga i ti tshazi uku i bona, ya nyamalala. Nga pinda nga tulisa ame*h*lo, nga i bona, nga ti, "Nembala." Nga bona nezinkanyezi—ya ba nye kuk*q*ala; za za za ba ningi, ngi zi bona. Nga dela ukuba nembala inyanga ka i fi. I loko ke e ngi kw aziyo ngenyanga.

Ku tiwa i induna yelanga.

and says, "The moon is not dead, as they say it dies; there it is. Look up. Shade your eyes, and bring the eyelids together, and get accustomed to the sun, and then you will see it." And indeed he seeks and seeks until he sees it, and says, "Truly it is hidden by the rays."

Men saw the stars too during the day; and I too have seen them. We were living on the Umbava. At midday I too disputed and said, "The moon really dies." But we were herding when the sun was very high; we were in the shade, lying on our backs without sleeping, and looking upwards. My brother said to me, "You see the moon. There it is; it is close to the edge of the sun." I contradicted him. He said, "Look hard; you will soon see it." And indeed I fixed my eyes, and looked earnestly at the sun and at the edge of the sun; I saw the moon for a moment; I again fixed my eyes, and saw it clearly, and said, "It is true." I saw also the stars—at first one; at last I saw many. So I was satisfied that the moon does not die. That is what I know about the moon.

The moon is said to be the sun's officer.

The Male and Female Heavens.

Izulu abantu ba l' a*h*lukanisa kabili; li linye ku tiwa izulu eli duma ngemvunga enkulu, ku tiwa elenduna lelo; a l' esabeki, a l' oni 'luto; ngokuba lona, noma li duma, into yalo imvula 'kupela. Uma li duma ngelenduna si ti, "Nonyaka nje izulu li bekile, ngokuba li nga dumi ngokona."

Elensikazi ku tshiwo lona ukuduma kwalo li bonakala ngezinyazi na ngesik*q*oto; nomoyana o fika umubana. Abantu ba baleke, ba ngene masinyane. Unyazi lwalo lu zinge lu ti nso masinyane, lu nga libali; umuntu u ya k*q*ala 'etuka, se lu kade lu d*h*lulile; umbala walo lu lu*h*lazana nemikwazana ebomvana kancinane; ukuduma kwalo izulu eli njalo li ya nkenketeka kakulu; ku nga li za 'udabula amakanda; li duma kabi lelo ke.

Umuntu uma la m fumana end*h*le u ko*h*lwa nokuba a nga zifaka pi; na send*h*lini ind*h*lu i be ncinane, a fune ind*h*lu yesibili e vimbela unyazi; nom*h*laba u be muncinane ngaleso 'sikati sokunkenketeka kwalo, ku dingeke nendawo lapa abantu nga be zifaka kona. Lelo 'zulu lensikazi libu*h*lungu bukulu. Ubu*h*lungu balo ukuba li nga niki 'muntu isikati

The people speak of two heavens; the one which thunders with a deep roar is the male; it is not dreadful, it does no harm; for although it thunders, it causes nothing but rain. When the male heaven thunders we say, "This year the heaven is peaceful, for it does not thunder injuriously."

It is said of the female heaven that its thunder is attended with lightning and hail; and the breeze which comes with it is rather bad. And men run away and go into their houses at once. Its lightning is usually forked and rapid; as soon as a man starts it has passed; its colour is bluish, and has little reddish streaks; this kind of heaven thunders very shrilly; it is as though it would split the head; and so its thunder is bad.

If it meet with a man in the open country he cannot tell where to go; and even indoors the house seems small, and he wants a second house into which the lightning cannot enter; and the world itself seems small at the time of its shrill thunderings, and men seek for a place where they can hide themselves. The female heaven causes much pain. The pain it causes is that it does not give a

sokuma isibindi; li kandanisa masinyane li buyekeze; ngaloko ke li dabule umuntu ngovalo; ingomuso umuntu a nga li boni ukuba li ya 'kuba kona; a ti, "Kqa; ingomuso a li se ko;" nokusa a nga be e sa ku bona ukuba li ya 'kusa, li d/dule; a bone ukuba li ya 'ud/dlula naye.

Into e si y aziko ngezulu lensikazi ukona; ukuba okwalo ukona 'kupela ezinkomeni na sebantwini na semitini. Ngemva kwalo ku gcina ukuba li balele kakulu. Si y' esaba uma izulu lensikazi ku vame lona; ngalo 'nyaka si ti, "Ilanga li ya 'uke li ku tshise ukud/da; umuva waleli 'zulu mubi."

man time to take courage; it presses upon him suddenly with constant repetition; it therefore tears a man with terror, and a man cannot see that to-morrow will ever come; he says, "No; there is no to-morrow;" and he can no longer see that the light of another day will shine in the heaven and pass away; he sees that the heaven will pass away with him.

What we know of the female heaven is the injury that it does; that it belongs to it only to injure cattle, and men, and trees. After it there follows intense heat. We are afraid if the female heaven occurs again and again; in such a year we say, "The sun will burn up our crops; this heaven is followed by evil."

The Smiting of the Heaven.

UMA ku kona izinkomo ezi tshaywe unyazi, kulukuni kubantu ukusondela kulezo 'nkomo uma be nge 'zinyanga; ngokuba ba ti, "Uma si sondele kuzo lezi 'nkomo, se si ya 'kuba se si zibizele unyazi lu ze kutina; a si nga yi, kona lu nga yi 'kuza kutina." Kepa inyanga i ya ya kuzo; um/daumbe i ti, "A zi d/diwe."

Ukud/dliwa kwazo zi d/dliwa ku

IF there are cattle which have been struck by the lightning, it is difficult for the people to approach them unless they are heaven-doctors; for they say, "If we approach these cattle, we shall be calling the heaven to come to us; do not let us go, then it will not come to us." But the doctor goes to them; perhaps he says, "Let them be eaten."

The mode of eating them is

hlanzwa njaloujalo; uma se ku pelile ukuhlanza, abantu ba yogeza; y elape inyanga, ukuba i ti i vimbela ukuza konyazi.

Kepa konke loko kwokwesaba izinkomo ezi tshaywe unyazi, labo 'bantu abesabayo a b' esabi ngokuba be ti unyazi lu ya 'kuza kubona ngezinkomo; b' esaba kakulu ngokuba uma be yile ezinkomeni, uma li ya duma ngemva kwaloko, a ba sa yi 'kukcabanga, ba ya 'kuti ngezwi eli nga li kqinisile, ba ti, "Si ya 'kubona impela." Ngokuba be ti ngokuya ezinkomeni, "Si l' onile izulu; li ya 'ku si sola ngoku si tshaya njengezinkomo." I loko ke oku veza ukwesaba kubantu, ngokuba lobu 'bunzima b' ehlela emakanda, a bu veli pansi; uma bu vela pansi, umuntu nga e ti, "Ngi ya 'ubona lu vela ngakuleya intaba, ugi lu gudhlukele." I loko ke ukwesaba kwabantu; b' esaba into e s' engeme sonke; a ku veli loko ngokuba ku ya 'kwenzeka impela; ku vezwa ukukcabanga loko, ngokuba le into i ngapezulu kwetu; a si namandhla oku i vika njengetshe li ponswa omunye umuntu.

this:—The people eat them, and take emetics continually; when they leave off emetics, they go and wash; and the doctor gives them medicines, that he may prevent the lightning from coming.

But as to all that fear of eating cattle which have been struck by the lightning, the people are not afraid because they suppose that it will come to them on account of the cattle; but they are afraid especially because if they have gone to the cattle, and it thunders after that, they will no longer think, but will say what is apparently true, "We shall now really see it come to us." For they say that by going to the cattle they have sinned against the heaven; and it will punish them by striking them as it struck the cattle. It is this then that causes fear in men, because the dreaded thing comes from above and not from below; if it come from below, a man might say, "I shall see it coming from yonder mountain, and avoid it." This then is the fear of men; they are afraid of something that looks down upon all of us; the fear does not arise because it will really strike; but it arises from thinking that it is a thing above us; we cannot defend ourselves from it as from a stone thrown by another.

Treating the Heaven.

Abantu uma izulu li duma, ba puma, ba kuze; ba tate induku, ba ti, ba za 'utshaya ubane lwezulu. Ba ti ba namandhla okwahlula izulu. Ba ti ba ya memeza, ba tate amahau nezinduku; ba tshaye emahaweni, ba memeze. Li ti izulu se li sile, ba ti, "Si l' ahlulile." Ba ti ba namandhla okwahlula izulu. Uma li duma izulu, ba tata imiti, ba i base emlilweni; ba ti, ba tunyisela izulu. Uma li nga dumi, l' esabe ngaleyo 'miti, ba ti ba ya jabula ngokumemeza izulu; ba ti, inhliziyo zabo zi ya jabula, be l' ahlula izulu. Ba ti, ba ya l' ahlula izulu ngemiti yabo.

Uma indhlu i tshile ngobane lwezulu, ba ya ezinyangeni ez' aziyo ukupata izulu, zi fike nemiti, z' elape abantu bonke bakulowo 'muzi lapo izulu li tshaye kona. B' elatshwe kakulu; ba geatshwe, ku ncindwe umsizi; ku betelwe izikonkwane enhla kwomuzi, na ngapambili kwomuzi, ezindhleleni zonke, na seminyango yezindhlu, na pezu kwezindhlu, na sesangweni

When it thunders the doctors go out and scold it; they take a stick, and say they are going to beat the lightning of heaven. They say they can overcome the lightning. They shout and take shields and sticks; they strike on their shields and shout. And when it clears away again, they say, "We have conquered it." They say they can overcome the heaven. When it thunders they take medicines and burn them in the fire; they say, they are smoking the heaven. If it does not thunder, but is afraid of the medicines, they are glad because they shout to the heaven; and their heart is glad when they overcome the heaven. They say they overcome the heaven with their medicines.

If a house is burnt by the lightning, they go to doctors who know how to treat the heaven, and they come with their medicines, and treat all the inhabitants of the village where the lightning has struck. They are treated very much; they are scarified and take umsizi; and little rods are driven into the ground on the upper side of the village, and in front of the village in all the paths, and near the doorways of the houses, and on the tops of the houses, and near the entrance of the cattle pen.

lezinkomo. Kw elatshwe ugemvu emnyama, ukuze izulu li be mnyama, li nga tandi ukutshaya kona futi; ngokuba uma be hlaba imvu emhlope li ya 'kupinda li tshaye futi ekaya. Ba tanda ukwenza ngemvu emnyama, ukuze izulu li nga be li sa pinda li tshayo ekaya.

Inyanga yokwelapa izulu i ya nemvu emnyama; uma ku nge ko imvu emnyama, a ba namandhla okwelapa; ngokuba be funa imvu emnyama. Inyanga i ya i gwaza; inyama yayo i hlanganiswe nemiti, ku gcatshwe abantu, ku bekewe izikonkwane, zi bekewe ngomuti, zi gcunyekwe, zi botelwe ezindhleleni.

They are treated with a black sheep,[60] that the heaven may be dark[61] and not wish to strike there again; for if they kill a white sheep it will again strike in that homestead. They wish to work with a black sheep, that the lightning may not strike that homestead again.

The doctor who treats the heaven goes with a black sheep; if he has not a black sheep, they cannot treat the heaven; for they require a black sheep. The doctor kills it; its flesh is mixed with medicines, and the people are scarified, and the little rods are smeared with medicine and fixed and driven into the paths.

Heaven-Medicines.

Umabope umuti wezulu o tshiswayo, o tshiswa esolweni, uma izulu li za kabi. Ubokqo futi u tunyisela izulu; nomhlonyane owezulu njalo uku li tunyisela; nomkatazo wona ke umuti o hlala ezikwiui zenyanga, ukuze ku ti uma ku ngena unyazi i lu kwife ngawo, e

Umabope is a heaven-medicine which is burnt in the isolo[62] when there is a threatening of a severe thunder storm.[63] Ubokqo also is used for smoking the heaven; and umthlonyane is used for the same purpose; and umkatazo is a medicine kept among the doctor's medicines, that if the lightning comes into the house he may

---

[60] The Ossetes, in the Caucasus, a half Christian race, sacrifice a black goat to Elias, and hang the skin on a pole, when any one is struck by lightning. (*Thorpe. Op. cit. Vol. I., p.* 173.)

[61] That is, unable to see clearly, so as to strike again where the black sheep has been sacrificed.

[62] See p. 376, note 22.

[63] Lit., If the heaven is coming badly.

u hlanganise nemiuyo ke imiti; amagama ayo a ngi w' azi. I leyo ke e ngi y aziyo imiti yezulu.

Omunye umuti wezulu u be isibetelelo; ku tatwe amafuta alo, a hlanganiswe nemiti yalo, kw enziwe isivimbelo eziuhlangotini zonke zomuzi; ngenhla ku be kona isikonkwane, ohlangotini lomuzi ku be kona ezinye futi; lezo ke z' alusile, z' aluse umuzi, na sesangweni; umuzi wonke, ku be na sezindhlini na ngapezu kwezindhlu. Li ya vinjelwa ke ngaloko, ukuba li kohlwe ukuba li ya 'ungena ngapi na. I loko ke e ngi kw aziyo.

Ku ti njalo ekupeleni konyaka lezo 'zikonkwane zi vuselelwe ngeziutsha; kw aziwa ukuti elidala izulu lonyaka o dhlulile li dhlule nawo; kodwa lo li za ngokwalo. Ku njalo ke ku vela izikonkwane iminyaka yonke.

Ku ti inyanga ey alusa izulu ngamhla i dhla imifino yonyaka

puff[64] at it with this medicine, which he mixes with other medicines, whose names I do not know. These then are the heaven-medicines which I know.

Another heaven-medicine is isibetelelo; its oil is taken and mixed with other heaven-medicines, and obstructions are made on every side of the village; rods to which these medicines are applied are placed above the village, and others at the side; so these rods herd the village; they are placed too at the entrance of the cattle-pen; the whole village is thus herded; and inside the houses, and on the tops of the houses these rods are placed. And the heaven is shut out by these means, that it may be unable to find a place where it can enter. This then is what I know.

And at the end of the year the rods are renewed by setting new ones in their place; it being known that the old heaven of the year which has passed away has passed away with the old year; but the present year has its own heaven.[65] Hence new rods are set up every year.

When a doctor who herds the heaven eats green food of the new

---

[64] The medicine is chewed, and whilst the breath is saturated with it, the doctor puffs at it.

[65] That is, each year has a character of weather peculiar to itself. This is remarkably true of Natal, no two years being alike.

omutsha, ku tiwe i y' eshwama, ku zilwe ku nga setshenzwa; abantu ba *h*lale emakaya, ba nga sebenzi. Futi ku ti uma li wisa isik*q*oto, ba nga sebenzi, ba zile ngokuti, "O, uma si sebenza si banga izulu." Konke loko a kw e-nziwa. Noma li vunguza umoya ngesikati sokuba se ku linywa, ku njalo futi a ku linywa, ku ya zilwa njalo, ngokuti, "Uma si lima si ya zibangela. Ku*h*le ukuba si zile, kona umoya ngomso u nga yi 'kufika ngamand*h*la."

I loko ke e ngi kw aziyo ngezulu. Kepa imiti yona e patwa izinyanga miningi, eminingi e ngi nga y azi uma imiti mini na.

year, and the people are told that he is eating new food, they leave off work on that day, and stay at home without working. And if it hails they do not work, but leave off, saying, "O, if we work we summon the lightning." All the works of men are omitted. Or if a great wind arises during the digging season, they leave off digging in like manner; thinking that if they work they summon the lightning to smite them. It is proper for them to leave off, and then the violent wind will not come again.

This is what I know of the heaven. But heaven-medicines which are used by the doctors are many, many of which I do not know.

The Insingizi and Ingqungqulu.

INDABA ngensingizi. Insingizi inyoni yezulu, inyoni enkulu. Ku ti uma izulu li balele kakulu, li tshise amabele ngelanga, ku yiwe ezinyangeni zemvula; abanye ba pange ukufuna insingizi ngokuti, "Uma si tole insingizi, sa i bulala, izulu li ya 'kuna, i fakwe esizibeni." Nembala i bulawe, i fakwe esizibeni. Ku ti uma li na, ku tiwe li na ngensingizi e buleweyo. Ku tiwa izulu li ya tamba naa ku

THE account of the Insingizi. The Insingizi is a heaven-bird; it is a large bird. If the heaven is scorching, and the sun burns up the corn, the people go to rain-doctors; others hasten to find an Insingizi, thinking that if they find one, and kill it, the heaven will rain, when the bird has been thrown into a pool of the river. And indeed it is killed and thrown into a pool. And if it rains, it is said it rains for the sake of the Insingizi which has been killed. It is said the heaven becomes soft

bulewe insingizi; li y' ezwela, a li bi lukuni; li ya i kalela ngemvula, li kala isililo. Abantu ba sinde ngokudhla amabele. I loko ke e ngi kw aziyo ngensingizi.

I yona e inyoni e funwayo kunezinye izinyoni; ngokuba ku ti nonza li balele izulu, uma ku bonwa izinsingizi zi hamba obala zi kala, abantu ku nga ti lapo ba bona isibonakaliso semvula ngokubona insingizi, ba tembe ukuba li za 'kuna, loku izinsingizi zi kala kangaka.

Enye inyoni, ingqungqulu, inyoni enkulu ezinyonini zonke; nensingizi i landela ingqungqulu. Kepa insingizi i dhlule, ngokuba umhlola wayo munye nje, imvula 'kupela,—ukuba izulu li ne uma i bulewe. Kepa ingqungqulu i nemihlola eminingi. Uma i tshekele umuntu, a li yi 'kutshona ilanga umuntu lowo e nga gijime nezindhlela e funa izinyanga zoku m elapa, ku be indaba enkulu, ku bhekwe into embi e za 'uvela kulowo 'muntu. Futi imihlola yengqungqulu ukuba uma i kala pezulu, ku tiwa li za 'kuna. Futi uma i hamba i tshaya amapiko, ku tiwa i bika impi.

if an Insingizi is killed; it sympathises with it, and ceases to be hard; it wails for it by raining, wailing a funeral wail. And so the people are saved by having corn to eat. This then is what I know about the Insingizi.

It is this bird which is sought for more than all others; for although the heaven be dry and scorching, if the people see many Izinsingizi walking in the open country and crying, it seems to men that they see a sign of rain because they see the Izinsingizi, and they trust that it will rain because they cry so much.

Another bird, the Ingqungqulu, is larger than all other birds; the Insingizi is next in size to it. But the Insingizi is of more importance, because it gives but one kind of omen, that of rain,—that the heaven will rain if it is killed. But the Ingqungqulu gives omens of many things. If it drops its dung on a man, the sun will not set before that man has run in all directions looking for a doctor to treat him; and it is a matter of great consequence, and men expect some evil to happen to him. Another sign which the Ingqungqulu gives is, that if it cries whilst flying, it is said it will rain. And if as it goes along it smites its wings together, it is said it reports the arrival of an enemy.

Magical Songs.

IN the *Zulu Nursery Tales* we meet with an instance of the use of an incantation or magical song to produce a storm. Umkʋakaza-wakogingʋwayo sung her song, and raised the tempest which destroyed the Amadhlungundhlebe. (*P*. 203). In another case, Ubongopa-kamagadhlela raised a storm by spitting on the ground. The spittle boiled up and saluted him; a great storm arose, from which every one suffered but himself. (*P*. 228). Every tribe has its tribal or national song, which is called "The chief's song." This song is sung on two occasions only; on the feast of firstfruits, when, if there has been a continued drought, it is supposed to be capable of causing rain; it is also sung by an army if overtaken with continuous rain on the march; on singing the chief's song the rain ceases, and the army is able to go on its way. Thus the national song is an incantation supposed to be capable of producing rain, or causing it to cease. The song of the Amapepete is given in the following account; its meaning is scarcely understood.

Ku kona kwabamnyama abantu amahhubo a imilingo, e ku ti ngamhla ku dhlala umkosi izulu li balele i bonwe imvula ngalelo 'langa, ku tiwe, "Izulu li na ngakona, ngokuba, li gqiba izinyawo zenkosi, ukuze zi nga bonakali lapa i b' i mi kona; zi kqedwe imvula."

Abantu ba ya hlakazeka, be ya emakaya; ba hamba be netile, be panga imifula, ukuze ba nga gcwalelwa.

Uma li nga sa ni ngalolo 'lusuku, ba ti, " Li kude ukuna, loku li nga zi gqibanga izinyawo zenkosi."

Njengaloku kwa ti mhla ku kupuka inkosi yakwiti, emapepeteni,

THERE are among black men magical songs, by singing which it happens on the day of the great festival,[66] although the sun has been for a long time scorching, that rain comes, and it is said, " The heaven rains with reason, for it is filling up the footprints of the chief, that they may no longer appear where he stood, but be obliterated by the rain."

The people are scattered to their homes; they set out already drenched, hastening to reach the rivers before they are flooded.

If it does not rain on the day of the festival, the people say, " It will not rain for a long time, for it has not filled up the footprints of the chief."

As it happened when Umyeka, the chief of our people, among

---
[66] That is, the great festival of firstfruits.

Umyeka, e ya en.riweni lakubo lapa kwa kw ake Umzimvubu, igama lomuzi; ku tiwa uyise o itongo ka vumanga ukwe/da ukuya cnanda, wa sala en.riweni. Kwa ti ngókuvama kwezifo endodaneni Umyeka, wa kupuka, e ti, "Nam-/da nje ngi za 'kulanda ubaba, e zokumela umuzi. Kwa ku nge nje ukufa ngi s' ake embava."

Kwa kupuka abantu abaningi, isizwe sonke, amadoda namake/da nezinsizwa; kwa hanjwa ku lalwa, kwa za kwa fikwa eduze nen.riwa, kwa lalwa emzini kasisila. Ku te ku sa kusasa wa e puma Umyeka, e se ya kona en.riweni; kwa ti ukuba a vele en/da kwalo in.riwa, kw' enziwa amaviyo njengempi; amadoda a hamba ngokwawo, namake/la ngokwawo, nezinsizwa.

Kwa ba njalo ke loku ku njalo-njalo izulu li balele kakulu ngesi-kati sokungena kwokwin/la, nge-nyanga e Ungcela, lapa nga se ku d/iliwa uma ka li balelanga. B' e-

the Amapepete, went up to the old site of his father's village, which was called Umzimvubu; for it was said his father, who was now an Itongo, did not wish to go down to the Inanda, but staid at the old site. But in consequence of the constant illness of the son Umyeka, Umyeka went up to the old site, saying, "To-day I am going to fetch my father, for him to come and protect the village. It was not thus when I was living on the Umbava." [67]

There went up with him many people, the whole nation, old men, and young men and youths; they went, sleeping in the way till they came near the old site, when they slept at the village of Usisila. On the following morning Umyeka set out to go to the old site; when he reached the hill overlooking it, they were divided into regiments as though they were an army; the men went by themselves, and the young men by themselves, and the youths by themselves.

It so happened that the sun had been very scorching at the time of eating new food, in the month called Ungcela,[68] when they would have been eating new food if there had not been so much drought.

---

[67] Umbava, a river, on which Umzimvubu was built. It is near Table Mountain, and runs into the Umgeni. Umzimvubu, if interpreted, means the Hippopotamus-village.

[68] January.

HEAVEN-DOCTORS, ETC.

Hla ke, se be ya kona en*r*iweni, Umyeka e hamba pambili, e landelwa impi yake; kw' enziwa lona ihhubo lelo likayise uku m vusa ngalo, ukuze a *h*langane nabo. Imbongi se inye e bongayo i bonga uyise noyisemkulu nendodana Umyeka. Kwa t' uba ku fikwe esibayeni emk*q*ubeni, kw' emiwa kona, kw' akiwa umkumbu; kwa fika nesizwe e sa sala kuleyo 'ndawo, loku usuku lwa lw aziwa, kwa se ku *h*leziwe eduze nen*r*iwa, ku *h*lomelwe inkosi; ba fika kona kanye nabesifazana, abafazi nezintombi, ku twelwe ukud*h*la, utshwala. Kwa *h*langanwa kona ke, kwa gujwa kakulu kakulu; ekupeleni kw' enziwa lona ihhubo likayise lokuti :—

They went on towards the old site, Umyeka going first, followed by his soldiers; they sung the song of his father to arouse him by it, that he might unite with them. The lauders[69] who lauded the father, and grandfather, and the son Umyeka, were innumerable. When they reached the cattle-pen, they halted there, and formed a circle; there came too the portion of the tribe which still lived in that neighbourhood, for they knew the day when Umyeka would come, and were staying near the old site, waiting for the chief; they came with the women, their wives and their daughters carrying beer. Thus then they assembled, and danced the shield-dance for a long, long time; after dancing they sang their father's song :—

"Limel' u *h*lole amazimw[70] etu asesiwandiye.

"Dig for[71] the chief, and watch our gardens which are at Isiwandiye.[72]

Amanga lawo.

Those words are naught.[73]

Limel' u *h*lole amazimw etu asesiwandiye.

Dig for the chief, and watch our gardens which are at Isiwandiye.

Amanga lawo.

Those words are naught.

---

[69] *Imbongi se inye*, the lauders were one; that is, the lauders were innumerable. Just as in such sentences as the following :—*A ku se si yo nembongi e bongayo*, There is not now even one lauder lauding; that is, the lauders are very many.

[70] Amazimu *for* amasimu; the z being used for s to give weight to the sound; the u changed into w before the vowel in the following word.

[71] *Limel'*—dig for, not known for whom, but probably, as here translated, the chief.

[72] *Asesiwandiye.*—Isiwandiye *for* Isiwandile. The name of a place, as if of a place where there were many gardens.

[73] *Those words are naught*,—that is, we object to dig at Isiwandile.

"Asesiwandiye, I-i-i-zi—asesiwandiye.
Amanga lawo."

Ku te ku se pakati li hhutshwa izulu la hloma, la duma; a ku yekwanga ngokuti, "O, a si baleke si y' ekaya, loku si za 'uneta." Izalukazi za ti, "Namhla nje i fikile inkosi yomhlaba wakwiti; si za 'ubona nemvula."

Kwa hlatshwa imikosi isifazana; kwa nga ti si ya hlanya lapa si bona izulu li futuzela, li za ngamandhla. Kwa hhutshwa njalo, abantu se be juluka kakulu ngokufudumala kwelanga. La i tela; ya gijima pansi; kwa sinwa nje, ku jabulwa, kwa tiwa, "Namuhla itongo lakwiti si hlangene nalo, loku si bona itonsi lemvula."

Umyeka wa tata isihlangu sake, wa ya 'kuma pansi kwomuti. Ba katala ukusina. Wa ti, "A ku godukwe." Ba hlala pansi kwomuti, kwa puzwa utshwala, ba kqedwa, kw' esukwa ke, kwa godukwa.

Lelo 'hhubo li ng' enziwa kabili ku be ukupela; a l' enziwa ku nga

"Which are at Isiwandiye, 1-i-i-zi[74]—which are at Isiwandiye. Those words are naught."

Whilst in the midst of the song the heaven became clouded, and thundered; they did not leave off, neither did they say, "O, let us run home, for we shall get wet." The old women said, "This day there has come the chief of our land[75] where our nation dwells; we shall see rain also."

The women shouted; it was as though they were mad when they saw the clouds gathering tumultuously and rapidly coming on. They continued singing, the people now sweating exceedingly through the heat of the sun. It poured; the rain ran on the ground; they still went on dancing and rejoicing, and saying, "This day the Itongo of our people has united with us, for we see a drop of rain."[76]

Umyeka took his shield and went and stood under a tree. The people tired of dancing. He told them to go home. They sat under the tree, and drank all the beer, and then went towards their homes.

This song is sung only on two occasions; it is not sung before

---

[74] *I-i-i-zi.* Z in zi pronounced as in azure. This chorus is used for the purpose of emphatically asserting the subject of the song.

[75] *Inkosi yomhlaba*, The chief to whom the land belongs,—an *inkosi yohlanga*, or chief descended from a race of primitive chiefs.

[76] *Itonsi lemvula.*—Here again a drop of rain means abundance of rain.

fikile isikati sonyaka omutsha e l' enziwa ngaso. Futi l' enziwa, ku pume impi, ya kandaniswa imvula endhleleni, i hamba izulu la na kakulu. A la vuma ukusa ku ze kw enziwe lona; izulu li se, ku punywe, ku yiwe lapa ku yiwa kona.

A njalo ke amagama amakosi. A wa bi mabili; igama elidala lamakosi onke akona.

the new year,[77] when it is sung. It is also sung when, if an army has gone out, it has been overtaken by rain[78] in the way, and as it is travelling it rains excessively. It will not become bright until this song is sung; then the heaven clears, and they go whither they wish to go.

Such then are the songs of chiefs. A chief has not two songs; each has his own, the ancient song of the chiefs of the several nations.[79]

---

[77] The feast of firstfruits.
[78] Lit., heaven.
[79] These are national songs.

The national song of the Amazulu consists of a number of musical sounds only, without any meaning, and which cannot be committed to writing. Each tribe has its own chief's song; some of these consist of words more or less intelligible, and once had doubtless a well understood meaning; others of mere musical sounds which have no meaning whatever.

PART IV.

ABATAKATI;
OR,
MEDICAL MAGIC, AND WITCHCRAFT.

ABATAKATI;

OR,

MEDICAL MAGIC, AND WITCHCRAFT.

The Strength of Medicines.

Ku kona imiti e misa amakosi; umuntu nje ka namand*h*la ukupata lowo 'muti, e nge 'nkosi, e nge 'nyanga futi; uma lowo 'muti u bonwa kumuntu nje kulabo 'bantu benkosi, u be bulawa; ku tiwe, "U za 'kwenza ni ngawo na?" Ngokuba inkosi i ya mu zwa umuntu o pata imiti emikulu ngomzimba; ku ti lowo 'muntu uma 'emi pambi kwayo, lowo 'muntu a sinde; ku nga ti inkosi i m etwele, i zwe se ku fika nencakcamba yokujuluka; i ze i suke i muke i ye 'kuzilungisa. Uma lowo 'muntu

There are medicines which give chiefs strength and presence;[80] a common man, who is neither a chief nor a doctor, cannot touch this kind of medicine; if any one among the chief's men were seen with it, he used to be killed; it was said, "What are you intending to do with that?" For a chief feels with his body a man who has great medicines; and when such a man stands in his presence he is oppressive; it is as though the chief was bearing him, and he feels a perspiration breaking out; and he starts up and goes away to strengthen himself with his medicines. If that man does not leave

---

[80] Lit., which make a chief stand, or which establish a chief; that is, make him strong in the face of danger, or give him presence before others, by which he is recognised at once as the chief.

e nga i la*h*li leyo 'miti, u ya 'kufa. Leyo 'nkosi i ya 'ku m tshela, i ti, "Mfana kabani, loku 'kuhamba kwako uma u nga ku yeki, se u file. Ngi nike imiti yako yonke, ngi bone imiti o i patayo." Nembala lowo 'muntu a i veze, ngokuba u se nukiwe ngokuzwakala kwake emzimbeni wenkosi. Kepa uma i fumana ikubalo elikulu kulo 'muntu, i buze, i ti, "Lo 'muti w enza ni ngawo na? wa u tata kubani?" A ti, "Nga u tenga kubani." I ti, "U za 'wenza ni ngawo?" A ku lande loko a u tenga e za 'kwenza; noma a tsho izintombi, a ti, "Nga u tengela izintombi." I u tabate inkosi lowo 'muti, u buyele ngakuyo.

Ukuzwakala kwomuntu e pete imiti e namand*h*la, indaba e ngi y aziyo.

Kwa ti ngolunye usuku kwa ku *h*langene abantu eketweni; kepa amadoda e *h*lezi esibayeni e buka intombi i sina; ku te ku se njalo, loku ba *h*lezi nje, ba ya buka, a ku ko 'keala, ba bona pakati kwabo umuntu omunye o nga ti u godole, ba m bona e wa pansi—insizwa yakwanomsimekwane, inkosi yakwamkeoseli, isizwe. Kepa kwa

these medicines, he will die. The chief will say to him, "Son of So-and-so, if you do not leave off this conduct of yours, you are already dead. Give me all your medicines, that I may see those which you have about you." And indeed the man does not conceal them, because he has been discovered by being felt by the chief's body. And if the chief finds a great medicine on him, he asks what he does with it, and from whom he got it. He says he purchased it from So-and-so. The chief asks what he was about to do with it. And he explains what he wished to do when he bought it; perhaps he says to make damsels love him. The chief takes the medicine, and places it among his own.

As to the possibility of a man who carries powerful medicines being felt, this is what I know.

It happened one day the people assembled at a dance; and the men were sitting in the cattle-pen looking at the damsel dancing; and then, as the men were sitting and looking on without there being anything the matter, they saw one among them who appeared to be cold, and saw him fall down—a young man of the people of Unomsimekwane, the chief of the nation of Umkcoseli.[81] And

---

[81] *Umkcoseli*, the unkulunkulu or founder of the tribe.

buzwana ngokuti, "Lo 'muntu u nani?" Abantu ba bhekana, ba buza ukuti, "U nani na?"

Wa ti, "Ai. Ngi zwa umzimba wami u shiyana; se ngi tambile; a ng' azi uma ngi nani na. Ngi zwe se ku ti futu ukufudumala, nga ba se ngi ya wa."

Kwa ba mnyama emehlweni ake. Umne wetu w' esuka wa tata izikqu zake, wa m lumisa emakubalweni ake, wa m pepeta na ngezindhlebe na ngamakala; kwa umzuzwana lowo 'muntu wa buya wa luluma, wa kqina. I loko ke e nga ku bonayo.

Okuningi ngi be ngi ku zwa ngendhlebe ukuti, "Au, Ubanibani w enze into e mangalisayo; si te si sa fika emtimbeni, si nga ka hlali nokuhlala, sa bona ugomuntu e se wa nje; u ze wa vuswa Ubani." Kuningi loko.

Ku ti uma lowo 'muntu b' ahluleka uku m vusa, ku ze ku be indaba na kubantu abakulu; abantu abanjalo ba sizwa inkosi, i yoku m lungisa lowo 'muntu, a vuke.

the people asked, "What is the matter with the man?" And they looked at each other, and asked, "What is the matter with you?"

He replied, "No. I feel different sensations in different parts of my body; I am weak; I do not know what is the matter with me. I felt myself become suddenly hot, and then fell."

He was unable to see. My brother went and took his medicines, and choosing from among them told him to bite off a portion, and he himself, having chewed some, puffed into his ears and nostrils; and in a little while the man rose up again and was strong. This is what I saw.

I heard the people talking much, saying, "O, So-and-so did a wonderful thing; as we were arriving at the wedding, before we had sat down any time, we saw a man fall without apparent reason; and So-and-so at last restored him." There was much talk of that kind.

If common men are unable to restore such a person, it at length becomes known to the great men; and people suffering in this way are helped by the chief; he will cure him.[82]

---

[82] The chief collects to himself all medicines of known power; each doctor has his own special medicine or medicines, and treats some special form of disease, and the knowledge of such medicines is trans-

Kepa pakati kwetu a si tsho ukuti lowo 'muntu owayo ku ng' enziwe 'luto, u wa isifo. Ai, si y' a*h*lukanisa isifo esi nga wisa umuntu. Ngokuba pakati kwetu, uma umuntu e nengozi i ya mu wisa, ku be mnyama 'me*h*lo, kakulu lapa ilanga li balele. Kepa u ti u ya zelula kakulu, a be se u ya wa; si ti okwengozi loko.

Futi a si tsho kumuntu owayo ukuti, "U wa nje; ka nakcala;" si y' azi masinyane ngokwenza kwake ukuti, naye u ya i pata imiti; kuloko e nga si ye umuntu o k*q*inileyo emitini, ku ngaloko ke ukubulawa kwemiti yake i bulawa e namand*h*la kunayo, ku ya 'kuwa umniniyo.

But we do not say amongst ourselves that nothing has been done to the man that falls, he falls from mere disease. No, we distinguish diseases which cause a man to fall. For amongst us if a man has an old injury of the head[83] it may cause him to fall, and be affected with blindness, especially when the sun is intensely bright. And he stretches himself and falls; we say, that is occasioned by the old accident.

Further, we do not say of a man that falls, "He merely falls; he has done nothing wrong;" we know at once by his conduct that he has medicines about him; for as he is not one who is thoroughly acquainted with medicines, therefore his medicines are overcome by others which are stronger than they, and the owner of the medicines falls.[84]

---

mitted as a portion of the inheritance to the eldest son. When a chief hears that any doctor has proved successful in treating some case where others have failed, he calls him and demands the medicine, which is given up to him. Thus the chief becomes the great medicine-man of his tribe, and the ultimate reference is to him. If he fail, the case is given up as incurable. It is said that when a chief has obtained some medicine of real or supposed great power from a doctor, he manages to poison the doctor, lest he should carry the secret to another and it be used against himself.

[83] An injury of the head is always a cause of anxiety to natives, especially one which has caused depression of the bone, which the natives usually treat by cutting down to the bone, and scraping it, often leaving a deep depression. Such injuries are always referred to as the cause of all future diseases.

[84] That is, an inexperienced man bears about him powerful medicines, and therefore the medicines of another become aware that there is an opponent at hand, and contend with the medicines till they are

Njengaloku e*h*lauzeni lakwiti, emkambatini, ku kona izinyanga ezimbili eza pikisana ugobunyanga. Ya ti onye, " Bani, u nge ze wa u ka umd*h*lebe, noma u inyanga." Wa ti omunye, " Ngi uga u ka ngesikatshana nje ngi sa fika." Wa ti, (ngokuba labo 'bantu boba-bili ngi ya b' azi ; omunye Uso-petu, omunye Upeteni,)—wa ti Usopetu kupeteni, "Peteni, hamba si ye enzansi nomlazi ; lowo 'muti ngi ya w azi, si ze si yeke izinka-ni ; nawe ngi kw azi ukuba u inyanga ; nami u ng' azi uma se si fikile kulowo 'muti."

Nembala ke ba hamba ba ya ba fika. Ku te uma ba fike wa u komba Usopetu, wa ti, " Peteni, nanku. A si *h*lale pansi."

Loku pela lowo 'muti ku ya liwa nawo ; impi enkulu ; umuntu a nge u ke e nga lwanga nawo. Ku tiwa futi pansi kwawo mani-ngi amatambo ezilwane ezifayo ; nezinyoni uma zi ti zi ya *h*lala, zi

Just as in the thorn-country where our tribe lived, at Table Mountain, there are two doctors who disputed with each other about their skill. One said to the other, " So-and-so, you are utterly unable to pluck umdhlebe,[85] though you are a doctor." The other said, " I can pluck it at once, as soon as I reach it." I know both these men ; one is called Uso-petu, and the other Upeteni. Usopetu said to Upeteni, " Upe-teni, let us go together to the Umlazi near the sea ; the tree you mention I know, that our conten-tions may cease ; as for you I know you are a doctor ; and you will know me when we reach the tree."

And truly they went till they came to the tree. When they came to it Usopetu said, " Upe-teni, there it is. Let us sit down."

But men contend with this tree ; it is a powerful opponent ; a man cannot pluck it before he has fought with it. It is also said that beneath it there are many bones of animals which die there ; and birds if they pitch on it, die. It

---

overcome, and he who carries them is seized with illness. By bearing medicines he becomes a centre of influence and attraction, and is, as it were, attacked by another. One who bears no such medicine does not suffer ; not being a centre of influence, he is not a centre of attraction, and so, being neutral, escapes.

[85] *Umdhlebe*, a tree, which is probably a kind of Aspen. In some respects it reminds us of the Upas. But much that is said about it is doubtless fabulous and wholly untrustworthy.

fe. Ku tiwa futi lowo 'muti u ya kala njengemvu. Miningi imidhlebe, a u munye; eminye mincinane; o wona umkulu kuyo yonke u senhlwengeni.

Wa ti Usopetu, "Peteni, u kqale." Lokupela ku ti noma izulu li bekile, ku nge ko 'moya, u zamazame, w enza umsindo ngokuzamazama; ku zamazama amahlamvu. Wa ti kupeteni, "U kqale wena, loku u ti u inyanga. U ngi kelele, u ngi pe."

Masinyane Upeteni wa tukulula izikqu zake, wa zi lungisa; wa zi lumula yena. W' esuka, wa ti, u ya 'kuka. Lokupela u pete umkonto, ukuze a u hlabe, wa u hlaba; wa zamazama kakulu; kw' ala ukuba a sondele. Wa buyela ezikqwini ezinye, wa zi lumula; wa buya wa ya kuwo, wa u gwaza; wa bila ngamandhla; wa bo sa te ka sondele, kw' aleka; wa buyela emuva, wa kqala ukufoma naye ubuso.

is also said that the tree cries like a sheep. There are several kinds of umdhlebe, not one kind only; some are small; the largest of all is that which grows among the Amanthlwenga.

Usopetu said, "Upeteni, begin." But although the heaven is still, and there is no wind, the tree moves, and makes a noise by moving; its leaves move. Usopetu said, "Upeteni, do you begin, since you say you are a doctor. Pluck for me, and give me."

At once Upeteni untied his medicines, and selected what was proper; he chewed them and puffed on his body. He arose, thinking to go and pluck from the tree. And as he carried his assagais that he might stab it, he stabbed it;[86] it moved violently; and would not allow him to approach it. He went back to other medicines, and chewed them and puffed upon his body; and again went to the tree, and stabbed it; it made a great noise; again and again he tried to approach it, but he was unable; he went back again, and his face began to be suffused with perspiration.

Wa tsho Usopetu, wa ti, "Peteni, u ke, si hambe."

Usopetu said, "Pluck from the tree, and let us go home."

---

[86] He stabbed it by throwing his assagai, standing at a distance, not by approaching it so as to stab it without throwing. When the tree is pierced, it is said to throw out of the wound a water, with a hissing noise; and if the juice fall on the body of a man, it will produce a deep wound, and kill him if he is not treated by a skilful

Wa ya kwezinye izikqu zake; kwa ba se kw alekile. Ka b' e sa buyela; wa ngenwa amakaza; loku li balele, wa godola, wa kqala ukutsho kusopetu ukuti, "Au, ng' ahlulekile." Futi, "Ngi size; se ngi ya fa."

Wa ti Usopetu, "Ehe! U za 'u ngi dela namhla nje ukuba ngi inyanga; wena umfana wami." Wa tukulula izikqu zake Usopetu, wa m lumula, wa m siza. Wa zi tata, wa hamba nazo, wa ya kuwo; wa u hlaba, wa bila ngamandhla; wa buyela emuva, wa lungisa, wa ya kuwo; wa u hlaba, wa tula; w' ehla, wa ya, wa w' apula amagaba awo.

Wa tsho nopeteni, wa ti, "O, ngi patele nami." Wa mu pa ke. Wa tata imikonto, wa buya nayo.

Wa ti Upeteni, "Sopetu, u inyanga. U ng' ahlulile namhla nje."

I lowo ke umuti o bulala abantu, e ku ti uma u telwe pakati kwomuzi, lowo 'muzi u bube; ku ngene umkuhlane omkulu; umuntu a fe e kqakqamba amatambo

He applied to other medicines; but he was still unable to pluck from the tree. And he was no longer able to quit the place; cold entered into him; although there was a cloudless, bright sun, he was cold, and began to say to Usopetu, "O, I am conquered. Help me; I am now ill."

Usopetu replied, "Yes! yes! You are about to be satisfied to-day that I am a doctor; you are my boy."[87] Usopetu untied his medicines, and chewed some and puffed on Upeteni, and cured him. He took his medicines, and went with them to the tree; he stabbed it, and it made a great noise; he went back from it, and took other medicines and went to it again; he stabbed it; it was silent; he went down to it, and plucked its branches.

And Upeteni said, "Pluck for me also." He gave him some of the branches of the tree. He took up the assagais and came back with them.

Upeteni said, "Usopetu, you are a doctor. You have conquered me this day."

This, then, is the tree which kills people, which if cast into the midst of a village, that village perishes; a great fever arises; and a man dies with all his bones

---

[87] You are my boy. That is, I am a man in my knowledge; you are but a boy. You are my pupil.

ngobu*hl*ungu; a nga bi nasikund*hl*a lapa e nga *hl*ala kona, a be loku e tshoba njalo. Ku ze ku fike inyanga, i m bone ukuba lo 'muntu u bulelwe ngombulelo, ukuti umd*hl*ebe; i mu size. Uku m elapa kwayo i m n*q*umisela amanzi, i ti, a nga wa puzi; futi namasi a nga wa d*hl*i.

Njengaloku labo 'bantu nga ba bona ngame*hl*o ami aba bulawa umd*hl*ebe en*hl*wengeni, be ye 'kuzingela izind*hl*ovu. Omunye ku umfo wetu. Wa ka wa fika na lapa, e tshayela in*q*ola inyanga ya ba nye; ike*hl*a lide, limnyama, li nesilevu eside. Be hamba nebunu; ku tiwa lelo 'bunu ibizo lalo Umkosi.

B' emuka, ba ya kona, ba zi fumana izind*hl*ovu, ba zi bulala eziningi; ba za ba fika lapo umd*hl*ebe u kona; lapa ku nga fuyiwa 'nkomo, 'kupela izimbuzi zodwa. Kepa ba tshaya inyati ntambama, b' ezwa be lambile; ya fa, ba ba se ba i *hl*inza, se ba ya y osa. Uku y osa kwabo ba y osa ngawo umd*hl*ebe, be nga w azi. Kepa leyo 'nyama a ba i k*q*edanga. Umdava wa k*q*ala ukuzibika ngokuti, "Hau, ku k*q*ak*q*amba amatambo ami." Nonofi*hl*lela futi naye

racked with pain; there is no place where he can rest, but he moves up and down continually. At length a doctor comes, and sees that the man has been made ill by umbulelo,[88] that is, umdhlebe; he cures him. His treatment consists in ordering him to abstain from drinking water, and not to eat amasi.

Just as I saw with my own eyes those men who were killed by umdhlebe among the Amanthlwenga, they having gone to hunt elephants. One of them was my brother. He once came here driving the waggon for one month; a tall man, with very black skin, and tall, and a long beard. They went with a Dutchman; the name of the Dutchman was Umkosi.

They set out and went to the Amanthlwenga; they met with elephants and killed many; at length they reached a place where umdhlebe grows; where the people cannot keep cattle, but only goats. And one afternoon, feeling hungry, they killed a buffalo; when it was dead, they skinned it and roasted it. They used umdhlebe to roast it with, not being acquainted with the tree. But they did not eat all the meat. Umdava first began to complain, saying, "O, my bones are racked with pain." Then Unofithlela complained, saying,

---

[88] *Umbulelo*, a gen. term for destructive medicines, of which *umdhlebe* is one.

wa zibika ukuti, "Na kumi ku njalo." Kepa leyo 'nyama a ba i k*q*edanga, ba ba se be bulawa na amakanda; kwa ba se ku ukungena kwokugula njalo.

Lokupela Aman*h*lwenga a ya s' azi leso 'sifo uku s' elapa. Unofi*h*lela wa k*q*ala ukuk*q*umba, isisu a sa be si sa pela ; wa ba loku 'esuti njalo. Nomndava wa ba njalo; kwa za kwa ba bhudisa loko 'kufa.

U te umlungu wabo, um' a bone ukuba ku njalo, abantu be za 'kufa; lokupela baningi, kwa ba *h*laba bonke, ukupela umlungu lowo e ku nga m *h*labanga ; (kanti naye wa ka wa gula pambili ngokuya kwake kwokuk*q*ala, w' elatshwa; kanti u se pinda ukuya;) wa biza izinyanga zakona, za b' elapa. Kepa ekufikeni kwabo kuman*h*lwenga, ba fika abanye be nga se ko, se be file. Kepa labo abab' elapayo ba ba tshela ukuti, "Ni nga wa puzi amanzi, futi ni nga wa d*h*li amasi; uma ni d*h*la amasi, ni ya 'kufa ezind*h*leleni ; a ni yi 'kufika."

Nembala ke, lokupela ba ti be s' elatshwa, ibunu la tanda ukupenduka, li goduke, la ba faka ezin*q*oleni. O, ekuhambeni kwabo, be d*h*lula emizini yakwazulu, ba bona amasi, ba d*h*la. Abaningi balabo aba d*h*la amasi ba fa kona end*h*leleni ; ba za ba fika kwaba-

"And I too am suffering in the same way." So they did not eat all that meat, but were seized with pain also in their heads ; and the disease continually attacked others.

But the Amanthlwenga know how to treat this disease. Unofithlela began to swell, and his abdomen continued tumid ; he was as if he was constantly full. And Umndava was the same ; and at length they had diarrhœa.

When the white man saw how it was, and that the people would die ; for they were many, and all were attacked except himself; (but he too was formerly ill when he went there the first time, and was cured; but he went again notwithstanding;) he called the doctors of the place, and they treated the people. But when they reached the Amanthlwenga some had already died. And those who treated them told them not to drink water nor to eat amasi; and that if they ate amasi they would die in the way and not reach home.

And indeed whilst under treatment, the Dutchman wished to return home, and put them in his waggons. O, as they journeyed they passed through the villages of the Amazulu, and saw amasi and ate. Many of those who ate amasi died there in the way ; and at last the others reached our village.

c c c

kwiti. Be fika izisu se ku impalapala, imizimba i nga se ko, se be sindwa izisu. O, sa koh̬lwa uma labo 'bantu ba ya 'kwenziwa njani ukwelatshwa. Sa ba nika amasi; b' ala, ba ti, "Inyanga i te, a si nga wa dh̬li, so ze si pile; s' and' uba si wa dh̬le."

Kwa be ku kona inyanga enkulu kwiti e umukwe wetu; ibizo layo Umjiya. Wa bizwa masinyane ubabekazi; wa b' elapa; ka godukanga ukuya emzini wake, wa lala kona njalo. Nembala kwa ti izinsukwana zi nga ka bi ngaki, sa bona ukuba ameh̬lo a buya a ba awabantu; loku sa se si ti b' eza 'kufa impela; nezisu lezo wa zi budh̬luza, za pela, ba sinda. Ba se kona na namh̬la nje.

Leso 'sifo sasenh̬lwengeni si ya s' azisisa, a si koh̬lwa i so. Ibizo laso ukuti imbo. Ku h̬lonitshwa ukuti umdh̬lebe! ngokuba a u gazulwa ukubizwa, ngokuba umuti owesabekayo; njengokuba ibubesi li be li nga gazulwa, ku be ku tiwa ingonyama.

When they came they had tumid abdomens, their bodies were wasted to nothing, and their abdomens were a burden to them. O, we did not know how to treat these people. We offered them amasi; they refused, saying, "The doctor told us not to eat amasi till we are well; then we may eat it."

There was a great doctor among our people, whose daughter had married among us; his name was Umjiya. My uncle at once called him; he treated them; he did not go home to his own village, but slept there continually. And indeed after a very few days we saw that their eyes again were like the eyes of men; for we thought they would really die; and the tumid abdomens were reduced, and they got well. And they are living to this day.

That disease of the Amanthlwenga we are thoroughly acquainted with, and know that it is a deadly disease. Its name is imbo.[89] We abstain from calling[90] the tree umdhlebe; for we do not take its name in vain, for it is an awful tree; just as the term ibubesi was not used, but we used to say ingonyama.[91]

---

[89] *Imbo* is a term applied to any severe epidemic or endemic disease, as acute dysentery, fever, &c.

[90] That is, its name is *h̬lonipa'd*. It is "tapu," and must not be called by name.

[91] *Ibubesi*, a lion; *ingonyama*, the name by which it is usually spoken of.

It is difficult to drink out of the Cup of a Chief.

Ku tiwa kulukuni ukupuza esitsheni senkosi kubantu aba ti ba izazi nabo; ngokuba uma e ti naye u ya s' amukela leso 'sitsha senkosi, kanti ka namand/la emakubalweni ake oku wa temba; ku nga ti uma e ti u ya puza, ku be njengokuba umuntu e k.rakwe uti empinjeni; utshwala bu nga vumi ukwe/la; l' ale lona lelo 'tamana lokuk*r*ala ukwe/la ; a ze a bu kipele pansi.

Ku bhekwane ngame/lo abantu end/lini, ba ko/lwe ukuti ni. Kepa lobo 'tshwala bu ze bu buyele kumninibo; uma e bu nika umuntu o nge nakcala a puze nje, bw e/le. Ku tiwe kulo 'muntu, " Hau ! Ukuhamba kwako kubi. Ini uma u bindwe ukud/la kwenkosi na ? "

Njengaloku futi ku te ngesikati sempi e kwa tiwa i ya kwahha-

It is said it is difficult even for men who consider themselves knowing ones[92] to drink out of the cup of a chief; for if one thinks that he too is taking the cup, yet forsooth there is not among his medicines one which he can trust; and when he thinks he is about to drink, it is as if he had a stick obstructing his swallow; the beer will not go down; the first mouthful cannot be swallowed ; and at last he spits it out upon the ground.

The men in the house look at each other, and do not know what to say. And the beer is handed back to the chief; and if he give it to a man who is faultless,[93] he just drinks it, and it goes down. And they say to the first, "O ! Your conduct is evil. Why could you not eat the food[94] of the chief ? "

As it happened also when it was said an army was about to go to

---

[92] *Izazi*, knowing ones, magicians.

[93] *Who is faultless*, that is, to one who does not use those strong medicines which are supposed to be possessed of magical properties. The doctor is using medicines similar in character to those which the chief is using, but those of the chief are the stronger of the two, and the doctor feels their power. He is, as it were, an enemy in the presence of an enemy more powerful than himself. The common man not being under the influence of medicines is not in a state of antagonism with those who use them.

[94] *Food*. Beer, *utshwala*, is called food, and is said to be eaten ; to distinguish it from solid food, it is sometimes called *ukudhlana*—light food ; or *amanzana*—waterish food.

hhaba. Usomseu wa tuma abantu ukuya kudumisa, ngokuba leyo 'mpi ya i menywe indawo zonke lezi ezi nganeno kwomkomanzi; kepa nganeno kwomgeni kwa ba Umk*q*undane; petsheya kwomgeni kwa ba Ungoza. Kwa ti labo 'bantu aba tunywa Usomseu kudumisa—kepa umuntu e ngi m aziyo munye Umanyosi, ngokuba owakwiti—ba fika kona. Ngomkuba wabantu abamnyama, uma umuntu e vela enkosini, e tunywe i yo, ku fanele ukuba a m etuke ngoku m *h*labisa. W' enza njalo ke naye Udumisa; wa ba *h*labisa itole lenduna. Kepa ba ti ba ya li peka, ba basela—nya ukuvutshwa. Ba pinda ba fumbela izinkuni ukuti, "M*h*laumbe umlilo u be umncinyane." Ai, kwa ba njalo. Ba za ba bona ku d*h*lula isikati sokuvutwa; ba k*q*ala ukukumbula ukuti, " Hau, kanene Udumisa a nga ba w enze, e si ke si ku zwe ukuba ku tiwa inkosi

fight against the Amahhahhaba.[95] Usomseu[96] sent men to Udumisa, for the army was mustered out of all the tribes on this side the Umkomanzi; and on this side the Umgeni Umk*q*undane was chief officer; and on the other side the Umgeni, Ungoza. And the men who were sent by Usomseu—and one of the men I knew was Umanyosi, for he was one of our tribe—arrived at Udumisa's. According to the custom of black men, when one comes who is sent by the chief, it is proper to honour him by killing a bullock for him. Udumisa did so; he killed for the messengers a young ox. And they set about boiling it, and kindled a great fire, that it might be thoroughly dressed. They collected a second time a great deal of firewood, saying, perhaps there is not enough fire. No, there was enough. At length they saw that more time had passed than was required to cook the meat; they began to remember, and say one to another, " Oh, can it be that Udumisa is doing that which we have heard mentioned, viz., that if a chief has prac-

---

[95] *Amahhahhaba*, a tribe among the Amakxosa Kafirs, probably a sub-tribe of the Amagcaleka, called by Dugmore, Amakhakhabe. (*Compendium of Kafir Laws and Customs, p. 10.*)

[96] *Usomseu*, Mr. Shepstone.

uma i linge inkomo, a i vutwa, ku ze ku pele amagok*q*o ezinkuni ? I kona loku, loku izinkuni se zi pelile ; amanzi si ya wa tela, a tshe, s' engeze amanzi njalo. Uma si funa ukubona, si bone ukuba i se njengaloku i be i njalo." Ba za ba y epula, ba zilalela.

tised magic on a bullock,[97] it does not get cooked, until heaps of firewood are burnt ? This is what it is, for all the firewood is burnt ; we pour water into the pot, and it boils away, and we add continually more water. When we wish to see, we see that the meat is just as it was at first." At length they took the meat out of the pot, and slept without eating.

---

[97] Ukulinga inkomo, ukuba i gud*h*lulwe ekumeni kwayo e i mi ngako, y enziwe ukuba ku ti uma i ya *h*latshwa, abantu ba nga kcabangi aba nga y aziko, ukwenziwa ey enziwe ngako, ba *h*labe nje, be ti, i za 'kuwa masinyane ; kepa ba bone se ku za 'kupelela amak*c*ebo abo oknketa izindawo zokufa ; ba k*q*ale ukuba "Le 'nkomo a i lingiwe na ? " I loko ke ukulinga inkomo. Ku njalo ke noma i za 'upekwa ; uma i lingwe ngokungavutwa, ba ya 'ku i *h*laba, i we masinyane ; uma i lingwe ngoku*h*latshwa, ba ya 'ku i *h*laba, i nga wi. I loko ukulinga. Uma e tanda ukuba leyo 'nkomo i nga wi, u ya 'kutata ikubalo lake elitile, a li lume, a zipepete esand*h*leni ; uma ku inkomo e isidanda, a hambe a ye kuyo, a i n*w*en*c*e ; i me, a i pulule o*h*langotini lapo i za 'ku*h*latshwa ngakona, a yeke ke. Uma e i linge ngokuvutwa, a nga pepeta imbiza yokupeka. Ku pela ke.

Ukulinga inkomo—to bewitch or practise magic on a bullock—is for the purpose of causing it to lose its natural properties; it is done in order that when it is stabbed, those who do not know what has been done to it, may without thinking just stab it, expecting it at once to drop ; but when they see all their skill in choosing fatal points for stabbing is near being exhausted, they begin to ask whether it has not been bewitched. This is what is meant by practising magic on a bullock. In like manner, when it is to be boiled, if it has been bewitched for the purpose of preventing its becoming cooked, they will stab it, and it will at once drop; if it is bewitched for the purpose of preventing its being fatally stabbed, it will not fall. This is what is meant by ukulinga. If a man wishes that the bullock should not drop when stabbed, he will take a certain medicine which he has, and chew it, and breathe it on his hand ; if the bullock is tame he goes to it, and scratches it; it stands still, and he rubs its side in the place where it will be stabbed ; and so leaves it. If he practises magic to prevent its being cooked, he may breathe on the pot in which it is to be cooked. That is all.

Kepa kwa ku 'bu*h*lungu loko kubo ukuti, "Ini ukuba Udumisa 'enze nje? loku e nge si yo impi nati. Loku si kw azi kw enziwa inkosi, y enzela enye inkosi, ukuze i bone ukuti, ' Uma ngi ya lwa nobani, ka yi 'kuvutwa; mina ngi ya 'kuvutwa.'"

Ba goduka ke. Ku te uma ba fike ekaya enkosini, ba i simza leyo 'ndaba. Kepa ku te uma inkosi i ku zwe ukuba Udumisa w enze njalo, wa ya wa bizwa. Ku te ukuba a fike, kwa tiwa, "Dumisa, si ku bizela le 'ndaba, ukuba ku k*q*inisile ini ukuba abantu u ba nike inkomo, ba i peka, a ya ze ya vutwa na?"

Kepa Udumisa, ukupendula kwake, wa ti, "O, makosi, a ng' azi uma ngi za 'uti ni, loku ngi ba nikile inkomo. Kepa uma be be nga i baseli, ni ti u mina nga ngi pume nga ya 'ku ba tezela ini na?"

Kepa amakosi a m vumela Udumisa, a ti, "Inyama a i vutwanga ngobuvila babo."

Kepa kubona, noma Udumisa wa kuluma ngezwi lobuk*q*ili, ama-

But that was a trouble to them, and they said, "Why has Udumisa done this? for he is not our enemy. For we know that this is done by one chief to another, that he may see and say, ' If I fight with So-and-so he will not be conquered,[98] but it is I myself that shall be conquered.'"

So they returned, and went at once to the chief.[99] And when the chief heard that Udumisa had done this, he summoned him to appear before him. When he came, it was said to him, "Udumisa, we have summoned you on account of this report, to know whether it is true that you gave the men a bullock, and that they boiled it, but it could not be thoroughly cooked?"

But Udumisa said in reply, "O, chiefs,[1] I do not know what to say, for I gave them a bullock. But if they did not kindle a fire to cook it, do you say that it is I who ought to have gone out and fetched firewood for them?"

And the chiefs agreed with Udumisa, and said, "The meat was not cooked because the men were idle."

But in their opinion, although Udumisa spoke cunningly, and

---

[98] Lit., cooked, or boiled.

[99] *The chief*, Mr. Shepstone.

[1] *Chiefs.*—All superior white men are so called, especially those sitting with a magistrate; and government officials.

kosi a m vumela, a ku banga njalo kubo; ngokuba ba ti, "Eh! Udumisa w' enza ni ukuba a ti inkomo a si i baselanga? U tsho oku njani uku i basela, loku ku pele izinkuni namanzi, s' a/iluleka na? I kona ini inkomo e pekwa nam/ila nje, i vutwe ngomso na? uma a ti a si i baselanga na?"

Ya pela leyo 'ndaba; kwa vunyelwa Udumisa; kepa kubona na nam/ila nje a ba pendukeki kuloko 'kubona kwabo, noma be la-/ilwa.

the chiefs agreed with him, it was not so; for they said, "Eh! what does Udumisa mean by saying that we did not kindle sufficient fire for the bullock? What does he understand by kindling fire enough, when both the firewood and the water were consumed, and we could do nothing more? Is there any bullock which one begins to boil on one day, and it is cooked on the morrow? We ask him this, when he says we did not kindle fire enough for it."

The matter ended; the chiefs agreed with Udumisa; but the others have in no way altered their opinion, though they lost the case.

The Magic of Ufaku.

INDABA yokulumba kukafaku kang*/*ung*/*ushe, e lumba Uncapayi kamadikane.

Uncapayi wa zeka indodakazi kafaku, udade wabo 'ndamase. Kwa ti ngolunye usuku Ufaku wa tuma umuntu wake ukuya kuncapayi ebusuku e se lele. Wa kumula itusi lake li sengalweni;

THE account of the magic of Ufaku,[2] the son of Ung*/*ung*/*ushe, which he practised on Uncapayi,[3] the son of Umadikane.

Uncapayi married a daughter of Ufaku, the sister of Undamase. One day Ufaku sent one of his men to go to Uncapayi by night whilst he was asleep. He took a brass ornament which was on his arm, without his hearing; neither

---

[2] Ufaku, a great chief of the Amampondo, now dead.

[3] Uncapayi, by descent a chief of a tribe of Amabakca, who raised himself to some position by his personal qualities as a leader.

k' ezwanga, nomkake k' ezwanga. Wa puma nalo, wa li yisa kufaku.

Ufaku wa li sebenza lelo 'tusi ngokwazi kwake. Kwa ti ngoluny' usuku wa m biza Uncapayi pakati kwobusuku, e se m lumbile; wa m biza ngegama, e nga memezi, e m biza, e pete imiti yokwazi kwake Ufaku.

Uncapayi wa vuka ebusuku, wa vata. Wa buza umkake ukuti, " U ya ngapi, nkosi ? "

Wa ti, " Ngi y' enkosini, kufaku."

Wa ti owesifazana, " Ebusuku nje na ? "

Wa ti, " Yebo."

Wa ti owesifazana, " A ku sa yi 'kusa ini na, u hambe ? "

Wa ti, " Kqa, ngi hamba kona manje."

Nembala wa puma, wa hamba

did his wife hear. He left their hut, and brought the ornament to Ufaku.

Ufaku worked on the ornament with his magical knowledge. And one night he called Uncapayi, having practised magic on him; he called him by name,[4] not shouting aloud, but calling him, and using the medicines with which he was acquainted.

Uncapayi awoke in the night, and clothed himself. His wife said to him, " Where are you going, O chief ? "

He replied, " I am going to the chief, to Ufaku."

The woman said, " When it is still night ? "

He said, " Yes."

The woman asked, " Will it never be daylight, that you may go then ? "

He replied, " No, I am going now."

And indeed he quitted the

---

[4] Calling him by name; that is, whilst practising magical arts he called Uncapayi by name, that the magic might take effect on him, and not on another.

In the Legends of Iceland we meet with several instances of persons being "called" or forced by magical means to go to a certain place, where their enemies were awaiting them. Thus Olafr says to Gudmundr:—"My father lives at a farm not far from hence; he has charmed you hither, for he wants to repay you the slaying of his son." (*Legends of Iceland. Second Series, p.* 103.) Again, the farmer having unsuccessfully attempted to kill Oddr, says :—" Great is thy luck, Oddr, to have escaped scatheless, for thou shalt know that, by my charms, thou art here, as I intended to kill thee." (*Id., p.* 123.) See also p. 132 and p. 153.

ngamand*h*la. Owesifazana wa sala. Wa vus' abantu ukuti, "Inkosi i mukile. I landele ni." Nembala abantu ba puma kona ebusuku; kwa za kwa sa be landela. Wa fika kona, kona ebusuku. Wa bikwa, kwa tiwa, "Nangu Uncapayi."

Wa buza, wa ti, "U ya ngapi na?"
Wa ti Uncapayi, "Ngi ze kona lapa."
"U zotata ni na?"

Wa ti, "Ngi be ngi ti, ngi biziwe inkosi."
Inkosi ya ti, "K*q*a. Kodwa mu yise ni end*h*lini etile. Si ya 'ukuluma kusasa." Kwa lalwa ke.

Kwa ti ku sa Ufaku wa e *h*langanisa impi yake, i *h*lasele. Kepa ekancapayi impi ya incane, i nge ngakanani. Wa ti Ufaku, "Ngi nge m bulale umyeni womntanami. Ka goduke."

Kepa Uncapayi ngaleso 'sikati wa e nge nampi enkulu; kodwa

house, and went on his way speedily. His wife remained behind. She roused the people and said to them, "Your chief has departed. Follow him." And the people left their home at once during the night, and followed him till the morning. Uncapayi reached the village of Ufaku during the night. Ufaku was told that Uncapayi had arrived.

Ufaku asked, "Where is he going?"
Uncapayi replied, "I have come to this place."
Ufaku said, "What has he come to fetch?"
He replied, "I thought I was called by the chief."
The chief said, "No. But take him to such and such a house. We will talk in the morning." So they went to sleep.

In the morning Ufaku assembled his troops that they might go out to battle.[5] But the soldiers of Uncapayi which followed him were very few in number. Ufaku said, "I cannot kill my child's husband. Let him go home."

But at that time Uncapayi had not a large army; but he was

---

[5] Although, as is supposed, Ufaku had by magical charms forced Uncapayi to come to him alone, yet when he was there in his power, Ufaku relented, and was unable to kill his son-in-law. But he could not be comfortable till he had vented his anger on someone, so he collected his troops and sent them out on a raid against some neighbouring tribe.

wa e namandhla eziteni; kodwa e pansi kukafaku, e nga buseki kahle, e nomlomo; ku nga ti a nga lwa nofaku. Kepa Ufaku e tanda uku m bulala ngesiny' isikati, a sinde ngobuyeni. Kepa noko Uncapayi wa za wa fa ngokuweliselwa impi esiweni kanye nempi yake, e zile 'kulwa nofaku.

mighty in battle with the enemy; but he was subject to Ufaku, but he did not readily submit to be governed, but disputed Ufaku's word, and appeared as though he would fight with him. And sometimes when Ufaku wished to kill him, he escaped because he was his daughter's husband. But notwithstanding at last Uncapayi was hurled by the army of Ufaku over a precipice together with his soldiers with which he had come to fight with Ufaku.

Intelezi.

Ku kona izinhlobo eziningi zemiti e ku tiwa intelezi. Intelezi into e ku ti uma umuntu womlisa e ya 'ugeza, a nga gezi ngamanzi odwa njengowesifazana; owesifazana yedwa o geza ngamanzi odwa; umlisa ku ti lapa e ya 'ugeza a hamb' 'apule izintelezi eziningana; ku ti uma e se e fikile emfuleni a fune imbokondo, a hlale pansi, a zi kande; uma e se zi kandile, a tele amanzi kancinane, a zi fumbate ngezandhla zombili; a zi bhekise pezulu izandhla; ku ti ukwehla

There are many kinds of plants which are called intelezi. Intelezi is a thing of this kind:[6] when a man goes to wash he does not wash with water only, like women; it is women only who wash with water only; when a man goes to wash he picks several kinds of intelezi; and when he has come to the river he looks for a pebble, and sits down and bruises the intelezi;[7] when he has bruised them he pours a little water on them, and squeezes them in both his hands; he raises his hands over his head; and as the water

---

[6] This cannot be rendered literally, so as to be intelligible to the English reader. It is very common for the Zulu thus to introduce a subject in an elliptical manner, "Intelezi is a thing which:—when a man goes to wash," &c.

[7] Properly *izintelezi*, the plural, for there are many kinds.

kwamanzi e puma ekambini lezintelezi 'e*h*le ngemikono yombili, a ze a pume ngezinyawo; futi na semlonyeni a ti fokco ukukamela, ukuze a kcinse ngalapa e petwe kabi ngakona; uma e nga zondeki ka kw enzi loku 'kukcinsa; a be ke se u ya *h*liki*h*la umzimba wonke, u se zi falaka*h*la esikoteni lezo 'ntelezi. U se li geza ngamanzi lelo 'tshe nembokondo, u se i fi*h*la, ngokuba na ngangomso u ya 'ku i swela; a zitele ke ngamanzi.

Ukugeza kwendoda a i k*q*ali ngomzimba wonke kubantu abamnyama; i k*q*ale ngemikono, ngemva kwaloko ke i wa tele emzimbeni ngezand*h*la zombili; i wa ponse ngalapa kwe*h*lombe na ngalapa kwelinye, i ze i k*q*ede ke, i vate, i kupuke njalo.

Y enzela ngaloko 'kugeza ngentelezi, ukuti u kona ku ya 'kuti noma u ya hamba a velelwe ingozi,

which runs out of the bruised leaves and stalks[8] of the intelezi descends by both his arms, it escapes at his feet; and he pours some into his mouth, that he may squirt it in the direction of where he has received an injury;[9] if he has no enemy he does not squirt in this manner; he then rubs his whole body, and throws the remains on the grass. He then washes the pebble with which he bruised the intelezi, and the rock on which he bruised it, and hides the pebble, because tomorrow also he may want it; he then washes himself with water.

As to the mode in which a man washes himself among black men, he does not begin to wash every part of the body indifferently; he begins with his arms, after that he pours water over his body with both his hands; then throws it over each shoulder, until he has washed the whole body, when he dresses and goes out of the water.[10]

He washes himself therefore with intelezi, that though he should meet with danger whilst travelling,

---

[8] By *ikambi lezintelezi* we are to understand the green portions of the plants, leaves, and stalks, when bruised.

[9] This system of squirting water containing medicine from the mouth, is a very common custom among the natives, in the efficacy of which they have great faith. It is practised to ward off a danger which might arise from the magical practices of another; it is also a defiance, and a means of sending evil to another. The custom of spitting in contempt is probably connected with some such superstition.

[10] The native dress is very simple, and during washing is placed on a rock close at hand; and the man stands in the water whilst washing, and does not go out of the water till he has dressed.

a nga tshetshi a limalo, a punyuke njalo engozini, noma eyokuwa noma eyokulwa ; a nga velelwa ingozi masinyane.

Intelezi kubantu abamnyama into e tembekayo kakulu ; ngokuba ku ti ngezikati zonke lapa umuntu e ya 'ugeza, a pate intelezi njalo. Kodwa uma e ye ezibukweni ka i pati, u geza ngamanzi nje ; ngokuba u puma ku se luvivi, a nge zi bone izintelezi ; futi a nge geze ngentelezi uma e ye ezibukweni, ngokuba ku tiwa izibuko li into embi ; noma umuntu e nemiti yake a i tembayo, a nge ye kuyo uku i pata ; ku ti uma u ya swela kakulu ukupata imiti yake, a func emakubalweni ake izilumulo, a i lumule, a be se u ya tukulula ke, u se i lungisile ke, a i se nakcala leyo 'miti.

I njalo ke intelezi. Ba kona abanye ab' azi intelezi enkulu e geza abantu aba izinyanga. Ku ti

he may not be quickly injured, but escape constantly from danger which may arise either from falling or from fighting ; and that he might not suddenly fall into danger.

Black men trust very much to intelezi ; for at all times when a man is about to wash he takes intelezi. But when he has gone to the ford[11] he does not take intelezi, but washes with water only ; for he quits his hut when it is still dark, and he cannot see intelezi ;[12] further, he does not wash with intelezi under such circumstances, because the ford is said to be a bad thing ;[13] and although a man has medicines to which he trusts, he cannot go to them to touch them ; and if he has great need to touch his medicines, he searches for izilumulo[14] among them, and uses them, and then he will untie his medicines, having put them in safety, and then his medicines come to no harm.

Such then is intelezi. There are some who are acquainted with powerful intelezi with which doctors wash themselves. If a man

---

[11] I do not explain this. The Zulu scholar will understand the meaning of the metaphor.

[12] That is, distinguish it from other plants.

[13] Influences other things for evil, and if the medicines be touched, their properties will be injuriously affected.

[14] *Izilumulo*, a class of medicines which are chewed *(luma)*, and the breath thus saturated by them puffed on the body, on medicines, &c., to protect them from evil.

uma omunye e dhlala nomunye, kanti lowo u gezo ngentelezi, a tole ingozi omunye kakulu ngokudhlala nalowo 'muntu; 'aziswe, ku tiwe, "O, lo 'muntu intelezi yake i namandhla. Ini ukuti e dhlala nje nomunye, be nga lwi, a be lo u se u tola ingozi engaka na? Kqa; intelezi yalo 'muntu inkulu."

plays with another who has washed with intelezi, and meets with some severe injury from merely playing with the man, the man is dreaded, and it is said, "O, the intelezi of that man is powerful. Why, when he is merely playing with another and not fighting, has he met with so severe an injury as this? No; the intelezi of that man is powerful."

Intelezi for Soldiers.

Ku ti uma inkosi i ya 'kulwa nenye, i bize inyanga yayo e pata impi. I ze nentelezi yayo, i i kande, i fakwe embizeni, ku telwe amanzi, ku be se ku ya kxovwa, i hlaganiswe namanzi. Lokupela ku kona itshoba lenyamazane ey aziwayo, ku tiwa inkonkoni; leyo 'nyamazane itshoba layo lide; se li fakwa esitsheni leso sentelezi, inyanga se i tata isitsha. Loku impi i se y enze umkumbu; a ku se ko 'muntu o kulumayo; se ku te nya; ngokuba pela uma se i puma impi a ku ko 'muntu o nga kuluma indatshana nje; ku suka ku kubi ngalolo 'lusuku, ngokuba ku ya 'kufa abantu; nokudhla a ku ngeni. I fafaza ke inyanga, i zungeza yonke, i ze i u hlanganise umkumbu. Loku pela uma y' enziwa njalo impi, a ku ko 'muntu kulabo aba ya empini o se nama-

WHEN a chief is about to fight with another, he calls his armydoctor. He brings intelezi, which he bruises, places in a pot, pours water on it, and then squeezes it with his hands, and mixes it with the water. And he has the tail of a large animal, which is well known, called the gnu; its tail is long; it is placed in the vessel of intelezi, and the doctor takes the vessel. The army forms a semicircle; no man speaks; there is perfect silence; for indeed when an army is being led out to war no one speaks even a little; it is an evil day, for men are going to die; and they eat nothing. The doctor sprinkles the whole army, going round it, until he has gone round the whole circle. And when an army has had this done to it, no one among them is able

ndhla okuhlangana nomfazi wake; ku ya zilwa kakulu; ngokuba uma umuntu ngesikati lapa kw a-luka impi, abantu se be petwe ngentelezi, a hlangane nomfazi, u ya zibulala, u zenzela amehlo a-mnyama. Intelezi a y ekqiwa umuntu; uma e y ekqile, u zibu-lala yena. Ngokuba ku ti ngam-hla i se i menywa impi, i hlangane kwomkulu, ku hlatshwe izinkomo inkosi; zi hlinzwe ngaleso 'sikati; inyama yokukqala a ba i dhlayo, ba i dhla imnyama, ngokuba i bu-kqwa emsizini njalo. Ba dhle bonke leyo 'nyama, amakqata nga-manye, uku b' emisa isibindi, ukuze ba ng' esabi. Ku ti uma a i kqede ngoku i fafaza, a ngene umniniyo, a tete nayo, e bonga amadhlozi akubo. U ya 'kuti e kqeda umniniyo ukuteta nayo, a be tsho e ti, "Mabandhla akwetu, a tize a ti, ngo'uke ngi zwe ke. Nanti ilanga pezulu; impi namhla nje ngi i nika ukuti," (u tsho ibu-to elitile;) "ngi ti ngemva kwako

to associate with his wife; they abstain excessively; for if a man, when the army is going out, and the men have been treated with intelezi, associate with his wife, he kills himself, making his own eyes dark.[15] No man sins against the law of intelezi; if he does, he kills himself. For on the day the army is summoned and assembles at the chief's, the chief slaughters cattle, and they are then skinned; the first meat they eat is black, being always smeared with umsizi."[16] All eat the meat, each a slice, that they may be brave, and not fear-ful. When the doctor has finished sprinkling the army, the chief[17] comes into the midst of it and talks with it, lauding the Amato-ngo of their people. In conclusion the chief says, "Troops of our peo-ple, who did such and such great ac-tions,[18] I shall hear of your doings. There is the sun in the sky; I have this day given the enemy into the hands of such and such a regiment; and I direct such and

---

[15] That is, if he break the law of the intelezi-sprinkling or bap-tism, it is to his own injury, and when he goes into battle, he loses all power of discrimination, and is soon killed.

[16] *Umsizi*, a powder made of the dried flesh of various wild beasts,—leopard, lion, elephant, snakes, &c.,—the natives intending by the administering this compound to impart to the men the qualities of the several animals. Sometimes if a man has killed a wild beast, a leopard for instance, he will give his children the blood to drink, and roast the heart for them to eat, expecting thereby to cause them to grow up brave and daring men. But it is said by others that this is dangerous, because it is apt to produce courage without prudence, and cause a man to rush on heedlessly to his death.

[17] Lit., the owner or master of the army, that is, the chief.

[18] Recounting the famous actions which they have done in battle.

ku landele ukuti. A ng' azi ke mina. Ni ya 'kuba ni ziḣleba nina. Ubaba wa e ikqawe; a ku bonanga kwiti ku be kona igwala. Imikonto a i ni ḣlabe ngapambili; ku nga bi ko 'nxeba ngemuva. Uma ngi bona ni buya n' aḣluliwe, ngi ya 'ku ni bulala; a ni yi 'kufumana 'ndawo lapa ekaya; ngi impi nami uma n' esaba."

Lapo ke ukugwiya a ku sa nqamuki. Abanye ba beka imizi yaoyise, ukuti, " Mina, uma ngi nga gwazanga, ngi ku nika umuzi wakwetu wonke." Kepa uma ku inkosi e nga tandi ukuba umfana a beke ngomuzi kayise, uyise e se kona, i ti, " Kqabo. Musa ni ukubeka ngemizi yamanye amadoda." Omunye a ti, " U kqinisile, silo. Ngi ti mina e ngi beka ngako, ngi beka ngekanda lami, ukuba uma ngi ng' enzanga 'luto, u ngi nqume; kupela. Nako e ngi beka ngako." Ba tsho njalo bonke. Abanye ba koḣlwe loko a ba nga ku tshoyo, ba tula nje.

Kepa ngaleso 'sikati sokubeka, ku bekwe enkosini, kubi, a ku ta-

such a regiment to follow it. I do not know for my part what more I could do. If you do not conquer, you will disgrace yourselves.[19] My father was a brave; there was never known to be a coward amongst us. Let the assagais wound you in front; let there be no wound in the back. If I see you coming back conquered I will kill you; you will find no place for you here at home; I too am an enemy if you are cowards."

Then there is no end of leaping and brandishing of weapons. Some devote[20] the villages of their fathers, saying, " For my part, if I do not stab the enemy, I give you the whole village of my family." But if it is a chief who does not wish a boy to devote his father's village whilst his father is living, he says, " No. Do not devote the villages of other men." Another says, " You speak the truth, leopard.[21] For my part I devote my own head, that if I do nothing, you may kill me; that is all. That is what I devote." All say the same. Some do not know what to say, and are silent.

And when they are devoting themselves to the chief, it is a bad

---

[19] He means that he has done all that a chief can do to ensure them victory; and if they fail the fault will be their own, because it will arise from their having in some way failed to observe the conditions upon which the efficacy of the intelezi-baptism depends.

[20] Devote,—or promise to give,—or vow to give,—*lay down* as a votive offering.

[21] *Leopard.* The natives magnify their chiefs by this title.

ndcki; ku ya gwiywa, kw apulwa izinti ebusweni bayo. Ukwapula uti ebusweni benkosi kubantu abamnyama ukufunga okukulu, ukuti, "U ya 'u ngi buza, uma u ng' ezwanga indaba yami."

Ngaleso 'sikati a i fani nenkosi a ba i *h*lonipayo; a ba sa y esabi ngaleso 'sikati. Abanye ba i tu*nq*isela ngotuli, be ti, "Leli 'gwalana el' efuza unina! I pi impi o si nika yona? Si ya tanda uku i bona ngame*h*lo etu." A i kupe impi yake.

Lokupela ngaleso 'sikati bonke abesifazana abamnyama a ba sondeli, se be hambela kude; aba sondelayo abafazi abakulu aba nga se nako ukupotela, se kw amadoda; i labo aba sondelayo empini; bonke abatsha ba hambela kude kuyo.

I hambe ke, i puma ekaya ngehhubo layo, loku pela se ku nga ti ba nga i bona masinyane. I hambe ke. Emakaya ku sale abagulayo, ku be ukupela.

Ngaleso 'sikati sokwaluka kwe-

and unpleasant time; the men leap and brandish their weapons, and break rods in the face of the chief. To break a rod in the face of the chief is a great oath among black people, and a man means to say by it, "You will take me to task, if you do not hear some great thing that I have done."

At that time he does not resemble a chief whom they reverence; they are not afraid of him at that time. Some throw dust on him, saying, "This little coward who resembles his mother! Where is the enemy which you give us to fight with? We wish to see it with our eyes." He then sends out his army.[22]

Under these circumstances no black woman draws near, but they go to a distance; those who approach are old women who have passed the time of childbearing, and have become men;[23] it is they only who go near the army; all the young women go to a distance from it.

So the army sets out from home singing its song, for it is as if they could see the enemy at once. So the army sets out. And the sick only remain at home.

When the army is in the field

---

[22] *Impi* is used in this paragraph in the double sense of the enemy—*impi kubo*; and the chief's army—*impi yayo*.

[23] Old women are called men, and no longer act as women, nor observe the customs of *h*lonipa in relation to the men.

mpi abafazi a ba zinaki ngokuzilungisa; ngokuba ku tiwa, a ku lungile ukuba owesifazana, uma indoda yake y alukile, a sale 'enze imikutshana eminingi neyokuzivunulisa. Futi ka gezi futifuti; ku y' aziwa njalonjalo ukuti indoda yake i seziteni; u ya linda ngako konke ukwenza kwake.

Ku ti uma ku kona o be e s' and' ukwendiswa, uma lowo 'muntu impi ya m ḣlaba ku sa ḣlanganwa, ku tiwe, "Amatanga alowo 'wesifazana mabi. Ini ukuba indoda yake i fe ku nga k' enziwa 'luto na? Mabi amatang' ake."

Ku njalo ke ukuma kwentelezi yokukcela impi.

Inyanga i ya tsho ukuti, "Naṁḣla, ngi ti a ni sa 'uze na ḣlatshwa; i ya 'uzinge i tshaya eziḣlangwini imikonto yezita, i dḣlule."

Ku kona umkuba ow enziwayo inyanga uma ku za 'upuma impi, isibonakaliso sokuti noma impi i

the women take no pains to keep themselves tidy; for it is said, it is not proper that a woman, when her husband is out with the army, should continue many little habits, not even those of adorning herself. And she does not often wash; she continually remembers that her husband is with the enemy; she watches herself in all she does.

And if there is any one who has just been married, and the enemy stabs him at the very first onset, it is said, "The lap of that woman is unlucky.[24] Why has her husband died before any thing was done? Her lap is unlucky."

Such is what is done with intelezi in sprinkling an army.

The doctor says, "I say that now you will not be stabbed at all; the enemies' assagais will constantly strike on the shields and glance off."

There is a custom[25] which is carried out by the doctor when an army is about to take the field, which is a sign by which it is

---

[24] It is said of such, *U 'matanga 'mabi.*

[25] This custom is that of churning medicine in a pot of water. Two medicines are chosen; one represents the chief, the other the enemy. These medicines are placed in separate vessels; if that representing the enemy froths up suddenly, whilst that representing the chief does not froth, they regard it as a sign that the enemy will prove too strong for them if they attack him at that time, and the army is not allowed to go out to battle. The same trial is repeated again and again, it may be for months or even years, and the army is allowed to go out to battle only when the sign is reversed, and the chief's vessel froths up, and that of the enemy does not froth.

ya 'kwaḥlulwa, noma i ya 'kwaḥlula. Ngokuba ku ti uma se i ḥlangene, ku be kona abantu aba izazi zokubhekisisa, b' emi kude nayo impi, be funa uku i bona ukuba impi impela na. Ku ti uma be i bona y edeleleka emeḥlweni, ba tsho enkosini, ba ti, " Kqa, nkosi! Le 'mpi yanamḥla nje a si i boni ; ibomvana. Ini ukuba impi i nga bi mnyama, i sinde emeḥlweni na? Kqa; a si boni impi. I lula; a i patwanga kaḥle. Buyela, u i lungise impi, ukuze i be nesitunzi, a ti umuntu uma e i bheka a nga i jwayeli, a y esabe. A ku 'mpi le." Nembala i buyekezwe ngokwelatshwa, ukuze i be nesitunzi.

Ku ti kubantu abamnyama, uma umuntu e s' and' ukwendiswa, a ku tandeki uma a pume impi; ngokuba ku tiwa, " A ku lungile ukuba ku ti umakoti e se gubuzele, ukuti e sa ḥlonipile, indoda i m

known whether the army will be conquered or conquer. For when the army is assembled there are wise men appointed to look earnestly, who stand at a distance from it, endeavouring to discover whether it is a trustworthy army or not. And if they see that it is contemptible in their eyes, they say to the chief, " No, O chief! The army which is assembled this day we cannot see; it is contemptible.[26] How is it that the army is without awfulness, and weight in our sight? No; we do not see an army. It is light; it has not been properly handled.[27] Return and set the army to rights, that it may be awful, that if one look on it, it may not appear a common thing to him, but strike him with awe. This is not an army." And indeed they again sprinkle it with intelezi, that it may be awful.

And among black men if a man has just married, it is not liked that he should go out with the army; for it is said, " It is not proper that the husband should leave the bride as soon as she has covered her head,"[28] that is, manifested respect for her husband's

---

[26] Lit., *reddish*,—having nothing awful about it,—a thing we can look at without fear. And *awful*—lit., black, or dark—resembling the sky which is being overcast with dark clouds which threaten a coming tempest. But all this is a matter of *feeling* with the wise men.

[27] Viz., by the doctor.

[28] A young bride, on reaching her husband's village, covers her head, as an intimation of respect for her husband's relatives, especially for his father.

shiye." Kwa ku ng' enziwa, ngokuba ku tiwa i ya tshetsha impi uku m ḥlaba o gubuzelisileyo, ukuti umakoti. Ku ngaloko ke ku be kona indoda e m tshelayo umlisa lowo, noma uyise, a ti, "Wena, u nga yi; ḥlala," e tsho ngasese.

Kepa loko kwamazulu kwa pela; ngokuba amabuto onke a ku tandwanga ukuba a ganwe; kwa tiwa bonke a ba nga ganwa, ukuze ba ng' esabi. Ku be ku njalo pakati kwetu; kwa kw esatshwa uma umuntu e puma impi e shiya e gobisile. Kwa yekwa ngokuti, "O, ai! loku abantu ba ya 'kuti, 'Umuntu o gobisileyo u y' esaba; u tanda umfazi kunobukqawe.' " Se ku pelile manje; a ku se ko.

Futi into e se kona ukuba uma umfazi e nesisu, ku tiwa, noma umuntu e inyanga yamanzi, u fanele uku wa ḥlonipa, ngokuba ku tiwa umfazi wake u miti; u ya 'utshetsha ukumuka namanzi.

people. He was not allowed to go out with the army, because it was said, the enemy quickly stabs the man who has made his bride cover her head. Therefore some man, perhaps his father, tells him secretly not to go, but to stay at home.

But that custom ceased among the Amazulu; for it was not wished that any of the soldiers should marry; all were commanded not to marry, that they might not be afraid. It used to be so amongst us, and we were afraid for one to go out with the army leaving his young wife behind.[29] Marriage was given up, because it was said, "O, no! for men will say, 'A man who has a young bride will be afraid, because he loves his wife rather than bravery.' " But there is now no longer the custom amongst us.

But there is still this custom: If a woman is pregnant, it is said, even though a man is a waterdoctor,[30] it is proper that he should abstain from going into the water, for it is said he will be quickly carried away by the water if his wife is pregnant.

---

[29] *Gobisile*, who has taken a young wife.

[30] Not a hydropathic doctor; but a man whose occupation it is to enable others to cross deep rivers.

The Bird-doctor.

Ku kona indaba e mangalisayo ngomuntu o inyanga yezinyoni ezi dhla amabele. Ngokuba ku ti ngesikati sokukahlela kwamabele, uma e kqala ukuti fokeo izinhlamvu, a lindwe kakulu; kw akiwe amakxiba okulinda izinyoni; umuntu a vuke ku se luvivi, a ze a buye ekutshoneni kwelanga; uma ku ti zwakea se zi godukile.

Ku ti uma e kqala ukubonakala izinhlamvu, ku bizwe inyanga, ngokuba se be bona ukuti nokuvuka a ku sizi 'luto, zi lala pakati, a zi sa pumi emasimini ngaleso 'sikati. Umfazi nendoda a ba sa tandani; ngokuba izinyoni uma zi vamile z' ahlukanisa izitandani; ku pele nesikati sokuhlala 'ndawo nye, abantu ba kulume indaba. Uma indoda i nga lindi, ku katazeke umfazi yedwa, indoda a i hlangani nomfazi, ngokuba umfazi ka sa peki; indoda i funa ukudhla, umfazi a ti, "Pela, wena, ukudhla u ya ku dhla ini na? Loku naku ku kqedwa izilwane nje na! Ngi si tata pi isikati sokufuna ukudhla, uma ngi hlupeka kangaka na? Izinyoni zi ya ngi nika ini isikati

There is a remarkable account of a man who was a doctor of those birds which eat the corn. For at the time of the blossoming of the amabele, when the grain begins to set, it is diligently watched; and watch-houses are built for the purpose of watching the birds; and people arise whilst it is still very early in the morning, and return at sunset; when it is dark the birds go to their roosts.

When the grain begins to appear, a doctor is called, for the people see that even early rising is of no use, since the birds sleep in the midst of the garden, and never quit it at the time of the setting of the grain. The wife and husband no longer love one another; for when the birds are numerous they separate lovers; and there is no time for sitting in one place, that the people may talk about the news. If the husband does not watch, and the wife alone is harassed, the husband does not associate with his wife, for she no longer cooks food; if the husband ask for food, the wife says, "As for you forsooth, do you eat food? For see there are those little beasts destroying it in this way! When can I find time to look for food, if I am harassed in this way? Do the birds allow me to have any

na? Loku ku ba kuhle uma ku ti emini ke zi bunge, anduba umuntu a ke a be nesikati sokuya 'kuzifuuela ukudhla na?"

Ngaleso 'sikati indoda uma i nga pumi ukuya 'kusiza umkayo i zakce; ngokuba ukudhla a i ku fumani 'ndawo uma indhlu nye. Ku ti amadoda, noma e hlala ekaya, ku ti ngokulamba na ngokuvukelwa abafazi be katazwa izinyoni, se be 'nhliziyo 'bomvu, a ze a pume amadoda a ye 'kweleka kuleyo 'mpi e liwa isifazana; anduba owesifazana a shiye indoda ensimini, a ye 'kufuna ukudhla esifeni, ku dhliwe ke ngaleyo 'mini. Amadoda a buye imikono i vuvukile ngokuponsa amatshe seloku ku sile ku ze ku tshone ilanga; izinyoni zi nga bungi.

Ku ze amadoda a hlangane nomninimuzi ukuti, "Hau, mngane, u tula nje, u ti ni? Lok' u bona nje ukuba si ya fa indhlala, nabantwana betu a ba sa sengelwa 'luto, abantu ba tunjwe izinyoni."

time? Since it is well if at noon they just leave off eating for a little while, can a person then find time to go and seek food for himself?"

At that time, if the husband does not go out to help his wife, he gets thin; for he cannot get any food anywhere if he has but one wife. And the husbands, although at first they stay at home, yet because of hunger and the anger of their wives, who are harassed by the birds and have now bleeding[31] hearts, at length go out to assist the women against the enemy which is fighting with them; and then the woman leaves her husband in the garden, and goes to seek for food in a small garden plot which is more forward than the rest, and then they eat food. And the men return home with their arms swollen with throwing stones at the birds from earliest dawn to sunset; the birds not leaving off eating for a little time.

At length the men go to the chief of the village, and say, "O, dear sir, what do you mean by remaining silent? For you see clearly that we are dying of want, and the cows are no longer milked for our children, for the people are taken captive by the birds."

---

[31] That is, are very angry.

Ku be njalo ke umnumuzane nembala a kumbule inyanga a y aziko, ukuba i y' azi ukuvimba izinyoni, a ti, "Hamba ni, ni ye kubani, ni ye 'ku m biza, 'eze namhla nje, ezo' ng' elamulela, ngokuba ugi ya dhliwa izilwane."

Nembala ke ku ti uma inyanga i fika, i fike nemifunzi yemiti emidala nemitsha, nokokoti inyoka e yona ku vinjwa ngayo izinyoni. Inyanga i bize inkomo, i ti, "Ngi kombise inkomo yami." Umninimuzi a ti, "U ti uma u goduse abantwana bami ba ye ekaya, ngi ya 'ute ng' ahlulwe u we? U ngakauani na? Kqeda izinyoni lezi lapa emasimini, ngi ku tshayele inkomo. A ku yi 'kuba ko 'nkani uma u kipe izinyoni lezi."

I tsho ke i ti, "Amadoda a wa hlangane onke, a gaule izinkuni ezimanzi; abafazi a ba yeke izinyoni namhla, zi dhle, ukuze ngi tole ukqakqa pansi; kona ngi ya 'ku z' elapa kahle." I ti, "Funa ni iselesele elikulu, ukuze ngi zi vimbe ngalo."

Nembala ngalolu 'suku izinyoni zi wa nikiza amabele; zi wa kqale kusasa ku ze ku tshone ila-

And so the chief of the village remembers a doctor whom he knows is skilful to prevent birds from entering the garden, and says, "Go and call So-and-so, to come here to-day to help me, for I am devoured by little beasts."

And indeed when the doctor comes he brings with him bundles of dried and green medicines, and a snake which is called Ukokoti, with which birds are kept out of the garden. The doctor demands a head of cattle, saying, "Point out my bullock to me." The chief of the village says, "Do you think if you cause my children to come home, that it will be possible for me to be excelled by you? How great are you? Destroy the birds which are in the garden, and I will give you a bullock. There will be no disputing when you have taken away the birds."

So the doctor gives directions, saying, "Let all the men come together, and cut green firewood; let the women leave the birds to-day, that they may eat, that I may be able to find the chaff of the amabele on the ground; then I shall be able to treat them well. Find a great frog, that I may shut out the birds by means of it."

Indeed on that day the birds eat the amabele excessively; they begin in the morning and leave off

nga. I ti inyanga ntambama, a ba bute izikoba nok*q*ak*q*a olutsha, ba lu lete kuye,—konke ngalolu 'lusuku oku d*h*liwe izinyoni amasimu onke. Nembala ke ku *h*langaniswe 'ndawo nye, ku gaywe; ku funwe isele, li *h*lo*h*lwe, li be umk*q*umbalala; nesinana; ku be se ku mbelwa pansi loko, se ku baswa ngapezulu umlilo, kw enziwe iziko elikulu; u vute ke umlilo ebusuku ku ze ku se. I tsho ukuti, "A no zi linda ngomso na ngom*h*l' omunye, ni bheke uma z' enza njani, ni zi yeke. Kona ni ya 'ubona ukuba ngi inyanga."

Nembala ke ku be njalo; ba zi bhekisise. I ba tshele nokuti iziko li nga loti, li vute njalo ebusuku na semini, ku ze kw a*h*luleke izinyoni, u nga keimi ku ze ku vutwe amabele. Li ng' enziwa eduze kwamasimu, li bekwe kudana kancinane.

I ti ke, " Ngi ti mina ukuze ni ngi dele, ni za 'ngoduka, ni ye emakaya; izinyoni z' a*h*lulekile. Ni nga zi bona zi k*q*ala ukuya at sunset. In the afternoon the doctor tells the people to collect the ears which the birds have left, and the chaff which has recently fallen on the ground, and bring it to him,—every thing that has been eaten on that day by the birds. And it is all collected, and ground; a frog is found, and stuffed till it is like a stuffed sack; and the same is done to an isinana;[32] and then all is buried together, and a fire is kindled on the top, and a large fireplace is made; and the fire is kept up all night until morning. The doctor says, "Watch the birds to-morrow and the day after, and see what they do, and then leave them alone. Then you will see that I am a doctor."

And indeed so it is; they watch them earnestly. The doctor tells them not to let the fire go out, but to keep it up day and night, until the birds are conquered, and not to put it out until the amabele is ripe. The fire is not made near the garden, but is placed at a little distance from it.

And the doctor says, "I say that you may be satisfied with me, you will go home; the birds are conquered. When you see them

---

[32] *Isinana* is a Batrachian, which is found under stones. It has an almost globular body, and small short legs; it is covered with papillæ, which give out a milky fluid when touched. It is slow in its movements, not leaping, but crawling. It is used much by the doctors.

'uhlala eziko ; a no te n' azi ukuba ngi za 'u z' ahlula. Uku zi kuza kwenu emasimini, ni ti,

Buba, buba, mbalane ;
Buba, hlokohloko."
Nembala ke i ti futi, " Ni ze nami ni ngi lindele, ku nga bi ko 'ndoda e ya endhlini ; kuhle ni ze ni ng' a- lusele ; kona ni ya 'ubona ubunya- nga bami."

Nembala ke amasuku a be ma- bili be zi vimbele, ku ti ngolobu- tatu ku potulwe, i ba pe intelezi yokugeza. Ba ya 'ugeza emfuleni. I ti, " Ni ze ni ti uma ni geze, ekukupukeni kwenu emfuleni ni ya emasimini, n' enze igama lo- kuti,
O, buba, mbalane ;
O, buba, hlokohloko.
Ni tsho njalo, ni bone uma ni ya 'ufika zi dhle kangakanani na."

Abanye ba kqale ukuti, " O, mina, bonyoko, se i ke i hlale nje inyoni. Ngi kokobe ngi yo'ubhe- ka, ngi bone i nga dhli ; i kamise umlomo nje." Nembala izinyoni

begin to come and sit by the fire, then you will know that I am about to conquer them. When you drive them away you shall say,
Die, die, mbalane ;
Die, thlokothloko."
He says further, " Do you watch yourselves for my sake ; let no man of you go to his house ;[33] it is proper that you should guard your heart for my sake ; then you will see my skill."

And having shut out the birds for two days, on the third they wash, the doctor having given them intelezi to wash with. They go to the river to wash. He says to them, " When you have washed, and are going up from the river to the gardens, sing this song,
O, die, mbalane ;
O, die, thlokothloko.
When you say thus, see on reach- ing the gardens how much they have eaten."

Some begin to say, " O, for my part, women, I see the birds doing nothing but sit still. I creep stealthily along to go and see, and I see the birds not eating ; they merely open their mouths." And indeed the birds begin to collect in

---

[33] That is, they are to abstain from their wives. Comp. Exodus xix. 15. They also all abstain from eating any thing growing in the gardens whilst the doctor is treating them, until they have washed. These are no doubt religious observances connected with some old and now forgotten superstition.

INDEX.

Abyssinians, the Bouda an evil spirit among the, 281
Adam, Biblical tradition of, quoted, 40, 99
Address, mode of, 334
Affliction, effect of, on religious ideas, 30-31
Age, influence of, in Zulu legends, 48
———, traditions applied to, 7
Agricultural periods, 397
Agriculture, origin of, 77
Allom's *China*, quoted, 308
American Indian legends about thunder birds, 381
——————— tribes, ideas of, on races of man, 82
Ancestor worship, 1, 5, 12, 17, 27, 28, 33, 54, 75, 110, 129-227, 410-411; *see* "Sacrifice"
Ancestral spirit, words for, 148
——————— ———, divination by, 348-374
Animal, a small, used for divination, 339
———, bones used in divination, 327, 332-336, 337
Animals sent by ancestral spirits, 152
———, cause of disease by, 286
———, man turned into, 200-202
———, qualities of, imparted to men, 438
———, tradition as to origin of, 41
———; *see* "bird," "buffalo," "bullock," "cattle," "chameleon," "cow," "dog," "domestic," "eagle," "elephant," "frog," "gall," "goat," "hare," "herds," "horns," "horse," "hyena," "leopard," "lion," "lizard," "sacrifice," "sheep," "snake," "wasp"
Ant-hill used by doctors for curing disease, 315
Apparitions or dreams, 228-252
Appleyard's *Kafir Grammar* quoted, 105, 110
Arab idea of the sky, 394

Arbousset's *Exploratory Tour in South Africa* quoted 60, 76, 100, 109, 117, 123
Army, ceremonies of the, 437
Arthur, legend of, quoted, 166
Aspen tree, notions concerning, 421-424
Assagais, origin of, 77
Assembly of chiefs, 92
Atheism of African tribes, 107-108; of Zulus, 29-30

Bacon (Roger), story of, 385
Baperis, legend of, quoted, 77
Baptismal ritual, omission of portion, cause of death (New Zealand), 4
Basutos, legend of, quoted, 51, 60, 76, 100
——— religious ideas parallel to Zulus, 3
Battle, omens of, 441
——— sacrifices, 131-133
Bechuanas, legend of, quoted, 50, 60
Bedouins, custom of heaping stones among the, 66
Bible, comparisons made with, 254
——— quoted, 14, 40, 47, 66, 341, 374, 377, 379, 393, 394, 448
———; *see* "Hebrew"
Biblical divination by looking into cup, 341
Bird of heaven, 119, 380, 381
——————, killing of, for rain, 407-408
Bird of lightning, 381-383
Bird-doctor, 444-448
Birds; *see* "Eagle"
Birth, notions concerning, 3
Bladder, disease of the, 337
Bleek's *Comparative Grammar* quoted, 105, 106, 107
——— *Hottentot Fables* quoted, 4, 66, 112
Blood of sacrificial animal, 180-181
Boiling, magical art of, 336

INDEX.

Bones, use of, in divination, 327, 332-336, 337
Bravery of animals transferred to men, 438
Bridal customs, 442; see " Marriage"
Bridge, making of, 207
Brinton's *Myths of the New World* quoted, 381
Brother (eldest), reverence for, 146-149
———, marriage of widow by younger brother, 348
Buddhist beliefs in power of nats, 268-269
Buffalo hunting, 234
Building of a village, 367, 368, 369, 373
Bullock sacrificed for cure of illness, 5-6, 12; see " Cattle "
Burial of live horse and man among the Comans, 100-101
Burning of dead man's property, 13
Burton (Captain), *Mission to the King of Dahome* quoted, 19, 92, 93, 118

Campbell's *Highland Tales* quoted, 227. 235, 336
——— *Travels in South Africa* quoted, 77
Casalis (M.), *Basutos*, quoted, 3, 51, 60, 100, 108
Catlin's *Life among the Indians* quoted, 382
Cattle disease, cures of, 162, 163
Cattle, origin of, 77, 129
——— purchasing, customs at, 298
——— sacrifice, 157, 158; sacrifice of, to ancestral spirits, 141
——— slaughtering, 11; see " Bullock "
——— struck by lightning, eating of, 403
Caucasus, custom in the, when any one is struck by lightning, 405
Cave dwellers, fairies are, 227
——— dwelling legends, 50, 51, 76, 77
——— dwellings; see " Habitations "
Chameleon, tradition concerning, 3, 15, 100, 138
Chief, medical functions of, 420, 427-431
———, sacrifice of bullock in honour of, 428
———, sacrifices at funeral of, 213
———, village, 173, 328
Chiefs, divination by, 340-347
———, election of, by diviners, 340
———, exaltation of, 121-123
———, family, 144

Chiefs, oaths taken in the name of the, 121
———, songs of, 409-413
———, salutation of, 92
Chieftainship, legend of the origin of, 57
Child, progress of in life, 364, 374
Children, fiction practised upon in the name of Unkulunkulu, 72-74
——— protection of, by father's spirit, 161
——— position of, in village affairs, 176
Chinese snake doctor, 308
——— myth on the sky, 394
Christianity, influence of among Zulus, 68-69
Circumcision, 58
Cloud birds (American Indian), 381
Contrary meaning of dreams, 241
Cold, spirits die of, when village is broken up, 225
Corn, origin of, 77, 89
———, origin of as food, 52
———, legend as to introduction of, 34, 41, 45
———, thanksgiving for to ancestral spirits, 179
Costume; see " Dress "
Councils; see " Assembly "
Cow, mankind belched up by, 34
———, tradition of its origin, 45
Creation, ideas as to the, 1, 7, 135-140
——— of man, 16, 40, 46, 50, 51, 76-77
Croker's *Fairy Legends* quoted, 227, 354

Dahoman notion of thunder, 117; of lightning, 118; of rainbow, 124
Dahoman's salutation of king, 92; ancestral ghosts, 93
Dancing, 411, 418
Danish traditions quoted, 270
Dawn, saying to express the, 278
Dead, battle of the, 354-356
———, spirits of the, used for divination, 348-374
———, worship of the, 28
Death, lucky to dream of, 236, 237, 244
———, mourning for, 13, 27, 28
———, prognosticated by lizard, 216
Death of man, tradition of origin of, 3, 4, 100, 138
Disease, cure of, 8, 9, 12; see " Medicine "
———, cause of, 286

Divination by shadow, 126; by snakes, 200
——— of blood sacrifice, 120
Diviners and their cult, 153, 259-374
Diviners, origin of, 5
———, functions of, 12, 28
———, offices of, in sickness, 172, 173
Doctors, origin of, 5
Dog, tradition of its origin, 45
Dog mounting on a hut, omen, 28
Domestic animals, 46
Dreams or apparitions, 228-252
———, ancestral spirits produce, 270
———, cures for, 160, 316-318
———, medicine revealed by, 162
———, origin of, 6
———, plants eaten to influence, 322
———, significance of, 134, 146
Drinking with the chief, 427-431
Dress, 245
Du Chaillu, *Equatorial Africa* quoted, 112

Eagle of Jupiter, probable connection of, with savage myths, 382
Earth, legends of man originating from, 76, 77
———, medicines dug up from, 219
———, ceremonies concerning, 220
———, striking the, in divination, 281, 284, 299, 313, 323-324, 367-368
———, tradition as to existence of, before man, 41
———; *see* "Hades"
Eastman (Mrs. M.), *Dacotah* quoted, 382
Ecstasy, 232-235
Elephant, bones of, used for divination, 332
Ellis's *Specimens* quoted, 166
English folk-lore quoted; *see* "Arthur," "Bacon," "Campbell," "Croker," "Fairies," "Good people," "Hardwick," "Harland," "Irish," "Jack," "Lancashire," "Milton," "parsley," "Scotch"
Evil, Zulu idea of, 24-25, 84

Fairies, Scotch and Irish, 226-227
Families, growth of, 18
Family ceremony for cure of disease, 9
——— chief, when dead worshipped by children, 144
——— divisions at an assembly, 93
——— divisions by the, at sacrificial feasts, 181
——— god, 32, 33

Family spirit, 27
——— succession, desire of, 225
——— worship, 17, 18
Fasting, custom of, 387-389
Father, relationship of, 348
———, reverence for, 145
Feast, sacrificial, 179
Female genealogy, 90-91
——— heaven, 401-402
——— spirit, worship of a, 253-256
——— in Zulu tradition, 42, 43, 45
Festival of the first fruits, 409
——— of harvest, 389
Fidelity of wife, how tested, 287
Fighting ceremonies, 437
Fire, ceremony with the spirits at the, 356-357
———, medicines burnt in the, 376
———, obtained by friction, 46
———, origin of, 41, 77
———, sacrifice against birds, 447
First fruits, festival of the, 409
Fog, tradition of man descending in a, 38
Food, diviners eat only certain kinds of, 259
———, legend as to how man first knew of, 35
———, origin of knowledge of, 52, 57
——— partaken of as a sacrificial feast, 182
Footmarks in rock (Bechuanas), 50
Foundation of new village, 212
France, burial of knight in, 100-101
Frog used for carrying away disease, 316
Funeral ceremonies, 213

Gall, use of, in ceremonial sacrifices, 178
——— of bullock, use of, in illness, 6
——— of cattle poured out for sacrifice, 132
——— of goat used for convulsions, 368
——— bladder of goat used in divination, 299
Gardiner (Capt. A. F.), *Journey in Zoolu Country* quoted, 54, 85, 87
Genealogy, ancestral, examples of, 86-88, 96, 97, 98
Ghosts, form of, 231
Goat, bones of, used for divination, 335
———, gall bladders of, used in divination, 299
———, sacrifice of, for convulsions, 368
———, sacrifice of, to snake, 12

INDEX.

God, notions of, by the people of Lake Nyassa, 124
——, Hottentot name for, 105-116
——, the Zulu notions of, 20, 21
Goel, custom of, 348
"Good people," or fairies, Scotch and Irish, 226-227
Grand-mother, position of, in family worship, 208
Greek idea of the sky, 394
Greek myth quoted, 43, 47
Grey (Sir G.), *Polynesian Mythology* quoted, 5, 388
Grave, ceremonies at the, 141-142
Grinding of corn, 46
Growth of children denoted by sneezing, 223

Habitations (underground), legend as to, 36, 37
Hades, traces of belief in, 13
Hail, 56
——, myth connected with, 375
Hare, vicarious use of, in sorcery, 270
Hardwick ( ) quoted, 43
Harland and Wilkinson's *Lancashire Folk-Lore* quoted, 315
Harvest festival, 389
Headman; *see* "Chief"
Health, sneezing a sign of, 223
Hearth, ceremony with the spirits at the, 356, 357
Heaven, King of, 20
——, Lord of, 50, 53, 56, 59, 65, 92, 117-126
——, non-belief in Lord of, 44
——, male and female, 401, 402
——, doctors, 375, 413
Heavens, legend of reaching the, by a rope, 56
Hebrew divination by looking into cup, 341
—— parallels to Zulu customs, 14
—— soothsayer, 374
——; *see* "Bible"
Herds of the Heavens, 375
Hereditary functions of medicine men, 419, 420
Hero legend, 166-168
—— worship, 113, 116, 148
Hiccup, cure of, 288-291
Hindu idea of the sky, 394
—— legend quoted, 43
—— storm gods, 381
Horns of bullock used as significant of dawn, 278
Horse, burial of with man, 100-101

Hottentot, religious ideas parallel to Zulu, 4
—————— word for God, and its meaning, 105-116
——————, custom of heaping stones among the, 68
——————, Zulu myth derived from the, 65
——————, Zulu word derived from, 105
House, ancestral spirits dwell therein, 177
——, ancestral worship performed in, 208
——, blood sprinkled for divination, 120
Houses (village) sprinkled with entrails of sacrifice, 178
Human sacrifices at chief's funeral, 213
Hyena, bones of, used for divination, 333
Hymn in use among the Zulus, 69

Icelandic fancies about yawning, 263
—————— legends quoted, 385, 432
—————— modes of laying ghosts or spirits, 314
Incantation to produce rain, 409
Indian (American); *see* "American"
—— (East); *see* "Hindu"
Inheritance from an elder brother, 156
——————; *see* "Succession"
Initiation of diviners, 259-267
Insects; *see* "Wasp"
Irish fairies, 226-227
Irish *Fairy Legends* quoted, 227, 354

Jack and the Bean Stalk legend, variant of, 56
Jews; *see* "Hebrews"
Jupiter's eagle, probable connection of with savage myths, 382

Kafir belief in spirits, 82
Kings; *see* "Chiefs"
Kneeling, sign of strength, 114, 121
Knowledge, diviners to "eat" of, 321
——————, Zulu ideas as to the origin of, 78-81, 94
Kolben (Peter), *Present State of Cape of Good Hope*, quoted, 105

Lancashire folk-lore, ghost laying, 315
Layard, *Nineveh* quoted, 111
Laying a spirit, 183, 184, 314, 316-318
Leopard, chiefs named as the, 439
Legerdemain, examples of, 336

INDEX.

Liar, characteristics of his spirit after death, 200
Lighoyas, superstition of the, 60
Lightning, 19, 53, 60, 117, 118
———, methods of stopping, 404, 405
———, myth connected with, 375, 380
———, proceeds from the female heaven, 401; smiting of cattle by, 402
Lightning-bird, 381-383
Lion, bones of, used for divination, 332
Lizard, an ancestral spirit, 215
———, man turn into, 200
———, a message of death, 3, 100, 138
Looking-back, prohibition against, during a charm, 315, 317
Looking-glass made by water in rock basin, 235
Love, divination, 343
Lucky omen from sneezing, 222

Magical songs, 409-413
——— practices, 336; see "Witchcraft"
Male heaven, 401
Man, God the ancestor of, 20, 21; see "Ancestor worship"
——; see "Birth," "Creation," "Death," "Marriage"
Marriage, legend of the origin of, 57
——— of widows, 161
——— custom, brother marries brother's widow, 348
———; see "Bridal," "Wedding"
Medical magic, 418-448
Medicine ceremonies, 219-221
———, chameleon used as, 3
——— for curing dreams, 160-161
——— (heaven), 405-407
———, legend as to finding of doctors, 37
———, origin of, 5
——— revealed in dreams, 162
———, use of for obtaining favours, 142-143
———, dug up by aid of spirits, 270, 272
Messengers, honour shown to, 428
Migration of chief from clan, 343, 367
Milton quoted, 47
Missionary, story of first labours of in Zululand, 68
Moffat, *Missionary Labour in South Africa* quoted, 51, 105, 107, 108

Moon, origin of, 59
———, a messenger of death (Hottentot), 4
———, ideas concerning, 395, 396, 399
Morality, Zulu idea of, 24, 84
Morning-star, myth concerning, 397
Mother, or chief wife, reverence for, 146
——— genealogy, 90-91
——— worship (ancestral), 223
Mountain, origin of man from, 99

Nails, vicarious use of, in sorcery, 270
Name, calling the, to practise magic on, 432
———, desire to perpetuate, 225
——— of family or tribe, 203
——— of house or tribe, 1
———; see "Surname"
Naming a husband, woman forbidden to, 316
——— of weapons, 166
Nats, beliefs as to, in Buddhist legends, 268-269
New year, new heaven comes with, 406
New Zealand tradition of death, 4

Oath taking, 440
Oaths "by the chief," 121
Omens, 28
———, lucky from sneezing, 222
——— of battle, 441
——— from birds for rain, 408
Ovid quoted, 43, 47

Parsley bed tradition, parallel to, 9
Picks (digging), origin of, 77
Plants used for carrying away disease, 317
Plants; see "aspen," "corn," "parsley," "reeds," "seed," "tree"
Pleiades, myth concerning, 397
Poison, beliefs as to power of, 351
———, corn and food first given for, 34, 36
Polygamy, 24, 84
Polynesians, custom of fasting amongst, 387-388
——— idea of the sky, 394
Population, large, desired by villages, 182
Pottery, making of, 46
———, origin of, 77
Powell and Magnusson, *Icelandic Legends* quoted, 263, 314
Praying to ancestral god, 33
Pregnancy, effect of on husband, 443
Presents given to diviners, 280

Priesthood, diviners assume functions of, 340
———, evidence of a, 385
———, relics of ancient, 130
Primogeniture, or allied ideas; see "Son (eldest)"
Pringle's *Narrative of his Residence in South Africa* quoted, 82
Prometheus, myth of, quoted, 43
Property, inheritance of, from an older brother, 156
———, personal, burial of with dead owner, 236
——— of dead man burnt, 13
——— of medicine man how acquired, 296
——— of the village chief, 173
Prosperity, effect of, on religious ideas, 30-31
Proverbial sayings, 171, 298

Quern for corn-grinding, 46

Race, differences of, savage ideas as to, 82
Rain, ceremony of praying for, 59, 125
——— doctors, 375
———, the heaven bird killed for, 407-408
———, incantation to produce, 409
———; see "Storm"
Rainbow called God by Nyassa tribe, 124
Reeds, bed of, creation of man in, 9, 15, 31, 35, 40, 41, 46, 52, 55, 88, 96
Relics of older worship, 253-256
Relations, names for ancestral, 86, 88, 90-91, 96, 97
Relationship, terms of, 48
River, ashes of dead chief thrown into, 214
Rock basin, water in, used for looking glass, 235
Roman idea of the sky, 394
——— men killed by lightning not buried, 118
———; see "Jupiter"
Rowley's *Story of the Mission to Central Africa* quoted, 124

Sacrifice to ancestral spirits, 55
——— of cattle, 132, 157-158, 174-178, 179, 428
——— of horse and man among the Comans, 100-101
———, human, at chief's funeral, 213

Sacrifice to the Itongo (spirit), 5, 6, 9, 11
——— to Lord of Heaven, 59
——— for rain, 93
Saints (Christian), parallels to experiences of, 252
Scotch fairies, 226, 227
——— tale quoted, 336; see "Campbell," "English"
Sea-side, first man born near, 33, 88
Seasons; see "festival," "first-fruits," "harvest," "new year," "seed time," "summer time," "year"
Seed-time observances, 444-448
Serpent or snake; see "Snake"
Shade, idea of spirit as, 91, 126
Shadow, dead body does not cast, 91
———, divination by, 126
Shaw, *Story of my Mission* quoted, 82, 108, 109
Sheep not a sacrificial animal, 143
Shooter ( ), *Natal* quoted, 85
Shoulders sensitive part of human body, 159
Sight the origin of thought, 22
Site of new villages, 210, 212, 410
Sky, ideas concerning the, 380, 393
Snake, connected with ancestral spirits, 130, 134, 140, 142, 196-200, 201, 205, 211, 231
———, dead men change to, 8, 12
——— used by diviners, 299
———, dreaming of, 183
———, man turn into, 200
———, taking up its abode in hut, omen, 28
———, power over, 305-311
———, worship of, 10, 11, 12
Sneezing, 64, 222-225, 234
Snuff-taking, 155; by diviners, 263, 283 284
Son (eldest), duties of in ancestor worship, 145
Songs, caused by Amatongo, 273
——— at ancestral worship ceremonial, 209
———, composition of, by diviners, 263
———, magical, 409-413
——— of prayer, 92
——— sung at sacrifice, 59
Southsea Islands, custom of heaping stones among the, 66
Spirit, ancestral, words for, 148
——— of departed, ceremony for recalling the, 141-144
——— of the dead, notions of, 5, 10, 28, 151-152, 165

Spirit of family or tribe, 27
Spitting in ceremonial practices, 160
———, custom of, 435
Spittle used as cure for dreams, 316
Stars, ideas concerning, 396, 397, 400
Stern's *Wanderings among the Falashas in Abyssinia* quoted, 281
Sticks, divination by, 330-332
Stitch in the side, Zulu beliefs concerning, 268
Stomach, contents of, used in spirit worship, 184
Stones, mankind derived from, 34
———, custom of heaping up, 65-66
———, power to remove great, 271
Storm gods, Hindu, 381
——— myths, 375-413
———; see "Rain"
Succession to the family, desire of, 225
———; see "Inheritance"
Summer, dreams in the, are true, 238
Sun, ideas concerning, 394, 395, 398
———, origin of, 10, 41, 59
Surnames, system of, 86-88
——— of family used as name of family god, 32
Survival; see "Relics"

Thorpe's *Northern Mythology* quoted, 271
Thought, Zulu process of, 22
Thumb-doctors, 327
Thunder, 53, 56, 57, 60, 117
———, prayer during time of, 34
——— of the male and female heaven, 401
Thunder-birds (American Indian), 381
Thunder-bolt, used as heaven medicine, 381
Thunder gods, 19
Time, reckoning of, 397
———; see "Seasons"
Transmigration, 196-202
Tree, eating fruit of, connected with man's origin, 3
———, a kind of aspen, notions concerning, 421-424
———, branches of, used in divination to smite the ground with, 281, 284, 299, 313
Trench, *Study of Words* quoted, 109
Tribal divisions at an assembly, 93
——— name, expression in usage of, 1
——— separations, 103-104
——— songs, 409-413
——— spirit, 27

Tribal usages, 2
——— worship, 17
Tribe, breaking up of into separate divisions, 51
———, deserters from one to another, 311
Tylor's *Early History of Mankind* quoted, 83

Umbrella-shield used by Zulus, 384
Uncle, position of in the family, 206
Uncles prayed to as fathers, 224
Underground habitations; see "Habitations"
Unkulunkulu, or the first man, 1-104
Urine, used as a means of injury, 351-352

Vessels used for divination, 341-343, 346
Vicarious objects used in divination, 343, 345, 346, 351
——— used for injuring, 351, 352
Vicarious sorcery, 270
Village building of a, 367, 368, 369, 373
———, property of, 173
———, site of, sanctified by ancestral spirit, 210, 212
Village-head, 328
Villages, clustering of, 357
Virtues of animals transferred to men, 438
Voices of spirits heard, 267
Vows to sacrifice, 225-226

Warts, charms for, 315
Washing, customs of, 434-437
Wasp, man turned into, 200, 202
Water, origin of all things from, 90
———, spirit unable to cross, 207
———, tradition of man being derived from, 44
———; see "River;" "Sea"
Weapons, naming of, 166
Wedding dance, unlucky to dream of, 237, 241
———; see "Marriage"
Whistling, 384
———, spirits speaking by, 265
———, tone of divination, 348, 374
Widows, marriage of, 161
Wife, fidelity of, how tested, 287
Will (human), Zulu ideas of, in moral influences, 24

Winter, dreams in the, are true, 238
Witchcraft, 28, 418-448; see "Magical"
Woman, the first, 40, 58; see "Female"
Women, ancestral spirit of, represented by lizard, 215, 217
—— eat by themselves, 183
——, position of, in village affairs, 176
—— (old) considered as men, 440
Work, suspension of, during storms, 407
Worship of the dead, 28

Yawning, a sign of diviner, 234, 263
————, Icelandic fancies about, 263

Year, new heaven comes with the new, 406

Zulus, age, influence of, 48
——, atheism of, 29-30
——, Christian influences among, 68, 69
—— evil, idea of, 24-25, 84
—— God, notions of, 20, 21
— ——, hymn used by the, 69
—— knowledge, ideas as to origin of, 78-91, 94
—— morality, idea of, 24, 84
——, myths of, parallel to Hottentot, 4, 65, 105
—— thought, process of, 22
—— will (human), idea of, 24

www.ingramcontent.com/pod-product-compliance
Lightning Source LLC
Chambersburg PA
CBHW031957300426
44117CB00008B/799